This volume of es[…] ctual context of the Anglo-Scotti[…] ved view of the Union as a simp[…] e Union was a landmark in the history of political thought. The opening contributions investigate the ideas of union, universal monarchy and empire current in Europe and Britain before 1707. There follow chapters devoted to intellectual and religious developments in Scotland between the Restoration and the Union, before attention is focused on the issues of sovereignty at the centre of the Union debate itself. The volume concludes by studying the aftermath of the debate in eighteenth-century discussions of Britain's relations with Ireland and the North American Colonies.

Underlining the vitality of Scottish intellectual life before the Enlightenment, the volume also gives unprecedented attention to the English view of the Union, to its European setting and to its consequences for the subsequent understanding of the British Empire. The result is a major contribution to the history of British (including Anglo-Irish and American) political thought, and more generally to the history of ideas of union and empire, which will be of wide interest.

A UNION FOR EMPIRE

A UNION FOR EMPIRE

POLITICAL THOUGHT AND THE BRITISH UNION OF 1707

EDITED BY

JOHN ROBERTSON

Lecturer in Modern History, University of Oxford, and Fellow of St Hugh's College

PUBLISHED IN ASSOCIATION WITH THE FOLGER INSTITUTE, WASHINGTON, DC

CAMBRIDGE
UNIVERSITY PRESS

CAMBRIDGE UNIVERSITY PRESS
Cambridge, New York, Melbourne, Madrid, Cape Town, Singapore, São Paulo

Cambridge University Press
The Edinburgh Building, Cambridge CB2 2RU, UK

Published in the United States of America by Cambridge University Press, New York

www.cambridge.org
Information on this title: www.cambridge.org/9780521431132

First published 1995
This digitally printed first paperback version 2006

A catalogue record for this publication is available from the British Library

Library of Congress Cataloguing in Publication data

A union for empire: political thought and the British Union of 1707 /
edited by John Robertson.
p. cm.
Includes index.
ISBN 0–521–43113–1
1. Political science – Great Britain – History – 17th century – Congresses.
2. Political science – Great Britain – History – 18th century – Congresses.
3. Political science – Scotland – History – 17th century – Congresses.
4. Political science – Scotland – History – 18th century – Congresses.
5. Scotland – History – The Union, 1707 – Congresses.
6. Great Britain – Politics and government – 1660–1714 – Congresses.
I. Robertson, John, 1951– .
JA84.G7U55 1995
320.441′09′033 – dc20 94–17184 CIP

ISBN-13 978-0-521-43113-2 hardback
ISBN-10 0-521-43113-1 hardback

ISBN-13 978-0-521-02988-9 paperback
ISBN-10 0-521-02988-0 paperback

CONTENTS

PART III THE ISSUES OF SOVEREIGNTY

PART IV UNION AND EMPIRE IN THE EIGHTEENTH-CENTURY BRITISH WORLD

NOTES ON CONTRIBUTORS

DAVID ARMITAGE is an Assistant Professor of History at Columbia University. He is the co-editor (with Armand Himy and Quentin Skinner) of *Milton and Republicanism* (forthcoming 1995). He is currently at work on a study of the ideological origins of the British Empire, and is preparing an edition of Viscount Bolingbroke's *Political Writings* for Cambridge Texts in the History of Political Thought.

JOHN W. CAIRNS is a Senior Lecturer in Private Law in the University of Edinburgh. He has published numerous articles in the field of eighteenth-century legal history, and is currently completing a book on legal education, legal philosophy and the legal profession in Scotland.

LAURENCE DICKEY is a Professor of History at the University of Wisconsin, Madison. He is the author of *Hegel: Religion, Economics and the Politics of the Spirit 1770–1807* (1987), and editor of Adam Smith, *The Wealth of Nations*, abridged with a commentary (1993).

ROGER L. EMERSON is Professor of History at the University of Western Ontario. He is the author of *Professors, Patronage and Politics: The Aberdeen Universities in the Eighteenth Century* (1992), and of many articles on the Scottish Enlightenment and its antecedents in late seventeenth-century Scottish culture.

JACQUELINE R. HILL is a Senior Lecturer in Modern History, St Patrick's College, Maynooth. She is the author of several articles on religion and politics in Ireland from the seventeenth to the nineteenth centuries, including 'Popery and Protestantism, civil and religious liberty: the disputed lessons of Irish History 1690–1812', in *Past and Present*, 118 (1988), and is completing a book on Dublin civic politics 1660–1840.

COLIN KIDD is a Lecturer in Scottish History at the University of Glasgow, and the author of *Subverting Scotland's Past. Scottish Whig Historians and the Creation of an Anglo-British Identity* (1993). He is now preparing a comparative study of the construction of ethnic and national identities in the seventeenth and eighteenth centuries.

NED C. LANDSMAN is an Associate Professor of History at the State University of New York at Stony Brook. He is the author of *Scotland and its first American Colony 1680–1765* (1985), and numerous articles on religion and Enlightenment in the provincial cultures of eighteenth-century Britain, and is currently working on a book entitled *From Colonials to Provincials: American Thought and Culture 1680–1760*.

JAMES MOORE is an Associate Professor of Political Science at Concordia University, Montreal. He has written on Locke, Carmichael, Hutcheson and Hume. He is currently writing a book on natural law in the age of Enlightenment, and preparing (with Michael Silverthorne) an edition of the juridical and theological writings of Gershom Carmichael.

KATHERINE R. PENOVICH is an Assistant Professor of History at the University of La Verne, California. She is completing her doctorate at the Johns Hopkins University, with a thesis on Daniel Defoe's conceptions of history, commercial humanism and social process.

STEVEN PINCUS is an Assistant Professor of History at the University of Chicago. He is the author of *Protestantism and Patriotism: Ideologies and the Making of English Foreign Policy 1650–1668* (1994), and is now at work on a book on the English pre-occupation with universal monarchy in the seventeenth century.

J.G.A. POCOCK is Professor Emeritus of History at the Johns Hopkins University. His principal publications have been *The Ancient Constitution and the Feudal Law: A Study of English Historical Thought in the 17th century* (1957; re-issued with a Retrospect in 1987); *Politics, Language and Time: Essays in Political Thought and History* (1971); *The Machiavellian Moment: Florentine Political Thought and the Atlantic Republican Tradition* (1975); *The Political Works of James Harrington* (edited, 1977); *Virtue, Commerce and History: Essays on Political Thought and History* (1985); and (with Gordon Schochet & Lois Schwoerer) *The Varieties of British Political Thought 1500–1800* (1993), a volume derived from the seminars of the Folger Institute Center for the History of British Political Thought.

JOHN ROBERTSON is a Lecturer in Modern History and Fellow of St Hugh's College, Oxford. He is the author of *The Scottish Enlightenment and the Militia Issue* (1985). He is preparing a new edition of *The Political Works of Andrew Fletcher* for the Cambridge Texts in the History of Political Thought.

MICHAEL SILVERTHORNE is an Associate Professor of Classics at McGill University, Montreal. He has written on Greek political thought and its influence in the early modern period. He has also translated Samuel Pufendorf's *On the Duty of Man and Citizen* and Thomas Hobbes's *On the Citizen*, both for the Cambridge Texts in the History of Political Thought.

PREFACE

THE intention of this volume is to demonstrate that the Union negotiated between Scotland and England in 1707 should be understood within an intellectual as well as a political and economic context, and that it generated a significant body of political thought. So doing, the volume deliberately cuts across the grain of an existing consensus, scholarly and popular, about the nature of the Union. According to the now prevalent view, the Union was a simple political job, cobbled together by two sets of politicians whose ambition was set no higher than the confirmation of the Hanoverian succession in both countries. Having already decided on this succession for themselves, English ministers sought its acceptance by the Scots in return for the minimum of political and economic concessions, backed by a latent threat to use force. Following an initial outburst of indignation over English presumption, Scottish politicians and their followers quickly succumbed to this pressure, allowing whatever principles they professed to be bought off by straightforward financial inducements, amounting in many cases to outright bribery. In these circumstances, it is supposed, there can have been little opportunity for serious debate, and the arguments that were heard must have been of purely ephemeral significance.

The decisive step in the formation of the modern understanding of the Union was taken by William Ferguson, in an article published in 1964, which uncovered and documented the extent of the individual bribery involved in ensuring the passage of the Treaty through the Scottish Parliament.[1] Fierce as was the expression of his outrage, Ferguson himself remained curious about other aspects of the Union crisis, including its intellectual dimension. Ten years later he devoted an equally

[1] Williams Ferguson, 'The making of the Treaty of Union of 1707', *Scottish Historical Review*, 43 (1964), 89–110.

pioneering article to the historical controversy over Scotland's 'imperial' crown which was in many respects the starting-point for the Union debate proper;[2] and this was shortly followed by an overview, *Scotland's Relations with England: A Survey to 1707* (1977), which contains what is still the most rounded single account, at once vivid and querulous, of the Union crisis.[3] Working alongside Ferguson, however, was a scholar who consistently regarded the expression of ideas in politics with the utmost scepticism, the late P.W.J. Riley. Concentrating his attention exclusively upon the 'high political' dealings of politicians and their factions, Riley judged the pamphleteering which accompanied the Union crisis to be 'little more than a campaign of rationalisation and propaganda', of no independant intellectual interest whatsoever. However rigorous in its own scholarship and shrewd in many of its political judgements, Riley's *The Union of England and Scotland* (1978) stands as a monument to the anti-intellectual influence which Sir Lewis Namier once exerted upon eighteenth-century historical studies.[4] Perhaps only one trained in that severest of schools could sustain so all-embracing a cynicism. Most scholars are prepared to acknowledge the seriousness of at least some of the participants in the Union debate;[5] and those for whom scholarship comes second to national piety are as anxious to highlight the intellectual purity of the Union's opponents as to emphasise the corruption of its supporters.[6] Nevertheless, there remains a widespread conviction that political expediency and mercenary motives dominated the passage of the Union to the exclusion of significant intellectual debate.

A greater willingness to devote attention to the arguments over union may be found in the works of previous generations of historians – by no means all of whom were, as is often now assumed, uncritical exponents of the Union's benefits.[7] But their accounts of the debate tended to be descriptive and illustrative rather than analytical: there was no recognition that the Union might have been an episode in intellectual as well as political history. A partial exception was A.V. Dicey and R.S. Rait's remarkable

[2] William Ferguson, 'Imperial crowns: a neglected facet of the background the Treaty of Union', *Scottish Historical Review*, 53 (1974), 22–44.

[3] William Ferguson, *Scotland's Relations with England: a Survey to 1707* (Edinburgh, 1977), esp. chs 9–14.

[4] P.W.J. Riley, *The Union of England and Scotland. A Study in Anglo-Scottish Politics of the Eighteenth Century* (Manchester 1978): the quotation is from p. 197.

[5] Michael Lynch, *Scotland. A New History* (London, 1991), pp. 310–17, is a recent example of temperate judgement.

[6] For example, P.H. Scott, *1707. The Union of Scotland and England* (Edinburgh, 1979); and *Andrew Fletcher and the Treaty of Union* (Edinburgh, 1992).

[7] James Mackinnon ended his (significantly entitled) *The Union of England and Scotland. A Study of International History* (London, New York and Bombay, 1896), with a sympathetic statement of the case for a national parliament for Scotland, to co-exist with one imperial legislative body. See esp. Ch. 15, 'Nationality and the Union'.

Thoughts on the Union between England and Scotland (1920), whose stated purpose was to demonstrate the 'extraordinary wisdom' of the constitutional principles on which the Act of Union had been framed. As the authors were at pains to emphasise, however, this was a work of commentary rather than of historical research. It was not the contemporary debate which interested Dicey and Rait, but the inferences which could be drawn from the act and its aftermath: the unstated implication was that this was a union in which the British should continue to have confidence, at a time when they faced a renewed threat of nationalist secession in Ireland.[8]

While a consensus of opinion discounts the intellectual significance of the debate which preceded the Union of 1707, the past ten years have seen a new interest in the debate a century earlier over the union proposals of James VI and I. Publication by the Scottish Historical Society in 1985 of an edition by B.R. Galloway and B.P. Levack of six tracts from the Jacobean debate offered clear evidence of the potential interest of the subject (and demonstrated that Sir Thomas Craig's *De Unione Regnorum Britanniae Tractatus* (1605), which the Society had published in 1909, was not an isolated achievement).[9] The point was reinforced in separate monographs by the two editors; and Levack's *The Formation of the British State. England, Scotland and the Union 1603–1707* (1987) in particular broke fresh ground by tracing the themes of the Jacobean debate across the seventeenth century and into the debate immediately preceding 1707.[10] By its nature, such an approach tended to emphasise continuities, and to diminish the impact of the new ideas which (this volume will suggest) were to re-invigorate the debate at the end of the century. But even if the suggested assimilation of two debates is to be resisted, the investigation of the Jacobean debate has already indicated the possible rewards of adopting a more intellectual approach to the history of the union question. Just how great those rewards may be should be even clearer following the publication of the volume edited by Roger Mason, *Scots and Britons: Scottish Political Thought and the Union of 1603* (1994), a volume to which this work is offered as a companion.[11]

[8] A.V. Dicey and R.S. Rait, *Thoughts on the Union between England and Scotland* (London, 1920), esp. pp. v–ix, and 361–2.

[9] B.R. Galloway and B.P. Levack (eds.), *The Jacobean Union, Six Tracts of 1604*, Scottish History Society, Fourth Series, xxi (Edinburgh, 1985); Sir Thomas Craig, *De Unione Regnorum Britanniae Tractatus*, ed. and trans. C. Sanford Terry, Scottish History Society, lx (Edinburgh, 1909).

[10] Brian P. Levack, *The Formation of the British State. England, Scotland, and the Union 1603–1707* (Oxford, 1987); by contrast, Bruce Galloway, *The Union of England and Scotland 1603–1608* (Edinburgh, 1986), concentrates upon James's proposals and their reception.

[11] Roger A. Mason (ed.), *Scots and Britons. Scottish Political Thought and the Union of 1603* (Cambridge, 1994).

Like *Scots and Britons*, *A Union for Empire* originated in a Seminar held at the Folger Institute Center for the History of British Political Thought, at the Folger Shakespeare Library in Washington, in May and June 1991. While the present volume may be regarded as a companion to *Scots and Britons*, however, it is not strictly a sequel, since it addresses the Union of 1707 from different, less exclusively Scottish, angles. More attention is devoted to the Scottish setting than to any other, since debate before 1707 was more thoroughgoing, and attracted many more participants, in Scotland than across the border. But as its title is intended to convey, *A Union for Empire* ranges furth of Scotland, to examine not only the English dimension of the debate, but also its wider European setting, and finally its implications for contemporaries' understanding of other parts of the eighteenth-century British world, the Kingdom of Ireland and the colonial empire in North America. The result is a volume only some of whose chapters contribute directly to a history of Scottish political thought, but which reflects its editor's conviction that the debate over the British Union of 1707 was also a European and an imperial event, with an intellectual significance extending far beyond Scotland.

The structure of the volume reflects these priorities. Opening part I, an introductory chapter by the editor outlines the complex connections established between the concepts of empire and union in European political thinking over the sixteenth and seventeenth centuries, and suggests that the parameters of the Anglo-Scottish Union debate were set by this inheritance. The two following chapters investigate the framework of assumptions within which the English were to approach the problem of union: Steven Pincus demonstrates the depth of the English obsession with the threat of a French universal monarchy, tracing its emergence to the years 1672–1688; and Laurence Dickey then explores the way in which the threat was taken up by Daniel Defoe in the years after 1698, and used to reinforce arguments on behalf of both commercial empire overseas and union with Scotland. As David Armitage demonstrates in the final chapter of part I, however, the Scots involved in the Darien venture of 1698 were simultaneously developing their own, very different ideas as to the form of commercial empire they should seek to acquire. Although the fear of a French universal monarchy was shared by many Scots, they were by no means simply beholden to the English for their conceptions of either union or empire: challenging the arguments of Defoe, the Darien projectors and Andrew Fletcher were to ensure that the Union debate confronted the Scots with genuine choices.

Focusing directly upon Scotland, the chapters in part II examine salient developments in Scottish intellectual and religious culture in the period between the Restoration and the Union. Roger Emerson charts the growing intellectual connections between Scotland, England and Europe after 1660: what he reveals is an intellectual culture in the throes of rapid, fertile change, in which it was taken for granted that closer connections with England and with Europe were complementary rather than antithetical objectives. Colin Kidd outlines the course of religious realignment over the same period, as it affected both Episcopalians and Presbyterians. On both sides, but crucially among Presbyterian moderates, it would seem that *jure divino* ecclesiastical principles were being compromised by an implicitly erastian acceptance of the advantages of government support, a development which goes far to explain the willingness of the Kirk to come to terms with political union.

The chapters in part III are concerned with the central constitutional issues of the Union debate, those of sovereignty. Underlining the extent to which academic natural jurisprudence was grounded in theology, James Moore and Michael Silverthorne explore the adaptation by Gershom Carmichael of Pufendorf's and Huber's discussions of sovereignty in the context of the German and Dutch unions. What characterised this tradition of Protestant jurisprudence, it is suggested, was its reluctance to think in terms of absolute sovereignties, its preference for limitations, and its emphasis upon the benefits of civil government. Convergent conclusions emerge from the outline of the course of the Scottish Union debate in the following chapter by the editor. Here the theme is the elusiveness of Scotland's sovereignty, understood as the Kingdom's historic independence: as even opponents of the proposed union acknowledged, it was a sovereignty almost impossible to put into a viable constitutional form, while the Union's supporters urged the advantages that would follow from acceptance of a new, shared sovereignty with England. This account of the Union debate is amplified by a further, short chapter on Defoe by Katherine Penovich, analysing his specific intervention in the later stages of the Scottish debate. Finally John Cairns re-opens the question of the Union's implications for Scots' Law, and suggests that the Treaty's preservation of a separate legal system by no means excluded a continuing openness to good legal practice elsewhere, including England. The Scots certainly did not accept the loss of their independent sovereignty without deep misgivings; what these chapters demonstrate, however, is the intellectual resilience with which they interpreted that loss as an opportunity to obtain fresh, substantive benefits for Scottish society.

The volume ends in part IV with three chapters which reflect on the implications of the Union of 1707 for subsequent discussion of the relations between Britain and the different parts of its eighteenth-century Empire. Jacqueline Hill considers the case of Ireland from the viewpoint of the most significant Anglo-Irish political thinker, William Molyneux: confident of the historic grounds of Protestant Anglo-Irish authority, Molyneux may be seen to have explored the extent to which political and legislative autonomy might continue to be exercised in the shadow of an incorporated British sovereignty. Ned Landsman then examines the neglected but distinctive understanding of the empire in North America held by Scots who became prominent as merchants and colonial administrators, and, after 1776, as revolutionary leaders. A final chapter by John Pocock looks back over the historical relation between the ideas of union and empire from the vantage point of 1776: the firmly Anglo-American terms in which this chapter concludes the volume stand in a – perhaps revealing – contrast to the Scottish–European perspective of the editor's introduction.

Despite – or because of – its range, this volume is by no means a comprehensive treatment of its subject. While it is meant to make it impossible for any future general study of the Union to ignore its intellectual dimension, this is not itself such a study. The Union remains a political as well as an intellectual event: if a recognition of the significance of the debate ought to enlarge our understanding of the politics of the Union, these do not lose their importance. There are, moreover, several aspects of the intellectual story which merit further investigation.

One which receives only passing mention in this volume is the Jacobite contribution to the debate. There is a sense in which the Union was not an issue for Jacobites: in their eyes the whole problem only arose from a failure to accept the succession of the main Stuart line, and would presumably disappear if this was restored. Jacobites might see tactical advantages in intervening in the debate, but there would be little point in their making a constructive contribution. Nevertheless, the studies of Bruce Lenman have demonstrated the existence of a distinctive Jacobite ideology;[12] and there are individual Jacobite participants in the Union debate, notably George Lockhart of Carnwath and Patrick Abercromby, whose political thinking would almost certainly repay further investigation.[13] Another aspect of the debate which needs more attention than it receives here is the economic. An outline of the economic arguments

[12] Bruce Lenman, *The Jacobite Risings in Britain 1689–1746* (London, 1980); and specifically, 'The Scottish Episcopal clergy and the ideology of Jacobitism', in Evelyn Cruikshanks (ed.), *Ideology and Conspiracy: Aspects of Jacobitism 1689–1759* (Edinburgh, 1982).

[13] On Lockhart of Carnwath, see *Letters of George Lockhart of Carnwath 1698–1732*, ed. with intro. Daniel Szechi, Scottish History Society, Fifth Series, ii (Edinburgh, 1989); several indications of Abercromby's interest are to be found in Colin Kidd, *Subverting Scotland's Past. Scottish Whig Historians and the Creation of an Anglo-British Identity 1689–c.1830* (Cambridge, 1993).

deployed, and an indication of their interest, was offered many years ago by T.C. Smout; their sophistication has since been underlined by Istvan Hont, who recognised in the Union debate an early expression of eighteenth-century political economy's preoccupation with the 'rich country–poor country' problem.[14] The chapters below by Dickey and Armitage trace the origins of the economic debate back into the 1690s: but there is still room for further and fuller study of the arguments of such as John Law, William Paterson and Hugh Chamberlen between 1700 and 1707. A third area which this volume positively opens up for research is the intellectual world of London Nonconformity, and its relations with Scottish Presbyterianism. As Penovich reminds us in her chapter, this was the world of Defoe; but it was also the world of those he recognised as his sharpest antagonists in the Union debate, the London Scots James Hodges and George Ridpath.

A much larger gap should also be highlighted. Between the debate which is the subject of this volume and that studied in Roger Mason's volume lies an interval in which the history of Scottish political thought has barely begun to be explored. There is a pressing need for further research into the discussions of union which occurred during this interval, in the 1640s and again in the 1650s, in 1667–70 and, above all, in 1688–90.

Finally, a rather different disclaimer may be advisable. This volume is not intended to serve as an argument either for or against the Union as it stands today. Like all scholarly writing, the contributions to the volume are liable to be informed by underlying preoccupations of their authors: but since the contributors include citizens of Canada and the United States as well as British subjects, such preoccupations are as likely to be with the prospects of the Canadian and American unions as with those of the Union of Britain. It may be that simply by taking the political thought associated with the Union of 1707 seriously, the volume will add to the credibility of the event. But this admission does not necessarily strengthen the case for the Union now. What is arguable is that modern criticism of the Union has failed to admit the strengths of the original case in its favour, and the weaknesses of the alternatives canvassed at the time. Insofar as it offers a better historical understanding of those strengths and weaknesses, therefore, this volume might even help to clear the way for the formation of a viable modern alternative to the Union.

[14] T.C. Smout, *Scottish Trade on the Eve of Union* (Edinburgh and London, 1963), pp. 257–75; Istvan Hont, 'The "rich country–poor country" debate in Scottish classical political economy', in Istvan Hont and Michael Ignatieff (eds.), *Wealth and Virtue. The Shaping of Political Economy in the Scottish Enlightenment* (Cambridge, 1983), pp. 276–80. The most recent discussion of the nature and role of economic issues in the passage of the Union is by C.A. Whatley, 'Economic causes and consequences of the Union of 1707: a survey', *Scottish Historical Review*, 68 (1989).

PREFACE

The editor of a collaborative volume such as this must depend on the support and goodwill of many. Both as director of the Folger Seminar and as editor my first and greatest debt is to John Pocock. As a member of the Steering Committee of the Folger Institute Center for the History of British Political Thought, he not only suggested the Seminar and encouraged and facilitated its planning, but offered constant stimulus to its proceedings by his participation; subsequently he has given every support to the volume. I am likewise most grateful to the staff of the Folger Institute: to its Executive Director, Dr Lena Cowen Orlin, for the efficiency and courtesy with which she handled every aspect of the Seminar's administration, its finances not least; and to Carol Brobeck, the Program Administrator, for the speed and good humour with which she and her assistants responded to many calls for help. My direction of the Seminar was made possible by the grant of a term's sabbatical leave by the Governing Body of St Hugh's College; I am, as ever, grateful to my colleagues Colin Matthew and George Garnett for much intellectual support, as well as for taking over my administrative chores.

The papers delivered to the Seminar, and the discussions which followed, were regularly of a high quality. I would like to thank particularly those who presented papers but who are not contributors to the volume, Professor Franz Bosbach of the University of Bayreuth, Professor Bernd Roeck of the University of Bonn, and Dr Eligah H. Gould, then of Johns Hopkins, now at the University of New Hampshire. The expertise of the first two added greatly to the Seminar's appreciation of the Union's European context, while in addition to his paper Dr Gould was a most helpful leader of discussion. The regular members of the Seminar sustained an encouraging level of intellectual curiosity; and the proceedings further benefited from the participation at different times of speakers to the previous Seminar, Brian Levack, Arthur Williamson, and Roger Mason.

To my contributors I am grateful for the trouble they have taken in re-writing their papers, and in the cases of Colin Kidd, Jacqueline Hill and John Pocock, for writing entirely new chapters. I also appreciate their patience with editorial delays. Roger Mason, as director of the previous seminar and editor of the ensuing volume, has been a constant help. So has Richard Fisher, exercising a judicious blend of patience and direction as the volume's editor at the Press. Most forbearing of all, however, have been my wife, Maxine Berg, and our daughters, whose support is always the strongest of encouragements.

John Robertson
Oxford

Part I

UNIONS, UNIVERSAL MONARCHY AND EMPIRE

I

EMPIRE AND UNION: TWO CONCEPTS OF THE EARLY MODERN EUROPEAN POLITICAL ORDER

JOHN ROBERTSON

I

FROM a purely British vantage point, the relation between union and empire is likely to seem quite straightforward. The formation of the United Kingdom of Great Britain in 1707 was so quickly followed by the expansion of British commerce and the acquisition of territory overseas, in North America and India, that a close, even a causal, connection between the Union and the British Empire could be taken for granted. Few might go as far as to claim that the achievement of Anglo-Scottish Union was a sufficient explanation for the acquisition of empire: both English and Scottish historians would wish to trace the roots of overseas imperial enterprise in the two countries back into the seventeenth and even the sixteenth centuries. But the disproportionate numbers in which Scots merchants, soldiers and administrators contributed to – and benefited from – imperial activity in the eighteenth century were to ensure that the Empire acquired its 'British' identity earlier and with fewer reservations than many of the domestic institutions of the newly united state.

The assumption of a straightforward correlation between union and empire has been strengthened by the conviction that the union was a one-off occurence, a singular British solution to the anomaly of two neighbour kingdoms sharing the same monarch. The anomaly had threatened the sovereign statehood which independent kingdoms were

Versions of this chapter were given as papers to the Early Modern Europe Seminar at Oxford and the Seminars in European and British History 1500–1800 at the Institute of Historical Research, London, and as lectures in the Universities of Bonn and Bayreuth: I am grateful to participants on these occasions for their helpful comments. I am more particularly indebted to Franz Bosbach, J.H. Burns, J.H. Elliott, George Garnett and H.G. Koenigsberger for specific observations. Responsibility for the judgements made, however, is entirely mine.

supposed to enjoy; but by forming a new, unitary state, the Union of 1707 enabled the British to gain the advantage over their continental rivals, the French above all, whose aspirations to such statehood were still compromised by the archaic political structures of *ancien régime* monarchy. Viewed in this light, the Union was not only the foundation of the Empire; it was itself an exceptional achievement, confirming and enlarging the gulf between British and continental patterns of political development.[1]

Indispensable as it may have become to a British historical consciousness, this is an understanding of the relation between union and empire whose historical supports are fast dissolving. The predicament in which England and Scotland found themselves in the seventeenth century, sharing the same monarch, was by no means as anomalous as the conventional account would suppose. On the contrary, historians now suggest, 'composite' monarchy was the European norm: almost every ruling dynasty of consequence – Habsburg, Bourbon and Vasa as well as Stuart – had acquired multiple titles, and exercised authority over a number of territories, which might not even be contiguous.[2] The potential advantages of closer unity between their territories were, moreover, well known to these rulers: over the sixteenth and seventeenth centuries there were many examples of the imposition or negotiation of more formal unions.[3] The belief that the British problem was exceptional, and that its solution, a negotiated union, was unique, can no longer be sustained. The Union of 1707 belongs within a European setting, and should be thought of as the British variant of a wider pattern.[4]

While the structural characteristics of composite monarchy have been re- assessed by modern historians, however, much less attention has been devoted to the terms in which contemporaries themselves understood and discussed the European political order, and forms of union in particular. Without a knowledge of these, it is impossible to gauge the extent to which union was discussed in the same terms in England and Scotland as elsewhere in Europe. As J.H. Elliott has commented,

[1] An assumption still to be found in the otherwise valuable work of Brian P. Levack, *The Formation of the British State. England, Scotland, and the Union 1603–1707* (Oxford, 1987), p. vi.

[2] The most prominent and persuasive exponents of this new understanding of early modern Europe have been H.G. Koenigsberger and J.H. Elliott. See H.G. Koenigsberger, '*Dominium regale* or *Dominium politicum et regale*', in his *Politicians and Virtuosi. Essays in Early Modern History* (London, 1986): also his 'Composite states, representative institutions and the American Revolution', *Historical Research*, 62, 148 (1989); and J.H. Elliott, 'A Europe of composite monarchies', *Past and Present*, 137 (1992).

[3] Elliott, 'A Europe of composite monarchies', pp. 62–8. Also, Mark Greengrass (ed.), *Conquest and Coalescence: The Shaping of the State in Early Modern Europe* (London, 1991).

[4] I have previously attempted to develop such an approach in: John Robertson, 'Union, state and empire: the Britain of 1707 in its European setting', in Lawrence Stone (ed.), *An Imperial State at War: Britain from 1689 to 1815* (London, 1994).

historians of political thought have hitherto offered little help, their pre-occupation with the concept of sovereignty leading them to neglect investigation of concepts more appropriate to the phenomenon of composite monarchy.[5] It is to such an investigation that this introductory chapter is intended to contribute.

At the centre of my inquiry will be the ways in which contemporaries understood the two concepts of 'empire' and 'union'. Not only was there more than one understanding of each; the concepts themselves were closely associated with others in current usage. The development of the concept of empire in particular was complicated by the existence of the – Holy Roman – Empire, an association which encouraged the elaboration of a synonym, 'universal monarchy', to convey the more general idea of rule over extensive territory.[6] Meanwhile 'empire' itself continued to be used in another, apparently contrary sense, to indicate the autonomy of individual kingdoms. I shall argue none the less that the two ideas shared a common emphasis on the territorial extent of a monarch's authority, and further that they were associated with a specific idea of union as 'incorporation' under one ruling head. This association of ideas crystallised during the first half of the sixteenth century, under the monarchies of Charles V and Henry VIII, and provided the conceptual framework for the Anglo-Scottish Union debate initiated by James VI and I in the opening decade of the seventeenth century.

From the 1620s, however, this pattern of ideas was to be shaken by new developments in political thinking, developments which altered and enlarged contemporaries' understanding of the concepts of empire and union. There emerged a new doctrine of pre-emptive defence and legitimate conquest, yielding an approach to union considerably more aggressive than that hitherto associated with the idea of universal monarchy. On the other hand, there also emerged a second, rival concept of union, understood as a confederation of more or less equal states. By contrast with the idea of incorporating union, confederal union was represented as antagonistic to extensive territorial empire.[7] As the case of

[5] Elliot, 'A Europe of composite monarchies', pp. 48–50, 52–4.

[6] Study of the idea of universal monarchy has until now been almost exclusively the preserve of German scholars (who should be exempted from Elliott's strictures): most recently: Franz Bosbach, *Monarchia Universalis. Ein politischer Leitbegriff der frühen Neuzeit* (Göttingen, 1988).

[7] This too has long been a subject of interest to German scholars. Perhaps the best-known German student of federalism is Otto Gierke (1841–1921): in English are *Natural Law and the Theory of Society 1500–1800*, trans. Ernest Barker, 2 vols. (Cambridge, 1934), and *Community in Historical Perspective*, trans. Mary Fischer, ed. Antony Black (Cambridge, 1990). But see now also: Reinhart Koselleck, 'Bund, Bündnis, Föderalismus, Bundesstaat', in Otto Brunner, Werner Conze and Reinhart Koselleck (eds.), *Geschichtliche Grundbegriffe. Historisches Lexicon zur politisch-sozialen Sprache in Deutschland*, vol. I: A–D (Stuttgart, 1972).

the United Provinces demonstrated, however, confederal union was not thereby incompatible with another, novel, concept of the empire, that of the empire of the seas, pursuit of which might be distinguished from the territorial ambition of universal monarchy. Thus by the time that the Scots and the English returned to the issue of the union, in the last decade of the seventeenth century and the first of the eighteenth, the interrelation of ideas of empire and union had been both reinforced and opened to new and divergent interpretations. The debate which preceded the Union of 1707 will be understood only if it is recognised as an outcome of an already long and complex discussion of the place of empire and union in the European political order.

II

The Monarchy of Charles V recast the mould of European politics. Modern historians may wish to emphasise the limits upon the effective exercise of his authority, but Charles himself, his advisers, alarmed contemporaries and later, more impartial observers (up to Montesquieu and Hume in the mid eighteenth century) had no doubt that the sheer extent of his inheritance made possible monarchy on a scale not seen since the Roman Empire. What Charles could not do was entitle the Monarchy as a whole an 'Empire'. Election as Holy Roman Emperor in 1519 rounded off his inheritance, but his other kingdoms, Castile at their head, insisted that the Imperial title would not have precedence in their territories. Limits on his use of the title, however, did not prevent Charles and his supporters from exploiting the universal associations of the Roman idea of empire.[8]

The image of Charles as a Roman emperor was variously portrayed. The biographical *Istoria Imperial y Cesarea* (1547) by the Spanish historian Pedro Mexia (subsequently translated as *The Imperiall History: or Lives of the Emperors, from Julius Caesar, the First Founder of the Roman Monarchy* (1623)) cast Charles V as the direct successor of the Roman Emperors.[9] Titian's great equestrian portrait of Charles after Muhlberg in the same year made the identical point, with rather more style. Well before then, as John Headley has argued, the Imperial Chancellor Gattinara had been making sophisticated political use of the Roman imperial model. Forced to abandon his early belief that Roman

[8] Frances Yates, *Astraea. The Imperial Theme in the Sixteenth Century* (London, 1975, pbk repr. of 1985), part I: 'Charles V and the idea of empire'.

[9] Pedro Mexia, *Istoria Imperial y Cesarea* (1547), trans. as *The Imperiall History: Or Lives of the Emperors, from Julius Caesar, the First Founder of the Roman Monarchy*, translation by W.T., corrected by Edward Grimeston (London, 1623).

Law would provide a single, universal basis for Charles' authority, Gattinara had adapted the Roman idea of 'client kingdoms' to accommodate individual states within an imperial framework.[10] Most evocative of all, however, was Charles's choice of emblem, the ship sailing beyond the Columns of Hercules, with the motto *'plus ultra'*: testimony to an ambition even more universal than the Roman.

Charles V was also the beneficiary of the recent revival of another imperial tradition, that forged in the great conflict between the Holy Roman Emperor and the Papacy. This might be a conflict in which few Emperors had gained the advantage; simply by joining the conflict, however, they had continued to associate their title with the pretension to universal authority, eliciting such powerful intellectual supports as Dante's *Monarchia*. In the fifteenth century, moreover, Empire and Papacy had temporarily made common cause against the 'national' monarchies and the Conciliar Movement. From this convergence had come a 'dualist' case for the universal authority of Emperor and Pope, as in the *Monarchia* (*c.*1430–43) of Antonio Roselli, who borrowed many of Dante's arguments, and in the still more enthusiastic imperialism of Roselli's pupil, Aeneas Sylvius Piccolomini, later Pope Pius II.[11] By the early sixteenth century Papal publicists such as Cajetan once again had the confidence to proclaim their master's supreme authority.[12] But the dualist argument continued to enjoy support, being restated in Spain in 1525, in the *Catholicum Opus Imperiale Regiminis Mundi* of Michael of Ulcurrunus.[13] More aggressively, Gattinara encouraged renewed interest in Dante's *Monarchia*, and there were publicists at Charles V's court who would justify even the Sack of Rome in 1527.[14] Prophecy offered a further

[10] John M. Headley, 'The Habsburg world empire and the revival of Ghibellinism', *Mediaevul and Renaissance Studies* (Chapel Hill, 1978), pp. 93–127.
For accounts of the Romans' own understanding of their '*imperium*': Richard Koebner, *Empire* (Cambridge, 1961), pp. 1–17; and Andrew Lintott, 'What was the '*Imperium Romanorum*'?', *Greece and Rome*, 28, 1, (1981), 53–67. Koebner's pioneering account of the history of the concept of 'empire' was, unfortunately, thinnest in relation to the period covered by this chapter.

[11] J.H. Burns, *Lordship, Kingship and Empire. The Idea of Monarchy 1400–1525* (Oxford, 1992), ch. 5, 'Monarchy: Papacy and empire'. Roselli's *Monarchia* was first printed in 1487, and republished in Germany in 1611, in a collection of texts which served as sources for the seventeenth-century debate over the Imperial constitution. Piccolomini's *De ortu et authoritate Romani Imperii* is dated to 1446.

[12] Burns, *Lordship, Kingship, and Empire*, pp. 138–45; Paolo Prodi, *The Papal Prince. One Body and Two Souls: The Papal Monarchy in Early Modern Europe*, trans. Susan Haskins (Cambridge, 1987), p. 24.

[13] Diana Perry, ' "*Catholicum Opus Imperiale Regiminis Mundi*" . An early sixteenth-century restatement of Empire', *History of Political Thought*, 2, 2, (1981).

[14] Headley, 'Habsburg world empire', pp. 104–7; J.A. Fernandez-Santamaria, *The State, War and Peace. Spanish Political Thought in the Renaissance 1516–1559* (Cambridge, 1977), pp. 38–49; Marcel Bataillon, *Erasme et L'Espagne* (Paris, 1937), ch. 5.

justification for universal pretensions. Gattinara set the idea of a crusade against the Turk in this perspective in the 1530s;[15] but it was most fully developed in the work of the Lutheran Johann Sleidan, whose *Quattuor summis imperiis* (1556) cast the Empire as the harbinger of the Fifth Monarchy foretold in *Daniel*.[16] The willingness of even the Lutherans to accept the Empire's universal mission offers powerful testimony to its continued appeal. By exploiting anew the universal associations of the imperial idea, in both its Roman and its Christian forms, Charles V and his publicists re-established its identification with the exercise of authority over extended territory: if the concept of empire, *imperium*, was itself no longer used exclusively in this sense, that of 'universal monarchy' became its recognised synonym.[17]

Significant as this reaffirmation of the idea of empire would be, it may be thought to have been offset by the simultaneous consolidation of another usage of the concept, that embodied in the phrase '*rex in regno suo est imperator in regno suo*'. Of twelfth-century origin, and often coupled with another, '*rex qui superiorem non recognoscit*', the phrase had been deployed since the thirteenth century by the Kings of France and Naples in particular at the expense of the Emperor's authority. By the late fifteenth century many of Europe's monarchies, including the Scottish, had claimed for themselves the status of an imperial crown. But the most resonant statement of the claim was still to come, in 1533. In the words of the preamble to the Act in Restraint of Appeals:

> Where by dyvers sundrie old autentike histories and cronicles it is manifestly declared and expressed that this Realme of Englond is an Impire, and so hath ben accepted in the worlde, governed by oon supreme heede and King having the dignitie and roiall estate of the Imperiall Crowne of the same, unto whom a Body politike, compacte of all sortes and degrees of people . . . ben bounden and owen to bere next to God a naturall and humble obedience.[18]

That these few words were sufficient to give the idea of empire a lasting place in English political thinking is not in doubt; less clear, perhaps, is what that idea signified. The common view is that this was a straightforward declaration of national sovereignty, and further, by virtue of its inclusion in a statute, of parliamentary participation in that sovereignty. Recent

[15] Headley, 'Habsburg world empire', pp. 114–15.

[16] J. Sleidan, *Quattuor summis imperiis* (1556).

[17] On the promotion of Charles V as a universal monarch: Bosbach, *Monarchia Universalis*, ch. 3: 'Die Universalmonarchie Karls V'.

[18] *An Acte that the Appeles in suche cases as have ben used to be pursued to the See of Rome shall not be from hensforth had ne used but wythin this Realme* (1533: 24 Henry VIII, c. 12), in *The Statutes of the Realm*, vol. III (1817), p. 427.

studies of the Act's intellectual genesis suggest, however, that the matter was considerably more complicated.

A number of strands of contemporary 'imperial' thinking can be identified in the preamble. One, elucidated by Walter Ullmann, was the Roman Law argument that since the *ecclesia* had been constituted by authority of the Emperor, his *imperium* rightly extended to all ecclesiastical matters.[19] When this claim seemed insufficient, Henry VIII's advisers turned to a second, native source of imperial inspiration: the historic pretension of the English Monarchy to exercise rule by lordship or conquest over others, and in particular over Scotland and Ireland. Coupled with the supposition of England's historic independence from papal jurisdication, Graham Nicholson has suggested, it was these territorial claims which informed the anglicising of the formula '*Rex est imperator in regno suo*'.[20] Thus while the claim of empire was designed to exclude the jurisdiction of the Pope, and, by extension, of the Emperor, it did not entail a repudiation of the 'universal' associations of imperial authority.[21] To the contrary, the preamble implied a reassertion of the English Crown's ambition to extend its territorial authority at the expense of its neighbours.

A further dimension to the language of the Act of Appeals underlines the territorial aspect of empire. The realm of England was also characterised as a 'body politic'. This concept too had strong mediaeval roots. It was a term which evoked both the religious imagery of the *corpus mysticum* (an imagery exploited by jurists no less than by theologians) and the more strictly juridical attributes of the corporation.[22] In the fifteenth century, J.H. Burns has argued, it had become central to discussions of monarchy. It underlay Sir John Fortescue's distinction between *dominium regale* and *dominium politicum et regale*, permitting him to accommodate parliament as an organ of the body politic of which the king was the head. But the concept had other implications besides, as both Fortescue and contemporary French theorists appreciated. The image of the body naturally placed a

19 Walter Ullmann, 'This Realm of England is an Empire', *Journal of Ecclesiastical History*, 30, 2 (1979), 175–203.

20 Graham Nicholson, 'The Act of Appeals and the English Reformation', in C. Cross, D. Loades and J.J. Scarisbrick (eds.), *Law and Government under the Tudors* (Cambridge, 1988); also John Guy, 'Thomas Cromwell and the intellectual origins of the Henrician Revolution', in A. Fox and J. Guy, *Reassessing the Henrician Age* (Oxford, 1986).

21 See J.P. Canning, 'Law, sovereignty and corporation theory, 1300–1450', in J.H. Burns (ed.), *The Cambridge History of Medieval Political Thought* c.350–c.1450 (Cambridge, 1988), pp. 464–73, on the possibility of distinguishing the claim to be an emperor in one's kingdom from the claim not to acknowledge a superior.

22 Ernst Kantorowicz, *The King's Two Bodies. A Study in Medieval Political Theology* (Princeton, 1957); J.P. Canning, 'Law, sovereignty and corporation theory', in *Cambridge History of Medieval Political Thought*, pp. 473–6.

premium on the unity of the realm: a monarchy ought to be 'incorporating'.[23] If therefore the realm was an empire as well as a body politic, as the Act of Appeals proclaimed in the case of England, it would seem to follow that such a realm should incorporate the territories over which it exercised imperial authority. Through the concept of the body politic, in short, empire was drawn into association with union by incorporation.

In the event neither the Scots nor the Irish had to wait long to feel the consequences of such thinking. To the Irish, Henry and his advisers carefully spelt out their understanding of the logic of his imperial status. By the Act of the Irish Parliament which in 1541 elevated Henry from Lord to King, the crown of Ireland was itself declared to be imperial, but one none the less 'united and knit to the imperiall crown of England'.[24] A year later the Scots were treated more bluntly, their (rather older) claim to possess an imperial crown being swept aside by a renewed declaration of the English King's claim to superiority – and hence, implicitly, to a superior 'empire'. Explicit, aggressive use of imperial rhetoric was then made by Somerset, in pursuit of a dynastic union between Edward VI and Mary Stuart. The idea had some enthusiastic Scottish supporters, but to many more it seemed a cover for the traditional English pretension to superiority.[25] Elizabeth eschewed imperial designs upon Scotland (having to be cajoled into limited intervention by Cecil) – but endorsed them in Ireland, where settlement schemes were likened to Roman colonisations.[26] More generally, as Frances Yates demonstrated in her classic study, the Queen and her image-makers proved themselves to be imaginative exponents of the imperial theme. Elizabeth might herself prefer to be cast as Astraea, the virgin goddess whose return to the world heralded the fifth and final age of empire, an age of union and peace. But the original theme of independence from the Papacy was renewed by Protestant apologists, while others made free use of the columnar device of Charles V to assert a pretension to independent maritime empire.[27]

[23] J.H. Burns, 'Fortescue and the political theory of *Dominium*', *Historical Journal*, 28 (1985); *Lordship, Kingship and Empire*, ch. 3: 'Lordship and Kingship: France and England' – a discussion to which this paper is greatly indebted.

[24] M. Perceval-Maxwell, 'Ireland and the monarchy in the early Stuart multiple Kingdom', *Historical Journal*, 34, 2 (1991), p. 280.

[25] For the claim against the Scots: *A Declaration, conteynyng the iust causes and consyderations, of this present warre with the Scottis, wherein also appereth the trewe and right title, that the Kinges most royall majesty hath to the soverayntie of Scotlande* (1542), repr. in J.A.H. Murray (ed.), *The Complaynt of Scotland* (London, for the Early English Text Society, 1882), pp. 191–206, and set in context by Roger A. Mason, 'The Scottish Reformation and the origins of Anglo-British imperialism', in Roger A. Mason (ed.), *Scots and Britons: Scottish Political Thought and the Union of 1603* (Cambridge, 1994), pp. 168–70.

[26] Mason, 'The Scottish Reformation and the origins of Anglo-British imperialism' p. 181; Nicholas Canny, *Kingdom and Colony. Ireland in the Atlantic World 1560–1800* (Baltimore and London, 1988), chs. 1–2.

[27] Yates, *Astraea*, part II: 'The Tudor Imperial Reform'.

A similar exploitation of the imperial idea, Yates also observed, was occurring in late sixteenth-century France. Represented between columns as the Gallic Hercules in the age of Astraea, Henri IV posed as the reconciler of Europe; and his minister Sully prepared his 'Grand Dessein' by which the French Monarchy would guarantee this peaceful new order. Behind these professions of pacific intent, however, might be thought to lie more familiar universal pretensions. With the title *Rex Christianissimus,* and a descent from Charlemagne, King of the Franks before he had had himself crowned Emperor, the King of France had an older and better claim to universal monarchy than any so far mustered by a King or Queen of England. His assassination may have left Henri IV's own intentions unclear; but his Bourbon heirs left no doubt which of the two French imperial traditions was to be taken more seriously.[28]

It is none the less a mistake to suppose – as Yates appears to have done – that the mantle of empire had simply been passed from Charles V to the national monarchies of England and France. There was no doubt among contemporary observers, in these countries and throughout Europe, that the leading imperial power of the age, the current aspirant to universal monarchy, was one of the two monarchies between which Charles V had divided the Habsburg inheritance: specifically, the Spanish Monarchy of Philip II. Even if the Spanish Habsburgs scrupulously avoided any pretension to the title of Emperor, out of respect for their Austrian cousins, their publicists readily exploited the universal associations of the imperial idea.

One of these was Giovanni Botero, the Piedmontese ex-Jesuit whose *Della Ragion di Stato* (1589) gave its name to a genre of political writing that in the early seventeenth century became particularly asssociated with Catholic monarchies.[29] Deliberately reversing Machiavelli's order of preference, Botero put the preservation of states, *'il conservare',* before conquest, *'l'aggrandire'* – a choice clearly more suited to the circumstances of the Spanish Monarchy in the later sixteenth century.[30] Botero also suggested that 'disunited' states were not necessarily at a disadvantage compared to those whose territories were joined together. Unity might

[28] Yates, *Astraea*, part III: 'The French Monarchy'; Maximilian de Bethune, Duc de Sully, *Memoires ou Oeconomies Royales d'Estat Domestiques, Politiques et Militaires de Henry le Grand* (Paris, 1644), IV, pp. 57–89, esp. pp. 77–89; 'Discours sur les Magnifiques Desseins du Roy Henry le Grand'. Sully characterised his new European order as 'cette Republique Monarchie Tres-Chrestienne' (p. 79).

[29] Robert Bireley, *The Counter-Reformation Prince. Anti-Machiavellianism or Catholic Statecraft in early modern Europe* (Chapel Hill and London, 1990).

[30] Giovanni Botero, *Della Ragion di Stato* (1589), Bk I, ch. 5, edn of Luigi Firpo (Turin, 1948), pp. 58–60, trans. by P.J. and D.P. Waley as *The Reason of State* (London, 1956), pp. 5–7. On the appropriateness of the theme: J.H. Elliott, 'Foreign policy and domestic crisis: Spain 1598–1659', in his *Spain and its World 1500–1700* (New Haven and London, 1989), p. 114.

give strength to an empire (*imperio*), but it also rendered it more vulnerable to corruption. By contrast if the parts of an '*imperio disunito*' could stand separately, and assist each other, the empire might be as strong as if it were united. As an example, Botero pointed to '*Il Dominio di Spagna*', whose separate states formed an empire joined by the sea.[31]

A separate *Relationi del Mare* (1598) clarified the importance which Botero attached to the sea. Distinguishing between 'oceans' and 'Mediterraneans' (the latter being defined as great lakes joined to oceans by a Straits of Gibraltar), Botero pointed to the situation of the Mediterranean between Africa, Asia and Europe, and to its concentration of cities and traffic, as the explanation for Europe's leadership of the rest of the world in commerce.[32] This suggests a view of the Spanish Monarchy as founding its empire primarily upon a Mediterranean base – a view in line with the priority which Botero attached to unifying Europe to meet the threat from the infidel Turk.[33]

Botero's preference for '*il conservare*' did not mean that he ignored conquest. Recognising that it occurred, he recommended means to consolidate authority over territories so acquired, and particularly recommended a policy of assimilation, such as the Romans had offered the Albans and the Sabines. An instance from modern times was provided by the Poles, whose '*imperio*' had been enlarged by their having incorporated ('*incorporato*') the territories of their foreign-born monarchs into the Crown of Poland.[34] The physical unity of a monarchy's parts might not be essential to its preservation; but in a case of conquest it was none the less desirable that the territories be juridically 'incorporated' within the monarchy's empire.

The case for the Spanish Monarchy was put still more aggressively by the Neapolitan Tommaso Campanella. Mixing reason of state with astrology and imperial prophecy, his *Monarchia di Spagna* (composed 1600 – 1) was the least inhibited of proposals for a universal monarchy in Europe.[35] Perhaps because it was too aggressive, however, Campanella's

[31] Botero, *Della Ragion di Stato*, Bk I, chs 7, 8, pp. 63–8; *Reason of State*, pp. 9–13.

[32] Giovanni Botero, *Relationi del Mare*, in *Aggiunte di Gio. Botero benese alla sua Ragion di Stato* (Pavia, 1598), pp. 81–95. Other examples of 'Mediterraneans' were the Baltic, Red, Caspian and Persian Seas.

[33] Richard Tuck, *Philosophy and Government 1572–1651* (Cambridge, 1993), pp. 65–7.

[34] Botero, *Della Ragion di Stato*, Bk V, chs 1, 7; Bk VIII, chs 6, 7, 18, pp. 175–9, 190–5, 255–8, 268; *Reason of State*, pp. 95–8, 107–8, 157–8, 167.

[35] Tommaso Campanella, 'Della Monarchia di Spagna' (1600–1), published in German in 1620 (see below, note 47), in Latin as *De Monarchia Hispanica* (Amsterdam, 1640), and in English as *A Discourse touching the Spanish Monarchy*, [trans. Edmund Chilmead] (London, 1654; repr. 1660 with a Preface by William Prynne); on the composition and publication of the work, L. Firpo, *Bibliografia degli scritti di Tommaso Campanella* (Turin, 1940), pp. 56–67, is indispensable. Recent studies are: Anthony Pagden, 'Campanella and the universal monarchy of Spain', in his *Spanish Imperialism and the*

work did not find official favour, and remained unpublished for twenty years; in its own kingdoms, that of Naples not least, the acceptability of the Monarchy continued to lie in its willingness to respect local privileges. The point, as Elliott has observed, was rendered with particular clarity by the Castilian jurist Juan de Solórzano Pereira, when he described the European kingdoms of the Monarchy as forming a union of equals, *aeque principaliter*.[36] But the jurist made this concession the better to insist upon the primacy of Castilian authority in the Indies. In the *De Indiarum Iure* (1629), and again in the *Política Indiana* (1647), Solórzano Pereira expressly characterised the Indies as 'provinces', 'united and incorporated' by accession to the Crown of Castile. If it had to be acknowledged that the Indies had originally been granted to Castile by Papal donation, this did not mean that they were held on the same terms of vassalage as the Kingdom of Naples.[37] Solórzano Pereira used the term *imperium* only occasionally in relation to the Monarchy, but 'province' had obvious imperial associations, and was now explicitly connected to the idea of union by incorporation. Out in the Indies, at least, ideas of empire and incorporating union could be regarded as correlative. As we shall now see, the point was not lost on contemporary European observers, despite the Spanish Monarchy's continued profession of very different principles as the basis of its rule within Europe.

III

The association of the ideas of empire and union by incorporation was a prominent feature of the first Anglo-Scottish Union debate, initiated by James VI of Scotland on his accession to the thrones of England and Ireland in 1603. James entered his long-awaited inheritance with a strong sense that a mere dynastic union must be consolidated if it was to last, and with clear views of his own as to how to achieve this. As he lost no time in telling his first English Parliament, in March 1604, only an incorporating union made sense. Joined as they were by nature, religion, language and manners, the two Kingdoms of Scotland and England – Ireland had no part in his proposal – ought to regard themselves as one wife to James as their husband, one body to the King their head – for surely no reasonable man would wish James to be a polygamist, or to have a divided and monstrous body. Where the Saxon Kingdoms had been united by

Political Imagination (New Haven and London, 1990), and Tuck, *Philosophy and Government*, pp. 69–72.

[36] Juan de Solórzano y Pereira, *Política Indiana* (1647, Madrid, 1972), Bk IV, ch. xix, s. 37. Elliott, 'Composite monarchies', pp. 52–3.

[37] Johannes de Solórzano Pereira, *Disputationem de Indiarum Jure* (Madrid, 1629), Bk III, ss. 46, 47, 67; *Política Indiana*, Bk V, ch. xvi, s. 12.

Bellona, he added, this would be a peaceful union, fastened by the ring of Astraea.[38] When he returned to the matter in 1607, James again argued in corporeal terms, for one body under his headship. But having in the meantime encountered English opposition, James now emphasised that such a union would be tantamount to a peaceful conquest of Scotland by England, since the latter would always be the seat of the Court and government. Only the English should not treat Scotland 'like a naked province': 'I hope you meane not I should set Garrisons over them, as the Spaniards doe over Sicily and Naples, or governe them by Commissioners . . .'. Avoid this, and the union would 'advance the greatnesse of your Empire seated here in England', providing security against both 'intestine Rebellion' and enemies abroad.[39] Among those enemies was of course the Papacy; but although James would show himself as defiantly imperial towards papal pretensions as any Tudor, he clearly wished to distinguish the ecclesiological from the territorial connotations of the term. It should be possible to join two imperial crowns without subordinating one kingdom to the other. As James presented it, union by incorporation would be the basis of a British empire, but the empire he had in mind was an empire of peace, an empire without a province.

The responses to James's proposal ranged from the enthusiastic to the obstructive, and indicate a wider spectrum of conceptions of union's relation to empire. Prominent among the enthusiastic were Francis Bacon and Sir Thomas Craig, both of whom viewed the union as an opportunity for empire in a more expansive sense. In an early contribution to the debate, Bacon drew a distinction between unions '*compositio*' and '*mistio*'. Composite unions, in which the political bodies remained separate under one sovereignty, were the more usual; but the late revolt of Aragon in defence of its liberties had demonstrated their vulnerability. Much happier, therefore, were mixed unions, by which political bodies were joined under a new form. To Bacon there had been no better exponents of such unions than the Romans, who had freely naturalised all with whom they had incorporated. Just as in nature the greater draws the lesser, so had the Romans united with the Sabines, and so should England unite with Scotland.[40] Anglo-Scottish union would in turn be the prelude to the plantation of Ireland, and hence the union of all three of James's

[38] James I, 'A Speach . . . delivered . . . on Monday the xix day of March 1604, being the First Day of the First Parliament', in C.H. McIlwain (ed.), *The Political Works of James I* (Harvard, 1918, repr. New York, 1965), pp. 269–80.

[39] 'A Speach to both the Houses of Parliament, the last day of March 1607', in McIlwain (ed.), *Political Works of James I*, pp. 290–305.

[40] Francis Bacon, *A Brief Discourse of the Happy Union Betwixt the two Kingdoms of Scotland and England* (1702), in *The Works of Francis Bacon*, ed. J. Spedding, R.L. Ellis and D.N. Heath (London, 1857–74), X: *The Letters and the Life*, III, pp. 90–9.

kingdoms, 'such a trefoil as no prince except yourself (who are worthiest) weareth in his crown . . .'.[41] Later Bacon was to elaborate the implications of this conception of union in still more expansive terms in the essay 'Of the true Greatnesse of Kingdomes and Estates', endorsing Machiavelli's idea of empire as increase, and expressing particular admiration for the imperial prowess of the Spaniard.[42]

Still more was made of the Spanish example by Thomas Craig in his *De Unione Regnorum Britanniae Tractatus* (1605). *Hispaniae Regnum* was explicitly characterised as an *Imperium*, the most powerful in existence. As such, it was the model to be followed by Britain. By fusing the two *regna* of Scotland and England, each with its *jura majestatis*, into *unius Regis imperium*, Craig argued, the British would achieve a union truly *incorporationis*. This would be the case even if, as in the Spanish Monarchy, or in the Polish – Lithuanian Union, there was no union of the two kingdoms' laws: while Craig believed that their common basis in feudal law ought to facilitate their assimilation, it was not a necessary condition of an incorporating, imperial union. Likewise, Craig saw no reason why the creation of *unum Regnum et Imperium* should be incompatible with the retention of the two kingdoms' separate offices. Like James, Craig urged the English to recognise that they would gain much more by such a union than if they conquered Scotland; but he was convinced that it would be equally to Scotland's advantage to be part of an imperial British Monarchy. United, Britain had the potential to be at least as formidable as *Hispanicum Imperium* itself.[43]

Not all responses to James's proposal were as sanguine as this. Many Scots feared that the Union would reduce their kingdom to 'ane pendicle' of England, endangering the liberties on which its own 'impyir' depended.[44] Two ways of avoiding that fate were canvassed. One was to

[41] Francis Bacon, *Certain Considerations touching the Plantation in Ireland* (1606/9), in *Works*, XI: *Letters and Life*, IV, pp. 114–26, quotation on p. 114. Bacon crowned this flattery by adding 'for indeed unions and plantations are the very nativities or birthdays of kingdoms' (p. 116).

[42] Francis Bacon, 'Of the true Greatnesse of Kingdomes and Estates', *Works*, VI, pp. 444–52; Recent studies of Bacon's treatment of empire are J.H. Martin, *Francis Bacon, the State and the Reform of Natural Philosophy* (Cambridge, 1992) esp. pp. 129–40; and Markku Peltonen, 'Politics and science: Francis Bacon and the greatness of states', *Historical Journal*, 35, 2 (1992).

[43] Sir Thomas Craig, *De Unione Regnorum Britanniae Tractatus* (1605), ed. and trans. C. Sanford Terry, *Scottish History Society*, vol. LX (Edinburgh, 1909): pp. 40–2 (Latin), 261–2 (English), 57–9 (Latin), 283–5 (English), 73 (Latin), 303 (English), 139–55 esp. 153 (Latin), 390–411 esp. 408 (English), pp. 170–93 (Latin), pp. 431–60 (English).

[44] John Russell, 'A Treatise of the Happie and Blissed Union' (1604), in *The Jacobean Union. Six Tracts of 1604*, edited B.R. Galloway and B.P. Levack for the *Scottish History Society*, Fourth Series, vol. XXI (Edinburgh, 1985), pp. 89–91, 97. A similar sentiment was expressed by the Scottish Estates, when in August 1607 it responded to reports of

ensure that political union was accompanied by complete religious and ecclesiastical union, on Scottish terms. Later the object of the Solemn League and Covenant, this was advocated at the time by millenarian mathematician Robert Pont.[45] The other was to settle for what an anonymous commentator termed an 'imperfect incorporation', such as the Romans had agreed with the Tuscans, and the Poles with the Lithuanians. While stopping short of what was imposed upon the vanquished Sabines, this ought to be sufficient to secure a common naturalisation, and hence access to each other's commerce, without sacrificing the two kingdoms' separate laws and customs.[46]

Justification for these Scottish apprehensions was provided by the response of most English commentators. English obstruction of James's proposals, it should be emphasised, was not all gratuitous. As the well-informed Sir Henry Savile pointed out, a dynastic union was unlikely to be perpetual: successful unions required a stronger basis, such as could only be provided by conquest, or by the authority of a parliament. 'For . . . I am of opinion', he wrote, 'that by the authority of the parliament with us, or an assembly of estates elsewhere, a state inferiour may be inseparably united to his superiour.'[47] More directly, this was to say that England already possessed the authority to impose union upon Scotland; and until union was accepted on English terms, there was no reason to compromise existing English liberties. Implicitly aligning the Henrician claim of empire with parliament as much as with the crown, Savile and the English parliamentarians held out for a union that would simply incorporate Scotland into an English empire.[48]

James's speech to the English parliament by advising him that:

> . . . we nevir meant . . . to except aganis onie confounding as it wer of these two befoir separated kingdomes in one glorious monarchie and impyre of the whole Yle, but onlie that this your Majesteis antient and native Kingdome sould not be so disordourit and made confusit by turneing of it, in place of a trew and freindlie Unioun, into a conquered and slavish province to be governed by a Viceroy or Deputye, lyke suche of the King of Spaynes provinceis as your Majestie in your Heynes said speech maid mentioun of.

in *The Register of the Privy Council of Scotland: Vol VII 1604–1607* (Edinburgh, 1885), pp. 535–6.

45 Robert Pont, 'Of the Union of Britayne' (1604), in *The Jacobean Union*, pp. 1–38; on Pont see Arthur H. Williamson, 'Number and national consciousness: the Edinburgh Mathematicians and Scottish political culture at the union of the crowns', in Mason (ed.), *Scots and Britons* pp. 193–7.

46 'A Treatise about the Union of England and Scotland, to King James the 1st' (1604), in *The Jacobean Union*, pp. 39–74, esp. 56–61.

47 Sir Henry Savile, 'Historicall Collections left to be considerd of, for the better perfecting of this intended union between England and Scotland' (1604), in *The Jacobean Union*, p. 193.

48 As Conrad Russell points out, 'The Anglo-Scottish Union 1603–1643: a success?' in A. Fletcher and P. Roberts (eds.), *Religion, Culture and Society in Early Modern Britain: Essays in Honour of Patrick Collinson* (Cambridge, 1994), the clear implication of this position was that there had been no union at all in 1603. See also: Jenny Wormald,

IV

The political and intellectual horizons of the Jacobean Union debate were those of the era of Spanish hegemony. That era came to an abrupt end after 1618, in the protracted conflicts which resulted from the challenge to Habsburg authority in Bohemia, and the lapsing of the Twelve Years' Truce between the Spanish Crown and the rebel United Provinces. At first, in the 1620s, the Habsburgs held their ground, intellectually as well as militarily. Campanella's *Monarchia di Spagna* was finally translated and published in Germany, probably by Besold, even as Imperial and Spanish armies were driving James's son-in-law Frederick Palatine from his Kingdom and his Electorate.[49] From 1630, however, both the course of the war and the discussion of empire were summarily transformed by the intervention of a new and unanticipated belligerent, the Vasa Monarchy of Sweden.

Veiled behind almost two centuries of modern Swedish neutrality, the devastating impact and predatory opportunism of the Vasa Monarchy are still too easily missed. Hugh Trevor-Roper has drawn attention to the ruthless taste with which the Swedish armies plundered the artistic wealth of Habsburg Europe, culminating in the gratuitous looting of Prague in 1648.[50] But there has been no comparable study of the intellectual world of Vasa aggression, even though the dynasty was as determined in its head-hunting of philosophers as it was in its plundering of the arts. What can be identified are two very different lines of justification for Swedish aggression; their inconsistency may be regarded as characteristic of Vasa opportunism.

One source of inspiration on which the Vasas were always happy to draw was the national identity myth, which cast the Swedes as descendents of the Goths, who in turn stemmed from the earliest people of the Bible.[51] Among the most ambitious exponents of this idea, it seems, was Gustav Adolf's tutor Johann Bure, or Bureus. His writings set runic and linguistic scholarship to work to render the Gothic origin myth compatible

'The creation of Britain: multiple kingdoms or core and colonies?', *Transactions of the Royal Historical Society*, Sixth Series, II (1992); Bruce Galloway, *The Union of England and Scotland 1603–1608* (Edinburgh, 1986), esp. pp. 30–57, 93–136; and Levack, *The Formation of the British State*, esp. pp. 31–48, 51–8.

[49] Thomas Campanella, *Von der spanischen Monarchy* (Frankfurt, 1620 and 1623); on these German editions: Firpo, *Ricerche Campanelliane*, pp. 56–67.

[50] Hugh Trevor-Roper, *The Plunder of the Arts in the Seventeenth Century* (London, 1970), pp. 40–51, reprinted in his *From Counter-Reformation to Glorious Revolution* (London, 1992), pp. 125–7.

[51] Michael Roberts, *The Swedish Imperial Experience 1560–1720* (Cambridge, 1979), pp. 70–5; and B. Ankarloo, 'Europe and the glory of Sweden: the emergence of a Swedish self-image in the early seventeenth century', in Goran Rystad (ed.), *Europe and Scandinavia. Aspects of the Process of Integration in the Seventeenth Century* (Lund, 1983), pp. 237–44.

with the prophetic framework of Daniel's Four Monarchies, and to present the Vasas as the heirs to the *translatio imperium* by which the Goths had succeeded the Romans.[52]

When the exigencies of policy-making while on campaign demanded arguments more likely to make an immediate impression on German foes and allies, however, Gustav Adolf could turn for justification to a quite different, and on the face of it improbable, authority: Hugo Grotius' *De Jure Belli ac Pacis* (1625). The received picture of Grotius is of course that of the peace-maker; and it is true that he ended this work with an admonition to preserve peace.[53] It is also true that Grotius rejected as grounds for just war the very arguments which Bureus found so compelling: the pursuit of universal empire, and the call to fulfil biblical prophecies.[54] But elsewhere in Grotius's discussion of what constitutes a just war, and of what is permissible in such a war, Gustav Adolf had no difficulty finding other grounds to justify his actions. For in identifying war between sovereigns with the conflict of individuals in the state of nature, Grotius had made two critical concessions. He construed the right of self-defence as extending to pre-emptive action, and he admitted a right to exact punishment.[55] Once a just war had been initiated, moreover, Grotius allowed that it might be pursued until the enemy had been conquered, his property taken, and the conquered people absorbed by the victors.[56] Grotius did urge clemency towards the conquered: the example to be followed was that of the Romans, who had admitted their former enemies the Albans, the Sabines and the Latins to membership of the *civitas*.[57] In the case of the Sabines in particular Grotius believed that there had been a *de jure* union, with a full communication of rights between the two peoples.[58] But it remained clear that that union was the result of conquest: in context, the mutual communication of rights appears as no more than a wise concession by the victors to the

[52] Johannes Bureus (1568–1652) is mentioned by Roberts, *Swedish Imperial Experiences*, pp. 72–3, and is discussed at various points in Susanna Åkerman, *Queen Christina of Sweden and her Circle. The Transformation of a Seventeenth-Century Philosophical Libertine* (Leiden, 1991), pp. 92–3, 114, 198.

[53] Hugo Grotius, *De Jure Belli ac Pacis Libri Tres* (1625), Bk III, ch. xxv. In the series *Classics of International Law, Carnegie Endowment for International Peace*, 2 vols. (Oxford, 1925): vol. I: the 1646 edition; vol. II: trans. F.W. Kelsey.

[54] *De Jure Belli*, II, xxii, 13–15.

[55] *De Jure Belli*, II, i, 2, 16; the implications of these concessions have been pointed up by Richard Tuck, *Sorry Comforters. Political Thought and the International Order from Grotius to Kant* (Oxford, forthcoming).

[56] *De Jure Belli*, III, iv–viii. It was these arguments that Gustav Adolf found particularly helpful when negotiating under pressure on campaign in Germany: Michael Roberts, 'The political objectives of Gustavus Adolphus in Germany 1630–32', in his *Essays in Swedish History* (London, 1967), p. 95.

[57] *De Jure Belli*, III, xv, 3.

[58] *De Jure Belli*, II, ix, 9.

vanquished. Not since Machiavelli had conquest been justified so aggressively: Grotius had certainly earned his reward of appointment in 1635 as Swedish ambassador to the Court of France.[59] Disdaining almost all the existing arguments for empire, whether from prophecy, reason of state or scholastic jurisprudence, the *De Jure Belli* offered instead a straightforward argument for union by right of conquest.

Following the Peace of 1648, the focus of the debate shifted away from Sweden. The young Queen Christina appears to have repudiated her father's aggression, converting to Rome and abdicating in search of an alternative, eirenic cenception of universal monarchy, for which the thrones of Naples or of Poland appeared more suitable than the Swedish.[60] Conquest theory was nevertheless made welcome by others, nowhere more so than in England. In 1651 Hobbes's *Leviathan* offered a justification of power based on conquest even starker than that conceded by Grotius. Not only did Hobbes argue that contracts of obedience to a conqueror were as valid as any other; redeploying the language of the body politic to insist upon the unitary character of a commonwealth, he determined that all separated territories of a commonwealth must be regarded as 'provinces', being but subordinate 'systems' of the sovereign body.[61] Over the 1650s a number of English political writers, notably Marchmont Nedham and James Harrington, were to revive the older, Machiavellian idea of empire by 'increase' or conquest: Rome, they reminded readers, was most aggressively imperial as a republic.[62] But it was Hobbes who was at the leading edge of conquest theory, reinforcing

[59] On his conduct in the post, which was hardly what Öxenstierna desired: Hugh Trevor-Roper, 'Hugo Grotius and England', in *From Counter-Reformation to Glorious Revolution*, pp. 65–77.

[60] Åkerman, *Queen Christina of Sweden and her Circle*, esp. part IV.

[61] Hobbes, *Leviathan* (1651), ed. Richard Tuck, (Cambridge, 1991), chs xx, xxii, and 'A Review, and Conclusion', pp. 138–9, 155–60, 485–6. Hobbes wrote

> This word Province signifies a charge, or care of businesse, which he whose businesse it is, committeth to another man, to be administered for, and under him; and therefore when in one Common-wealth there be divers Countries, that have their Lawes distinct one from another, or are farre distant in place, the Administration of the Government being committed to divers persons, those Countries where the Soveraign is not resident, but governs by Commission, are called Provinces. (pp. 158–9)

[62] James Harrington, *Oceana* (1656), in *The Political Works of James Harrington*, ed. J.G.A. Pocock (Cambridge, 1977), pp. 320–33. David Armitage has sought to qualify Harrington's enthusiasm for empire, in 'The Cromwellian Protectorate and the languages of Empire', *Historical Journal*, 35, 3 (1992). But the distinction which Harrington draws between the 'patronage' and the 'empire' of the world (*Oceana*, p. 323) seems to me to be no more than the republican obverse of the distinction between a beneficent and a harmful universal monarchy; a little later Harrington simply refers to 'the empire of the world' as appertaining to 'a well-ordered commonwealth' such as he is proposing (*ibid.*, p. 329). For a comment on the imperialism of English republicans: A.B. Worden, 'English Republicanism', in J.H. Burns with Mark Goldie (ed.) *The Cambridge History of Political Thought 1450–1700*, (Cambridge, 1991), pp. 466–7.

Grotius's challenge to the traditional Habsburg idea of a dynastic territorial *imperium*.

The awakening of English interest in conquest theories had a specific context. In 1650–51, even as Hobbes was writing *Leviathan*, the armies of the Commonwealth succeeded where so many kings had failed, and summarily conquered both Ireland and Scotland. The experience of defeat, followed by enforced union, changed for ever the relationship of each country to England. In Ireland a lasting wedge was driven between Protestant settlers and the indigenous and 'Old English' Catholics. In Scotland it would be widely if grudgingly acknowledged that the union offered some benefits; but never again could the Scots deceive themselves that the English lacked the will or the means to conquer them. The conquest of the 1650s would hang heavily over all the subsequent Scottish discussion of union, up to 1707.

The advent of Grotian conquest theory did not, however, mark the end of the idea of universal monarchy. On the contrary, it too was to be restated, after 1660, in terms more aggressive than ever before. Set on campaigns of territorial acquisition in the Low Countries and the Rhineland, Louis XIV seems to have been the first ruler since Charles V to sanction the explicit presentation of himself as an aspirant to universal monarchy. His case was made by Antoine d'Aubery, in his *Justes Pretentions du Roi sur l'Empire*, a work which so appalled the Imperial Librarian that he promptly re-issued it for the edification of Europe in a Latin abridgement as *Axiomata politica Gallicana* (1667).[63] This was a quite unrestrained statement of the dynastic priority of the French Monarchy, whose claims to an *imperium* without limit between the heavens and the oceans were traced back to Charlemagne. As King of the Franks, Charlemagne had been the heir to the Empire of Rome, ruler of Germany as well as of France, and *Dominus* of the city of Rome and the Papacy within it. In his case, therefore, the papal conferral of the title of Emperor had been but an acceptance of his rightful overlordship. When later the German kings had received the title, however, it had been an acknowledgement of their inferior status, and the closed imperial crown had been a mark of their subordination to the Pope and to the King of France. On these grounds, Aubery maintained, most of Germany was justly subject to Louis already: and when the happy dynastic union of Louis to his Spanish Queen bore fruit, the Dauphin would inherit 'the

[63] For the relationship between the *Justes Pretentions* and the *Axiomata politica Gallicana*: Franz Bosbach, 'Eine französische Universalmonarchie? Deutsche Reaktionen auf die europäische Politik Ludwigs XIV', in Jochen Schlobach (ed.), *Vermittlungen. Aspekte der deutsch-franzosischen Beziehungen vom 17. Jahrhundert bis zur Gegenwart* (Berne, 1992), pp. 56–7.

Empire of the entire sea and the entire earth, and consequently a Universal Monarchy'.[64]

It was to similarly brazen statements of Bourbon dynastic ambition that Franz von Lisola responded in his *Bouclier d'Estat et de Justice, contre le dessein manifestement découvert de la Monarchie Universelle, sous le vain pretexte des pretentions de la Reyne de France* (1667). The aim of the French King, Lisola demonstrated, was far more than the conquest of a few provinces. It should be likened to a Vesuvian eruption, which would give him 'l'empire absolue' within Europe, and make him 'maitresse absolue de commerce'. To maintain the liberty of Europe against such a danger, Lisola invoked the Duc de Rohan's principle of a balance between the powers of France and the House of Austria. Claiming that the Habsburgs had historically been Europe's bulwark against universal monarchy, he urged the members of the Empire to unite behind them to resist the French.[65]

Lisola's tract was only the first and most famous of a flood of denunciations of Louis XIV as a universal monarch, from every corner of Europe. As an argument on behalf of the Habsburgs, however, its significance lay rather in marking the close of the tradition which had supported their pretension to imperial monarchy. Shattered politically by Vasa and Bourbon aggression, bypassed intellectually by a new strain of conquest theory, a monarchy which had aspired to be Roman while putting dynastic right before conquest was now being presented, however improbably, as the guardian of Europe's liberty. Nor, despite the best efforts of Lisola and, later, Leibniz, could even that role be credibly sustained. For Habsburg authority within the Empire itself rested, after 1648, on a new basis, while the ambitions of Louis XIV would only be frustrated if an alliance could be made with the United Provinces and the Stuart Monarchy in Britain. And in this new political context the discussion of empire had finally to come to terms with the existence of an alternative idea of union, by leagues or confederations. There had emerged in early modern Europe, we now need to recognise,

[64] Antoine D'Aubery, *Axiomata politica Gallicana* (1667), Lib. I, cap. i; II, i–iii; III, i, 10–11, ii, iii, esp. 35: 'Delphino Franciae, ex matrimonio Regis, Ludovici XIV & Reginae, Maria Theresiae, nato, promittunt omnes rerum circumstantiae infallibilitur futurum Imperium totius maris & totius terrae, & consequenter Monarchiam Universalem.'

[65] [Franz von Lisola], *Bouclier d'Estat et de Justice. Contre le dessein manifestement découvert de la Monarchie Universelle, sous le vain pretexte des pretentions de la Reyne de France*, (1667), Articles I, VI; for a fuller analysis of the arguments of Aubery and Lisola, Bosbach, 'Eine französische Universalmonarchie?', pp. 54–68, and *Monarchia Universalis*, ch. 6: 'Die Universalmonarchie Ludwigs XIV'; and for the range of other devices by which Louis' aggrandisement was portrayed: Peter Burke, *The Fabrication of Louis XIV* (New Haven and London, 1992), pp. 71–83, 179–80.

another form of union besides incorporation into a territorial *imperium*, and another form of empire besides the territorial.

V

Leagues of cities or nobles were widespread in mediaeval Europe, where they offset the hierarchic but fractious structures of vassalage; the concept itself existed in a range of synonyms, in Latin and in the vernaculars.[66] Leagues were particularly prevalent, however, in the German territories of the Empire. The most successful had been the Hanseatic League, in the north, and the Swiss Confederation, or Eidgenossenschaft, in the South. The member cities of the Hanse were renowned for their devotion to commerce rather than territorial aggrandisement; but even at its strongest, in the fourteenth century, the co-ordinating powers of their Diet, the *Hansetag*, had been limited. By contrast the Swiss Confederation, a composite league of Alpine communities and riverine cities, had grown steadily in extent and cohesion since the thirteenth century; early in the sixteenth century its independence was recognised by its nominal overlords, the Habsburgs, (although it remained formally within the Empire until 1648). Despite briefly threatening to dominate northern Italy, the Confederation, like the Hanseatic League, was averse to territorial expansion. Adjoining the Confederation in south-western Germany was the more recently formed Swabian League (1488–1534), whose willingness to accept Maximilian and then Charles V as its head indicated that leagues might also be used to strengthen Imperial authority. The experiment, however, was cut short by the Reformation, and the ensuing confessionalisation of leagues. The activities of the Lutheran Schmalkaldic League (1530–47), and later of the Huguenot and Catholic Leagues in France, left monarchs and their jurists no reason to suppose that leagues were other than undesirable agents of religious division and political subversion.[67] Nevertheless, the confederal idea survived. The successive leagues formed from the 1560s by the aggrieved provinces of the Netherlands might be subversive of the Habsburgs' authority; but the Dutch resisted confessionalisation, despite the prominence of calvinists in the revolt, and in the Union of Utrecht (1579) they committed themselves to both provincial autonomy and religious freedom. Although it required another three decades to determine exactly which

[66] Koselleck, 'Bund, Bündnis, Föderalismus, Bundesstaat', *Geschichtliche Grundbegriffe*, I, pp. 582–600.

[67] H.G. Koenigsberger, 'Liga, Ligadisziplin und Treue zum Fursten im Westeuropa der frühen Neuzeit', in Paolo Prodi (ed.), *Glaube und Eid. Treueformeln, Glaubensbekenntnisse und Sozialdisziplinierung zwischen Mittelalter und Neuzeit* (Munich, 1993), pp. 173–8.

provinces would belong to the Union, the growing likelihood of its success, culminating in the Spanish concession of a Twelve Years' Truce in 1609, did much to restore the credibility of confederal leagues as alternatives to imperial and incorporating monarchy.

The potential of these leagues was noted with particular enthusiasm by the Venetian political writer, Trajano Boccalini, whose *Ragguagli di Parnasso* (1612–13) repeatedly attacked the Spanish pretension to universal monarchy, along with the arguments of supporters such as Botero. Suggesting that the monarchies of Europe had every reason to regard such leagues as a greater threat than individual republics, Boccalini pointed to the strict equality maintained between their members, and to the attraction they exerted over their neighbours precisely because they showed no inclination to make slaves of others.[68]

For a short time at the outset of the seventeenth century it did indeed seem that the age of the confederation might be at hand. While the Spanish Habsburgs remained unable to overcome the Union of the Netherlands, the Austrian Habsburgs found themselves facing a grand Confederation of their Bohemian, Moravian, Austrian and Hungarian Estates. Modelling itself on the constitution of the Polish–Lithuanian Commonwealth, the Confederation declared its intention in 1619 to make the Bohemian Crown, and hence the Empire itself, genuinely rather than formally elective, and to uphold the principle of religious liberty.[69] In the event the Confederation quickly went down to defeat in 1620, but its inspiration, the Polish–Lithuanian Commonwealth, survived. Despite the repeated assaults of Gustav Adolf, the Commonwealth continued to offer a working example of a large-scale territorial union. Here, if anywhere, was an indication of what the alternative to territorial monarchic *imperium* might look like. The Commonwealth was based upon a formal union, negotiated with unusual care; its structure was egalitarian and radically decentralised, most powers lying in the regional Dietines (Sejmiki), which chose and mandated the delegates to the common Diet (Sejm), whose decisions in turn required unanimity; and it was committed to religious toleration.

It is by no means clear, however, that the Commonwealth was actually

[68] Trajano Boccalini, *I Ragguagli di Parnasso* (1612–13), in the translation by Henry [Carey] Earl of Monmouth, *Advertisements from Parnassus: in Two Centuries, with the Politick Touchstone* (London, 1674), pp. 138–46. On Boccalini, Tuck, *Philosophy and Government*, pp. 101–3.

[69] See the important articles by Gottfried Schramm, 'Armed conflict in east-central Europe: Protestant noble opposition and Catholic royalist factions 1604–20', and especially Inge Auerbach, 'The Bohemian Opposition, Poland-Lithuania, and the outbreak of the Thirty Years War', both in R.J.W. Evans and T.V. Thomas (eds.), *Crown, Church and Estates. Central European Politics in the Sixteenth and Seventeenth Centuries* (London, 1991).

understood as an alternative form of union, either by its members or by external observers. The terms of the Union of Lublin, agreed in 1569 after the Diets of the Kingdom of Poland and the Grand Duchy of Lithuania had accepted separate Acts of Union, were themselves indicative. While the title, laws and offices of the Grand Duchy were retained, the union was none the less declared incorporating: Kingdom and Duchy were to become 'one inseparable and indistinguishable body . . . one united Commonwealth', with one Diet and one elected ruler.[70] This would ensure the naturalisation of the two nobilities as equal citizens of one Commonwealth. Contempory observers, such as Botero, evidently had no difficulty in accepting this account of the Union. A further obstacle to understanding the Commonwealth as a new kind of union was the persistence of Aristotelian categories of political interpretation. In these terms it was obvious to Bodin, as later to the German Hermann Conring, that the Polish constitution was aristocratic. To the Poles, by contrast, it was a matter of honour that the Commonwealth was counted as a monarchy. That the crown was strictly elective (with no allowance for pre-election), that the nobility possessed rights of resistance unknown anywhere else, made no difference: Poland remained a monarchy. (The extent to which there was a separate Lithuanian view of these matters is unclear.) In this Aristotelian framework the application of the concept of confederation was limited to the legitimation of resistance, and did not refer to the more general structure of the union; in so far as Polish commentators referred to the union with Lithuania at all, it was to the original dynastic union under the Jagiellons in 1385.[71]

The possibility that the Polish – Lithuanian Commonwealth might come to be regarded as an alternative model of union was in any case destroyed by the calamities which befell it in the 1640s and 1650s. Following the revolt in the Ukraine in 1647 and the subsequent political crisis, the reputation of the Polish nobility and their 'liberties' was irretrievably damaged. Far from offering a model of union, the Commonwealth had by 1700 become a byword for feudal anarchy.

Yet just as one apparent opportunity was lost, the middle years of the

[70] H.E. Dembkowski, *The Union of Lublin. Polish Federalism in the Golden Age* (Boulder and New York, 1982), quotation from the Act of Union, p. 175.

[71] Jean Bodin, *Six Livres de la Republique* (1576), in the trans. by Richard Knolles, corrected by K.D. McRae, *The Six Bookes of a Commonweale* (Cambridge, MA, 1962), Bks I, ch. x, and IV, ch. iii, pp. 166, 472. The persistence of the Polish commitment to monarchy is illustrated by Francisco Marinio [Johann Sachs], *De Scopo Reipublicae Poloniae adversus Hermannum Conringium* (Warsaw, 1665), and Christoph Hartknoch, *De Republica Polonica Libri Duo* (Frankfurt and Leipzig, 1678). For comment, Robert Frost, '"Liberty without License?" The failure of Polish democratic thought in the seventeenth century', in M.B. Biskupski and James S. Pula (eds.), *Polish Democratic Thought from the Renaissance to the Great Emigration* (New York, 1990), pp. 29–54.

century saw the idea of equal union gain new strength elsewhere – ironically in the very monarchy which the Polish model had been used to challenge in 1619, the Empire itself. The Peace of Westphalia in 1648 not only ended the Thirty Years' War, it wrought a fundamental change in the status of the Empire. In political terms, the main beneficiaries of the Peace were of course the Princes, whose powers were enhanced at the expense of the Emperor. But the Peace also reaffirmed the unity of the Empire under the Emperor, and gave it a formal juridical status which it had hitherto lacked. Signed by the various members of the Empire as independent states, the Peace constituted a treaty *jure gentium*; as such, German jurists proceeded to argue, it should be regarded as a Fundamental Law for the Empire, the basis of a specifically Imperial Public Law or ReichsRecht. The ascription of a specific juridical status to the Empire was reinforced by Conring's assault on the historical thesis that there had been a *translatio imperii* from the Roman to the German Emperors. There was an increasing tendency for jurists and publicists to abandon the prefix 'Holy Roman', with its universal pretensions, and to identify the Empire exclusively with the German territory.[72] So understood, the Peace of Westphalia effectively marked the end of the Empire (though not of course of the larger, Central European Habsburg Monarchy) as a monarchic *'imperium'*, and its reconstitution on a basis much more akin to a juridical union of equals, whose relations with each other and with the Emperor were governed by a common Public Law.

In the Empire as in Poland, however, discussion of the constitution as a form of union was still impeded by adherence to Aristotelian political categories. Again Bodin was the *bête noir*, his insistence that the Empire too was an aristocracy provoking fierce controversy among German thinkers, controversy happily fanned by interested outsiders like the Swedes.[73] What transformed this debate was the appearance in 1667, the same year as the exchange between Aubery and Lisola, of Samuel Pufendorf's *De Statu Imperii Germanici*. Written in the guise of reflections by a travelling Italian, Severino da Monzambano, the book was a deliberately provocative assault on the shibboleths of Imperial

[72] On Westphalia: Hanns Gross, *Empire and Sovereignty. A History of the Public Law Literature in the Holy Roman Empire 1599–1804* (Chicago and London, 1973, repr. 1975), pp. 293–310; on the supposed *translatio imperii*: K.O. Freiherr von Aretin, 'Il problema della *Renovatio Imperii Romanorum*. Pretese universali e realtà costituzionale del sacro romano impero dal xvi al xviii secolo', in *La Nozione di Romano tra cittadinanza e universalità*, Da Roma alla Terza Roma, Documenti e Studi, Studi II (Naples, 1984), pp. 73–87.

[73] Julian H. Franklin, 'Sovereignty and the mixed constitution: Bodin and his critics', in *The Cambridge History of Political Thought 1450–1700*, pp. 298–328, though with an anachronistic tendency to arraign the Germans for failing to understand the modern theory of sovereignty; Tuck, *Philosophy and Government*, pp. 124–7.

constitutionalism. After an historical introduction in which he virtually admitted the justice of the French claim that Charlemagne had held Germany as part of the Kingdom of France, Pufendorf proceeded systematically to expose the inadequacy of the traditional Aristotelian categories of analysis. In those terms, Pufendorf argued, the Empire could only ever be regarded as an 'irregular' form, a constitutional 'monster'.[74] The scandal caused by this one simile made the book's reputation – but was soon regretted by its author, since it distracted attention from his attempt to construct an alternative account of the Empire as a particular form of union.

Pufendorf deferred to monarchy to the extent of admitting that the most perfect union *(perfectissima unio)* would be achieved in a well-ordered kingdom. But Germany could not now be reformed into a monarchy without enormous upheaval. The direction in which it tended was, rather, towards a system of confederates or allies *(systema foederatorum* or *sociorum*), united in an unequal league.[75] The *De Statu Imperii* closed with an impassioned argument that the 'state interest' of the German Empire lay in the continuation of this process, until it formed a true 'system of states' *(systema civitatum)*. In an Empire so constituted, the Princes would treat each other as equals, while the Emperor would be bounded by the law and by a perpetual council. Liberty of religion would be secure, and the defence of Germany provided for.[76]

In later works of general jurisprudence Pufendorf further clarified the principles behind the idea of 'systems of states', and openly acknowledged its derivation from Hobbes. A system of states existed when several states were joined by a league so as to appear to constitute one body, but each none the less retained sovereign power.[77] On the last point Pufendorf was particularly insistent: a state which lost its sovereignty would be reduced to a 'province'. Those which had come closest to forming a 'system of

[74] Severino da Monzambano, [i.e. Samuel Pufendorf], *De Statu Imperii Germanici* (1667, in the revised edition of 1684), chs. I, sects. viii, xii–xv, and VI, sect. ix; translated as *The Present State of Germany, or an Account of the Extent, Rise, Form, Wealth, Strength, Weaknesses and Interests of that Empire*, by Edmund Bohun, (London, 1690, 1696), pp. 11–13, 18–24, 152–4.

[75] *De Statu Imperii Germanici*, VI.ix, VII.vii, pp. 237–40, 265–8; *Present State of Germany*, pp. 153–4, 175–7.

[76] *De Statu Imperii Germanici*, VIII.iv–x, esp. pp. 289–94; *Present State of Germany*, pp. 192–6; Gross, *Empire and Sovereignty*, pp. 311–23. See also James Moore and Michael Silverthorne, 'Protestant theologies, limited sovereignties: natural law and conditions of union in the German Empire, the Netherlands and Great Britain', below, pp. 178–84.

[77] 'Systemata civitatum nobis appellantur plures una civitates, vinculo aliquo ita inter se connexae, ut unum corpus videantur constituere; quarum singulae tamen summum in sese imperium retineant.' Samuel Pufendorf, *De Systematibus Civitatum*, in *Dissertationes Academicae Selectiores* (Uppsala, 1677), and in *Politica Inculpata* (Lund, 1679), p. 228 of the latter edition.

states' in Pufendorf's terms were the Achaian League in the ancient world, and the Union of the Netherlands in the modern.[78]

Once the scandal of the monster simile wore off, Pufendof's ideas exerted considerable influence upon jurists attracted by the idea of a Reichssystem.[79] But there were also critics, notably Leibniz. In his *Caesarinus Fürstenerius* (1677) (itself but one chapter in an epic challenge to every aspect of Pufendorf's philosophy), Leibniz attacked Pufendorf's simple Hobbesian insistence on the indivisibility of sovereign power, in order to argue that the 'territorial superiority' of the German Princes remained compatible with the continued ascription of a universal authority to the Empire. In the course of this argument, Leibniz expressly distinguished a confederation (*confoederatio*) from a union (*unione*): a confederation might be likened to a *societas*, but only a union formed a body (*corporis*), and hence a new *persona civilis* or *respublica*. Any comparison of the Dutch confederation with the German Empire was accordingly invalid.[80] Perhaps what is most revealing about this exchange, however, is the move that neither participant was able to make. Neither Pufendorf, with his clear-cut alternatives of monarchy and a system of states, nor Leibniz, with his refusal to admit that a confederation was a union, was in a position to draw the modern distinction between a 'confederal' and a 'federal' union. This conceptual incapacity may be thought at odds with German reality, since the Emperor still possessed important powers; nevertheless, the distinction would not begin to be drawn for another hundred years. In the meantime, despite Leibniz's criticism, it was Pufendorf's straightforward definition of union as either confederal or monarchic that won general acceptance.

The conviction that only a strict confederation offered a coherent alternative to monarchy was powerfully reinforced by the seventeenth-century achievements of the United Provinces or States of the Netherlands – and by the terms in which it was defined as a union by contemporaries. The Union of Utrecht in 1579, to which the United Provinces traced its foundation, had itself been little more than a defensive league, a step towards the formation of a General Union of all the Netherlands. It did not repudiate the Habsburgs' sovereignty, and fell short of a comprehensive

[78] *De Systematibus Civitatum*, in *Politica Inculpata*, pp. 226–83; more concisely in Samuel Pufendorf, *De Jure Naturae et Gentium* (1672, in the edition of Amsterdam, 1698), Bk VII, cap. v, ss. xvi–xxi, pp. 714–21, and in the translation *Of the Law of Nature and Nations*, (London, 1703), pp. 184–89.

[79] Bernd Roeck, *Reichssystem und Reichsherkommen. Die Diskussion uber die Staatlichkeit des Reiches in der politischen Publizistik des 17. und 18. Jahrhunderts* (Stuttgart, 1984).

[80] G.W. Leibniz, *Caesarini Furstenerini Tractatus de Jure Suprematus ac Legationum Principum Germaniae* (1677), in *Gothofredi Guillelmi Leibnitii . . . Opera omnia* (Geneva, 1768), vol. III, part iii, caps x–xi, pp. 357–61; trans. in *The Political Writings of Leibniz*, trans. and ed. Patrick Riley, (Cambridge, 1972), pp. 114–20.

constitution. It did, however, enunciate two clear principles, guaranteeing the traditional privileges and freedoms of each province and town, and securing individual religious freedom.[81] As the Revolt took hold in the seven northern provinces, and these won the breathing space of the Twelve Years' Truce in 1609, institutional consolidation gradually followed. Each province had its own Estates and Stadtholder, and sent delegates to the Estates General, which proceeded by unanimity. The formal equality of the Union was of course complicated by the real pre-eminence of Holland; but while Holland's leaders might sometimes treat the other six provinces as their inferior allies, they were always careful to exert their influence from within the institutions of the Union. A potentially greater complication was the independent role of the House of Orange, whose head was by tradition Captain-General of the Union's armies and navy, and whose exact constitutional relation to the Estates General was never strictly defined.[82]

To begin with, the political theory of the Dutch Revolt was that of resistance against tyranny, political and religious; and when the rebellious provinces sought a collective identity, they found it in the myth of the ancient Batavians, who had heroically defied Roman imperial despotism.[83] From the 1580s, however, a debate developed on the implications of the Union of Utrecht's reservation of provincial liberties; and a number of writers began to articulate the principle that sovereignty lay in the individual states.[84] There are signs that Grotius contemplated the qualification of this principle, either through the emergence of superiors within a league, or through the strengthening of the central institutions of the Union (but not the House of Orange).[85] But the principle of States'

[81] A translated version of the Treaty of Utrecht is given in E.H. Kossman and A.F. Mellink (eds.), *Texts concerning the Revolt of the Netherlands* (Cambridge, 1974), pp. 165–73; J.C. Boogman, 'The Union of Utrecht: its genesis and consequences', in J.C. Boogman and G.N. van der Plaat (eds.), *Federalism. History and Current Significance of a Form of Government* (The Hague, 1980), pp. 5–35.

[82] H. Wansink, 'Holland and six allies: the Republic of the seven United Provinces', in J.S. Bromley and E.H. Kossman (eds.), *Britain and the Netherlands, Vol. IV Metropolis, Dominion and Province* (London, 1971).

[83] Martin van Gelderen, *The Political Theory of the Dutch Revolt* (Cambridge, 1992). E.H.N. Mout, 'Ni Prince ni Etat', in André Stegman (ed.), *Pouvoir et Institutions en Europe au XVIième Sièle* (Paris, 1987), pp. 117–30; and 'Ideales Muster oder erfundene Eigenart. Republikanische Theorien während des niederländischen Aufstands', in H.G. Koenigsberger (ed.), *Republiken und Republikanismus im Europa der Frühen Neuzeit* (Munich, 1988).

[84] *Texts concerning the Revolt of the Netherlands*, pp. 255–9: 'About the present condition of government in the Netherlands, 1583', and pp. 274–81: 'A short exposition of the rights . . . of Holland and West Friesland . . . 16 October 1587', by Francis Vranck.

[85] Grotius, *De Jure Belli*, I.iii.21; and other writings discussed by Tuck, *Philosophy and Government*, pp. 162–4, (though cf. pp. 192–3 for later arguments apparently upholding the principle of States' sovereignty).

sovereignty became widely accepted, and later in the century was powerfully endorsed by the Friesland jurist Ulrik Huber, possibly under the influence of Pufendorf. Given this principle, Huber was clear that the Union must be regarded as a *foedus aequale*: in effect, as a confederation.[86] There was also general agreement that such a union was defensive only, on the model of the Achaian League in ancient Greece, with no interest in territorial acquisition.[87]

Foreign observers who overcame their anti-republican prejudices sufficiently to examine the Dutch constitution sometimes showed the beginnings of a subtler understanding. Both Cardinal Bentivoglio, in the first half of the century, and, later, Sir William Temple appreciated that sovereign power was in practice divided between the Provinces and the Estates General. Even so, Temple still believed it impossible to range the United Provinces (like the state of Poland) 'under any particular names of goverment that have yet been invented'.[88] In the absence of a coherent account of the division of powers within the Union, it was the jurists' understanding which seems to have prevailed.[89] As in the case of the Empire, this understanding may have done less than justice to the complex reality of Dutch politics; but the impression that the only form of union coherent enough to withstand imperial monarchy was a confederation of equal, sovereign states had gained still more ground. Well before 1700, it seems, it had been accepted that confederation was the (sole) alternative to incorporation.

If the Dutch was, within Europe, a purely defensive union – a union against territorial empire – its relation to empire overseas was another

86 Ulrik Huber, *De Jure Civitatis libri tres* (Franeker, 1684, 3rd edn 1698), Bk I. ch. xvii, paras. 8–14. In 1698 Huber added a discussion of the German constitution, suggesting that the Empire too should be regarded as a *foedus aequale*: Bk I, sect. iii, ch. 3, paras. 17–19. Cf. Moore and Silverthrone, 'Protestant theologies, limited sovereignties', below, pp. 184–9.

87 Huber, *De Jure Civitatis*, I.xvii.10; for the identification of the Dutch with the Achaians, cf. Boccalini, *Ragguagli di Parnasso*, (in the 1674 translation), pp. 175, 197–8, 201–2, and Henry Stubbe, *The History of the United Provinces of Achaia* (London, 1673), 'To the Reader'. What was known about the Achaian League derived from Polybius: see W. Den Boer, 'The Dutch Republic and Antiquity', in Boogman and van der Plaat, *Federalism*, pp. 47–64.

88 Guido Bentivoglio, *Historicall Relations of the United Provinces of Flanders*, trans. Henry [Cary], Earl of Monmouth, (London, 1652), Bks I, chs iv, v, and III, vii, pp. 4, 7, 45–8. Sir William Temple, *Observations upon the United Provinces of the Netherlands* (1673), ed. Sir George Clark (Oxford, 1971), pp. 52 (ch. ii), 127–8 (ch. vii), 133–5 (ch. viii); and *An Essay upon the Original and Nature of Government* (1672), in *The Works of Sir William Temple*, 2 vols. (London, 1720), 1, p. 96.

89 The caution of this judgement reflects my inability to read the vernacular literature. The *Bibliography of Dutch Seventeenth-Century Political Thought. An Annotated Inventory, 1581–1710*, comp. G.O. van de Klashorst, H.W. Blom and E.O.G. Haitsma Mulier (Amsterdam and Maarssen, 1986), indicates the existence of a limited amount of further material.

matter. There, as Richard Tuck has pointed out, the Dutch were ruthless in deploying the arguments of Grotius to proclaim their freedom to sail and trade there they would, to use pre-emptive force whenever necessary, and to assume the rights of conquest over the goods of those they overpowered.[90] In their own eyes, the Dutch sought no more than – in Grotius's phrase – the 'freedom of the seas', and that on behalf not of the state but of private bodies, the East and the West India Companies. But by treating goods at sea equally with those on land as open to pre-emptive conquest, Grotius's doctrine went far further than previous accounts of the sea as a basis for empire. It eliminated Botero's distinction between 'mediterraneans' and 'oceans', with its implication (also evident in Charles V's columnar emblem) that empire overseas depended upon, and was an offshoot of, empire within Europe. Equally, it dispensed with Solórzano Pereira's assumption that territories acquired overseas must be 'provinces' of a specific European monarchy, held by an 'incorporating' union. Goods and territory could legitimately be acquired anywhere in their own right, without having to be regarded as an extension of a prior European *imperium*. Within Europe itself, the aggressive edge of Grotius's theories might be masked by the United Provinces' deliberate repudiation of territorial acquisition on their own account; overseas, the Dutch had no such inhibitions.

Not surprisingly, the point was appreciated most clearly by the main rivals to the Dutch for maritime supremacy, the English. Long remembering that they had been the victims of an early instance of Dutch ruthlessness, the Amboyna massacre of 1623, the English regarded it as obvious that what the Dutch sought was the 'empire of the seas'. Hostility to the Dutch on this account reached a peak in the anti-republican climate of the 1660s, when a spate of pamphlets accused them of attempting to establish no less than a universal monarchy by sea.[91] But this was name-calling, since the English by no means rejected the pursuit of maritime empire on their own account. In John Evelyn's words, 'a spirit of commerce, and strength at sea to project it, are the most certain marks of greatness of empire'.[92] Just as the English had shown none of the restraint of the Dutch in acting on the implications of Grotian-Hobbesian conquest theory at the expense of their neighbours, so they showed a similar impatience with the doctrine of the freedom of the seas, countering it with a succession of Navigation Acts, and a frank avowal of

[90] Tuck, 'Grotius and Selden', in *The Cambridge History of Political Thought 1450–1700*, pp. 503–4; more fully in *Sorry Comforters*, ch. 2.

[91] S.C.A. Pincus, 'Popery, trade and universal monarchy: the ideological context of the outbreak of the second Anglo-Dutch War', *English Historical Review*, 422 (1992), pp. 1–29.

[92] J. Evelyn, *Navigation and Commerce, Their Original and Progress* (London, 1674), p. 15.

their own maritime imperial ambitions. By 1700 it was common ground in English political and economic debate that the sea was England's natural empire, and that the interest of state must be identified with that of commerce.[93] Between them, the Dutch and the English thus added a new dimension to the concept of empire, making it possible to detach it from its previous identification with the territorial ideal of universal monarchy.

VI

1672 was the decisive year for the empires and unions of early modern Europe. By gratuitously invading and almost over-running the entire Netherlands, Louis XIV had come within an ace of accomplishing both his own univeral monarchy and the ruin of the United Provinces and its commerce. Even in failure, he transformed the alignment of forces in Europe, and the relation between the United Provinces and England in particular.

Somehow the Province of Holland held out, but the republican regime of de Witt was brought down, and with it the policy of preserving diplomatic independence. In its place the newly restored Stadtholder William of Orange set about constructing the alliances which would secure both his own country and Europe from the French King's dreadful ambition. Above all he looked to England, and when his Stuart cousins denied him, he took the extraordinary risk of invading England to secure the crown. The risk was offset, however, by the knowledge that English public opinion now regarded France, not the United Provinces, as the pre-eminent enemy. After 1672, as Steven Pincus will show in the following chapter, relentless pamphleteering stirred the British into an obsession with the threat of a French universal monarchy, an obsession which contributed strongly to the acceptance of the invasion and revolution of 1688, and which continued unabated into the 1690s.[94] Exploiting this climate of Francophobia, William proceeded to devote himself to harnessing the resources of all three of his kingdoms for the ultimate struggle over the Spanish Succession, which was expected to follow the now imminent death of Charles II, the last Spanish Habsburg.

[93] For some (chronologically rather scattered) expressions of this idea: Koebner, *Empire*, pp. 68–77; for a much more systematic account of the key economic arguments: Istvan Hont, 'Free trade and the economic limits to national politics: neo-Machiavellian political economy reconsidered', in John Dunn (ed.), *The Economic Limits to Modern Politics* (Cambridge, 1990).

[94] Steven Pincus, 'The English debate over universal monarchy', below pp. 37–62: until Pincus uncovered the evidence, the scale of pamphleteering on this subject had passed virtually unnoticed.

At stake in the conflict, it was anticipated, would be no less than the preservation of the 'Liberties of Europe' from a Bourbon universal monarchy, and, closely related to those liberties, England's own freedom to pursue its natural empire of the sea.

It was in this European setting that the question of union returned to Britain after 1688. Over the course of this volume, contributors will explore in greater detail a number of specific ways in which this setting was understood, alongside the concerns, cultural, religious and legal as well as political, which informed the Scottish response to it. In the remainder of this introductory chapter, I shall confine myself to outlining the extent to which the Anglo-Scottish Union debate of 1698–1707 exploited the conceptual resources made available by two centuries of European discussion of empire and union.

Perplexed by the erratic, mercenary behaviour of Scottish politicians, William had by his death reached the conclusion that further union of the two kingdoms was desirable, and he and his ministers expected it to take the form of an incorporating union of parliaments. Additional urgency was lent by the realisation that his successor, Anne, would have no heirs, creating an opportunity for a return of the exiled heirs of James II. Even so, it appears to have been assumed that the Scots would simply accept the English Parliament's choice of the Hanoverian succession, and that they would be content with the minimum of economic concessions.

The Scots, however, believed that there was room for manoeuvre. Resentful of the ever-mounting pressure on the historic sovereignty of their kingdom, the Scottish elite was persuaded to support, in quick succession, two initiatives designed to restore its economic and political autonomy. The first was the Darien Scheme of 1698–1700, an attempt to establish a commercial *entrepôt* on the isthmus of Panama. As David Armitage demonstrates, the venture embodied a distinct and original conception of commercial empire, in which trade would not be concentrated in the hands of metropolitan merchant monopolies.[95] The flaw in the scheme was the Scots' inability to give military support to the Darien colonists: an intensely irritated William and an enraged London merchant community simply left the colonists to their fate at the hands of the Spanish. Nevertheless, the Scots' commitment to the scheme was a strong indication that closer union of the British kingdoms would be hard to reconcile with an exclusively English empire of the sea.

Frustrated in this attempt to develop an independent maritime empire, the Scottish elite was the more easily persuaded to take advantage of the political opportunity provided by the prospect of an open succession.

[95] David Armitage, 'The Scottish vision of empire: intellectual origins of the Darien venture', below, pp. 97–118.

Deferring to the intelligence of Andrew Fletcher, the Scottish Parliament signalled that it would only accept the Hanoverian successsion if the crown's powers were curtailed. Parliament should become the guarantor of Scotland's sovereignty. This was not a declaration of independence as such: what Fletcher and his allies sought was a re–negotiation of the terms of the union between the two kingdoms, reconstituting it as, in effect, an equal or confederal union. Informing their argument, it is clear, was the now well–established conviction that confederal union was the one coherent alternative to incorporation: what was envisaged was a sort of United Provinces of Great Britain.[96]

Fletcher's initiative ensured that the Scots were presented with a choice: there was, in principle, a geniune alternative to the offer of incorporation emanating from London. Unfortunately, the confederal idea faced a crucial difficulty: the requirement of equality. Within a union of the three Kingdoms as they stood England would inevitably continue to predominate; but to create equal units would require the break–up of all three Kingdoms, with (as Fletcher tacitly admitted) the consequent sacrifice of the historic sovereignties which confederal union was supposed to preserve. Here, perhaps, Pufendorf's pre-emption of a distinction between 'confederal' and 'federal' union proved critical. When they had the opportunity, in 1703–4, the Scottish advocates of confederation were reluctant to qualify their insistence on equality as a condition of such a union with any admission that there might also be central or 'federal' institutions with distinct powers. There was a definite sense in which the adherents of confederal union allowed themselves to be hoist by the rigidity of their conceptual inheritance.[97]

Increasingly aware of the dangers of keeping the succession open when there was no credible Protestant alternative to the Hanoverians, Scottish political opinion had by late 1705 swung back to those making the case for an incorporating union of parliaments. The strength of this case lay in its promise to exchange political weakness for civil, and especially economic, benefits. Relentlessly the advocates of incorporation criticised the existing Scottish Parliament as little better than a Polish Diet, whose survival was too high a price to pay for a notional independent 'sovereignty'. (So far had Poland now fallen from offering a model of a successful union.) Once they shared a common legislature with the English, however, the Scots would gain the same security for their liberty

[96] John Robertson, 'Andrew Fletcher's vision of Union', in R.A. Mason (ed.), *Scotland and England 1286–1815* (Edinburgh, 1987); and 'An elusive sovereignty: the course of the Union debate in Scotland 1698–1707', below, pp. 205–7.

[97] As two of Fletcher's early associates, James Hodges and George Ridpath, were later to acknowledge, by moving away from the idea of confederation: see Robertson, 'An elusive sovereignty', below, pp. 208–10, 213–15.

and property as the English, and the same economic opportunities. Specifically, England's maritime empire would be open to their participation. Although this was not the form of empire which the Darien projectors had had in mind, the belated concession by English negotiators of free trade with England and its overseas colonies could be presented as generous compensation for the sabotage of the Darien Scheme.[98] Empire was, finally, being offered to the Scots in return for incorporating union.

Nevertheless, the term chosen to characterise this 'exchange' of incorporating union for maritime empire contained a critical ambiguity. For the preferred reference of the incorporating unionists was to Grotius's definition of union as a 'communication' of rights, such as the Romans had offered the Sabines. This was repeatedly cited as authoritative re-assurance that an incorporating union entailed no surrender of sovereignty, but its transfer into a new body politic.[99] As Fletcher early pointed out, however, the reference was flawed: Grotius himself had presented Rome as conquering the Sabines before incorporating them into its empire.[100] Behind the reassuring concept of 'communication' there lay the dark shadow of Grotian conquest theory. In the event, the threat of conquest was played down during the debate. Protestant opponents of the Union feared to provoke an English invasion, since it would only give the Jacobites their chance; the English, meanwhile, had no wish to be diverted from the war on the continent. But the threat was none the less present – and drawn to the Scots' attention at strategic moments by English minsters:[101] after Cromwell's success in the 1650s, it was an unavoidable, intrinsic dimension of Anglo-Scottish relations. In Grotian (and *a fortiori* in Hobbesian) terms, the English possessed both the power and the right to have enforced the process of Anglo-Scottish 'communication' by a simple pre-emptive strike. There was more justice than even King James had supposed in his remark, 100 years earlier, that an incorporating union was tantamount to the peaceful conquest of Scotland by England.

The implication is reinforced when the Union of 1707 is viewed from the perspective of the English parliament. For the Parliament which accepted the Treaty of Union was the direct descendant of the Parliament

[98] Laurence Dickey, 'Power, commerce and natural law in Daniel Defoe's political writings 1698–1707', below, p. 95; Armitage, 'Scottish Vision of Empire', below, pp. 116–18.

[99] See above for the Grotian doctrine, pp. 18–19; and for the use of it in the Union Debate, Robertson, 'An elusive sovereignty', below, p. 221 and n 78.

[100] Andrew Fletcher, *An Account of a Conversation concerning a Right Regulation of Governments for the Common Good of Mankind* (Edinburgh, 1704), in *The Political Works of Andrew Fletcher* (London, 1732), pp. 408–9; also Robertson, 'Andrew Fletcher's vision of Union', pp. 213–14.

[101] For examples, Robertson, 'An elusive sovereignty', below pp. 204, 211n.40.

which had proclaimed the imperial status of the realm of England in 1533, and to which in 1604 Sir Henry Savile had confidently ascribed the power of uniting an inferior state to its superior. If it now accepted an Act of Union which formally ended its independent existence, it did so knowing that in every respect bar its style and a limited addition to its membership the new Parliament of Great Britain would be as its English predecessor. In this perspective, incorporating union was, as James's critics had insisted it must be, a straightforward enlargement of England's 'empire'. The Scots may have accepted union in return for the prospect of empire overseas; but the English Parliament was at least equally interested in the empire to which it had laid claim since 1533, an empire of territory within Britain, now afforced by the threat of conquest. From this point of view the limited concession of a new style, unacceptable a century earlier, was now worthwhile, since English interests would remain predominant in a British parliament, while the resources of Scotland would be added to the struggle against French universal monarchy in Europe, and to the defence and enlargement of empire overseas.

The debate preceeding the Union of Scotland and England in 1707 was thus one outcome of two centuries of European discussion of the ideas of empire and union, ideas constitutive of the early modern European political order. Far from being *sui generis*, the formation of Britain, its Union and its Empire in the eighteenth century can only be appreciated in the European context. A union which it was suggested might be confederal, but was in the event incorporating, though on a parliamentary rather than a dynastic basis; a union intended to facilitate the pursuit of maritime, commercial empire, but which was also, in historical effect, an extension of the territorial empire of one party over the other: this was a union framed in terms reaching far back into history of European political thought. In its principles as well as in its circumstances, British union was a thoroughly European event.

The union agreed in 1707 was of course only one of several eighteenth-century outcomes of the early modern debate over empire and union. Among others whose accompanying debates are equally in need of investigation, two which stand out are the Spanish Monarchy's *Nueva Planta* of 1707–16, uniting Aragon with Castile, and, at the other end of the century, Joseph II's remarkable attempt to remodel the Austrian Habsburg Monarchy. Of more direct concern to this volume, however, are the outcomes of the British Union itself, outcomes explored in the final three chapters. One was in Ireland. At the turn of the seventeenth century incoporating union was the ideal of the Protestant Anglo-Irish; but the English Parliament saw no advantage, and some economic disadvantage, in absorbing its Irish counterpart. Anticipating this rebuff,

Molyneux encouraged his fellow Protestants to reassert their parliament's autonomy on the basis of a distinctively Anglo-Irish version of Grotian conquest theory.[102] But the question of Ireland's relation to the British Empire remained: and when the Anglo-Irish Ascendancy as well as the Empire were threatened at the end of the eighteenth century, incorporating union would offer both Dublin and Westminster an all too ready-made outcome to the crisis.

By contrast, incorporating union did not offer a solution to the crisis in relations between Britain and its North American colonies. While Scottish settlers and administrators in the colonies strove to interpret the imperial union in terms similiar to those of mutual 'communication', at Westminster the Parliament of Great Britain remained adamant in its refusal to compromise its imperial sovereignty.[103] Faced with such rigidity, the colonists were reluctantly obliged to form themselves into a union. At first this took the conventional form for a union against empire, a confederation. But when the constraints of confederation quickly became apparent, a new distinction began to be drawn. A union of states, it was suggested, might be 'federal' as well as 'confederal' – and might then aspire to an 'empire' of it own. In the words with which Alexander Hamilton addressed his fellow Americans in 1787, as they prepared to draw up the constitution of this new union:

> . . . you are invited to deliberate a new Constitution for the United States of America. The subject speaks its own importance; comprehending in its consequences, nothing less than the existence of the Union – the safety and welfare of the parts of which it is composed – the fate of an empire, in many respects, the most interesting in the world.[104]

The creation of the United States of America would simply give the age-old association of union and empire a new lease of life.

[102] Jacqueline R. Hill, 'Ireland without Union: Molyneux and his legacy', below, pp. 277–84.

[103] Ned Landsman, 'The legacy of the British Union for the North American Colonies: provincial elites and the problem of Imperial Union', below, pp. 304–11; J.G.A. Pocock, 'Empire, state and confederation: the War of American Independence as a crisis in multiple monarchy', below pp. 346–7.

[104] Alexander Hamilton, *The Federalist*, no. 1, 27 October 1787.

2

THE ENGLISH DEBATE OVER UNIVERSAL MONARCHY

STEVEN PINCUS

'THE welfare of England', one polemicist observed shortly after the Glorious Revolution, 'is involved in the common fate of Europe'. Though living on an island, the English knew that they were not self-sufficient. The need to trade, thought another pamphleteer, made the English 'citizens of the world', necessarily interested in political and cultural developments occurring beyond the English Channel.[1]

Historians of England have traditionally denied the essential Europeanness of their subject, preferring instead to explain the causes and consequences of English political and cultural transformations without reference to developments across the Channel or the North Sea. European culture and politics did intervene, but only as a sort of *Deus ex machina* propelling change.[2] Recently, however, a group of historians has argued that Restoration Englishmen and women where deeply concerned with, and implicated in, European developments. But the Europe in which England participated was not a Europe of nations. Rather it was a Europe divided by one single issue: the issue of religion. The seventeenth century, Dr Jonathan Scott – the most eloquent proponent of this interpretation – insists, 'was the century of the victories of the Counter-Reformation. It was a century of disaster for European

I am grateful to Bernard Bailyn, Toby Barnard, Tom Cogswell, Mark Goldie, Tim Harris, Wallace MacCaffrey, Peter Miller, Jenny Paxton, Jennifer Poulos, John Robertson, and Blair Worden for their comments and criticisms of this essay in its various forms.

1 *Nero Gallicanus: Or, The True Pourtraicture of Louis XIV* (London: R. Taylor, 1690),p. 29; *The Cities Great Concern* (London: William Godbid, 1674), sig. Alv.

2 This position has been expressed by a wide variety of scholars. See for example: Ronald Hutton, *The Restoration* (Oxford, 1985); J.R. Jones, *Britain and The World* (Glasgow, 1980); J.L. Price, 'Restoration England and Europe', in J.R. Jones (ed.), *The Restored Monarchy*. (London, 1979), pp. 118–35.

Protestantism.'[3] In this context seventeenth-century English history should be read as a continuous struggle against the menacing tide of the Counter-Reformation. 'It was concern about religion, not about politics or economics,' Jonathan Scott proclaims, 'which drove seventeenth-century English people to compromise their political allegiances and mire themselves in one another's blood.'[4]

Against these views, I will maintain that the English in the Restoration period – from a wide variety of social classes and geographical milieus – participated actively in a European debate, and that European debate was about universal monarchy, not about the true religion. While religious concerns often played a vital role in English political discourse, a narrowly confessional focus is unable to explain why parts of the English political nation demanded war against the Protestant Dutch in the 1660s and an attack on France in the later seventeenth century. An examination of the argument about European affairs over the entire course of the Restoration reveals that far from being an anachronistic imposition of Whig historians, the definition of national interest and integrity was at the centre of English political polemic. By attempting to recover and analyse the complex Restoration discussion of universal monarchy I hope to cast the Glorious Revolution in a fresh light, and to suggest that the Augustan state was not forced upon the English by an outsider but was essential to achieve European ends to which most of the English people were committed.

I

By 1660, most members of the political nation knew that England had spent the better part of the past century trying to prevent the Habsburgs from achieving their goal of universal monarchy. The works of Traiano Boccalini, Henri Duc de Rohan and Tommaso Campanella – all of which outlined the Spanish pretensions to 'the Universal Monarchy, which only

[3] Jonathan Scott, *Algernon Sidney and the Restoration Crisis, 1677–1683* (Cambridge, 1991), p. 8. Few have written explicitly about Restoration foreign affairs; however, there are other important exponents of the religious war thesis. They include J.C.D. Clark, *Revolution and Rebellion* (Cambridge, 1986), esp. pp. 64–7; Conal Condren, *George Lawson's politica and the English Revolution.* (Cambridge, 1989); Conal Condren, 'Andrew Marvell as polemicist: his account of the growth of Popery and arbitrary government', in Conal Condren and A.D. Cousins (eds.), *The Political Identity of Andrew Marvell* (Aldershot, Hampshire, 1990).

[4] Jonathan Scott, 'Radicalism and Restoration: the shape of the Stuart experience', *Historical Journal*, V 31 (1988), 458–62; Scott, 'England's troubles: exhuming the Popish Plot', in Tim Harris, Mark Goldie and Paul Seaward (eds.), *The Politics of Religion in Restoration England* (Oxford, 1990), p. 110.

the Romans arrived unto' – were very familiar to English audiences.[5] These classics were assiduously read, commented upon, and cited throughout the later seventeenth century. Their arguments became part of the stock of popular knowledge.[6] The English might have disagreed about the relative merits of Elizabethan and early Stuart foreign policy, but they all concurred that the Habsburgs had 'for a long time aspired after an Universal Monarchy', and that their forefathers had done all they could to prevent the Spanish and Austrians from achieving their aim.[7]

Charles I's failure to stem the tide of the Habsburg advance played a large role in Parliamentarian and moderate Royalist criticisms of his regime. Unsurprisingly, then, the newly created English Republic quickly began considering proposals to thwart the Austrian family's universalist designs. The publication in late 1651 of Fulke Greville's popular *Life of Sidney* provided its readers with a guide to action. The pamphlets eponymous hero, Sir Philip Sidney, devoted his life to ensuring that the House of Austria did not achieve 'her long affected Monarchy over the West'.[8] Sir Philip's epic efforts ended with his death at Zutphen, fighting in alliance with the Dutch against the forces of the Habsburg monarch. For supporters of the Rump, the time had come to revivify this heroic alliance, this alliance between the English Republic and the 'popular estate' of the Dutch Republic.[9] Both the Rump and the Nominated Parliament advanced proposals so 'both these commonwealths

[5] All of them were published in English translations in the seventeenth century. For their discussions of the Spanish pretensions see: Traiano Boccalini (trans. Henry Earl of Monmouth), *I Ragguagli di Parnasso: Or, Advertisements from Parnassus*, 2nd edn. (London: T. Dring, J. Starkey, T. Basset, 1669), pp. 327, 333; Tomasso Campanella (trans. Edmund Chilmead, preface by William Prynne), *Thomas Campanella An Italian Friar and Second Machiavel His Advice to the King of Spain for Attaining the Universal Monarchy of the World* (London: Philamon Stephens, 1660), sig. A4v; Henri Duc de Rohan (trans. Henry Hunt), *A treatise of the Interest of the Princes and States of Christendom* (London: Ric. Hodgkinsonne, 1641), sig. A8, pp. 25–7, 74-5.

[6] *Europae Modernae Speculum: Or, A View of the Empires, Kingdoms, Principalities and Common-Wealths of Europe*. Printed by Order of Secretary Morrice (London: T. Leach for Tho. Johnson, 1665), pp. 104–5. See also Edmund Everard, *Discourses of the Present State of the Protestant Princes of Europe* (London: Dorman Newman, 1679), p. 5; Sir William Temple, *Miscellanae* (London: A.M. and R.R. for Edward Gellibrand, 1680), pp. 19–20.

[7] *French Intrigues; Or, The History of their Delusory Promises Since the Pyrenean Treaty* (London: W. Hensman, 1685), p. 3.

[8] Mark Caldwell (ed.), *The Prose of Fulke Greville Lord Brooke* (New York, 1987), p. 17. Sidney's and Queen Elizabeth's efforts to thwart Spanish universal monarchy are the overarching theme of the entire pamphlet.

[9] Greville, 'Life of Sidney', Caldwell (ed.), *Prose of Fulke Greville*, p. 15. Greville's William of Orange was very much a republican leader. His political role came from his 'inward greatness' not his birth, which was natural in the Netherlands where 'no pedigree, but worth could possibly make a man a Prince.' Greville also emphasises William of Orange's unprincely attire. ibid., pp. 14–5.

might become one, and be under one supreme power' in order to prevent a Spanish universal monarchy.[10] No doubt it was this failure to achieve a republican union in the face of the universalist threat of the Habsburgs which led Algernon Sidney, an active participant in these events as well as a descendant of Sir Philip, to create a new category of republics for the Dutch – neither a commonwealth for increase nor a commonwealth for preservation – 'one composed of many cities associated together . . . every one retaining and exercising a sovereign power within itself'.[11]

After 1660, however, Spanish power was clearly on the wane. Although English commentators fiercely debated the origin of Spain's decline, the reality was undeniable. 'The Spanish Monarchy, and the House of Austria (whose great accessions of territory gave rise to those observations on which the policy of the last age was founded),' noted the author of *Europae Modernae Speculum*, 'are concluded to be consumptive and to stand merely on the defensive part.'[12] The problem now was to identify and deter the next aspirant.

The most enthusiastic supporters of the Restored Monarchy, the Anglican Royalists, quickly became convinced that the Dutch Republic was seeking universal dominion.[13] Although no one can doubt the cultural and economic vitality of the Dutch polity, some might question the imperial potential of a small cluster of watery provinces, so recently emancipated from the clutches of the Habsburg Monarchy.[14] Why did this Protestant trading republic evoke so much fear and loathing from the now triumphantly restored English Monarchy?

Much of the answer lies in the seventeenth-century conviction that

[10] John Thurloe (?), 'A Review of Several Treaties with the Dutch', 26 March 1661, National Maritime Museum, Clifford Papers, vol. I, Dw32. I have described the struggle against Spanish universal monarchy in the 1650s in 'England and the world in the 1650s', in John Morrill (ed.) *Revolution and Restoration* (London, 1992), pp. 129–47. The proposals of republican union are described in my *Protestantism and Patriotism: Ideology and the Making of English Foreign Policy 1650–1668* (Cambridge, 1994).

[11] Thomas G. West (ed.) *Discourses Concerning Government by Algernon Sidney* (Indianapolis, 1990), pp. 206–7, pp. 564–5. This is the retrospective explanation for their refusal to form a sovereign unit; the Dutch themselves were not a single sovereign unit. Algernon Sidney also recalled that the house of Austria was 'thought to have effected the universal monarchy'. *Discourses*, p. 215.

[12] *Europae Modernae Speculum*, pp. 4, 103; Everard, *Discourses*, p. 37; *French Intrigues*, p. 8.

[13] The third section of *Protestantism and Patriotism: Ideology and the Making of English Foreign Policy*, goes some way, I hope, to substantiate my claims for Anglican Royalist antipathy towards the Dutch with respect to the outbreak of the second Anglo-Dutch War.

[14] Charles Molloy, *De Jure Maritimo et Navali* (London: John Bellinger, 1676), sig. A6r; *The French Intrigues Discovered* (London: R. Baldwin, 1681), p. 23; William Aglionby, *The Present State of the United Provinces of the Low Countries* (London: John Starkey, 1669), p. 154. It is important to note that Dr Aglionby was a close friend of, and tutor for, the 'rabidly Anglican' Robert Paston, Earl of Yarmouth. See William Aglionby to Mr. Arundel, 26 May 1671, Cambridge University Library, MSS Dd.11.57, f. 67v. On Yarmouth see John Miller, *Charles II* (London, 1991), p. 249.

trade was the key to power and dominion. Seventeenth-century Europeans felt certain that the most lucrative commercial endeavours were the new long-distance maritime trades. Control of the sea became the key to the universal monarchy. After all, Columbus's discovery of the New World, and the resulting Spanish claims to the monopoly of the South American silver mines, had led the Habsburgs to think 'of no less than an Universal Monarchy'. 'Whosoever commands the sea, commands the trade', Sir Walter Raleigh had noted long before, 'whosoever commands the trade of the world commands the riches of the world and consequently the world itself.'[15] By the 1670s it was a 'maxim as true as common, that he who is master of the sea, carries the keys of the world in his hand'.[16] Clearly, control of the sea was widely felt to be the first and essential step towards the universal monarchy.

The Dutch, it was argued, were not merely eager and aggressive merchants seeking to trade in new territories, they were grasping for a monopoly of all the world's trade. Like the King of Spain in the sixteenth century, the Dutch 'stretched their power to the East and West Indies; in many places whereof they are Lords of the sea-coasts, and have likewise fortified on the main, where king and people are subject to their devotion, and our countrymen the English, lying open to all the outrages a cruel and insulting tyrant can inflict upon them', explained one Restoration pamphleteer.[17] Anglican Royalist opinion at Court, on the London exchange, in the provinces, even in Persia, was unanimous in this interpretation of Dutch economic strategy. The court poet John Dryden expressed the sentiment most eloquently: 'Trade, which like blood should circularly flow, / Stop'd in their Channels, found its freedom lost: / Thither the wealth of all the world did go, / And seem's but shipwreck'd on so base a coast.'[18]

Anglican Royalists were convinced that once the Dutch had control of the seas, they would have all but established the universal monarchy.

[15] Sir Walter Raleigh, *Judicious and Select Essays and Observations* (London: A.M., 1667), p. 20. Sir John Evelyn plagiarised this passage in the preface to his intended history of the Anglo-Dutch Wars, *Navigation and Commerce, Their Original and Progress*. Dedicated to Charles II (London: Benjamin Tooke, 1674), pp. 15–17.

[16] 'A letter from a Gentleman in Holland to a Worthy Member of the House of Commons', 13/23 December 1677, British Library, Add. MSS 28092, f. 11r. See also Sir William Temple, 'A Survey of the Constitutions and Interests', May 1671, in Sir William Temple, *The Works* (London, 1814), II, p. 210; *The Character and Qualifications of an Honest Loyal Merchant* (London: Robert Roberts, 1686), p. 13.

[17] *A Discourse Written by Sir George Downing* (London: John Littone, 1672), pp. 44–5.

[18] John Dryden, 'Annus Mirabilis', in Edward Niles Hooker and H.T. Swedenberg, Jr. (eds.), *The Works of John Dryden*. Vol. I: Poems 1649–1689 (Berkeley, 1956), pp. 59–60, lines 5–9. Similar points are made in *Hogan-Moganides: Or, The Dutch Hudibras* (London: William Cademan, 1674), p. 112; *The Dutch Design Anatomized*. With allowance (London: Randal Taylor, 1688), p. 18.

'The world is now at that pass, that he who is Lord of the Sea, is also of the shore', averred the loyalist and future poet laureate James Howell in his elaborate political allegory *Dodona's Grove*, 'nor, I dare avouch did the Roman Republic, though as well swaddled in her infancy as any ever that was, come near to [the Dutch Republic] in so short a time.'[19] It had become a commonplace that the Dutch 'thought to grasp a pow'r great as old Rome, / Striving to carry all commerce away, / And make the universe their only prey.'[20] When a Dutchman in a tavern asked why the English insisted on calling his compatriots butterboxes, he was reputedly told, because 'you are so apt to spread everywhere, and for your sauciness must be melted down'.[21] Although 'no nation can be rich that abounds not in some part of his dominions in shipping, or who neglects trade', the moderate Anglican Royalist Sir Philip Warwick insisted, 'yet it is no policy to think to engross it, or be monarchs of it, as Holland hath for a time affected, & pursued that Sea-Monarchy as eagerly as Charles the Fifth or Francis the First did the Land Monarchy.'[22]

For Anglican Royalists – whether at the Council table, in trade company committee rooms, or in country taverns – the Dutch needed to be fought not because they were England's greatest economic rivals, but because they threatened to subvert the entire nexus of ideas upon which Restoration England was based. Their republicanism was a cancer which ate away at monarchy. Their religious pluralism and nominal Calvinism threatened to replace religion with atheism and grasping ambition. It was the moral failings of the Dutch that generated the economic threat to England. The Anglican Royalists complained not that the Dutch were making use of vastly superior economic resources, but that 'they treacherously burnt our stores, and murdered our men, committing outrages that the world cannot parallel'.[23] 'We are now chastising the

[19] James Howell, *Dodona's Grove, or the Vocall Forrest*, 3rd edn (Cambridge: R.D. for Humphrey Moseley, 1645), p. 22. The same point was made by the Swedish ambassador at the Hague. M. Appelbome to Chancellor of Sweden, 6/16 October 1665, Bodleian Library, Clarendon MSS 83, f. 251.

[20] Robert Wild, *A Panegyricke Humbly Addresst to the King's Most Excellent Majesty* (London: A.P. for Philip Brooksby, 1673), p. 3. Similar points were made by Edmund Waller in 'Instructions to a Painter', 1665, in George DeF. Lord, *Poems on Affairs of State*. Vol. I 1660–1678 (New Haven, 1963), p. 25, lines 69–70; John Crouch, *The Dutch Imbergo, Upon the State Fleet* (London: Edward Crowch, 1665), p. 7; and John Ogilby, *The Frog, or The Low-Countrey Nightingale, Sweet Singer of Amsterdam*. Based on Aesop's Fable of the Frogs (?1672), pp. 1–2.

[21] *The Complaisant Companion* (London: H.B., 1674), part II, p. 32.

[22] Sir Philip Warwick, 'Of Government', 28 August 1679, Huntington Library, MSS HM 41956, p. 182. Warwick did not believe, in 1679, that the Dutch were still pursuing that policy. I owe this reference to the kindness and generosity of Dr Blair Worden.

[23] *A Prophecie Lately Transcribed From an Old Manuscript of Dr. Barnaby Googe* (London: J.C. for R. Robinson, 1672), p. 3; Edward Hyde, Earl of Clarendon, 'A Brief Narrative of Late Passages', 1664, Bodleian Library, Clarendon MSS 83, f. 377.

Dutch', one pamphleteer explained during the third Anglo-Dutch War, 'not for their industry . . . but for their ingratitude, incivility, and rag-manners.'[24] Anglican Royalist merchants wanted to fight the Dutch not because they thought they would be able to seize new trade routes, nor to pursue their short-term economic self-interest – indeed many of them knew that an Anglo-Dutch War would be disastrous for their particular trades – but because they thought their long-term economic survival was at stake.

II

The Anglo-Dutch War of 1672–1674 was nevertheless a turning-point. Immediately after the Restoration, while memories of the anarchy and confusion of the later 1650s were still fresh in the minds of most Englishmen and women, the Anglican Royalist case had seemed particularly strong. A broad range of moderate opinion, including many who had opposed the King in the 1640s or who had accommodated themselves to the Protectorate, had been convinced that the threats from the radical sects and from the republicans demanded a foreign policy directed against their European allies, the Dutch. Louis XIV's invasion of the United Provinces in the Dutch Year of Wonders in 1672, however, changed their thinking. The image of the Dutch forced to slit the dykes in a desperate attempt to prevent French armies from overrunning the country made claims that the Dutch were seeking universal monarchy seem incredible.[25] More importantly, the demise of the Dutch republican regime and William III's consequent assumption of the offices of Captain General and Stadholder alleviated English fears of the ideological threat posed by the United Provinces. Once again led by a Prince of Orange against a power which sought to dominate Europe, the Dutch now sparked memories of Elizabeth's virtuous comrades in arms.

English moderates had supported war against the Dutch in the 1660s and early 1670s because the Dutch republican party, led by John de Witt, appeared to be ideologically committed to the overthrow of the English monarchy. It was this republican faction, not their domestic enemies the Orangists, who had fallen from Protestant virtue, replacing godly

[24] *A Discourse Written by George Downing*, p. 50.

[25] After the States of the United Provinces had by their powerful arms constrained Spain to acknowledge them a free state . . . they were for a time the object of their neighbour's admiration and envy, every one endeavouring to court and make alliances with this growing state, which began to be looked upon as the umpire of Europe,' recalled one observer from the perspective of the 1680s, 'but this high reputation of theirs has suffered notable eclipse since the war of 1672, when France . . . brought them to the very brink of destruction.' (*The Designs of France Against England and Holland*. [1686], p. 7)

worship with a base materialism. All of the Dutch infringements on the English fishing trade, the atrocities perpetrated in the East Indies, the casuistical application of treaties, even the ideological justification for Dutch mercantile policy – Grotius's *Mare Liberum* – indeed 'all the mischief which hath befallen this nation, hath ever been occasioned, or fomented by that [republican] party'.[26] Consequently, the moderates had never wanted to destroy the Dutch, but only the republican faction. 'We may hope for a better neighborhood when persons of honor and integrity shall rule their Councils, and the Government be reduced into some rational form', argued Henry Stubbe, who was at the time a client of the moderate Royalist Edward Conway, 'but certain it is that most of the mischiefs which have befallen Europe during the last century have had their original from this perfidious faction of Oldenbarnevelt'.[27] English moderates, then, were fighting the Dutch on behalf of the Prince of Orange and rational government. 'Be just to him, and us, the quarrel ends', one poet simply put it.[28]

The sensational demise of the republican party in the United Provinces coming, as it did, in the wake of the spectacular successes of the French armies, made the Nonconformist and radical claim – a claim made persistently and with increasing frequency throughout the 1660s – that the French had been seeking universal monarchy all along seem all the more credible. This grouping in the English political nation had always denied that the Dutch were seeking universal monarchy. Instead, the success of Dutch commerce, the republican Slingsby Bethel insisted, could only result from 'industry and ingenuity'.[29] In this view the wars against the Dutch made no economic sense. The Nonconformist divine Joseph Hill derided 'the senseless clamor of men' for war, crying 'We are competitors for trade! It's our interest! Our interest! Down with the Dutch!' because it was manifestly clear that 'the world is wide enough, and the sea large enough for both nations to exercise their skill and industry.'[30] The only explanation for the Anglo-Dutch wars, Nonconformists and their ideological fellow travellers had claimed, was that they were part of the French grand strategy, a strategy designed to achieve the universal monarchy. The massive French naval build-up, Colbert's mercantilist policies, and the duplicitous French mediation between the English and

[26] Henry Stubbe, *A Further Justification of the Present War Against the United Netherlands* (London: Henry Hills and John Starkey, 1673), sig. C1.

[27] Stubbe, *A Further Justification*, sigs C3–C4.

[28] Crouch, *The Dutch Imbergo*, p. 8. See also: Robert Wild, *A Panegyricke Humbly Addresst to the King's Most Excellent Majesty*, pp. 4–5.

[29] Slingsby Bethel, *The Present Interest of England Stated* (London: D.B., 1671), pp. 30–1.

[30] Joseph Hill, *The Interest of these United Provinces*. 30 November 1672 (Amsterdam: Thomas Berry, 1673), sig. G2.

the Dutch were all of a piece. It was clear that Louis XIV had 'no greater desire than to take the Dominion of the Sea from us, and the precedency in commerce'.[31] The net result would be ominous indeed. 'France has been dangerous enough to the rest of Europe, whilst they were in a manner without shipping', the author of the *Discourses Upon the Modern Affairs of Europe* wrote with trepidation, but now nothing seemed to prevent them from driving 'on that huge design of ambition for the Universal Monarchy which has so long swelled their hearts'.[32] No one could now doubt that they were 'setting up an Universal Monarchy of commerce'.[33]

In the 1670s, while French armies seemed poised to overrun all Europe, the English began to ask themselves how they had been duped into fighting wars so manifestly against their interest. The answer was omnipresent in Restoration England: the French had successfully implemented a policy of cultural subversion. The French, cognizant that it would be 'a hard matter' to conquer England, had discovered 'finer ways to victory than by force of arms, and their gold has done them better service than their iron'.[34] Indeed, French inducements had been so successful that the English court was overflowing with French agents. 'Neither you, nor any man', confided the author of *The French Politician Found Out*, 'can know all the Papists, French and other disaffected, pre-engaged, innovators and pensioners in England, who Proteus-like can change themselves to all figures.'[35] It was precisely these 'French counsels', these men who 'applied themselves to France', these men who scrutinised 'all over the kingdom to find out men of arbitrary principles, that will bow the knee to Baal, in order to their promotion to all public commissions and employments', these men who have 'undertaken and do make it their business, under so legal and perfect a government, to introduce a French slavery, and instead of so pure a religion, to establish the Roman idolatry' whom Andrew Marvell blamed in his classic *Account of the Growth and Popery and Arbitrary Government* for England's failure to prevent the growing power of France and for attempting to make the English Monarchy 'absolute'.[36]

[31] *Popery and Tyranny: Or, The Present State of France* (London, 1679), pp. 9–11; *A Free Conference Touching the Present State of England Both at Home and Abroad: In Order to the Designs of France* (London: E.T. for R. Royston, 1668), pp. 38–9, 49–50.

[32] *Discourses Upon the Modern Affairs of Europe* (1680), p. 3; *Europae Modernae Speculum*, pp. 91–2.

[33] *French Intrigues Discovered*, p. 5.

[34] Slingsby Bethel, *The Present State of Christendome and the Interest of England, With a Regard to France* (London: J.B. for H. Brome, 1677), pp. 24–5; Slingsby Bethel, *The Interest of Princes and States* (London: John Wickins, 1680), sigs. A4v–A5r.

[35] *The French Politician Found Out* (London: Robert Harford, 1680), p. 9.

[36] Andrew Marvell, *An Account of the Growth of Popery, And Arbitrary Government in England* (Amsterdam, 1677), pp. 14, 16, 100, 151, 154.

The powerful and cunning Louis XIV had a wide variety of means to infiltrate the English political nation. French women were well known to be 'engines of the state', who brought with them 'corresponding colonies of that restless, ambitious and intriguing nation, to make the interest of that court where they go bend to that of their native country'.[37] Charles II's well publicised affairs with French women, principally Louise de Kerouaille, Duchess of Portsmouth, led at least one Member of Parliament to exclaim that 'he cannot repose any confidence in the King, if he puts his counsel into "strange women".[38] This was hardly surprising since the Duchess of Portsmouth, 'who like a Dalilah passed from France to lull asleep the [English] Sampson', was popularly thought to have persuaded Charles II to break the Triple Alliance.[39] After his fall from power, even the Earl of Danby was certain that 'the French interest was chiefly supported by my Lady Portsmouth'.[40]

More subtle, yet perhaps more dangerous than French embraces were French dresses and French manners. French romances, French dances,

[37] *The Politician Discovered* (London: Langley Curtis, 1681), first discourse, pp. 24–5.

[38] Michael Mallet, 23 May 1677, in Anchitell Grey, *Debates of the House of Commons From the Year 1667 to the Year 1694* (London: D. Henry and R. Love, 1763), IV, p. 367. Mallet was drawing an explicit parallel to Solomon's loving many foreign women and the consequent demise of Israel detailed in 1 Kings 11. See also James J. Cartwright (ed.), *The Memoirs of Sir John Reresby* (London: Longman, Green, and Co., 1875), p. 191. One popular poem of 1679 'The Dissolution', made a similar point:

When French runs through the Prince's veins
And he by theirs not our law reigns
When French creeps into the Royal bed
First charming codpiece then the head
And Monarchs swives on good behaviour
But as he'll show dear Monsieur favour
When female buttocks dictate thus
Good Lord what will become of us?
Is there no end of monarch's itch
who lolls upon a fulsome bitch
Who ranker as the adder grows
Ferreting her belly with his nose
And swears upon her bawdy skin
He'll let the mass & French troops in
Assign his crown & regal power
To be disposed of by a whore. (British Library, Add. MSS 34362, f. 49r)

[39] *The Present Policies of France and the Maxims of Lewis XIV Plainly Laid Open* (London, 1689). Exactly reprinted as *The Present French King Drawn to the Life* (London: R. Baldwin, 1689), p. 6; *The Design of France Against England and Holland* [1686], p. 6.

[40] Earl of Danby, 'Memorandums about the Duke of York', September 1679, in Andrew Browning, *Thomas Osborne Earl of Danby and Duke of Leeds 1632–1712* (Glasgow, 1944), II (Letters), p. 88. See also Danby's similar comments from the same period on p. 91. Shaftesbury made an identical remark about Portsmouth in a paper of 1679 quoted in W.D. Christie, *A Life of Anthony Ashley Cooper, First Earl of Shaftesbury* (New York: Macmillan and Co., 1871), II, pp. 311–12.

French plays – alas, even French fruit – were all the rage. 'A Curse on these French cheats', swore one of Thomas Shadwell's stage creations, 'they begin to be as rife amongst us as their country disease, and do almost as much mischief too: No corner, without French tailors, weavers, milliners, strong water-men, perfumers, and surgeons.'[41] 'We must have all French about us', seethed another pamphleteer in mock disbelief:

> their behaviour, their fashions, their garb in wearing them, their mean way of house-keeping (to the utter extinguishment of the noble way of Old English Hospitality), their needy men for servants, their mere dietary leeches or scholastic methodists (no better than most of our own) for physicians; their cast tooth-drawers and barbers that had not worth enough to earn bread at home, to become our admired surgeons; French music, French dancing-masters, French air in our very countenances, French legs, French hats, French compliments, French grimaces.

'Such is the witchcraft also upon other nations of Europe,' this author warned, 'that having made the French language and humors universal, I cannot but look on it as a sad omen of Universal Slavery' since 'a nation's taking of a language from another nation, and preferring it before their own, hath usually been a forerunner of, and prepared the way for, its conquest.'[42]

When in the early 1670s the English attempted to emancipate themselves from French fashion and reassert the native style of wearing vests, the French were furious, and sent Charles's sister, the Duchess of Orleans, to 'laugh us out of these vests'. The French placed a high value on this minor incident, the Marquis of Halifax recalled, because they knew well 'that it is a natural introduction first to make the world their apes, that they may be afterwards their slaves'.[43] Though English attempts 'to ape the French' had only rendered them 'ridiculous', it brought 'great pride' to the French because they realised it allowed them

[41] Thomas Shadwell, *The Humorists* (London: Henry Herringman, 1671), p. 2.

[42] Marchamont Nedham, *Christianissimus Christianandus. Or, Reason for the Reduction of France to a More Christian State in Europe* (London: Henry Hills, 1678), pp. 37–8. The significance of Nedham's anti-French arguments will be discussed in the next section. An almost identical argument was made about the 1670s in the post revolutionary pamphlet *Nero Gallicanus: Or, The True Pourtraicture of Louis XIV*, p. 13.

[43] Halifax, 'Character of a Trimmer', M.B. Brown (ed.), *The Works of George Savile Marquis of Halifax* (Oxford, 1989), I, p. 227. The same story about the vests is repeated in *Nero Gallicanus*, p. 67. For discussions of the emergence of the vest, and its resubmergence under the weight of French style see Esmond S. De Beer, 'King Charles II's Own Fashion: An Episode in Anglo-French Relations 1660–1670', in *Journal of the Warburg Institute*, 2 (1938–39), pp. 105–15; Diana de Marly, 'King Charles II's Own Fashion: The Theatrical Origins of the English Vest', in *Journal of the Courtauld and Warburg Institutes*, 37 (1974), 378–82; David M. Kuchta, '"Graceful, Virile, and Useful": the origins of the three-piece suit', in *Dress*, 17 (1990), pp. 118–26.

to 'preside over our genius, and to guide it into all the fashions which their rambling fancies take'.[44]

Along with French fashions came French principles. 'That same legereté, on which the French so value themselves,' and which had so recently become the fashion in London as well as Paris, 'is but in plain English, a lightness of humor, by the which they are easily piped into a new mode of government.'[45] Algernon Sidney complained that 'French lackeys, valet de chambres, tailors, and others like them in wisdom, learning and policy . . . when they fly to England for fear of a well-deserved galley, gibbet or wheel, are ready to say *Il faut que le roy soit absolu, autrement il n'est point roy*'.[46] 'Who is so blind not to see what further steps have been taken by conspirators', Robert Ferguson asked, 'not only to be in love with the French mode and manners, but also with the very French yoke of slavery put about the necks of their own natives, longing for that day to come, when the same yoke of tyranny and slavery, shall be fitted upon the Englishmen's shoulders, as now upon the French asses'.[47]

After the Dutch revolution of 1672 large numbers of Presbyterian Royalists and moderate Anglicans, those who had loathed and feared the aggressive republicanism of the de Witt faction, could now join their more radical Protestant brethren in denouncing the political machinations of the King of France. They felt free to call for a new Dutch alliance, an alliance which they very much hoped would bring as much glory as had the old Elizabethan Anglo-Dutch alliance, because their quarrel had been with a corrupt political party, not with Dutch political or religious culture.

The Presbyterian Royalist Anthony Ashley Cooper, Earl of Shaftesbury, was merely the most flamboyant of those who shifted from an anti-Dutch to an anti-French alignment in the early 1670s. As Lord Chancellor, and member of the infamous Cabal, the Earl of Shaftesbury delivered the single most celebrated piece of Restoration oratory. Comparing England to Rome, the United Provinces to Carthage and himself to Cato, he exclaimed '*Delenda est Carthago*'.[48] 'Let this be remembered', Shaftesbury thundered, 'the States of Holland are England's eternal enemy both by interest and inclination'. This, he explained, was because they were 'the

[44] *Remarques on the Humours and Conversation of the Town* (London: Allen Banks, 1673), pp. 97–8.

[45] *A Prospect of Government in Europe* (London: Daniel Brown, 1681), pp. 66–7.

[46] Sidney, *Discourses*, p. 287.

[47] Robert Ferguson, *The Second Part of the Growth of Popery and Arbitrary Government* (Cologne: Philliotus, 1682), pp. 159–60; T. De Hay, *A Letter from Paris* (1681), pp. 1–2; *The Catholick Ballad: Or, An Invitation to Popery, Upon Considerable Grounds and Reasons, to the Tune of 88* (London: Henry Brome, 1674), broadside.

[48] Grey, *Debates of the House of Commons*, 5 February 1673, II, p. 2.

common enemies to all monarchies, and I may say especially to ours, their only competitors for trade and power at sea, and who only stand in their way to an universal empire, as great as Rome'.[49] Although this speech has usually been interpreted as a spectacular piece of Hollandophobic rhetoric, Shaftesbury was at pains to make clear that he attributed Dutch policy not to the nation as a whole but to the republican faction. England declared war against the Dutch Republic, Shaftesbury made clear in the autumn of 1673, because 'the king was obliged for the security of a lasting peace, as also by the laws of gratitude and relation, to see the House of Orange settled, and the Loevestein, that Carthaginian party brought down'.[50]

Shaftesbury was not being inconsistent, nor displaying pique for having dismissed from the Privy Council, when in 1675 he warned that the King of France 'is grown the most potent of us all at sea'. 'Tis incredible the money he hath, and is bestowing in making harbors, he makes nature itself give way to the vastness of his expense', marvelled Shaftesbury,

> and after all this, shall a Prince so wise, so intent upon his affairs, be thought to make all these preparations to sail over land and fall on the back of Hungary, and batter the walls of Kaminitz, or is it possible he should oversee his interest in seizing Ireland, a thing so feasible to him, if he be master of the seas, as he certainly now is; and which when attained gives him all the Southern Mediterranean, East and West India trade and renders him both by situation and excellent harbors, perpetual Master of the Seas without dispute.

The only hope for 'disengagement from the French interest', Shaftesbury insisted, lay in the 'two Houses differing from the sense and opinion of Whitehall'.[51] Upon the signing of the Treaty of Nijmegen Shaftesbury was furious, exclaiming that that peace, concluded 'by the mediation of the English Court, and, to speak truly, enforced by them', was one by which 'the Crown of England hath neither honour nor visible advantage, but is exposed, as well as the Emperor, the King of Spain, the States of the United Provinces, to the mercy of the French'.[52] Indeed, in 1680 when he

[49] Anthony Ashley Cooper, Earl of Shaftesbury, *Journal of the House of Lords*, 5 February 1673, XII, pp. 525–6.

[50] *Journal of the House of Lords*, 27 October 1673, XII, p. 589. The Dutch republican party were known as the Loevesteiners because the supporters of Jan van Oldenbarnevelt, including John de Witt's father and Hugo Grotius, had been imprisoned in Loevestein castle by Prince Maurice.

[51] Shaftesbury's Speech, 20 October 1675, *Two Speeches* (Amsterdam, 1675), pp. 8–9.

[52] Shaftesbury's paper, quoted in Christie, *Life*, II, p. 281. It is certainly true that Shaftesbury expresses a real fear of Popery in this paper, but he did not conceive of the international struggle as one between Catholicism and Protestantism. It is hard to understand why the Emperor or the King of Spain would be aligned with England against France in a war of religion.

felt compelled to explain Parliament's reticence to vote money for a war against France, Shaftesbury insisted that 'nothing ever shut the English purses but the fears of having their money used against them'.[53] Who were these men who prevented England from going to war against France? This pernicious 'French interest' and 'opinion of Whitehall', Shaftesbury identified as 'some of the Episcopal clergy of our British isles' as well as the 'High Episcopal Man and the Old Cavalier'. These men wanted 'to fight the old quarrel all over again' in defence of the principle that 'monarchy is of divine right'. 'Our statesmen and bishops', insisted Shaftesbury drawing the most frightening of parallels, are 'now as well agreed as in old Laud's time, on the same principles with the same passion to attain their end'.[54]

John Milton's godson and nephew John Phillips, who catered to more popular audiences than Shaftesbury, also shifted in the 1670s from castigating Dutch designs on universal dominion to excoriating the French pretensions upon universal monarchy. In his almanac for 1672 Phillips claimed that the 'hogen States' were no 'more likely' to achieve their design to 'establish the fifth monarchy in an Universal Commonwealth, than Sabbothy Levy to receive and recollect the ten scattered tribes, for taking posssession of the Holy Land'.[55] A decade later, Phillips published a popular dialogue between the devil and his servants delineating the French strategy for achieving the universal monarchy. Louis XIV 'no more dreaming of mortality, than you of dying', Belsagor explained to Pluto, 'is resolved to make himself the Universal Monarch . . . to which purpose he goes daily on, vexing, tormenting and encroaching upon his neighbours, that nobody can live in quiet for him. No leagues will hold him, no faith will bind him up'. Indeed, the treaty of Nijmegen (1678) had hardly slowed Louis XIV's advance. Louis XIV, Phillips had an English agent of the French King remark, 'conquers more in the times of Peace, than all the European Princes besides can do, by the greatest face of war they are able to make'. Phillips's Frenchman, 'Monsieur Francois',

[53] *A Speech Lately Made By A Noble Peer of the Realm.* [Shaftesbury] (London: F.S., 1681). Narcissus Luttrell, *A Brief Historical Relation of State Affairs from September 1678 to April 1714*, (Oxford, 1857), I, 31 December 1680, p. 2.

[54] Shaftesbury's Speech, *Two Speeches*, pp. 10–11; Earl of Shaftesbury, *A Letter from a Person of Quality to his Friend in the Country* (1675), pp. 1, 7, 34. Henry Stubbe undertook a similar ideological odyssey to that of Shaftesbury. I hope to discuss that further elsewhere. See James Jacob in *Henry Stubbe, Radical Protestantism and the Early Enlightenment* (Cambridge, 1983), pp. 117–18, 131–2; Henry Stubbe, *A Justification of the Present War Against the United Netherlands* (London: Henry Hills and John Starkey, 1672); Henry Stubbe, *A Further Justification*; Henry Stubbe, *The History of the United Provinces of Achaia*. Based on Jacobus Gothofredus, but significantly altered (London: Andrew Clark for Jonathan Edwin, 1673).

[55] Phillips, *Montelions Predictions, or the Hogen Mogen Fortune Teller*. 11 May 1672 (London: S. and B. Griffin, 1672), p. 6.

neatly summarised the inevitable consequence: 'my master will have all or none; for though he may be constrained to use the Turk, you may be sure he'll give him Polyphemus's Law, devour him last, for he hates competitors'.[56]

French economic policies, French military victories, and manifest French perfidy convinced all but the hottest Cavalier, all but the most extreme Tory, in short all but the Duke of York and his immediate supporters, that England needed to join the European struggle against the intended French universal monarchy.[57] Throughout the 1670s anti-French sentiment was building in a powerful crescendo of vituperation. 'If his Majesty will give up all such as speak with fredom of the French', the English envoy John Dodington reported as early as 1670, 'for anything I know he must part with most of his subjects.'[58] William Garroway informed Parliament that 'our fears of ruin from the French are in everybody's mouth.'[59] 'There are ninety in a hundred against France, all England over', chimed in Colonel Birch.[60] The London weavers were said to be 'in a mutiny against the French'.[61] Sir John Reresby was certain that 'the nation did much desire a war with France'.[62] 'God be thanked we are at present very quiet', wrote one court newsletter writer on the eve of the Popish Plot, 'and people seem only dissatisfied with the greatness of French, which is still increased.'[63] Indeed, it was well known that the fateful last session of the Cavalier Parliament was called principally 'to alarm the French'.[64] 'There is no discourse here but of war', the Earl of Huntingdon reported from London in the Winter of 1678.'[65] As Colonel Birch returned to London for the Parliamentary

[56] Phillips, *A pleasant Conference Upon the Observator and Heraclitus*. (London: H. Jones, 1682), pp. 2, 28–9, 38.

[57] For York's insistence on a pro-French alignment see *Memoirs of Sir John Reresby*, pp. 115–16, 118; see also Sir William Coventry to Halifax, 27 May 1677, British Library, Althorp MSS C18, ff 16v–17r. James's Francophilia was, of course, proverbial. See 'The Duke of York's Farewell Speech to his Friends, ca. 1679–80', Folger MSS G.c.2; and 'Hodge's Vision', which accused him of being addicted to 'France and Rome', Huntington Library, MSS STT Lit (7).

[58] John Dodington to Joseph Williamson, 27 June 1670, Huntington Library, MSS STT 625; see also Dodington to the Earl of Arlington, 20 June 1670, Huntington Library, MSS STT 625. Unsurprisingly, Dodington was relieved of his post for expressing these views in an inn in Savoy.

[59] William Garroway, 19 April 1675, Grey, *Debates of the House of Commons*, III, p. 8.

[60] Colonel Birch, 10 May 1675, Grey, *Debates of the House of Commons*, p. 127.

[61] 'A Letter from a Gentleman in Holland to a Worthy Member of the House of Commons', 13/23 December 1677, British Library, Add. MSS 28092, f. 15r.

[62] *Memoirs of Sir John Reresby*, 28 May 1677, p. 118.

[63] Francis Benson, to Leoline Jenkins, 10 July 1677, Huntington Library, MSS HM 30314, unfoliated.

[64] Henry Thynne to Francis Parry, 20 December 1677, Folger Library, MSS V.b. 285.

[65] Earl of Huntingdon to John Geary, 24 January 1678, Huntington Library, MSS HA 5943; see also Huntingdon to Geary, 10 January 1678, Huntington Library, MSS HA 5942.

session people everywhere cried, 'God bless you, you are going to fight against the French'.[66] The Earl of Danby, who was in a position to know, wrote to the Earl of Essex that 'truly things appear to me more like a war with France than otherwise'.[67] Nor were the English unaware of the costs involved in fighting the world's greatest power. 'They of the country seem not to be afraid of war, nor what is the necessary concomitant of it, taxes', Thomas Thynne informed Halifax, 'so universal is their dread of the growth of France.'[68] Indeed, so certain was one English army officer that there would be war with France that he prepared and published an inspirational speech for his troops.[69] In this context, it does not seem that Marchamont Nedham was exaggerating by much when he claimed 'that if it were put to the vote of the people, whether a war or no war with France, I believe not one in a thousand, but would be for a war'.[70]

III

While Charles II never did begin the much desired war against France, he at least promised to do so as soon as the country was again united. James II, however, never felt it necesssary even to make a rhetorical concession to public opinion. Instead, he made every effort to suppress public discussion of European affairs.

The Tory reaction of the 1680s had provided James II with a remarkably loyal and united political nation. The ease with which he suppressed Monmouth's rebellion convinced all who cared to comment that the time was right for James to take on the great European menace, Louis XIV. Instead of opposing French tyranny, however, James appeared to adopt the French style of government. Instead of sending English redcoats to resurrect the glories of Crecy, Poitiers and Agincourt, James II burdened his own people with a standing army, violated parliamentary prohibitions against employment of Papists, and made every effort to make parliament itself subservient to his will. Consequently, the English people throughout the country welcomed William III's intervention. Far from expressing a traditional xenophobia, the English were well aware that in the autumn of 1688 the battle for the mastery of Europe was being fought in England. In Yorkshire 'neither the gentry nor

[66] Colonel Birch, 14 March 1678, Grey, *Debates of the House of Commons*, V, pp. 238–9.

[67] Danby to Essex, 4 December 1677, Browning, *Thomas Osborne*, II, p. 62.

[68] Thomas Thynne to Halifax, 9 December 1677, British Library, Althorp MSS C5, unfoliated.

[69] *Advice to a Souldier* (London: John Shadd for John Gay, 1680).

[70] Nedham, *The Pacquet-Boat Advice* (London: Jonathan Edwin, 1678), p. 6; see also Nedham, *Christianissimus*, p. 72. Whig propagandists made similar claims.

the common people seemed much afraid or concerned', marvelled the loyalist Sir John Reresby.[71] The Earl of Dorset, a political moderate, was heard to say 'that if they come it may be called the Merry Invasion'.[72] A pamphleteer friendly to James could not but admit that the people 'are running headlong into a slavery to the Dutch'.[73] When discussing the intended Dutch invasion the 'people yet speak of it smilingly', reported the Londoner William Westby, 'the reigning humor of the present time being so that the people believe if the Dutch should come . . . that as they & we are Protestants that they will not do us any hurt.'[74] Reflecting on the events of 1688 over a decade later, Charles Davenant explained William's popular support in the simplest of terms: he had achieved the desired ends. 'The Late Revolution, and the war that happened upon it', Davenant recalled, 'were both carried on upon the same foot of opposing the growth of the French Monarchy.'[75]

IV

Was the Restoration debate about foreign policy, then, a debate over religion? Was Louis XIV opposed exclusively because he was a Roman Catholic? Did Englishmen and women desert James II in 1688 because he was a Catholic who was pursuing a Catholic foreign policy? In short, were the events of 1688 merely a rerun of those of 1588 with Louis XIV replacing Philip II as the Catholic arch-villain?

A close examination of the language of political discussion makes one doubt the veracity of this argument. Although it is true that both those in favour of war against the Dutch and those insistent upon doing battle with the French thought that their policies would reduce the risk from Popery, Popery no longer had a predominantly theological meaning. A term so flexible as to embrace the predominantly Calvinist Dutch and the largely Roman Catholic French commented on more than just religious proclivities. Indeed, it is clear that in Restoration England the competing definitions Popery turned on political and cultural as well as religious associations. The Dutch, the Anglican Royalists pointed out, were Papists because they endorsed king-killing, something that no good Protestant could stomach. In the view of the Nonconformists and their allies the French Monarchy was Papist, despite its celebrated Gallicanism

[71] *Memoirs of Sir John Reresby*, 17 October 1688, p. 408.

[72] William Westby, Memorandum Book, 20 October 1688, Folger Shakespeare Library, MSS V.a. 469, f. 40.

[73] *The Dutch Design Anatomized*, p. 32.

[74] Westby, Memorandum Book, September 1688, Folger MSS V.a. 469, f. 37r.

[75] Charles Davenant, *Essays Upon I. The Ballance of Power. II The Right of Making War, Peace, and Alliances. III Universal Monarchy* (London: James Knapton, 1701), p. 28.

and spectacular squabbles with the Pope, because it was willing to use the power of priestcraft to promote absolute power and arbitrary government. Indeed, even those who saw Popery in the policies of the Restoration government did not believe that the Stuart brothers – two men more celebrated for their sexual exploits than their personal piety – were religious enthusiasts. Instead, it was claimed, Charles II and James II derived their religious principles from their politics. The two brothers in exile 'suffered their heads to be intoxicated with a necessity of absolute power, looking upon it as the only remedy to prevent the frequent revolutions in England', maintained one pamphleteer, and they soon realised 'that the only means to bring about their ends upon the English, and to free the Crown from depending upon Parliaments, was to introduce Popery by degrees into the island; for that under pretence of those insensible changes which religion would suffer, it would be easy to alter the laws and form of government.' In short, they determined 'that of all the Christian sects, the Roman is that which best agrees with arbitrary dominion, and is most proper to blind obedience'.[76]

Nor did the English perceive their historic role in Europe in confessional terms. England's place was not to lead Protestant crusades, but to prevent any other state from achieving the universal monarchy. Since 'England cannot pretend to such hopes of a universal monarchy', noted Algernon Sidney, and since 'France and Spain have long contended for it, therefore, 'tis best for England that no one in Europe attain unto it.'[77] 'That righteous maxim of holding the balance of Europe steady', agreed one pamphleteer, was a maxim the English 'took up above six hundred years ago.'[78]

Seventeenth-century European politics, in the eyes of Restoration Englishmen and women, then, was a stuggle to maintain national integrities against aspiring universal monarchs, not an unending series of religious wars.[79] Protestant England had a special role to play in this international power game, but it was not a confessional role. England should maintain a Protestant foreign policy only in that it should protect Protestantism where it was established by national laws; very few still called for crusades

[76] *The Happy Union of England and Holland* (London: Richard Baldwin, 1689), pp. 1, 13–14.

[77] Algernon Sidney, 'Court Maxims', Warwick County Record Office, p. 152.

[78] *Discourses Upon the Modern Affairs of Europe* (1680), p. 16. This observation was commonplace among commentators of all political stripes. See, for example, Hill, *The Interest of these United Provinces*, sig. O2r; *A Free Conference*, pp. 20–1; *French Intrigues Discovered*, p. 2; Marquis of Halifax, 'Character of a Trimmer', p. 223; Denzil Holles, 'Letter to Van Beuningen', p. 460; *The Design of France Against England and Holland*, p. 1.

[79] The rhetoric of balance of power is necessarily incompatible with a confessional foreign policy. An eschatological struggle between the forces of the Reformation and Counter-Reformation, between the forces of good and evil, can brook no compromise. It had to be a fight to the death.

against Rome. During the Thirty Years War a wide variety of European princes united 'against the aspiring House of Austria for the general good and liberty of all Europe'. 'Some ascribe all this to controversies in religion,' Algernon Sidney admitted, 'but besides many reasons that persuade me to believe that even Urban VIII, then Pope, did at first favour the design of Gustavus; no man can continue in that opinion who considers that France, Venice, and Savoy three Popish states were the contrivers and advancers of it.'[80] Supporters of the restored Monarchy understood international conflicts in the same terms. 'Wars for religion', maintained one 1660s' polemicist, are 'but a speculation, an imagery thing or as some problems in the metaphysic, astrology, or chimie, which wise or rather cunning men make use of to abuse fools, and that in truth there never was nor ever will be any.'[81] It was the historical role of maintaining the European balance, of preventing the growth of a universal monarchy, which, their critics claimed, the Restored Stuarts had abdicated. 'That equality between the two monarchies which we might forever have preserved', mourned the Marquis of Halifax, 'hath been chiefly broken by us, whose interest it was above all others to maintain.'[82]

Not only did the English deny that their own role in European politics was primarily confessional, but they insisted that Louis XIV's drive towards the universal monarchy had precious little to do with religion. It was true that Louis XIV mercilessly persecuted his Protestant subjects but, Sir William Coventry was quick to point out, 'the rigours in religion, in states, arise from interest rather than religion; formerly Spain was more rigorous in religion, and now France.'[83] The implication could not have been clearer. Religious persecution was a means to appear holy, while actually following the precepts of Machiavelli. The totality of Louis XIV's actions made a mockery of his claim to be *dévot*. 'Most evident it is that both priests and ministers are banished alike; that religious houses are dissolved as well as the Reformed Churches, that monasteries are sacked and destroyed as well as Temples, and that they

[80] Algernon Sidney, 'Court Maxims', Warwick County Record Office, pp. 153–4. Clearly Algernon Sidney understood foreign policy in terms of opposition to universal monarchy not in terms of 'uniting the Protestant cause in Europe' as Jonathan Scott claims. Apparently Dr Scott has based his analysis on the same pages from the 'Court Maxims'. See Jonathan Scott, *Algernon Sidney and the English Republic 1623–77* (Cambridge: Cambridge University Press, 1988), pp. 204–6. My reading of this document is much closer to that offered by Alan Houston in *Algernon Sidney and the Republican Heritage in England and America*. (Princeton, 1991).

[81] MSS Pamphlet by Sir Thomas Clifford (?), 1665, National Maritime Museum, Clifford Papers, vol. 3, Dw100, p. 5.

[82] Halifax, 'Character of a Trimmer', p. 224.

[83] Sir William Coventry, 31 October 1673, Grey, *Debates of the House of Commons*, II, p. 203. The same point was made about Spain in Boccalini, *Ragguagli di Parnasso*, p. 328.

make war with the same violence upon those that adhere to the Pope, as upon those that side with Calvin', recounted the author of *The Happy Union*.[84] Since the French King was not above weakening the Catholic Church 'especially in secular advantages of wealth and power', argued Marchamont Nedham, 'it almost equally concerns both Papist and Protestant, in reference to religion, to adventure their distinct powers and interests in one common bottom and resolution, to war with him, and to hinder the obstinate pursuit of an Universal Monarchy.'[85] Neither Protestant nor Catholic polemicists believed that they were engaged in the last phases of the great struggle between the Reformation and the Counter-Reformation.

Philip II of Spain might have seen himself as the secular arm of the Papacy, but it was pure anachronism to describe Louis XIV in those terms. 'Nobody thinks that France in its intentions of conquering us, ever thought of the church', scoffed one Orangist, 'or that the Emperor troubled his head about religion, when he designed our assistance; this was frequent pretence about a hundred years ago; but time and experience has taught us all wit.'[86] 'The question now on foot is a communion of state, not of faith', argued the author of a print distributed in 1688.[87] Clearly 'the main business is not now either about Calvinists or Catholics' but rather about 'the restitution to everyone of that which belongs to him; and to prevent the further usurpation of Louis XIV'.[88]

In this context, it is hardly surprising to discover that the alliance against France was multi-confessional. Though it is true, of course, that the Dutch and the English were particularly concerned to protect the Protestant religion, this was only because it was the religion by law established in their dominions. Freedom of Protestant worship was but one of the plethora of the liberties threatened by the French. 'For though

[84] *The Happy Union*, p. 29.

[85] Nedham, *Christianissimus Christianandus*, p. 72. Roman Catholic pamphleteers made the same point. See *The Present Policies of France and the Maxims of Lewis the XIV Plainly Laid Open*, pp. 19–20. The author of this pamphlet is a professed Catholic.

[86] *Two Letters: The One from a Dutch-Man to his Correspondent in England, The Other an Answer from the Said Correspondent* (1673), p. 9.

[87] *A Short Discourse Upon the Designs, Practices & Counsels of France* (first printed 1677. 29 December 1688), pp. 4–5.

[88] *The Present French King Demonstrated an Enemy to the Catholick as well as Protestant Religion.* Licensed 10 June 1691 (London: Tom Goodwin, 1691), pp. 18–19. See also *Nero Gallicanus*, p. 4; John Yalden, *Machiavil Redivivus* (London: Will. Cademan, 1681), sig. B3; *A New Discovery of the Private Methods of France* (London: J. Weld, 1691), p. 4; Gerald Aylmer (ed.), *The Diary of William Lawrence* (1679; Beaminster, Dorset, 1961), pp. 38–9; *A Learned Discourse on Various Subjects.* Dated 4 January 1678 (London: H. Sawbridge, 1685). This is a reprint with similar pagination of the 1677 pamphlet: *A Discourse of the Rise and Power of Parliaments*, pp. 130–1; *A View of the True Interest of the Several States of Europe* (London: Thomas Newborough, 1689), p. 58.

the preservation of the Protestant religion be most the concernment of England and Holland', elaborated one observer of the European scene, 'yet the special and immediate end of the preservation of Flanders, and the general end of holding the balance of Europe is Universal.'[89] Such a multi-confessional alliance was possible because England and its Protestant allies, unlike the French, were firmly committed to national self-determination in matters of religion. As early as the 1660s the country MP Sir Richard Temple had argued that 'foreign alliances' are to be secured 'with respect to the balance of monarchy & obviating that design [for universal monarchy]'. Therefore, Temple concluded, 'not only the Protestants but all who are on a distinct foot as the Portugal, the Catholic Princes of Germany, Dutch and Italian Princes not dependent on Spain, nay the Pope himself, *qua* Prince are to be united in this common bottom'.[90]

Religion formed but one part of the national identities threatened by France. Consequently a war against France was a war to protect national integrities, not a war of religion. 'The grand concern is now to support the right of nations, which is common to all', explained one particularly eloquent polemicist,

> and to prevent the introducing of maxims into the world which destroy all commerce among men, and will certainly render humane society no less dangerous and insupportable than that of lions and tigers; to defend the public faith of treaties, and remove from the sight of Christendom a scandalous example, which, by the fatal consequence of it, will surrender the most feeble to the will and pleasure of the strongest and most potent; to stop the inundation of a rapid torrent against the impetuosity of which neither leagues nor marriages, neither oaths nor ties of blood and parentage, neither amity nor condescensions, are mounds or dams sufficient to defend the common bulwark of Christendom against a vast design, which has no other ground but the insatiable thirst of conquest, no other end than despotic domination by clout of arms and slight of intrigue, nor any limits but such as fortune shall prescibe. In short, England is now to decide the fate of Europe, and to pronounce the sentence of her liberty or bondage.[91]

This language was not a 'xerox copy' of early seventeenth-century religious enthusiasm.[92] The European experience in the Thirty Years War and the English experience during the Interregnum had taught them all the impossibility of ever concluding a war of religion. 'If you make this a war of religion', warned the Parliamentary moderate Sir Thomas Lee

[89] *Discourses Upon the Modern Affairs of Europe*, pp. 9–10.

[90] Sir Richard Temple, 'An Essay Upon Government', 1667?, Bodleian Library MS Eng. Hist. c. 201, f. 13^r.

[91] *Nero Gallicanus*, pp. 63–4.

[92] The phrase is Jonathan Scott's in *Algernon Sidney and the Restoration Crisis*, p. 6.

when considering war against France, 'you will never have done.'[93]

In the later seventeenth century the defence of national identities and not the propagation of the true religion had become the organising principle of English political discourse. While English society remained profoundly religious, as the reformation of manners movement amply demonstrates, English political debate was taking place in increasingly erastian terms. The Protestant religion now made up but one element of the national interest.[94] Interest had replaced religious enthusiasm, ideas of English liberty had displaced conceptions of apocalyptic Protestant internationalism, as the dominant themes of Restoration political discourse. 'The genius and disposition of the times', the courtier Samuel Fortrey found soon after the Restoration, was 'to study more the interest and improvement of the nation than usually heretofore.'[95] Slingsby Bethel, who was more likely to speak a popular than a courtly language, agreed that 'the prosperity or adversity, if not the life and death of a State, is bound up in the observing or neglecting of its interest'.[96] Sir Heneage Finch, who agreed with Bethel about little else, emphasised that 'joint interests have often secured the peace of differing religions, but agreeing professions hath no example of preserving the peace of different interests. Religion never united those whose interests were divided'.[97] It was to this language of interest, not to the obsolete language of confessional strife, that polemicists appealed when they suggested that war against the Dutch or French would protect England's trade.[98]

[93] Sir Thomas Lee, 14 March 1678, Grey, *Debates of the House of Commons*, V, p. 242.

[94] Let me emphasize that I am not arguing that religion was unimportant, that religious proclivities had nothing to do with political alignments. Indeed, I am convinced that Nonconformists were far more likely to be Whigs, and High Churchmen tended to be Tories. Rather, I am trying to highlight an important phase in the *process* of secularisation. For other comments on secularisation of political language, see Steven N. Zwicker, 'England, Israel and the Triumph of Roman Virtue', in Richard H. Popkin (ed.), *Millenarianism and Messianism in English Literature and Thought 1650–1800* (Leiden, 1988), pp. 37–64: Blair Worden, 'Introduction' to his edition of Edmund Ludlow's *A Voyce from the Watch Tower* (London: Royal Historical Society, 1978), especially pp. 5–16, 51–5; A.D.T. Cromartie, *Sir Matthew Hale 1609–76*, unpublished PhD thesis, 1991, University of Cambridge, p. 152. Alan Houston has shown that for Algernon Sidney 'separating religion and politics . . . made it possible to preserve the integrity of each'. *Algernon Sidney and the Republican Heritage*, p. 125; in another sphere see the useful discussion in Paul Slack, *The Impact of Plague in Tudor and Stuart England* (Oxford, 1985), ch. 9.

[95] Jacob H. Hollander (ed.), *Samuel Fortrey on England's Interest and Improvement 1663*. (Baltimore, 1907), p. 9.

[96] Bethel, *The Present Interest of England Stated*, sig. A2r.

[97] Sir Heneage Finch, 'Speech for Supply', 31 October 1673, Leicestershire Record Office, D.G. 7/Box 4957/p. 33.

[98] In addition to the extensive discussion above, see Don Pedro de Ronquillo, *The Last Memorial of the Spanish Ambassador Faithfully Translated Into English* (London: Francis Smith, 1681). Luttrell, *Historical Relation*, 26 January 1681, p. 2.

The nation, not Scripture, determined the proper interest of the government. Indeed, though government itself existed by divine right, the form was necessarily a national creation.[99] 'But where this high power and sovereignty rests, in whom 'tis lodged, this is a point not so obvious: nor can the [saints] or holy Fathers any way help us in the discovery', observed one commentator; 'the customs and particular laws of every nation, are only capable to direct us in that scrutiny.'[100] 'There can be no universal rule', agreed Daniel Defoe in his justly famous *Reflections on the Late Great Revolution*, 'because that the laws vary according to the differing constitution of government that is in several nations.'[101] Because governments existed to serve the nation, though they were not necessarily created by the people, it was absolutely incumbent upon them to adopt a foreign policy which was in the best interest of the nation. In the English case, this precept necessarily elevated the importance of the Parliament, the national assembly. 'Now since interest will not lie, how is it morally possible, that the major part of the nation so qualified should act contrary to the true and proper interest of their country?' asked one controversialist. 'For tho' particular men may be imposed upon by artifice, or deluded with pretences, or biassed by private advantages, yet 'tis not imaginable, that the whole body should be so infatuated as not to see or so stupidly tame as not to oppose, as far as lawfully they may, what tends their universal ruin.'[102] The application to England's role in European affairs was obvious. 'This House has many years now advised the King to suppress the growing greatness of France, and the ministers would not', complained Sir Thomas Meres whose principles were sufficiently moderate to receive approbation from both Whigs and Tories, 'the interest of the nation is in this House, and the ministers are of another interest.'[103]

The centre of later seventeeth-century political discussion was captured by those who understood the world in national rather than religious terms. Naturally there were extremists on either end of the political

[99] The idea of unique national interests was central to later seventeenth-century defences of monarchy. See Houston, *Algernon Sidney and the Republican Heritage*, p. 81.

[100] *A Prospect of Government in Europe*, p. 6. This same point is made repeatedly by Algernon Sidney in his *Discourses*, see for example pp. 99, 502–10. I therefore find it difficult to accept Jonathan Scott's claim that Sidney had an 'exceedingly incomplete' notion of 'where the boundaries between nation states lay'. Scott, *Sidney and the Restoration Crisis*, p. 87. The notion of nation and national interest is central to Sidney's critique of absolute monarchy.

[101] Daniel Defoe, *Reflections Upon the Late Great Revolution*. (London: Richard Chisniell, 1689), pp. 56–7.

[102] *Vox Patriae*, sig. A1v.

[103] Sir Thomas Meres, 7 May 1678, Grey, *Debates of the House of Commons*, V, p. 357. It is important to note that Meres ended his career as a country Tory. He was no extremist.

spectrum who persisted in describing domestic politics in exclusively religious terms, and who demanded an international crusade against the anti-Christ.[104] But these men and women were already marginal to a debate conducted fundamentally about interest. Halifax's Trimmer, an imaginary Restoration moderate, came very close to expressing the typical worldview. 'Our Trimmer is far from idolatry in other things, in one thing only he cometh near it, his country is in some degree his idol', elaborated Marquis of Halifax,

> he doth not worship the Sun, because it is not peculiar to us, it rambleth about the world and is less kind to us than it is to other countries; but for the earth of England, though perhaps inferior to that of many places abroad, to him there is divinity in it, and he had rather die than see a spire of English grass trampled upon by a foreign trespasser.

The conclusion was clear: 'before the French blood can be let into our bodies, every drop of our own must be drawn out.'[105]

After decades of debate and discussion in coffee houses, playhouses, country taverns, Anglican churches and Dissenting meeting houses, the English knew what was at stake in their struggle with France. 'Tis true this war must needs be prodigiously expensive,' admitted the author of one pamphlet distributed soon after William of Orange had arrived in London, but 'in cases of this quality, people must do so as in a storm at sea, rather throw part of the lading overboard, than founder the vessel.'[106] 'France does endeavour by certain emissaries that are never wanting to her, cunningly to persuade everyone, that the war, besides the blood of part of their best soldiers, will cost them vast sums of money', sneered another defender of the Revolution, but

> one must needs have a mean opinion of that generous people, to think that they are either so covetous as to be thus wrought upon, or so simple, as for the saving their money and sparing the blood of some few, to do that which would most certainly be the cause of both their lives and fortunes, or plunge them at least into a constant misery.[107]

Englishmen and women were willing to suffer through the infringements

[104] Both Non-Jurors and extreme Dissenters, like William Penn, continued to place religion first on their lists of political objectives. Unsurprisingly both groups became Jacobites.

[105] Halifax, 'Character of a Trimmer', p. 237. Halifax was clearly not a Protestant internationalist. This is significant in the light of Dr Scott's arguments for the similarity between Halifax's and Sidney's views in *Algernon Sidney and the Restoration Crisis*, pp. 140–4.

[106] *A Short Discourse Upon the Designs, Practices & Counsels of France* (first printed 1677. 29 December 1688), p. 16.

[107] *The Fate of France* (London: Richard Baldwin, 1690), sig. A2v.

upon their personal liberty implicit in the Augustan state because they knew the alternative was subjugation to a universal monarch.[108]

Just as English republicans had hoped that a union with their Dutch brethren would thwart the ambition of one grasping monarch, so English Whigs and moderates hoped that a different sort of union – a dynastic union – would foil the aspirations of the new aspirant to universal monarchy. Before the third Anglo-Dutch War came to a close, Edmund Verney gushed that a marriage between William and Mary, an 'incorporation' of the two peoples, would 'give us the universal empire of the sea'.[109] Half a year later William Coventry thought the Prince of Orange 'is now at the head of all the business of Christendom' leading the crusade against Louis XIV, leadership which could only be confirmed by 'that match which the people of this nation so much wish & which he hath much reason to desire'.[110] These hopes and expectations were finally realised in the autumn of 1688. 'The grand complaint against France is for pretending to the Universal Monarchy', enthused the author of the aptly titled *Happy Union*, 'and I dare affirm, that had it not been for the great revolution in England, that France was upon the point of obtaining what she had been so long thirsting after.'[111] 'This news will be most of all amazing in France', the conservative Robert Southwell wrote of the revolution to the Duke of Beaufort, 'all our thunderbolts will light there, besides what might fall from the rest of Europe. They have great desolations and inhumanities to account for.'[112] Now that William III had liberated England, if the Christian Princes would 'cleave to his interests, the project of France concerning the Universal Monarchy of Christendom will fall to the ground'.[113] The English and Dutch allied together, predicted one polemicist, 'may be the restorers of Europe to her liberties'.[114]

James, it becomes clear, lost his crown not because of his religious belief, but because he had foresaken the national interest. Englishmen and women rallied around James, despite his known Catholicism in 1681

[108] In a sense, then, this essay can be read as the ideological backdrop to the developments chronicled in John Brewer's *The Sinews of Power: War, Money and the English State 1688–1783* (London, 1989).

[109] Edmund Verney to Sir Ralph Verney, 23 February 1674, Princeton University, Firestone Library, Verney MSS Microfilm, Reel 27 (unfoliated).

[110] William Coventry to Thomas Thynne, 11 November 1674, Longleat House, Thynne MSS 16, f. 202.

[111] *The Happy Union*, p. 50; See also *The Deliverance* (London: R. Baldwin, 1689), pp. 3, 7.

[112] Robert Southwell to the Duke of Beaufort, 14 December 1688, HMC, Twelfth Report, Appendix part IX, p. 94.

[113] *A View of the True Interest*, p. 45.

[114] *The Happy Union*, p. 4. See also *The Present Policies of France and the Maxims of Lewis XIV Plainly Laid Open*, p. 5.

and 1685, because they hoped he, as the rightful heir to the throne, would maintain the ancient constitution and protect England against the aspiring universal monarch. 'I am not of the opinion that the King being a Papist, has made himself incapable of the Crown', argued the Whig jurist Serjeant Maynard.[115] A polemicist friendly to James also knew that 'it is not Roman Catholic or Protestant religion is the quarrel'.[116] Instead, the Stuart brothers' crime was they have 'forsaken their true interest, blindly to follow that of France'. 'Tis an untruth that the new King of England is an usurper under the pretence of religion', insisted one of William's supporters, 'James II, seduced by the crafty and violent counsels of the French, together with his own haughty and capricious humour, had violated the laws of which he was the Protector and not the sovereign.'[117] 'If this King had followed his true interest', concluded one post-revolutionary pamphleteer,

> it is certain, as great a Catholic as he was, he might have peaceably enjoyed his three kingdoms; might have been the arbitrator of all Christendom, might have maintained peace and tranquility throughout Europe, might have openly professed his religion, favoured his Catholic subjects, and might even have placed some of them in public employments, especially military, without much offending his Protestant subjects.'[118]

But James chose instead to mimic Louis XIV at home, and appease him abroad. In so doing, he united Whigs, Trimmers, and moderate Tories in a fragile, yet potent alliance. The events of 1688 – 1689, then, should not be seen as yet another in a long string of religious wars, but as a permanent redefinition of English political culture, a final rejection of the French style of government.[119] Implicit in this cultural redefinition was an assumption that only unions of nations could prevent aspiring universal monarchs from achieving their ambitious aims. A Glorious Revolution indeed.

[115] Serjeant Maynard, 28 January 1689, Grey, *Debates of the House of Commons*, IX, p. 17.

[116] *Dutch Design Anatomized*, p. 21.

[117] *The Present French King Demonstrated an Enemy*, p. 19. Algernon Sidney had predicted that James would 'rather be a tributary to France than a lawful king of England'. *Discourses*, p. 265.

[118] *A View of the True Interest*, pp. 37, 43.

[119] This was the point the Earl of Danby made to the Earl of Chesterfield in September 1688: 'I confess as to my own part I had rather lose my life in the field than live under an arbitrary power, and see our laws and religion changed, which is now visibly the King's intention', in Browning, *Thomas Osborne*, II, p. 135.

3

POWER, COMMERCE, AND NATURAL LAW IN DANIEL DEFOE'S POLITICAL WRITINGS 1698–1707

LAURENCE DICKEY

IN this essay, I wish to make three claims about Daniel Defoe (1660 – 1731) during a specific period of his life. First, I wish to argue that in the late 1690s Defoe articulated a theory of power that had economic, political, and historical dimensions. Next, I wish to show how this theory of power, which is clearly expressed in the 'Standing Army' essay of 1698, informed the arguments Defoe would advance seven years later when he began to participate in the English – Scottish debate that culminated in the Union of 1707. Finally, I wish to demonstrate how, while trying to bring his theory of power to bear on the Union issue, Defoe began to recognise how his theory of power had to be adjusted so that it could take adequate account of the disparities of economic power between the two countries. While making this adjustment, I want to suggest, Defoe developed subtle distinctions in his theory of power which illuminate some of the strains that the economic realities of empire placed on the natural jurisprudential aspects of Defoe's pro-union arguments.

In approaching Defoe this way, I am attempting to do something that John Pocock urged Defoe scholars to do some time ago: namely, to take Defoe seriously as a social and political thinker as well as a famous novelist and key figure in the history of English literature.[1] Since that challenge was issued, very little has been done in that area of Defoe scholarship. Among political theorists, only Martyn Thompson seems to have responded to Pocock's promptings, offering us in the process a richly textured view of the context in which Defoe worked around 1700.[2]

I wish to dedicate this essay to Istvan Hont and John Pocock, friends and scholars who have taught me so much about the intellectual history of early modern Europe.

[1] J.G.A. Pocock, *The Machiavellian Moment* (Princeton, 1975), pp. 426ff.

[2] M. Thompson, *The Author of the True-Born Englishman*, Habilitationschrift der Neuphilologischen Fakultät (Tübingen, 1984); This is a spectacular work on several different levels and may be rewardingly consulted by historians, literary theorists, historians of literature, and political theorists.

As an intellectual historian, I have long been committed to the methodological strategy of contextualism – that is, to explaining thinkers and their texts in terms of their context.[3] To that end, I propose to examine a period in Defoe's life – roughly the ten-year period that runs from 1697 to 1707 – that provides a particularly fruitful context for evaluating Defoe as a social and political thinker. At the beginning of this period, Defoe was extensively involved in the standing army debate. As Pocock has taught us, that debate constitutes a defining moment in the history of English political thought. At the end of this period, Defoe was a leading figure in the Union debate. That, too, as is testified to by several essays in this volume, was a pivotal moment in eighteenth-century 'British' political thought. If our aim, then, is to begin to measure Defoe as a social and political thinker, this period would seem to recommend itself as a compelling unit for study.

Defoe's theory of power: the 'Standing Army' essay (1698)

In the 'Standing Army' essay, Defoe developed a theory of power which held that a nation's 'strength' lay more in its commercial wealth than in the martial valour of its people. Defoe enunciated this position, moreover, in an ideological context which for a variety of reasons forced him to question the Gothic version of English history in which the martial prowess of the militia – of the sword in the hands of the citizens – figured prominently.[4] As is well known to students of English history, anti-army writers of the so-called 'new country party' immediately opposed William III's request to Parliament to fund a standing army after the signing of the Peace of Ryswick in September, 1697.[5] Since the peace had brought the long war with France to an end, Parliament wished to reduce the forces William currently had under his command. For his part, William, anticipating a future military confrontation with France over the Spanish Succession, wished to be prepared for that eventuality.

Working from within and without Parliament, the leaders of the country party (respectively Robert Harley and John Trenchard), orchestrated a propaganda campaign against William's army initiative. Thus, as Parliament was about to meet to vote on William's request, the

[3] Laurence Dickey, *Hegel* (Cambridge, 1987), pp. vii–xiii.

[4] In addition to J.G.A. Pocock, *Politics, Language, and Time* (New York, 1973), pp. 104–47, see most recently R.J. Smith, *The Gothic Bequest* (Cambridge, 1987). An excellent insight into Gothicism in seventeenth-century English thought can be found in M. Goldie, 'The Roots of True Whiggism 1688–1694', in *History of Political Thought*, I (1980), 212–5.

[5] For details, consult L. Schwoerer, *No Standing Armies* (London, 1974) and J. Downie, *Robert Harley and the Press* (Cambridge, 1979).

anti-army pamphlets of Trenchard, Walter Moyle, and Andrew Fletcher began to appear. Although it is not at all clear how Defoe initially became involved in this debate, he quite certainly was writing for William and against the country party when he published the 'Standing Army' essay in early 1698.

In this essay, Defoe approaches the standing army issue from two different but related perspectives. On the one hand, he objected to the anti-army writers' refusal to acknowledge how changes in the exigencies of modern warfare had rendered arguments that linked national security to militia forces quite dubious. On the other hand, Defoe detected in the anti-army writers' fascination with England's 'Gothic' constitution a deep-seated ideological obstacle to the modernisation of England's fighting forces. The connection Defoe posits between the one and the other, between inner-and outer-*politik*, is the hinge upon which the 'Standing Army' essay turns.

Defoe admitted that the militia had once served the cause of English liberty well: indeed, it had allowed feudal barons to call out their forces to check the designs of kings with absolutist ambitions. But that was a circumstance, Defoe said, that was only appropriate to 'England formerly' – when it was a martial society.[6] By contrast, 'England now' was quite differently constituted – a trading empire existing in a commercial world of large and expanding nation states. Moreover, changes in the power relations among European nations, especially since the 1650s, had made England quite vulnerable to attack by sea. The Dutch wars, of course, had recently and graphically testified to that possibilty. But it was the French, who under Colbert had become a 'sea' as well as 'land' power, that truly threatened England's security – in interlocked commercial and military senses.[7] An invasion from France or blockades at sea were real possibilities, ones that Defoe contended had to be included in national security calculations of any English government. The anti-army writers, Defoe charged, had not done this, preferring instead to define the standing army issue as an internal constitutional matter rather than as an external problem of national security. On the first reading, one that Defoe regarded as incredibly insular, William III, who had only recently 'delivered' England from tyranny, was perceived as a threat to 'enslave the nation' with his standing army.[8] On Defoe's reading, Louis XIV, who

[6] Daniel Defoe, 'An Argument Shewing, that a Standing Army, with Consent of Parliament is not Inconsistent with a Free Government', in J. Boulton (ed.), *Daniel Defoe* (London,1965), pp. 35–50.

[7] Defoe had argued this point in *The Englishman's Clear, and True Interest* (London, 1694). Also see S. Bethel, *The Interest of Princes and States* (London, 1680), pp. 1–73.

[8] Defoe, 'Standing Army', p. 38.

had been at war with Europe for years, was the enemy with whom England still had to reckon.

Given these larger considerations, Defoe started his essay by situating the standing army issue in the context of new and emergent power relations among the European states. Speaking of 'England now', Defoe deliberately contested the main assumption of the anti-army writers by declaring that, 'while our peace at home seems secure' under William's leadership, the matter of maintaining 'our peace abroad' is something else again.[9] Focusing on France, Defoe warned that 'Here is a neighbour grown too great for all the rest', that is, too great unless all the rest enter into 'leagues and confederacies . . . to mate' the French king.[10] To begrudge a standing army to William in these circumstances, Defoe complained, was tantamount to condoning Louis XIV's attempt to establish France as the successor to the 'universal monarchy' Charles V had tried to establish for sixteenth century Spain. Looking ahead to the crisis in the Spanish Succession that would surely arise when the sickly Charles II died, Defoe used the occasion of 'the pen and ink war' over the army to argue for allowing William to continue as head of a coalition of nations whose mission was to ensure preservation of a 'balance of power in Europe'.[11]

On the surface, Defoe's decision to approach the standing army controversy from the perspective of 'French power', from outside in, as it were, looks transparently political. Writing at the court's request, Defoe chose as the new party 'hack' to support William's foreign policy line – the balance of power line that William had advocated long before becoming King of England.[12] But the concern with French power – with Louis XIV's aspiration to install himself at the head of a universal monarchy – had agitated English thinkers since the late 1660s. As the writings of Slingsby Bethel (among numerous others) reveal, there were English writers, especially among the Dissenters, who had perceived the need for England to align herself with the Dutch in order to preserve the balance of power in Europe. In the 1660s and 1670s, of course, this entailed a *rapprochement* with the Dutch; and, as several of the essays in

[9] Defoe, 'Standing Army', p.39. [10] Defoe, 'Standing Army', p. 39.

[11] Defoe used the phrase in two other tracts from this period: *The Interests of the Several Princes and States of Europe* (London, 1698), p. 29; and *Two Great Questions Considered* (London, 1700), pp. 14–5. Defoe acknowledged his debt to Rohan for the reason of state argument in *True Interest*, p. 25. On Rohan's long-term influence on English thinkers, see J. Gunn, "Interest will not lie", *Journal of the History of Ideas*, 29 (1968), pp. 551–64, and A.B. Worden, 'Classical republicanism and the Puritan revolution', in H. Lloyd-Jones, V. Pearl, and A.B. Worden (eds.), *History and Imagination* (London, 1982), pp. 182–200.

[12] As I shall argue throughout this essay, I believe that Defoe was a more 'principled' writer than has hitherto been appreciated. In this, I concur with W. Ferguson, 'Imperial crowns: a neglected facet of the background to the Treaty of Union 1707', in *Scottish Historical Review*, 53 (1974), 31.

this volume note, this was precisely what emerges as a main tendency of English political thought during the 1670s and 1680s.[13] As a Dissenter, who had close ties with London's radical community, Defoe would have long been familiar with this line of argument, and there is evidence that he had advocated pro-Dutch views from at least 1689 on. Thus, the fact that Defoe was a party-writer in 1698 does not mean that the argument advanced in the 'Standing Army' essay was not his own, however 'commonplace' the argument might have otherwise been.

What was surely not commonplace about the 'Standing Army' essay was the range of issues Defoe managed to work into his criticism of the anti-army writers. As we shall see, in this endeavour to refute the perennial wisdom upon which the anti-army position was based, Defoe wove together a series of arguments which, I shall argue, add up to a coherent natural jurisprudential defence of William III's policy – at home and abroad.

Defoe begins his repudiation of the anti-army writers by reminding readers of the lesson Europeans had drawn from the United Provinces' successful revolt against Spain earlier in the century. What that major event in European history showed – and this was evident to thinkers from Giovanni Botero, Francis Bacon, and Walter Raleigh on – was that the creation, projection, and preservation of power in the modern world depended heavily on a nation's economic prosperity.[14] More specifically, it depended on trade, on the kind of trade that had brought so much wealth to industrious Dutch in the seventeenth century. As Defoe saw it, profits generated by Dutch trade had bankrolled the long war against Spain, a war which eventually led to the economic exhaustion of the latter.

> The Spaniards were once the most powerful people in Europe . . . The Dutch . . . were then . . . [Spain's] subjects . . . [The Dutch] are now the richest people in the world; and the Spaniard is now become the meanest and most despicable people in Europe, and that only because they are the poorest.[15]

Given this startling reversal of power, Defoe concluded that, in modern

[13] See any of the following works by S. Bethel: *The World's Mistake in Oliver Cromwell* (London, 1668); *The Present Interest of the English State* (London, 1671); *Princes and States*. Some of the connections between London radicals and pro-Dutch dissenters in England and Scotland are discusssed in G. De Krey, 'London radicals and revolutionary politics, 1675–1683', in M. Goldie, T. Harris and P. Seward (eds.), *The Politics of Religion in Restoration England* (Oxford, 1990), pp. 134–51.

[14] See G. Botero, *The Reason of State*, trans. P.J. and D.P. Waley, (New Haven, CN 1956); F. Bacon, 'Of the True Greatness of the Kingdom of Britain', in D. Montagu (ed.), *The Works of Francis Bacon* (Philadelphia, 1850), II, pp. 222–9; and W. Raleigh, *The Works of Walter Raleigh* (Oxford, 1839), VIII, pp. 299–316.

[15] Defoe, 'Standing Army', p. 47.

warfare, 'he who has the longest sword has yielded to them who had the longest purse'.[16]

Within the context of widespread European appreciation of the long-term implications of the so-called 'Dutch miracle', the longest purse argument also had a long history in English political thought. For example, as early as 1608, Bacon had outlined the main features of the argument while discussing the truth or falsehood of the old saying: 'money was the sinews of war'.[17] From at least that time on, the argument runs through the writings of such thinkers as Lewes Roberts, Henry Parker, and William Temple, right down to the 1690s when Defoe's fellow projectors, Nicholas Barbon and Dalby Thomas, underscored the connections between trade, wealth, and power.[18]

On Defoe's own testimony, we have it that he was writing this way early in the 1690s – at a time when he was a 'projector' and working with Thomas, the man to whom he dedicated his *Essay Upon Projects* in 1697.[19] In that essay – five years in the writing, Defoe said – there is much discussion of what Defoe termed the 'art' of modern warfare.[20] Commenting upon this art, Defoe noted how 'new inventions' (many of which he lists) had made warfare more expensive as well as more destructive.[21] Developing trained personnel with expertise in the various new technologies of modern warfare cost money, Defoe said. To that end, he proposed establishing a military academy for the training of a cadre of professional military officers.[22] While outlining what the course of study at such an academy might look like, and while estimating the cost of such an undertaking, Defoe offered the observation 'that 'tis not he who has the longest sword so much as he who has the longest purse, will hold the war out best'.[23]

As several informed commentators have pointed out, Defoe's appreciation of the exigencies of modern warfare sets off his position on the standing army from that of Trenchard and other anti-army writers who, in Lois Schwoerer's words, displayed 'surprising naiveté' on this subject.[24] As

[16] Defoe, 'Standing Army', p. 48. Defoe used this phrase repeatedly throughout his life. For earlier uses, see S. Clement, *A Discourse of the General Notions of Money, Trade, and Exchange,* (London, 1695), p. 32; and [Philanglus], 'Britannia Languens, Or A Discourse of Trade', in J. McCulloch (ed.), *Early English Tracts on Commerce* (Cambridge, 1952), p. 293.

[17] Bacon, 'True Greatness', p. 225.

[18] See L. Roberts, 'The Treasure of Traffic', in J. McCulloch (ed.) *Early English Tracts on Commerce* (Cambridge, 1952), pp. 50–119; H. Parker, *Of a Free Trade* (London, 1648); W. Temple, *The Works of Sir William Temple* (New York, 1968), I, pp. 31–203; N. Barbon, *A Discourse of Trade,* ed. J. Hollander (Baltimore, 1905); and D. Thomas, 'An Historical Account of the Rise and Growth of the West-Indian Colonies', in *Harleian Miscellany*, 2 (1809), pp. 357–87.

[19] Defoe, *An Essay Upon Projects* (London, 1969), p. iii.

[20] Defoe, *Projects*, p. 3. [21] Defoe, *Projects*, p. 3.

[22] Defoe, *Projects*, pp. 252ff. [23] Defoe, *Projects*, p. 258.

[24] Schwoerer, *No Standing Armies*, p. 182.

Schwoerer has also noted, Trenchard approached the army issue as an internal constitutional matter.[25] Defoe, by contrast, defined the army issue in terms of national security. For him, of course, that was the equivalent of making it an economic matter as well – which is precisely why Defoe states in the *Projects* essay that 'the sinews (of war) fail' when money is in short supply.[26]

In drawing connections between money and warfare, trade and power, Defoe subtly shifted the focus of the standing army debate from the domestic to the international level. On those terms, instead of being at the centre of an internal constitutional struggle between William and parliament, the standing army issue became a matter of national security, of 'reason of state' in a Machiavellian sense.[27] English 'liberty', to be sure, was at stake in both frameworks. But on Defoe's terms the national security focus had the added advantage of allowing him to use the longest purse argument to stress the need for increased parliamentary attention to England's commercial development and long term economic interests.

Thus, the 'Standing Army' essay challenged the anti-army writers on two levels at once. On the one hand, it implored them to be realistic about the French threat to England's security. On the other hand, the essay called on these self-proclaimed English 'patriots' – many who were country gentlemen and members of the majority opposition party in the Commons – to articulate a policy for English commercial development that would ensure English commercial wherewithal in the future.[28] If France intended to incorporate the sea into her plan for universal monarchy, then surely, Defoe reasoned, the anti-army writers would have to support William III's policy – for long-term economic reasons, if for nothing else.

Two points about Defoe's two-tier argument need to occupy us here. First of all, Defoe's longest purse argument would seem to suggest that establishing a commercial 'empire on the sea', to use John Somers' phrase,[29] was in England's national interest, for the wealth derived from trade would assure 'power and plenty' for England as she entered the eighteenth century.[30] Many of Defoe's contemporaries – some quite close

[25] Schwoerer, *No Standing Armies*, p. 180. [26] Defoe, *Projects*, p. 258.

[27] For Defoe's use of reason of state arguments earlier in the 1690s, see J. Moore, 'Daniel Defoe: King William's Pamphleteer and intelligent agent', in *Huntington Library Quarterly*, 34 (1971), pp. 251–60. More generally, Gunn, 'Interest', is helpful on the reason of state argument in seventeenth-century thought.

[28] Defoe's tirades against the 'pretended zeal' of English 'patriots' start in 1694, in the *True Interest*, pp. 3–5.

[29] J. Somers, *A Letter, Balancing the Necessity of Keeping a Force in Time of Peace* (London, 1697), pp. 1–2.

[30] J. Viner, *Essays on the Intellectual History of Economics*, ed. D.A. Irvin (Princeton, 1991), pp. 128–53.

to him – emphasised this point as well, often doing so in the language of 'reason of state'.

A problem, though, arises when this Machiavellian view of economic relation among nations is juxtaposed with Defoe's stated concern with balancing French power within the family of European (i.e., Protestant) nations. With regard to France, the concerns of reason of state are defensive – aiming at negating French power through a system of alliances, especially with the Dutch. In the context of the former, however, the idea of a defensive alliance vanishes as reason of state principles are invoked to justify policies that prevent rivals, even Protestant ones, from penetrating England's markets. In 1698, Defoe's argument for a standing army encompasses both possibilities. As we shall see shortly, the Union debate of a few years later will oblige Defoe to deal with the problem in a more explicit way.[31]

The second aspect of Defoe's argument that calls for further comment has to do with the way Defoe's longest purse argument threatened the country opposition to William III at a strategic institutional point. As has previously been noted, the country party was generally composed of independent country gentlemen with landed interests. In the 1690s, however, the Commons contained interest groups – dissenters, London merchants, projectors, and war financiers – that not only had stakes in commercial expansion but were eager to win governmental support for such expansion. In that context, Defoe's commercial challenge to the country party – like Bethel's, Algernon Sidney's, and John Wildman's before him – was calculated to present the Commons with a choice between a Gothic and a commercial future. In that respect, the 'Standing Army' essay may be read as an expression of the emerging commercialisation of a strain of radical Whiggism in England after the Revolution.

That Defoe attached great importance to the last consideration becomes strikingly evident over the last half of the 'Standing Army' essay. There, in an attempt to discredit the anti-army writers further, Defoe attacked the country opposition on the grounds that its Gothic conception of English liberty distorted English history and trivialised the role of the Commons in it. To support this accusation, Defoe closely

[31] The larger issue that arises here can be seen in the complexities of the language Viner, *Essays*, pp. 39–54, uses to discuss seventeenth-century economic thinking. On the one hand, the thinking is identified both as mercantilist and as oscillating between universalistic and nationalistic extremes. On the other hand, Viner generally associates mercantilism with the latter alone. The up-shot of this is that mercantilism as an economic discourse (as distinct from a policy) becomes dissociated from economic universalism. That, in turn, involves de-emphasising the close connection in seventeenth-century thinking both between natural law and economics and between certain liberalising tendencies in Protestantism and emerging economic thinking.

examined Trenchard's 'Argument' of late 1697. In that pamphlet, Defoe argued, the author's equation of 'sword' and 'sovereignty' was based on out-dated republican wisdom that had no relevance to the modern world.[32] All the same, anti-army writers clung vigorously to that wisdom, insisting that so long as the sword remained in the hands of citizens England would be free from tyranny. Appealing to the teachings of Machiavelli, Bacon, James Harrington, and Robert Molesworth, Trenchard claimed that the preservation of liberty in England required a 'Gothic constitution' in which freeholders, by assuming the responsibilities of citizen-soldiers, would ensure that 'limited' government would continue to be the measure of political life in England.[33]

To discredit this argument, Defoe developed an alternative perspective on the forces that had sustained liberty in England since 1500. He did this by directly contesting the Gothic version of English history that informed the arguments of his opponents. Availing himself once again of the power of the purse argument, only this time in the context of domestic politics, Defoe tried to demonstrate two things: first, that a standing army was not, in his words, 'inconsistent with a free government'; and, second, that the Gothic conception of English liberty and English history had become an obstacle to both the preservation and the spread of English liberty in the modern world.[34]

With regard to the first task, Defoe is most cursory, asserting rather than arguing his case. Focusing attention on the title of Trenchard's pamphlet, Defoe simply declared: 'I do confute the assertion in [Trenchard's] title . . . that a standing army is inconsistent with a free government'.[35] He then added: 'I shall further do it by the authority of Parliament' – by which he meant he would show his readers that the keeping of an army 'with consent of Parliament' is neither 'against law' nor inconsistent with the principles of 'free' government.[36] In fact, as Defoe saw it, the 'true balance' of the English constitution required the sword to be 'trusted in the hands of the king, and the purse in the hands of the people'.[37]

On the surface, this might appear to be but a variation on the formula for a 'limited' government, a formula in which institutional forces check the political power of each other. But in the light of the commercial basis of Defoe's theory of power another reading suggests itself. For would it not follow from his argument that, if a government were organised

[32] For Trenchard's remarks: see, 'An Argument Shewing, that a Standing Army is Inconsistent with a Parliamentary Government', in *A Collection of State Tracts Published During the Reign of William III* (London, 1706), II p.567.

[33] Trenchard, 'Inconsistent', p. 568.

[34] Defoe, 'Standing Army', pp. 44–5.

[35] Defoe, 'Standing Army', pp. 41, 38.

[36] Defoe, 'Standing Army', p. 43.

[37] Defoe, 'Standing Army', pp. 45–6.

around a 'true balance', the 'power of the purse' would have precedence over that of the 'sword'?[38]

As with so much else that Defoe wrote on politics in the 1690s, there was a long 'pro and con' history behind the Parliamentary purse argument. As several entries in Thomas Burton's diary account of the English Parliamentary debates of the late 1650s show, the notion that the purse was more essential to the power of the Commons than the sword had been discussed much earlier.[39] Bethel, for example, observed that

> in giving (up) the purse . . . the people . . . give away all the security they have for their rights and liberties; because, having the purse [gives its holder] power to raise what forces he pleases, and having that, all bounding him signifies no more than bounding a lion with paper chains.[40]

Trenchard, of course, explicitly rebutted the logic of this argument, exhibiting a realistic streak of his own when he noted how easily James II had managed to find extra-Parliamentary means to fund troops under his sole command.[41] Though Defoe conceded this point to Trenchard with regard to James specifically, he none the less dismissed Trenchard's point overall, suggesting rather that James was the exception that proved the rule.[42] Thus, Defoe was perfectly willing to associate himself with Bethel's view of the power of the purse, especially since Bethel had impeccable radical credentials (among Whigs and Dissenters) and had relatively recently tried himself to identify Whiggism with a programme of commercial expansion.[43]

In the light of this background information, it is easier to understand the connection Defoe posited between England's commercial development and the power of the purse argument on the one hand and the growing political power of the Commons on the other. Moreover, with these affinities in his mind, it is easier to see why and how Defoe proposed to de-legitimise Gothicism as a mode of political and cultural discourse in late seventeenth century England. And insofar as late seventeenth-century English Gothicism relied on what Pocock has called the neo-Harringtonian conception of history to sustain it, Defoe's attack on Gothicism obliged him to contest that influential conception of English history too.[44]

[38] Defoe, 'Standing Army', p. 50.

[39] Consult Thomas Burton, *Diary of Thomas Burton*, ed. J. Rutt (London, 1828), III, pp. 88, 124, 179, 421, and 534n.

[40] S. Bethel, quoted in T. Burton, *Diary*, III, p. 534n.

[41] Trenchard, 'Inconsistent', p. 571.

[42] Defoe, 'Standing Army', pp. 47–8.

[43] R. Ashcraft, *Revolutionary Politics and Locke's 'Two Treatises of Government'* (Princeton, 1986), p. 228.

[44] On this theme, see Pocock, *Politics*, pp. 104–47. As Goldie, 'True whiggism', has shown, John Wildman, whom Defoe knew, is an important figure in this development.

Defoe begins his criticism of Trenchard, Gothicism, and neo-Harringtonianism with a simple chronological distinction. Trenchard's view of English history, Defoe said, expressed values that were appropriate to 'England formerly' but not to 'England now'.[45] What is more, Defoe held that Trenchard's history was flawed because it 'came to omit giving us an account' of that part of English history that had led to the present – that is, it neglected to explain the gradual emergence of the House of Commons as the dominant force in Parliamentary government.[46]

After establishing a 'then versus now' framework for his discussion of English history, Defoe proceeded to insert into that framework the 'power of the sword' vesus the 'power of the purse' argument. Trenchard, needless to say, personified the former, Defoe the latter. By implication, moreover, Defoe intended both sets of associations to be homologous with the all- important opposition he wished to establish between older Gothic and newer commercial tendencies in the commons.

From this point on in the essay, Defoe's strategy is to show how Trenchard's celebration of Gothic balance distorted 'our English story'.[47] It did so, Defoe argued, by representing England's feudal barons, who collectively possessed the martial might to check the king's exercise of 'arbitrary power', as the mainstays of English liberty.[48] As Defoe saw it, however, the real consequence of the barons' martial power lay elsewhere – less in their capacity to fustrate the political designs of absolute kings than in the unabashed way the barons wreaked havoc on each other during a long period of 'commotions, civil wars and battles'.[49]

In a highly revealing passage, Defoe refers to the 'tyranny of the barons' and to how the barons inflicted 'misery and slavery' on the 'common people'.[50] Indeed, from Defoe's perspective there was little to choose between the rule of 'one tyrant' and that of 'three hundred' barons.[51] So much, Defoe facetiously said, for the security of English liberty under the auspices of the 'old Gothic model of Government'.[52]

If one of Defoe's debating strategies in the 'Standing Army' essay was to associate the Gothic balance with anarchy rather than stability – was, in Pocock's sense, to pit Harrington against the neo-Harringtonians – another strategy was to explain how the House of Commons came to be an intitutional source of political stability during the tumultuous years of the barons' rule.[53] As Defoe explained, what 'we call a Parliament' arose when 'the people . . . obliged the king and barons to accept of an

[45] Defoe, 'Standing Army'. p. 38.
[46] Defoe, 'Standing Army', p. 44.
[47] Defoe, 'Standing Army', p. 49.
[48] Defoe, 'Standing Army', p. 45.
[49] Defoe, 'Standing Army', pp. 44–5.
[50] Defoe, 'Standing Army', p. 45.
[51] Defoe, 'Standing Army', p. 45.
[52] Defoe, 'Standing Army', p. 45.
[53] Defoe, 'Standing Army', p. 45.

equilibrium . . . [a] due balance, . . . the foundation on which we now stand'.[54] Referring to this 'balance' as 'a much nobler constitution in all its points than the old Gothic model of government', Defoe insisted, as several important radicals before him had, that this 'alteration' marked the ascendancy of parliament as the guardian of English liberties.[55]

The radicalism that is implicit in the distinction Defoe draws between Gothicism and commercialism becomes all the more important because of the way he works the theme of 200 years of English commercial expansion into it. His view of this expansion was that it coincided with the emergence of 'the people' and the demise of the barons as political forces in English political life. And to underscore the role commerce played in the rising and declining fortunes of these two social groups, Defoe specifically said that the spendthrift ways of the latter were in large part responsible for the growing wealth and power of the former.[56] From this appraisal of the shifting grounds of domestic political power in England from 1500 on, Defoe drew the conclusion that the increasing power of parliament in general and that of the House of Commons in particular had been driven by England's commercial expansion, the implication being that the growing commercialisation of English society rendered Gothicism increasingly irrelevant to the political life of the nation.

At this point, I think, we can see that Defoe availed himself of a strategy of historicisation both to de-legitimize Gothicism and to celebrate the political benefits of commercialism. On the one hand, insofar as he was successful in associating Gothicism with 'England formerly', he could equate Gothicism with political disorder and incessant violence. And since both these conditions were in his mind inimical to commercial activity, Defoe implied that Gothicism represented the values of a martial rather than a commercial society.[57] On the other hand, the clear links he established between increased trade, the decline of the barons, and the emergence of the House of Commons as the institutional expression of those changes, enabled Defoe to represent 'England now' as a commercial

[54] Defoe, 'Standing Army', p. 45.

[55] Defoe, 'Standing Army', p. 45.

[56] Defoe, 'Standing Army', p. 45. Pocock, *Politics*, p. 139, and John Robertson, *The Scottish Enlightenment and the Militia Issue* (Edinburgh, 1985), pp. 22–59, have discussed the 'dialectical' implications of this historical focus. Much of the argument of Bk III of Adam Smith's *Wealth of Nations* turns on this issue.

[57] The larger issue is to determine when the Gothic became associated exclusively with martial society. In 1690, N. Barbon, *Discourse*, p. 27, regarded Gothicism as compatible with commercialism. As J.G.A. Pocock (ed.), *The Political Works of James Harrington*, (Cambridge, 1977), pp. 82ff and 137ff, has explained, the association of Gothicism with the martial dates from at least the 1650s. By the time of Hume and Smith, the Gothic has become indistinguishable from 'feudal anarchy'.

society whose 'long purse' ensured its military security among the nations of Europe. At the same time, the role the Commons now played in English political life guaranteed that England's commercial classes would exercise control of the military through the power they had over the purse. On those terms, the theory of power that informs Defoe's view of English history relies heavily on the commercialisation argument to make it historically persuasive. That triangular interplay – between power, commerce, and history – is what ultimately gives the 'Standing Army' essay its coherence.

The Union debate, I: the language of liberty in Defoe's Review, *1705–1707*

As his biographers have documented, Defoe's life from 1698 to 1704 oscillated between experiences of exhilarating literary success and depressing business failures.[58] As the widely acclaimed author of 'The True-Born Englishman' (1701) Defoe achieved public recognition that matched the ambitions he had for himself as a writer and a gentleman;[59] but as a bankrupt merchant, who had engaged in many shady dealings (even with members of his own family), Defoe was put into jail in 1702 and pilloried and imprisoned again in 1703 for libel.

Throughout these difficult years, Defoe continued to write, but it was not until 1704, just after his release from prison, that he re-established writing momentum. To be sure, writing was almost forced upon him by his personal circumstances, for as a religious Dissenter he was prohibited from holding certain positions in society and as a debtor many business opportunities were foreclosed to him. Given these circumstances, it was natural for Defoe to turn to writing as a means of livelihood – which explains, Paula Backscheider argues, why Defoe produced '400,000' words in 1704.[60]

To gain his release from prison, moreover, Defoe had to give Harley, now a member of the government with responsibility for Scottish affairs, certain assurances about his willingness to write political propaganda for the administration. In these circumstances, Defoe's *Review* began to appear in February 1704. For the next nine years, Defoe single-handedly produced the *Review* – by all accounts a prodigious effort as well as a tremendous contribution to the beginnings of modern journalism.[61]

More relevant to our purposes here, though, is that by the autumn of

[58] P. Backscheider, *Daniel Defoe* (London, 1989), part 1.
[59] M. Shinagel, *Daniel Defoe and Middle-Class Gentility* (Cambridge MA, 1968).
[60] Backscheider, *Defoe*, pp. 139ff.
[61] J. Sutherland, *Defoe*, (London, 1937), pp. 105ff, and Downie, *Harley*, ch. 3.

1706, Defoe's *Review* was aggressively calling for Scotland to ratify the terms of the treaty that had been negotiated in London earlier in the year. Since we know in retrospect that Defoe was 'Harley's man' at the time, it has always been assumed that Defoe pursued this line because he had agreed with Harley to use the *Review* as a propaganda agent for disseminating the government's pro-union views in England.[62] There is, of course, no doubt about Defoe's relations with Harley from at least 1703 on.[63] Nor can it be gainsaid that the *Review* played an important role in promoting the Union – more so in England, where the *Review* was widely distributed, than in Scotland, where it was not readily available.[64] But as Backscheider has recently shown, there is much evidence to suggest that there is more to Defoe's participation in the Union debate than can be accounted for by his employment status.[65] In what follows, I want to explain both why that is the case and how our initial concern with Defoe's theory of power fits into that argument.

There is little evidence in the *Review*'s first year of publication to suggest that Defoe had much interest in Scottish affairs at that time. As English – Scottish relations deteriorated in 1704-5, however, the matter of Union began to dominate the pages of the *Review*, especially from late 1706 on.[66] That can hardly be surprising, since Defoe had been secretly sent to Scotland by Harley in mid-September, 1706, to keep the government informed on Scottish attitudes towards Union.

Harley's decision to send Defoe to Scotland was calculated to take advantage of both Defoe's journalistic talent and his unique qualifications for reporting on Scottish affairs.[67] Though evidence is hard to come by, it would appear that Defoe had been well known in the Scottish community in London before Harley dispatched him to Scotland.[68] He certainly knew William Paterson, a fellow projector in the 1690s' and probably William Carstares.[69] Paterson and Carstares, moreover, were advising Harley in 1702–4 – at the time Harley was arranging for Defoe's release from prison. And it was about this time that Charles Davenant, who was also advising Harley during these years,[70] wrote his so-called 'Memorial' of 1705 – in which he urged the government to send a secret agent to

[62] 'Harley's man' is the title of chapter 5 of Sutherland's book, *Defoe*.

[63] Backscheider, *Defoe*, pp. 153ff; and Downie, *Harley*, pp. 57ff.

[64] J. Downie, 'Daniel Defoe and the general election of 1708 in Scotland', in *Eighteenth Century Studies*, 8 (1975), pp. 315–28, and J. Moore, *Daniel Defoe. Citizen of the World* (Chicago, 1958), disagree about Defoe' influence on the Union.

[65] Backscheider, *Defoe*, pp. 152, 208.

[66] Backscheider, *Defoe*, pp. 195–252.

[67] Appreciated by Moore, *Citizen*, ch. XV.

[68] Backscheider, *Defoe*, pp. 203ff.

[69] F. Bastian, *Defoe's Early Life* (London, 1981), pp. 119, 229.

[70] Downie, *Harley*.

Scotland to help gather information for supporters of Union.[71] Why Harley eventually chose Defoe rather than Davenant for that task is unclear, but Backscheider thinks that Defoe's close relations with the Scottish business community in London might explain Harley's choice.

There is considerable evidence that Defoe's interest in Scotland and the Union issue grew steadily in 1705. In early March 1705, Defoe's *The Consolidator* was published. Among other things, it offered a politically transparent rendering of English – Scottish relations at the beginning of the eighteenth century.[72] And, as Backscheider has appreciated, the book is (in spots) pro-Union and extremely sympathetic to Scottish complaints about England's effort to bully the Scots into a Union agreement.[73]

Furthermore, by April 1706, at the very time English and Scottish commissioners were beginning to meet in London to negotiate the articles upon which the Treaty of Union would be based, Defoe had accepted a 'request' from pro-Union members of the Scottish community living in London to write a series of tracts promoting Union.[74] Hence the publication in May of two of Defoe's early essays on Union.[75] Defoe's interest in Scottish affairs, then, had been building for almost a year and a half before the Harley assignment. And, if we add to this evidence the testimony of Defoe's Scottish friends that, in July 1706, they had prevailed upon him to travel to Scotland in order to promote Union from there, it would seen most misleading to regard him as no more than Harley's stooge in late 1706.[76]

Defoe arrived in Edinburgh in early October 1706, after two weeks of travel. Although his official assignment was to keep Harley abreast of the ins-and-outs of the Scottish Parliamentary debates on Union, Defoe used the occasion of his stay in Scotland to begin an extensive discussion of the Union in the *Review*.[77] He did so, it would appear, without instructions to do so from Harley.

[71] C. Davenant, 'Memorial', in D. Waddel, 'An English economist's view of the Union', *Scottish Historical Review*, 35 (1956), 148–9.

[72] Daniel Defoe, 'The Consolidator', in *The Novels and Miscellaneous Works of Daniel Defoe*' (Oxford, 1840), pp. 346ff, 402–7.

[73] Backscheider (*Defoe*, pp. 145–6, 206) discusses the Scottish references in *The Consolidator*. I have not been able to ascertain whether there are significant differences between the early and late 1705 editions of *The Consolidator*. As the Alien Act was passed in between, there may be important differences.

[74] Backscheider, *Defoe*, pp. 207–8.

[75] Defoe, *An Essay at Removing National Prejudice Against a Union with Scotland* (Edinburgh, 1706), in four parts. I have used the Edinburgh publication of late 1706 in which the four parts are published in one edition. Parts I and II were initially published in London in May 1706.

[76] Backscheider, *Defoe*, pp. 208, 218, 222.

[77] All citations to the *Review* refer to the facsimile edition: ed. A. Secord (New York, 1938). Citation of the volume will be followed by page references. I have modernised the Old Calendar datings.

He opens the *Review* discussion of Union with testimonials from famous European military figures as to the martial prowess of the Scottish people,[78] a strategy he likewise used in his long poem, *Caledonia*, published shortly thereafter and aimed exclusively at Scottish readers.[79] He follows this up with a qualifying statement:

> the way of fighting in the world is very altered; and the longest purse has now so much more influence in matters of war than the longest sword, that I believe, the Scots themselves will own, they are no match for us that way.[80]

That, too, is a theme he develops in *Caledonia*.[81]

From what we have learned from Defoe's previous writings, the longest purse reference here is not without significance. It alerts us to Defoe's intention to discuss the Union in terms of his theory of power, especially in its commercial aspects. Indeed, it would not be too much to say that Defoe's recommendations for Union are wholly consistent with the perspective on power he had developed in the 'Standing Army' essay almost ten years earlier. And, as we shall see, as Defoe applies the theory to the cicumstances of the Union, he expands the power argument into a full-blown theory of how martial and commercial societies differ in the modern world.[82] It is the prospect of the latter, and of the power, peace, and plenty that goes with it, that Defoe holds out to the Scots as a material benefit of Union.[83]

That Defoe approached the matter of Union with his theory of power in mind is important for two reasons. First of all, carry over of the power argument from the earlier to the latter context obliged Defoe, at least initially, to frame the Union issue in martial versus commercial terms – in terms of arms versus trade.[84] On that score, Defoe pitted Scottish opportunity for economic development against Scottish pride in the nation's martial heritage. Presenting the Union as a choice between the one and the other enabled him rhetorically to associate the pro-Union argument with the former and anti-Unionism with the latter.

Having the power thesis at hand, moreover, also permitted Defoe to

[78] *Review*, III pp. 447–8.

[79] Defoe, *Caledonia* (Edinburgh, 1706). pp. 27–36.

[80] *Review*, III, p. 477.

[81] Defoe, *Caledonia*, p. 31.

[82] A general issue arises here, for the shift from martial to civil and from martial to commercial conceals the tension between civil and commercial that arises later in the eighteenth century. Pocock, 'Paradigms', discusses the long-term ramifications of this tension.

[83] Variations on the power, peace, and plenty theme appear repeatedly in England's seventeenth-century discourse of trade literature.

[84] This, too, is a wide-spread theme of the discourse of trade literature. See, e.g., (Philanglus), *Trade*, pp. 291–3.

rebut Scottish anti-Union writers who wished to preserve the martial values associated with 'Caledonian glory'.[85] To that end, Defoe willingly accepted at face value this group's twin conceptions of Scotland as a martial culture and its people as brave and warrior-like. He did this in order to explain why Scotland was 'a brave . . . but poor nation'[86] whose 'fame' lay in the 'valour' its citizens showed in serving as mercenaries in the armies of other European nations.[87] According to Defoe, however, a 'constitution' which allowed this to happen – this trafficking in men's lives rather than in goods – was 'unqualified to make a nation rich or happy'.[88] Without Union, he suggested, Scottish prospects for a qualitatively different future would remain bleak.

Given the hold the martial/commercial typology had on Defoe's mind, it is easy to see what he was doing in *Caledonia* and the *Review* when he juxtaposed Scotland's and England's constitutions.[89] The latter, Defoe reiterated time and again in the *Review*, had the constitution of a 'free' nation. And since it was the 'very nature' of a free nation both to 'encourage all manner of virtue . . . and [to] promote universal industry' among her citizens, England's constitution provided her citizens with the kind of 'liberty' that made the people 'thrive' and the nation 'rich and strong'.

In light of this delineation of the 'natural' attributes of 'free' nations, Defoe conjectured that were Scotland to agree to Union she would become part of a constitutional arrangement that would facilitate her future economic development. What Scotland needed to reverse a century of economic decline, Defoe argued, was 'liberty and industry'.[90] Using what we now recognise is an integral part of natural jurisprudential political discourse, Defoe noted that 'Liberty makes nations thrive . . . for liberty encourages industry' in the same way that 'slavery' encourages 'sloth'.[91] On those grounds, therefore, Defoe thought Union would secure for Scotland the kind of liberty she needed to overcome her depressed economic condition.

It is worth observing here that the commercial versus martial thrust of Defoe's pro-Union argument was less effective against anti-Union Scottish writers who, like Andrew Fletcher, had been aware since the mid-1690s of Scotland's need to commercialise. Indeed, it would not be too much to say that such thinkers as Fletcher and Paterson, both of

[85] Defoe, *Caledonia*, p. 41. Robertson, *Militia*, pp. 43–4, discusses the theme with reference to Belhaven.

[86] *Review*, III, p. 478. [87] Defoe, *Caledonia*, pp. 27–31.

[88] *Review*, III, p. 671.

[89] For what follows, see *Review*, III, p. 647; cf. pp. 650, 671.

[90] *Review*, III, p. 650. [91] *Review*, III, p. 671.

whom had staked much on the Darien venture, had prepared the ideological ground in Scotland for Defoe's commercialisation argument. As we shall see, however, it was precisely because Fletcher operated within the frame of commercial discourse itself that his economic and political objections to Union so unsettled the pro-Union writers – whether English or Scottish.

The second reason Defoe's theory of power is important to his pro-Union position has to do with the meaning of the language he used in the *Review* in late 1706 to discuss the mutual benefits Scotland and England would derive from Union. This is a complicated issue – one that will be dealt with in this as well as in the next two sections of this essay. What makes the matter of the meaning of Defoe's language so complicated is that the *Review*'s pro-Union arguments were directed almost exclusively to English readers (when Defoe wished to address the Scots specifically, he would publish something – like 'Caledonia' – in Edinburgh).

Given these considerations of audience, several points need to be made. First, it would seem to follow that, when Defoe reminded *Review* readers that modern societies ought to expand by means of 'commerce' rather than 'conquest', he was rebuking certain English groups for contemplating military action against Scotland under the auspices of the Alien Act.[92] As early as December, 1705, Defoe had used the *Review* to criticise this legislative 'act of war' against Scotland.[93] Moreover, it was at that time that Defoe announced his unswerving support for Union, arguing that Union would solve simultaneously England's so-called 'backdoor' security problem *vis-à-vis* France and Scotland's economic problems. In a sense, then, the conquest to commerce argument, which had been a common theme in seventeenth-century English economic writings,[94] and which fitted nicely into Defoe's martial/commercial typology, would seem to have been employed in the *Review* less to convince the Scots about their post-Union commercial prospects than to dissuade the English from undermining their reputation as a freedom-loving people by resorting to military means to solve their Scottish security problem.

A second point about the *Review* and its audience follows from the first. This point has to do with the language of liberty Defoe developed in the *Review* to buttress the pro-Union argument. As we have seen, throughout the autumn and winter of 1706-7 Defoe repeatedly referred to England as

[92] *Review*, III, p. 647.

[93] *Review*, II, pp. 478–80; cf. Defoe, *Removing*, I, p. 8. There are parallels between what Defoe says in the December *Review* and certain passages in *The Consolidator*.

[94] The phrase, e.g., appears in Roberts, *Traffic*, p. 92. Needless to say, use of the phrase raises questions about mercantilistic thinking as war-oriented.

a 'free' nation. By contrast, he unfailingly traced present day Scottish 'misery' – its 'tyranny, cruelty, and bondage' – to the martial character of its 'constitution'.[95]

In this context, it is easy to misconstrue the meaning of Defoe's references to England as 'free'. True, on the surface the juxtaposition of the two nation's constitutions would seem to confirm what Defoe thought was at stake for the Scots in the Union debate. But the real point of presenting this juxtaposition to an English audience was to remind England of its future legal and moral obligations to Scotland were a British nation to be formed out of Union. As a minority in the 'Parliament of Britain', the Scots would be vulnerable to English tyranny in the form of majority rule; Defoe as well as the Scots realised that clearly. So, in a series of writings published in Edinburgh in late 1706, Defoe assured the Scots that the tradition of liberty in England – equal protection under the law for every citizen – obviated legal tyranny of that sort.[96] Concurrently, Defoe used the *Review* to impress that point on the English. William Molyneax had employed that strategy in 1698 while arguing the case for Ireland; [97]and there are traces of the same argument in a piece Fletcher wrote in 1704.[98] What the three thinkers have in common is the belief that invocation of natural jurisprudential principles of liberty and justice would inhibit the English from abandoning these principles for the sake of advancing strictly English interests at Scotland's expence. By the same token, by honouring these principles the English would create a bond of trust that would give Scotland the confidence to undertake economic initiatives without fear of English intervention in its affairs.

To English readers of the *Review*, then, Defoe carefully cast his pro-Union arguments in natural jurisprudential form. This can hardly be surprising; after all, Defoe had long been convinced that peace and security were synonymous with the rule of law.[99] Likewise, he placed great store in the rule of law both as a precondition for, and as a 'spur to industry'.[100] Not coincidentally, therefore, words like 'peace, commerce, plenty, [industry], and liberty' repeatedly cluster in Defoe's *Review* pieces to form a discursive configuration which is as much a prescription for a commercial society as a recognisable natural jurisprudential discourse.[101] Accordingly, in Defoe's thought commerce stands to conquest, peace to war, industry to sloth, wealth to poverty, liberty to slavery, and freedom to tyranny, as civil stands to martial.

95 *Review*, III, p. 671; cf. Defoe, *Removing*, II, p. 33.
96 Defoe, *Removing*, parts III–IV.
97 W. Molyneux, *The Case of Ireland Being Bound* (Dublin, 1698), pp. 50–3.
98 Andrew Fletcher, *Selected Political Writings and Speeches*, ed. D. Daiches (Edinburgh, 1979), p. 127.
99 *Review*, III, p. 510. 100 *Review*, III, p. 510. 101 *Review*, III, p. 647.

And yet, for all its symmetry, the binary oppositions around which Defoe organised his discourse failed to convince those anti-Union writers who, like Fletcher, regarded such assurances as merely rhetorical – that is, as hollow promises that did not entail long-term English commitments to ensuring that the disparities of power between rich England and poor Scotland would not always be resolved in favour of Scotland's dominant partner in Union.[102] In the final two sections of this essay, I wish (in the third section) to ground Fletcher's reservations about Union in Scottish economic and political circumstances of the years 1697–1707 and then (in the fourth section) to show how Defoe expanded natural jurisprudential discourse so as to take specific economic account of Fletcher's economic objections to Union.

The Union debate, II: rich-country/poor-country and the theory of empire

That Defoe's theory of power permeated his writings between 1697 and 1707 should now be obvious. Equally as obviously he grounded his theory in a binary view of the differences between martial and commercial societies. Defoe, moreover, historicised these differences by placing them in a 'then versus now' historical framework. At the same time, he politicised these differences by associating the martial with tyrannical and the commercial with free government. And because he also posited connections between martial and commercial regimes on the one hand and poverty and prosperity on the other, we have interpreted his theory of power overall as offering a rather comprehensive commercial view of history and much else besides.

Now, it seems safe to say that much of Defoe's commercialisation argument was based on lessons drawn from English history – lessons which Defoe thought could be applied to Scotland in the form of generalisations about how commercial development subverts martial regimes.[103] Defoe had made that point in the 'Standing Army' essay of 1698 when he pitted commercialism against Gothicism; and we have just seen him do the same thing in several of his pro-Union pieces. Again, Defoe was not alone in this, for Davenant, who worked for Harley and who had a reputation of being something of a party-writer himself, exhibited similar inclinations in the 'Memorial':

[102] Fletcher, *Speeches*, p. 32. In Grotius's terms, *De Jure Belli Ac Pacis Libri Tres*, trans. F. Kelsey (Oxford, 1925), II, pp. 328–47, the matter turns on the difference between promises of short-term 'display' and of long-term 'purpose'.

[103] Later, Defoe, *A Plan of the English Commerce*, 2nd edn [1730] (New York, 1967), p. 50 will say just this.

> The advantages accruing to the [commons from Union] are immense . . . and they may in a few years gather such wealth as shall exempt them from the bondage they now lie under . . . and they have the example of England before their eyes, when the nobility and gentry had almost the same power over their tenants, as is now exercised in Scotland, till our commons became enriched by foreign traffic.[104]

In this respect, a main sub-text of the pro-Union argument was that Scottish access to England's trading empire would trigger Scottish commercial expansion: this, in turn, would hasten the subversion of the martial values that had sustained Scotland's 'brave' but 'poor' people for so many centuries.

To appreciate how compelling the commercialisation strategy was as a pro-Union and anti-Gothic argument, we need only take note of the famous pro-Union speech which William Seton delivered to the Scottish Parliament in November, 1706, in the midst of the Union debate.[105] There, Seton equated Scotland's own tradition of 'Gothic' government with 'feuds, murders, deprecations, and rebellions' – in effect, with what later Scottish theorists of commercial society would call 'feudal anarchy'.[106] Without Union, Seton argued, Scotland would be unable either to 'expand its trade' or 'raise its power'; with Union, it would gain 'security' both from belligerent neighbours and for 'our liberty, property, and religion' at home. What is more, Seton said, Union would allow Scotland to 'flourish in wealth' in proportion to 'the industry of its inhabitants'.[107]

Because the parallels between Seton's speech and his own position were so pronounced, Defoe highlighted Seton's remarks in his *The History of the Union* (1709).[108] And it is surely no accident that in the *History* Seton's speech is followed by one against Union delivered by Lord Belhaven, a speech in which Scotland's martial heritage is glorified in the name of "Mother Caledonia".[109]

[104] Davenant, 'Memoir', p. 147. On the subversion theme, see Robertson, *Militia*, pp. 31, 35. Early foreshadowings of this theme can be found in the 1650s in the works of M. Nedham and 'RG'. Pocock, *Harrington*, esp. pp. 35, 43, 58, discusses both thinkers.

[105] W. Seton, 'Speech', in Daniel Defoe, *The History of the Union Between England and Scotland* (London, 1786), pp. 312–16.

[106] Seton, 'Speech', p. 314. Quotations from other Scottish thinkers on this issue can be found in Robertson, *Militia*, p. 47, and N. Phillipson, 'The Scottish Enlightenment', in R. Porter and M. Teich (eds.), in *The Enlightenment in National Context* (Cambridge, 1981), pp. 25–6. [107] Seton, 'Speech', pp. 313, 316.

[108] Riley, *The Union of England and Scotland* (Manchester, 1978), downplays the importance of Defoe's *History*.

[109] Lord Belhaven, 'Speech', in Daniel Defoe, *The History of the Union Between England and Scotland* (London, 1786), pp. 316–28. Even before the publication of *Caledonia*, Defoe had ridiculed Belhaven's speech in verse. See Defoe, 'The Vision', in G. de F Lord (ed.), *Anthology of Poems on Affairs of State* (New Haven CN, 1975), pp. 691–8.

The deliberate juxtaposition of Seton's and Belhaven's speeches in the *History* captures what Defoe thought was ultimately at stake for Scotland in the Union debate: namely, choosing between becoming a commercial people or remaining a martial one. To that end, Seton's speech is sprinkled with familiar Defovian buzzwords: 'industry', 'trade', 'wealth', 'power', and 'security'. At the antipode, we find Belhaven talking about 'valiant' and 'honorable barons', ancient martial 'glory', the 'independence' of 'our *Patria*', and so on.

On the surface, of course, these two speeches dovetail nicely with Defoe's attempt to present Union as a choice between commercial and martial societies. But if we look more closely at Belhaven's and Seton's speeches another ideological dimension of the Union debate emerges, disrupting the neat symmetry of Defoe's commercial versus martial discursive framework. And it is this dimension – one that Istvan Hont's work has done so much to illuminate – that explains why Defoe addressed certain other themes in his pro-Union writings.[110]

The dimension I have in mind is hinted at in Belhaven's speech – in a section in which he conjectures about English – Scottish relations *after* Union. In two carefully worded paragraphs Belhaven elaborated a response to a simply put rhetorical question: why would England, a rich and powerful commercial nation, with a 'capital city [that was] the *Emporium*' of the world, ever agree to honour a Treaty of Union which required so much English 'self-denial'?[111] Relative to England, Belhaven said, 'we are an obscure, poor people', living in 'a *remote* corner of the world without name and without allies'. Given these disparities of wealth and power, Belhaven asks, why would England ever agree to a fully 'equal' Union in which she had to moderate her power to accommodate Scottish interests?

The questions Belhaven raised and the language in which he framed them addressed assertions Seton and other pro-Union writers had made about the benefits of a fully 'incorporating Union'. In his speech, for example, Seton had insisted that 'every part' in the new Union, however 'far removed from the seat of the government' in London, would eventually flourish 'in wealth, in proportion to the value of its natural product, or the industry of its inhabitants'.[112] From this premise, Seton drew a further conclusion:

[110] See Istvan Hont, '"The rich country–poor country" debate in Scottish classical Political economy', in I. Hont and M. Ignatieff (eds.), *Wealth and Virtue* (Cambridge, 1983); and 'Free trade and the economic limits to national politics: neo-Machiavellian political economy reconsidered', in J. Dunn (ed.), *The Economic Limits to Modern Politics* (Cambridge, 1990).

[111] Belhaven, 'Speech', p. 323.

[112] Seton, 'Speech', pp. 315–16.

> that by this union we will have access to all the advantages in commerce the English enjoy: we will be capable, by a good government (centred in London), to improve our natural product, for the benefit of the whole island: and we will have our liberty, property, and religion, secured under . . . one Parliament of Great Britain.[113]

Defoe's Scottish friend, John Clerk, had used identical language in his own 1706 pro-Union pamphlet, claiming that despite Scotland's remoteness from the 'seat of government' she would 'thrive' economically.[114] The same point was made by the Earl of Cromarty who, in a 1706 pamphlet of his own, insisted that Scotland 'will . . . draw riches from the center' once Union has been achieved.[115] W. Paterson held similar views, too.[116]

The different views expressed by Seton and Belhaven on how Scottish economic interests would fare in the context of a British trading empire, whose centre was London, had a history – a shorter one that Hont has traced to the debates over Irish – English relations in the late 1690s;[117] and a longer one that goes back to Matthew Wren's exchanges with Harrington in the late 1650s over the centralising tendencies of commercial empires.[118] In that regard, two general points about the larger ideological context of Seton's and Belhaven's speeches need to be made.

First, Belhaven's decision to discuss Scottish-English relations in terms of disparites of power between the centre and the periphery of empire echoed concerns voiced earlier by Fletcher. In several essays written between 1698 and 1704, Fletcher had stated that Scotland's incorporation into a British empire, whose 'seat of government' was centred in London, would not result in robust Scottish economic development.[119] Pointing to recent developments in Irish – English relations, Fletcher wondered why Scottish industries, were they to begin to prosper after Union, would not be subjected to the kind of crippling legislation England had passed to curtail the development of Irish industries that had threatened English economic interests. Within the legal framework of empire, Fletcher observed, there was precious little the Scottish minority in a unified Parliament could do to prevent heavy-handed legislation of this sort.

[113] Seton, 'Speech', pp. 315–16. It is worth noting that Seton's remark would seem to confirm Pocock's (*Harrington*, p. 151) and Robertson's (*Militia*, pp. 49–50) arguments about Scottish willingness to de-emphasise political participation as essential to life in a 'civil society'.

[114] J. Clerk, *A Letter to a Friend* (Edinburgh, 1706), p. 19.

[115] Earl of Cromarty, *Two Letters Concerning the Prospect of Union* (Edinburgh, 1706), pp. 7–10.

[116] W. Paterson, *The Works of William Paterson*, 3 vols., 2nd edn [1859], ed. S. Bannister (New York, 1968), I, pp. 147–60.

[117] Hont, 'Limits'.

[118] See Pocock, *Harrington*, pp. 82ff, 137ff. For Wren on this, see M. Wren, *Considerations on Mr. Harrington's 'Common-Wealth of Oceana*, (London, 1657), pp. 85ff.

[119] Fletcher, *Speeches*, pp. 32, 65, 117–36.

Indeed, Fletcher's fear of London's hegemony can be detected in the following statement: 'Trade is now become the golden ball, for which all nations of the world are contending, and the occasion of so great particularities, that not only every nation is endeavoring to possess trade, but every city to draw all to itself.'[120] Hence, his grave reservations about leaving 'poor, remote, and barren' Scotland at the mercy of Machiavellian-like policy makers residing in the imperial centre.[121]

The second point I wish to make about the larger ideological context of Seton's and Belhaven's speeches has to do with Davenant, a thinker whose importance has been amplified in the work of Pocock and Hont.[122] As Hont has shown, Davenant developed a theory of empire between 1697 and 1702 that had conflicting tendencies, ones which could be used to support either positive or negative views of Union. On the one hand, Davenant recognised that relations between large nation states in the modern world made centralisation of economic and political power – in a 'seat of empire' – a matter of reason of state.[123] Thus, Davenant subscribed to the concentration of power in London, England's great 'Emporium', he said.[124] On the other hand, and here Botero anticipated him by almost a century,[125] Davenant acknowledged that the centralising process would have adverse effects within the English trading empire itself, creating disparities of power between London and the regions remote from the imperial centre.[126]

In the context of Union, it proved easy to generate as well as resolve tensions between England and Scotland by selective use of Davenant's work. Anti-Union writers, for example, seized upon Davenant's admissions about power disparities within the empire to fan Scottish fears of London's hegemony in 'British' affairs.[127] Pro-Union writers, by contrast, gave Davenant's argument a startlingly modern economic twist, pointing out how the logic of markets in England's trading empire would foster price and wage differences between London and the remoter regions of the empire. Accordingly, they reasoned, the latter would gain a competitive economic advantage relative to the former.[128]

Fletcher, of course, would have none of this, citing the Irish case as an instance of how far England could be trusted to honour the Union's free

[120] Fletcher, *Speeches*, p. 120. [121] Fletcher, *Speeches*, p. 119.

[122] Pocock, *Machiavellian*, pp. 436ff; and Hont, 'Limits'.

[123] Charles Davenant, *An Essay Upon the Probable Methods of Making a People Gainers in the Balance of Trade* (London, 1699), pp. 101, 120.

[124] Davenant, *Essay*, p. 102. [125] Botero, *Reason*, p. 258.

[126] Davenant, *Essay*, pp. 122ff. [127] Fletcher, *Speeches*, pp. 106ff.

[128] I discuss Defoe's view of this below. Others who made the same point: S. Clement, *Discourse*, pp. 10, 29–30; R. Coxe, *Some Thoughts on the Bill Pending* (Dublin, 1698), p. 11; H. Maxwell, *An Essay Towards an Union of Ireland with England* (London, 1703), p. 49; and J. Cary, *An Essay on the State of England* (London, 1695), pp. 91–5.

trade provisions were its economic interests to be threatened by a competitor.[129] This was a subject Belhaven too had broached in the speech he gave to the Scottish Parliament in November, 1706. Conversely, pro-Union writers, Defoe and Seton among them, sought to allay this concern by insisting that the very idea of a British empire, in which freedom was measured in natural jurisprudential terms, ruled out the possibility of England's reneging on any of the terms of Union.

Be that as it may, the point of discussing Davenant here has been to illuminate the larger ideological issues that surrounded the exchange between Seton and Belhaven on the meaning of London as the imperial centre of a British Empire. In that context, the Union debate became re-figured, for the main questions now became these: would the English majority in a unified Parliament, whose interests lay in keeping the imperial centre rich and powerful, create legislative obstacles to economic competition from the Empire's 'poor, remote, and barren' regions; or would the majority uphold the right of Scotland to a free communication of trade in an imperial market system in which the benefits of economic mutualism out-weighed those to be secured by unilateral English abridgement of Scottish rights to participate in that trade?

Hont's important work on Davenant as well as on the so-called 'rich-country/poor-country problem' allows us to establish a different ideological context for assessing certain aspects of Defoe's view of Union.[130] For Defoe had much to say about the issues raised by Davenant. That context, however, does not turn on the same ideological axis as the martial/commercial one we have been exploring. Rather, it turns on a theory of commercial empire in which questions of power and security in a 'neo-Machiavellian' sense and the dynamics of economic markets in a natural jurisprudential sense not only come into conflict with each other but do so in the context of relations between richer and poorer commercial societies.[131] I wish to end this chapter by discussing how Defoe's writings on Union fit into this context.

Natural law economised: Defoe on the 'automatic mechanism' of wage and price adjustments

The place to begin is with Defoe's notion that commercial societies are not only the antithesis of martial ones but subvert them as well. Based on the English pattern of development, Defoe offered a commercial version of Harrington's dictum that 'power follows property'. Defoe did this by

[129] Fletcher, *Speeches*, p. 32.
[130] See Hont, 'The "Rich country-poor country debate"'.
[131] The point I made above about Viner (n 31 above) is pertinent here.

explaining the increasing power of the Commons in parliament in terms of the growing power of commerce in English affairs. This sort of generalisation, we know, later became popular among thinkers of the Scottish Enlightenment who skillfully used it in their ideological assaults on the idea of feudal society; and through them the idea became a basic trope of modern historical consciousness.

When the generalisation is applied to Scotland, however, a problem arises – because absorption of the Scottish parliament into a unified British one ruled out the possibility of a straightforward transfer of Scottish economic interests into Scottish political power. In terms of the economic mutualism of natural jurisprudential modes of thought and discourse, this would not be a problem; for, supposedly, in a unified parliament English and Scottish commercial interests would combine to form one interest bloc whose policies were designed, in Seton's words, to 'benefit . . . the whole island'.[132]

However, in the context of Davenant's theory of empire, which we have seen was pervaded by 'reason of state' considerations, Scottish – English relations could generate tensions in Britain, especially were the promise of Union to be realised in Scottish economic development. Defoe's pro-Union writings indicate that he recognised the possibility of this.[133] To his credit, he dealt with it in the *Review*; and on two different levels – one political; the other economic.

First of all, and like so many other pro-Union Scottish writers, Defoe insisted that Union would create a new British parliament of 'equal communication'.[134] In that context, *legal* oppression of Scotland by England was impossible.[135] Appealing to history, Defoe noted in one *Review* issue how his 'equal' conception of Union was modelled after that used by Rome to incorporate different peoples into its expanding empire.[136] To this end, Defoe said that Rome had employed a 'communicating' rather than a 'subjecting' model of incorporation.[137] As he remarked, ''Tis plain here is no subjecting on either hand, and indeed there is no room for a possibilty of subjection in the nature of [this kind of] Union [between England and Scotland]'.[138]

What Defoe meant to say here – and this is evident from what follows this statement in the *Review* – is that there is no room for 'legal' subjection in this kind of Union. Indeed, as Defoe argued, 'when [separate] nations agree to be governed by [a common set of] laws', it is understood that the

[132] Seton, 'Speeches', p. 316. [133] Defoe, *Removing*, II, p. 29.

[134] *Review*, III, pp. 677–8. Others who thought this way: Cromarty, *Two Letters*, pp. 6ff, 22–3; Clerk, *Letter*, p. 15; Paterson, *Works*, I, pp. 176–83.

[135] *Review*, III, 650, 605–14. [136] *Review*, III, pp. 645–7. [137] *Review*, III, p. 647.

[138] *Review*, III, 647.

'very nature' of such a Union guarantees equal protection for all under the law.[139] Since in Defoe's view England was a 'free' nation ruled by laws, it followed for him that an English 'majority' could never 'tyrannise' a Scottish minority within the framework of Union. The 'legal foundation' of the British empire precluded that. Summing-up, Defoe contended:

> should England under the shelter of . . . majority attempt the enslaving Scotland and assault the Articles of Stipulation, invade the Treaty, and break in upon the conditions by (legal) violence . . . the Union is dissolved . . . and the invaders become tyrants and oppressors.[140]

True, an English-dominated Parliament could act in an oppressive and unilateral way towards Scotland, but it could not do so legally and without subverting the rule of law throughout the British empire.

Two things about Defoe's argument here are revealing. First of all, Defoe's view of Rome's policy of incorporation directly contested Fletcher's (and Machiavelli's) interpretation of it.[141] Where Defoe saw extension of Roman citizenship to incorporated peoples as a communication of equal rights to all, Fletcher saw it as a pretext for the city of Rome to make claims on the wealth and manpower of non-Roman peoples everywhere. In this, Defoe's interpretation of Rome coincided with that of Paterson, Clerk, and Cromarty as well as with that of Henry Maxwell who, in a 1703 pamphlet on Irish-English relations, distinguished between Unions of 'subjection' and ones founded on communication of 'interest'.[142] Rome, Maxwell said, operated in accordance with the latter procedure.[143]

Second, it is highly revealing for our understanding of the meaning of his language that Defoe invoked the authority of Grotius (and Livy) to add legitimacy to his legalistic interpretation of union. Clerk had resorted to this strategy in his own 1706 pamphlet.[144] Both, moreover, cited the same passage from Grotius to confirm the relevance of his natural jurisprudential style of thinking to the Scottish situation. The passage is one in which Grotius comments favorably on Rome's policy for incorporating the Sabines and Albans into the Empire. As Grotius wrote,

> if two nations be united, the rights of neither of them shall be lost, but become common . . . as Sabines first, and afterwards the Albans, were

[139] *Review*, III, p. 647. [140] *Review*, III, p. 609.

[141] Fletcher, *Speeches*, pp. 122, 126–7. For Machiavelli, see *The Prince and the Discourses* (New York, 1950), pp. 105–17, 288–96.

[142] Paterson, *Works*, I, pp. 149–53, 176–9; Clerk, *Letter*, pp. 10–11; Cromarty, *Parainesis Pacifica; Or a Perswasive to the Union of Britain* (Edinburgh, 1702), pp. 10–12; and Maxwell, *Essay*, pp. 5–6. [143] Maxwell, *Essay*, p. 18. [144] Clerk, *Letter*, pp. 10–11.

> incorporated with the Romans, and so they were made one state, as Livy (Lib. I) expresses it.[145]

Livy, for his part, while acknowledging that Rome was unquestionably the 'seat of power' in the Empire after Roman – Sabine union, only recognised Rome as a 'civilising influence' in the Empire when, under Numa's leadership, it abandoned 'force of arms' for the rule of 'law'.[146] On that reading, and Grotius seems to have interpreted Livy this way,[147] Rome administered the Empire from the centre but never claimed sovereignty for the capital city over the Empire as a whole. At any rate, Livy and Grotius provided pro-Union writers with arguments and language with which to calm Scottish fears about legal oppression. That is why Defoe referred to them in the *Review* issues of late 1706 and early 1707.

As a background figure in Defoe's life, Grotius is also important to the economic response Defoe devised to meet the challenge of the anti-Union writers' concerns over London as a hegemonic force within the empire. Grotius, we should recall, was famous in the seventeenth century (among other things) for his views on the natural right of all nations to use the seas to facilitate their trade.[148] His argument – and it is an early jurisprudential rendering of what we now call the *doux-commerce* thesis of international trade[149] – was that commerce was a divinely ordained agent of 'human fellowship' – a 'bond' that tied different peoples together in a network of 'reciprocal commercial relations' and 'mutual service'.[150] And because Grotius depicted the Dutch as the agents of this Providential design versus the Spanish, the free trade argument tended in the seventeenth century to have a Protestant versus Catholic dimension to it (that point was not lost on English writers, among them Defoe).[151] On Grotius's terms, then, 'justice' was served when nations recognised free communication of trade as a natural right of every nation. Conversely, he

[145] Grotius, *De Jure Belli*, II. ix 9, p. 315: see, John Robertson 'Empire and union: two concepts of the early modern European political order', above pp. 18–19.

[146] T. Livy, *The Early History of Rome*, trans. A. de Selincourt (New York, 1960), pp. 48, 51.

[147] H. Grotius, *A Treatise of the Antiquity of the Common-Wealth of the Battavers*, trans. T. Wood (London, 1649), pp. 130–1.

[148] H. Grotius, *The Freedom of the Seas*, trans. D. McGoffin (New York, 1916).

[149] A. Hirschman, *The Passions and the Interests* (Princeton, 1977), brought the *doux-commerce* theme to our attention. As a discourse, however, it is much older. See, e.g., Grotius's notes *(De Jure Belli*, pp. 199–200) for the ancient antecedents.

[150] Grotius, *Freedom*, pp. 1–2, 7, 60–3, and 70–6.

[151] Defoe, 'Giving Alms No Charity', in J. McCulloch (ed.), *A Select Collection of Scarce and Valuable Economic Tracts*, pp. 32–3. Maxwell, *Essay*, pp. 23, 40. In Defoe's case, there are frequent references to the same theme in later issues of the *Review*: e.g., IV, pp. 134–6; IX, pp. 107–10.

regarded attempts to abridge such a natural right as a 'power' play which violated the natural order of things.[152]

If we turn to Defoe with Grotius's distinctions and language in mind, we see that throughout his life Defoe discussed trade between nations in natural jurisprudential terms. Thus in 1706, just before he began to work with the Scots on a strategy for union, Defoe talked in the *Review* about God's reasons for distributing the world's resources over such geographically diverse areas.[153] Like Grotius's, Defoe's view was that this was God's way of ensuring that the people of the world would be 'of mutual assistance' to 'one another'.[154] Whether by sea or river, Defoe said, trade made 'communication' between the 'remote' parts of the world possible. Then, while shifting from a religious to a more natural-scientific mode of discourse, Defoe likened the commercial circulation of goods among nations to the way 'blood' circulated through and invigorated all parts of the body.

Defoe's shift in language is not without economic significance for our purposes here. For two years earlier, in 1704, he had talked about blood and trade in similar terms.[155] In 1704, however, the meaning of this discussion is much plainer, for at that time Defoe was talking about London's commercial relations with the remoter 'corners of the kingdom'. 'London', he asserted, stood to 'the other parts of the kingdom' as 'the heart' stood to the circulation of blood in the body.[156] Other writers – John Cary, Davenant, George Mackenzie, Henry Mackworth, and John Toland – had also used the circulation of blood image in 1690s to explain the dynamics of commerce.[157] Toland was the most specific of all, likening London simultaneously to the 'heart' and to the centre of a new Roman-like empire in the West.[158] But in developing his own version of this, Defoe took exception to Toland's (and Davenant's) view, for he argued that, in order for a body to remain healthy, blood had to *circulate* through the heart not *concentrate* in it. If the latter should occur, 'distemper' would follow for the whole body, Defoe said.[159] Hence, Defoe's caveat against London's hegemony in the empire.

In late 1706, while living in Scotland, Defoe reiterated the natural jurisprudential argument for economic mutualism. He began by admitting

[152] H. Grotius, *De Rebus Belgicis; Or the Annals and History of the Low-Country Warres*, trans. T. Manley (London, 1665), p. 922.

[153] *Review*, III, pp. 5–8. [154] *Review*, III, pp. 6–7.

[155] Defoe, 'Alms', pp. 46–7. For additional references, see *Review*, II, p. 459; VI, p. 166.

[156] Defoe, 'Alms', pp. 46–7, 38.

[157] Cary, *Essay*, p. 1; Davenant, *Essay*, pp. 7–8, 101; G. Mackenzie, *The Moral History of Frugality* (London, 1691), pp.11–12; H. Mackworth, *England's Glory* (London, 1694); and J. Toland, 'Dedication', *The Works of James Harrington*, ed. J. Toland (London, 1700), p. iii. [158] Toland, 'Dedication', pp. i–iv.

[159] Defoe, 'Alms', p. 49. 'Distemper' is Davenant's word (*Essay*, p. 8).

that it is impossible to determine whether England or Scotland would gain more of 'a particular advantage' from Union.[160] In his view, though, Union promised 'mutual security, mutual improvements, and mutual prosperity' for 'both sides'.[161] More specifically, he thought that 'Scotland will increase in wealth, England in strength, both in tranquility'.[162] In this respect, Defoe envisaged Union in terms of a 'mutual incorporation' in which a 'communicating of [legal] priviledges and [economic] interests' between the two nations would occur.[163]

At the core of Defoe's pro-Union views, therefore, were two arguments for mutualism, both of which had deep roots in natural jurisprudential modes of thought and value.[164] The rule of law allowed for peace and security in a political sense. Natural jurisprudential notions of the interplay between security, free trade, industry, and the advance of mutual understanding among the nations of the world facilitated Scottish economic development. Peace, plenty, and power, the often stated aims of much seventeenth century economic writing, is a phrase that expresses this mutualism very well.

However helpful Grotius might have been to Defoe in formulating a coherent economic and political response to the arguments of the anti-Union writers, there were few resources either in Grotius or in the natural law tradition to help Defoe deal with the wage and price aspects of Davenant's theory of empire. As we have seen, the problem was starkly posed in the Irish debate, a curiosity of which was that writers such as Molyneux and Maxwell had appealed to the natural law tradition to try to shame England into conducting her relations with Ireland on a level appropriate to a free nation whose people were proud of living in liberty and under the rule of law.[165] Defoe, obviously, had the same aim in mind. None the less, Defoe's experience as a propagandist must have told him to address the wage and price issue more substantially, for he did so in a relatively original way from 1704 on.

In 1704, in the long essay entitled 'Giving Alms no Charity', Defoe had attempted to render the differences between martial and commercial societies in economic terms by examining their respective wage structures.[166] His reason for this lay in his conviction that men chose to be tradesmen rather than soldiers because of the wage differential between the two occupations.[167] Later, in the *Review* he explained: 'our people are too

[160] *Review*, III, p. 557. [161] *Review*, III, p. 558. [162] *Review*, III, p. 506.

[163] *Review*, III, 646. [164] Also see: Paterson, *Works*, I, pp. 130, 153, 159, 176, 214–15.

[165] Molyneax, *Case*, pp. 2, 93; Maxwell, *Essay*, pp. 7, 21.

[166] I regard this as a signal 'move' in eighteenth-century thinking, for it explains the shift from the martial to the civil-commercial in terms of economic processes. Earlier hints of this can be found in [Philanglus], *Trade*, p. 291, and Barbon, *Discourse*, p.23.

[167] Defoe, 'Alms', pp.54–5.

rich, our poor have too great wages, and live too well' to accept 'a soldier's pay' as a means of livelihood.[168] Assuming the posture of a realist, Defoe contended that, although men would rather 'serve [in the military] . . . than starve', they would pursue other options were 'better employment' opportunities available to them.[169] And because such options abounded in commercial societies, Defoe argued that commercial development in an economic sense deterred the institutionalisation of tyrannical government in a politico-martial sense.[170] Similarly, when such opportunities were foreclosed to men, soldiering became a form of commerce – as had been the case in Scotland for some time.

Along these lines, it is of some chronological interest that Defoe was talking this way about wages and commerce as early as 1704. At that time, though, Defoe employed the different wage structures of martial and commercial societies to explain the differences both between tyrannical France and free England and between Catholic and Protestant countries in Europe.[171] In a clever but self-serving historical argument, one which was common among English dissenters,[172] Defoe argued that Catholic 'tyranny and persecution, the one an oppression of property, the other of conscience', had curtailed 'trade' throughout Europe. 'The consequence of this', Defoe then wrote, 'was . . . the people fled and scattered themselves in their neighbours countries . . . bringing the wealth of England, and the power of Holland into the world'. In the wake of this population shift, 'trade and liberty' throughout Catholic Europe were further ruined. Attributing the dynamic for all of this to 'the secret overruling hand' of 'Providence', Defoe suggested that 'God Almighty' had used Catholic 'oppression and tyranny' to put 'the great machine of trade' in the hands of Protestants who, according to Defoe, would be 'the chief bulwarks of . . . liberty' for 'ages to come'.

There is a good deal that is interesting about this argument in its own right, for it clearly shows – as Jacob Viner appreciated years ago – how Providential and commercial discourses could be combined in seventeenth-century Protestant interpretation of the history of early modern Europe.[173] For our purposes, however, what needs to be noted is that Defoe proceeds in the 'Alms' text to relate 'the growth of England . . . in trade, wealth and people', to corresponding up-swings in national employment opportunities

[168] *Review*, II, p. 46. [169] *Review*, II, p. 46.

[170] A point later made by Montesquieu, *The Spirit of the Laws*, trans. T. Nugent (New York, 1949), I, pp. 364–6.

[171] For the following, see Defoe, 'Alms', pp. 32–5.

[172] See, e.g., Bethel, *Princes and States*, pp. 123–4.

[173] See J. Viner, *The Role of Providence in the Social Order* (Princeton, 1972).

and the wages of workers.[174] The result: soldering became an unattractive career for Englishmen of all social groups. Defoe put it this way:

> . . . poverty makes men soldiers, and drives crowds into the armies, and the difficulties to get Englishmen to list is, because they live in plenty and ease, and he that can earn 20s. per week at an easier, steady employment, must be drunk or mad when he lists for a soldier . . . for 3s.6d. per week . . .[175]

As early as 1704, then, Defoe had worked out in his mind a rather comprehensive theory of power in which the differences between martial and commercial societies could be discussed in terms of their respective wage scales.

As Defoe's involvement in the Union issue intensified in 1705 and 1706, we observe him sliding the argument about wage differences between martial and commercial societies into a discussion of the relationship between rich England and poor Scotland in the context of Union. In making the case for Union to the Scots, Defoe obviously did not wish to dwell on the hegemonic role London might economically play in the empire. To down-play this, therefore, he chose to stress the economic advantages Scotland would enjoy as a low-wage country relative to England. Here, of course, is where Defoe's liberty and industry argument fits into his larger pro-Union perspective, for in his view Scotland would become prosperous were its people to become industrious within the context of the competitive economic advantage their low-wage scale gave them. On these terms, Defoe could tell the Scots with confidence that the matter of the nation's future economic prosperity was within their own hands.

Now, in the context of the rich-country/poor-country debate of 1698–1707, this argument might appear quite disingenuous. The Irish case, after all, which Defoe had commented upon in Davenantian terms in the *Review* in 1705,[176] had demonstrated that for reasons of state England would not abide economic competition from a low-wage country even if it meant England's adopting an imperial attitude towards Ireland politically and forsaking the principles of free trade economically.[177]

In the *Review* issues devoted to Union, however, Defoe does, in fact, confront this issue, albeit in a roundabout way – roundabout because the argument is directed to English rather than Scottish readers. What Defoe does – and it is a strategy that Richard Coxe and Maxwell had employed earlier[178]– is to try to persuade his English audience that the Scots

[174] Defoe, 'Alms', pp. 54–5. [175] Defoe, 'Alms', p. 55.

[176] *Review*, II, p. 89.

[177] Davenant, *Essay*, p. 103–4, regarded his change of mind about Ireland as a reflection of his own growing 'maturity'.

[178] Coxe, *Some Thoughts*, pp. 10–11; Maxwell, *Essay*, pp. 53–4.

low-wage advantage will not threaten English prosperity in the long run. To re-assure the English on this matter, he advances several arguments.[179] First, on several occasions in late 1706 he claims that neither the 'nature of their country' nor the 'genius of their people' would allow the Scots to compete directly with the English businesses for market shares or with English workers for jobs.[180] 'They have'. Defoe wrote, 'manufactures enough of their own to encourage trade sufficient' to employ and enrich themselves. Consequently, he concluded, Scottish manufactures 'shall be . . . remote from your manufactures'.[181]

Second, Defoe maintained that the low-wage advantage that a poor-country held *vis-à-vis* a rich one would be only a temporary benefit.[182] Hinting at what we would call today the 'automatic mechanism' of wage and price adjustments,[183] Defoe implied that as Scotland began to experience economic prosperity her wage scale would gradually come into equilibrium with that of England. Given that premise, Defoe counselled his English audience against cutting wages in England in order to remain competitive with Scottish producers. Going one step further, he even suggested that in the short run a little belt-tightening (Davenantian public frugality) would not hurt English producers either.[184]

Above all, however, Defoe warned the English against politically intervening in the economic affairs of Scotland for the purpose of eliminating economic competition. Defoe is quite explicit about this, writing in late 1706 that ''tis evident the English cannot invade or oppress [the Scots] in trade, because an open free communication of trade . . . is a capitulation of the treaty, and cannot be altered'.[185] Defoe, moreover, continued to talk this way about England's obligation to maintain an open trade with the Scots long after the Treaty of Union had been ratified by both Parliaments and signed by Queen Anne. As numerous post-Union issues of the *Review* attest,[186] Defoe regarded unimpeded Scottish access to all English markets as England's 'debt to the Scots by promise'.[187]

Defoe should be given his due: in the *Review* he made an attempt to confront the rich-country/poor-country problem within the twin-contexts of Davenant's complex theory of empire and of a Treaty of Union that Defoe interpreted in natural jurisprudential terms. In that framework,

[179] See, e.g., *Review*, III, pp. 467, 517.

[180] *Review*, III, p. 467. [181] *Review*, III, p. 517. [182] *Review*, II, pp. 44–5.

[183] J. Viner, *Studies in the Theory of International Trade* (New York, 1937), discusses the automatic mechanism.

[184] *Review*, II, pp. 57–9. [185] *Review*, III, p. 517.

[186] *Review*, VI, pp. 191, 231–2, 235–6.

[187] *Review*, VI, p. 167. Grotius's ideas on promises (n 102 above) are relevant here, for Defoe's idea of a promise obliged the English to make an ethical commitment of 'will' to realise the purpose of Union.

Defoe's theory of wages and prices allowed him to maintain the latter position in the face of the former's neo-Machiavellian principles of state.

Within that general discursive framework, however, Defoe's pro-Union writings speak with two clearly discernible voices, each of which addresses a different audience. On the one hand, to the Scots Defoe makes the Union's promise of prosperity contingent upon Scottish industriousness. On the other hand, he urges restraint and patience to his English readers – restraint with regard to seeking (self-destructive) quick fix political solutions to the matter of Scottish economic competition; and patience enough to realise that in the long-run the advantage that low-wage countries enjoy relative to rich ones not only is temporary but will eventually put Scotland in a position to become a major consumer of English goods. That is to say, Defoe's conception of Union had a time factor built into it; and it is around that time factor that he developed his strategy for showing Englishmen as well as Scots how Union promised *doux-commerce* for all Britains if each were willing to accept the obligation that the free communication of rights between the two nations entailed.

Deep within Defoe's understanding of the promise of Union, then, was an economic argument that at once reinforced key aspects of natural jurisprudential arguments for Union and responded to anti-Union concerns about rich-country/poor-country relations within a market context. Though not unique to Defoe, this argument was novel in its day; and Defoe showed profound strategic insight in incorporating it into his pro-Union position.

4
THE SCOTTISH VISION OF EMPIRE: INTELLECTUAL ORIGINS OF THE DARIEN VENTURE

DAVID ARMITAGE

By the Union of 1707 Scotland lost its hopes of a colony, but gained an empire. At least, so the traditional story goes. The costly failure of the attempt to plant a settlement on the isthmus of Panama made Union if not necessary, then at least thinkable.[1] The Scots gambled their all in a desperate bid to build a commercial empire centred on Darien, but threw it away on a project 'big with necessary abortions', as Daniel Defoe called it with sour English hindsight.[2] The country lost the shirt off its back, and had to go begging to be let into the gates of the English empire. England demanded that Scotland sell the sovereign independence of its parliament in return for free trade to the plantations. Penury, bribery and self-interest drove the Scots to capitulate, but before too long they were congratulating themselves on the bargain they had driven. Once within the imperial fold, the Scots achieved success in Britain's overseas dominions of which they could never have dreamed within Britain itself. The wealth of Glasgow and

Earlier versions of this essay were presented in Pittsburgh, Washington, DC, Cambridge, Edinburgh, and London. As well as to the audiences on those occasions, I am particularly grateful to Tomás Carruthers, Joyce E. Chaplin, István Hont, John Robertson, and Quentin Skinner for their help and comments. The John Carter Brown Library, the British Academy, and the Institute for Advanced Studies in the Humanities, Edinburgh University, together made my research possible.

[1] On Darien and the Union, see, for example, Gilbert Burnet, *History of His Own Time*, 6 vols. (Oxford, 1823), V, p. 291; James Mackinnon, *The Union of England and Scotland* (London, 1896), pp. 15–59; Albert V. Dicey and Robert S. Rait, *Thoughts on the Union Between England and Scotland* (London, 1920), p. 151; T.C. Smout, *Scottish Trade on the Eve of Union 1660–1707* (Edinburgh, 1963), p. 253; Nicholas Phillipson, 'Culture and society in the 18th century province: the case of Edinburgh and the Scottish Enlightenment', in Lawrence Stone (ed.), *The University in Society*, 2 vols. (Princeton, 1974), II, p. 417; George Davie, *The Scottish Enlightenment and Other Essays* (Edinburgh, 1991), p. 3.

[2] Daniel Defoe, *The History of the Union Between England and Scotland* (London, 1786), pp. 66–7.

a leading part in the pan-British imperial elite were the ample rewards for the loss of a precarious trading-post in a virulent central-American swamp.[3]

The benefits of Union in the aftermath of Empire now seem much less clear than they once did, and even the most sanguine accountants of Scotland's eighteenth-century economy recognise that any profits took almost four decades to start flowing.[4] The Union was no clear gateway to imperial exaltation, and there was no high road from Darien to the Union. The Act of 1707 provided the most persuasive solution to the problems which Darien itself had made evident in the constitutional relationships between two Parliaments which promoted competitive economic interests while being headed by a single monarch. It also attempted to solve the wider strategic problems of poverty, defence and the European balance of power which Darien itself had been meant to determine in the interests of Scotland alone. The architects of the Union did not design it as the Scots' consolation prize for their abandoned emporium, nor did the Scots join it hoping to gather the fruits of empire. Instead, it gave them the means to strengthen and enforce their sovereign *imperium* within a British state. The Empire may now be unthinkable except as a British entity, but its creation was no aim of the framers of the Union.[5]

The story which sees the Darien venture as a frivolous and desperate episode, only of interest as a motive for Union, has distorted our sense of what the venture meant to those who promoted and invested in it. Because it failed, with great loss of blood and treasure, it has always been seen as doomed to fail: but how then do we explain the hostility of other European nations to the plan? Similarly, because in retrospect it seemed to show Scotland's incapacity for any form of economic modernisation without English partnership, it has been unclear why it was taken seriously, and why any sane Scot should have wanted to invest in it at all. Yet it was taken seriously by the English Board of Trade, on whose behalf John Locke investigated it; it was taken seriously enough for perhaps the most creative political analyst in Britain, Andrew Fletcher of Saltoun, to sink his money into the venture; and it was promoted by William Paterson, who lives to fame as the founder of the Bank of England. The interventions of three such thinkers should be enough to commend the

[3] A recent restatement is Eric Richards, 'Scotland and the uses of the Atlantic empire', in Bernard Bailyn and Philip D. Morgan (eds), *Strangers within the Realm: Cultural Margins of the First British Empire* (Williamsburg, 1991), pp. 68–70.

[4] R.H. Campbell, 'The Anglo-Scottish Union of 1707: II. The economic consequences', *Economic History Review*, 16 (1964), 468–77; Christopher A. Whatley, 'Economic causes and consequences of the Union of 1707: a survey', *Scottish Historical Review*, 68 (1989), 150–81.

[5] On the necessary Britishness of the Empire, see Linda Colley, *Britons: Forging the Nation 1707–1837* (New Haven, 1992), p. 130.

debate on Darien to the attention of intellectual history, but it has gone almost entirely unexamined, overshadowed it seems by the argument over Union and Empire which succeeded it.[6]

The history of the Darien venture begins in the head of William Paterson, some time in the mid-1680s, and in the aspirations of a group of London and Edinburgh merchants in 1693. Paterson's plan to settle a trading-post on the isthmus of Panama was one of the guiding motives of his life as an economic projector, and his persistence in promoting it was only matched by his insouciance about who should be the beneficiary. He told King William he had been promoting the plan since 1685; in 1687 he was heard in the coffee-houses of Amsterdam hawking his plan 'to Erect a Common Wealth and Free port in the Emperour of Dariens Countrey (as he was pleased to Call that poor Miserable prince)'; and it was still in his mind long after the collapse of the Scottish attempt to settle there, as we shall see.[7] The Company of Scotland Trading to Africa and the Indies which eventually took up Paterson's plan was incorporated under patent by an Act of the Scottish Parliament in June 1695. The Company itself had been the brainchild of a group of Anglo-Scottish merchants who had pressed for the earlier 'Act for Encouraging of Forraigne Trade' of 1693 allowing companies trading to foreign regions to be established in an effort to circumvent the East India Company's monopoly. The 1695 Act empowered the Company to make treaties and plant colonies, and gave it the exclusive trade with the Americas for thirty-one years. It was to be capitalised both in England and in Scotland, and Paterson's name appeared as one of the ten London directors named by the Act.[8]

The Company of Scotland publicly acknowledged no colonial plans in 1695. Though it followed three-quarters of a century's effort by Scots to establish a foothold in the Americas, in Nova Scotia, Cape Breton Island, East New Jersey, and South Carolina, the Company's foundation was almost entirely discontinuous with these earlier efforts.[9] Instead, it was

[6] The only treatment of the debate is as part of an empirical attempt to test the Weber thesis: Gordon Marshall, *Presbyteries and Profits: Calvinism and the Development of Capitalism in Scotland, 1560–1707* (Oxford, 1980), pp. 198–207.

[7] Paterson, 'To the King' [1 January 1701/2], in Saxe Bannister (ed.), *The Writings of William Paterson*, 2nd edn, 3 vols. (London, 1859), I, r. 118; *ibid.*, I, pp. xxvi, cxvii–cxviii; Robert Douglas [to the Company of Scotland?], 5 September 1696, NLS MS Adv. 83. 7. 4, ff. 23^{v}–24^{r}.

[8] *Acts of the Parliament of Scotland*, IX (London, 1822), pp. 314–15, 377–81; see G.P. Insh, 'The founding of the Company of Scotland trading to Africa and the Indies', *Scottish Historical Review*, 21 (1924), 288–95; Insh, 'The founders of the Company of Scotland', *Scottish Historical Review*, 25 (1928), 241–54.

[9] G.P. Insh, *Scottish Colonial Schemes 1620–1686* (Glasgow, 1922); only one of the original investors in the Scots Company (Robert Blackwood) had also been among the proprietors of East New Jersey, and less than 10 per cent of East New Jersey's proprietorial group ultimately invested in the Company, for example: see 'Subscriptions for Careing on a

originally intended to be a joint-stock venture on the model of the East India Company, open to investment from both English and Scots. In this it was naturally perceived as a threat both to the East India Company's monopoly (renewed in 1695) and to the Navigation Acts which had ring-fenced the English mercantile empire since the Restoration. In response, the East India Company lobbied the English Parliament for countermeasures, and an Address of both Houses informed the King that under the provisions of the 1695 Act Scotland could become a free port channelling East India goods into Europe, with Scottish plantations undercutting the English colonies' prices in the Americas. Yet if the Company was perceived as a threat to England's commercial empire, its origins also threatened the relationship between William's two imperial crowns. The Act of 1695 had been passed in William's absence (he was besieging Namur at the time), and he was furious that a measure so potentially damaging to English commercial interests should have been passed by one of his Parliaments. It was as if the Scots Parliament had assumed an ancient constitutionalist sovereignty, rather than the dependent sovereignty of King-in-Parliament which had been confirmed in the English Revolution Settlement. Accordingly, William felt that the Scots Act granted 'such powers priviledges and soveraignties as iff there had been no King of Scotland', and hence as if there were no imperial crown such as that in England. He distanced himself from the Act with curt wrath: 'I have been ill served in Scotland'.[10] Under the threat of legal sanctions from the English Parliament, the Company closed its subscription books in London and withdrew to Scotland in 1696 in search of capital and a purpose.

Thereafter the Darien venture, for good and ill, was Scotland's alone. Reason of state had demanded that William's two kingdoms, each competing for the trade on which their prosperity and security depended, should collide rather than coincide in their commercial interests. In February 1696, subscription books opened in Edinburgh with £400,000 of capital on offer, and the total was achieved by the following August. Even at this late stage, no concrete plans for any colonial or trading venture had been publicly proposed, and the Company had no ships at its

Trade to the Africa and Indies', NLS MS 3582, f. 188 (printed in Insh, 'Founders of the Company of Scotland', pp. 253–4); Ned C. Landsman, *Scotland and its First American Colony 1683–1765* (Princeton, 1985), App. B, pp. 275–8; *A Perfect List of all the Several Persons Residenters in Scotland, Who Have Subscribed as Adventurers in the Joynt-Stock of the Company of Scotland* (Edinburgh, 1696).

[10] P.W.J. Riley, *King William and the Scottish Politicians* (Edinburgh, 1979), pp. 98–9; Marquess of Annandale to Marquess of Tweeddale, 9 December 1695, NLS MS 7019, f. 154[r]; *The Parliamentary History of England, V: A.D. 1688–1702* (London, 1809), cols. 975–6.

disposal. Subscriptions came in from burgh corporations, from professionals in Edinburgh, Dundee and Glasgow, and from wealthy Lowland magnates; only the central Highlands and the Hebrides were conspicuously stinting in their contributions.[11] Many motives encouraged eminent Scots to invest. The Marquess of Tweeddale thought that 'the ill usage it hath mett with in the House of Commons' was quite enough to commend the Company to most people; the Earl of Leven subscribed £2,000 despite being advised 'mr Paterson talks too much' and that the Bank of Scotland would be a safer investment; the Earl of Tullibardine said he had put up £500, 'by which means I shall have the more influence to hinder any designs that may prove uneasy to his Majesty.'[12] The Scots were not investing in the Darien venture, nor indeed were they putting any hard cash down at this stage. Yet they were all for their various reasons showing support for the idea of a Scottish trading venture, whether in the interests of national prosperity, personal investment, or defiance of English interference.

The decision to use the Company to plant a settlement in Africa or the Indies was not officially made until July 1696. Its prime mover was William Paterson, who was called before the Company to make a presentation from various books and manuscripts of 'Discovery in Africa and the East and West Indies,' with a recommendation of which discoveries seemed most profitable for the Company to follow. The Company was warned comprehensively against accepting Paterson's scheme to colonise Darien because it would excite English opposition and encroach upon the Spanish territories, thereby offending William's major ally in the war against Louis XIV.[13] All of these strictures turned out to be correct, but evidently the force of Paterson's personality (to which all attested, even those with most cause to be suspicious of his motives) and the testimonies of such travellers as Lionel Wafer and William Dampier were enough to persuade the Company that its best returns could be had from a West Indian expedition. The intentions of the Company were clear to outsiders early in 1697, as the Scots (led by Paterson) went to northern Europe to organise the construction of a fleet

[11] See *A Perfect List of all the . . . Adventurers in the Joynt-Stock of the Company of Scotland*; Smout, *Scottish Trade on the Eve of Union*, pp. 150–1; Bruce Lenman, The highland aristocracy and North America, 1603–1784', in Loraine Maclean (ed.), *The Seventeenth Century in the Highlands* (Inverness, 1986), p. 179.

[12] Marquess of Tweeddale to Lord Yester, 28 February 1696, NLS MS 7030, f. 69r; David Nairn to Earl of Leven, 16 June 1696, SRO GD 26/13/43/27; Earl of Tullibardine to William Cartstares, 24 July 1697, in Joseph M'Cormick (ed.), *State-Papers and Letters Addressed to William Carstares* (Edinburgh, 1774), p. 322.

[13] Committee of Foreign Trade of the Company of Scotland, 23 July 1696, NLS MS Adv. 83. 7.4, f. 12r–v; Robert Douglas [to the Company of Scotland], 5 September 1696, NLS Adv. MS 83. 7. 4, f. 26r.

and to muster investment. Though opposed by a propaganda campaign masterminded by Sir Paul Rycaut, the English representative in Hamburg, the Company did manage to get the core of a fleet built.[14] By July 1698 the first 1,200 planters had been assembled to sail to Darien, Paterson among them (though as a volunteer, not as a Company representative). The fleet sailed hopefully from Leith on July 1698, and reached the Gulf of Darien the following October.[15]

Yet what did all this mean to the Scots? How did they explain to themselves what they were doing? And what did they think they could achieve by such an enterprise? These questions are less easy to answer than they might be because the Company produced almost no promotional literature for its design.[16] For the investors, who had already had a quarter of their subscriptions called in, there was of course the desire for a return on their money. For the settlers who embarked on the ships for Panama, the Darien venture held out the chance of land and homes for their families – fifty acres to plant, and fifty feet of ground for a house in the colony's capital – albeit on an unfamiliar shore.[17] Yet for Scotland, there was the opportunity of economic modernisation and of being able to compete on an equal footing with the other nations of Europe for whom trade was now the major reason of state. There was the possibility of self-defence through prosperity, an escape from the metropolitan dominance of England, and the hope of economic growth without the attendant dangers of corruption. In sum, the Darien venture was an alternative to dependency and corruption within Britain, and to poverty and universal monarchy within Europe.

The Darien colony was justified as a necessity in a world where the longest purse and the largest population guaranteed military success, and in which the greatest empire to be captured was the empire of the seas. In an era of standing armies financed by public debt, money was now the sinews of war, and trade was the most reliable means of creating national wealth. 'It's now beyond all Controversie,' wrote one defender of the

[14] Sir Paul Rycaut to William Blathwayt, 16 February 1697, 30 March 1697, 30 April 1697, Firestone Library, Princeton University, General MSS: Rycaut-Blathwayt Correspondence, ff. 145, 149, 154; see also Rycaut-Trumbull correspondence in G.P. Insh (ed.), *Papers Relating to the Ships and Voyages of the Company of Scotland Trading to Africa and the Indies 1696–1707* (Edinburgh, 1924), pp. 6–48.

[15] For general accounts of the course of the venture see G.P. Insh, *The Company of Scotland Trading to Africa and the Indies* (London, 1932); John Prebble, *The Darien Disaster* (London, 1968).

[16] The only publications detailing the composition and aims of the Company in its first year were alarmingly brief: see *Proposals for a Fond to Cary on a Plantation* (n.p., 1695); *Constitutions of the Company of Scotland Trading to Africa and the Indies* (Edinburgh, 1696).

[17] Company broadsheet, 12 March 1698, reprinted in John Scott and George P. Johnston, *A Bibliography of Books Relating to the Darien Company*, rev. edn (Edinburgh, 1906), pp. 15–16.

Scots Company, 'that it is in the Interest of all Nations to increase their Trade; the Increase of which begetteth Wealth, and Riches, which now in the time of Warr doth more contribute to the preservation of a Nation, then the multitude and valour of it's Men.' Though commerce had once been seen as the enemy of martial hardiness, particularly within a tradition of Machiavellian moralising, it had become the only way to finance military establishments in a brutally competitive world: 'the posture and condition of other countries considered', thought Charles Davenant, swallowing his fears of greed and luxury, 'it is become with us a necessary evil'. Yet if trade was necessary for national defence, it could also be the way to international eminence, 'For as *Trade* is a richer and more dureable *Mine* than any in *Mexico* or *Peru* . . . so in proportion to its plenty of Money, will . . . [a nation] flourish at Home, and be terrible Abroad.'[18] Since a large population would be needed to sustain such an enterprise, any foreigners should be granted rights of citizenship by general naturalisation as had been done by the Roman Republic. Contemporary Spain had failed to follow such a policy, and as a result had been impoverished by emigration.[19] Yet times had changed since Roman days, and a universal monarchy on the classical model would have to be maritime not territorial if it were to be truly global. Any nation that could capture the empire of the seas could dictate terms to the rest of the world and would achieve for itself 'An Empire not less Glorious, and of a much larger Extent, than either *Alexander's* or *Caesar's*'.[20]

With these shibboleths of late seventeenth-century economics and the admonitory example of Spain firmly in mind, William Paterson justified the Darien colony as a free port, sustained by general naturalisation, its

[18] *A Letter from a Gentleman in the Country to His Friend at Edinburgh: Wherein it is Clearly Proved, That the Scottish African and Indian Company is Exactly Calculated for the Interest of Scotland* (Edinburgh, 1696), p. 3; Charles Davenant, *An Essay Upon the Probable Means of Making the People Gainers in the Balance of Trade* [1699], in Charles Whitworth (ed.), *The Political and Commercial Works of Charles D'Avenant LL.D.*, 5 vols. (London, 1771), II, p. 275; C.K., *Some Seasonable and Modest Thoughts Partly Occasioned By, and Partly Concerning the Scots East-India Company* (Edinburgh, 1696), p. 4; see also István Hont, 'Free trade and the economic limits to national politics: neo-Machiavellian political economy reconsidered', in John Dunn (ed.), *The Economic Limits to Modern Politics* (Cambridge, 1990), pp. 41–120.

[19] On general naturalisation, see N[icholas] B[arbon,] *A Discourse of Trade* (London, 1690), p. 60; Charles Davenant, *Essay Upon the Probable Means of Making the People Gainers in the Balance of Trade*, in Whitworth (ed.), *Works of Charles D'Avenant*, II, p. 186; Walter Moyle, *An Essay upon the Constitution of the Roman Government* [*c.* 1699] in Caroline Robbins (ed.), *Two English Republican Tracts* (Cambridge, 1969), pp. 228–9; Daniel Statt, 'The controversy over the naturalization of foreigners in England, 1660–1760', PhD thesis, University of Cambridge, 1987, esp. ch. 4; on Spain, see e.g. John Locke, 'For a Generall Naturalization' [1693], in Patrick Kelly (ed.), *Locke on Money*, 2 vols. (Oxford, 1991), II, p. 487.

[20] Barbon, *Discourse of Trade*, pp. 40–1, 61.

commercial wealth providing the key to the empire of the seas. The Scots argued that the isthmus between Portobello and Cartagena had not been continuously occupied by the Spanish, whose rights had thereby lapsed, and that sovereignty might be passed to any European nation which could make an agreement with the native peoples of the area, in accord with natural law.[21] The strategic importance of the isthmus as a crossing-point between the two hemispheres and as a shaft into the heart of the Spanish American empire had long been recognised. Darien could be 'the door of Commerce to *China* and *Japan*, and the Emporium and Staple for the Trade of both *Indies*'.[22] To exploit the potential of the isthmus, Paterson argued, English and Dutch models of exclusive trading-companies could not be followed, 'but of whatever Nation or Religion a Man be (if one of Us) he ought to be look'd upon to be of the same Interest and Inclination.' Spain and Portugal had become depopulated and impoverished because they barred foreign immigrants from their overseas dominions, 'So that the Indies have rather conquered *Spain* and *Portugall*, then they have Conquered the Indies . . . People and their industry are the true Riches of a prince or Nation.' Rome rose by a policy of general naturalisation, liberty of conscience, and freedom of government, and the Company should follow such a course in Darien. With the large population such a policy would create, Scotland need have no fear of depopulation, 'Trade will increass Trade . . . money will begett money', and Scotland would have the command of a benign universal empire of the seas: 'Thus this Door of the Seas, and the key of the universe with any thing of a Reasonable management will of Course enable its proprietors to give Laws to both Oceans and to become Arbitrators of the Commerciall world, without being liable to the fatigues, expences and dangers, or contracting the Guilt and blood of Alexander and Cesar.'[23]

It was left to the shrewdest Scottish political analyst of the time, Andrew Fletcher of Saltoun, to place the Darien venture into the wider

[21] The arguments for and against the Scots claim are usefully summarised in 'The Spanish Reasons against The Scotch invasion of Darien. Offer'd to his Maj^{ty}' [1700?], BL MS Harl. 2071, ff. 275^{r}–277^{v}.

[22] See e.g. Philippe Du Plessis-Mornay, 'Discours sur les moyens de diminuer l'Espaignol' [24 April 1584], in P.R. Auguis and A.D. La Fontenelle de Vaudoré (eds), *Mémoires et correspondance de Duplessis-Mornay*, (Paris, 1824), II, p. 590; *Caledonia. The Declaration of the Council Constituted by the Indian and African Company of Scotland; For the Government and Direction of their Colonies, and Settlements in the Indies* (Boston, [May 15] 1699), p. 3. British settlement on Darien (based on the Scots' claim) as a check to Spain was still being proposed in 1738–9: BL Add. MS 32694, ff. 9^{r}–12^{v}, 22^{r-v}, 31^{r}–32^{v}.

[23] Paterson to Sir Robert Chiesly, 9 July 1695, NLS MS Adv. 83. 7. 4, f. 4^{v}; Paterson to Company of Scotland, 17 January 1700, NLS MS Adv. 83. 7. 5, f. 56^{r} (cf. Paterson *et al.*, 'The Council of Caledonia's Address to the King's Most Excellent Majesty' [1698], in *A Full and Exact Collection of All the Considerable Addresses . . . and Other Publick Papers Relating to the Company of Scotland* (np, 1700), pp. 75–6).

context of the debates in contemporary Britain on the standing army, the necessity of trade, and the threat of universal monarchy. Fletcher pledged £1,000 to the Company of Scotland on the very day that the books opened, and until 1700, when the last shares were called in, he was notably punctual in paying his subscriptions.[24] He also kept up thoroughly with the printed debate in 1699–1700.[25] Tradition holds that Fletcher convened a meeting between Paterson and the Marquess of Tweeddale at Saltoun to help the passage of the Company's legislation through the Scottish Parliament, and that Fletcher was instrumental in obtaining Lionel Wafer's knowledge of central America for the Company of Scotland. Neither story can be corroborated.[26] However, Fletcher and Paterson were linked intellectually, not solely by an interest in Scottish prosperity and a patriotic commitment to the Company of Scotland, but also by the belief that the design of Darien could offer Scotland the possibility of economic growth without the danger of corruption – in short, of an emporium without the costs of an empire. This is evident from the cluster of *Discourses* on militias, on the affairs of Scotland, and on those of Spain, which Fletcher published in 1697–98, his most fertile period, as well as from Paterson's later proposals for reviving the Darien scheme as a British venture and for the institution of a Council of Trade which he proposed in the aftermath of Scotland's failure. Scotland's economic adversity in the 1690s made strange bedfellows of these men, and as we shall see they were to diverge sharply in their recommendations for remedying Scotland's crisis after Darien.

Andrew Fletcher was a political interventionist as much as an analyst. Almost all of his published works were intended as contributions to debate, particularly because he had to conduct his political campaigns from outside the Scottish Parliament in the years between 1685 and 1703. His earliest certain publication, *A Discourse of Government with Relation to Militia's*, was published in both London and Edinburgh in 1697–1698 as a shot in the battle over the fate of King William's armed forces in the

[24] NLS MS Adv. 83. 1. 1, f. 3^{r} (subscription book 1696); MS Adv. 83. 2. 5, ff. 55^{r}, 114^{v}, 299^{v}, 341^{r}, 383^{r}, 439^{r} (Company journal 1696–1700).

[25] NLS MS Saltoun 17863 (Fletcher's library catalogue), ff. 12^{r} (*An Enquiry into the Causes of the Miscarriage of the Scots Colony at Darien* (Glasgow, 1700); *Scotland's Grievances, Relating to Darien* (np, 1700)), 18^{r} (Lionel Wafer, *A New Voyage and Description of the Isthmus of America* (London, 1699), 65^{v} ([Walter Herries,] *A Defence of the Scots Abdicating Darien* (np, 1700); *An Enquiry into the Causes of the Miscarriage*), 70^{r} (*A Defence of the Scots Settlement at Darien* (Edinburgh, 1699); [Robert Ferguson,] *A Just and Modest Vindication of the Scots Design, for Having established a Colony at Darien* (np, 1699)).

[26] Sir John Dalrymple, *Memoirs of Great Britain and Ireland*, 2 vols. (London, 1771–1788), II, pp. 95–9; [Walter Herries,] *A Defence of the Scots Abdicating Darien* (np, 1700), pp. 38–44; cf. the reply to Herries in *An Enquiry into the Causes of the Miscarriage of the Scots Colony at Darien* (Glasgow, 1700), pp. 97–8, where Fletcher goes unmentioned.

aftermath of the Treaty of Ryswick (1697).[27] Fletcher argued that since the late fifteenth century the feudal baronage had been so softened by the luxury brought in by the discoveries of America and the East Indies, that the kings of Europe had had to take on responsibility for national defence with standing armies. This caused a shift in the balance of power in favour of increasingly absolute monarchs who taxed their people to provide for the armies, which in turn stood fair to enslave the enfeebled and impoverished people under martial tyranny, as had happened in ancient Rome. This historical argument supported Fletcher's more timely recommendation that Britain had no need for such a standing army because it was protected by its natural maritime defences, and should not be involved in continental wars. This would also lessen the tax burden on Scotland, which had been sending its money and men to support a specifically English war effort. A militia at home and fleets abroad would be all that was needed to protect British interests and the balance of power in Europe: 'The Sea is the only Empire that can naturally belong to us. Conquest is not in our Interest, much less to consume our People in conquering for others.'[28]

Fletcher extended the arguments of his intervention in the standing army debate with two further pamphlets in the summer of 1698 which gave intellectual sustenance to the Darien venture. The first of Fletcher's *Two Discourses Concerning the Affairs of Scotland* was the only substantial publication (apart from the official statements of the Company) to deal with the Darien venture in the time between the Act of 1695 and the storm which broke upon the news of the collapse of the first colony in 1699. 'The Ships of the Company are sailed', he wrote, and 'Scotland has now a greater venture at Sea than at any time since we have bin a Nation . . . I may well say all our hopes of ever being any other than a poor and inconsiderable People are imbarked with them.' The precariousness of the enterprise and its urgent need for supplies meant that its political importance was greater even that the question of the standing army, though Fletcher's arguments from that debate underpinned his reasons for the long-term necessity of the Darien venture. The standing armies which replaced the feudal militias could now only be supported

[27] On this debate, see Lois G. Schwoerer, *'No Standing Armies!' The Antiarmy Ideology in Seventeenth-Century England* (Baltimore, 1974), pp. 155–87, and on Fletcher's place within it John Robertson, *The Scottish Enlightenment and the Militia Issue* (Edinburgh, 1985), pp. 22–59.

[28] [Andrew Fletcher,] *A Discourse of Government with Relation to Militia's* (Edinburgh, 1698), pp. 11–12, 15, 25, 45, 46, 63; compare [John Trenchard and Walter Moyle,] *An Argument, Shewing, that a Standing Army Is inconsistent with a Free Government, and absolutely destructive to the Constitution of the English Monarchy* (London, 1697), p. 18 ('The Sea is our element').

financially from the proceeds of trade. However, Scotland had been left behind in the race for commerce which had followed the great discoveries of the fifteenth century. As Scotland's great chance to enter that race, the Darien venture was 'the only means to recover us from our miserable and despicable condition'. Scotland had received no peace dividend in the aftermath of the Treaty of Ryswick: why then should it be taxed to pay for forces (manned by a great many Scots who could otherwise be helping to boost Scottish prosperity) to defend England and Holland's competitive trading interests? 'From all these Considerations I say, That the keeping up of any Standing Forces in time of Peace is not only useless, but destructive to the well being of this Nation.'[29]

The commercial prosperity hoped for from the success of the Darien venture was to be both the alternative to fiscal dependence on London and to impoverishment in the new Europe of trading nations defended by standing armies. Yet how could a plantation on the isthmus of Darien hope to solve such global predicaments? Fletcher supplied an answer in his other work of the summer of 1698, the teasing Italian pamphlet entitled *Discorso delle Cose di Spagna*. The dispute over the Spanish Succession and the fear of universal monarchy provided the shifting diplomatic, strategic and ideological context for much of the Darien debate, from the sailing of the expedition, through the vain attempts by Paterson to resuscitate its aim before the death of William in March 1702. The *Discorso* was an early intervention in this debate, though it also had a pointed application to the fortunes of the Darien venture. According to its title-page, the *Discorso* was 'written in the month of July 1698' ('*Scritto nel mese di Luglio 1698*'), just as the first ships sailed forth from Leith to Darien, and a few months before the first Partition Treaty in October 1698. It brought fears of the tyrannical force of empire up to date with an ironic and admonitory programme by which Spain might obtain universal monarchy. It was obvious to outside observers that Spain had long since missed her chance for an independent universal monarchy, despite her huge dominions in Europe and the preponderant wealth derived from the Indies. This was a matter of wonder as much as a cause of relief, and in the debates over the Partition Treaties, three pre-eminent British economic writers – Andrew Fletcher, Charles Davenant,[30] and

[29] [Andrew Fletcher,] *Two Discourses Concerning the Affairs of Scotland; Written in the Year 1698* (Edinburgh, 1698), pp. 9–10, 12, 19, 26, 28. Fletcher's solicitude for the recently departed colonists was echoed in Sir Robert Sibbald, 'Discourse Anent the improvements may be made in Scotland for advancing the Wealth of the Kingdome in these Parts' [12 September 1698], NLS MS Adv. 33. 5. 16, f. 27^{v}.

[30] Davenant, *An Essay Upon Universal Monarchy* [1701] in *Essays Upon I. The Ballance of Power. II. The Right of Making War, Peace, and Alliances. III. Universal Monarchy* (London, 1701).

William Paterson[31] – anatomised, advised and moralised upon Spain's wasted opportunity, not least to instruct their own countries in the dangers still present and the opportunities to hand.

The *Discorso* was the first, and most sophisticated, of the tracts in this sub-genre of universal monarchist literature. Fletcher stressed that his aim was not to support Spain's claim to universal monarchy, but rather to warn her neighbours how easily, and by what methods, Spain might gain the 'empire of the world' (*'insignorirsi del Mondo'*); how the rest of Europe might 'avert from the world so terrible a ruin'; and how the people of Spain might establish a form of government 'tending to nourish the virtues' (*'che nutriscoro le virtù'*) and 'enjoy the blessings of peace, liberty and good government' after the death of their King if they so chose.[32] The means by which the successor to the dying King Carlos II might obtain universal monarchy, Fletcher wrote, would be an expedition against Africa, the reformation of the affairs of his kingdom, and the acquisition of the empire of the sea (*'l'aquisto dell' imperio del mare'*); without maritime supremacy 'it would be the greatest absurdity for him to think of extending his empire'. Spain's success so far depended on her position, straddling two seas over the Straits of Gibraltar; the northern nations had largely failed to acquire empire because their people could only expand their power by emigration. Fletcher speculated that Egypt might be as great an empire as Spain if it had a Suez canal to link two seas as Spain controlled Mediterranean and Atlantic trade.[33]

The argument that to straddle the junction of two oceans was the key to the empire of the seas was, of course, the heart of the strategic justification for Scotland's expedition to the isthmus of Panama: to plant a colony in Darien would be to hold the world's *entrepôt* between east and west. Spain had also bled itself of men and money to keep up distant possessions by force of arms and absolute government, when it should have secured new territory by colonies and retained the good-will of its people by looking after their ancient privileges. Spain could only repopulate its overseas possessions by granting freedom of conscience in the Indies. The Darien venture went unmentioned in Fletcher's teasing

[31] Paterson, 'Proposal for settling on the Isthmus of Darien, releasing the nations from the Tyranny of Spain by throwing open the Trade of S[ou]th America to all Nations. – [1 January] 1701[/2]', BL Add. MS 12437, printed in Bannister (ed.), *Writings of William Paterson*, I, pp. 117–60.

[32] [Andrew Fletcher,] 'Auviso' to *Discorso delle Cose di Spagna, Scritto nel mese di Luglio 1698* (Naples [s, Edinburgh], 1698), trans. as *A Discourse Concerning the Affairs of Spain*, in *The Political Works of Andrew Fletcher, Esq; of Saltoun* (Glasgow, 1749), pp. 125–6. On the significance of Fletcher's Neapolitan imprint, see John Robertson, 'Andrew Fletcher's vision of Union', in Roger A. Mason (ed.), *Scotland and England 1286–1815* (Edinburgh, 1987), pp. 216–18.

[33] Fletcher, *Political Works*, pp. 129, 172, 129–30.

text, but the implications were clear for Scotland. Any nation which could sit astride two oceans might control world trade; with freedom of conscience and a liberal immigration policy it could people its colonies without debilitating mass emigration; and with the empire of the seas, it could both avoid suspicion of aggressive motives within Europe and ensure the economic dependence of its far-flung dominions.[34] Here was Paterson's proposal for a free port on the isthmus of Panama transformed by Fletcher's ironic intelligence into a plan for Spanish regeneration, whose outlines might just as easily be followed by the British monarchies without the dangers of depopulation, impoverishment, and the tyranny of standing armies.

The response of the English Board of Trade to the Darien venture showed that the Scots were not alone in believing that the isthmus of Panama could hold the key to national regeneration. In May 1697 rumour reached the Board that the Scots were intending to settle Darien and attack the Spanish on the isthmus, and they were asked 'what you think fit to be done for preventing the Scotch East India Company from carrying on any Designs that may be to the Injury of the Spanyardes, or prejudicial to the Trade of this Kingdome'. In its reply of August 1697 the Board thought 'it would be no very difficult matter for any European Prince or State to make some secure settlement' on the isthmus, and feared that if the Scots were the ones to succeed it would hurt Spanish interests in the Americas, and potentially draw away the inhabitants of the English colonies, in the Caribbean especially, 'with hopes of Mines and Treasures'. English subjects should therefore be forbidden to give any assistance to the Scots, and any Scottish ships on the high seas should be searched lest they be going to Darien. By September, the Board had interviewed William Dampier and Lionel Wafer, and they were so sure that a Darien colony was viable that they recommended an expedition should be sent to capture Golden Island, and the port on the mainland of Darien opposite, for the English Crown. 'This work seems to us to require all possible despatch, lest the Scotch Company be there before us, which is of the utmost importance to the trade of England.'[35]

[34] Fletcher, *Political Works*, pp. 136–7; cf. Davenant, *Essay Upon Universal Monarchy*, pp. 253–6 (quoting Machiavelli, *Discorsi*, II, iii, *ibid.*, p. 255).

[35] James Vernon to Board of Trade, 20 May 1697, Bod. MS Locke c. 30, f. 47; 'Copy of a Representation relating to the Designes of the Scotch East India Company upon the Isthmus of Darien in America, Augt 10th 1697', Bod. MS Locke c. 30, ff. 49^{r}–51^{r}; Insh (ed.), *Papers Relating to . . . the Company of Scotland*, pp. 49–54; Board of Trade Journal, 10 September 1697, in *Calendar of State Papers, Colonial Series, America and West Indies 1696–1697*, ed. Cecil Headlam (London, 1904), p. 599; Board of Trade to Lords Justices, 16 September 1697, in Bannister (ed.), *Writings of William Paterson*, III, p. 261; cf. W.T., 'A Memoriall concerning the setling a Colony on the Istmus of Darien in America', Bod. MS Locke c. 30, ff. 127^{r}–128^{v}.

The English never sent an expedition to Darien, probably because of the rising concern over the partition of the Spanish Empire on the death of Carlos II. Yet this did not diminish the Board of Trade's interest in the infant Scottish colony. It seems that John Locke was delegated to gather information on the position of the colony and on the provisions of the Navigation Acts. He took note of Dampier's testimony on the position of Golden Island and the mainland port, and he went to St Paul's churchyard to pick up a copy of Lionel Wafer's newly published book on the isthmus.[36] The publication of *An Enquiry into the Causes of the Miscarriages of the Scots Colony in Darien* (references in which to designing English opponents of the Scots Locke seems to have taken personally) in January 1700, spurred Parliament to ask the Board 'how consistent the Colony at Darien may be with the [1670] Treaty with Spaine, and the Trade of this Kingdom'. Once again, the Board decided that only the Spanish claim to Darien could be respected, and that Scotland's actions threatened to involve the King in war with Spain.[37] Yet it was not long before news came back to Britain that the Spanish had routed the Scots, and that the Darien venture was effectively dead.

The news of failure arrived too late in Scotland to forestall a second expedition which sailed hopefully in June 1699 to New Caledonia, urged on by (amongst others) John Locke's intermittent correspondent, Andrew Fletcher, who refused to believe the reports of the desertion.[38] Congratulatory poems poured off the presses, and thanks were given to God in all of Edinburgh's churches at the news of the success. At the Edinburgh University graduation ceremony that summer the Regent, William Scot, 'declam'd an Elegant Harangue on an unusual Subject for that place, *Viz* Our *Indian* and *African* Company's settlement in *America*,' a full-dress natural law defence of the colony which was

[36] Bod. MS Locke c. 30, ff. 125^r, 40^r. Locke's copy of Lionel Wafer, *A New Voyage and Description of the Isthmus of America* (London, 1699), remained in his library, along with *The History of Caledonia: or, the Scots Colony in Darien in the West Indies* (London, 1699): see John Harrison and Peter Laslett, *The Library of John Locke*, 2nd edn (Oxford, 1971), items 3121, 2597. On Locke and Darien see Maurice Cranston, *John Locke: A Biography* (London, 1957), pp. 444–6.

[37] *An Enquiry into the Causes of the Miscarriages of the Scots Colony at Darien*, pp. 16, 41–2; Locke to Edward Clarke, 19 January 1700, in E.S. de Beer (ed.), *The Correspondence of John Locke*, 8 vols. (Oxford, 1976–89), VI, pp. 771–2; Bod. MS Locke c. 30, ff. 116, 117^r–118^v.

[38] [Fletcher to Lord Yester], 23 September 1699, NLS MS 7020, ff. 169^r–170^v. (My thanks to John Robertson for this reference.) Locke had heard news of the desertion of the first colony a week earlier: Locke to Edward Clarke, 16 September 1699, *Correspondence of John Locke*, VI, p. 683. For the correspondence between Fletcher and Locke (mostly on medical matters) see *Correspondence of John Locke*, V, pp. 82–3, 274–5; VI, pp. 303–4, 314; VII, pp. 471–2; VIII, pp. 434–6.

repeated in the student's printed theses for debate.[39] Carried by this wave of enthusiasm and support from home, the second party of Scots settlers arrived in Panama only to find the houses of New Caledonia abandoned and the settlement in ruins. As Macaulay put it, 'The site marked out for the proud capital which was to have been the Tyre, the Venice, the Amsterdam of the eighteenth century was overgrown with jungle, and inhabited only by the sloth and the baboon'.[40] The new settlers still decided to stay and, led by Alexander Campbell of Fonab, they routed a Spanish camp at Toubacanti. A week later, a Spanish flotilla arrived to take revenge, and after two weeks of attack, the Scots admitted defeat and left the isthmus for good in April 1700; none of the four ships made it back home. It was probably also about this time that the young John Clerk of Penicuik, whose brother Robert had accompanied the first expedition, composed a defiantly martial cantata, *Leo Scotiæ Irritatus*, on a libretto by the Leyden chemistry professor William Boerhaave, which urged the Scots to fight off their enemies so that they might enjoy an idyll on the 'sweet isle of Darien' ('Suavis insula Daria').[41] When Scotland heard of the retreat and desertion of the only colony, the response was a storm of recrimination, against the Company, the Spanish, and the King who had signally failed to promote – indeed, had openly blocked – the welfare of his northern kingdom. Presbyterians saw God's anger visited upon his errant nation in the disaster in Panama as in the great Edinburgh fire of February 1700. The Church of Scotland ordered days of fasting and humiliation, as God's purposes were vainly sought.[42]

After the collapse of the colony, the Darien venture returned to the

[39] *The Edinburgh Gazette* 36 (26–29 June 1699); [William Scott,] *Amplissimis Senatui Edinburgeno . . . Theses Hasce Philosophicas . . . ad XXVI Diem Junii propugnandas* (Edinburgh, 1699); C.P. Finlayson, 'Edinburgh University and the Darien scheme', *Scottish Historical Review*, 34 (1955), 97–102.

[40] Lord Macaulay, *The History of England from the Accession of James the Second*, ed. C.H. Firth, 6 vols. (Oxford, 1915), VI, p. 2,932. Darien was the only colonial enterprise Macaulay treated in his history: J.W. Burrow, *A Liberal Descent: Victorian Historians and the English Past* (Cambridge, 1981), p. 233.

[41] SRO GD 18/4538/4/1 (libretto 'by Doctor Bourhaven'), GD 18/4538/4/2–3 (music by 'Gio Clerk'). (My thanks to Sir John Clerk of Penicuik, Bt., for permission to cite these manuscripts, and to the Scottish Music Information Centre for a recording of the cantata.) On the date of *Leo Scotiæ Irritatus*, see Iain Gordon Brown, 'Sir John Clerk of Penicuik (1675–1755); Aspects of a Virtuoso Life', PhD thesis, University of Cambridge, 1980, p. 310, n. 137.

[42] *Scotland's Lament for Their Misfortunes* (np, nd [1700]); *The Sighs and Groans of a Sinking Kingdom, In an Humble Address To the Parliament of Scotland* (np, 1700), sig. [*]^{V}, 6, 11; 'Act, Anent a Solemn National Fast and Humiliation. At Edinburgh, 14. February 1700', in *The Principal Acts of the General Assembly of the Church of Scotland; Convened at Edinburgh, Feb. 2 1700* (Edinburgh, 1700), pp. 8–11; Robert Wodrow to James Wallace, 16 July 1700, in L.W. Sharp (ed.) *Early Letters of Robert Wodrow 1698–1709* (Edinburgh, 1937), pp. 92–93.

realm of argument. The shifting context of national and international politics had made the alternatives for Scotland, among which was its claim to Darien, all the sharper. In the parliamentary session of 1700 two major issues divided the House: should the claim to Darien be insisted upon, in the face of the Crown's opposition, and should the parliament vote William the supply he needed to keep up his army? The two questions became dependent upon one another. Addresses flooded into Parliament urging retaliation for the humiliation of Scotland, the burdens of the standing army, and the poverty of the nation. As the alternatives were debated in the course of the stormy session, matters grew so heated that one excitable witness exclaimed, 'God help us, we ripening for destruction. It looks very like Forty-one . . . They talk publickly that unless the King will grant them the legal settlement of Caledonia, that they will address him with forty thousand hands at it.' The claim to Darien had become at worst a forlorn grievance, which should not be allowed to distract from the more pressing issue of the standing army.[43] The death of the Duke of Gloucester in August 1700, which threw the question of the succession further into confusion, and the accession of Philip of Anjou to the throne of Spain as Philip V in November 1700 fuelled the tension. For William Seton of Pitmedden, these two events could only point one way: to a full incorporating Union between England and Scotland. Not only would this settle the succession, it would prevent internal disputes about Britain's claim on Darien as a bulwark against the possibility of a Franco-Spanish universal monarchy in the New World: 'how much it were for the Interest of Great-Britain, to be Master of that Isthmus, is obvious to every Coffee-house Politician, in spight of all our more refined wits.[44]

By February 1701, when Louis XIV registered Philip V in the succession to the French throne, the nightmare of Bourbon universal monarchy seemed all too possible. George Ridpath urged William to recognise Scotland's claim to Darien to ensure enthusiastic Scottish support for his fight against the Bourbon universal monarch.[45] William

[43] Colonel Ferguson to William Carstares, 15 June 1700, in *State-Papers . . . Addressed to William Carstares*, p. 527; *A Letter from a Gentleman at London to His Friend at Edinburgh* (np, 1700); [George Ridpath?] *Scotland's Grievances Relating to Darien &c. Humbly offered to the Consideration of the Parliament* (np, 1700); for the progress of the issues, see, e.g. John Home (ed.), *A Diary of the Proceedings in the Parliament and Privy Council of Scotland. May 21, MDCC. – March 7, MDCCII. By Sir David Hume of Crossrigg* (Edinburgh, 1828), pp. 5–6, 45, 61. William ordered that no royal assent should be given to any Act asserting Scotland's right to Darien: William to Marquess of Queensberry, 25 April 1700, BL Add. MS 6420, f. 28^{r}.

[44] [William Seton of Pitmedden,] *The Interest of Scotland in Three Essays* (np, 1700), p. 60.

[45] [George Ridpath,] *The Great Reasons and Interests Consider'd Anent the Spanish Monarchy* (np, 1701), pp. 36–7. Paterson owned a copy of this work: see Bannister (ed.), *Writings of William Paterson*, III, p. 71, item 245.

Paterson, following Pitmedden and Ridpath, also used the Spanish Succession crisis as the reason to press for the resumption of the claim to Darien, but this time as a British venture. In 1700 he had proposed to the Scottish Parliament a detailed *dirigiste* plan for national economic revitalisation under a Council of Trade, a quarter of whose members should be directors of the Company of Scotland. Paterson's plea to Parliament fell on deaf ears, and in January 1702, he addressed himself directly to King William with a plan for the settlement of Darien to be taken up once more, as a whole-heartedly British venture. In the proposals for a Council of Trade, Paterson had fearfully awaited 'that dreadful storm which is so openly arising against the Protestant religion and liberties of Europe; all [Holland's] progress and ours united is like to be little enough to balance that growing greatness of the popish world which at this day stands so formidably ranged under the banners of the House of Bourbon.'[46] By the time he presented his memorial to William, Paterson found an expedition to Darien 'much more heavy and pressing upon my Spirit since the Late Accession of Spain, and consequently of the Indies, to the House of Bourbon'. The aim now was not the economic regeneration of Scotland, but rather 'so to Byas and alter the Ballance of wealth and Power' in the world as to put Britain on a proper footing for war with the Bourbons.[47]

Paterson cynically cannibalised the very document which he had used to reinvigorate to the Company of Scotland in January 1700 to urge William to capture 'the keys of the Indies and doors of the world' at Darien and prevent the imperial nightmare which would become flesh if the Spanish were to new-model the Indies (along much the same lines that Fletcher had ironically proposed in his *Discorso delle Cose di Spagna*). The riches of trade which would flow from the isthmus would also ensure that commerce might at last become the band of union, not the bone of contention, between William's British kingdoms. No longer would an emporium be the alternative to *imperium*; under Paterson's new plan for a pan-British enterprise they would be united, as sovereignty became merged and trade flowed through the isthmus to London. United 'into one empire, whereof England [is] to be the centre country, and London to be the centre city . . . this island, as it seems by nature designed, will of course become the emporium of Europe'. The logical accompaniment to the capture of Darien would be Union with Scotland, for the glory of William and the safety of Britain against the designs of

[46] William Paterson, *Proposals and Reasons for Constituting a Council of Trade* [1701], in Bannister (ed)., *Writings of William Paterson*, I, p. 60; [Paterson,] 'Heads of things fitt to be granted and Done in the ensuing Session of Parliam: 1700', NLS MS Adv. 83. 7. 6, ff. 154^{r}–158^{v}.

[47] Paterson to William III, 24 November 1701, Bod. MS Rawl. D. 132, fol. $1.^{r}$.

France.[48] Paterson turned thereafter firmly to the side of England and the Union. The Marquess of Queensberry thought he would be just the man to write against the Darien venture to defuse tension over the issue in 1700, and by 1705 Paterson called the Company of Scotland 'a weapon which I was misfortunately concerned in the forming'. A year later he was back in Edinburgh as an agent of Harley, writing pro-Unionist propaganda, keeping an eye on the debates of the Scottish Parliament for his London paymasters, and acting as one of the statisticians calculating the Equivalent. Never one to let an obsession drop, however, he was still insisting to Harley in 1710 that 'in all my thoughts for the good of this Island the Indies is always included'.[49]

Andrew Fletcher's only recorded responses to the failure of the Darien venture were to lament that Scotland had 'suffer'd so great a Loss both in Men and Mony, as to put us almost beyond hope of ever having any considerable Trade' and to suspect that the English Board of Trade had been hand-in-glove with France in opposing Scottish economic interests. Yet Fletcher was looking forward, and he said repeatedly that he would no longer insist upon the affair of Darien.[50] Unlike Paterson, he had no desire to fall in with King William, whom he suspected of aiming to become a universal monarch himself, by uniting England, Scotland and Ireland to his Dutch dominions, thereby capturing 'the Empire of the Sea, with an Intire Monopoly of Trade'. Trade was now 'the Golden Ball' which all nations, and all cities, were fighting to monopolise, and 'the *English* are no less guilty of these Partialities than any other trading Nation.'[51] Though with hindsight after 1707, it seemed to many that a full

[48] Paterson, 'Proposal for settling on the Isthmus of Darien', in Bannister (ed.), *Writings of William Paterson*, I, pp. 147, 132, 156; Paterson to Lord Treasurer Godolphin, 12 December 1709, in Abel Boyer, *Quadriennium Annæ Postremum; or The Political State of Great Britain* (London, 1711), p. 271.

[49] Marquess of Queensberry to William Carstares, 31 July 1700, in M'Cormick (ed.), *State-Papers . . . Addressed to William Carstares*, p. 584; [William Paterson to Robert Harley,] 23 April 1705, in Historical Manuscripts Commission, *Report on the Manuscripts of His Grace the Duke of Portland, K.G., Preserved at Welbeck Abbey*, VIII (London, 1907), p. 179; [Paterson,] *An Inquiry into the Reasonableness and Consequences of an Union with Scotland* (London, 1706); [Paterson,] 'A Brief View of the Present Treaty of Union in five Letters. Edinburgh, 1706', BL Add. MS 10403, ff. 6^r–35^v, printed in Bannister (ed.), *Writings of William Paterson*, III, pp. 5–25; Paterson to [Robert Harley,] 4 September 1710, in HMC, 15th Report, *The Manuscripts of His Grace the Duke of Portland*, IV (London, 1897), pp. 583–4. No works on Darien were, however, to be found in Paterson's 'Catalogue of Books and Pamphlets Relating to Trade, Revenue, Navigation &c^a.' [23 August 1703], BL MS Harl. 4654, printed in Bannister (ed.), *Writings of William Paterson*, III, pp. 49–72.

[50] [Andrew Fletcher,] *Speeches, By a Member of the Parliament, Which Began at Edinburgh the 6th of May 1703* (Edinburgh, 1703), p. 38; [Fletcher,] *An Account of a Conversation Concerning a Right Regulation of Governments for the Common Good of Mankind* (Edinburgh, 1704), p. 31.

[51] [Andrew Fletcher,] *A Speech Upon the State of the Nation, In April 1701* (np, nd), p. 22; *Account of a Conversation*, pp. 30–1.

incorporating Union was the only solution to the conflicts of interest made evident by the Darien episode, the range of options presented between 1702 and 1705 was much wider, and Fletcher's political vision encompassed two of them. In 1703, his proposals for limitations upon any monarch who succeeded Anne demanded parliamentary control over the monarch's prerogative rights to declare peace and war or make treaties. Such provisions were an implicit acknowledgement that the sovereignty of the Scottish parliament had not been enough to legitimate the Acts which supported the Darien venture. The Limitations also proposed to prevent the English Court determining policy in Scotland through placemen. As Fletcher argued, such a limitation 'does not flatter us with the hopes of Riches by an uncertain project' but would mean that 'our Trade [would be] intirely in our own Hands and not under the Power of the Court, as it was in the Affair of Darien'. When the Scottish Parliament passed the Act of Security in 1703, the confirmation of any successor was made dependent on the assertion of the parliament's sovereignty, religious liberty and freedom of cross-border trade with England: a clause demanding access to the English plantations as well was omitted from the final version of the Act.[52]

More boldly still, in his *Account of a Conversation Concerning a Right Regulation of Governments for the Good of Mankind* (1704), Fletcher proposed a complete re-imagining of Europe along federalist lines which would allow Scotland its rightful place in an irenic, self-sustaining *Europe des patries*. This was to be a system of states in which none of the conditions which had created the necessity for Scotland's commercial emporium would any longer be in place. The confederations of city-states Fletcher proposed would be defended by militias, so there would be no standing armies; they would be balanced and with no aspiration for conquest, so there would be no danger of universal monarchy; above all, they would be largely agrarian, so commerce would no longer be a reason of state pitting countries' interests in mutual hostility against one another: 'Trade is not the only thing to be considered in the Goverment of nations; and Justice is due, even in point of Trade, from one nation to another.'[53] In the union debate, Fletcher continued to protest that a communication of trade with England would be no solution to Scotland's problems because a metropolitan emporium would always overpower

[52] Fletcher, *Speeches, By a Member of the Parliament . . . 1703*, p. 76; P.W.J. Riley, *The Union of England and Scotland: A Study of Anglo-Scottish Politics of the Eighteenth Century* (Manchester, 1978), pp. 57–8; Paul H. Scott, *Andrew Fletcher and the Treaty of Union* (Edinburgh, 1992), pp. 80–90.

[53] Fletcher, *Account of a Conversation*, p. 41; on the *Account of a Conversation* in the context of civic thought, see John Robertson, 'The Scottish Enlightenment at the limits of the civic tradition', in István Hont and Michael Ignatieff (eds), *Wealth and Virtue: The Shaping of Political Economy in the Scottish Enlightenment* (Cambridge, 1983), pp. 146–51.

and impoverish a provincial market. In the *Account of a Conversation*, Fletcher had turned to his imagination, and the civic tradition, for comfort; in the final stages of the debate on the Treaty in November 1706, he turned to history and

> w*ith* all the Rhetorick, Art & force of the argument the subject could bear, and (*whi*ch is not his ordinary) w*ith* great Calmnesse too – He alledged from history *tha*t the Condition of the governments of Flanders, Milan & the Kingdoms of Spain enjoyed more wealth freedom & power *tha*n since they were United in Castile, and *tha*t the fate of all weaker States after ane Union w*ith* greater Kingdoms, was, to be at length swallowed up and enslaved by *the*m.

It is ironic that the testimony of Fletcher's last-ditch defence of provincial autonomy – the only verbatim report of his speeches in those crucial days – may have come from the pen of his former ally in promoting Darien, now the turncoat spokesman for England, the court, and the metropolis, William Paterson.[54]

The shadow cast by the Darien affair over the final stages of the Union negotiations was in the shape of reparations for the Company's losses, not as a grievance about access to the English empire. By the fifteenth Article of the Treaty of Union, Scotland was to be paid the 'Equivalent' of £390,085 10/-, in recompense for the share of the English public debt it would have to take on, for the rise in excise and customs payments once English rates were introduced, and for the loss sustained by the Company of Scotland. By this expedient, the English in effect admitted and made reparation for their blocking of the Company's plans and the fiscal impact their opposition had cost the Scots. The motives which impelled a majority of the members of the last Scottish Parliament to vote in favour of Union are, of course, unrecoverable but it was frequently charged by anti-Unionist writers that their thoughts of compliance 'were much quickened by the prospect of recovering what they had lost in the ill-concerted undertaking of Darien' by means of the payments paid under the Equivalent.[55] It is difficult to correlate voting patterns on the Treaty of Union with support for the Company of Scotland twelve years earlier.[56] For example, the Queen's Commissioner,

[54] BL Add. MS 70039, f. 87^{v}, 5 November 1706. This report is calendared in HMC *Portland*, VIII, p. 261, where it is attributed to William Paterson, though it is not in his hand. See also Hume of Crossrigg, *Diary*, p. 184 (19 November 1706): 'Salton had a long discourse, showing the Disadvantages of a Communication of Trade.'

[55] Burnet, *History of His Own Time*, V, p. 292; compare [George Lockhart of Carnwath,] *Memoirs Concerning the Affairs of Scotland* (London, 1714), pp. 213, 272; 'The articles of the Union unmasqued', NLS MS Saltoun 17802, f. 192^{v}; Scott, *Andrew Fletcher and the Treaty of Union*, pp. 158–9, 164.

[56] Though there had been a large turnover in the Scottish nobility and gentry between 1695

the Marquess of Queensberry, had subscribed for £3,000 in the Company, but so had one of the most passionate opponents of the Union, the Earl of Belhaven.[57] (We might also wonder whether John Clerk of Penicuik recalled *Leo Scotiæ Irritatus* while he laboured over the calculations for the Equivalent as a Union Commissioner.[58]) A vote against the Union was, however, a stand on principle with the prospect of financial loss for those who had been investors. Andrew Fletcher received his payments out of the Equivalent in 1707, but the potential loss of them would never have been enough to sway him from his conviction. Perhaps this is what Lockhart of Carnwath (who had himself subscribed for £1,000 in 1695) meant when he applauded Fletcher for being 'so Stedfast to what he thought Right, that no Hazard nor Advantage, no not the Universal Empire, nor the Gold of *America*, could tempt him to yield or desert it'.[59]

The Darien venture and the Union of 1707 were both intended as solutions to the same structural problems in the relationship between the two British kingdoms. The Scots had been emboldened to exercise their parliamentary sovereignty in pursuit of an emporium which would enrich their provincial economy and provide it with independent defences in a world of aspiring universal monarchs. The failure of the attempt did not lead them to demand access to the English commercial empire, but rather to bemoan the abuse of their *imperium* at the expense of English trading interests. It also narrowed the field of possible solutions to the unequal distribution of power enshrined in the Union of the Crowns. Without a sense of what those possibilities were, it is hard to understand how the Scottish parliament came to the point where it had to consider incorporating Union, let alone how it came to decide that such a Union was the only plausible alternative left. It is in this sense that the reconstruction of a failed enterprise such as the Darien venture is historically important.

and 1707, compare the voting lists on the Union Treaty in Riley, *The Union of England and Scotland*, pp. 330–4, with *A Perfect List of all the . . . Adventurers in the Joynt-Stock of the Company of Scotland*.

57 See [John Hamilton, Lord Belhaven,] *A Speech in Parliament on the 10th. day of January 1701, By the Lord Belhaven, On the Affair of the Indian and African Company, and its Colony of Caledonia* (Edinburgh, 1701); *The Lord Beilhaven's Speech in Parliament Saturday the Second of November, On the Subject-Matter of an Union Betwixt the Two Kingdoms of Scotland and England* (np, 1706), pp. 18–19.

58 For Clerk's later views on the venture, see [John Clerk,] *The Circumstances of Scotland Consider'd, With Respect to the present Scarcity of Money* (Edinburgh, 1705), p. 4; [Clerk,] *An Essay Upon the XV. Article of The Treaty of Union* (Edinburgh, 1706), pp. 20–1; T.C. Smout (ed.), 'Sir John Clerk's Observations on the Present Circumstances of Scotland, 1730', *Miscellany of the Scottish History Society*, 10 (1965), 189–91.

59 See NLS MS 83.2.6, ff. 510, 566, 609 (Company journal 1700–1707), for the progress of payments to Andrew Fletcher out of the Equivalent; Lockhart of Carnwath, *Memoirs*, pp. 69–70.

Only by recovering the dilemmas it was intended to resolve, the avenues its failure closed off, and the new possibilities it created, can we understand how the Scots in 1707 came to calculate that their vision of empire could only be realised by Union, and within a British state.

Part II
THE SCOTTISH SETTING

5
SCOTTISH CULTURAL CHANGE 1660–1710 AND THE UNION OF 1707

ROGER L. EMERSON

I

SEVENTEENTH-CENTURY Scotland has been described as a backward land made dull and benighted by repressive Calvinists and politically turbulent by ministers and a greedy aristocracy. Those who wish to see it in these ways can and easily do find evidence of even greater savagery beyond the Highland Line. But Scotland was not alone in being backward, uncouth and even savage in the seventeenth century. Descriptions of France show as great a range of manners, intellectual attainments and cultivation and an even more complex linguistic situation than obtained in Scotland. No one who has read much about the Thirty Years War thinks even Highlanders were unduly savage. And there was another Scotland, albeit small, whose members belonged and knew they belonged to a European world of learning and civility. This was a thin slice of the Scottish social elite and one constantly attenuated by emigration. Nevertheless, its members were influential, reasonably well educated and articulate and interesting. They shared the culture of Europeans, read the same books, and confronted many of the same problems. In doing so, they also increasingly shared a common culture with the English. How these Scots thought and felt bears upon the Union of 1707 which was in part made feasible by the convergence of ideas and feelings in both Scots and Englishmen.

II

One area in which such convergence was notable was religion, which in both countries and throughout Europe was still deeply politicised. Scots as well as English participated in the great religious debates about the nature of the church and its relation to societies and states. Both kingdoms saw the Whigs triumph politically in 1688–9. Protestant Europe applauded as Calvinist political theory was transformed into

Whiggery of various sorts. Both Scots and Englishmen argued vociferously at Dort, at Westminster and in books often printed in Holland and read in France about the mysteries of their religion and the terms in which these could be discussed. As they did so, the epistemological and metaphysical commitments of Boyle, Tillotson or Locke tended to converge with those of Bayle and Desmaizeau – all were read in Scotland. Calvinist scepticism about human nature was related to the careful qualifications given to knowledge claims by Bayle, Locke and Newton whose world, like Calvin's, was designed by and was known to point toward an unfathomable Creator. Rational theologies were possible as the *virtuosi* of all nations agreed by the 1690s. By 1700 religious and philosophical controversy in both countries had prepared Scots for the rapid assimilation of the views of Newton and Locke who entered Scottish classrooms between *c.* 1690 and 1715. In moral theology similar trends had also been at work. English Puritans such as Richard Baxter had come in round-about ways to emphasise works as the Anglicans always had. But so too had the Scottish divines for whom 1688–9 opened the way to power in the colleges and Kirk. In both England and Scotland the bases of morality had shifted somewhat from the Two Tables of the Law to reason, conscience and the passions. As that happened, moralists had again to examine Calvinist activism. This had traditionally seen naturally social beings cherishing and regulating their societies for the glory of God and the improvement of man's fallen estate. By 1700 this meant not only the maintainance of liberty but the pursuit and use of science and state power to effect improvements.

As the religious situation in both England and Scotland cooled and moderated, it also produced more Vicars of Bray and more cynics and sceptics. In the last generation of the seventeenth century such figures abounded at the court in London and in city taverns frequented by the likes of Dryden, Charles Blount or John Toland, who also had been a student at Glasgow and Edinburgh. English sceptics, deists and atheists found Scottish counterparts in Sir Robert Sibbald, Thomas Halyburton, Archibald Pitcairne, MD and Thomas Aikenhead. Sibbald's doubts led him to Episcopacy *via* Catholicism. Halyburton's were resolved through prayer and determined efforts to believe; they led to the St Andrews divinity chair. Pitcairne, a reputed deist, attended Episcopal services. Aikenhead's atheism, however, ended at the Grassmarket scaffold in Edinburgh in January 1697. The presence of such men amongst the Scottish elite in the 1690s shows how much Scotland had changed since 1660 when its saints were driven from power. It should come as no surprise that by the 1680s Scots were reading Father Richard Simon or ten years later worrying about deists. Their reading habits had changed remarkably since 1660. To understand that shift one must look briefly at what had gone on in the universities.[1]

III

Throughout the seventeenth century, Scots students, like those elsewhere, got a good deal of Latin, Greek and religion. Aristotle's metaphysics, logic, ethics and physics bulked large in the syllabus until *c.*1680. In this respect Scots most resembled the Dutch: 'The theses for disputation at Leiden, for example, are very similar to the Scottish graduation theses, while most of the authorities whose works were debated are the same as those quoted by the Scottish university teachers.' By the 1670s or 1680s the logic and metaphysics dictates of the Scottish regents often had references to modern philosophers including Bacon, Descartes and the Port Royal Fathers.[2] Aristotelian moral philosophy had been enriched by the moral theology and casuistry of Puritan divines, by the works of some Cambridge Platonists, such as Henry More whose *Enchiridion ethicum* was sometimes read, and, by the 1680s, by some of the natural lawyers – Grotius, Cumberland and Pufendorf. Until *c.*1660 the natural science of the Scots was largely based on Aristotle's *Physics* taught with some modern criticisms. Between *c.*1660 and 1700 this was radically changed. Copernican cosmology and the new astronomy appeared in the 1660s. 'The sudden appearance of the mechanistic philosophy of Descartes and Boyle about 1670 in theses from St. Andrews, Aberdeen and Edinburgh, marked a break with the old tradition, and favoured the espousal of Descartes' vortex theory.' By 1700 'scientific teaching in the Scottish universities was thoroughly up to date and probably as good as was to be

[1] I have addressed some of these issues elsewhere: R.L. Emerson, 'Calvinism in the Scottish Enlightenment', in Joachim Schwend, Susanne Hagemann, Hermann Völkel (eds.), *Literatur in Kontext – Literature in Context: Festschrift für Horst W. Drescher* (Frankfurt-on-Main, 1992), pp. 19–28; R.L. Emerson, 'Science and moral philosophy in the Scottish Enlightenment', in M.A. Stewart (ed.), *Studies in the Philosophy of the Scottish Enlightenment* (Oxford, 1990), pp. 11–36; R.L. Emerson, 'The religious, the secular and the worldly: Scotland 1680–1800', in James E. Crimmins (ed.), *Religion, Secularization and Political Thought: Thomas Hobbes to J.S. Mill* (London, 1989), pp. 68–89; R.L. Emerson, 'Science and the origins and concerns of the Scottish Enlightenment', *History of Science*, 26 (1988), 333–66. See also: David C. Lachman, *The Marrow Controversy 1718–1723* (Edinburgh, 1988); Eric G. Forbes, 'Philosophy and science teaching in the seventeenth century', in Gordon Donaldson (ed.), *Four Centuries: Edinburgh University Life 1583–1983*, (Edinburgh, 1983); Gordon Marshall, *Presbyteries and Profits: Calvinism and the Development of Capitalism in Scotland, 1560–1707* (Oxford, 1980), especially pp. 65–112; Brian G. Armstrong, *Calvinism and the Amyraut Heresy* (Madison, 1969); H.R. McAdoo, *The Structure of Caroline Moral Theology* (London, 1949).

[2] Forbes, 'Philosophy and science teaching', pp. 28–37, 28, 31. See also Norman Fiering, *Moral Philosophy at Seventeenth-Century Harvard* (Chapel Hill, 1981).

found anywhere in Europe'.[3] By then, when Scots graduated they were likely to know something about Copernicus, Kepler, Brahe and even Newton; about Galileo, Toricelli, Borelli; about van Guericke, Huygens, Leeuwenhoeck, Gassendi, Mersenne and Mariotte; and about various French and Dutch textbook writers like Jacques Rohault and Jean LeClerc. The story was much the same in all the colleges save Glasgow which was slower to adopt the new science.[4] Even there by 1691 a professorship of mathematics had been created and the College had begun to look more modern and less poor. Change in the colleges was real and important but we do not yet know exactly how and when it came and who brought it about.

Innovators in Scottish thought at the mid-century everywhere included men from both the Presbyterian and Episcopalian wings of Scottish Christianity, from the King's friends and from his foes. At Glasgow the faculty between 1640 and 1670 included at one time or another James Dalrymple (1619–1695), later 1st Viscount Stair, George Sinclair (? – 1696 or 1699) and Gilbert Burnet (1643–1715), later Bishop of Salisbury. Sinclair was a mathematician, engineer and experimentalist best known for his defence of the belief in witchcraft. *Satan's Invisible World Discovered* (1685) was in part an attempt to justify the witch-hunting activities of his relatives, in part his attempt to be a Scottish Glanvill proving empirically the existence of a spirit world. Sinclair was a Presbyterian outed from his Glasgow regency in 1666. He was re-admitted in 1689 after the Glorious Revolution. Stair began as a Covenanter, soldiered between 1639 and 1641 and then served Glasgow as a regent for six years. After a year of private study, the one-time infantry captain 'passed advocate' in 1648 and thereafter was active as a lawyer, judge and politician who served Cromwell, Monck, Charles II and eventually James VII and William and Mary. He is best known for his *Institutions of the Laws of Scotland* (1681); Stair also published other legal and political works and a treatise on natural philosophy. He trimmed with each regime and ministry but always managed to retain the respect of most Presbyterians throughout the grim years of the 1660s, 1670s and 1680s. Burnet too was a trimmer but he was much more. An able theologian, something of a philosopher, an early member of the Royal Society of London and a good historian, he was also a fair-minded and astute politician. All three men were remarkable and all three produced works in more than one field. Dalrymple and Sinclair were educated in Scotland; Burnet studied in Cambridge, Oxford, London, Amsterdam and Paris before teaching at Glasgow. All three were later abroad, two certainly as political refugees,

[3] Forbes, 'Philosophy and science teaching', p. 35.

[4] J.D. Mackie, *The University of Glasgow 1451–1951* (Glasgow, 1954), pp. 144–5.

which was probably Sinclair's status too when he visited Holland in 1681.

What was true in Glasgow was equally so in Edinburgh. There during the 1650s the teachers included Robert Leighton (1611–1684), sometimes called the Scottish Pascal, Thomas Crawford (*c.*1620–62), and John Wishart. Leighton impressed upon his students a relatively tolerant view of things rooted not only in the love of God and men but also in the limited capacity of men to know anything by natural means. Crawford taught mathematics but is also remarkable for having written a *History of the University of Edinburgh from 1580 to 1646* (published in 1808), a work indicative of an increasing concern in Scotland both with antiquities and history and with the old theme of vindicating the honour of the kingdom.[5] Wishart was an Aristotelian who by the 1670s was prelecting on Descartes and mentioning or alluding to the optical theories of Sir Isaac Newton.[6] When Sir Robert Sibbald (1641–1723) looked back at Edinburgh University in the late 1650s he remembered Leighton with fondness and respect but mentioned learning modern philosophy from the works of two of Galileo's correspondents and defenders, Sir Kenelm Digby (1603–65) and Thomas White (1593–1676), two English Catholic philosophers who then worked abroad in France and Spain. That his experience in a Presbyterian college was not unique is suggested by what little is known about the extra-curricular reading of other Edinburgh students.[7]

At St Andrews there was probably no brilliant teacher at the mid-century save Samuel Rutherford (1600–61). There was, however, by 1668 a regius chair of mathematics filled by the first of a long line of academic Gregories.

In Aberdeen things were different. The King's College Principal during the 1650s was John Row (1598–1672), the author of a Hebrew grammar and dictionary and the continuer of his father's *History of the Kirk of Scotland 1558–1637*. At the Restoration he was sacked and succeeded by Alexander Middleton who by the 1680s was known to

5 Sir Robert Sibbald, MD, studied mathematics with Crawford and noted of Leighton, then Principal, that he 'had excellent discourses to us in the Common Hall, sometymes in Latine, sometymes in English, which, with the blessing of God upon y^{m}, gave me strong inclinations to a serious and good lyfe. I shunned the plays and divertisements the other students followed, and reach much in my study, for which my fellowes gave me the name of Diogenes in Dolio'. *The Memoirs of Sir Robert Sibbald (1641–1722)*, ed. Francis P. Hett (London, 1932), pp. 54–5. Later in life Sibbald became a patriotic antiquary and, like Leighton, a seeker whose religious career led him from Presbyterianism to Episcopacy, to Rome and finally again to the Scottish Episcopal Church to which he remained loyal after 1689. Crawford seems to have discussed some natural historical topics with his students; Sir Robert Sibbald, 'Ane Essay Relating to the Natural History of Scotland'. Advocates MSS. National Library of Scotland, MS 33.5.19, pp. 59, 212.

6 Forbes, 'Philosophy and science teaching', p. 34.

7 Jonquil Bevan, 'Seventeenth-century students and their books', in Donaldson (ed.), *Edinburgh University Life 1583–1983*, pp. 16–27.

members of the Oxford Philosophical Society as a *virtuoso*. By that time King's had others who had contacts with English *virtuosi*. Among them were Henry Scougal (1650–78), the Principal's son George Middleton (1645–1726), and James Garden (1647–1726) whose brother George (1649–1733) sold the College a telescope in 1712.[8] Throughout the century, King's possessed an instrument collection.[9] Earlier George Gordon, 1st Earl of Aberdeen (1637–1720), had taught at King's before leaving to make a career as a lawyer, judge and statesman too tolerant to serve King James VII. At neighbouring Marischal College the Principal during the 1650s, William Moir (*c.* 1600–after 1661), also held the chair of mathematics. Moir published on mathematics and mechanics. In 1661 he was replaced as Principal by James Leslie, MD, a physician educated on the continent. His place as mathematics professor was taken by Duncan Liddell (1667–?) who had 'taught Geometry, Navigation, and Gunnery, for several years in London'.[10] At both Aberdeen colleges the tolerant views of the 'Aberdeen Doctors' continued to be discussed and, after 1660, were again promoted as was somewhat later the mystical piety exemplified in Henry Scougal's *The Life of God in The Soul of Man* (1677).[11]

In all the colleges during the 1650s and 1660s, Scots students were kept abreast of currents of thought and discussion elsewhere. Moreover, English political and religious discussions were hardly irrelevant to Scots ruled first by their own covenanting 'Saints' and then by Cromwell's Major-Generals. Cromwellian government had also been stimulating in other ways. Sectarian and Quaker views circulated within the kingdom and unorthodox Calvinist ideas were uttered in the schools. Historians, antiquaries and lawyers were stimulated to think and write as they reflected upon the Union which had been forced upon them. Englishmen more determined to rule in the Highlands than Scots had ever been were also more successful. Even medical men found some stimulus in the works of men such as Richard Wiseman. Scots might have found the English obnoxious but contact with them was not wholly useless. It taught some Scots one thing, some another; others it provoked to

[8] Curricular change at Aberdeen has been most recently discussed by P.B. Wood, *The Aberdeen Enlightenment: The Arts Curriculum in the Aberdeen Universities 1717–1800*, (Aberdeen, 1993), ch. 1.

[9] Emerson, 'Natural philosophy and the problem of the Scottish Enlightenment', *Studies on Voltaire and the eighteenth century*, 242 (1986), pp. 243–91, 258, 268.

[10] *Officers and Graduates of University & King's College Aberdeen MVD–MDCCCLX* (1495–1860), ed. Peter John Anderson (Aberdeen, New Spalding Club, 1893), *passim.*; *Fasti academiae Mariscallanae Aberdonensis*, 3 vols., ed. P.J. Anderson (Aberdeen, New Spalding Club, 1889–1898), *passim*; the quote is from p. 53.

[11] W.G. Sinclair Snow, *The Times, Life and Thought of Patrick Forbes, Bishop of Aberdeen, 1618–1635* (London, 1952), pp. 142–78; G.D. Henderson, *Mystics of the North-East* (Aberdeen, Spalding Club, 1934), pp. 1–70.

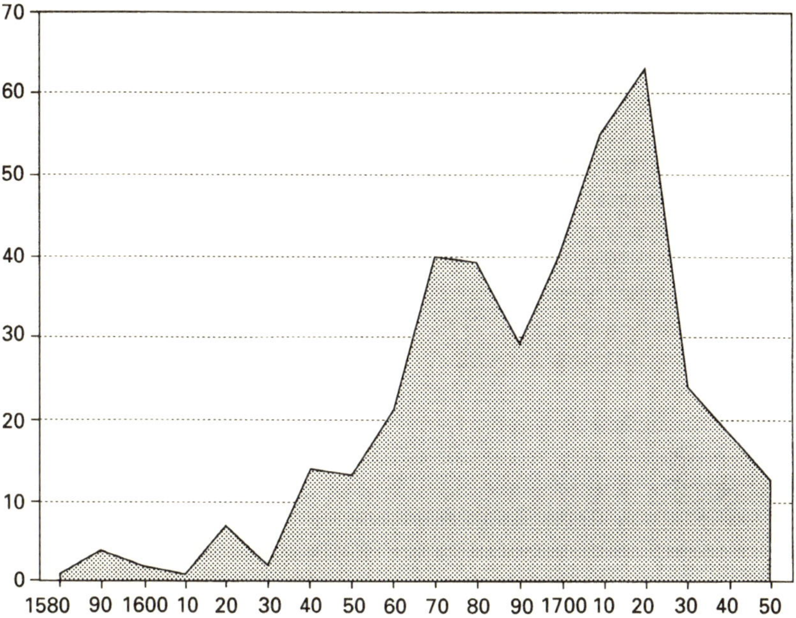

Figure 5.1 Scottish Maticulants at Leyden University 1580–1749 (sample based on letters, A, M, S in Edward Peacock, *Index to English Speaking Students who have Graduated* [Matriculated] *at Leyden University*.

defences of their nation's honour and to attempts to recover and write a more adequate natural and civil history of the Kingdom, a project which had already engaged Drummond of Hawthornden and Sir James Balfour of Denmiln.[12] Finally, that period was in an odd way to be repeated *c.*1685–1707 when again uncertainties about the church, state and universities revived old arguments which the prospects of war and disorder made urgent.

IV

Outside the colleges there are other clear indicators (*pace* Trevor-Roper[13]) that during these years Scots did not remain excluded from important

[12] Sir James Balfour of Denmylne, *The Historical Work of*, ed. James Hais (Edinburgh, 1824), pp. x–xxiv; Gordon Donaldson, 'A Lang pedigree', *Scottish Historical Review*, 65 (1986), 1–16.

[13] Hugh Trevor-Roper, 'The Scottish Enlightenment', in *Studies on Voltaire*, 58 (1967), 1,935–58; 'The Scottish Enlightenment', *Blackwood's Magazine*, 322 (1977), 371–88.

currents of European thought. A sampling of the published matriculation list for Leyden[14] shows a continuous increase in the numbers of Scottish students from 1640–50 into the 1690s with numbers increasing again after 1710. Leyden figures may understate the number of those going abroad from Scotland before 1650. Other universities were more distinguished, better and more orthodox. What these figures also suggest is that warfare and unrest in Scotland and on the continent had as much to do with student numbers as ideology and ties to England. Be that as it may, by the 1680s there was clearly in Scotland a 'critical mass' of foreign-educated Scots who could respond to calls to imitate or emulate what they had seen abroad.[15] Those calls were increasingly made by Scots concerned with economic improvements but also by intellectuals and professionals.

Between the late 1660s and 1700 the Scots copied others in many fields. They produced a more powerful parliament, mercantilist legislation, banking and colonising schemes. They strengthened professional bodies for lawyers, physicians, and surgeons; created the Order of the Thistle (1687–8) and clubs and societies such as the Royal Company of Archers (1676)[16] or Dr Sibbald's antiquarian and natural history societies (1680–?1703). Even the universities in the 1680s and 1690s began to be reformed in ways which would keep students at home by giving them what they could have found abroad – polite education in the classics and history, training in law and medicine and in the disciplines ancillary to those fields. Most of these initiatives were related to the political needs of the Stuart kings or the Whigs after 1689–90. They were mostly imitative of developments elsewhere and indicated that by the 1680s many Scots were familiar with foreign institutions and ideas and were prepared to

[14] For Scots abroad in foreign universities see: John Durkan, 'The French connection in the sixteenth and seventeenth Centuries', in T.C. Smout (ed.), *Scotland and Europe 1200–1850* (Edinburgh, 1986), pp. 19–44; Paul Nève, 'Disputations of Scots students attending universities in the northern Netherlands', in W.M. Gordon and T.D. Fergus (eds.), *Legal History in the Making: Proceedings of the Ninth British Legal History Conference, Glasgow 1989* (London and Rio Grande, 1991), pp. 95–108, especially 96–9. My own figures are taken from Edward Peacock, *Index to English Speaking Students who have Graduated* [read: *matriculated*] *at Leyden University* (London, Index Society, 1883). These are perhaps less accurate than those given in the studies mentioned above but the unknown numbers of unmatriculated students makes accuracy in this matter impossible. What figure 5.1 shows are the decennial totals of Scots matriculants based on a sample drawn from the letters, A, M, S in Peacock's work. These give a better indication of short-run movement and are not incompatible with the trends discerned in the studies listed above.

[15] According to figure 5.1, 27 per cent of the Leyden men 1580–1749 had matriculated by 1680. Others had doubtless attended classes without matriculating.

[16] Hugh Ouston, 'York in Edinburgh: James VII and the patronage of learning in Scotland, 1679–1688', in J. Dwyer, R.A. Mason, A. Murdoch (eds.), *New Perspectives on the Politics and Culture of Early Modern Scotland* (Edinburgh, nd [1982]), pp. 133–55.

copy them. They had adopted new attitudes toward knowledge and its uses and were seeking ways to institutionalise and perpetuate their new outlook on knowledge, themselves and their country. Important to that transition were not only those who studied abroad but those who left Scotland for long periods to work in other lands but who did not sever their ties with Scotland.

Scots abroad included some who held important or interesting intellectual posts. Scottish science might have looked considerably different if men such as John Wedderburn (1583–*c*.1654), an early defender of Galileo, had found places at home rather than in Padua and Moravia.[17] Similar cases could be made using others whose careers were mostly made outside Scotland, for example Robert Morrison (1620–83), professor of botany at Oxford, or Ninian Campbell who was for some time professor of rhetoric at Saumur. Others like Duncan Liddell (1561–1613) who founded the mathematics chair at Marischal College, to which he also left his instrument collection, returned only after years abroad. With him or with a political exile like Thomas Forbes, MD, who had taught philosophy and medicine at Pisa between 1659 and 1662, came new ideas which would eventually influence Scottish university teaching. The Reformation had not kept these men out of Catholic Europe, which like the Protestant states also welcomed Scottish soldiers. Gordon Donaldson has estimated the numbers of Scottish mercenaries as peaking between 1600 and 1620 at over 10,000 in the Baltic region alone.[18] In the 1630s the French also had about 10,000 Scottish troops. The officers among these men were often educated and cultivated and would have been another source of intellectual change in Scotland. Moreover these men, in the mid seventeenth century, were often exiles who when they returned came back to status and power. There could not have been many among them as brilliant as Sir Robert Moray (1608–73) but he is unlikely to have been unique.

Sir Robert Moray was an extraordinary mercenary soldier who left Britain for France in the 1640s. Before he did so he had probably been connected with others seeking esoteric wisdom in the masonic lodge of Edinburgh. In Europe Sir Robert had contacts with a surprising number of intellectuals. They ranged from the Jesuit polymath Athanasius Kircher to the Huguenot ministers Jean Daillé, Charles Drelincourt and Raymond Gaches; from the French academician Christian Huygens to the Anglo-Irish projector Sir William Petty. Even before he became a Fellow of the Royal Society of London, Moray's correspondence came from European capitals, the Caribbean, North America, Africa and the

[17] I thank Paul Wood for this information.

[18] Gordon Donaldson, *The Scots Overseas* (London, 1966), pp. 30–1.

East Indies. When he was sent to Scotland to rule it for Lauderdale in 1663 he found it a dull place with few interested in the subjects which excited him – natural history, chemistry, mechanics and improvements based on new knowledge.[19] But 'few' at least implies that some, such as the apothecary Matthew Mackaile, the mathematician and astronomer James Gregory and Andrew Balfour, MD, were interested.

Perhaps the best evidence of how much Scottish opinion was to shift in the later seventeenth century is provided by what is known of private libraries and Scottish publishing. These show Scots to have been anything but isolated. They followed European and English debates on issues which were perplexing to men everywhere. Medical men, divines and lawyers clearly situated themselves in a European cultural world to which by the 1680s they also sought to contribute. How they oriented themselves at the Restoration may be seen in two libraries gathered before 1685, those of Thomas Kincaid Sr. (1620–91) and Robert Leighton (1611–84).

Kincaid was an Edinburgh surgeon whose career began in the late 1630s. He was notable enough to win appointment as a regimental surgeon to a regiment which marched south into England in 1644. After the civil wars, Kincaid settled into a civilian practice as a surgeon-apothecary. He died in 1691 leaving a valuable library of which his son Thomas gave 228 books (titles) to the Edinburgh Incorporation of Chirurgeons in 1709.[20] These volumes provide clues to what a medical man the mid-seventeenth century knew and whence his information came.[21]

Kincaid's books (41 folios, 48 quartos, 97 octavos and 42 duodecimos) mostly dated from the period 1630 to 1670, the years in which most of the volumes must also have been purchased. The latest work was issued in 1685 and only a handful of his books were published after 1674. Most deal with modern medicine, anatomy, surgery, botany, chemistry and pharmacy. If his whole library was given,[22] then Kincaid had relatively few volumes dealing with magic, alchemy, astrology or the ancients, no incunables and

19 Alexander Robertson, *The Life of Sir Robert Moray . . . 1609–1673* (London, 1922); David Stevenson, *The Origins of Free Masonry. Scotland's Century, 1590–1710* (Cambridge, 1988), ch. 3.

20 *List of Fellows of the Royal College of Surgeons of Edinburgh* (Edinburgh, 1874). Andrew Cunningham, 'The medical professions and pattern of medical care: the case of Edinburgh, *c.*1670–*c.*1700', in Wolfgang Eckart and Johanna Geyer-Kordesch (eds.), *Heilberufe und Kranke im 17. und 18. Jahrhundert* (Munster, *Munstersche Beitrage zur Geschichte und Theorie der Medizin*, 18, 1982), 9–28, 20; John D. Comrie, *History of Scottish Medicine*, 2 vols. (London, Wellcome Historical Medical Museum, 1932), I, pp. 231, 246; Minute books of the Royal College of Surgeons of Edinburgh, College Library, IV, p. 18.

21 I am grateful to Dr Rosalie Stott for having made available to me this library list with her annotations. She is presently writing an extended analysis of this collection.

22 It is likely that Kincaid's son Thomas retained a portion of his father's books.

only forty-one volumes (19 per cent) published during the sixteenth century. Those were mostly classical texts or landmark works such as those by Fallopius, Paracelsius or Libavius. This was clearly the working library of an up-to-date general practitioner. While we can only speculate about where he purchased his books, we know where they were published. The largest number were printed in Holland; Germany and France ranked second and third. These were also his most modern books. Those from Italy tended to pre-date 1620. The collection is surprisingly lacking in works of general natural philosophy and contains gaps which are puzzling. There are few volumes by famous seventeenth-century physicians and surgeons whose reputations came from particular studies and practice rather than teaching. It is also curious that Kincaid lacked the works of Harvey and Richard Wiseman even though he may have known the latter. Despite these peculiarities, this collection is interesting. Those using it would have found works by Cartesians, iatro-mechanists, iatro-chemists, books by medical 'positivists' like Sylvius (but not Sydenham) and ecclectic synthesisers 'who tried to harmonize neo-Galenic doctrine and Paracelsian chemistry'.[23] When these books were purchased they had related Mr Kincaid to a very European medical world, one in which there were no certainties but controversy and disputes over methods, facts, remedies and the basic processes by which life was sustained. He was open to debates whose participants came from everywhere in Europe: Uppsalla and Salerno, London and Riga and many places in between. Kincaid may have made only one trip outside Scotland – to England – but he was certainly part of a European medical world throughout his career. This was a world where Scots would not figure as innovators until the 1680s and 1690s. Those who did so then had generally read more iatro-mechanists than iatro-chemists.[24] In short, they had changed with the times.

Another indicator of what moved Scots can be found in the gift of 1390 volumes made by Archbishop Robert Leighton (1611–84) to the clergy of the diocese of Dunblane. This was a library oriented toward classics, divinity and philosophy, but one which did not exclude science and medicine. Leighton owned a lot of classical and scholastic philosophy, much divinity but also works by Bacon, the Fathers of Port Royal, the Cambridge Platonists, Hobbes' *Leviathan* and works against it, many of the great natural lawyers, Samuel Rutherford's *Lex Rex* and a great deal

[23] Lester King, *The Road to Medical Enlightenment, 1650–1695* (New York, 1970), p. 94; and King, *The Philosophy of Medicine: The Early Eighteenth Century* (Cambridge and London, 1978), p. 82.

[24] Lester King dates the division between the schools to *c.* 1675, in *Philosophy of Medicine*, p. 98; see also Antonia J. Bunch, *Hospital and Medical Libraries in Scotland* (Glasgow, 1975).

Table 5.1 *The library of Thomas Kincaid, senior surgeon-apothecary of Edinburgh: place of publication of books by number and per cent*

Place	No.	%
Holland	73	32
Germany	49	21
France	42	18
Switzerland	23	10
England	14	6
Italy	11	5
Spanish Netherlands	4	2
Scotland	2	1
Denmark	1	0.66
Poland	1	0.66
Sweden	1	0.66
Unknown	6	3
Total	227	100

of Anglican divinity much of which was tinged with the irenical spirit for which Jeremy Taylor was famous. Leighton had some history books and late in life clearly bought latitudinarian works. Books of mystical piety were, however, about as numerous as these and came from Catholic as well as Protestant pens. Leighton's views were shaped in England where he grew up, in France where he travelled, but also at Edinburgh where he studied. His books seem to reflect a taste and an outlook fixed by the 1660s to which Puritans, Covenanters, Catholics and Anglicans had contributed.[25]

Scottish intellectuals born in the 1630s and 1640s continued to depend upon English and continental thinkers for new ideas but their libraries suggest that they also had deeper interests in novel philosophical ideas.

Sir Robert Sibbald left a collection of over 4,000 volumes of which perhaps 75 per cent were in Latin.[26] About 20–30 per cent of his books were published in the sixteenth century with a somewhat smaller number purchased in his old age during the eighteenth century. The remaining 60–70 per cent were issued in the seventeenth century, generally in its second half. He had a good collection of the classics, a little scholastic philosophy and theology but a distribution of modern volumes which one would expect from a *virtuoso*. History, antiquities, natural history, natural philosophy, the various sciences, medicine, the improving and scientific literature of the time were all well represented as was modern

[25] D. Butler, *The Life and Letters of Robert Leighton* (London, 1903), pp. 590–2.

[26] 'Bibliotheca Sibbaldiana . . . with A curious Collection of Historical and other Manuscripts', Sibbald MSS, Library of the Royal College of Physicians, Edinburgh. Bunch, *Hospital and Medical Libraries*, pp. 18–19, gives a rough subject catalogue of the library worked out from the published catalogue of 1722.

literature. Among the modern philosophers one notes Bacon, Descartes, the Port Royal Fathers, Kenelm Digby, Thomas White, Athanasius Kircher, George Sinclair and his opponent, James Gregory, but also a host of men who belonged to the Royal Society of London or to some comparable foreign body. Here *virtuosi* and natural theologians such as Walter Charleton, John Ray, Edward Lhuyd, Francis Willughby, Nehemiah Grew, Robert Hooke, John Woodward, Hans Sloane, Edmund Halley and William Whiston (but not Newton) gave a distinctly modern and scientific flavour to his list of the erudite. Sibbald had formed and sold an earlier collection of books so this one may not wholly reflect his earlier taste. Surviving manuscripts suggest that in only one respect might the earlier collection have been much different. He probably had had more works written by sixteenth-century Scots.

Sir James Lauder of Fountainhall (1646–1722) also left a particularly good indicator of what a genteel Scots lawyer was likely to buy and read during the period 1667–79. In those years Lauder bought or was presented with about 500 volumes. He recorded the titles or subject of 478 of these which are distributed into categories in table 5.2.[27] This table separates his earlier purchases (1667–75), made when he was a student and establishing a law practice, from the later ones of a rising young advocate (1675–9). Again, what is most significant about Lauder's list is its modernity. While he was not much interested in science and natural philosophy, he owned works by John Dee, Bacon, Hobbes, Boyle, Glanvill and Stillingfleet. This suggests at least a slight interest in epistemology and mitigated scepticism, an interest also supported by his ownership of the principal works of Gassendi. He possessed few books on mathematics and the sciences but among them were three on hydrostatics and a mathematics text by John Wallis. He bought volumes by Augustine and Aquinas and read Thomas à Kempis, but his taste in divinity ran more toward the works of Jean Daillé, Hugo Grotius, Jeremy Taylor, Richard Baxter, Edward Stillingfleet, Gilbert Burnet, and John Tillotson, all forerunners or sources of the Scottish Moderates. Lauder was a latitudinarian who cared little about the forms of Kirk government. His law books included editions of Grotius and other natural lawyers, but

[27] *Journals of Sir John Lauder, Lord Fountainhall*, ed. Donald Crawford (Edinburgh, Scottish History Society, 1st series 36, 1900), pp. 283–99; see also Thomas I. Rae, 'The origins of the Advocates' Library', in Patrick Cadell and Ann Matheson (eds.), *For The Encouragement of Learning: Scotland's National Library 1689–1989* (Edinburgh, HMSO, 1989), pp. 1–22, 13–14. Crawford reproduced the list of purchases made between 1667 and 1679. In addition to these, Lauder had earlier acquired 536 books many of whose titles are noted in the *Journals*. My total for his purchases 1667–1679 differs from Rae's (456 titles) probably because where Lauder gave no title but listed the topic of a book I have counted it in the appropriate category.

Table 5.2 *The libraries of James Lauder of Fountainhall, and John Spotiswoode of that ilk*

Category of book	Lauder of Fountainhall Purchased 1667 to June 1675 (%)	Purchased 1675 to 1679 (%)	1667–1679 (%)	Spotiswoode 1728 (%)
Theology, sermons	21 (11)	79 (27)	100 (21)	37 (19)*
Natural philosophy and astronomy	3 (2)	1	4 (1)	7 (4)
Mathematics	1 (1)	4 (1)	5 (1)	1 (1)
Medicine	4 (2)	1	5 (1)	2 (1)
Military and naval	1 (1)	2 (1)	3 (1)	1 (1)
Geography	3 (2)		3 (1)	2 (1)
History	19 (10)	24 (8)	43 (9)	13 (7)
Biography	1 (1)	7 (2)	3 (2)	
Moral philosophy and manners	18 (10)	20 (7)	38 (8)	7 (4)
Law	35 (19)	61 (21)	96 (20)	84 (44)
Acts, etc.	13 (9)	2 (1)	15 (3)	
Political theory and pamphlets	23 (12)	6 (2)	29 (6)	8 (4)
Heraldry	1 (1)		1	
Reference books	1 (1)		1	
Texts	4 (2)	5 (2)	9 (2)	
Language books	2 (1)	5 (2)	7 (1)	6 (3)
Classics	7 (4)	15 (5)	22 (5)	8 (4)
Essays and romances		2 (1)	2	4 (2)
Plays	11 (6)	9 (3)	20 (4)	
Poetry and songs	9 (5)	8 (3)	17 (4)	10 (5)
News	3 (2)	5 (2)	8 (2)	
Miscellaneous	8 (4)	35 (12)	44 (9)	
Improvements	1 (1)			1 (1)
University materials				
Unknown	3 (2)	4 (1)	7 (1)	
Totals	188 (100)	290 (100)	478 (100)	191 (100)

*Percentages in this column are based on a total which excludes acts, proclamations, etc.

most of them seem technical and not oriented toward political theory. *Belles lettres* are represented not only by the ancients but by such moderns as Shakespeare, Milton, Dryden, Shadwell, Settle, Wycherly, Behn, Sir George Mackenzie, Sir William Temple and a few other poets and playwrights. Like other Scots, he also enjoyed the old works of 'Blind Harry' and Sir David Lindsay. Lauder had a fondness for history. In an assortment of volumes written by Polydore Vergil, Holinshed, Sir Richard Baker, Francis Bacon, Lord Herbert of Cherbury, William Camden, John Rushworth and modern memorialists of the reigns of

James VI and Charles I he could follow the course of English history. His collection of French historians was not quite so good but he presumably knew a good deal about France from *c.*1480 to his own time. Scottish history was represented by Knox, Leslie, Buchanan and a few other writers, but we know that he hoped it would improve since he was one of several lawyers to give Sir Robert Sibbald 'Ane Account of Manuscript Histories' then held in private hands.[28] Perhaps equally good guides to his outlook are books difficult to categorise such as More's *Utopia*, Burton's *Anatomy of Melancholie* and Montaigne's *Essays*. He also liked joke books and owned at least five.

Fountainhall's library by 1680 is a good guide to the taste of those who projected the Advocates' Library in July of that year. Foremost among these men was George (later Sir George) Mackenzie of Rosehaugh (1636–1690). Mackenzie was prolific. His works include a book on rhetoric and eloquence, poetry, a novel, history, legal compilations and commentaries, political pamphlets, a study of heraldry, and even a treatise on natural philosophy. All these made him welcome amongst the London wits and, after his retirement (really exile) from Scotland in 1689, in Oxford where he became a member of the Philosophical Society. The Library which he promoted and justified had from its inception a broad definition of what lawyers needed to read and to know. This of course gave primacy to books on the law, but it also found plenty of room for the 'three branches of learning [which] are the handmaidens of Jurisprudence, namely, History, Criticism and Rhetoric' not only in the ancient but in the modern worlds.[29] Mackenzie had somewhat earlier noted that '[b]eing bred to the law . . . requires a whole Man and his whole Age'. 'The knowledge of the Law is not easy and . . . none should pretend to it, but such as have illuminated their excellent natural Parts with laborious learning, and have polish'd that Learning by long Experience.'[30] Within a few years the Library was purchasing in a wide range of fields which included philosophy and natural history. Setting up such a library institutionalised a conception of learning which made lawyers *virtuosi*. It also gave Scotland a model of what polite and useful learning was. That was carried into the eighteenth century and promoted by extra-mural law teachers in Edinburgh such as John Spotiswoode (1666–1728), and it undoubtedly helped to push the colleges toward reforms which allowed them to serve the needs of the upper-class

[28] *Remains of Sir Robert Sibbald, Knt, M.D. Containing His Autobiography . . . and an Account of his MSS* (Edinburgh, 1837), p. 4.

[29] 'Sir George Mackenzie's speech', trans. James H. Loudon in J[ohn].W. Cairns and A.M. Cain (eds.), *Oratio Inauguralis in Aperienda Jurisconsultorum Bibliotheca: Sir George Mackenzie*, (Edinburgh, 1989), p. 73.

[30] John Cairns, 'Sir George Mackenzie, the Faculty of Advocates, & The Advocates Library', in *Oratio*, pp. 18–35, 26.

boys who attended them but expected to go on to study medicine or law in Holland or France where this polite mode of education was already in place. This programme of modernisation and reform received political support in the 1680s from men in the entourage of James, Duke of Albany (James VII).[31]

It was not only lawyers and physicians who prized innovation. The Reverend William Carstares (1649–1715), a Calvinist plotter from the 1680s who became chaplain to William III and Principal of Edinburgh University (1703–15), also left a library of some interest. It had a great deal of divinity but one might not have expected so much church history. Carstares had a personal interest in this topic and seems to have possessed numerous books on the ancient churches and on the spread of Christianity. Among those books is found Richard Simon's *Critical History of the New Testament*. All this was supplemented by ancient and modern historians ranging from Livy and Polybius to Samuel Pufendorf, Louis de Maimbourg, Bishop Bossuet and William Nicolson, whose *Scots Historical Library* (1702) had been produced with the help of Edinburgh antiquaries. Carstares had known many of the English latitudinarians and he owned their works. His collection of Boyle Lectures was complete to 1714; he also possessed other works by Newtonians such as James Keill.[32] After he came to Edinburgh as Principal of its university in 1703, its standard of teaching improved and ecclesiastical history was added to the complement of chairs. He probably also tried to found a civil history chair. When one was created in 1717 it went to a member of his family.[33]

The library lists of two men much younger than Sibbald and Carstares survive to show that by the early eighteenth century Scottish tastes were becoming more catholic and current – those of John Spotiswoode and Charles Erskine (1680–1763). Spotiswoode's library is that of an erudite *virtuoso*; Erskine's is that of an enlightened gentleman. In those descriptions is symbolised the transformation of the Scottish intelligentsia between *c.*1690 and 1730.

[31] Ouston, 'York in Edinburgh', pp. 133–55.

[32] I have not found a complete catalogue of this library but my comments are supported by 'The correspondence of Andrew and William Dunlop 1715–1720', preserved at Glasgow University Library, MS Gen. 83. The Dunlops were his nephews.

[33] A. Ian Dunlop, *William Carstares and the Kirk by Law Established* (Edinburgh, 1967), p. 105, n2; D.B. Horn, 'The University of Edinburgh and the teaching of history', *University of Edinburgh Journal*, 17 (1953–4), 161–76, especially p. 161. The first professor of Ecclesiastical History, John Cuming of Relugas (*c.*1641–1714) was interested in Scottish antiquities and may have belonged to the antiquarian club existing in Edinburgh for some time after 1702, *Early Letters of Robert Wodrow 1698–1709*, ed. L.W. Sharp, Scottish History Society, 3rd series, 23 (Edinburgh, 1937), pp. 191, 261–2. Cumin's successor was Carstares's nephew, William Dunlop. Charles Mackie, the first professor of civil history, was Carstares's nephew by marriage.

Spotiswoode[34] was a lawyer educated in Edinburgh and Leyden who for many years taught law extra-murally in Edinburgh but never gained the university chair he sought. He was polymathic in his interests and reading and encouraged his students to make grammar, rhetoric, logic, history and philology their especial studies.[35] This did not mean a neglect of philosophy, science, mathematics, modern literature or of the law which required all the other sciences in the successful scholar and practitioner.[36] The spur to the efforts to master all these was in part the patriotic determination to improve, modernise and make respectable his own kingdom which seemed so negligible in the republic of letters. He was full of projects to effect the changes which seemed to be required in Scotland.[37] Like others of his time, his allegiances were complex. He seems to have sympathised with the Stuart cause but he chose his 'spiritual guide[s]' from amongst the evangelical clerics of Edinburgh, although those might not have approved his reading in the mystical divinity of the French.[38]

The catalogue of Spotiswoode's books made in 1728 listed 2,982 titles of which some were collections containing several items.[39] Of these titles 401 were folios, 741 quartos and the rest (1840) octavos and duodecimos. A sampling of his collection suggests that it was distributed as shown in table 5.3.

The number of Latin volumes in his library might suggest that Spotiswoode was a late humanist of sorts. He can more fairly be described as a *virtuoso* whose interests were serious and professional. Latin places him not among philologists and humanists but among scholars of every sort. Secondly, one is struck by the range of the man's interests. He possessed some of the early Fathers of the Church but also religious works by Cicero, Erasmus, Luther, Calvin, Guillaume Viret, Theodore

[34] John Cairns, 'John Spotiswoode, Professor of Law: A Preliminary Sketch', *The Stair-Society Miscellany Three*, XXXIX (Edinburgh, 1992), pp. 131–59; see also, Cairns, 'Rhetoric, language and Roman Law: legal education and improvement in eighteenth-century Scotland', *Law and History Review*, 9 (1991), 31–58.

[35] Spotiswoode MSS, NLS MS 2934.

[36] Spotiswoode MSS, NLS MS 658, John Spotiswoode, *A Discourse Shewing the Necessary Qualifications of a Student of the Laws and What is Propos'd in the Colleges of Law, History & Philology, Establish'd at Edinburgh* (Edinburgh, 1704).

[37] NLS MS 2934 ff. 92, 105, 108, 121, 123–4; 125–6; 137. Elsewhere Spotiswoode made proposals for studies of Scottish coins, weights and measures, great men, topography and history. He possessed an outlook much like Sir Robert Sibbald's. See R.L. Emerson, 'Sir Robert Sibbald, Kt., The Royal Society of Scotland and the origins of the Scottish Enlightenment', *Annals of Science*, 45 (1988), 41–72. Spotiswoode's name clearly belongs on the list given there on p. 71.

[38] NLS MS 658, ff. 18–20.

[39] 'A Catalogue of Curious and Valuable Books, Being the Library of Mr. John Spotiswoode' (Edinburgh, 1728); NLS Ms. Bc. 5. 1(1).

Table 5.3 *The library of John Spotiswoode, 1728*

Books printed in:	1400s	1500s	1600s	1700s
	—	17%	78%	4%

Books in:	Latin	French	English	Italian	Dutch	Greek	Hebrew
	67%	12%	13%	3%		2%	

Books by subject:*	f°		4°		8 & 12°		Totals	
	No.	%	No.	%	No.	%	No.	%
Religion	9	14	12	20	16	24	37	19
Philosophy	1	2	4	7	4	6	9	4
Law	42	65	16	27	26	39	84	44
Politics	1	2	5	8	2	3	8	4
Science and technology	—	—	5	8	—	—	5	3
Mathematics	—	—	—	—	1	2	1	1
Medicine	1	2	1	2	—	—	2	1
Military and naval	1	2	—	—	—	—	1	1
Classics	2	3	2	3	4	6	8	4
Languages	—	—	2	3	4	6	6	3
Belles lettres	4	6	6	10	4	6	14	7
Trade and geography	—	—	2	3	1	2	3	2
History	4	6	6	9	4	6	13	7
Other								
Totals	65	100	60	100	66	100	191	100

*This sample of 191 titles probably understates his interests in mathematics, sciences (especially chemistry), medicine and military matters.

Beza, Joseph Hall, Moïse Amyrault and a collection of modern free thinkers which included Richard Simon, Charles Blount, John Toland and other English deists. Those who wrote against the deists were represented by Robert Burton, Richard Baxter, Edward Stillingfleet, John Tillotson and Charles Leslie. His philosophers included Plato, Aristotle, Epicurus, Cicero, Augustine, Duns Scotus and Thomas Aquinas. Other traditions among the moderns were represented by Montaigne, Charron and Naudé; Silhon and Gassendi; Descartes and Malebranche; Bacon, Boyle and Fellows of the Royal Society; Chillingworth, Stillingfleet and Tillotson; Henry More, Cudworth and other Cambridge Platonists. There were, surprisingly, no volumes by Locke or Newton. All of the great natural lawyers were there but so too were Machiavelli, Hobbes, Harrington and Andrew Fletcher of Saltoun. Spotiswoode possessed the works of Buchanan and continental *monarchomachi*. His natural philosophy shelves were loaded with physico-theological books by Ray, Grew, Charlton, Boyle and some of the Boyle lecturers. Spotiswoode also had many works on astronomy, dialling, physics, chemistry and pure mathematics. Here Archimedes,

Galileo, Boyle, Huygens, Mariotte and Swammerdam rubbed shoulders with LeMort, Rohault, Lemery, Steno and an impressive collection of mathematical writers which included Barrow, Stevin, various of the Gregories and some ancients. This lawyer owned enough medical works to have taught himself to practice. They included some anatomical books, systematic works by Sanctorius, Senert, Hoffman, Wecker and Borelli; Sydenham and even recent texts on midwifery by Mauriceau and Glisson. Harvey jostled Scots writers on fevers and medical Newtonians associated with Archibald Pitcairne. Modern botany books included ones by Robert Morrison and James Sutherland, both Scots; he had many more on pharmacy and chemistry. Spotiswoode also possessed a considerable collection of works on fortification and other military and naval topics. He had, in effect, complete histories of Greece, Rome, France, England and Scotland with many miscellaneous volumes on special topics and peoples. In the works of Bodin, Bayle and a few other moderns, he possessed works on historical method and the purposes to be realized by antiquaries and historians such as he and his friends aspired to be. His interests were catholic but he had also bought many Scottish authors.

Charles Erskine (1680–1763) was educated at Edinburgh, Utrecht and Leyden (1708) and had in 1699 sought a St Andrews regency.[40] He served as an Edinburgh regent from 1701 to 1707 and then until 1734 held the largely sinecure post of Professor of Public Law. Erskine qualified as an advocate in 1711 and thereafter was active as a lawyer, MP, Solicitor-General, Lord Advocate and judge in the Courts of Session and Justiciary. He was connected politically with his kinsman John Erskine, the 10th Earl of Mar, and from *c.*1726 on with the Argathelian interest which looked after him very well.[41] He was clearly a bookish man with a library of 1,361 volumes catalogued principally in 1731 but with additions still being made to it until 1762.[42] It was much like Spotiswoode's but there were also clear signs of change. Of 68 quartos sampled (he had 470) half were written in English and the other half in Italian (29, 43 per cent), French (3, 4 per cent) and Spanish (2,3 per cent). His shelves, predictably, had far more editions printed after 1680 and the earliest of his books were almost all works standard for lawyers. He read a lot of history and *belles lettres*, was interested in the deistic controversy and certainly kept up his philosophy, including natural philosophy or

[40] St Andrews University Minutes, 10 June 1699, St Andrews Muniment Room.

[41] John Stuart Shaw, *The Management of Scottish Society 1707–1764* (Edinburgh, 1983), pp. 49, 68–81 *passim*; *The History of Parliament, The House of Commons 1715–1754*, 3 vols., ed. Romney Sedgwick (New York, 1970), I, pp. 420–1.

[42] 'Tinwald Library', Erskine-Murray MSS, NLS MS 3283.

science.[43] He possessed editions of Locke, Newton, Colin MacLaurin, Lord Shaftesbury, Francis Hutcheson, Duncan Forbes, David Hume, Lord Kames and some FRS's while continental philosophy was represented by Charron, Descartes, Pascal, Malebranche, père Buffier, the abbé Pluche and Mandeville. Erskine bought works on Scottish history including those by Thomas Innes and William Robertson. His books are those of a man who started out an *érudit* and *virtuoso* but ended up as an enlightened and polite member of the fashionable Edinburgh clubs to which Hume and his friends also belonged.

What these libraries show is that by 1707 the outlook of well-educated Scots had much in common with their counterparts elsewhere, especially those in England. This was particularly true of medical men, lawyers, educators, some soldiers and almost certainly of those who sought to make careers which depended on English patronage. Even the ministers were not as inward looking as is sometimes assumed. This is also borne out by what Scots published in the latter seventeenth century.

Most of what Scottish printers produced is contained in Harry G. Aldis's *A List of Books Printed in Scotland Before 1700* (Edinburgh, 1904, 2nd edn, 1970).[44] From 1650 to 1699 the total number of imprints counted is only 3,901 of which 36 per cent were produced in the 1690s and 64 per cent in the last two decades of the period. From 1630 to 1680 the Scottish printers had produced on average 46 titles each year with highs coming in the 1638 (55 imprints), 1643 (69), 1660 (138) and 1679 (71) for political and economic reasons. A sustained but uneven rise in publications began only after 1677. The Restoration appears not to have had any immediately stirring effect upon Scottish thinkers but it did change the political and religious orientation of local publications. It also introduced more news and publications which foreshadowed secularisation. Between 1660 and 1689 there was clearly a new category for Scottish printers which we might anachronistically and euphemistically call 'science'. Many almanacs were produced by Scots. Works on mathematics and natural philosophy by George Sinclair, James Corss (Corse or Cross), James and David Gregorie, Matthew Mackaile, Sir Robert Sibbald, James Sutherland, William Saunders and James Paterson had appeared before 1689 as had a few medical items. These were novel publications

[43] One of Erskine's colleagues at Edinburgh University, Robert Steuart (1675–1747), professor of natural philosophy, left a remarkable memorial in the form of 'the Physiological Library'. This has been analysed by Michael Barfoot: 'Hume and the culture of science in the early eighteenth century', in Stewart (ed.), *Studies in the Philosophy of the Scottish Enlightenment*, pp. 152–60.

[44] I have used the second edition prepared by the National Library of Scotland (Edinburgh, 1970). My categorisation of books listed by Aldis is rough: one cannot always judge a book by its title.

and probably more numerous than works of Scottish latinity or translations from Latin or Greek into English. Scots published classical authors as well as works written by Erasmus, Castellio, and Buchanan, while *The Westminster Confession* and portions of the Bible were put into Latin for schoolboys. So much for Scottish humanism in the local press![45] There were other signs of encroaching modernity in the various items by Francis Bacon, Robert Boyle and some of the Latitudinarian divines; certainly Richard Simon's *Opuscula critica adversus Isaacus Vossium* (1685) belongs here. Most years saw books or pamphlets against Quakers and Covenanters and numerous political polemics, proclamations and news items. Bits of Dryden, Settle and other English poets had appeared but Scots probably preferred and bought more copies of the poems of Sir David Lindsay, 'Blind Harry', John Barbour and Robert Henryson or of 'The Flyting of Polwart and Montgomery' and 'the Salms [*sic*] newly translated'. Judged by these lists the average Scottish mind by 1688 had not shifted over much but it had evinced some interests in science and modern literature and it had been forced to hear Episcopalian and Royalist, even Romanist arguments after a steady diet of Presbyterian views from the 1630s until 1660. If there was a Royalist Enlightenment beginning *c.*1680, only one of its exponents, Sir George Mackenzie, bulked large in this index. He was the most frequently published Scottish writer and published at least twenty-one items between 1660 and 1689. A change in this pattern came in 1688–9 with the Revolution.

In those years there was an outpouring of printed matter double that of most of the decade's earlier years. Once again the political-religious pendulum swung back to the Presbyterians and the royalist press at Holyrood House, like the 'college' there, disappeared.[46] *Salus populi suprema lex* could again be printed and Sir James Steuart, its author, like many other exiles could come home again.

The 1690s saw other signs of change. Deism which had been noticed earlier found a local martyr in Thomas Aikenhead, a student executed for blasphemy in Edinburgh in 1697.[47] Behind his death there was a certain amount of local printed discussion of deism. Edmund Hickeringill's *The*

[45] This is not of course the whole story since I have not touched upon works printed outside Scotland. For a partial list of these, see J.F. Kellar Johnstone and A. Webster Robertson, *Bibliographia Aberdonensis . . . 1641–1700*, 2 vols. (Aberdeen, 3rd Spalding Club, 1930). Their entries often show Scots intellectually active and important in English and continental contexts.

[46] The Duke of York set up a Catholic school within the precincts of Holyrood Palace; his printer working within the same bounds was James Watson.

[47] Michael Hunter, '"Aikenhead the Atheist": the context and consequences of articulate irreligion in the late seventeenth century', in Michael Hunter and David Wootton (eds.), *Atheism from the Reformation to the Enlightenment* (Oxford, 1992), pp. 221–54.

Table 5.4 *Scottish imprints: the Aldis List (1970)*

	1660s		1670s		1680s		1690s		Totals	
Category	No.	%	No.	%	No.	%	No.	%	No.	%
Sermons	14	3/4*	10	2/3	21	2/3	33	2/3	78	2/3
Religious works	59	11/15	139	28/40	156	14/22	162	12/17	516	15/21
Moral philosophy	12	2/3	2	–/1	3		3		20	1/1
Law			2	–/1	16	1/2	62	4/6	80	2/3
Law cases	2	–/1	8	2/2	41	4/6	39	3/4	90	3/4
Acts, proclamations, etc.	141	27/–	158	31/–	394	36/–	427	31/–	1,120	32/–
Politics and polemics	66	12/17	38	8/11	168	15/24	74	5/8	346	10/14
Political economy			3	1/1	8	1/1	24	2/2	35	1/1
Natural history and philosophy	1		1		3		6	–/1	11	
Mathematics	2	–/1			8	1/1	4		14	
Astronomy	1				1		1		3	
Almanacs	12	2/3	15	3/4	38	3/5	36	3/4	101	3/4
Technology, military, naval	1				2		3		6	
Medicine and pharmacy	7	1/2	1		2		22	2/2	32	1/1
Surgery and anatomy			1				4		5	
Botany					2		4		6	
Chemistry	2	–/1	1		2				5	
Zoology							1		1	
Improvements							49	4/5	49	1/2
Agriculture							2		2	
Metaphysics										
Logic and philosophy of mind					3		1		4	
Rhetoric and criticism	7	1/2	3	1/1	1		5	–/1	16	–/1
Poetry and song	25	5/6	31	6/9	46	4/6	51	4/5	153	4/6
Plays	1				1				2	
Tales, novels, essays	6	1/2	1		3		6	–/1	16	–/1
Geography			1		10	1/1	6	–/1	17	–/1
History and antiquities	8	1/2	4	1/1	8	1/1	8	–/1	28	1/1
Biography	1				7	1/1	7	–/1	15	–/1
Education					2		4		6	
Periodicals and news	112	21/29	20	4/6	84	8/12	213	15/22	429	12/18
Dictionaries	1		1		3		3		8	
Grammars	9	2/2	14	3/4	7	1/1	17	1/2	47	1/2
Classics	7	1/2	12	2/3	2		9	1/1	30	1/1
Textbooks	5	1/1	10	2/3	2		12	1/1	29	1/1
University materials	16	3/4	17	3/5	27	2/4	32	2/3	92	3/4

Table 5.4 (*cont.*)

	1660s		1670s		1680s		1690s		Totals	
Miscellaneous	10	2/3	5	1/1	22	2/3	44	3/5	81	2/3
Unknown	3	1/1	5	1/1	13	1/2	25	2/3	46	1/2
Total Imprints	531	100	503	100	1,106	100	1,399	100	3,539	100
Imprints excluding Acts, etc.	390	100	345	100	712	100	972	100	2,419	100

*The 'numerator' is the % of total imprints; the 'denominator' is the % of imprints excluding Acts, etc.

Ceremony-Monger had been printed in 1689, a year after Dryden's *Hind and the Panther* which had argued for the need of an infallible teaching church just as his earlier poem, *Religio laici* (1682) had justified the rational theology of latitudinarian divines. A number of other titles refer to deism in 1695 and, a year after Aikenhead's death, Charles Leslie's *Short and Easie Method with the Deists* (1698) was printed in Edinburgh. Sir William Anstruther's essays against 'atheists' appeared three years later. By then Scots had also had a taste of the controversies in England over the nature of the church and the state's right to alter its established position and privileges. By the 1690s the Scots were also discussing their economic life and how it might be improved. That too was a new topic for their printers.[48] Equally furious, if not more numerous, were medical publications in which Newtonian and Jacobite physicians attacked and ridiculed others who were Whigs but perhaps less medically up-to-date. The nosology, causes, prognoses and treatments of fevers would concern Edinburgh physicians for 100 years.[49] So too would agriculture which also figures in the titles of the 1690s.[50] Some antiquarian and historical titles also show a broadened interest in the Scottish past. That this had a modern counterpart is indicated by an attempt to print in Edinburgh the *Bibliotheca Universalis* (1688) and the *History of the Works of the Learned* (1699). Law theses were now being regularly printed and more theses were coming from university regents now teaching more modern topics. These books, mostly printed in Edinburgh, contain few real novelties but

[48] These debates are noticed in William Ferguson, *Scotland's Relations with England: A Survey to 1707* (Edinburgh, 1977), pp. 180–253, *passim*.

[49] Andrew Cunningham, 'Sydenham *versus* Newton: the Edinburgh fever dispute of the 1690s between Andrew Brown and Archibald Pitcairne', *Medical History*, Supplement 1 (1981), 71–98; Cunningham also believes the Edinburgh medical community was restructured in the period 1670–1700; see: Cunningham, 'The medical professions'.

[50] Ian Whyte, *Agriculture and Society in Seventeenth-Century Scotland* (Edinburgh, 1979), pp. 252–5.

they clearly show that Scots were aware of and now themselves contributing to discussions which would be formative of the Scottish, even the European Enlightenment.

By the early 1700s both the lists of books in private libraries and the titles of Scottish imprints suggest that significant shifts had come in Scottish thinking. Scots were interested in a wider range of things and they were clearly trying harder to participate in the republic of letters. They were also far better prepared to do so than they had been for a very long time. But that only means that more of them were thinking like men in England, France, Holland and Germany. The patterns of cultural unity and convergence were not only British but also European.

This convergence of outlook among Scots and Englishmen may have been a pre-condition for the Union of 1707; certainly it helped to make union a success. But there was something else which marked the attitudes of many Scots in the latter seventeenth century. That was a new confidence that they could emulate as well as imitate others. It is evident in the projects of Sir Robert Sibbald and his friends but it is equally apparent in the patriotic and improving works of many others. The Union of 1707 was aided by this change of spirit. Without it, interest in improvements and the confidence that Scots could equal or outstrip the English would have been lacking and the Union would have been like earlier ones an unwelcome exercise of force or royal power.

6

RELIGIOUS REALIGNMENT BETWEEN THE RESTORATION AND UNION

COLIN KIDD

SCOTLAND'S ecclesiastical politics were central to the debates which preceded the Anglo-Scottish Union of 1707. In terms of contemporary political thought, this incorporating union of civil governments unaccompanied by a union of religious establishments was a solecism.[1] Uniconfessional states predominated in early modern Christendom, not only in unitary kingdoms but also in composite dynastic states. Although there were looser confederal unions, such as the Swiss cantons and the Holy Roman Empire, in which different confessions were established, and there existed successful experiments in toleration, in England and in the confederal United Provinces of the Netherlands, there were nevertheless no states with plural church establishments. Only in an attenuated and highly devolved form in the exceptional context of some of England's North American colonies, such as New York, were there multiple establishments. These derived from the limited freedom of townships to choose their own form of Protestant worship, and to support their different choices with local religious taxes.[2] However, the case of a multiconfessional British unitary state with opposed Church establishments, Episcopalian in England, Presbyterian in Scotland, was a much more dramatic assault on the axioms of contemporary political wisdom.

Thus the most likely consequence of the Union was that the Presbyterian Kirk would be absorbed within a pan-Britannic Episcopalian Church. The reasonable fear that Britain would inevitably become a uniconfessional Episcopalian state meant that for Scots Presbyterians unresolved questions

[1] *A Letter from Mr. Scrupulous, to Trialogus Concerning the Union* (Edinburgh, 1706), p. 3; *The Restoration of Episcopacy in Scotland, The only sure foundation for a lasting Union with England In a letter to Sir J.P. Bart.* (London, 1705).

[2] L.W. Levy, *The Establishment Clause: Religion and the First Amendment* (New York, 1986), pp. 10–24.

about the constitutional nature of the new British Union were far from theoretical, but touched on the very preservation of their long-embattled Kirk. There was some uncertainty whether the Scottish Presbyterian establishment was firmly secured as part of an unalterable international agreement which was constitutive of the new British state, or vulnerable to the sovereign legislative will of an Episcopalian-leaning British crown-in-parliament.

Religious ideas also gave rise to different conceptions of Scottish national identity and of Scotland's proper relationship with England. Indeed it is important to remember that in the pre-modern world, national identity was often inextricably linked to confessional identity. The role of religion was important in determining preferences for different constitutional arrangements to settle the Anglo-Scottish relationship.

There were also important religious dimensions to the concepts of 'empire' which are now acknowledged to have been central to the political thought of the Union debates.[3] The claim that the English crown had imperial authority over Scotland as a dependent homager kingdom was paralleled by an assertion of English ecclesiastical superiority over the Scottish Church. Secondly, fear of Louis XIV's ambitions to create a Counter-Reformation Catholic empire in western Europe led to a realisation that Union was a strategic necessity for Protestantism as a whole.

This essay will investigate these central features of the Union debates in terms of changes in Scots Presbyterian and Episcopalian thought from the era of the Restoration. It will concentrate on the role of different forms of religious moderation in creating an ideological environment in which a multiconfessional state was conceivable, and the status of the churches in the proposed united Britain could be debated in an idiom at least partially liberated from the absolutes of divine right assertion. Latitude helped to soften partisanship, and to redirect the intellectual energies of Scottish *literati* trapped in a society sharply divided between warring Presbyterians and Episcopalians. Traditions of religious moderation, although still outweighed by the continuing hostility of committed Episcopalians and Presbyterians, assisted the development of a more sophisticated political culture. Thus in the first decade of the eighteenth century the Scots political nation found itself able to discuss the alternative schemes of Anglo-Scottish affiliation proposed during the Union debates, in terms of the evolution of the post-medieval European state system and of the growth of trade in the overseas empires of its

[3] W. Ferguson, 'Imperial crowns: a neglected facet of the background to the Treaty of Union of 1707', *Scottish Historical Review*, 53 (1974).

maritime powers. A crucial part of this new realism in Scottish political writing came from a trend away from an understanding of the church in terms of uncompromising *ius divinum* standards towards the spheres of constitutionalism and the language of interests.

Episcopalian latitude

Scotland's Restoration ecclesiastical settlement was, like England's, a predominantly lay political affair, carried out in the Scots parliament. This body was hijacked by a resentful cavalier party led by John, 1st Earl of Middleton (*c.*1608–74), which militated against comprehension.[4] The Covenants were rejected as a basis for the restored Scottish Church and Presbyterianism was replaced by an episcopal system in which the majority of bishops were confirmed prelatists.[5] The lower church courts of synods, presbyteries and sessions still sat, but by the grace of the episcopate rather than in their own right. Moreover, under Middleton's vigorous enforcement of an act of 1662 requiring ministers admitted since 1649 to obtain both presentation from a patron and collation from a bishop, around 270 ministers, mainly in the south-west, were purged from the Church.[6] Thus, from the start, the Restoration era was dogged with the problem of presbyterian nonconformity.

However, a spirit of latitude – the acceptance that there were occasions when the civil peace took priority over certain second-order religious conflicts – was already apparent among some of the politicians and clergy of both ecclesiastical persuasions. Although its adherents were defeated in the crucial manoeuvrings to determine the shape of the restored church, this spirit was eventually to be important in winning sufficient Scottish support for the erastian and indifferentist establishment of the Scottish and English Churches in the Union of 1707. In the 1660s a latitudinarian disposition was most associated with the group of politicians in the orbit of John Maitland, 2nd earl of Lauderdale (1616–82). These included John Hay, 2nd earl of Tweeddale (1625–97), Alexander Bruce, 2nd earl of Kincardine (*c.*1629–80), and Sir Robert Moray (*c.*1600–73). Lauderdale was a former Covenanter, but as the scion of the Maitland dynasty, which owed its rise to crown service in administration, he now subordinated his presbyterian sympathies to political pragmatism.[7] Some of his allies were *politiques* of a less opportunistic cast. Moray, an early

[4] J. Buckroyd, *Church and State in Scotland 1660–1681* (Edinburgh, 1980), pp. 2, 20–1, 29–30.

[5] Buckroyd, *Church and State*, p. 4.

[6] G. Donaldson (ed.), *Scottish Historical Documents* (Edinburgh and London, 1970), pp. 228–9; Donaldson, *Scotland James V to VII* (Edinburgh and London, 1965), p. 365.

[7] Buckroyd, *Church and State*, pp. 3, 17, 23–4.

Royal Society Fellow, was renowned for an open disposition and ideological quietism.[8] Tweeddale, according to the later testimony of Gilbert Burnet, one of his ecclesiastical contemporaries, had 'loose thoughts both of civil and ecclesiastical government; and seemed to think, that what form soever was uppermost was to be complied with'.[9] These politicians engineered the Indulgences of 1669 and 1672, when a small minority of the deprived Presbyterian ministers accepted the state's terms for their restoration to selected parishes.[10]

There was also some support for moderation within the restored Episcopal Church, many of whose clergy were former Presbyterians. The Archbishop of St Andrews, James Sharp (1618–79), a former Covenanter who was later in his disillusionment with uncompromising nonconformity to become the leading scourge of Covenanting dissent, was in the early years of the Restoration a proponent of comprehension and an episcopacy justified on the *politique* grounds of convenience and necessity.[11] More committed to moderation as an ideal was the Bishop of Dunblane, Robert Leighton (1611–84), an Engager or royalist Covenanter in the late 1640s who had broken with the Presbyterians, according to Burnet, because of their 'narrow' thoughts and 'fury against all who differed from them'.[12] Leighton inspired a number of younger disciples including Gilbert Burnet (1643–1715), Laurence Charteris (1625–1700) and Henry Scougal (1650–1678): they constituted the Scottish school of latitudinarian theology.[13] Leighton was influenced by Bishop Patrick Forbes (1564–1635) and his followers, the Aberdeen Doctors, and by the scheme proposed by James Ussher, Archbishop of Armagh, for a reduced episcopacy likely to be acceptable to puritans. Forbes and the Aberdeen Doctors had distinguished between the essentials of faith and second-order things indifferent. Church government was of this second order. Episcopacy was not, they felt, essential to the Church, though it was of its '*melius esse*' – extremely useful to the preservation of its unity and order. Their labours in patristic research had convinced them that modern episcopacy was not identical to the government of the primitive church, and that agreement in the fundamentals of faith rather than descent from the apostolic succession of bishops was the sign of a true church.[14] Ussher,

[8] David Stevenson, *The Origins of Freemasonry: Scotland's Century 1590–1710* (Cambridge, 1988), pp. 166–89.

[9] Gilbert Burnet, *History of His Own Time*, 2 vols. (London, 1724, 1734), I, p. 102. Spelling and capitalisation in quotations have been modernised throughout.

[10] Buckroyd, *Church and State*, pp. 77–8.

[11] Buckroyd, *Church and State*, pp. 12, 49; J. Buckroyd, *The Life of James Sharp Archbishop of St. Andrews 1618–1679* (Edinburgh, 1987).

[12] Burnet, *History*, I, p. 135.

[13] W.G.S. Snow, *The Times, Life and Thought of Patrick Forbes* (London, 1952), pp. 168–70.

[14] Snow, *Forbes*, pp. 153–5.

also steeped in patristic scholarship, had sought to reconcile the fierce religious divisions which had led to the Civil Wars by arguing for a reduced episcopate which partook less of the character of lordly Laudian prelacy. Ussher's proposal instead transformed bishops into presidents or moderators of diocesan synods, which accorded with their status in the early church.[15]

Leighton and the Scottish latitude-men tended more towards the reduction of episcopacy as a means of winning over Presbyterian nonconformists to the Church than to the Indulgence schemes of the *politiques*. Nevertheless, these were complementary strategies of a comprehensive middle ground in Scottish Restoration politics, in which the Lauderdale and Leighton groups overlapped. Leighton, after his translation to the Archbishopric of Glasgow, launched an abortive scheme for an Accommodation with the nonconformists in the south-west based on an Ussherian remodelling of episcopacy. This Accommodation of 1670 had official approval, and was tried after the relative failure of Lauderdale's Indulgence of 1669. Leighton's position for negotiation appears to have been that only prelacy had been abjured by the National Covenant – and not episcopacy in its moderate primitive form. Bishops ruling as permanent synodical presidents in conjunction with a Presbyterian court structure seemed to offer a practical institutional solution to the grievances of Dissenters. However, despite considerable Presbyterian interest the discussions fell through.[16]

Leighton's ideas, nevertheless, outlived his practical influence on church policy, most notably in the works of Gilbert Burnet, whose use of dialogue forms allowed him to advance the full range of positions associated with the middle ground.[17] In one set of dialogues, Burnet's principal mouthpiece Eudaimon, 'a moderate man', aspired to impose a civility of conversation on the debate between Philarchaeus, 'an episcopal man', and Isotimus, who advanced the presbyterian case. Eudaimon was assisted by Polyhistor, a patristic expert who made the case for a revived primitive episcopacy acting with 'the concurrence of presbyters', and by Criticus, a scholar well-versed in the Scriptures who refuted the case for a *ius divinum* prelatical episcopacy: 'churchmen have not by Christ a lordly

[15] James Ussher, *The Reduction of Episcopacie unto the Form of Synodical Government Received in the Antient Church* (London, 1656), p. 7.

[16] Robert Leighton, *The Whole Works*, 4 vols. (London, 1830), I, pp. clxxxi–cxcii; Buckroyd, *Church and State*, pp. 95–100; D.S. Hopkirk, 'A study of accommodation movements between Presbytery and Episcopacy in the seventeenth century in Scotland, England and Ireland', PhD thesis, University of Edinburgh, 1946, pp. 147–73.

[17] [Gilbert Burnet], *A Modest and Free Conference Betwixt A Conformist and a Nonconformist* (1669); Gilbert Burnet, *A Vindication of the Authority, Constitution and Laws of the Church and State of Scotland* (Glasgow, 1673).

or despotic dominion over Christians committed to them, but a paternal and brotherly one'.[18]

The Reverend James Gordon was deprived for his discussion of the conduct he expected from a reformed episcopate modelled on the primitive pattern. Gordon argued that no minister should be appointed to the episcopate who had not already pledged to devote his revenues to 'pious and charitable uses'. The prelatical practice of bishops 'immersing themselves in secular affairs' Gordon denounced as a 'scandal of the first magnitude', a position not far removed from the presbyterian abhorrence of the clerical assumption of civil offices. Gordon indicated his admiration for the modest way in which the bishops of antiquity had conversed with their colleges of presbyters, and, arguing that 'a general convocation' was 'the true sole representative of a national church', he propounded a conciliarist position on the authority of such assemblies to overrule episcopal hierarchies.[19]

James Garden (1647–1726), who was professor of divinity at King's College, Aberdeen until his deprivation in 1696, argued that 'Absolute Theology', the study of what had been enjoined by God, needed to be balanced by what he called 'Comparative Theology', which 'teacheth us, how to distinguish between the essential or fundamental principles of religion, and those that are not fundamental'. Garden maintained that the end of religion was the love of God, and that there was a hierarchy of means to that end. These ranged from those which were 'necessary, sure and infallible', such as faith in Christ the mediator and the need to wean the heart from worldly concerns, down to those which had 'no sure and infallible connexion with the salvation of men', including church government.[20]

On a more elevated plane, disengaged from the hostilities raging over church government, Henry Scougal, whose thought bears the hallmarks of the Scottish latitudinarian tradition and of the Cambridge Platonists, encouraged a return to true religion. This was not to be found in the 'fierce wrath, and bitter rage' of sectarian enthusiasts, but in an inward life infused with divine love, 'an union of the soul with God, a real participation of the divine nature, the very image of God drawn upon the soul'. The outward manifestations of true religion were charity, a 'frank

[18] Burnet, *Vindication*, pp. 325–6.

[19] James Gordon, *The Reformed Bishop* (1679), pp. 22–3, 113, 137, 180–3; T. Clarke, 'The Williamite Episcopalians and the Glorious Revolution in Scotland', *Records of the Scottish Church History Society*, 24, Pt. I (1990), 43.

[20] [James Garden], *Comparative Theology* (1700: Edinburgh, 1707), pp. 3, 7, 19–20, 45, 49–53, 71, 81. See also Laurence Charteris, *The Difference between True and False Christianity Plainly Represented* (Edinburgh, 1703), pp. 35–54, 70–9.

and liberal' spirit and 'a sincere and unbounded affection' to all men.[21]

By the time of the Union debates the Episcopalian establishment in Scotland had been toppled by the Revolution, in large part because the strict adherence of its bishops to the principles of passive obedience and non-resistance left the bulk of Episcopalians tainted with Jacobitism.[22] This meant that although a small number of latitudinarian Episcopalian ministers were either comprehended or left unmolested in their parishes, by the time of the Union the Episcopalians as a party were a minor force in the process for winning its ratification in Scotland. However, the ideas of Restoration latitude were to have considerable impact on the views of two of the most convinced incorporating Unionists, William Seton of Pitmedden (1673–1744), and George Mackenzie, Viscount Tarbat and Earl of Cromarty (1630–1714), who might well stand representative for a larger and less articulate body of nobles and gentry: perhaps Episcopalian in sympathy, but prepared to establish the Kirk in an erastian union if only to quash once and for all the religious conflicts which had bedevilled the seventeenth century.[23]

Seton, although he supported Scotland's Presbyterian establishment, was from the Episcopalian north-east and advanced arguments bearing some resemblance to those of the Aberdeen Doctors and their Restoration successors. He denied that any type of church government could be plausibly claimed as *ius divinum*: 'That church government which is from God, must be revealed by him to his people some way or other; but no scheme of church government hath as yet been revealed: therefore all church government must be of human institution.'[24] Seton also maintained that neither modern presbytery nor modern episcopacy 'as they are now constitute, was in fashion in the primitive ages'. Seton argued that there were three basic types of ecclesiastical government – an episcopal hierarchy, the superintendency of the Church by an administrative cadre resembling a reduced episcopacy, and presbytery – best suited to civil government by absolute monarchy, aristocracy and democracy respectively. As mixed governments, Scotland and England, Seton believed, were best suited either to presbytery or to superintendency. Owing to an affinity of form, the episcopal hierarchy of the Church of England was a potential tool of despotism, and posed a threat to England's liberties and mixed constitution. Seton claimed that the best preservative of British liberties

[21] Henry Scougal, *The Life of God in the Soul of Man* (London, 1677), pp. 4–5, 11.

[22] D.H. Whiteford, 'Jacobitism as a factor in Presbyterian–Episcopalian relationships in Scotland, 1689–90', *Records of the Scottish Church History Society*, 16, pt II (1967), 129–49.

[23] For the subordination of ecclesiastical to lay politics, see P.W.J. Riley, *King William and the Scottish Politicians* (Edinburgh, 1979), pp. 6–7; Riley, *The Union of England and Scotland* (Manchester, 1978), p. 10.

[24] [William Seton], *The Interest of Scotland* (1700), p. 11.

was an erastian union of Scotland and England under either presbytery or a set of superintendents.[25]

Cromarty was an enigma. Associated throughout the Restoration era with strongly pro-Episcopalian cavalier politics, he also maintained links to the new science of the Royal Society. A notorious political opportunist, he also found time to pen a series of judicious and learned treatises on questions of religion, history and public policy.[26] In these he adopted latitudinarian positions. In one of his more eccentric essays, Cromarty, advancing ideas associated with the sixteenth-century Italian irenicist, Jacobus Acontius, argued that the sectarian divisions of Christendom could be traced to the Devil, who had used theologians to introduce 'human explanations', 'inconsistencies', and 'clouds of metaphysical notions' into 'the divine and plain system of the Messiah's gospel'.[27] Moreover, at the time of the Revolution, Cromarty advanced a broad comprehension scheme for the Church of Scotland on the grounds that: 'The matter of church government hath been made a pretence for the troubles of Scotland now for a hundred years.'[28] He was sceptical about the chances of stability in a divided Scotland for an establishment built on the single foundation of either presbytery or episcopacy. Cromarty suggested the experiment of uniting the loyal Williamite clergy of both parties together in a national church embracing two types of church courts. He proposed a system of Presbyterian synods operating alongside synods with permanent moderators whose stipends would be paid out of the former bishops' rents. There would be no General Assemblies, except by the 'special call' of the monarch. It would also be laid down: 'That both models forbear to preach against either model, or to preach against the models of other reformed churches, and to be advised to entertain Christian charity and communion, though of different modes of government.'[29]

The scheme did not come to fruition, but its principles informed Cromarty's erastian unionism. Cromarty believed that differences in church government were too insubstantial to stand in the way of union: 'no indifferent thing should hinder so uncontroverted a good'. The religions of Scotland and England were 'the same in all fundamentals',

[25] [Seton], *Interest*, pp. 1–35.

[26] Riley, *Union*, pp. 40–1; W. Fraser, *The Earls of Cromartie*, 2 vols. (Edinburgh, 1876), I, pp. lxvii–cxciv, 20–3. For another Cavalier associated with persecution who subscribed to latitudinarian views, see [Sir George Mackenzie of Rosehaugh], *Religio Stoici* (1663: Edinburgh, 1665), pp. 37, 39–41, 46–7, 51–2.

[27] [Cromarty], *A Bundle of Positions* (London, 1705), 'An Essay on the Nature of a Church', pp. 1–6; N. Tyacke, *Anti-Calvinists* (Oxford, 1987), p. 82.

[28] Cromarty, 'Memorial', June ?1689, *Leven and Melville Papers* (Edinburgh, 1843), pp. 125.

[29] Cromarty, 'Memorial', pp. 126–7.

and though they differed in 'praeter-fundamentals', these ought by definition to be 'subjected to charity'. Cromarty argued that the 'modal difference' of church government, 'being neither essential nor unalterable', should not hinder 'essential unity'.[30] A political realist, Cromarty realised that a sovereign united parliament could not in practice be bound by a union treaty, but that, built on explicitly erastian foundations, the legislature would be relatively immune from clericalist pressures of whatever persuasion.[31] Having advocated the granting of a measure of toleration to Scots Episcopalians, Cromarty also hoped that Union would liberalise Scotland's ecclesiastical polity.[32]

It is hard to quantify the importance of the tradition of Scots episcopal latitude and moderate episcopacy-leaning *politique* views in the Union debates. However, it does seem probable given contemporary comment about the mild Episcopalian sympathies of many of the nobles and gentlemen, and Riley's assessment of the subordination of confessional differences to magnate feuds in post-Revolution Scottish politics, that there was at least a hard-headed erastianism common to the political elite whose expression in policy bore a strong resemblance to the preferences of the latitude-men. It also suggests that for many of the members of Scotland's first and second Estates there was no insuperable ecclesiastical objection to incorporating Union.[33]

The Covenanting tradition

There was, by contrast, no equivalent latitudinarian high road from Restoration to Union among Scots Presbyterians. Since the post-Revolution Kirk which was involved in the Union debate was established in 1690 around the core of the Antediluvians, the sixty survivors among the deprived ministers of 1662, it is necessary to concentrate on the nonconformist tradition in Restoration Scotland rather than on those Presbyterians who compromised with the Episcopalian regime. The ideology of the nonconforming Presbyterians was dominated by commit-

[30] Cromarty, *Paraneisis Pacifica* (London, 1702), pp. 7, 18–19.

[31] Cromarty, *Paraneisis*, pp. 10–11.

[32] [Cromarty], *A Few Brief and Modest Reflexions Perswading a Just Indulgence To be Granted to the Episcopal Clergy and People in Scotland* (1703); Cromarty, *Several Proposals conducing to a farther Union of Britain* (London, 1711), pp. 16–22. See also John Arbuthnot, *A Sermon Preached to the People at the Mercat Cross of Edinburgh* (1706: London, 1707), p. 15. There was, of course, no necessary connection between latitude and support for incorporation; see, e.g., [Archibald Sinclair], *Some Thoughts on the Present State of Affairs* (1703), pp. 10–12; [Sinclair], *The State of the Nation enquir'd into* (1705?).

[33] T. Clarke, 'The Scottish Episcopalians 1688–1720', PhD thesis, University of Edinburgh, 1987, pp. 73–6, 138.

ment to the National Covenant (1638) and the Solemn League and Covenant (1643).[34] Most of these Presbyterians were firmly opposed to erastianism as an anti-christian usurpation by the monarch or the state on Christ's headship of the Church. Thus only a small minority accepted the state's erastian condition for compliance with the Indulgence of 1669, whose basis in the royal ecclesiastical supremacy was denounced as 'a plain dethroning of Christ'.[35] These Presbyterians had a rigorous body of ecclesiology, and detected anti-christian deviance even in the idea of toleration, despite its potential practical benefits to their cause. However, their hostility to latitudinarian ideas did not mean that they were intellectually bereft. In the vanguard of resistance theory, Scots Presbyterian ideology remained for most of the Restoration era vigorous, illiberal, democratic and hostile to pragmatic engagement with an uncovenanted state.

The principal Presbyterian theorist was James Steuart (1635–1713), a layman exiled in the United Provinces whose tracts, *Naphtali* (1667), co-written with James Stirling, and *Ius Populi Vindicatum* (1669), justified the assumption of defensive arms by private individuals against a malignant uncovenanted state. This was a dramatic radicalisation of the earlier Scots Calvinist resistance theories of George Buchanan (1506–82), who defended the legitimacy of popular resistance when sponsored by responsible aristocratic leadership, and of Samuel Rutherford (1600–61), who argued for popular sovereignty in the broadest sense, including the right of the people as a whole to resist a parliament which had betrayed their trust. Steuart's radicalism led him to a position where he deconstructed the authority even of the body of the people and justified secession from a malignant and ungodly community:

> That through the manifest and notorious perversion of the great ends of society and government, the bond thereof being dissolved, the persons, one or more thus liberated therefrom, do relapse into their primeval liberty and privilege, and accordingly as the similitude of their case and exigence of their cause doth require, may upon the very same principles again join and associate for their better defence and preservation, as they did at first enter into societies.[36]

Drafted as a theoretical defence of armed conventicling and of the Presbyterian uprising of 1666, this controversial argument sheds considerable light on conceptions of national identity held by Covenanting Presbyterians. In Steuart's scheme, if Scotland failed to live up to its Covenanted pledges, then the national community was no longer

[34] For the Covenants, see Donaldson (ed.), *Documents*, pp. 194–201, 208–10.

[35] [James Brown], *The History of the Indulgence* (1678), p. 87.

[36] [James Steuart and James Stirling], *Naphtali* (1667), p. 150.

sacrosanct. His view owed a great deal to the federalist theories of the German Calvinist Johannes Althusius (*c.*1577–1638), who had shown how commonwealths were constructed as a series of layers of civil association. At the lowest level were guilds and corporations; these could be associated into cities; cities leagued into provinces; and eventually, the combination of provinces resulted in commonwealths. Each level of collectivity was constituted on the basis of a paction with clearly defined ends. The fulfillment of these ends defined the legitimacy of the association; for Althusius, politics was the art of preserving in a community the shared pursuit of certain goals or ideals. Among the proper ends of a commonwealth Althusius included the pure and uncorrupted worship of God. The perversion of the purposes of an association amounted to tyranny and justified the secession of the partners from what was no longer a legitimate community.[37] Steuart appeared to be claiming that Scotland no longer served the goals of the Covenants, and that an Althusian secession and recombination was required. The anti-Covenanting bishop, Andrew Honyman (1619–76), denounced his scheme as an attempt to 'dissipate and dissolve the immemorially settled frame of this nation and kingdom': under Steuart's radical doctrine the people of every little parish in the Covenanting south west could 'cantonise' themselves into free republics.[38]

The Scottish Covenanting tradition thus came to subordinate the ideal of nationhood to the religious aims of the Covenants themselves. This created a tension on the question of national identity which was to complicate Presbyterian views during the Union debates. As it was, the Covenants did not simply validate bold assertions of Scotland as a nation providentially appointed for a special role in the work of reformation. The National Covenant, which was composed in opposition to the imposition of Anglicising Laudian innovations in the Kirk, and has recently been described as 'a nationalist manifesto asserting the independence of a sovereign people under God',[39] had a strong unionist counterweight in the Solemn League and Covenant. The Solemn League was an alliance of 1643 between the Scottish Covenanters and English parliamentarians to promote godliness throughout the British Isles by means of Presbyterian discipline. Scholars have also drawn attention to the co-existence of patriotic Scottish shibboleths derived from the national past, with British unionist and universalist perspectives, in the

[37] *The Politics of Johannes Althusius*, ed. and trans. F.S. Carney (London, 1965).

[38] Andrew Honyman, *A Survey of the Insolent and Infamous Libel entituled Naphtali* (1668), pp. 9–10.

[39] A. Macinnes, 'The Scottish Constitution, 1638–51', in J. Morrill (ed.), *The Scottish Covenant in its British Context 1638–51* (Edinburgh, 1990), p. 108.

thought of the Scottish Reformers of the sixteenth and seventeenth centuries.[40] Steuart's arguments for secession added a third strand to the understanding of nationhood within the Covenanting tradition.

The unreconstructed Covenanting wing of the Kirk and its allies outside the Church, the Cameronians – Covenanters who rejected the erastian compromise of the 1690 establishment[41] – firmly opposed the Union proposed in 1706. Although these Presbyterians utilised the national past to argue against the pollution of Scotland's remarkable providential history of religious purity by a union with an unreformed and malignant England, their objections were not founded on a wholesale Scotocentric anti-unionism. Covenanters did not like the terms of the Union proposed in 1706, but they remained committed in principle to the Solemn League and Covenant and the ideal of a pan-Britannic union along strict Presbyterian lines. However, Union with a lame equivocating 'reformed' church like England's, except on the basis of a Scottish-inspired agenda for further reform, was anathema.[42]

Covenanting hostility to Union was essentially religious, and not founded in a secular conception of Anglo-Scottish relations. The apparent contradictions of Scottish, British unionist, and secessionist visions were reconcilable as strategic concerns secondary to the primary aspiration of state rededication to the Covenants. Within the Covenanting idiom, anti-Unionism was predicated not so much on the preservation of Scotland as a nation *per se*, as on upholding 'Christ's rights in Scotland', and the Scottish people's 'national engagements' with God.[43] The Union would involve the nation not so much in bondage to an English majority as in the sin of abjuring the Covenants. The Reverend James Webster (1658–1720), the leading anti-Unionist of the Kirk's traditionalists, rejected Union as a 'manifold breach of the Solemn League', by whose first article Scots had sworn to 'reform England in worship and government', since the proposed Union laid an 'eternal embargo upon all such endeavours'.[44] This widespread popular Presbyterian anti-Unionism

[40] A. Williamson, *Scottish National Consciousness in the Reign of James VI* (Edinburgh, 1979); S.A. Burrell, 'The apocalyptic vision of the early Covenanters', *Scottish Historical Review*, 43 (1964), 24.

[41] *The Nonconformists Vindication* (1700).

[42] *The Smoaking Flax Unquenchable* (1706); *To His Grace, Her Majesties High Commissioner. . . . The Humble Address of a Considerable Body of People in the South and Western Shires* (1706?).

[43] *A Speech in season against the Union or a smoking furnace and a burning lamp* (np, nd), p. 8; and see, e.g., *To His Grace, Her Majesties High Commissioner, and the . . . Estates of Parliament, The Humble Address of the Presbytery of Dumblane* (1706); *Unto His Grace, Her Majesties High Commissioner . . . The Humble Address of the Presbytery of Hamilton* (1706).

[44] James Webster, *Lawful Prejudices against an Incorporating Union with England* (Edinburgh, 1707), pp. 4–5.

also dwelt on the horror of incorporation with a nation so prey to religious errors and sinful manners as England. James Hodges, the Presbyterian federalist pamphleteer, contrasted the 'slackness of ecclesiastical discipline, drinking in of false doctrines and spreading of erroneous opinions' of England with a Scotland whose efficient Presbyterian court system had 'Satan's kingdom' under 'powerful and awful checks'.[45] For many Presbyterian traditionalists the main problem with the future British parliament was not the threat its Anglican majority would pose to the security of the Kirk, but the incurring of national guilt, in particular by the acceptance, in clear defiance of the Covenanted prohibition on the civil offices of clergymen, of bishops in the British House of Lords.[46]

Presbyterian moderation

By the time of the Union debates, the leadership of the Kirk and a number of Presbyterian pamphleteers were, without openly breaking with Covenanting standards, operating within a more secular constitutionalist idiom of political thought. There had been divisions in the Presbyterian tradition between extremist theocrats and orthodox Covenanters, as in 1648 between the rigid opponents of the Engagement with Charles I in the Second Civil War and its royalist-Covenanting supporters, and throughout the 1650s between Remonstrants, or Protesters, who had tried to exclude the Engagers from public life, and less intolerant Resolutioners.[47] A number of the Presbyterians who joined the Episcopalian Church at the Restoration, including Sharp, were from the Resolutioner wing of the Presbyterian tradition; and so were those nonconformist Presbyterian ministers, led by the Reverend George Hutcheson (1616–74), who accepted the terms of the Indulgence in 1669.[48] Nevertheless, a real division between Covenanting and an orthodox yet compromising Presbyterianism emerges only at the time of the 1679 Covenanter uprising. In the aftermath of the rebellion it was clear that the poor bleeding remnant of Cameronian Covenanters with their outrageous manifestos renouncing allegiance to Charles II, promulgated without the sanction of Presbyterian courts, had alienated the mainstream of

[45] [James Hodges], *The Rights and Interests of the two British Monarchies . . . Treatise III* (London, 1706), p. 49. See also M. Hunter, '"Aikenhead the atheist": the context and consequences of articulate religion in the late seventeenth century', in M. Hunter and D. Wootton (eds.), *Atheism from the Reformation to the Enlightenment* (Oxford, 1992), p. 239.

[46] Webster, *Lawful Prejudices*, p. 4; Robert Wyllie, *A Letter from a member of the Commission of the late General Assembly to a Minister in the Country concerning present dangers* (Edinburgh, 1707), p. 4.

[47] Hopkirk, 'Accommodation movements', p. 76.

[48] Hew Scott, *Fasti Ecclesiae Scoticanae*, new edn, 7 vols. (Edinburgh, 1915–28), III, p. 99.

nonconformity.[49] By 1687 the bulk of the Presbyterian mainstream had come out of the cold to accept James VII's Second Indulgence of that year, despite its erastian basis.[50] The establishment of 1690, although formed around the deprived Antediluvians of 1662, and hostile to latitude and toleration, was none the less unburdened of the most extreme Covenanters, and since it was founded on an erastian compromise, its leaders were prepared to trim some principles for power.

William II and III (1650–1702), a *politique* whose political and strategic priorities rendered him keen to unite as many Scots as possible in a broad-based national church, and who was aware of the historical argument for an original Knoxian Reformation in Scotland by superintendents, was reluctant to establish a narrow Presbyterian Kirk. However, the nonjuring intransigence of the bishops and the uncertain flux of war and politics in the summer of 1690 pressured a reluctant William into accepting a Presbyterian establishment.[51] Nevertheless, he would not accept a *ius divinum* establishment, and the formula 'the only government of Christ's church in this kingdom' was rejected for: 'the government of the church in this kingdom established by law'.[52] In his address to the first General Assembly of the new Kirk in October 1690, William made it clear that he would have no truck with presbyterian extremism; the Kirk was on probation, and he would not stand for 'irregular passions' from any ecclesiastical party.[53] In the early 1690s William kept up sufficient pressure on the Kirk to comprehend loyal former Episcopalians for kirkmen to remain aware of the precarious standing of their establishment.[54] In 1697 a worried General Assembly passed the Barrier Act by which any changes in the government, doctrine or worship of the Kirk had first to be approved by her local presbytery courts, thus 'preventing any sudden alteration or innovation, or other prejudice to the church'.[55] From 1702 Queen Anne, whose commitment to episcopacy was well known, posed perhaps an even greater threat to the Kirk establishment.

Such pressures produced a change of tone in the arguments of several influential kirkmen in the post-Revolution era, and laid the groundwork for the Kirk's grudging acceptance of the unpropitious incorporating

[49] For Cameronian manifestos, see Donaldson (ed.), *Documents*, pp. 239–43.

[50] I.B. Cowan, *The Scottish Covenanters 1660–1688* (London, 1976), pp. 130–1.

[51] J. Israel, 'William III and Toleration', in O. Grell, J. Israel and N. Tyacke (eds.), *From Persecution to Toleration* (Oxford, 1991).

[52] William to Melville, 22 May 1690, *Leven and Melville Papers*, p. 437.

[53] *Acts of the General Assembly of the Church of Scotland, 1638–1842* (Edinburgh, 1843), p. 222.

[54] A. Drummond and J. Bulloch, *The Scottish Church 1688–1843* (Edinburgh, 1973), pp. 7, 15; T. Maxwell, 'The Presbyterian–Episcopalian controversy in Scotland from the Revolution settlement till the accession of George I'; PhD thesis, University of Edinburgh, 1954, pp. 1–9, 48, 51.

[55] *Acts of the General Assembly*, pp. 260–1.

Union of 1707 as a political necessity. Without making explicit concessions, and while still fighting a bitter pamphlet war against the many deprived Episcopalians keen to win over elite opinion in Scotland and England against the unstable Presbyterian establishment, these Presbyterians tried to distance themselves from the radicalism, rebellions, assassinations and extremist Covenanting of their heritage.

The new breed of apologists came from different branches of the Presbyterian tradition. The Reverend Gilbert Rule (?1629–1701), who became the Principal of Edinburgh University in 1690, was a former field preacher who had been imprisoned on the Bass Rock. The Reverend Thomas Forrester (?1635–1706) had been admitted as a minister under the Episcopalian regime in 1664, but had later renounced episcopacy to become a nonconformist field preacher; after the Revolution he became a professor at St Andrews. The Reverend William Carstares (1649–1715) was the son of a Remonstrant minister and had spent most of the Restoration era in exile in the United Provinces, where he had learnt as an intimate of William's court the importance of expediency in politics. The Reverend George Meldrum (?1635–1709) was raised in the north-east and became a Presbyterian minister at Aberdeen in 1658. After an initial suspension at the Restoration, he complied with the new regime, accepting Episcopacy as far as it was consistent with presbyteries and synods, but was deprived again in 1681 after refusing the Test. Meldrum was admitted to a charge in Ayrshire under the Indulgence of 1687. After the Revolution he became the Moderator of the General Assembly twice, in 1698 and 1703, despite his equivocal past. Meldrum's nephew, Francis Grant (*c.*1660–1726) was an important pamphleteer during the Union debates, advancing a moderate erastian Presbyterian case. The Reverend David Williamson, who became moderator in 1702, had been deprived in 1662, but was of moderate inclinations and held the Cameronians in low esteem. These men did not form a coherent party in the Kirk, nor were they of equal degrees of moderation. However, in their published works and political practice they helped to lower the temperature of Presbyterianism.[56]

Rule and Forrester were prominent in debates with Episcopalians on the subject of church government. Neither was prepared to concede the

[56] For the Presbyterian moderates mentioned, see J. Warrick, *The Moderators of the Church of Scotland from 1690 to 1740* (Edinburgh and London, 1913), pp. 94–5, 103, 140, 145–6; Maxwell, 'Presbyterian–Episcopalian controversy', p. 352; Drummond and Bulloch, *Scottish Church 1688–1843*, pp. 1–2, 9, 12, 20–1; A.I. Dunlop, *William Carstares and the Kirk by Law Established* (Edinburgh, 1967); Scott, *Fasti*, I, pp. 39–40, 66–7, 96, 139–40; IV, p. 296. But see also David Williamson, *Scotland's Sin, Danger, and Duty, Faithfully Represented In a Sermon Preach'd at the West-Kirk, August 23d, 1696* (Edinburgh, 1720) for the limits to their moderation; note also in the case of Williamson that there was no inevitable link between moderation and unionism – see Maxwell, 'Presbyterian–Episcopalian controversy', p. 137.

divine right of Presbytery (though the recent research of Spurr on English Restoration ecclesiology indicates that *ius divinum* was a much vaguer concept and covered a wider spectrum of ecclesiastical commitment than has previously been thought).[57] Yet Forrester and Rule did, by existing Presbyterian standards, clearly indicate a disposition to moderation. Forrester admitted that Christ 'did not forbid all imparity and jurisdiction among church officers'.[58] To counter the charge that the Presbyterian Kirk was a dangerous democracy incompatible with monarchy and the social hierarchy, Forrester declared: 'we own and maintain a beautiful subordination, both of officers and church government'.[59] Forrester conceded that exceptional circumstances had permitted a *ius divinum* hierarchy in the early church of twelve apostles ruling over seventy disciples; but these apostles had been 'extraordinary expired messengers' and their authority had only been intended 'for modelling churches as yet *in fieri*', and could not be used to justify an apostolic succession.[60] Although Rule had attacked the indifferentist ecclesiology of the English theologian Edward Stillingfleet, he was keen to differentiate the Scottish Kirk from the extremism of the Cameronians, and to strike a pose of moderation. Rule offered an explicit defence of the Kirk as a civil religion, showing how presbyterian ecclesiology more clearly regulated the bounds of the Church than episcopacy, by forbidding clergy to interfere in the workings of the state.[61]

The use of arguments for presbytery culled from patristics and ancient Scottish history made presbyterian ecclesiology appear less threatening, especially to Anglicans who remembered the commitment in the Solemn League to extirpate prelacy in England. The argument for a Presbyterian Kirk on the grounds of an ancient Scottish constitution of church government by colleges of proto-presbyterian monks, or Culdees, could be used to suggest a mere particularist claim involving only the Scottish church, and that there was no longer any imperialist intent to reform England as there had been in the 1640s.[62] This was reinforced by a number of presbyterian civil religionists who interpreted the Solemn

[57] J. Spurr, *The Restoration Church of England 1646–1689* (New Haven and London, 1991), pp. 134–7, 141, 151–2.

[58] Thomas Forrester, *The Hierarchical Bishop's Claim to A Divine Right tried at the Scripture-Bar* (Edinburgh, 1699), pt. II, p. 27.

[59] Forrester, *Hierarchical Bishop's Claim*, pt. I, p. 2.

[60] [Forrester], *A Counter-Essay: or a Vindication and Assertion of Calvin and Beza's Presbyterian Judgment and Principles* (Edinburgh, 1692), pp. 47–50, 54; Forrester, *Causa Episcopatus Hierarchici Lucifuga* (Edinburgh, 1706), p. 254.

[61] [Gilbert Rule], *A Modest Answer to Dr. Stillingfleet's Irenicum* (London, 1680); [Rule], *A True Representation of Presbyterian Government* (Edinburgh, 1690).

[62] C. Kidd, 'Scottish Whig historiography and the creation of an Anglo-British identity, 1689–*c.*1800', DPhil thesis, University of Oxford, 1991, pp. 55–80.

League to mean that the Kirk would assist England in the work of reformation only if asked. Williamson declared, 'I will not meddle with the neighbour nation, seeing they are pleased with their government as an easy yoke'.[63] Patristic argument also mellowed Presbyterian ideology because it enabled kirkmen to concede that they were for primitive episcopacy: the ancient Cyprianic *episcopos* bore more resemblance, however, to the modern presbyter than to the modern bishop who claimed to be his direct successor. These historical arguments were articulated in support of what were still *ius divinum* claims, but they drew attention away from the radical universalism which had been so apparent in divine right Presbyterianism when declaimed in the demanding voice of Covenanting.

The implication in Culdaic ancient constitutionalism that Scots Presbyterianism was a particularism whose limited establishment in Scotland would not ignite another war of religion within the British composite monarchy was reinforced by other positions adopted by the moderates. Several Presbyterian commentators indicated their acceptance of the very mild critique of episcopacy in the Claim of Right (1689) of the Scottish Revolution. It was argued that Scotland had a 'national aversion'[64] to prelacy, and that 'Scots soil could never agree with prelatic or erastian domination',[65] the suggestion being that what took place on English soil was irrelevant to Scots Presbyterians.

The gradual trend towards a Scots Presbyterian constitutionalism was evident in the Union debates. Although it tended to be used to advance anti-incorporationist arguments, none the less, by de-emphasising rigid Covenanting standards, it allowed a pragmatic Kirk leadership more ideological room in which to manoeuvre. In addition, it meant that for lay commentators who happened to be committed to the Kirk, there was no intellectual chasm between their kirkmanship and their analyses of other governmental and economic issues in the Union debates.

The Presbyterian debate about Union operated on two theoretical levels – it embraced the uncompromising idiom of the Covenanters, discussed above, as well as a debate about the constitutional status of the Scottish Church. However, there was in practice no neat divide between Covenanting and constitutionalist arguments. Some pamphleteers fused both in their work. Hodges combined a standard jeremiad about the betrayal of the Covenants with a much more sophisticated exploration of Anglo-Scottish relations and the arguments for a confederal as opposed

[63] David Williamson, *A Sermon Preached in Edinburgh at the opening of the General Assembly* (Edinburgh, 1703), p. 51.

[64] *A Farther Vindication of the Present Government of the Church of Scotland* (1691), p. 32.

[65] Williamson, *Sermon* (1703), p. 36.

to an incorporating union.[66] In addition, moderate Presbyterian unionists tried to answer the Covenanting case against incorporation. The Reverend William Adams (1670–?1720) denied that the National Covenant of 1638 had outlawed absolutely the holding of civil office by clergymen, and by extension a union of parliaments resulting in a British legislature where bishops would sit in the upper house. Rather the National Covenant had stopped short of a blanket condemnation, and had conceded its approval of the civil power of clergymen 'if the parliament and Assembly should allow of it, or find it expedient'. Thus the nation would not be perjuring itself by uniting with England in a parliament containing bishops.[67]

In general, though, the Covenanting debate was an exclusive and parochial Presbyterian sideshow; while the constitutionalist arguments of Presbyterians intersected with the larger debate in Anglo-Scottish politics involving lay politicians, Episcopalians and Englishmen. The status of the Presbyterian Kirk and the unusual prospect of a British state founded on two conflicting ecclesiastical constitutions were issues central to the whole discussion of Union. There was a Presbyterian consensus that the Union of the Crowns had also failed to guarantee the interests of the Kirk, and would have to be reformed. However, the preferred solutions seem to have been a confederal union or the acceptance of the Hanoverian succession in Scotland only on the basis of a scheme of limitations, such as Charles I had been forced to concede in 1641.

The experience of a century of the Union of the Crowns had left Scots Presbyterians sceptical of their Kirk's prospects within any arrangement with England which did not include institutional controls for the protection of Presbyterianism. This came to a head before the Union in the toleration debate of 1703. The heated response to the attempts of the court-cavalier alliance to force a toleration for Episcopalians through the Scots Parliament indicated that Presbyterians feared that Episcopacy might be imposed on them by the back door. The failure of the proposals in the Scots Parliament reinforced that body's role as the institutional guardian of Presbyterianism.[68]

Incorporating Union seemed to hold out the prospect of toleration at least and possibly also the restoration of lay patronage and even Presbyterian disestablishment. In addition, the loss of the Scots Parliament meant that there would be little Scots themselves could do even to rectify in the long term the various hostile projects for Episcopalian relief,

[66] Hodges, *Rights and Interests III*.

[67] William Adams, *A letter from the Country containing some Remarks concerning the National Covenant and Solemn League* (Edinburgh, 1707), p. 7.

[68] Riley, *Union*, pp. 49–51; *A three-fold cord for ensuring and securing of Presbytery in Scotland* (1704?).

British ecclesiastical uniformity and more sensible lay control of enthusiastic clergymen being planned by the Kirk's assorted enemies. One federalist author concluded that a multiconfessional state was unworkable, and that there would be an inevitable drive towards religious uniformity. He feared a united parliament would very quickly 'reduce one of these incompatible establishments; which of these will fall is easy to guess'.[69]

There was a keen sense of the constitutional reality of parliamentary sovereignty, and a lack of trust in an Anglican-dominated British parliament. The English Tory members, with their strong commitment to hereditary monarchy and the Church of England, were declared enemies of Presbyterianism and its radical political theology of resistance theory and qualified allegiance. Nor could the English Whigs, who were more sympathetic to dissent, be trusted to support the Kirk. George Ridpath warned that the leading English Whig lords were 'men of no religion or common probity'.[70] Webster went further, claiming that the Kirk could not even trust her English Presbyterian brethren: they subscribed to the latitudinarian principles of Richard Baxter and could be easily drawn into the Church of England in a liberal comprehension scheme. The Kirk would be dependent on an England in which she had no staunch allies.[71]

The Kirk and the imperial crowns debate

This question of trusting English motivations proved to be central to the furore created in the tense atmosphere of Anglo-Scottish relations in the years preceding Union, which arose from historic English claims to an imperial suzerainty over the Kingdom of Scotland and a corresponding metropolitan authority over the Scottish Church. It was far from an antiquarian digression from the Union debates: it provoked a strong reaction in the Scottish Parliament, which voted funding for scholars to vindicate Scotland's *imperium*, and ordered the work of the leading English imperialist theorist, William Atwood (*c.*1650–1712), to be burnt by the public hangman.[72]

The claim that a metropolitan authority over Scotland resided in the Archbishop of York dated from a controversy in the twelfth century when it had led Scottish ecclesiastics to lobby Pope Celestine III for their national church to be declared a '*filia specialis*' of the papacy, as it was in

69 *State of the Controversy betwixt United and Separate Parliaments* (1706), p. 10.

70 Ridpath to Wodrow, 19 April 1706, *Miscellany of the Abbotsford Club* (Edinburgh, 1837), p. 389.

71 Webster, *Lawful Prejudices*, p. 8.

72 Ferguson, 'Imperial crowns'; *The Acts of the Parliaments of Scotland 1124–1707*, 11 vols. (Edinburgh, 1814–75), xi, pp. 85, 203, 221–2.

the bull *Cum universi* of 1192. The issue was exacerbated by Scotland's lack of an Archbishop till the elevation of the see of St Andrews in 1472, an omission which lent credence to the claim that the Scottish Church was not a full province.[73] Although a legacy of the pre-Reformation Catholic church, the issue had not died, and had in fact been revived by the royal policies of ecclesiastical uniformity which followed the Union of the Crowns. During the Jacobean reinstitution of episcopacy in Scotland in 1610, John Spottiswode (1565–1639) had avoided consecration by an English archbishop for fear of reviving an English archiepiscopal claim to an ecclesiastical authority over the whole island of Britain.[74] Later, Anglican ecclesiastical controversialists continued to assert the historic metropolitan and imperial claims of England over the institutions of church and state in Scotland.[75]

The issue erupted in 1704 when Atwood claimed that the imperial authority of the English crown was matched by a pan-Britannic metropolitan authority in the Archbishopric of Canterbury. The 'dependency' of the Scottish Church had meant that 'the bishops of Scotland were to obey the summons of the Archbishop of Canterbury to a national synod', paralleling Atwood's Whiggish imperialist claims about Scottish attendance at pan-Britannic folkmotes.[76] Presbyterians were keenly aware that their differences with the Church of England meant that the metropolitan claim was no idle jurisdictional question, but a real threat to their distinct religious forms. The Presbyterian controversialist James Dalrymple tried to demonstrate that the Scottish Church had always been free by her own inherent right as at different times either a self-governing church or as a body which was directly dependent on Rome.[77]

But it was not simply a Presbyterian issue. Scots Episcopalians, despite the realisation that the metropolitan claim would probably, if realised, benefit them to the detriment of their Presbyterian opponents, were not prepared to concede the autonomy of the Scottish Church to English metropolitan claims. Although the Scots Episcopalian pamphleteering campaign in the years preceding Union dovetailed tactically with the English Tory 'Church in Danger' movement, of which the plight of their northern brethren was a crucial dimension,[78] Scots Episcopalian identity

[73] M. Ash, 'The Church in the reign of Alexander III', in N. Reid (ed.), *Scotland in the Reign of Alexander III 1249–1286* (Edinburgh, 1990), pp. 33, 48 n6.

[74] C. Russell, *The Causes of the English Civil War* (Oxford, 1990), p. 49.

[75] Peter Heylyn, *Cosmographie* (London, 1652), pp. 298, 305–6; William Lloyd, *An Historical Account of Church-Government* (London, 1684), pp. 45–6.

[76] [William Atwood], *The Superiority and Direct Dominion of the Imperial Crown of England . . . Asserted* (1704), p. 541.

[77] James Dalrymple, *Collections concerning the Scottish History preceding the death of King David the First* (Edinburgh, 1705), pp. 301–36.

[78] Maxwell, 'Presbyterian–Episcopalian controversy', p. 10.

remained distinct from that of their English co-religionists and as patriotic as that of Scots Presbyterians. Scots Episcopalians remained committed to an autocephalous church headed by the Archbishop of St Andrews. Sir Robert Sibbald (1641–1722), an Episcopalian patriot who had briefly converted to Catholicism under James VII, argued that Scottish churchmen, before the elevation of St Andrews as an archbishopric, had governed their national church by provincial councils under the supervision of one of the bishops as conservator and that this body under papal licence had issued canons for the Scottish province.[79]

The doubt about whether Scotland was an imperial sovereign kingdom with its own autonomous national church raised fears about the nature of the proposed Union. On the basis of these English claims, a plausible case could be made that the Union was really the reintegration of a dependent Scottish church and state within pan-Britannic English institutions. William Nicolson (1655–1727), an English ecclesiastic and antiquarian hostile to Atwood, felt the need to stress that the commissioners for Union would 'treat as delegates on an equal foot' of two 'independent monarchies' and not 'as proctors and attorneys of a supreme lord of the fee and his vassals'.[80] One optimistic English unionist projected that after full incorporation the Queen would be elevated to the title of Empress; that in future the heir to the throne would be styled the King of England and his younger siblings, the Kings of Scotland and Ireland; and that at the centre of the Empire the see of London would be raised to 'a patriarchal dignity and jurisdiction'. The author also suggested that English divines might attempt 'to complete a union of the British churches at a proper season'.[81] Such insensitive remarks raised for Scots Presbyterians the spectre of their forcible absorption after Union under a British patriarchate resembling the traditional bogey of the English metropolitical claim. Such claims cast a blight over the Union for Scots of all persuasions: '[W]e must choose either to refute these libels, or be thought to confess our subjection. When these are made the preliminaries of the Union allowed to us, we ought well to consider what we do.'[82]

The winning of Union

The Scots Presbyterian moderates did not speak with one voice on Union, nor did they secure its passage in Scotland. Factional realignment

[79] Robert Sibbald, *The Liberty and Independency of the King and Church of Scotland asserted* (1702: Edinburgh, 1704), pt. I, p. 11.

[80] William Nicolson, *Leges Marchiarum* (London, 1705), p. vi.

[81] *The Queen an Empress, And her Three Kingdoms One Empire* (London, 1706), pp. 22–3, 27–31.

[82] Sibbald, *Liberty and Independency*, pt. II, p. 11.

in the Scots Parliament saw to that. Yet the group associated with Rev. William Carstares, denounced by Wodrow as 'modern presbyterians . . . of the court, [who] have got new light',[83] helped to minimise the opposition of the Kirk to Union. They achieved this in large part by devising a formula for the security of the Kirk acceptable to the English Parliament, and also by discountenancing violence and the radical anti-unionism of the southwest during the crucial months of the winter of 1706–7. It was a victory for political pragmatism.

In fact, church government had been excluded from the Treaty lest in England it 'give a handle to the tories, and high-church people, to reflect upon and oppose the treaty in their parliament'.[84] The Presbyterian sympathisers among the Scottish Commissioners for Union had been divided between either following their commission and saying nothing about church government in the draft of Union, and obtaining explicit guarantees in the Treaty for the Kirk.[85] What happened was that the Commissioners chose a strategy of silence, which meant that the Treaty and Act of Union ignored the church issue, but the Kirk itself insisted on guarantees, which were embodied in a separate Act. On 16 October 1706 the Commission of the General Assembly of the Kirk, opposed to the Treaty as it stood, applied to the Scots legislature for additional measures to safeguard the Church of Scotland within the incorporating Union. The Scots Parliament responded with the passage on 12 November of the Act for the Security of the Church of Scotland; this was matched by a similar measure in the English Parliament for the security of the Church of England. These came to be seen as essential parts of the Union agreement.[86] The immediate result in Scotland was to neutralise the institutional leadership of the Kirk, and to strengthen the position of the pragmatic Carstares on the Commission. Presbyterian hostility to the Union continued, but henceforth only the lower local courts of the church, the presbyteries, articulated a coherent anti-unionism, without an institutional voice at the national level. To reinforce this situation Carstares and the Commission urged presbyteries where anti-unionist feelings were running high to 'discountenance and discourage all irregularities and tumults'.[87] This negative inhibitory role was the major

[83] Wodrow to Ridpath, 21 June 1706, *Abbotsford Miscellany*, p. 397.

[84] Stair to Carstares, 26 April 1706, in Joseph McCormick (ed.), *State-Papers and Letters Addressed to William Carstares* (Edinburgh, 1774), p. 751.

[85] *Carstares State-Papers*, p. 750.

[86] W. Ferguson, *Scotland 1689 to the Present* (1968: Edinburgh, 1987), p. 50; Ferguson, *Scotland's Relations with England* (Edinburgh, 1977), p. 253; Donaldson (ed.), *Documents*, pp. 275–7.

[87] *A Letter from the Commission of the General Assembly, sent to the several Presbyteries within this National Church* (6 December, 1706); *A Letter from the Commission of the General Assembly, To the Presbytery of Hamilton* (1706).

contribution of moderate kirkmanship to the achievement of Union.

It was also supplemented by a more positive moderate Presbyterian case for incorporation. Francis Grant, a Presbyterian layman, had advanced in *An Essay for Peace, By Union in Judgement; about Church-Government in Scotland* (Edinburgh, 1703) an argument for ecclesiastical pluralism in Britain on the grounds that presbyterianism should be instituted where it was politically feasible, and that where exceptional circumstances, as in England, made presbyterianism a political impossibility, then episcopacy was a legitimate compromise. At the Union, Grant was to support incorporation as a measure in the best interests of Presbyterianism, which would not be protected in the Union as a mere 'simple' or 'mutable' law, but as a fundamental law of the new incorporated state. Grant's optimism about the fate of the Kirk within the incorporating Union was based on his version of Presbyterian latitude. He argued that so long as the fundamentals of religion, like the principles of justice, were preserved, men could tolerate established differences in the forms of religion and legal procedure among their fellows. Thus, drawing an analogy between minor variations in legal customs and inessentials in religion, he pointed to the way in which state formation had not necessitated the abolition of local customary laws, citing among other examples the tolerated existence within a part of the Scottish kingdom of Scandinavian udal law. Grant also advanced a *politique* case, that making religion unalterable by the Union ought to lead to religious peace. Religious conflicts fizzled out when sects no longer saw the possibility of winning political advantage: '[W]e see abroad, when they despair the subversion of one anothers constitution what calm there is betwixt Protestants and papists, Lutherans and Calvinists.'[88]

There was also a new form of latitude inspired by the international situation of beleaguered Protestant powers on the fringes of Europe struggling to thwart the ambitions for universal monarchy of an aggressively Catholic Louis XIV. Inspired by English pamphlets urging the union of Britain to lead the forces of Protestantism, several Scots, including Presbyterians and anti-incorporationists, began to speak of a common Protestant interest and of the liberties of Europe, a synonym for the balance of power threatened by Bourbon expansion.[89]

[88] Francis Grant, *The Patriot Resolved* (1707), pp. 12–18.

[89] Cromarty, *A Letter from E.C. to E.W. Concerning the Union* (Edinburgh, 1706), p. 3; Seton, *Interest*, pp. 59–62; Grant, *Patriot Resolved*, pp. 15, 17; [Defoe], *A Discourse upon an Union of the two kingdoms of England and Scotland* (London, 1707), pp. 12–13, 21; Peter Paxton, *A Scheme of Union between England and Scotland with advantages to both kingdoms* (London and Edinburgh, 1705), pp. 3–8, 22; [Andrew Brown], *Some Very Weighty and Seasonable Considerations* (1703), p. 4.

Despite Levack's argument that the issue of religious union became so contentious in the course of the seventeenth century that the ideal of British union became 'secularized',[90] religion was not peripheral to the Union of 1707. Contemporaries were not blinded to the unprecedented nature of an incorporated multiconfessional state by the conspiracy of silence on the subject of religion in the Treaty negotiated by the Commissioners for Union. The practical consequence was the Presbyterian demand for the Treaty to be complemented by the Act for the Security of the Kirk – at the very least. This measure of security was a qualified success: a Presbyterian establishment was preserved in Scotland, but quickly modified in the British Parliament during the Tory regime of 1710–14 by legislation for the restoration of lay patronage and a toleration for Episcopalians.[91]

Yet the role of religious moderation in its different forms had also been vital in creating an atmosphere in which the elites of Scotland and England could contemplate a Union whose very foundation was a Protestant indifference in the sphere of church government. A loud and uncompromising Covenanting voice was still heard during the Union debates, but its shrill dogmatism no longer drowned out a Presbyterian constitutionalism in which many commentators from both incorporationist and limitationist-federalist positions discussed the best way to protect the interests of the Kirk. For all moderates north and south of the border, the multiconfessional experiment combined with a united lay-dominated Parliament held out the prospect of ending the violence of the British wars of religion of the seventeenth century.

[90] B. Levack, *The Formation of the British State* (Oxford, 1987), p. 135.
[91] Ferguson, *Scotland 1689 to the Present*, pp. 59, 110–11.

Part III
THE ISSUES OF SOVEREIGNTY

7

PROTESTANT THEOLOGIES, LIMITED SOVEREIGNTIES: NATURAL LAW AND CONDITIONS OF UNION IN THE GERMAN EMPIRE, THE NETHERLANDS AND GREAT BRITAIN

JAMES MOORE AND

MICHAEL SILVERTHORNE

To discover the conditions and the constitutional arrangements which have persuaded men of different states and nations to unite in peaceful, prosperous and powerful unions is an undertaking which has taxed the imagination and the patience of legislators, jurists and philosophers over the centuries. In Europe, in the late seventeenth and early eighteenth centuries, there were different challenges of this kind in the German Empire, the Netherlands and Great Britain. These countries were quite unlike one another in their constitutional arrangements and conditions of life. The German Empire was a cluster of unstable and unequal territorial states. The Netherlands was a confederacy of almost sovereign provinces. Great Britain was a kingdom in which two previously sovereign parliaments had agreed to unite on certain conditions. Political systems as dissimilar as these do not present, at first glance, a promising prospect for comparative study. There was, however, a tradition of philosophical speculation which linked these experiences of union in a common scholarly pursuit. For these empires and unions were regarded as illustrative, in their different ways, of principles which followed from the elements of universal or natural jurisprudence. Each of these political systems had been made a subject of critical scrutiny by the most distinguished natural law theorist of his country at that time: Samuel Pufendorf, in Germany, Ulrik Huber, in the Netherlands, and Gershom Carmichael, in Great Britain.

Samuel Pufendorf (1632–94) and Ulrik Huber (1636–96) were contemporaries; the first editions of their comprehensive treaties of natural law were published in 1672;[1] both wrote in response to problems posed by their predecessors in the early modern natural law tradition, Hugo Grotius and Thomas Hobbes. Gershom Carmichael (1672–1729) belonged to a later generation; his judgement concerning the conditions of union of the Parliaments of Scotland and England was contained in his commentary on the natural law system of Pufendorf;[2] it was a commentary written in the light of the theological and political ideas of Ulrik Huber, among others.

Pufendorf, Huber and Carmichael were all devout Protestants, a circumstance of some importance for an understanding of their natural law theories and their ideas concerning the conditions of union in their respective commonwealths. Whatever may have been the intentions of certain writers in this tradition (of Hobbes, for example), with respect to natural and revealed religion, it was no part of Pufendorf's or Huber's or Carmichael's design to propose natural law theories which were in opposition to or which contradicted their Christian beliefs. Their religious convictions were significantly different from one another: Pufendorf was, throughout his life, a devout Lutheran; Huber was a member of the Dutch Reformed Church; Carmichael belonged to the Presbyterian Church of Scotland. Their understandings of the relation between man and God, of the natural condition of mankind, of the source of obligation and of rights may all be made more intelligible when examined in the light of the Protestant theologies to which they subscribed. Their respective theological convictions may also contribute to a better appreciation of their ideas on the subject of political union.

The most important condition of union of states and nations, in the minds of all three natural jurists, was a common understanding or agreement that sovereign power should be limited. Pufendorf thought sovereigns were limited in their power by the end of government, by their obligation to promote sociality or life in society. This obligation took on particular significance in his delineation of the conditions of a peaceful and prosperous union in the German Empire. Huber held that the manner in which sovereigns are instituted or accredited implied limitations on their power. He described the general nature of these limitations in the fundamental laws of the Netherlands and their specific application in his

[1] Samuel Pufendorf, *De Jure Naturae et Gentium* (1672): references are to the English translation by Basil Kennett, *Of the Law of Nature and Nations . . . to which are added all the large notes of Mr. Barbeyrac*, 4th edn (London, 1729). Ulricus Huber, *De Jure Civitatis* (1672): references are to the third edition: Ulrici Huberi, *De Jure Civitatis. Libri Tres. Novam Juris Publici Universalis disciplinam continentes.* (Franequerae, 1694).

[2] S. Puffendorfii, *De Officio Hominis et Civis, juxta Legem Naturalem, Libri Duo. Supplementis et Observationibus in Academicae Iuventutis usum auxit et illustravit Gerschomus Carmichael* (1718), 2nd edn (Edinburgh, 1724).

own state or province, Friesland. Carmichael contended that sovereigns inspire a sense of obligation in their subjects when they acknowledge and exercise limitations on their power. His natural law arguments reinforced demands made by his fellow Scots, on other grounds, for limitations on the powers of the recently united parliament of Great Britain.

I

Our understanding of Pufendorf's natural jurisprudence and its significance in early modern moral and political philosophy has undergone a substantial revision in the past ten or fifteen years. It is now generally known that Pufendorf's texts on moral philosophy and the law of nature were required reading for university students everywhere in Protestant Europe from the late seventeenth century to the middle of the eighteenth century. The religious bearing of Pufendorf's natural law theories is not as well understood. In a recent study of Pufendorf's theological and historical writings, it is argued that Pufendorf never ceased to be a devout Lutheran, one who sought to remain faithful to the spirit of Luther's own teaching, while repudiating, sometimes vigorously and intemperately, the scholastic or Aristotelian Lutheranism of contemporary German theologians.[3] This image of Pufendorf as an Evangelical Lutheran is consistent with the funeral oration pronounced by his friend, the German Pietist, Jacob Spener.[4] It is also consistent with a revealing description of his project as a natural law theorist, written late in life by Pufendorf himself.

In a letter written to Justus Christoph Schomer in 1690, Pufendorf declared that when he composed his work, *On the Duty of Man and Citizen* (1673), it had been his intention to add a third part to this book, on the duty of a Christian:

> At that time, my plan was to divide the whole of moral doctrine into three parts: on the duty of Man, Citizen and Christian . . . the reason I did not finish this third part on the duty of a Christian, which is the very heart of moral philosophy, was that under the pressure of war I was compelled to change my home and manner of life, being unexpectedly driven from the school to the court, where I had to give up those studies and apply myself to a new kind of activity. But the outline of that doctrine as I then conceived it, has stuck in my mind, which by your leave it is no trouble to include in this letter . . . I would have had to treat of the rigour of the divine law, of perfection under the law and under the gospel, of the worth which accrues

[3] Detlef Döring, *Pufendorf-Studien. Beiträge zur Biographie Samuel von Pufendorfs und zu seiner Entwicklung als Historiker und theologischer Schriftsteller* (Berlin, 1992).

[4] Philipp Jacob Spener, *Leich-Predigten. Sechste Abteilung* (Frankfurt-am-Main, 1696), pp. 218–48.

> to the actions of the faithful from the fact that they are members of Christ . . . And in a special section where the virtues commended to Christians would have been expounded one by one, I would also have to have shown how they promote sociability in the highest and most perfect degree; just as the vices opposed to them totally confound human society. Whence it follows that . . . men will lead the happiest lives in this world, if they carefully observe the moral precepts taught by Christ and the Apostles. At least there would be no quarrels then, no wars and the infinite calamities which are the consequence of wars; but perpetual peace, and an abundance of all things and secure enjoyment.[5]

As Pufendorf recalled the design of his work, in this letter to his friend, he perceived no contradiction between the duty of a man, a citizen and a Christian. He would have demonstrated, instead, if he had finished his work as he had planned, that it was the duty of a Christian to observe the law of nature and the civil law. But a Christian would be more conscientious and more rigorous in his observance of those laws, than one who was not a Christian.

In the Author's Preface to his book *On the Duty of Man and Citizen*, the same idea of Christian duty was clearly enunciated. Natural law, civil law and Holy Scripture or divine law were three distinct disciplines or fields of study; but it would be 'very ignorant to set these disciplines against each other or to imagine any contradiction between them'.[6] In natural jurisprudence, one reasons from the nature of things; in the study of civil law, one examines the laws of particular states: in both cases one abstracts from what is known by revelation. One also abstracts from the motives and intentions of men and citizens; in natural law and in civil law, the concern of the jurist is human conduct or behaviour. It is left to moral theology or to study of the divine law to provide a more searching inquiry into those motives that inspire men to live a good virtuous life. He summed up the contribution of moral theology and Christian duty to the duty of men and citizens by concluding:

> moral theology does most effectively encourage a good quality of civil life, since the Christian virtues too do as much as anything to dispose men's minds to sociality. And, vice versa, if you see anyone engaged in sedition and disrupting civil life, you may safely infer that the Christian religion may be on his lips but has never penetrated to his heart.[7]

[5] Letter from Pufendorf to Justus Christoph Schomer, Berlin, 6 October 1690. This letter, published originally in J.C. Schomer. *Theologia moralis* (Rostock and Leipzig, 1707), is reproduced by Döring, *Pufendorf-Studien*, pp. 188–90.

[6] Samuel Pufendorf, *On the Duty of Man and Citizen According to Natural Law* (1673), ed. James Tully, trans. Michael Silverthorne (Cambridge, 1991), p. 7.

[7] Pufendorf, *On the Duty of Man and Citizen*, p. 9.

Now when Pufendorf wrote that the Christian religion disposes men and citizens to perform their natural and civic duty most effectively, he did not mean that everyone who claimed to be a Christian was equally inclined to be dutiful. Many men and citizens, including some who pretended to be Christians might conform their behaviour with the rules of natural and civil law without any particular inclination to do so. Like Martin Luther, Pufendorf distinguished between true or sincere Christians and others. And, in Pufendorf's mind, as in Luther's, true or sincere Christians were, almost without exception, followers of Luther's theology or were at least, Protestant. It is in this light that one may best understand the basic principles of Pufendorf's natural jurisprudence: his distinction between the divine and human forum, his understanding of the natural condition of mankind and his theory of obligation and rights.

Pufendorf's distinction between the divine and the human forum was a methodical principle. It directed natural and civil lawyers to search for their ideas of legality in sources relevant to those disciplines: in the nature of things and in the laws of particular states, they were to abstract from revealed truths and the findings of moral theology. But we have seen that abstraction from revealed theology did not imply, in Pufendorf's mind, opposition to the truths of revelation; on the contrary, strict or rigorous adherence to Christian revelation, properly understood, complemented and reinforced natural and civil law.

A distinction between the divine and the human, between the kingdom of God and the kingdom of man, was also characteristic of Martin Luther's writings on secular authority or worldly government. It was a distinction which Luther took over from St Augustine, who adapted it from the writings of St Paul. This dichotomy allowed Luther to explain that in the kingdom of God or of the spirit, in a realm inhabited by true Christians, there is piety, love and forgiveness of others; but in the kingdom of man, in secular or worldly kingdoms, most subjects are not true Christians; they are either not Christians at all or they merely pretend to be Christians. In worldly kingdoms, the ruler or sovereign must first be punitive: seditious, unlawful behaviour must be punished; only then could the sovereign and his truly Christian, i.e. Lutheran subjects, enjoy the benefits which follow from Christian virtue.[8]

There was then no inconsistency between Pufendorf's distinction between the divine and human forum and Luther's thinking on the subject of divine and worldly government. Pufendorf's distinction abstracted from true or Lutheran theology so that Pufendorf could focus

[8] Martin Luther, 'Secular authority: to what extent it should be obeyed' (1523), in *Martin Luther: Selections from his Writings*, ed. John Dillenberger (New York, 1961), p. 368.

his attention as a natural jurist on the human forum, or, as Luther had called it, the kingdom of man. His theories of the natural condition of mankind and of obligation are consistent with the same Protestant theology. Pufendorf's description of the natural state of mankind as a condition of poverty, weakness and malice was a characterisation of human life considered apart from society. It was an account which was strongly indebted to the Epicurean tradition, to the writings of Lucretius, Gassendi and Hobbes.[9] It was also a description of the natural state of man considered in abstraction from God and the benefit of divine grace. It was not a morally or theologically neutral account. It assumed the fall of man and the presence of sinful or evil desires in human nature:

> natural law is not at all in conflict with the dogmas of true theology; it simply abstracts from certain theological dogmas which cannot be investigated by reason alone. Hence it is also obvious that man must now be regarded by the discipline of natural law as one whose nature has been corrupted and thus as an animal seething with evil desires.[10]

Nothing could have been further from his mind, he told his Lutheran scholastic critics, than to have supposed that human nature was naturally in a state of innocence, such as Adam is believed to have enjoyed before the fall. Natural law assumes that human nature is fallen; it does not explain how the fall of man occurred; for an account of that occurrence, one must turn to moral theology and revelation; natural law takes the fall of man as a given, and builds upon that assumption.[11]

How then do men and citizens become obliged? Two ingredients must always be present in Pufendorf's view for men to be obliged: there must be a rule or law imposed by a superior who has the power to punish subjects who disobey the law; and, subjects must derive a benefit from their obedience.[12] The same considerations were made by Luther, in his account of the divine law and the manner in which that law was supplemented by the Gospel. God's law was punitive, as applied to sinners; but obedience to or compliance with the law made it possible to

[9] The Epicurean dimension of Pufendorf's natural law theories has been presented persuasively by Fiametta Palladini, *Samuel Pufendorf Discepolo di Hobbes. Per una reinterpretazione del giusnaturalismo moderno* (Bologna, 1990). See also the fine edition and translation of Samuel Pufendorf's *On the Natural State of Men*, by Michael Seidler (Lewiston, NY, 1990).

[10] *On the Duty of Man and Citizen*, p. 10.

[11] Samuel Pufendorf, *Eris Scandica qua Adversus Libros De Jure Naturae et Gentium Objecta Diluuntur* (Frankfurt-am-Main, 1706), 'Apologia pro se et suo Libro', sections 11 and 12, pp. 17–19.

[12] Samuel Pufendorf, *Of the Law of Nature and Nations* (1729), I, VI, V ff. and XII, pp. 60, 67 and *On the Duty of Man and Citizen*, I, 2, 5, p. 28.

enjoy the benefits of the atonement made by Christ for human sins.[13] Pufendorf's natural law theory of obligation assigned a similar role to God as legislator of the law of nature. In our natural or fallen condition we live in misery; the remedy for this natural condition is the law of nature, imposed by a superior power, God, who punishes those who transgress the law of nature; the benefits of social living are conferred by God on those who observe the natural law.

Just as we are obliged as human beings to God by the law of nature and the benefits which follow from it, we are obliged as citizens to sovereigns, the rulers of civil states or commonwealths. As citizens, we are obliged by an original contract or agreement, made expressly or tacitly, to live in society, under a government which enjoys sovereign power. By sovereign power, Pufendorf meant that governments must have the power to punish uncivil or unsociable behaviour, and they must also have the power to confer the benefits of peace and prosperity upon their subjects: these were the attributes of sovereign power. In the absence of these characteristic features of sovereignty, governments were unable to govern in a manner consistent with the ends for which states or commonwealths were established. The subjects of such less than sovereign governments remained, accordingly, only imperfectly obliged to their rulers. Sovereign governments, by contrast, generated a perfect obligation; their subjects were obliged to offer no resistance to acts of the sovereign; at worst, and only if no other recourse was available to them, subjects might flee the commonwealth.[14]

But sovereign power was not in every case absolute power. A sovereign might be limited in his powers by the terms of the original contract or agreement. Such limitations might consist of laws or procedures which a sovereign would be obliged to observe in the conduct of his administrations. In addition, a sovereign might be obliged to obtain the consent of the people or their representatives for particular policy initiatives. Sovereigns which are limited in these ways do not cease to be sovereign; they remain sovereigns in respect of their power to promote sociability by punishing uncivil conduct and by providing the benefits of peace and prosperity. Such sovereigns are limited, however, in the manner in which they may exercise their sovereign powers. And Pufendorf considered these limitations self-imposed inasmuch as sovereigns might choose not to subject themselves to these limitations. But, he continued,

[13] Thomas M. McDonough, OP, *The Law and the Gospel in Luther* (Oxford, 1963), pp. 142–5, also J.S. Whale, *The Protestant Tradition: An Essay in Interpretation* (Cambridge, 1959), chapter 3.

[14] *On the Duty of Man and Citizen*, II, 9, 4, pp. 146–7.

> when they have once accepted of the Sovereignty under these Conditions, the solemn Oath by which they engage to observe the Conditions utterly forbids them to use any Means, whether of secret Contrivance or of open Violence, in order to subvert the Laws of the Kingdom and render themselves absolute.[15]

Pufendorf's theory of limited sovereignty, in which sovereigns agree to or assent to limitations upon the manner in which they exercise sovereign power, provoked different responses among his readers. His remarks on this subject were a source of great satisfaction to John Locke's friend, James Tyrrell, who found in Pufendorf's discussion of limited sovereignty reinforcement for his own arguments against Sir Robert Filmer's case for the absolute or patriarchal power of sovereigns. Tyrrell considered the best sovereigns to be those rulers who inspire the respect, esteem and affection of their subjects; absolute sovereigns, as defended by Filmer and by Hobbes, engendered not respect so much as 'slavish dread' in their subjects.[16] Other readers of Pufendorf were puzzled by the difficulty of reconciling Pufendorf's limited sovereignty with his theory of non-resistance to sovereigns. Jean Barbeyrac, the translator and most widely read commentator on Pufendorf's work, wondered how limitations on sovereignty could be enforced, if subjects had no right of resistance when the limits were exceeded?[17] Gershom Carmichael also thought that Pufendorf was inconsistent in his reasoning on the subjects of sovereign power and non-resistance.[18] Both men were thoughtful critics of Pufendorf's work. But Barbeyrac was writing in a tradition which judged resistance to sovereigns on grounds of conscience to be a natural right.[19] And Carmichael had his own reasons, theological and political, for limiting sovereignty and endorsing the rights of self-defence and resistance to sovereigns. Pufendorf's ideas on these subjects become more comprehensible when they are seen to have been inspired like much else in his natural jurisprudence by his own theological convictions, and by his continuing concerns about the disorderly constitution of his native country.

The significance of Pufendorf's study of the German Empire for

15 *Of the Law of Nature and Nations*, VII, VI, IX, p. 695 and *On the Duty of Man and Citizen*, II, 9, 6, p. 147.

16 James Tyrrell, *Patriarcha non Monarcha* . . . (London, 1681). Tyrrell wrote of Pufendorf: 'I know no man that hath writ more clearly of this Subject . . .'. He concluded his text (pp. 239–59) with an extended translation of those sections of Book VII, chapter VI, 7, 8, 9, 10 of *Of the Law of Nature and Nations*, where Pufendorf outlined the characteristics of limited sovereignties.

17 *Of the Law of Nature and Nations*, VII, VIII, V, p. 719 (Barbeyrac's note 2).

18 *De Officio Hominis et Civis . . . auxit et illustravit Gerschomus Carmichael* (1724), II, IX, IV, pp. 404 ff; and below, pp. 000–00.

19 See Tim Hochstrasser, 'Conscience and reason: the natural law theory of Jean Barbeyrac', in *The Historical Journal*, 36 (1993), 289–308.

contemporary historians is that his work, together with other juridical writings of the seventeenth and eighteenth centuries, demonstrated how the Empire could be understood as a judicial system of restraints.[20] Pufendorf's contemporaries found his work provocative and controversial; their reasons for considering his analysis disputable and troubling were many.[21] One of Pufendorf's contentions that particularly aroused his critics was his observation that the German Empire must be considered an irregular body politic, something like a monster: 'Germaniam esse irregulare aliquod corpus, monstro simile.'[22] He meant among other things that the government of the Empire could not be recognised as any one of the normal or typical or regular forms of government. It was certainly not a simple form of government: a monarchy or an aristocracy or a democracy. Nor was it a mixed government, as the Roman Republic was; for there was no orderly distribution of powers among the various governments which made up the Empire.[23] Indeed, it was not an empire at all in any of the usual or accepted senses of the term. There was an Emperor, but he lacked the basic attributes of *imperium* or sovereign power. The Emperor had no power to make or enforce laws; he did not appoint magistrates or punish subjects; he lacked the power to confer substantial benefits upon his subjects. The effective sovereigns of the Empire were the princes, the secular and ecclesiastical nobility, the territorial rulers of the states and free cities. These were the governments that made and enforced laws, that exercised the power of life and death over their subjects. These were rulers who determined the religion of the state, who levied taxes, minted money and generally provided for the peace and prosperity of their subjects. How had sovereignty devolved upon the states? A historical explanation was available in the distant German past.

The predecessors of the Emperor, the successors of Charlemagne, had allowed the many lords of the Empire to exercise power over the subjects of their respective domains. Some of these noble lords had served, since the eleventh century as the electors of the Emperor: they were the

[20] Hanns Gross, *Empire and Sovereignty. A History of the Public Law Literature in the Holy Roman Empire, 1599–1804* (Chicago, 1973), pp. 311–28. See also John G. Gagliardo, *Reich and Nation: The Holy Roman Empire as Idea and Reality, 1763–1806* (Bloomington,1980), p. 41.

[21] A summary of the controversial literature is provided by Fiametta Palladini, in *Discussioni seicentesche su Samuel Pufendorf. Scritti Latini 1663–1700* (Bologna, 1978), pp. 111–62.

[22] *De Statu Imperii Germanici* (1667) cited by Gross, *Empire and Sovereignty*, p. 321. Subsequent references to the *De Statu* will be to *The Present State of Germany. Written in Latin by the Learned Samuel Puffendorff, Under the Name of Severino de Monzambano Veronensis*. Made English and Continued by Edmund Bohun, Esq. (London, 1696).

[23] 'De Republica Irregulari' and 'De Forma Reipublicae Romanae', in *Dissertationes Academicae Selectiores* (Uppsala, 1678), pp. 301–57, 357–404.

Archbishops of Meinz, Trier and Cologne; the King of Bohemia; the Dukes of Saxony and Bavaria; the Marquess of Brandenburg, the Count Palatine of the Rhine. But the relationship between the Electors and the Emperor was not a feudal relationship; it was not that the Emperor conferred benefits, land and jurisdictions, in return for the allegiance of the Electors. It was the Electors who held land and power: the Emperor was expected merely to confirm his Electors in their possessions and their powers.[24] These Electors were merely the most notable of the territorial sovereigns; there were at least thirty-two barons known to Pufendorf, 'and perhaps many others whose Nobility is not to be prejudiced by my silence';[25] there were over twenty free cities, whose sovereignty was contested from time to time by noble rulers, not usually with success.

Pufendorf concluded that the government of the German Empire most closely approximated a system of states.[26] In such systems a number of sovereign states were united, typically, by a perpetually binding treaty or covenant or accord. The best illustrations of systems of this kind were the United Provinces of the Netherlands and the Helvetic Confederacy.[27] But the German Empire did not correspond precisely with these models either; in Germany there was no covenant or constitutional accord which enunciated the terms of union and outlined the powers and jurisdictions of the several states. It was also possible for a system of states to be united in their loyalty to a common monarch: this was the case in Great Britain in the seventeenth century, before 1707, when sovereign parliaments in England and in Scotland owed allegiance to a common monarch. But the difference between the British system of government and the German Empire was that the Emperor was not a sovereign, as the kings and queens of Great Britain were, when they exercised their prerogative powers and when they acted in conjunction with the respective parliaments of the kingdom.[28] The best course for the German Empire, Pufendorf thought, was to secure an agreement or accord among the various sovereigns of Germany, of the kind that pertained in Switzerland and in the Netherlands. He was also acutely aware of the difficulty of introducing a system of this kind in Germany.

The most formidable challenge to a system of states would not be presented by the states themselves; at least not by the greater number of the states. For an agreement could be achieved among them which would

[24] The historical background of these relations is narrated in chapters 1–5 of *The Present State of Germany*. See also Gross, *Empire and Sovereignty*, pp. 318ff.

[25] *The Present State of Germany*, p. 44.

[26] *The Present State of Germany*, p. 154.

[27] *Of the Law of Nature and Nations*, VII, X, XVIII, pp. 682ff.

[28] Samuel Pufendorf, 'De Systematibus Civitatum', in *Dissertationes Academicae Selectiores* (1678), sections 9–12; pp. 228–36.

secure the several states in the territories and powers they already enjoyed. They would be obliged, to be sure, to renounce any claims upon the territories and jurisdictions of other states. And the states would be further obliged to submit disputes among themselves to arbitration by other states. These limitations, albeit self-imposed, on the sovereign powers of the states, would be acceptable, or so Pufendorf believed, to most of the states. The principal objections to the introduction of such a system in Germany would be made not by the states but by the Emperor, who, unlike sovereigns of most states, would be almost certainly reluctant to relinquish the high dignity of the imperial office. An ideal system of states would be presided over by a prince whose powers would be limited 'by certain and accurate Laws in his Administration'.[29] And the powers of such a prince would also be limited by a council or assembly representing the states, which would assume responsibility for 'all foreign affairs which concern the whole body of the Empire'. An ideal prince in a system of states would agree to limitations of this kind; the Emperor, Pufendorf believed, would never agree to the diminution of dignity and curtailment of the imperial powers that a system of states would require. What was to be done? Pufendorf counselled resistance by the states, if a prince in such a system should attempt to assert a direct sovereignty over the subjects of the states: 'it will become the Princes manfully, and with united Hands and Hearts, to oppose and resist such Encroachments'.[30]

Pufendorf's analysis of the disorders of the Empire and his proposed conditions of union provoked a flurry of responses. It is an analysis which prompts a number of questions. Why would the states, or most of them, agree to limitations on their sovereign powers? Why did he suppose that the Emperor would not agree to the limiting conditions proposed, when the imperial powers had already been alienated or conceded for the most part to the states in earlier centuries? And how could he have recommended resistance to the Emperor, when he had maintained that subjects have an obligation of non-resistance to sovereign power? The last question may be answered most directly: the Emperor was not an actual or effective sovereign; accordingly, the obligation of subjects to the Emperor was very imperfect. Moreover, it was not the subjects of the states who were expected to initiate resistance to the Emperor, it was the sovereigns themselves who were to lead the resistance, in defence of their sovereignty. Why then would the same sovereigns be willing to limit their powers, while the Emperor would not? One influential reading of Pufendorf's work on the German Empire has proposed that his suspicion of the ambitions of the Emperor derived from 'the doctrine of interests' that

[29] *The Present State of Germany*, p. 194.

[30] *The Present State of Germany*, p. 195.

pervades his writings. Any prince in a German system of states would put the interest of his own state or principality above the interest of the Empire as a whole.[31] The difficulty with this interpretation is that it was not any possible prince who aroused Pufendorf's suspicions, it was specifically the Emperor who was the object of Pufendorf's concern. He was the most obvious personification or symbol of unity in the Empire, he was also severely disqualified from performance of the limited duties of a prince in a system of states. The problem for Pufendorf appears to have been not the 'interests' of the Emperor, for the same misgiving would apply to the sovereigns of the states: it was the theological persuasion of the Emperor that was the object of his anxieties.

'The Emperor and the rest of the Catholic Princes' had engendered in the German Empire those 'ill Humours which now oppress it'.[32] The oppressive influence of the Roman Catholic religion upon civil life derived from theological doctrines which inspired rulers, both secular and ecclesiastic, to pursue wealth and power for themselves, at the expense of their subjects. All the doctrines and practices of the Catholic religion seemed to conspire to promote the worldly grandeur of Catholic rulers and the Catholic Church. The doctrine that forgiveness of sins depends upon the mediation of priests afforded the Catholic Church an opportunity of increasing its revenues, while impoverishing the laity. The doctrine of good works contributed to the same result: 'The vast Force they ascribe to the Merit of Good Works, as it excites, like a Spur, the ambitions and vain-glorious Piety of Men; so [it] tends to the enriching of the Clergy, and doth most incomparably well agree with the rest of their Theological System'.[33] The mass and confession, the veneration of saints, further reinforced the authority of the clergy. Catholic rulers were prompted accordingly to seek ever greater wealth and power; not only to better serve the Church; but also to maintain the dignity and power of secular authority, which was constantly in danger of being overtaken by the grandeur and authority of the Church. There were good reasons then why Catholic rulers would be unwilling to accept limitations on their powers.

The implications of Protestant theologies for civil goverment were entirely different. Lutheran theology presented no problem at all for good government. As his spokesman put it: 'I could never yet find anything in their Doctrine which was contrary to the Principles of Civil Prudence and Government'.[34] The Lutheran doctrine that sins are forgiven directly by

[31] Friedrich Meinecke, *Machiavellism: The Doctrine of Raison D'Etat And Its Place in Modern History*, trans. Douglas Scott (New Haven, 1957), chapter 9, esp. pp. 231ff.

[32] *The Present State of Germany*, p. 220.

[33] *The Present State of Germany*, p. 208.

[34] *The Present State of Germany*, p. 200.

God permitted the clergy no opportunity to enrich themselves in the performance of their pastoral duties. The Lutheran emphasis on humility, as opposed to good works, provided no encouragement to ambition. The sovereigns of Lutheran subjects had no theologically inspired motive to seek territorial aggrandisement or power either on behalf of the Lutheran churches or in order to compete with them. There was no reason then why the sovereigns of Lutheran states should not have agreed to accept limitations on their powers. And the same considerations applied to Calvinists or the Reformed. They differed from Lutherans mainly in their more democratic form of church government and in their zeal to eradicate all signs of the Catholic liturgy. In other respects, their theological differences with Lutherans were not of great importance. It was the duty of Protestants, and especially their sovereigns 'to have laid these controversies asleep'.[35] This was also the theme of Pufendorf's last work, *Jus Feciale Divinum* (1695), in which, it should be added, his proposals for reconciling Protestants required the Reformed to abandon theological doctrines peculiar to themselves and embrace Lutheran principles on fundamentals: the availability of salvation to all, not merely to the chosen or elect; the ubiquity of Christ; the real presence of Christ in the Eucharist. With respect to liturgical differences with the Reformed, Pufendorf was prepared to abandon the Lutheran practice of exorcism in infant baptisms, but he remained firm on the use of the round wafer in communion and the enjoyment of harmonious music in church. He had no expectation at all, however, that non-Protestants, which is to say, Catholics, would find it possible to agree on any of these matters.[36]

Pufendorf's conditions for union in the German Empire involved an agreement on the part of sovereigns to limit their sovereignties by an accord or covenant in a system of states. It was an agreement which could be achieved more readily among Protestants, Lutheran or Reformed, than by the Emperor or by Catholic sovereigns. His remedy for the problem of union in the German Empire was very much a Protestant remedy; it seems clear that he regarded the Roman Catholic religion as quite simply an obstacle to union in the German Empire. This was no doubt a controversial judgement on Pufendorf's part; it was not an unreflective judgement, however, nor an opinion which belongs to his historical work but which has no connection with his work as a natural law

[35] *The Present State of Germany*, p. 204.

[36] *Jus Feciale Divinum* (1695), trans. as *The Divine Feudal Law: Or, Covenants with Mankind Represented. Together with Means for the Uniting of Protestants. In which also The Principles of the Lutheran Churches are Stated and Defended.* Translated from the Latin by Theophilus Dorrington, Rector of Winresham, in Kent (London: 1703). On differences of doctrine, see pp. 200ff; on liturgical differences, pp. 236ff; on the impossibility of a reconciliation between Protestants and Papists, pp. 41ff.

theorist. On the contrary, Pufendorf's thinking on the subject of German union follows from the elements of his natural jurisprudence, whose principles were designed, all along, it would appear, to be consistent with true Christian or Lutheran or Protestant theology.

II

Unlike the scholarly reputation of Pufendorf, now higher than at any time since the early eighteenth century, Ulrik Huber remains an almost entirely neglected thinker.[37] He lived and taught in the province of Friesland, at the University of Franeker, an institution of some distinction, not only in the Netherlands but in Europe, in the seventeenth century. Descartes fled to Franeker to begin his long exile and to escape from the persecution he feared in France.[38] Religious dissidents of various kinds (such as the Labbadists) found a refuge in Friesland.[39] The University provided a forum for theological controversy, in which Huber freely participated.[40] Huber wrote two major works: *De Jure Civitatis* (1672 and 1694) and *The Jurisprudence of My Time* (*Heedensdaegse Rechtsgeleertheyt*) (1686) and several other monographs on jurisprudence and theology.[41]

Huber's principal concern as a natural jurist was to distinguish the study of natural law and the right ordering of societies from the science of government or the art of ruling in the public interest. Although Grotius had distinguished these two studies very clearly in the Prolegomena to his work *On the Rights of War and Peace*, it was common practice, as in the work of Hobbes, and in some degree in the writings of Pufendorf and of Grotius himself, to confuse natural law with considerations of utility. The most effective way of avoiding this confusion was to trace the principles of natural jurisprudence to their ultimate source or foundation in the relationship between man and God.[42] Huber's understanding of his

[37] See, however, E.H. Kossmann, *Politike Theorie in Het Zeventiende – Eeuwse Nederland* (Amsterdam, 1960), pp. 82–103, and Theo. Veen, *Recht en Nut: Studien over en naar aanleiding van Ulrik Huber (1636–1694)* (Zwolle, 1976).

[38] For an account of Descartes' sojourn in Franeker, see Richard Watson, 'On the Zeedijk', *The Georgia Review*, 43 (1989), pp. 19–32. This article was drawn to our attention by Harry M. Bracken.

[39] Leszek Kolakowski, *Chrétiens sans Église* (traduit du Polanais par Ana Posmer) (Paris, 1969), ch. XI.

[40] An extended review of the theological controversies at Franeker was provided by Jean Le Clerc in the *Bibliotheque Universelle* (1687), pp. 368–435.

[41] References to the *Heedensdaegse Rechtsgeleertheyt* will be to the translation by Percival Gane, *The Jurisprudence of My Time* (Durban: Butterworth and Co. (Africa) Ltd., 1969), 2 volumes. A short bibliography of Huber's principal legal writings is prefaced to this edition, pp. xxi–xxii.

[42] *De Jure Civitatis*, I, I, I, para. 14–22, pp. 3–4.

relationship was much indebted to the dogmatic theology of the Reformed Church. Pufendorf had proposed that the differences between Lutheran and Reformed theology might be easily reconciled or 'put to sleep'. Even a brief consideration of Huber's theological jurisprudence may suggest that the theological gulf between Lutheran and Reformed doctrines was wider than Pufendorf's ecumenical project was designed to lead one to believe.

Reformed theology, like Luther's theology, takes its point of departure from the doctrine or assumption that the natural state or condition of mankind is a sinful or fallen condition. In this condition, we share the human weaknesses of understanding and will power that we have inherited from our first parents.[43] And although our faculties are merely diminished, not extinguished by the fall of man, we would never have had knowledge of the law of nature and the rights and obligations which follow from it, nor the will power to act consistently with this knowledge, if there had not been an atonement or satisfaction made to God for our sins. Huber understood the atonement or satisfaction made by Christ in a manner consistent with a powerful strain in Reformed theology, from at least the beginning of the seventeenth century, as the payment or restitution or satisfaction of a debt.[44] It was the sacrifice made by Christ for our sins that redeemed some, not all, of mankind. And the same sacrifice or atonement permits at least the redeemed or regenerate to understand the divine moral law as a law that obliges one to pay one's debts. This understanding and the attendant ability to act accordingly distinguish those persons in society who conduct themselves in a manner consistent with the law of nature and with a just idea of what it means to be obliged.

The inadequacy of even the most thoughtful juridical expositions of obligation derived from ignorance or neglect of the lesson of the atonement. For jurists were in agreement that the best way to understand the most basic of our obligations was to consider the nature of our obligation to God.[45] Hobbes had understood man's relation to God as submission to the irresistible power of God; but Huber observed that while irresistible power may force one to submit, it cannot of itself generate the idea that one is obliged. Pufendorf was right therefore to think that something must be added to God's irresistible power: he proposed (following Luther) that the benefits God bestows upon us are

[43] *De Jure Civitatis*, I, I, II, para. 1–10, pp. 4–6.

[44] *De Jure Civitatis*, I, IV, VI, 'De Satisfactione Christi', pp. 127–38. See also Heinrich Heppe, *Reformierte Dogmatik* (1861), trans. G.T. Thomson, as *Reformed Dogmatics, set out and illustrated from the sources*. (London, 1950), pp. 468ff.

[45] *De Jure Civitatis*, I, I, II, 1–22, pp. 4–7.

the source of our obligation to Him. But benefits, Huber argued, prompt one only to feel grateful to the benefactor, and while this feeling may enhance a sense of obligation, the obligation itself must rest on a different foundation. Some Reformed theologians (Carmichael, among them, as we will see) believed that God's eminence over all created things provided a better source of our obligation to God; but Huber countered that while eminence inspires in us a profound veneration, it lacks the compelling force of obligation. When we understand our relation to God as the obligation to satisfy or repay a debt, we discover what is missing in these alternate accounts: conviction (in the case of Hobbes) necessity (in the case of Pufendorf) and compelling force (in the case of some of the Reformed). When we are indebted to someone, we are convinced that the debt must be repaid; we believe that such satisfaction is necessary; and we accept the condition that compulsion or force may be applied to effect payment of the debt.[46]

The significance of this disagreement with his contemporaries for Huber's understanding of civil society and sovereign power may be simply stated. It was Huber's view that sinful men, and we are all sinful men, must be punished. Some men know that Christ has accepted this punishment on our behalf. But others, most persons in fact, do not have this knowledge; at least their conduct does not signify that they have such knowledge. And the prevalence of sin in the world obliges at least those men who know that debts must be paid and sins must be punished to institute government for the punishment of sin. And there is no orderly way by which this can be done except by an agreement to establish a civil society (*civitas*) ruled by a sovereign power (*summum imperium*) who has the power to punish sinful subjects.[47]

Huber's understanding of natural law, obligation and the origin of sovereign power owes much to an older tradition of Reformed or Calvinist jurisprudence and political thought. Many of the themes in Huber's work were taken over from such works as the *Vindiciae Contra Tyrannos* and the *Politica Methodice Digesta* of Johannes Althusius.[48] But Huber differed from this tradition in at least one notable respect. It had been the opinion of Althusius, and the Reformed tradition abridged methodically by him, that sovereignty remains with the people, with God's chosen people or elect. It could not be otherwise if the people had entered into a covenant with God, in which the people promised to obey

[46] *De Jure Civitatis*, I, IV, VI, 17ff., pp. 129–39.

[47] *De Jure Civitatis*, I, II, I, 'De Origine Civitatis ex consensu', pp. 28–31.

[48] See *Constitutionalism and Resistance in the Sixteenth Century*, trans. and ed. Julian H. Franklin (New York, 1969), and *The Politics of Johannes Althusius*, trans. and abridged Frederick S. Carney (London, 1965).

the laws of God, and God in turn promised His people a land, and sovereign power in that land. Huber offered a different construction of the origin of societies and sovereign power, in which it is not the people but the government that enjoys sovereign power. For it has been, he alleged, the experience of mankind that people generally behave badly. This was why multitudes or the majority of the people agree or ought to agree that sovereign power should be exercised by a government: of a monarch, or of a council of the nobility or of an assembly composed of representatives of the people. Huber's preference was for a council of the nobility. But whatever the form of government, sovereignty resided in the government; not in the people.[49]

In the Netherlands, as in Switzerland, each province or canton had its own sovereign government. Although the seven provinces of the Netherlands were united by a treaty of union, sovereign power remained with the states. In the state or province of Friesland, any subject who instituted a complaint against the state of Friesland to the States General of the Netherlands was guilty of high treason.[50] Why was it important that the several states retain their sovereign powers? One reason underlined by Huber was that the states understood sovereign power very differently. In Friesland, sovereignty resided in a council of the nobility, who enjoyed entire freedom of debate and action. In Holland, sovereignty was exercised by delegates or deputies of the people who were obliged to speak and act according to the instructions of their constituents.[51] And just as sovereignty was exercised differently in the states, sovereignty was also limited in different ways by the fundamental laws of the states. In Holland, the sovereignty of the state assembly was limited by the obligation of delegates to confer continually with their electors. In Friesland, the elected nobility had no obligation to confer with their constituents, although they were obliged to present themselves for election or re-election every year. But the same noblemen were expected to respect the right of every subject to think and to believe in whatever he understood to be the nature and attributes of God. This was, for Huber, the most fundamental law or limitation on goverment; he thought it should apply to all governments; but the laws of Friesland made liberty of belief particularly effective in that state or province.[52] The reason is consistent with the basic principles of Huber's natural jurisprudence.

In Friesland, the laws distinguished between natural right and utility.

[49] *De Jure Civitatis*, I, II, VI, 12–30, pp. 44–7; *The Jurisprudence of My Time*, IV, V (Vol. II, pp. 14–16); Kossmann, *Politike Theorie*, n42, pp. 91–2.
[50] *The Jurisprudence of My Time*, IV, VI, (Vol. II, p. 21).
[51] *The Jurisprudence of My Time*, IV, VI, (Vol. II, pp. 19–20).
[52] *The Jurisprudence of My Time*, IV, VII (Vol. II, p. 22) and IV, X, (Vol. II, pp. 35 ff).

It was never right to enforce religious belief; for 'no earthly creature or assembly is infallible, nor such that we ought or can resign ourselves to its judgment. Therefore no high authorities can bind a person to believe what a particular church or assemblage of men believes; for all men are liars . . .'[53] The limits on sovereign power regarding religion, did not follow, as with Pufendorf, from the self-imposed limitations practised by true Christians, inspired by the benefit of divine grace; nor did Huber think, like Locke, and the friends of Locke in Holland, that liberty of conscience was a right, analogous to the right of property which had never been transferred by consent to civil magistrates. Huber's respect for the heterodox beliefs of individuals derived from his understanding of the limits of fallen human nature. It was beyond the competence of governments to comprehend the beliefs of subjects; Huber was offering a justification of private heterodoxy or of the invisible church, a justification which may happen to explain why religious dissidents of various kinds found refuge in Friesland. Huber considered it entirely appropriate, on the other hand, for sovereigns to regulate the proceedings of visible churches, insofar as the activities of organised religions adversely affected the public interest. In the course of explaining why the court of Friesland would not punish a bookseller who had sold books of a Socinian persuasion, Huber commented:

> The punishment for heresy can only be determined by the law-giver, according to the degree of disturbance which it causes to the republic; for, so far as the mind is concerned, no man has jurisdiction over it; and as to overt actions, no fixed punishment can be settled for them, except in proportion as an upheaval of the commonwealth is produced, sometimes more and sometimes less.

The bookseller was accordingly acquitted, 'free of cost and penalty'.[54]

What recourse did subjects have against sovereigns who exceeded the limitations on their sovereignty? Huber's answer was that subjects in such cases have a right of resistance. He rejected the opinion of Grotius who thought that the right of resistance appeared to have been withdrawn by Christian revelation.[55] Given Huber's understanding of that revelation, it is clear that obligation derives from indebtedness. Subjects owe no debt to a ruler who has discredited himself by acting in disregard of the limitations of sovereignty (a tyrant); and subjects have no obligation to a sovereign who has never been properly accredited (a usurper). In such cases, subjects may not only resist, they may determine that they have a

[53] *The Jurisprudence of My Time*, IV, X, (Vol. II, p. 37).
[54] *The Jurisprudence of My Time*, IV, XX, (Vol. II, p. 450).
[55] *De Jure Civitatis*, I, IX, III, 32f, p. 257.

new debt to pay, that they have not only a right but an obligation to punish the tyrant or usurper. Huber took some pains to establish that punishment of discredited or unaccredited sovereigns is right and consistent with the law of nature; he left it an open question whether the public interest or utility is always best served by action of this kind.[56] In this matter, as in others, one must distinguish natural law considerations from considerations of utility.

III

Gershom Carmichael perceived himself and his fellow Scottish academics to belong to a European republic of letters. The great achievement of the natural law tradition, following Grotius, was that it made available to students of moral philosophy a compendium of the duties of men and citizens which transcended the boundaries of nations; in natural jurisprudence moral principles were founded upon the nature of man and of things. From the time of Grotius, 'the most erudite and celebrated scholars of Europe, as if aroused by the sound of a trumpet, have vied with one another in the study of this noblest and most useful branch of learning'.[57] He exchanged texts and insights in natural jurisprudence with Jean Barbeyrac of Groningen.[58] He corresponded on problems related to the teaching of natural philosophy with Willem J. van s'Gravesande, of Leiden.[59] But the European scholars to whom he was most profoundly indebted were, together with John Locke, Samuel Pufendorf and Ulrik Huber. His differences with his distinguished predecessors derive from the distinctive theological perspective Carmichael brought to the study of the law of nature.

Pufendorf had set out the principles of natural jurisprudence more logically and more completely than anyone before him. For this reason, his work provided the best syllabus or compendium available for students of moral philosophy. But notwithstanding the merits of his system, Pufendorf's understanding of the relation between God and man, and particularly the method of abstraction which Pufendorf employed to understand that relationship, had led him to controversial conclusions.

[56] *De Jure Civitatis*, I, IX, IV, 'De jure puniendi Tyrannos', pp. 259–63.

[57] S. Puffendorfii, *De Officio Hominis et Civis, Juxta Legem Naturalem, Libri Duo. Supplementis et Observationibus in Academicae Juventutis usum auxit et illustravit Gerschomus Carmichael* (Edinburgh: 1724), 'Address to the reader', p. vi.

[58] Letter from Barbeyrac to Patrick Simson, 3 February 1720. Glasgow University Library, Ms. Murray 660, fol. 1. See also Pufendorf, *Le Droit de la Nature et des Gens*, etc. . . . Traduit du Latin par Jean Barbeyrac (Basle, 1771), I, p. 650, note and *passim*.

[59] J.N.S. Allamand, 'La Vie de Mr. s'Gravesande', prefaced to *Oeuvres Philosophiques et Mathématiques de Mr. G.J. s'Gravesande* (Amsterdam: 1774), pp. xxxiii–xxxiv.

Pufendorf's method of abstraction was revealing in its depiction of the state of nature as a condition abstracted from the conveniences and refinements of life in society. The method of abstraction was not the method which was most conducive to an accurate understanding of the relation between God and mankind.[60] In the case of Pufendorf, this method had led him to distinguish too strictly between the divine and human forum, to the neglect of the former in his natural jurisprudence. Carmichael endeavoured to restore the divine forum to a place of first importance in moral philosophy: 'I have sought to elevate moral science from the human forum to which it has been too much reduced by Pufendorf to the loftier forum of God.'[61] The method he proposed for a better understanding of man's relation to the divine was the method of negation or *via negativa*, a method employed by Reformed scholastics to recognise the incommunicable attributes of God: those qualities of the divinity which cannot be shared with man.[62] Carmichael expatiated upon these attributes peculiar to God (omniscience, omnipotence, aseity or self-createdness) at length, in his theological work, to impress upon the reader the infinite superiority and eminence of God.[63] The distinctiveness of this theological perspective also becomes apparent when it is compared with the work of Ulrik Huber.

Carmichael was not reluctant to profess his indebtedness to Huber's work. He described *De Jure Civitatis* as a 'golden book' and Huber himself as 'much missed in the world of learning'.[64] He advised the reader that his discussion of rights bore obvious resemblances with Huber's presentation.[65] And he appealed to Huber's authority on the subject of the right to resist tyrants or sovereigns who ignore the limitations imposed by natural and fundamental laws.[66] But although both men wrote in the tradition of Reformed theology, their understanding of the relation between God and mankind was quite different. Carmichael was not concerned, as Huber was, with the payment of a debt to God, and with Christ's satisfaction of that debt. He perceived instead in the redemption offered by Jesus the possibility of beatitude or lasting happiness, which could be found only in union with God. Such a union or

[60] *De Officio Hominis et Civis . . . auxit et illustravit Gershomus Carmichael* (1724), II, I, III, pp. 310–11.

[61] *De Officio Hominis et Civis*, pp. xvi–xvii.

[62] Heppe, *Reformed Dogmatics*, n44, ch. V, esp. pp. 60ff.

[63] Gershom Carmichael, *Synopsis Theologiae Naturalis, sive Notitiae, De Existentia, Attributis et Operationibus Summi Numinis, ex ipsa rerum Natura, Studiosae Juventutis usibus accomodata* (Edinburgh, 1729).

[64] *De Officio Hominis et Civis . . . auxit et illustravit Gerschomus Carmichael* (1724), I, XV, XIV, p. 274, n2.

[65] *De Officio Hominis et Civis*, p. xx.

[66] *De Officio Hominis et Civis*, II, IX, IV, pp. 404ff.

complete communication was impossible in the imperfect condition of this life. But the longing for beatitude was characteristic, he thought, of all mankind. And to act in a manner consistent with this reverence for God was to act in accordance with the divine moral law or the law of nature.[67]

The obligations imposed by natural law followed neither from the power to punish nor from the power to confer a benefit nor from recognition of a debt that must be paid. The obligations of men and citizens derived from the reverence or veneration one must feel for God. This reverence could be signified directly to God, but also indirectly, by signs of respect for others who long for lasting happiness.[68] By conducting one's life in this spirit of reverence for God, for others and for oneself, a man or citizen might live in accordance with natural law. And by acting in the same spirit, a man might also generate a sense of obligation in others. This was the source of civic obligation and the origin of societies and of sovereign power.

In order for societies to be formed and governments instituted, some men must act in a manner which generates obligation in others. Such obligation can be prompted only by conduct inspired by a spirit of reverence for God, for others and oneself. Before the advent of societies and civil governments, there were persons who inspired this sense of obligation in others; they were men who acknowledged the right of others to aspire to lasting happiness, and who signified this acknowledgement by permitting others to occupy and use their land for the preservation of themselves and their families.[69] Such persons were typically great landlords; they enjoyed a form of sovereignty over the land (*imperium soli*) which derived from the recognition of all they had obliged. On this social foundation, the origins of civil sovereignty (*imperium civile*) could be traced to an original contract or agreement among men already recognised to enjoy a natural or pre-civil sovereignty. Implicit, then, in the origin of sovereignty was an understanding that sovereignty be exercised in a manner consistent with respect for the rights of others and reverence for God. In Carmichael's mind, this general theory of the origin of sovereignty was consistent with the manner in which sovereignty had been exercised in Scotland in centuries past. His Scottish contemporaries had reasons of their own for insisting upon an understanding of sovereignty that acknowledged limitations upon its exercise.

From the Revolution of 1688 to the Act of Union of 1707, Scottish legislators and publicists had asserted time and again that the form of

[67] *De Officio Hominis et Civis*, Supplementum I, pp. i–xi.

[68] *De Officio Hominis et Civis*, I, II, V, n2, p. 37 and Supplementum II, pp. 53–62.

[69] *De Officio Hominis et Civis*, II, VI, IX, pp. 373–9.

government in Scotland was and had always been a limited monarchy.[70] In the Declaration of the Estates of the Kingdom of Scotland containing the Claim of Right (1689), it was said of King James the Seventh, that he 'did, by the advice of wicked and evil counsellors, invade the fundamental constitution of this Kingdom, and altered it from a legal limited monarchy, to an arbitrary despotic power.'[71] He had also attempted to subvert the Protestant religion and had violated the laws and liberties of the Kingdom of Scotland. The determination of the Parliament of England to settle the succession in the House of Hanover elicited from Scottish politicians a renewal of the demand for limitations.[72] There were different understandings of the term 'limitations' in Scottish political discourse in this period. For some, limitations meant that Scotland must retain a parliament of its own; this argument was substantiated by appeals to an ancient Scottish constitution, to the Presbyterian theory of the Solemn League and Covenant, and to examples drawn from the leagues and federations devised by the ancients.[73] For others, notably Andrew Fletcher of Saltoun, 'limitations' meant the presence in Scotland of a national militia, annual parliaments, voting by ballot, and disqualification of officers of state from any place in the legislature. Fletcher's limitations may be properly described as classical republican, inasmuch as they were designed to permit greater scope for citizens to participate in the military and civic life of the nation.[74] But neither of these limitations would prove to be decisive for the Scottish Commissioners who negotiated the Act of Union. In the event, there would be no Scottish parliament; and thus there would be no distinctively Scottish public space in which civic virtue, as Fletcher conceived it, might be exercised. The limitations specified in An Act for an Union of the Two Kingdoms of England and Scotland reserved instead those 'twin palladia of the Scottish nation', the Protestant Religion with Presbyterian Church Government, and the

[70] W.L. Mathieson, *Scotland and the Union. A History of Scotland from 1695 to 1747* (Glasgow, 1905), ch. 2; William Ferguson, *Scotland's Relations with England: A Survey to 1707* (Edinburgh, 1977), ch. 11.

[71] D. Oswald Dykes, *Source Book of Constitutional History from 1660* (London, 1930), pp. 122ff.

[72] David Daiches, *Scotland and the Union* (London, 1977), p. 65: ' "Limitations" were the great argument among Scottish patriots: the word referred to the purely Scottish terms that would be insisted on before any successor to Queen Anne would be accepted.'

[73] George Ridpath, *Considerations upon the Union of the Two Kingdoms: with an Account of the Methods taken by Ancient and Modern Governments, to effect an Union, without endangering the fundamental Constitutions of the United Countries* (1706).

[74] Andrew Fletcher of Saltoun, *Selected Political Writings and Speeches*, ed. David Daiches (Edinburgh, 1979), pp. 94–9. See also John Robertson, 'Andrew Fletcher's vision of Union', in Roger Mason (ed.), *Scotland and England, 1286–1815* (Edinburgh, 1987), pp. 203–25.

Scottish legal system.[75] 'The Protestant Religion and Presbyterian Church Government' were 'expressly declared to be a fundamental and essential condition of the said Treaty of Union in all Times coming'. To better secure the Protestant religion in the United Kingdom, it was further specified that 'all Papists, and persons marrying Papists, shall be excluded from, and for ever incapable to inherit, possess, or enjoy the Imperial Crown of Great Britain' (Article II). There would be one Parliament of Great Britain (Article III). There would also be freedom of trade and a sharing of rights among all the subjects of the United Kingdom (Article IV). And Scotland would retain the Civil Law and its own system of administering justice.[76] These were the conditions of union which Carmichael had in mind when he presented his natural law arguments for limitations on sovereign power.

Carmichael agreed with contemporaries such as Fletcher that the form of government in Scotland had always been a limited monarchy. He thought it extraordinary that his countryman, George Mackenzie, should have praised the ancient Scots for having chosen absolute monarchy as their form of government. Mackenzie had surely contradicted himself when he derived absolute monarchy from the choice of the people, when he elsewhere discovered its origin in divine ordination and patriarchal right. But whatever Mackenzie might claim, it was never in the power of kings of Scotland, Carmichael claimed, to make laws or impose taxes unless the orders of the kingdom agreed.[77] The kings of Scotland had been limited sovereigns; they were none the less sovereigns; not merely chief magistrates, as they would have been if the republican form of government had prevailed in Scotland. In a government modelled after the Roman and other ancient republics, an act of the prince or of a chief magistrate might be declared null and void by the senate and people. This was not the case in either of the British kingdoms. Indeed, when Pufendorf had described the British form of government in the second half of the seventeenth century as a system of states united under a common monarch, he had recognised that the kings of Great Britain might exercise the power of war and peace and employ the forces of either kingdom to defend and promote the rights of the other. It was not difficult for a system of states of this kind to be consolidated into one united kingdom.[78]

The union of the two kingdoms had provided an opportunity to specify

[75] Hugh Trevor-Roper, 'The Anglo-Scottish Union', in *From Counter-Reformation to Glorious Revolution* (London, 1992), p. 294.

[76] Dykes, *Source Book of Constitutional History*, n73, pp. 144–56.

[77] *De Officio Hominis et Civis . . . auxit et illustravit Gerschomus Carmichael* (1724), II, IX, V, pp. 412–13.

[78] *De Officio Hominis et Civis*, II, VIII, XIV, p. 399.

the traditional limitations on sovereignty more precisely. When two kingdoms unite in one, each may reserve particular rights, which it does not subject to the jurisdiction of the government constituted by the union. Rights which are reserved in this way are not laws which may be abrogated or rescinded by some future act of the sovereign; they form an integral part of the union. And rights which are so reserved cannot be withdrawn by the legislature, even at the request of representatives from that part of the kingdom which had originally sought to have these rights reserved. For those representatives were empowered to determine only those matters which were left to the jurisdiction of the legislature.[79] Those rights, which were reserved by the Scots and the English in the Act of Union remained limiting conditions on the government which neither the Crown nor the Parliament might alter or retract.

It is not surprising then that the limitations or reservations specified in the Act of Union should have been consistent with the principles of Carmichael's natural jurisprudence. He considered a knowledge of Roman or civil law to be indispensable not only for use in Scottish courts of justice but also as an illustration of the principles of the natural law. As he put it,

> the science of natural law will never reach perfection or be culvitated with felicity, until the philosophers know more about the civil law and the jurists know more about philosophy; until, that is, the philosophers recover, or the jurists restore, the garments borrowed from philosophy which at one time added lustre to the attire of Roman jurisprudence.[80]

His natural jurisprudence was designed to provide strong arguments for a sharing of rights (notably the rights of self-defence and of property) and for the sanctity of contracts. The tradition in which Carmichael wrote, the tradition of Grotius, Pufendorf, Locke and Barbeyrac, was a tradition of finding arguments to justify the rights of property and the obligation of promises and contracts; they were arguments which could be used to reinforce Article No. 4 of the Act of Union securing freedom of trade and a communication of rights. But the provisions of the Act of Union which were of most fundamental importance to Carmichael were without doubt the guarantee of the Protestant religion and Presbyterian Church Government (the Preamble and Article XXV) and the disqualification of Catholics or Papists from succeeding to the Crown of Great Britain. It is always legitimate, he wrote, to exclude from the succession anyone who holds opinions which may cause him to govern in a manner that endangers public safety. Among these opinions none are more dangerous

[79] *De Officio Hominis et Civis*, II, IX, VI, p. 415.
[80] *De Officio Hominis et Civis*, pp. xiii–xiv.

than those religious doctrines which subvert the sacred civil rights of citizens and tend to erase any consciousness of obligation among them. He concluded this reflection, by observing that

> It was therefore a salutary counsel, and [one] no less consistent with the principles of universal law, by which the British nations, after excluding all who had surrendered themselves to the Roman Pontificate, conferred the succession of government among themselves on that most illustrious family, pointed out by the finger of Heaven to save them from death, a family which has given us the most serene King George, today happily ruling over us, and which will afford a line of pious Kings which will last, if the prayers of Britain have force, as long as the sun and the moon.[81]

What was to be done if a sovereign ignored or violated the fundamental laws or explicit limitations on the power of the sovereign? We have seen that Pufendorf thought that sovereignty, properly exercised, was self-limiting, that true Christians or Protestants had no motive or reason to exceed their self-imposed limitations. But it was also Pufendorf's view that subjects should bear the severities of harsh government with patience; rather than take arms against their sovereign, subjects should flee the country. Carmichael commented on this opinion at some length. His differences with Pufendorf on this matter were much indebted to the reasoning of Locke and Grotius, qualified, in the case of the latter, by remarks made by Huber. Following Locke, Carmichael held that no man has an unlimited right against another; and whenever a right is exceeded or abused, injury begins, and the injured has a right of resistance. When the injured party is an entire people, who have suffered from an abuse of power by their sovereign, a right of resistance may be exercised by that people.[82]

Who is to judge, Locke had asked, when a government has abused its power or exceeded its limits? His answer was that the people must judge. Carmichael agreed; indeed it was the people who must judge; but he was careful to qualify who should be included in the people.

> When I use the word *people* I mean the citizens who are so called in a more eminent sense, more or less as Pufendorf has described them, i.e. those who by direct consent and agreement entered into with the sovereign himself originally instituted the state and those who have succeeded to the rights they possessed, which relates to their public position . . . not all heads of households qualify. The composition of the citizens, properly so called, is to be gathered from the laws and customs of each state.[83]

What kind of judgement was it reasonable to suppose that a people so

81 *De Officio Hominis et Civis*, II, X, XII, pp. 434–5.
82 *De Officio Hominis et Civis*, II, IX, IV, pp. 404–5.
83 *De Officio Hominis et Civis*, II, IX, IV, p. 406.

constituted could make? It was not always a public declaration made by the people or their representatives in an assembly; under conditions of abuse of power, it might not be possible for the people to assemble. Secondly, it should not be a wilful decision, or lightly taken; there should be clear signs or indications of an abuse of power from the situation itself: 'from the fact that the sovereign has notoriously and persistently exceeded the limits of power conferred upon him, has abused it to bring disaster on the civil society, and has sufficiently revealed his intention of abusing it in future.'[84] It was not necessary that such a sovereign publicly declare his enmity towards his subjects, it was sufficient that the conduct of his administration should indicate a lack of reverence or respect for natural law and for the fundamental laws of the kingdom.

Carmichael's justification of the right to resist sovereigns who violate natural and fundamental laws was inspired, finally, by theological considerations. An abusive or tyrannical sovereign was one whose conduct signified a lack of reverence for God and for God's creatures. Accordingly, he found no contradiction, as Grotius had discovered, between the natural right to defend oneself and one's fellow citizens, and the Christian doctrine that one should suffer wrong rather than resist; like Huber, and also like Locke and Hoadly, Carmichael thought that it was entirely consistent not only with natural law but also with Protestant theology that citizens and Christians should resist abuses of power. But it was also consistent with an appropriate sense of reverence for God and for one's fellow creatures that resistance be itself limited to the exercise of only as much force by subjects as might be required to counter the abuse. Resistance, therefore, would always justify reinforcement of the limitations on sovereign power; subjects might also be justified in ensuring that a particularly abusive sovereign was never again permitted to rule; and a former sovereign might be expected to make reparation to the society and to particular citizens for injuries inflicted upon them. But further punishment of a deposed sovereign, such as the trial and execution of Charles I, conduct unheard of in any age (*ab omni aevo inauditum*) until the seventeenth century, is never consistent with natural law or the respect due to one who had held the office of sovereign.[85] In this respect, Carmichael's theory of punishment of abusive rulers was consistent with Locke's, who thought that the right to punish justified no more than reparation and restraint.

The absence of vindictiveness from Carmichael's theory of punishment affords further evidence of the dissimilarity between Carmichael's

[84] *De Officio Hominis et Civis*, II, IX, IV, p. 407.
[85] *De Officio Hominis et Civis*, II, IX, IV, p. 408.

natural law theory and traditional Calvinist or covenanter political thought. As long as sovereignty was believed to have been communicated by God to His elect or chosen people, it might be presumed to follow that the people would themselves exercise the attributes of sovereignty or rulership. Carmichael's natural law theory, like Locke's, entertained no such belief. It was not sovereignty which the people were expected to exercise, it was judgement: whether natural and fundamental laws were respected by the ruler; whether the natural and civil rights of subjects were secure; whether the government was conducted in a manner consistent with the end of government, with the liberty and prosperity of subjects and commonwealths.

The natural law theories of Pufendorf, Huber and Carmichael are illustrative in their different ways of the conditions which made or (in the case of the German Empire might have made) union possible in their different states or commonwealths. Their arguments were inspired by theological doctrines formulated in the era of the Protestant Reformation. But the themes of their respective arguments for union and for limitations on sovereign power may continue to have relevance for ourselves. In an era of resurgent claims for the sovereignty of separate nations, and the attendant fragmentation of once peaceful, sometimes prosperous, political unions, it may be salutary to be reminded that sovereignty has not always been considered the end of government. As we learn from the natural law theorists of the age of Union, there may be good reasons to limit sovereignty for considerations of more substantial worth: among them, the welfare of subjects, the liberty to hold heterodox opinions and respect for the aspirations of others.

8

AN ELUSIVE SOVEREIGNTY THE COURSE OF THE UNION DEBATE IN SCOTLAND 1698–1707

JOHN ROBERTSON

THE Union of 1707 was the climax of almost constant political upheaval in Scotland following James VII's flight into exile in 1688. Wilfully destabilised by James during the last two years of his reign, the Scottish political community was only further disorientated by the accession of William of Orange. This was not simply due to the virtually immediate mobilisation of Jacobite resistance by Viscount Dundee, or to the continuation of clan feuding in the Highlands. The more fundamental problems were the result of the failure of the Revolution 'Settlement' to establish a stable institutional framework for Scottish political life, and to stem the re-emergence of sharp divisions over the Church. In turn, these failures were exacerbated by the acute economic misfortunes of the mid–1690s. Who should be held responsible for the political failure was and remains disputed: the personal rivalries of the great nobility, the entrenched antagonisms of Presbyterian and Episcopalian clergy, and the arbitrary high-handedness of William and his chosen ministers were all in evidence.[1] But as the politicians squabbled, the Church and the universities were purged and the harvests failed, there was no denying that the 1690s were a dreadful decade for Scotland.

The disorientation of Scottish politics after 1688 was reflected in political thinking.[2] The *Claim of Right* and the accompanying *Articles of Grievances* agreed by the Convention of Estates might in some respects be more radical than their English model, the *Declaration of Right*. But it is unlikely that many of the nobility were comfortable with a rhetoric that

[1] For a powerful recent defence of the political realism of the nobility see, B.P. Lenman, 'The Scottish nobility and the Revolution of 1688–90', in Robert Beddard (ed.), *The Revolutions of 1688* (Oxford, 1991); by contrast, P.W.J. Riley, *King William and the Scottish Politicians* (Edinburgh, 1979), concentrated upon their failings.

[2] Bruce Lenman has written of 'The poverty of political theory in the Scottish Revolution 1688–1690', in Lois G. Schwoerer (ed.), *The Revolution of 1688–1689: Changing Perspectives* (Cambridge, 1992).

was rather too reminiscent of the Covenanters' demands in 1641. For good historical reasons, the nobility associated their own power with the continuity of the Scottish monarchy. This was true not only of committed Jacobites, on whom the purged Episcopalian clergy urged a hard-line theory of indefeasible hereditary right.[3] More fundamentally, the natural royalism of the nobility reflected the almost universal assumption that the dynastic continuity of the Scottish monarchy was central to the nation's political identity. That Scotland's was an 'imperial' crown, independent of any other and of England's in particular, and enjoying the longest recorded direct succession of holders, was accepted by Whigs and Jacobites alike, however much they disagreed about when and how the Scottish people might call a king to account. Without that crown, it was assumed, a Scottish political community could not exist. It was a conviction reinforced by the all too recent experience of the 1650s, when Scotland had effectively been conquered by the regicide Oliver Cromwell, and the Kingdom forcibly incorporated into the Commonwealth of England. Having accepted the *Claim of Right*, William of Orange had no pretence to rule Scotland by conquest; but his actions none the less revealed a disturbingly Cromwellian attitude. From the start, he seems to have regarded Scotland as no more than a troublesome provincial kingdom, the obvious and simple solution to whose problems was a firm hand and a union of parliaments.

In such an unsettled atmosphere, it is not surprising that Scots were acutely sensitive to any threat to the 'sovereignty' of their crown, its independent, 'imperial' status. The English antiquary Thomas Rymer had only to publish a Form of Homage supposed to have been performed by Malcolm III of Scots to Edward the Confessor for George Ridpath, a London-Scottish Presbyterian controversialist, to respond with a translation of Sir Thomas Craig's hitherto unpublished manuscript on Homage, under the title *Scotland's Sovereignty Asserted* (1695). Ridpath's explanation for the publication of a work written 100 years earlier was that he could see no reason why 'Scotsmen should not defend with their pens, what their ancestors maintained so gallantly with their swords'. To fail to respond to this forgery would be an admission of national degeneracy.[4]

[3] B.P. Lenman, 'The Scottish Episcopal clergy and the ideology of Jacobitism', in Evelyn Cruikshanks (ed.), *Ideology and Conspiracy: Aspects of Jacobitism 1689–1759* (Edinburgh 1982).

[4] *Scotland's Sovereignty Asserted. Being a Dispute concerning HOMAGE, against those who maintain that Scotland is a Feu, or Fee-liege of England, and that therefore the King of Scots owes Homage to the King of England . . . By Sir Thomas Craig, Author of the Book De Feudis. Translated from the Latin Manuscript, and a Preface added, with a short account of the Learned Author, and a Confutation of that Homage said to be performed by Malcolm III King of Scotland, to Edward the Confessor.* By Geo[rge] Ridpath, (London, 1695), pp. xii–xiv.

That the Scots had good reason for alarm was borne out by the simultaneous campaign waged by English publicists to assert the dependence of the Kingdom of Ireland upon that of England. Over the next twelve years the historical defence of the 'sovereignty' of the Scottish imperial crown would be taken up by a number of writers and scholars, and the controversy with their English antagonists formed part of the setting in which the union debate unfolded.[5]

By 1700, however, the issue of Scotland's sovereignty had also been posed in a more tangible form, over the matter of Darien. To its begetters, the Darien scheme was not an assertion of sovereignty as such. Its inspiration, as David Armitage has demonstrated in an earlier chapter, was an alternative vision of maritime, commercial empire, in which English merchants would be welcome to participate alongside Scots, but which would not be organised to the exclusive benefit of one metropolitan emporium.[6] What turned the venture into an issue of sovereignty was the success of English efforts to persuade William III, as King of England, to obstruct a scheme of which, as King of Scotland, he had formally approved. Even before the failure of the venture was certain, the author of *A Defence of the Scots Settlement at Darien* (1699), who may have been Lord Belhaven, thought it clear that Scotland's sovereignty had been 'trampled underfoot'. Identifying this sovereignty with the crown of Scotland, he observed that it 'hath alwise been held sacred by our ancestors, who were never sparing of their blood to defend it'.[7] A year later, in *Scotland's Grievances relating to Darien* (1700), Ridpath complained that the treatment of the Scots by the English King and Parliament was a greater invasion of 'our sovereignty and freedom' than any since our betrayal by Baliol.[8]

Such ancestral imprecations expressed real anger, but were barely adequate to a situation in which the territorial sovereignty of the crown within Scotland was not at issue. Although one of the largest individual investors in the Africa Company, Andrew Fletcher of Saltoun had from the first recognised the need to set the Darien venture in a wider context.

[5] William Ferguson, 'Imperial crowns: a neglected facet of the background to the Treaty of Union of 1707', *Scottish Historical Review*, 53 (1974); and now Colin Kidd, *Subverting Scotland's Past. Scottish Whig Historians and the Creation of an Anglo-British Identity* (Cambridge, 1993), pp. 43–50.

[6] David Armitage, 'The Scottish vision of empire: intellectual origins of the Darien Venture', above, ch. 4.

[7] [John Hamilton, Lord Belhaven?], *A Defence of the Scots Settlement at Darien. With an Answer to the Spanish Memorial against it. And Arguments to prove, that it is in the interest of England to join with the Scots, and protect it* (np, 1699). The quotations are from the Dedication to the King, and p. 42.

[8] [George Ridpath], *Scotland's Grievances relating to Darien. Humbly offered to the consideration of the Parliament* (np, 1700).

Support for the venture should be the first concern of the Scottish Parliament, he argued, but this should be accompanied by measures to reduce the standing army and refurbish the militia, to relieve the poor and to improve agriculture – in other words, by practical applications of sovereign authority within Scotland.[9] Simultaneously Fletcher emphasised the common strategic interests of Scotland and England in the face of the impending Spanish Succession crisis, with its threat of a Franco-Spanish universal monarchy; and his scheme for a reformed militia implied that its Scottish component would be subject to a unitary British command. To defeat France, as Ridpath too would soon acknowledge, the Scots and the English needed to reconcile, not enlarge their differences.[10] By 1699 Fletcher was clearly alarmed that the Scots' justified anger with William would turn into general Anglophobia. While in no doubt that the severe treatment of the English in the *Defence of the Scots Settlement at Darien* was justified, he urged Lord Yester to take steps to prevent the work from intensifying popular hostility towards them.[11]

By 1701, however, it was clear that the alteration of the succession in 1688 had resulted in a far more direct threat to the sovereignty of the Scottish crown than that presented by William's partiality towards English imperial interest. For it was now highly likely that William's sister-in-law and heir, the future Queen Anne, would herself have no living heirs. Immediately the Jacobite cause was revitalised, as the exiled Stuart line possessed by far the best hereditary claim to the British thrones. But what in England was an acute political embarassment, in Scotland threatened one of the essential shibboleths of the monarchy, its unbroken dynastic continuity. How was the sovereignty of Scotland's imperial crown to be upheld at the same time as the Jacobite Stuart claim to the throne was denied? The peremptory solution adopted by the English Parliament in 1701, the Act of Settlement which determined that the English throne would pass to the Electress of Hanover and her heirs,

[9] Andrew Fletcher, *Two Discourses concerning the Affairs of Scotland* (Edinburgh, 1698), in *The Political Works of Andrew Fletcher, Esq;* (London, 1732), and in *Andrew Fletcher of Saltoun: Selected Writings and Speeches*, (ed.) D. Daiches, (Edinburgh, 1979).

[10] [Andrew Fletcher], *Discorso delle cose di Spagna, scritto nel mese di Luglio 1698* (Napoli [i.e. Edinburgh], 1698); [Andrew Fletcher], *A Discourse of Government with relation to Militia's*, (Edinburgh, 1698), both in the *Political Works*, but only the latter in the *Selected Writings*. [George Ridpath], *The Great Reasons and Interests Consider'd, Anent the Spanish Monarchy* (np, 1701). On the Scots' awareness of the European context of their predicament, see further: John Robertson, 'Empire, state and union: the Britain of 1707 in its European setting', in Lawrence Stone (ed.), *An Imperial State at War: Britain from 1689 to 1815* (London, 1994), pp. 239–40.

[11] Andrew Fletcher to Lord Yester, London, 23 Sept. 1699, NLS Yester papers, Ms. 7020, ff. 169–70. The concern is also evident in a short pamphlet entitled *A letter from a Gentleman at London to his Friend at Edinburgh* (October 13, 1700), preserved in the Saltoun Papers (and just possibly written by Fletcher himself): NLS Ms 17498, f. 72.

only compounded the problem for the Scots. The Act made no mention of the Scottish – or the Irish – succession: clearly the English simply assumed that the other kingdoms would have no alternative but to follow suit and accept the Hanoverians. In the case of Ireland the assumption was justified: the Irish Parliament in due course accepted the Hanoverian succession, and its accompanying plea for a parliamentary union was easily ignored.[12] The Scots, however, were not to be disposed of so easily.

Already angry over Darien, the Scots were exasperated by the unilateral English attempt to settle the succession. Aware that there would be difficulty, William prompted Anne and the English and Scottish ministers to revive his proposal of a closer union. Authorisation to appoint union commissioners was obtained from both Parliaments (though in the Scottish case from the old Convention of Estates, the legality of whose continuation after Anne's succession was challenged); and talks proceeded intermittently between November 1702 and February 1703. But the support which ministers would have required to carry a treaty through the two Parliaments did not exist; and once elections for a new Scottish Parliament had taken place, it was still clearer that any agreement would be unacceptable. When the new Parliament opened in May 1703, ministers were hoping simply for an Act of the Scottish Parliament to endorse the Hanoverian succession.[13] This Parliament, however, not only proved even less tractable than its predecessor; it contained men willing at last to take the constitutional initiative. It was in the first session of the parliament, over the summer of 1703, that the Union debate properly began, as a group led by Andrew Fletcher sought to re-establish Scotland's sovereignty with a proposal of an alternative to the incorporating union of parliaments offered by the English.

In the remainder of this paper I shall outline the course of the ensuing debate. My first and perhaps most valuable objective is simply to give the debate itself a chronology. It will be seen that there were several distinct phases to the debate, which can be related to major political turning-points, the Acts of Security of 1703 and 1704, the Alien Act of 1705, the negotatiations for the Treaty of Union in the early summer of 1706, and the subsequent passage of the Treaty through the Scottish Parliament in the winter of 1706–7. While I certainly do not suggest that the course of debate explains the outcome of the Union crisis, I shall seek to show how the arguments illuminate the events, and even how they defined and

[12] See Jacqueline R. Hill, 'Ireland without Union: Molyneux and his legacy', below, pp. 288–9.

[13] On the political situation in 1702–3, the negotiations for union, and the Court's plans for the new Parliament, see: P.W.J. Riley, *The Union of England and Scotland* (Manchester, 1978), pp. 33–52, 177–82; William Ferguson, *Scotland's Relations with England: A Survey to 1707* (Edinburgh, 1977), pp. 196–206.

legitimated the options. Arguments may not be a reliable guide to motives;[14] nevertheless, there was a relationship between what was conceptually plausible and what was politically possible. A narrative of the debate thus leads to an interpretation: what is revealed by the exchange of arguments between 1703 and 1707, I shall argue, is a growing recognition of the elusiveness of Scotland's sovereignty. Radical and imaginative as their thinking was, those who would uphold Scotland's sovereignty, and preserve the kingdom from incorporating union, were faced with the frustration of their efforts to identify an institutional framework equal to the challenge. Meanwhile, those who favoured incorporating union weighed Scotland's sovereignty against the prospect of material improvement, internal stability, the maintenance of the balance of Europe and the extension of colonial settlement – in short, against all the apparent benefits of participation in a British empire – and concluded that the sovereignty might safely be transferred, with England's, to a British Parliament.

The quality of the Scottish union debate was due almost entirely to the inspiration of one man, Andrew Fletcher of Saltoun. Fletcher was not the first to discuss the issue directly, nor was he alone in bringing to the debate both intelligence and political knowledge: in varying degress, the same qualities distinguished Lord Belhaven, George Ridpath, James Hodges, William Seton of Pitmedden, George Mackenzie the Earl of Cromarty, Daniel Defoe and Francis Grant. But it was Fletcher's intervention in the new Parliament which gave the debate its initial focus, and an impetus substained until the ratification of the final treaty in 1707.[15]

The Parliament convened for its first session in May 1703 in an atmosphere charged with tension and resentment. Immediately the Court's attempt to manage the proceedings through an alliance of Queensberry's interest and the 'Cavaliers' broke down.[16] Commanding no interest but considerable respect, Fletcher seized the opportunity to explain the real nature of the crisis, and to offer a solution to it. The fundamental problem, he argued in a succession of subsequently published *Speeches*, lay not with England, but within the Scottish

[14] A point laboured by Riley in particular: *The Union of England and Scotland*, *passim*.

[15] Although purporting to restore his political role in the Union crisis to pride of place, the most recent study of Fletcher, P.H. Scott's *Andrew Fletcher and the Treaty of Union* (Edinburgh, 1992), altogether fails to capture his achievement. Unable to think in terms other than those of patriotic good intentions, Scott has no sense of the extent to which Fletcher's political impact depended on his willingness to take extraordinary intellectual risks.

[16] Ferguson, *Scotland's Relations with England*, pp. 206–7, emphasises the charged atmosphere; Riley, *The Union*, pp. 50–63, describes the breakdown of the Court's strategy.

Parliament itself. Removed from a distant court, it was being managed by magnates who made themselves subservient to English interests for their own and their followers' private benefit.

> And what less can be expected, unless we resolve to expect miracles, than that greedy, ambitious and for the most part necessitous men, involved in great debts, burdened with great families, and having titles to support, will lay down their places, rather than comply with an English interest in obedience to the Prince's commands?

No wonder, he observed, in terms whose significance was all too well understood, that Scotland now appeared to the rest of the world to be but a 'conquered province'. Repeatedly during the session he returned to this theme, emphasising that supposed religious divisions merely aggravated the underlying problem of dependence on courtier magnates. His solution was to propose an Act of Security, which (without mentioning the Hanoverians) stipulated that any successor to the imperial crown of Scotland who was also King of England would be subject to specified 'Limitations'. As spelt out by Fletcher, these Limitations would secure the independence of the Scottish parliament from the crown, the dependence of the Scottish administration on the parliament, and the defence of both parliament and administration by arming the 'Fencible' men of the nation.[17]

However persuasive the analysis, this was a bold prescription. Its starting point was a calculated bluff: to propose that Scotland should only accept the same succession as the English under specific limitations was to imply that if these were refused the Scots might proceed to choose a different succession. For a non-Jacobite, the bluff was two-fold: first, that a Protestant succession other than the Hanoverian could be found, and second, that after having had the Scottish king in London for 100 years the English would be prepared to accept a restored and separate Scottish monarchy. Neither eventuality was at all likely. The only identifiable Protestant claimant of the throne was the erratic Duke of Hamilton; as for the English, Lord Treasurer Godolphin sent a clear message to the Earl of Seafield, the Scottish Chancellor, during the session, warning that force would be used to bring the Scots into line if necessary.[18] What might reasonably be anticipated, however, was a reluctance by English ministers

[17] Andrew Fletcher, *Speeches by a Member of the Parliament which began at Edinburgh the 6th of May, 1703* (Edinburgh, 1703), in *Political Works*, pp. 270–306, with quotations on pp. 271, 274, and 'The Act of Security with Limitations' on pp. 281–8; and in *Selected Writings*, pp. 70–83, 86–99, quotations on pp. 70, 71, and Limitations on 74–6.

[18] Godolphin to the Earl of Seafield, 17 July 1703, *Historical Manuscripts Commission*, XIVth Report, Appendix III, *Manuscripts of the Duke of Roxburghe . . . and the Dowager Countess of Seafield* (London, 1894), pp. 198–9.

to divert men and resources away from the war on the continent in order to enforce the Hanoverian succession upon Scotland: to have to withdraw from the War of the Spanish Succession in order to fight a war over the British succession would involve a humiliating loss of status in Europe. To this extent the bluff was calculated, and the omission of any mention of the Hanoverians from the Act of Security skilfully maximised the Scottish Parliament's room for manoevre.

While he bought time over the succession, Fletcher was also advancing a much more substantial argument for shifting the focus of Scotland's sovereignty away from the crown and onto the parliament. The idea that the Estates should share sovereignty with the crown was not, of course, novel: as William Ferguson observed, the key Limitations reproduced the demands of the Covenanting Parliament of 1641 and of the Club in 1689.[19] That the Limitations should be understood as but renewing the Buchananite, Covenanter idea of the ancient Scottish constitution was powerfully argued at the time by George Ridpath, in *An Historical Account of the Ancient Rights and Power of the Parliament of Scotland*, published during 1703. Ridpath had to acknowledge the difficulties caused by a lack of records (which he blamed as much on royal suppression during the Union of the Crowns as on earlier English destruction); he also admitted that Scotland's leaders were much better known for martial feats than for pariliamentary commitment.[20] Nevertheless, Buchanan's *History* provided him with ample evidence that the nearer one approached the original fountains of Scottish government, the stronger one found the streams of liberty. From the outset the monarchy had been an office of trust, sharing with the three estates all the *jura majestatis*, including powers of legislation, taxation, peace and war, and the appointing of officers of law and state. Given the maxim that dominion follows property, Ridpath inferred that the barons and freeholders were truest to the interest of the Kingdom, and argued that they ought to be better represented in the Estates. But he was careful (in this work) not to suggest that sovereignty might lie outside the parliament itself, in the people.[21]

By comparison, Fletcher's own speeches in 1703 gave significantly less encouragement to these associations. Before the Union of the Crowns, indeed, 'no Monarchy in Europe was more limited, nor any people more jealous of liberty than the Scots'. But after that union first the prelatical

[19] Ferguson, *Scotland's Relations with England*, p. 209.

[20] [George Ridpath], *An Historical Account of the Ancient Rights and Power of the Parliament of Scotland* (1703); I have used the edition published in Aberdeen in 1823 and erroneously ascribed to Andrew Fletcher. The page references in this edition are 2–4, 8.

[21] [Ridpath], *Historical Account*, pp. 26–7, 62ff.

and then the Presbyterian parties had exalted the preogative power of the crown, for 'mean and fawning priests of any sort . . . are always disposed to place an absolute power in the prince, if he on his part will gratify their ambition, and by all means support their form of church government'.[22] No less compromised was the record of the Scottish parliament since the Revolution, the freedom won by the abolition of the Lords of the Articles (through which the crown had previously controlled proceedings) having been abused by the magnate politicians, whose penurious ambition Fletcher held responsible for Scotland's present dependence on the English court. If parliament had shared in the defence of Scotland's sovereignty before the Union of the Crowns, it had failed to do so in the seventeenth century. Fletcher's rhetoric might hark back to an ancient constitution, but to implement the Limitations would clearly require major institutional reform as well as an end to sectarian division.[23]

The Limitations presupposed, moreover, that a union of the crowns would continue: the demand that parliament reassume responsibility for Scotland's sovereignty was also, implicitly, a demand to renegotiate the terms of the existing union. Keeping attention focused upon the succession issue, Fletcher did not press this point during the 1703 Parliament; and Ridpath, who had previously urged caution over the negotiations of 1702–3, also declined to pursue it.[24] Those negotiations had, however, prompted James Hodges to write a much fuller treatise on the subject, which he was happy to publish in 1703 as *The Rights and Interests of the two British Monarchies, Inquir'd into, and Clear'd; with a special respect to an United or Separate State*. Carefully defining his terms, Hodges reduced the sense of the word 'union' to two principal heads, Incorporating and Federal. An incorporating union was one in which distinct and independent kingdoms parted with their independence, and so united with another, as to be embodied with it, becoming a part or province of the kingdom with which they united. Thus were united ten of the fourteen kingdoms of Spain, and the seven kingdoms of England. By contrast,

> a Confederate or Federal Union is that whereby distinct, free, and independent Kingdoms, Dominions or States do unite their separate interests into one common interest, for the mutual benefit of both, so far as

[22] Fletcher, *Speeches*, no. III (introducing his Act of Security), *Political Works*, pp. 276–80; *Selected Writings*, pp. 72–4.

[23] For an interpretation of Fletcher's proposals as a Machiavellian *rinnovazione*, see John Robertson 'The Scottish Enlightenment at the limits of the civic tradition', in Istvan Hont and Michael Ignatieff (eds.), *Wealth and Virtue. The Shaping of Political Economy in the Scottish Enlightenment* (Cambridge, 1983), pp. 142–51.

[24] [George Ridpath], *A Discourse upon the Union of Scotland and England. Humbly submitted to the Parliament of Scotland, by a Lover of his Country* (Edinburgh, 5 Oct. 1702).

relates to certain conditions and articles agreed upon betwixt them, retaining in the meantime their several independencies, national distinctions, and the different laws, customs, and government of each.

Hodges admitted, however, that in this federal sense the word union is 'a general term of very large comprehension', applying to all treaties of alliance. He thus acknowledged a whole spectrum of such unions (though without specifying very clearly wherein they differed), ranging from the ancient alliance of Scotland and France, through the union of the states of Holland, the unions of the thirteen Swiss Cantons and the ancient Greek republics, and the federal union of the two sovereign and independent kingdoms of Poland and Lithuania.[25] Quite which model Scotland and England ought to adopt Hodges was for the moment unsure, though he did suggest that the position of the crown ought to be regarded as that of the Stadtholder in the states of Holland, giving the monarchy a circumstantial rather than a fundamental part in the union.[26] The details of a Federal Union of the two Kingdoms he left to a second treatise, which he claimed was already written, but did not publish.[27] Instead, he devoted the remainder of the first *Treatise* to a critique of incorporating union as liable to insuperable difficulties (of which King James's imagining of the monstrosity of uniting two bodies was much the least), and as inconsistent with the rights and liberties of the Scottish people.[28]

The length at which Hodges criticised the case for incorporating union did indicate, however, that it too had its proponents. Not only had the English union commissioners made it clear that this was their preference during the negotiations of 1702–3, it already had able Scottish supporters in William Seton of Pitmedden and the Earl of Cromarty. These based their case on a critique of the status quo very similar to Fletcher's; in 1700 Seton had been imprisoned for the vehemence with which he had denounced the maladministration of the Court party.[29] At the same time,

[25] [James Hodges], *The Rights and Interests of the Two British Monarchies, Inquir'd into, and Clear'd; with a special respect to an United or Separate State. Treatise I, shewing the different Nature of an Incorporating and Federal Union; the Reasons why all Designs of Union have hitherto prov'd unsuccessful; and the Inconsistency of an Union by Incorporation with the Rights, Liberties, National Interests, and Publick Good of Both Kingdoms* (London, 1703), pp. 2–4. [26] [Hodges], *Rights and Interests*, pp. 15–18.

[27] [Hodges], *Rights and Interests*, 'The Preface', in which he informed readers that both treatises had been written before the last meeting of the parliament of Scotland in 1702.

[28] [Hodges], *Rights and Interests*, pp. 19–68, with the reference to James's problem on pp. 21–2. Support came from *Some very Weighty and Seasonable Considerations tending to Dispose, Excite and Qualify the Nation, for the more effectual treating with England in relation to an Union of Confederacy* (1703); attributed to Andrew Brown MD by W.R. and V.B. McLeod, *Anglo-Scottish Tracts 1701–1714: A Descriptive Checklist* (Lawrence, University of Kansas Libraries, 1979), who also date it after 2 November 1703.

[29] [Willam Seton of Pitmedden], *Memorial to the Members of Parliament of the Court Party* [1700]: the work was burnt by the hangman on 16 November 1700.

both Seton and Cromarty articulated a strong sense of opportunity. Could the English as well as the Scots but be made aware of the mutual benefits, the present need to harness the resources of both countries in the war against the Bourbon monarchies made this an excellent moment to secure a closer union. Seton was initially the more ambitious, calling in *The Interest of Scotland, in Three Essays* (1700) for a union of parliaments, peerages, laws and churches (a more open avowal of erastianism than would later be prudent).[30] In *Parainesis Pacifica* (1702), Cromarty had been keen to show that while free trade would give the Scots the advantage of lower costs, there was sufficient mutuality between the two economies for many English interests to benefit too. Anticipating English reluctance to grant the Scots complete freedom of trade, he would however be content for the moment with a perpetual confederation under the same succession.[31]

In the event the parliamentary session of 1703 was adjourned without a clear outcome. Fletcher's detailed Limitations were rejected in July, but in August there were majorities for both an Act of Security and an Act anent Peace and War. The former provided that the succession to the Scottish crown should not be the same as that to the English except on conditions that would secure the honour and independence of the crown, the freedom and power of the parliament, and a free communication of trade; the latter simply laid down that in the event of a common succession the right to declare war would lie in parliament. Only the second of these Acts received (reluctant) royal assent, but the idea of an Act of Security remained very much alive.[32]

Fletcher delivered his own comment on the *impasse* in an open letter, dated 1 December 1703 (but published in 1704), to the young nobles who had supported him during the Parliament, the Marquis of Montrose and the Earls of Rothes, Roxburgh and Haddington: *An Account of a Conversation concerning a Right Regulation of Governments for the common Good of Mankind.*[33] As I have sought to show elsewhere, this most

[30] [William Seton], *The Interest of Scotland in Three Essays* (1700; 2nd edn, London, 1702): 'II The Union of Scotland and England into one Monarchy'.

[31] [George Mackenzie, Earl of Cromarty], *Parainesis Pacifica; or a perswasive to the Union of Britain. By a Person of Quality* (Edinburgh, repr. London, 1702), pp. 6–16, 22. (Cromarty received his earldom in 1703, having previously been Viscount Tarbat.) As Cromarty feared, the English Union commissioners of 1702–3 were most unwilling to concede free trade: Riley, *The Union*, p. 181.

[32] Ferguson, *Scotland's Relations with England*, pp. 209–12.

[33] Andrew Fletcher, *An Account of a Conversation concerning a Right Regulation of Governments for the common Good of Mankind. In a Letter to the Marquiss of Montrose, the Earls of Rothes, Roxburg and Haddington, from London the first day of December, 1703* (Edinburgh, 1704), in both *Political Works* and *Selected Writings*. Publication may have been as late as May or June 1704, when the work is referred to in a letter from Fletcher to Montrose, from Saltoun on 9 June 1704: Scottish Record Office, Montrose Correspondence,

remarkable of Fletcher's writings may be read as a devastating critique of the case for incorporating union, anticipating several arguments which its exponents had yet to air in public, and as a visionary account of how the principle of confederal union might be extended throughout Europe.[34] Read in its specific place in the course of the union debate, however, the work – which was probably Fletcher's last published contribution to the debate – may also be taken as an acknowledgement that the best of the incorporating unionist case was yet to come, and as a characteristically ingenuous admission that however greater its advantages, not even a confederal union could preserve Scotland's sovereignty.

Drawn into a conversation in London with the Earl of Cromarty and two English Tories, Sir Christopher Musgrave and Sir Edward Seymour, Fletcher had been obliged (as he reported) to defend his conduct and proposals in the previous Parliament against Seymour's charge of recklessly framing utopias to mislead the inexperienced. Taking the initiative, Fletcher had then proceeded to expose the weaknesses in the case for incorporation. The economic arguments of Cromarty were countered, with Musgrave's involuntary assistance, from the case of Ireland; and on the constitutional front the proponents of incorporating union were challenged to say what guarantee Scotland would have of the observance of a treaty once there was a single parliament dominated by representatives from England.[35] When he came to expound his alternative idea of confederal union, however, Fletcher frankly acknowledged that this would involve the break up of the existing three Kingdoms of England, Scotland and Ireland into smaller political units. Within Scotland itself, Stirling and Inverness were suggested as the cities around which the territory might be divided. A similar process of division, he suggested, ought to occur across the continent, creating a Europe of confederations.[36]

Although Fletcher was careful to point up the visionary character of his scheme, its implications were hardly reassuring. He clearly assumed that equality between its constituent members was a precondition of a viable confederation. At the same time, he was insistent that within a confederation each constituent city or kingdom would have a distinct sovereignty: the reference to the Achaian League suggested that the United Provinces were his model, and the whole scheme was broadly consistent with the

GD 220/5/75; and in a letter from the Earl of Mar to his wife of 16 June 1704: *Historical Manuscripts Commission, Mar and Kellie Manuscripts* (London, 1904), p. 228.

[34] John Robertson, 'Andrew Fletcher's vision of Union', in R.A. Mason (ed.), *Scotland and England 1286–1815* (Edinburgh, 1987), pp. 212–19.

[35] *Account of a Conversation*, in *Political Works*, pp. 376–422, and *Selected Writings*, pp. 110–27.

[36] *Account of a Conversation*, in *Political Works*, pp. 422–48, and *Selected Writings*, pp. 127–37.

jurists' idea of a strictly confederal 'system of states'.[37] What such consistency entailed, however, was that there was no scope for a division or hierarchy of sovereignty, with some powers accorded to a common or, in the modern sense of the term, 'federal' authority. When coupled with the assumption of equality, this made it all but impossible for Fletcher to accommodate the existing kingdoms of Britain within a confederal union. As Fletcher understood it, a confederal union required a plurality of more or less equal states, and could not be achieved between England and Scotland (or Ireland) as they stood. Even if incorporation was averted, therefore, confederation would not necessarily secure Scotland's sovereignty.

The uncertainty, both about the succession and about the future form of union between the two countries, was to continue throughout 1704 and 1705, exacerbated by reciprocal provocations. The next session of the Scottish Parliament, in July and August 1704, was entrusted by the crown to the New Party, or Squadrone, whose leaders included Rothes and Roxburgh, associates of Fletcher in 1703, and recipients of his *Account of a Conversation*. These now sought compromise, in the form of agreement to the Hanoverian succession in return for conceding to parliament a role in appointment to offices. But compromise was still unacceptable to the Parliament: an Act of Security was once again voted, and since supply was effectively 'tacked' onto it, the crown was at last persuaded to give its assent. What conditions the Scots might make in return for accepting the Hanoverian Succession remained open for negotiation: limitations, free trade and incorporating union were all still in play.[38] The next move came from the English Parliament, which passed 'An Act for the effectual securing the Kingdom of England from the apparent dangers that may arise from several Acts lately passed in the Parliament of Scotland'. Approved by the Crown in March 1705, the Act provided that if the Scots did not settle the succession by 25 December 1705, they would be declared aliens in England, and the import of their coal, cattle and linen prohibited. At the same time the Act offered the Scots fresh negotiations for a union (although English political leaders were as yet far from agreed on whether this was necessary).[39] In Scotland

[37] For the jurists' concept of confederation, see Robertson, 'Empire and Union', above, pp. 26–9. Fletcher's willingness to envisage the fragmenting of the three kingdoms into smaller units may also be compared with the radical Covenanters' political thinking after the Restoration: on these, see Colin Kidd, 'Religious realignment between the Restoration and Union', above, pp. 154–6; but the language in which Fletcher presented his scheme is far removed from that of Althusius.

[38] Riley, *The Union*, pp. 85–6, 96–102; Ferguson, *Scotland's Relations with England*, pp. 216–22. [39] Riley, *The Union*, pp. 121–3.

the Alien Act was taken as a gross provocation. Outwith Parliament the immediate public outcry led, after a travesty of a trial, to the execution of an unfortunate captain and two of the crew of an English merchantman, the *Worcester*. In the longer run, the Act significantly altered the terms of public debate.

At one level, the Alien Act was interpreted as a potential declaration of war. That it might come to that had previously been intimated by ministers;[40] when coupled with the publication in the previous year of William Atwood's *Superiority and Direct Dominion of the Imperial Crown of England over the Crown and Kingdom of Scotland* (1704), the Act was understood to have cleared the way for an English conquest. The threat stirred predictable invocations of the martial ancestors,[41] but it also disconcerted all who were not Jacobites. Since it was clear that there could be no war without the involvement of the exiled Stuarts and the French, thereby enlarging the European conflict into one of the British as well as the Spanish Succession, Presbyterians such as Ridpath and Hodges made haste to acknowledge that war between the two kingdoms was unthinkable, and that a settlement was still possible. At most they warned that should England attempt to impose its will by force, it would have to do so by a standing army, which would threaten England's as well as Scotland's liberty. But at no point did they seriously suggest that Scotland should fight.[42]

There was, however, a second implication of the Alien Act. For if the Scots were to be declared aliens after Christmas 1705, they could not be so now – and therefore should not be treated as aliens under other, existing English legislation such as the Navigation Acts. The Alien Act was, in fact, an admission that the Navigation Acts breached the naturalisation which the Scots were supposed to have been granted as a result of Calvin's Case in 1608. The point had already been argued by

[40] Godolphin subsequently reiterated the threat: to Seafield, 9 August 1705, *HMC*, XIV, App. III, *Roxburghe . . . and Seafield Mss*, p. 207: 'England is not now in the condition it was when Scotland used to make inroads upon us. Wee have the power, and you may give us the will to return those visits . . . '

[41] As for example [William Forbes? or Alexander Penicuik?], *A Pill for Pork-Eaters: or, A Scots Lancet for an English Swelling* (Edinburgh, 1705): the title is its best feature.

[42] [James Hodges], *War betwixt the Two British Kingdoms Consider'd and the dangerous Circumstances of Each with regard thereto lay'd open; by a full view of the Consequences of it on Both Sides. Being Design'd as a Perpetual Standard, for Judging aright of that Event: and for promoting Peace, and Friendly Agreement betwixt them, by Reasonable Concessions from each to each, for the mutual Interest and Good of Both* (London, 1705); [George Ridpath], *The Reducing of Scotland by Arms, and annexing it to England as a Province, considered. With an historical account of the grievances the Scots complain they have suffer'd in their Religion, Liberty and Trade, since the Union of the Crowns; which they assign as the cause of their delay to come into the same succession with England, until they have a previous security against such grievances from time to time* (London, repr. Edinburgh, 1705).

Ridpath in a tract published in 1703: many thousands of Scots, he calculated, had already benefited England and its Plantations, 'the English Empire in America', by moving thither with their labour and capital.[43] As we shall see presently, both Ridpath and Hodges would make the Scots' naturalisation the basis for a significantly new approach to the question of union early in 1706.

In the meantime, the Scottish Parliament was convened again in June 1705 to consider its response to the English ultimatum. In some desperation the court summoned the second Duke of Argyll to manage the business; but the proceedings continued to be confused.[44] On the one hand, Scotland's sovereignty was vigorously reaffirmed. Both Hodges and James Anderson were thanked and rewarded for their writings, the latter for confuting Atwood, whose book was ordered to be burnt.[45] Sovereignty was also implicit in the parliament's consideration of a series of proposals for Scotland's economic improvement, including a Council of Trade, long advocated by William Paterson and now endorsed by Seton, and the credit schemes of Hugh Chamberlen and John Law.[46] But desperation was also apparent among the crown's opponents, and there was a slow, unsteady drift towards compromise. Perhaps significantly, Fletcher's interventions became increasingly erratic. At one point he suggested that Scotland should look to the Prince of Prussia as a successor to Anne, on the ground that this was a Calvinist line where the Hanoverians were Lutheran. Not surprisingly, there was little response: there could be no more candid admission of the bluff involved in threatening to find an alternative to the Hanoverians than the suggestion that the oldest continuously held crown in Europe should be transferred

[43] [George Ridpath], *The Case of Scots-men residing in England and in the English Plantations. Containing an Account of the Reasons in Law, why they look upon themsleves as Entituled to all the Priviledges of the Natives of England. Of the Difficulties they labour under, by a new construction of some late Acts of Parliament . . . and of the Reasons, why they think they are not excluded from the Priviledges of Englishmen by those Acts: And that it is not the Interest of England, they should be so* (Edinburgh, 1703). Attribution to Ridpath by the McLeods, *Anglo-Scottish Tracts*, no. 58.

[44] Ferguson, *Scotland's Relations with England*, pp. 226–31.

[45] A. Boyer, *The History of the Reign of Queen Anne, digested into Annals*, vol. IV (London 1706), p. 52: 'The Parliament of Scotland', 10 August 1705.

[46] Boyer, *Annals*, IV, pp. 40–1, 48–52: 10–13 July, 24 July–9 August, 1705. William Paterson, *Proposals and Reasons for Constituting a Council of Trade* (Edinburgh, 1701); [William Seton], *Some Thoughts, on Ways and Means of making this Nation a gainer in Foreign Commerce; and for Supplying its present Scarcity of Money* (Edinburgh, 1705); [Hugh Chamberlen], *A Few Proposals humbly recommending the Establishment of a Land Credit* (Edinburgh, 1700); [John Law], *Money and Trade Considered, with a Proposal for Supplying the Nation with Money* (Edinburgh, 1705); James Hodges, *Considerations and Proposals, for supplying the present Scarcity of Money, and advancing Trade* (Edinburgh, 1705).

to a dynasty whose royal title was just four years old.[47] On another occasion Fletcher denounced the proposals of Law and Chamberlen as 'gibberish', and then rounded on his erstwhile disciple Roxburgh for accusing him of ill manners. Defying the Commissioner's express orders, Fletcher proceeded to challenge Roxburgh to a duel (only just averted the following dawn).[48] Members were remarkably tolerant of Fletcher's intemperance, but no longer inclined to follow his lead. Sensing that an Act to treat with England would now lead to incorporating union, he tried again to insist on Limitations, only to have his addresses blocked.[49] By the end of August the decision to treat had been taken, and on 1 September the Duke of Hamilton made the fateful motion that nomination of the commissioners be left to the Queen. The political initiative had passed to those favouring incorporation.

It was against this discouraging movement of the political odds that Hodges and Ridpath now attempted to develop a fresh conception of an Anglo-Scottish union. Hodges' *Essay upon the Union, shewing that the subjects of both nations have been, by the Union of the two Crowns, justly intitled to all manner of privileges, which the ensuing Treaty can give them* appears to have been published in April 1706.[50] It opened, once again, with definitions of incorporation, confederacy and conquest. This time, however, Hodges argued that what had existed since the Union of the Crowns was actually an incorporating union, incorporation being entailed in mutual naturalisation. What had undermined that union was precisely the denial of that naturalisation in the Navigation Acts, the matter of Darien and the threatening clauses of the Alien Act – although

[47] *Historical Manuscripts Commission, Portland Papers*, IV, pp. 214–15: [William Greg] to [Robert Harley], 2 August 1705, reporting Fletcher's intervention on 31 July. The Elector Frederick III of Brandenburg-Prussia had had himself crowned as Frederick I, King of Prussia in 1701, following the Emperor's agreement to recognise the title.

[48] The incident was reported by [Mungo Graham of Gorthie] to [the Duke of Montrose], [13 July 1705], SRO GD 220/5/800/13; by [William Greg] to [Robert Harley], 14, 17 July 1705, *HMC Portland Papers*, IV, pp. 207–9; and by the Earl of Mar to his wife, 16 July 1705, *HMC Mar and Kellie*, p. 234.

[49] Boyer, *Annals*, IV, pp. 56–8: 28, 29 August, 1, 4 Sept. 1705.

[50] [James Hodges], *Essay upon the Union, shewing that the Subjects of both Nations have been, by the Union of the Two Crowns, justly Intitled to all manner of Privileges, which the ensuing Treaty can give them. Therefore the work of the Ensuing Treaty is not so much to treat of New Privileges, as to provide for the Security of Old Ones* (London, 1706). Ridpath drew the attention of the Rev. Alexander Wodrow to the pamphlet in a letter from London on 19 April 1706; he endorsed its sentiments as his own, though he thought it the work of a cavalier: 'Correspondence between George Ridpath and the Rev. Robert Wodrow', *Miscellany of the Abbotsford Club*, Vol. I (Edinburgh, 1837), pp. 388–91. Replying, the Rev. Robert Wodrow (Alexander's brother) reported that the Essay was said to be by Mr Hodges, and 'relishes much here': Wodrow to George Serle [i.e. Ridpath], 30 May 1706, in L.W. Sharp (ed.), *Early Letters of Robert Wodrow 1698–1709*, *Scottish History Society*, 3rd Series, 24 (Edinburgh, 1937). pp. 289–92.

the threat itself was an admission that the Scots should be entitled to the rights of natives. All that the forthcoming negotiations need do, therefore, was ensure that the existing incorporating union was strengthened by an agreement over which matters should be determined jointly, and which should be kept apart. The succession, naturalisation, war and peace, and trade and customs ought to be unified; but all other matters should be left to the separate parliaments, with a joint committee to meet beforehand to prepare overtures on matters of common concern.[51]

Ridpath's *Considerations upon the Union of the two Kingdoms* appeared later, perhaps as late as September, but may well have been drafted earlier.[52] Taking as his authorities the major contributors to the union debate of 100 years earlier, Bacon, Doddridge and Craig, Ridpath now sought to show that the Union of the Crowns had been designed according to the model of incorporation adopted by the greatest governments in Europe. Heeding the lesson taught the Romans by the Social War, these governments had made a general act of naturalisation the basis for uniting nations under the same allegiance. Not troubling over modern distinctions between federal and incorporating unions, they had thought it 'an intire and compleat union to all intents and purposes, which secur'd allegiance to the Sovreign with liberty, property and equality of privileges to the subject, without making their country their crime, or a bar to their preferment'.[53] Likening the existing union of England and Scotland to that of Poland and Lithuania, or of the German Empire, Ridpath underlined the extent to which their distinct dominions retained their 'respective sovereignties, constitutions and diets'.[54] He was prepared to envisage that there might be joint meetings of the Scottish and English parliaments to overcome serious disagreements; for the most part, however, he thought that deputations from one to the other, and a common Council of Trade, ought to be sufficient to manage affairs of common interest.[55] In any case, Ridpath no longer maintained that a nation's sovereignty stopped at parliament. The Scottish parliament in particular owed its existence to the rights of the freeholders; and as it had been entrusted by them with the preservation of the government and the

[51] [Hodges], *Essay upon the Union*, pp. 3–30.

[52] [George Ridpath], *Considerations upon the Union of the Two Kingdoms. With an Account of the Methods taken by Ancient and Modern Governments, to effect an Union, without endangering the Fundamental Constitutions of the United Countries* (1706). Dated to September by the McLeods, *Anglo-Scottish Tracts*; in his letter of 19 April to Alexander Wodrow, Ridpath reported that he would himself have written something on the union by the time parliament met: 'Correspondence between George Ridpath and the Rev. Robert Wodrow', pp. 388–91.

[53] [Ridpath], *Considerations upon the Union*, pp. 1–14.

[54] [Ridpath], *Considerations upon the Union*, pp. 36–8.

[55] [Ridpath], *Considerations upon the Union*, pp. 40–51.

property of the subject, the parliament had not the right to surrender these responsibilities without the freeholders' express commission. It was not for the Scottish parliament, in short, to surrender the 'legislature, and decisive judicature, which are Rights of Sovereignty'.[56]

It is possible simply to interpret these arguments as a belated attempt to shore up the Union of the Crowns in order to avert the loss of the Scottish parliament. Given the care which Hodges had previously taken over their definition, the redeployment of the terms 'federal' and 'incorporating' has an appearance of intellectual expediency. Ridpath's observation that unions such as the Polish-Lithuanian had been accepted as 'incorporating' was just – but this was the Polish understanding of the Union of Lublin, and the Scots were in the position of the Lithuanians. At the least, the attempt to argue that distinct sovereignties might be preserved in an incorporating union ran against the grain of the powerful conceptual association built up over the previous two centuries between 'incorporation' and territorial 'empire'.[57] Nevertheless, the arguments of Hodges and Ridpath do demonstrate a willingness to think again, and a new flexibility of conception. No longer bound, as Fletcher seems to have been, to a strict idea of confederation, they were now prepared to consider the distribution of powers between united and separate institutions. Above all, they showed a new awareness of the scope for institutional diversity provided by a common allegiance to one monarch: perhaps the best contemporary comparison is with Molyneux's case for the autonomy of the Irish Parliament under the monarchy.[58]

In the event, there was never an opportunity for this alternative conception of union to become a practical political proposition. Meeting between April and July 1706, the Union Commissioners worked quickly and decisively. Hopes that two treaties, one for a federal, the other for an incorporating union, might be negotiated simultaneously were dashed: the English Commissioners immediately insisted upon an incorporating union of parliaments. In return, however, the English were at last willing to make the offer of free trade unqualified, and to agree to a form of security for the Presbyterian Church of Scotland. A deal was struck to omit the question entirely from the Treaty itself, on the understanding that when the Scottish and English Parliaments came to enact the Treaty, they would

[56] [Ridpath], *Considerations upon the Union*, pp. 54–9.

[57] Robertson, 'Union and Empire', above, pp. 8–16, 19, 34–5.

[58] On Molyneux, see Hill, 'Ireland without Union', below, pp. 284–7; Cromarty criticised the *Considerations upon the Union* together with Molyneux's (newly republished) *Case of Ireland* in *A Friendly Return to a Letter concerning Sir George Mackenzie's and Sir John Nisbet's Observation and Responce on the matter of the Union, Letter Fourth*, (1706), pp. 5–6.

each also enact a separate statute securing, respectively, the Presbyterian Church Government and the Church of England as by Law Established. Detailed hard work, even if only intelligent guess-work, also went into the financial and fiscal clauses which formed the greater part of the Treaty.[59] The outcome was a 'Treaty' (as the 'Articles of Union' were generally known) in which almost all the safeguards were in favour of the Scots. This might well be regarded as an index of the Scottish negotiators' success; it was almost certainly essential to secure the passage of the Treaty through the Scottish Parliament. But the imbalance also carried the adverse implication that Scotland was intrinsically the weaker party.[60]

The Treaty was to be put to the Scottish Parliament first, and its passage was entrusted by the Queen to Queensberry, Argyll and the Old Party; since the Squadrone (the New Party) were likely to be acquiescent, there was some reason to expect it to pass virtually unscathed. Nevertheless, there were still circumstances in which it might come unstuck. Opponents in Parliament might succeed in introducing amendments to the Treaty which would make it unacceptable to the English Parliament, or pressure might build up in the country at large to a level which made withdrawal from the Treaty essential to the restoration of order. To pre-empt these possibilities, the crown and its supporters disposed of a number of resources. Most notoriously, ministers were able to use the crown's patronage, and to exploit the Equivalent as a slush fund, to induce supporters to stay in line. Extra precautions were also taken to prevent or contain disorder, particularly close contact being maintained with Church leaders. In addition to these measures, the Treaty's supporters were obliged to respond, in parliament and in pamphlet, to the fierce criticisms of its opponents: it was with the publication of the Treaty that the Union debate entered its final, climactic phase.[61]

Publication of the Treaty gave those opposed to an union of parliaments a clear target, although it also meant that constructive thinking about the alternatives all but ceased. One major line of objection (not pursued here) was economic;[62] the other, to which the issue of sovereignty was central, may broadly be termed constitutional. The most important single work was from the experienced hand of James Hodges, who now published the

59 The Minutes of the Commissioners and the agreed 'Articles of Union' were recorded by Daniel Defoe, *The History of the Union between England and Scotland* (London, 1786), pp. 107–96 (Minutes), 197–208 (Articles).

60 T.B. Smith, 'The Union of 1707 as Fundamental Law', *Public Law* (Summer 1957), 105–8.

61 Ferguson, *Scotland's Relations with England*, pp. 232–69, provides the most rounded account of the Treaty's passage; Riley, *The Union*, pp. 254–310, concentrates upon ministerial manoeuvring.

62 On the economic debate, not studied further here: T.C. Smout, *Scottish Trade on the Eve of the Union 1660–1707* (Edinburgh and London, 1963), pp. 261–70.

third of his treatises on *The Rights and Interests of the Two British Monarchies*: this enumerated thirty-one particular national interests infringed by the Treaty. (His second treatise, which was to have outlined the form of a federal union, was again deferred.)[63] A similar, more reflectively argued work, which reiterated the case for union with distinct parliaments, was the *State of the Controversy betwixt United and Separate Parliaments*.[64] These were now joined by contributions from opposite ends of the politico-religious spectrum. From the Jacobites came a rare, tactically intelligent tract by Patrick Abercromby, the *Advantages of the Act of Security, compar'd with these of the Intended Union*, urging that the succession should continue to be left open.[65] Much more numerous were the contributions of overtly Presbyterian writers, whose primary concerns were the security of the Church, or the inconsistency of the Treaty with the Covenants. These were also the most aggressively 'popular' in style. *Scotland's Speech to Her Sons*, possibly by the Glasgow minister James Clark, was a straightforward appeal (or incitement) to Scots to defend their 'INDEPENDENT SOVEREIGNTY'. Opting for burlesque, the writer of *The Comical History of the Marriage Union between Fergusia and Heptarchus* made Fergusia (Scotland) declare that she would rather let her sovereignty die like a candle than commit 'self-murther'. By contrast, the more radical author of *The Smoaking Flax Unquenchable* simply bypassed the secular issue of sovereignty to address 'the true subjects of the Covenanted Kingdom of Scotland': with the monarchy now likely to expire, these should take the opportunity to return to the form of godly commonwealth which had existed during Cromwell's usurpation.[66]

[63] [James Hodges], *The Rights and Interests of the Two British Monarchies. With Special Respect to an United or Separate State. Treatise III, containing Farther Inquiries into the Best Means for procuring a Happy Union betwixt the Two Kingdoms; with a special regard to the Argument, That the making Both Nations One People, must also make them One Interest* (London, 1706).

[64] *State of the Controversy betwixt United and Separate Parliaments* (1706): subsequently attributed to Andrew Fletcher on the authority of Thomas Ruddiman, and reprinted by Sir John Dalrymple in his *Memoirs of Great Britain and Ireland*, vol. II [i.e. III] (Edinburgh, 1788), Appendix III, pp. 55–84. Reprinted again by P.H. Scott in a Saltire Society pamphlet (Edinburgh, 1982); but Scott has subsequently retreated from the attribution: *Andrew Fletcher and the Treaty of Union*, pp. 174–5. See Robertson, 'Andrew Fletcher's vision of Union', p. 220, n2, for reasons for doubt.

[65] [Patrick Abercromby], *The Advantages of the Act of Security, Compar'd with these of the Intended Union: Founded on the Revolution Principles publish'd by Mr Daniel Defoe. Or, the Present Happy Condition of Scotland, with respect to the certainty of its Future Honourable and Advantageous Establishment, demonstrated. Wherein is shew'd, that both the Projected Union, and a Nomination of a Successor to the Crown, tho' with Limitations, cannot fail to compleat the Miseries of this Kingdom; but that the Act of Security alone, if adher'd to, will infallibly retrive our lost happiness, and make us a Rich and Glorious People.* (np, 1706).

[66] [James Clark?], *Scotland's Speech to her Sons* (np, ?1706); in November Clark preached a sermon which Defoe held responsible for an anti-Union riot in Glasgow: Defoe, *History*

There were two points at which the Treaty was believed to be particularly vulnerable. The first was the right of parliament to accept the Treaty, and hence to vote itself out of existence, without first consulting the freeholders who elected it. The idea of freeholder sovereignty owed much of its polemical force to the support it supposedly received from authors as different as the Tory Lord Advocate, Sir George Mackenzie, and the radical English Whig, Daniel Defoe. The Presbyterian Ridpath happily cited Mackenzie's opinion in his *Considerations upon the Union*, while the Jacobite Abercromby made a show of turning Defoe's 'Revolution Principles' against their author.[67] Strictly speaking, however, the idea of freeholder sovereignty was considerably less radical in the Scottish context than its English associations might suggest. 'Freeholder' in Scotland was a feudal status, enjoyed by only a small minority even of those recognised as landowners; that only 'freeholders' were entitled to vote in the counties ensured that the electorate was proportionally far smaller than in England. To claim that Scotland's sovereignty lay with the freeholders, therefore, was to continue to appeal to the old feudal political order, of which many anti-Unionists were themselves fierce critics. There were those who wished to interpret the concept more loosely: Hodges went so far as to suggest that Scotland's sovereignty could be given up only by the unanimous consent of all the freeborn, including freeborn women.[68] But there was no sustained attempt to argue that the nation's sovereignty should be identified with the people of Scotland as a whole: the Scottish Union debate generated no equivalent to Locke's *Two Treatises of Government*.[69]

of the Union, pp. 268–80. *The Comical History of the Marriage Union betwixt Fergusia and Heptarchus* (printed in Scotland and reprinted in England, 1706); attributed to the Rev. William Wright, minister in Kilmarnock, by the McLeods, *Anglo-Scottish Tracts*. *The Smoaking Flax Unquenchable; where the Union betwixt the two Kingdoms is dissecated, anatomized, confuted and annuled. Also, that good form and fabrick of civil government, intended and espoused by the true subjects of the land, is illustrated and held out* (np, 1706). The 'Smoaking Flax' was a reference to Isaiah 42.3. On this work's identification of the covenanted Scots with the biblical Israelites – a theme also present in the *Comical History* (in which Fergusia demands that Heptarchus be circumcised), *A Pil for Pork-Eaters*, and Ridpath's *Considerations upon the Union*, p. iii, see Arthur H. Williamson, 'A Pil for Pork Eaters': ethnic identity, apocalyptic promises and the strange creation of the Judeo-Scots', in Raymond Waddington and Arthur Williamson (eds.), *The Expulsion of the Jews: 1492 and After* (San Francisco, 1993). On the important differences between presbyterian writers, see Kidd, 'Religious realignment', above, pp. 156–63, 165–8.

[67] [Ridpath], *Considerations upon the Union*, pp. 56–7; [Abercromby], *Advantages of the Act of Security*, pp. 6–10. [68] [Hodges], *Rights and Interest*, pp. 73–4.

[69] Scots, moreover, were disinclined to read Locke in a radical vein: James Moore and Michael Silverthorne, 'Gershom Carmichael and the natural jurisprudence tradition in eighteenth-century Scotland', in Hont and Ignatieff, *Wealth and Virtue*. See also Moore and Silverthorne, 'Protestant Theologies, Unlimited Sovereignties', above, pp. 195–6.

The second issue repeatedly raised by the Treaty's opponents concerned the security which the Scots would enjoy once the new Parliament of Great Britain, with its overwhelmingly English membership, had assumed the sovereignty previously held by the Scottish parliament. It was the question on which Fletcher had seized in his *Account of a Conversation*; and its historical force was underlined by the publication of an extract from Pufendorf's *History of Sweden* describing how Denmark had exploited the Union of Calmar at Swedish expense.[70] What made the question of the utmost concern in 1706, however, was fear for the independence of the Scottish Church: for one parliament to support two different churches seemed too great an anomaly to be sustained. Without the guarantee that only a separate parliament could provide, a treaty of incorporating union must put Scotland and its Church at the mercy of another sovereignty, whose predominant inclination was in favour of the episcopal Church of England.[71]

When the Parliament opened on 3 October 1706, the Treaty's opponents did what they could to exploit these objections. Up against ruthless management by the crown, they were further hampered by the utter unreliability of their titular leader, the Duke of Hamilton. Fletcher continued unyielding, varying his tactics between intelligent obstructionism, intemperate accusations and studied oratory. He was received with respect and tolerance, but heeded by few.[72] The most memorable speech was Lord Belhaven's set-piece in opposition to the First Article of the Treaty, a rhetorical lament for the passing of 'Mother Caledonia'. Belhaven gave moving expression to the sense of loss which many doubtless felt, but did not quite hold the line between the sublime and the ridiculous. Much merriment ensued; the point, however, was that the speech was effectively an admission of defeat.[73]

70 *A Short Account of the Union betwixt Sweden, Denmark and Norway, which commenced about the year 1396, and was broke about the year 1523. Taken from Puffendorf's History of Sweden, p. 85, printed at London 1702. Fit to be perus'd by Scotsmen at this juncture; and published for the benefit of such as have not access to the Book* [Edinburgh, 1706].

71 [Ridpath], *Considerations upon the Union*, pp. 69–71; *State of the Controversy*, in Dalrymple, *Memoirs of Great Britain and Ireland*, III, App. III, pp. 57ff., on the Church in particular, pp. 63–73; [Abercromby], *Advantages of the Act of Security*, pp. 12–13; *Comical History*, pp. 16–19, 26–7.

72 For examples: *HMC Mar & Kellie Mss*, pp. 289–90: the Earl of Mar to Sir David Nairne, 13 Oct. 1706 (intelligent obstructionism); ibid., pp. 304–6: the same to the same, 29 Oct. 1706 (intemperate accusation, tolerantly received); ibid., pp. 308–9: the same to the same, 3 Nov. 1706, ('studied speeches'). Also *HMC, Portland Mss*, VIII, pp. 260–1: [William Paterson] to [Erasmus Lewis?], 5 Nov. 1706, (the only report of the content of his oratory, during the debate on the First Article).

73 Speech by Lord Belhaven on the First Article of the Union, reprinted by Defoe, *History of the Union*, pp. 317–27. Marchmont's one-line response – 'Behold he dreamed, but lo!

On the other side, the Scottish proponents of an incorporating union made the most of the opportunity which the successful completion of the treaty negotiations had afforded them. Cromarty was the most prolific, readier to mix it with opponents, and to adopt a popular style. His pamphlets appeared from the summer of 1706 through until virtually the end of the parliamentary proceedings, dealing with issues as they arose. Seton's manner was more elevated: he led for the Union in Parliament, in a series of thoughtful, elegant speeches, and contributed one telling pamphlet. Support also came from Sir John Clerk, one of the Union Commissioners, and William Paterson, both of whom had a detailed grasp of the economic issues.

Their case for the Treaty was marked by a clear-headed discussion of the issues associated with sovereignty. Once again Seton and Cromarty reminded the Scots of the inadequacies of their past, ruthlessly denigrating the sovereignty they had enjoyed by associating it with dependence under the Union of the Crowns or, worse still, with 'that Gothic constitution of government, wherein our forefathers were, which was frequently attended with feuds, murders, depredations and rebellions'.[74] Such sovereignty as Scotland did possess was lodged, the Unionists insisted, in crown and parliament together. There was no basis, therefore, for the idea of freeholder sovereignty. Scotland's government, Seton reassured parliament, was not 'a Polish aristocracy, founded upon *pacta conventa*, whereby all the gentry are empowered in their particular meetings, to prescribe rules to their representatives in a general Dyet'. Nor was it a common democracy, in which every subject could claim a vote in the legislature.[75] Commenting expressly upon the opinion of Sir George Mackenzie, Cromarty had earlier explained that in Scotland 'the supreme and sovereign power' had been devolved, not delegated, upon the crown and parliament, thus ensuring that the representatives of the barons and the burgesses were the 'true, integrant parts of the sovereign constituted body'.[76] Later in the same work Cromarty dismissed the claim that this

when he awoke, he found it was a dream' (p. 328) – offered immediate relief; for futher expressions of merriment: *HMC, Mar & Kellie Mss*, pp. 309, 329: Mar to Nairne, 3, 19 Nov. 1706; from England Nairne reported that the speech was being read there with incredulity: p. 320, 14 Nov. 1706.

74 Speech by William Seton of Pitmedden on the First Article of the Union, 2 November 1706, in Defoe, *History of the Union*, pp. 312–14. Also [Earl of Cromarty], *A Letter from E.C. to E. W. concerning the Union* [Edinburgh, 1706], pp. 3–5; and [Earl of Cromarty], *A Letter to a member of Parliament upon the 19th Article of the Treaty of Union between the two Kingdoms of Scotland and England* (np, 4 Dec. 1706), p. 4.

75 Speech by Seton of Pitmedden on the Third Article of the Union, 18 Nov. 1706, in Defoe, *History of the Union*, p. 360.

76 [Earl of Cromarty], *A Friendly Return to a Letter Concerning Sir George Mackenzie's and Sir John Nisbet's Observation and Responce on the matter of the Union* (np, 22 Aug. 1706), pp. 5–29.

sovereignty could be re-established in a federal union with separate parliaments: a federal union was 'so ambulatory and changeable, by the nature of treaties', there was no reason to suppose it would last. The alternative claim that two parliaments might be retained within an incorporating union made even less sense, since it was in the nature of an incorporating union to unify the supreme government.[77]

To these unionists, the point of the Treaty was that it did not involve a surrender of sovereignty, still less a conquest: as Grotius had explained, incorporation was a mutual communication of rights and privileges, by which a new and greater sovereignty was created without any loss of the rights and privileges enjoyed under its separate predecessors.[78] (Fletcher's sharp comment that the Roman examples on which Grotius based his argument showed conquest to have preceded this communication of rights was, not surprisingly, ignored).[79] The real justification for incorporating union, however, was not what it preserved, but what it created and made possible. Henceforth there should not be two peoples, but one, with a common interest and even a common name. Cromarty was particularly enthusiastic on the subject, urging Scots and English to rediscover their ancient common identity as Britons, and to adopt the name 'Britich'.[80] Much more important than the name, however, were the real benefits which the Union was expected to bring. The title of Seton's pamphlet, *Scotland's Great Advantages by an Union with England*, epitomised the argument. Greatest of these advantages would be the enjoyment of the rights of liberty and property as the English had asserted them, but now 'secured under the protection of one Sovereign, and one Parliament of Great Britain'. With these would come access to all the advantages in commerce which the English had possessed: the spirit of trade and industry would be encouraged, while tenants would no longer be tyrannised by their landlords. A common sovereignty, in short, would at last enable the Scots to modernise their economy and society.[81]

[77] [Cromarty], *Friendly Return Letter Fourth*, pp. 6–7. Cromarty was explicitly discussing [Ridpath's] *Considerations upon the Union*.

[78] 'I agree with the learned Grotius (Lib. 2. Cap. 9. Sect. 9)', Seton told parliament in his Speech on the Third Article, Defoe, *History of the Union*, p. 362; the reference was to the *De Iure Belli ac Pacis*. Another to refer to this passage in Grotius was Sir John Clerk, *A Letter to a Friend, Giving an Account how the Treaty of Union has been received here. And wherein are contained, Answers to the most material Objections against it, with some remarks upon what has been written by Mr. H. and Mr. R.* (Edinburgh, 1706), p. 10.

[79] Fletcher, *Account of a Conversation*, in *Political Works*, p. 409, and *Selected Writings*, p. 122. See Robertson, 'Empire and Union', above p. 34.

[80] [Cromarty], *A Letter from E.C. to E.W.*, pp. 5–7.

[81] [William Seton of Pitmedden], *Scotland's Great Advantages by an Union with England: showen in a Letter from the Country, to a Member of Parliament*, (np, 1706), esp. pp. 5–6, 12; Speeches on the first and Third Articles of Union, in Defoe, *History of the Union*, pp. 316, 361–2.

Even the distance from the new parliament would be to Scotland's advantage: as Cromarty shrewdly pointed out, the removal of government to England should rid the Scots of English ministerial interference in their affairs, and of the factions which resulted.[82] In his most popular work, the *Trialogus*, Cromarty repeatedly ridiculed those who insisted on 'the glory of being a kingdom per se', refusing to recognise that everything associated with an independent sovereignty – being part of a rich and great body politic with a king at its head, being safe from invaders and respected abroad – was as well or better secured by the Union. The 'notion of a kingdom per se' was an abstraction; what really mattered were 'the riches, honour and safety of all, and every individual'.[83] Such were its real advantages, Seton could argue, that the Treaty of Union had done more to assert 'our sovereignty and independency' than anything else the Scots had had occasion to do in a long time.[84]

This, however, was the confidence of the committed – and of the non-Presbyterian. Both Cromarty and Seton were Episcopalians of an erastian cast: and if they were careful not to be too explicit in 1706, the suggestion that a united parliament might use its sovereignty at least to enlarge the toleration enjoyed by Episcopalians was not far from the surface.[85] Neither, therefore, was well placed to assuage the doubts of Presbyterians about the security of their Church after the Union.[86] This was the specific contribution of Daniel Defoe, the English journalist who, with ministerial approval, came north in September 1706 to observe the progress and further the cause of the Union Treaty at first hand. As the contributions of Laurence Dickey and Katherine Penovich elsewhere in this volume indicate, Defoe approached the issue with an intellectual agenda of his own: he was not simply a hired hand.[87] His sense of the Union's importance was grounded on a continuing analysis of the need to deploy British resources to maintain the balance of Europe, and his first concern – as his writings both before and after his Scottish period testify –

[82] [Earl of Cromarty], *A Second Letter on the British Union* (np, nd [1706]), pp. 15–16.

[83] [Earl of Cromarty], *Trialogus. A Conference betwixt Mr Con, Mr Pro, and Mr Indifferent, concerning the Union* (np, 1706), pp. 5–6; also *Trialogus. A Second Conversation* (np, nd [1706]).

[84] [Seton], *Scotland's Great Advantages*, p. 11.

[85] Cromarty made it explicit a few years later: [Earl of Cromarty], *Several Proposals conducing to a farther Union of Britain. And pointing at some Advantages arising from it* (London, 1711); and *The Scottish Toleration Truly Stated in a Letter to a Peer* (London, 1712).

[86] Doubts voiced in *A Letter from Mr Scruplous to Trialogus concerning the Union* (Edinburgh, 21 October 1706). Admitting the other advantages of union, the writer was unable to accept that one parliament would support two different church governments.

[87] Laurence Dickey, 'Power, commerce and natural law in Daniel Defoe's political writings 1698–1707', above pp. 75–96; Katherine R. Penovich, 'From 'Revolution principles' to Union: Daniel Defoe's intervention in the Scottish debate', below, pp. 228–42.

remained the Union's consequences for the English, the Dissenters in particular.[88] Once in Scotland, however, he quickly brought to bear the professionalism and versatility of an experienced controversialist, identifying the several points, economic as well as constitutional, at which the case for the Union most needed reinforcement.

Defoe accepted that the Freeholders (who he apparently assumed to be the same in Scotland as in England) possessed an original right to make the laws by which they were governed. He denied, however, that their right was infringed by Parliament's ratification of the Union Treaty without consulting them. Parliament was not removing the original right of the people; it was simply altering the circumstances in which it would be exercised, by substituting one united parliament for two.[89] The further objection that the new parliament would have the power to break the terms of the Treaty was likewise a misunderstanding.

> The treaty is the foundation and constituent head of the parliament of Great Britain, and gives it a being, and therefore is so far superior in its power, as not to be destroyed by its own substitute, and . . . to breake the Treaty, is to dissolve the constitution and very being of the parliament, and overthrow the Union.[90]

Quite why the Treaty was to have the status of a 'fundamental' Defoe never fully explained. The relation between this argument and the Grotian formula of communication, also endorsed by Defoe, was not elaborated; and there was no suggestion that this was a treaty *jure gentium*, to be maintained within a framework of Public Law.[91] Further complicating the issue were Defoe's powerful endorsements of the principle of parliamentary supremacy in relation to the circumstances in which freeholders exercised their rights, and to responsibility for the army. Nevertheless, Defoe's affirmation of the fundamental status of the Treaty addressed and, in its own terms, met the most important single objection to the Union: how two Acts (the Treaty itself and the Act for securing Presbyterian Church Government) passed by a Scottish Parliament

[88] [Daniel Defoe], *An Essay at Removing National Prejudices against a Union with Scotland. Part I* (Edinburgh [also London], 1706, and *Part II*, (np, 1706): both published in May, and addressed to the English. Likewise, following the Treaty's ratification by the Scottish Parliament, [Daniel Defoe], *A Discourse upon an Union of the Two Kingdoms of England and Scotland* (London, 1707). Defoe also continued to publish the *Review*, with comment on the Union debate as well as on European affairs, throughout 1706–7.

[89] [Daniel Defoe], *A Fourth Essay at Removing National Prejudices; with some Reply to Mr Hodges and some other Authors, who have printed their Objections against an Union with England* (np, 1706), pp. 9–12. For a fuller discussion of Defoe's complex argument, see Penovich, 'From "Revolution principles" to Union', below, pp. 236–40.

[90] [Daniel Defoe], *An Essay at Removing National Prejudices against a Union with England. Part III* (np, 1706), pp. 10–33, with the quotation on p. 26.

[91] [Defoe], *A Fourth Essay*, p. 42, for the citation and endorsement of Grotius.

which then ceased to exist would continue to bind a new British Parliament, possessed of a fresh sovereign power of its own. Before Defoe's intervention, no one had offered an answer remotely as plausible as the one he outlined.

The importance of Defoe's argument to a committed Presbyterian Scot was illustrated in *The Patriot Resolved*, a pamphlet published early in 1707 by Francis Grant, a lawyer and future Lord of Session. At this late stage in the debate, Grant wrote expressly to explain why he had been persuaded by the case for united rather than separate parliaments. It was evident to him that the 'chain of Providence' had supported this outcome.[92] But he was also clear that preservation of Scotland's distinct sovereignty had become pointless. Under the Union of the Crowns a separate Scottish Parliament had protected neither religon nor trade; if a federal union were to be re-constituted, it would be as the unions of Spain and Portugal, Sweden and Denmark, in which the stronger enforced its will on the weaker. The objection to a federal union, he added, was still stronger now that nations stood by trade, and the stronger had to protect themselves against the lower costs of the weaker: a common legislature had become the precondition of enjoying a common market.[93] The proposed Union, however, involved no surrender of Scotland's sovereignty 'taking that word in its full import': a main part would remain with the Scots, while the rest was adjoined to England's. From such a union, Grant was confident, would follow many real advantages, both religious and secular. The Protestant Interest would be established throughout the world, while the 'substantials' of religion would be safe at home. The Queen would continue to hold the balance of Europe and the sea, justice would be secured in Scotland as it was in England, and Scottish trade encouraged in those several branches in which it did not interfere with England's. Set against these advantages, Grant asked, 'what was our nominal sovereignty? The phantom of a body . . . without a head.'[94]

What was crucial, however, was that the security of Scotland's interests would rest on more than their compatability with England's. For the Treaty of Union was different from most '*pacta conventa*' abroad, like the Union of Utrecht or the Pacification of Munster (the Treaty of Westphalia): it was to be the basis of a new government, in which Scotland's rights would be indefeasible. Specifically, the Protestant religion was made 'fundamental to the new constitution, and therefore

[92] [Francis Grant], *The Patriot Resolved; in a Letter to an Addresser, from his Friend; of the same sentiments with himself; concerning the Union* (np, 1707), pp. 5–7. Grant was elevated to the Bench in 1709 as Lord Cullen. On his Presbyterianism, see Kidd, 'Religious realignment', above, p. 167.

[93] [Grant], *Patriot Resolved*, pp. 14–16, 27.

[94] [Grant], *Patriot Resolved*, pp. 17–25, with the final quotation on p. 21.

not changeable'. (An understanding of the principles of the Treaty which Grant reinforced, however, with the shrewd prudential observation that any breach of it would open again 'the postern and hazard of Ireland'.[95]) It is perhaps significant that Grant, though a lawyer, was no clearer than Defoe as to the juridical basis for this characterisation of the treaty, and offered no more indication as to how its 'fundamentals' were to be upheld if the united parliament were to decide to alter them. What is plain, nevertheless, is Grant's conviction that the sovereignty assumed by the new British Parliament was less than absolute, and that certain basic Scottish interests could be regarded as entrenched by the Treaty of Union.

Not every Presbyterian, of course, was as persuaded as Grant. Even now the Rev. James Webster was denouncing the Treaty as a violation of the Covenants, and provoking Defoe into a fresh series of exchanges.[96] It was almost certainly fortunate too that the belief that the Treaty secured Presbyterian church government as a 'fundamental' was not immediately tested: when it was, by the Toleration and Patronage Acts passed by the Tory-dominated British Parliament in 1711–12, those who put their trust in it were quickly disabused.[97] At the time, however, Grant's pamphlet effectively marked the end of the Union debate. The treaty completed its passage through the Scottish Parliament on 16 January 1707; by early March it had also been ratified by the English Parliament.[98] With the Scottish Parliament dissolved for the last time on 28 April, the Union formally took effect on 1 May 1707.

[95] [Grant], *Patriot Resolved*, pp. 18, 25–6. Grant also answered the scruples of those who feared that the Treaty breached the Presbyterian principle of the separation of church and state, because it was made with a House of Lords containing bishops: in this respect, he believed, the Scots' position was no different from that of Dutch, German and Swiss Protestants who made pacts with Catholic states (pp. 29–31).

[96] [James Webster], *Lawful Prejudices against an Incorporating Union with England; or Some Modest Considerations on the Sinfulness of this Union, and the Danger Flowing from it to the Church of Scotland* (Edinburgh, 1707). Defoe replied with *The Dissenters in England Vindicated from the Reflections in a late Pamphlet, Entituled, Lawful Prejudices & c.* (Edinburgh, 1707), and the two exchanged at least one more pamphlet each.

[97] As William Carstares, no less, ruefully observed, 'if this, which is the most solemn and absolute condition of the Treaty, can admit of distinctions to defeat the interest of the Church, the Treaty will be of very small force or security in any part of it . . .': [William Carstares], *The Case of the Church of Scotland with relation to the Bill for a Toleration to the Episcopal Dissenters to set up Meeting Houses, and use the English Service in Scotland* (np, nd [1712]), p. 4. Likewise 'The Humble Representation of William Carstares . . . in the name . . . of the Commission of the late General Assembly . . . concerning the Bill for restoring Patronages', in *A Collection of Papers against the Scots Toleration and Patronages* (London, 1712), pp. 74–5.

[98] *Acts of the Parliament of Scotland, Vol XI: 1702–1707* (1824), pp. 402–14: 15, 16 January 1707 (with the text of the Act of Union and the Act for securing the Protestant Religion and Presbyterian Church Government).

That there was a genuine debate over the Union has not always been admitted by historians: this chapter has sought to demonstrate its existence, its scope and its interest. The better to do so, I have focused upon the issue of sovereignty, as a central thread of the debate from first to last. It was an issue forced on the Scots by the Revolution of 1688, the Darien fiasco of 1698–1700 and the Succession Crisis of 1701–2, and it necessarily led them to reassess their relationship with England. Given the historical identification of Scotland's sovereignty with its imperial crown, Anne's lack of heirs was especially critical: in 1702 those who would not accept the exiled Stuarts faced the shameful alternative of adopting a succession chosen for them by the English, an insult aggravated by the grudging terms of the accompanying offer of incorporation into England's parliament.

That the Scots were given an opportunity to turn the crisis to their advantage was the remarkable achievement of Andrew Fletcher, when he suggested that the (improbable) threat to find an alternative Protestant succession be used to win concessions that would restore the independence of the Scottish parliament. The strength of Fletcher's case lay in the thoroughness of his criticism of the experience of the existing Union of the Crowns (including the Covenanter period), which suggested that Scotland's sovereignty would only be re-established by a correspondingly radical reform of political institutions, accompanied by the establishment of a new, more equal form of union with England. That such reform was possible, that an alternative, confederal form of union did exist, was what Fletcher urged the Scottish Parliament to recognise in 1703. His case was not made easier, however, by his own admission that not even then would Scotland's sovereignty be guaranteed. Between two Kingdoms as unequal as Scotland and England, confederation would succeed only when the historic sovereignties of both were set aside, and divided between smaller regions and their cities. Hodges and Ridpath would later seek to retrieve this admission by pressing for reform within the existing framework of regnal union. Scotland's historic sovereignty might still be preserved, they argued, if Scottish subjects were free to benefit from their status as naturalised subjects of the crown in England and its colonies. But even had immediate political circumstances been more favourable to this case, it must be doubtful if the damage already done to the credibility of the Union of the Crowns could have been repaired.

As a viable Scottish sovereignty eluded even its ablest defenders, those who saw more posititive possibilities in an incorporating union of parliaments grew in confidence. The sovereignty of Scotland's imperial crown and independent parliament, they reasoned, was too compromised by its association with the poverty, political disorder and religious bigotry of the past century for an incorporating union to count as its surrender. In the reassuring Grotian formula, incorporation should be understood rather as a mutual communication of rights, strengthening those which the Scots wished to preserve, and giving them access to others which the English already enjoyed. For those Unionists who were confident of the benevolence of a predominantly Anglican parliament in Westminster, this was assurance enough; for those who still feared for the Presbyterian Church of Scotland, there was the additional rider, suggested by Defoe and taken up by Grant, that the sovereignty of the new British parliament would be qualified by the Treaty of Union itself, and by the accompanying Acts securing the respective Churches. The resulting Scottish understanding of the status of the Treaty as fundamental law was, and would remain, both unilateral and underdeveloped, with no support from a corpus of Public Law.[99] It did nothing to disturb the English constitutional conviction of the necessary connection between the sovereignty and the territorial 'empire' of the realm of England, a connection which it was taken for granted would continue to obtain within the new United Kingdom. Even if the Scots underestimated the strength of this conviction, however, they at least refused to be awed by it. Their own sovereignty might have proved too elusive to sustain; but no one else's was to be regarded as absolute.

Insofar as the Scottish Unionists were prepared to concede sovereignty, moreover, it was in return for the tangible advantages it was expected to bring. The lesson of Scotland's sovereignty was that its mere possession was no guarantee of peace and prosperity. What mattered about any sovereignty was what it enabled its subjects to do. The overriding justification for Scotland's now associating its sovereignty with England's was that it would make possible Scottish participation in England's markets – in its territorial and maritime 'empire', within, around and beyond the British Isles. To hold that sovereignty was justified by the advantages it secured, rather than of itself, however, was to imply that it should always be regarded as inherently conditional. Were the sovereignty of the British parliament ever to cease to offer such advantages, there would be no reason to regard it, or the Union which created it, as any more sacrosanct than Scotland's own sovereignty had become by 1707.

[99] See also John W. Cairns, 'Scottish Law, Scottish lawyers and the status of the Union', below, pp. 248–9. For a modern legal opinion: T.B. Smith, 'The Union of 1707 as Fundamental Law'.

9
FROM 'REVOLUTION PRINCIPLES' TO UNION: DANIEL DEFOE'S INTERVENTION IN THE SCOTTISH DEBATE

KATHERINE R. PENOVICH

DANIEL DEFOE left London in September 1706, posing and for the most part passing as an English businessman in search of economic opportunity in Edinburgh. The guise was a necessary and credible one; in the present crisis over the Anglo-Scottish Union, habitually peevish relations between the two kingdoms had deteriorated into rash belligerence. Defoe's recent ignominy as a debt-ridden entrepreneur helped to divert attention from his greater reputation as a trenchant political pen and from the real purpose of his expedition – to advance the cause of the Union. He spent fifteen months in Scotland, writing tracts in support of the treaty both before and after its ratification, gathering intelligence for the English ministry and materials for his lengthy *History of the Union of Great Britain*, and pursuing actual commercial ventures once political urgency and the pressing need for his talents had subsided.[1] Fortune, while perpetually eluding him as a businessman, favoured Defoe as a journalist and this point is as important to the political and cultural history of the period as it is to his biography.

Defoe described the part he played in the passage of the Act of Union in various ways: to his *Review* readers he rejoiced in being an instrument of God's providence; to readers of his *History of the Union*, he proclaimed his status as an 'Eye Witness to much of the General Transaction' with

[1] A fellow Unionist and Scottish acquaintance of Defoe's remarked that had Defoe been discovered as 'a Spy amongst us . . . the Mob of Edin[burgh would have] pulled him to pieces'. John M. Gray (ed.), *Memoirs of the Life of Sir John Clerk of Penicuik . . .*, Scottish Historical Society Publication, vol. 13 (Edinburgh, 1892), p. 67. Spiro Peterson examines the gradual fraying of Defoe's cover in 'Defoe in Edinburgh, 1707', *The Huntington Library Quarterly*, 38 (1974), 21–33. For additional biographical details of Defoe's financial difficulties and life in Scotland, see Paula Backscheider's *Daniel Defoe: His Life* (Baltimore, 1989) and two earlier articles 'Defoe and the Clerks of Penicuik', *Modern Philology*, 84 (1987), 372–81, and 'John Russell to Daniel Defoe: fifteen unpublished letters from Scotland', *Philosophical Quarterly*, 61 (1982), 161–77.

special access to documents furnished by 'the best Hands' as well as the 'publick registers'; to his sometime and secret patron, Robert Harley, he compared his operations to those of Cardinal Richelieu and confessed a Pauline devotion in being 'all to Every one That I might gain some'.[2] Though, in their proper contexts, these statements may best be explained respectively as measures of faith, historiographic convention, and subservience, modern historians have been inclined to diminish the importance of such a self-promoting actor. It may be argued, however, that as one of London's pioneering propagandists, Defoe brought an unmatched professionalism to the subsequent frenzy of opinion unleashed by the union controversy. In the 1701–2 paper war, in the bitter 1705 electoral campaign and as editor of the *Review*, Defoe had advanced the co-ordination of propaganda directed both in and out of parliamentary doors, the organisation of intelligence and distribution networks, and the production of sustained, serialised commentary, and these were the methods he now employed in support of the union.[3]

Until the Treaty Commissioners convened in London in April 1706, Defoe's observations on Scotland and union matters had been sympathetic but intermittent, a subtext in his disputes with Tories over trade, toleration, and war. Emerging bloodied but unbowed from prison and pillory for his pamphlet of 1702, *The Shortest Way with Dissenters* and with new success as 'Mr. Review', Defoe had established his reputation as a notorious Whiggish publicist whose chief targets were High Churchmen enraged by occasional conformity and Tories irritated by the cost of war against France. More often than not this arch-Anglicanism had combined with blue-water bias in attempts to impede various ministerial objectives. The opposition's strength was dramatically evident in the Parliament of 1705, when the House of Commons sought to force through the House of Lords a controversial measure outlawing occasional conformity by tacking it to the supply bill of that year. Amidst these controversies and the souring of relations with Scotland, the English court had renewed its

[2] Daniel Defoe, *The Review*, 1 February 1706, vol. III, Bk.8, no. 170, p. 678. Throughout I have used the Facsimile Text edited by Arthur Wellesley Secord (Columbia University Press, 1938). Volume, number, and page are original to Defoe's serialisation. The book number refers to the volume of Secord's edition, included as a convenience for the reader. Hereafter cited as *Review; History of the Union of Great Britain* (London, 1709), 'Of the Last Treaty, Properly Called The Union', p. 1 and 'Preface', p. 6; see also *Review*, 21 January 1706, vol. III, Bk. 8, no. 165, p. 658. Daniel Defoe to Robert Harley, 18 March 1706/7, p. 211; Defoe [to Robert Harley], 26 November 1706, p. 159 in George Healey (ed.), *The Letters of Daniel Defoe* (Oxford, 1955). Hereafter cited as Healey.

[3] J.A. Downie, *Robert Harley and the Press: Propaganda and Public Opinion in the Age of Swift and Defoe* (Cambridge, 1979). Ruth B. White examines Defoe's writings on the Union in the context of the growth of professional journalism: *Activities of Defoe Relating to the Act of Union, 1706–1707*, PhD thesis, Columbia University, 1966.

bid for an incorporation with neighbours maligned by many of the opposition for their Presbyterianism and poverty. Defoe's interest in Scottish issues prior to the summer of 1706, however, had extended only to those questions relevant to his preoccupation with safeguarding English Dissent and European Protestantism. Thus his use of the phrase 'Peace and Union' in this period, a deliberate echo of Queen Anne's own irenic plea, referred to relations not between the two kingdoms but between the Church of England and the Dissenters.

The limited nature of Defoe's early campaign on behalf of the Union is further attested by the fact that most of his references to Scotland in this period occur within the narrow compass of his debate with Lord Haversham.[4] In November 1705, Haversham had denounced the amelioration of England's pugnacious Alien Act, attacked the unco-operative Scots and avaricious Dutch for trading with France in wartime, and suggested that the Hanoverian Electress reside in England to secure the succession.[5] His speech was meant to embarrass the Whigs and court supporters but its printing was a bid to aggravate English bigotry against the Scots by depicting them as enemies of a blue-water policy towards France. Although Defoe warned his readers of the dangers in offending Scotland, he understood this skirmish as the denouement in the drama of the tack and not as his own *mise en scene* for union. Scottish violation of the Navigation Acts had piqued those who, in their aversion to Goldophin's and Marlborough's taxes and troops, preferred to check French aggression through the 'Police [of] Trade with our wooden walls'.[6] In confronting an entrenched naval chauvinism, Defoe once again found himself exhorting men like Haversham to relinquish comforting national mythologies in the face of fundamental structural change, just as he had done in supporting a standing army over a militia in 1698. As a defence of Protestant Europe against the latest threat of 'Universal Monarchy . . . and the tyranny of the House of *Bourbon*', Defoe argued that the Dutch and the Scots understood, as Haversham and his ilk did not, that wartime embargoes were as ineffective as 'a Hedge about the Cookoo'.[7]

Ineffective and even obscurantist, for, to Defoe's mind, the defence of commerce was not only of present purpose but of providential proportions.

[4] Defoe knew John Thompson in the 1690s. For his services to William, Thompson was made the first Baron Haversham and a Lord of the Admiralty in 1699. By 1704, however, he had jettisoned his Whig identity. Ever loyal to William's memory and to the Whig cause, Defoe's fortunes had been more mixed, prompting him to remark 'Fate . . . makes Footballs of Men, kicks some up Stairs and some down . . . and no man knows whether his Course shall issue in a PEERAGE or a PILLORY . . . ' [Defoe], *A Reply to a Pamphlet Entituled, the L[or]d H[aversham]'s Vindication of his Speech, &c.* (London, 1706), p. 8.

[5] *The Lord H[aver]sham's Speech in the House of Peers, November 15, 1705* (London, 1705).

[6] *Review*, 3 November 1705, vol. II, Bk. 5, no. 105, p. 419.

[7] *Review*, 6 January 1705, vol. I, Bk. 2, no. 88, p. 366.

Enthusiasm for trade has long been part of Defoe's contemporary and historiographical identity. As an alternative vision to the civic humanist model, Defoe's promotion of commerce as the basis for national strength in the modern age has been well-established.[8] But his wider application of the idea of exchange and his understanding of its religious foundations merit further attention. Defoe launched the *Review* as a serialised investigation of the rise of French power and Louis XIV's pretensions to universal monarchy through the establishment of a 'Universal Trade' which

> like a slow Poison [will be] Fatal to our Prosperity . . . and will in Time, if not prevented, as certainly work in Destruction of these Nations, as it if was wrought by immediate force.
>
> And what is still more Unhappy to us, the Mischief of this Encroachment is not discern'd; 'tis a Silent Evil, that creeps upon insensibly, like Dust upon our Cloaths, or Chronical Diseases upon the body, which consumes as surely tho', not so violently, as Fractures and Contusions on the Members and Feavours in the Blood.[9]

Even more important to Defoe's mind, French economic ambitions, and the ineffective blue-water strategies designed to hinder them, constituted a direct threat to God's order because he believed trade to be the key to the divinely ordained moral and material advance of human history:

> the Wisdom and Direction of *Nature Natureing*, which I call GOD, produced such differing Species of things, all of them in their kind equally Necessary, or at least Useful and Desirable; as insensibly preserves the Dependence, of the most Remote Part of the World upon one another; and at least makes them useful to each other, and Contributing to one anothers Convenience, Necessity, or Delight.
>
> The Variety, both of the Produce and Manufactures . . . are the Foundations of Trade, and I Entitle Providence to it; not only as it is found in Nature, but as it is found in Customs and Consequences of things; for GOD in whose Infinite foreknowledge, all the Accidents of Time are always present . . . must be suppos'd to foreknow that Natural Causes consider'd, *and to Natural Causes, he had in his Infinite Wisdom by Laws of Nature, submitted all the Variety of Consequences*; the Generations of the World, could not subsist in the Manner prescib'd, without the Mutual Assistance, and Concurrence of one another.[10]

The extent to which these ideas constituted an explicitly Protestant frame of reference needs further study, but Luther employed the same

[8] J.G.A. Pocock, *The Machiavellian Moment: Florentine Political Thought and the Atlantic Republican Tradition* (Princeton, 1975), ch. 13.

[9] *Review*, 23 January 1705, vol. I, Bk. 3, no. 93, pp. 385–6.

[10] *Review*, 3 Januuary 1706, vol. III, Bk. 6, no. 2, p. 6.

arguments in his celebrated debate with Erasmus on free will.[11] A connection to the ideas of Francis Bacon is more certain for implicit in this passage is the expectation that trade not only led to mutual assistance but also to mutual advancement. His own heavily annotated copy of Francis Bacon's *Advancement of Learning*, his indoctrination as a Dissenting academy student into the principles of the New Science, his correspondence with members of the Royal Society all certify to Defoe's predilection for a concept of human progress through the industry and exchange of men and women engaged in the pursuit of liberty and property.[12]

In May 1706 Defoe began to focus almost exclusively upon the Union question, publishing the first in a series of six essays 'at Removing National Prejudices against a Union with Scotland'. Ironically, Defoe's position as England's primary pro-Union pamphleteer began in the employ of Scottish negotiators who had been favourably impressed with his 'understand(ing) of trade and the interest of nations'.[13] That understanding had been shaped by Defoe's faith in the virtues of plurality and exchange and by his sensitivity to the structural changes through which commerce had supplanted conquest as the basis of national power. Talk of an English conquest of Scotland, though, was precisely what the recent exploitation of Anglo-Scottish hostilities for political gain had encourgaged. In hiring Defoe, the Scots had found a public voice sufficiently voluble to combat it.

Defoe responded to the increasingly belligerent tone of English public opinion by attacking the parochialism upon which it fed. The raillery with which he had satirised native xenophobia in his best-selling poem of 1702, *The True-Born Englishman*, gave way to an excoriation of 'National Prejudices' in both kingdoms as 'the worst sort of Humane Antipathies'. Since the reign of Edward I, their sorry legacy to the island of Britain had been one of depredation and bloodshed at home resulting in missed opportunities and a diminished stature abroad.[14] In one respect this opening was a cautionary tale, a response to the reciprocal provocations and bellicose rumors of the past year. Even pamphleteers sceptical of the

[11] 'God does not give everything to each and we cannot all do everything. As Paul says, 'Now there are varieties of gifts, but the same Spirit' (1 Corinthians 12, 4). It remains, therefore, that these gifts render a mutual service. One with his gift bears the burden of the other's lack. Thus we shall fulfill the law of Christ.' Ernst F. Winter (trans. and ed.), *Discourse on Free Will* (New York, 1992), p. 99.

[12] Ilse Vickers, 'The influence of the New Sciences on Defoe', *Literature and History*, 13, 2, (1987).

[13] Cited in Backscheider, *Daniel Defoe*, pp. 207–8.

[14] [Defoe], *An Essay at Removing National Prejudices against a Union with Scotland, Part I* (London, 1706), p. 11.

proposed union, notably George Ridpath and James Hodges, made efforts to steer their readers away from the polemics of men like William Atwood and from notions of another Anglo-Scottish armed conflict.[15] But Defoe's emotive rhetoric dramatised their more conventionally expressed warnings. The future novelist invited his readers to reflect upon the 'Consequences of Armies ranging [over] an open and defenceless Country', to hear the groans of widows and children, and to picture 'the *Despair* of flourishing Families . . . with their Fields *over run*, their Barns and Houses *plunder'd and burnt*, their Cattle *driven away*, and their whole Substance *destroy'd*'. On both sides of the Tweed, ploughshares frequently unearthed the 'miserable Antiquities of eternal Feuds', and he goaded more genteel readers to consider 'what noble Branches of their Ancestors spilt their Blood on the desolate Borders' who now lay 'buried [and] blended with the Carcasses of the Common People'.[16] No doubt Defoe's arduous ride through the northern counties some weeks later fortified his historical imagination as the first *Reviews* dispatched from Edinburgh continued to rue the days when 'the Borders were the Courts of Judicature' and 'the Rights of Families and Nations were tryed by the unequal Decision of the Sword'.[17]

Beneath the surface of this barbarous landscape, however, lay Defoe's bedrock belief in a providential theory of material progress. The essay unveiled Defoe's dogged attempt to construct a corresponding *British* identity, which he termed 'a New National Interest', predicated upon England's and Scotland's shared commercial future and Protestant past.[18] Other aspects of their past, therefore, were subject to revision: Bannockburn again was cited, along with Flodden, Musselburgh, and Dunbar, but with the intended message that these battles should not be remembered as respective national victories, but lamented as blots upon a British escutcheon. Moving from the historical to the statistical, Defoe then cited the trebling of land values, which the island's most recent period of peace had brought to England's northern counties, in order to demonstrate the 'Security and quiet Possession of . . . Wealth and Improvements' which union would afford the 'common man' on both sides of the Tweed.[19]

15 [George Ridpath], *The Reducing of Scotland by Arms, and annexing it to England as a Province considered* (London, 1705). [James Hodges], *War betwixt the Two British Kingdoms Consider'd, and the dangerous Circumstances of Each with regard thereto lay'd open; by a full view of the Consequences of it on Both Sides* (London, 1705). [William Atwood], *The Superiority and Direct Dominion of the Imperial Crown of England, over the Crown and Kingdom of Scotland . . . Asserted* (London, 1704).

16 [Defoe], *An Essay at Removing National Prejudices . . . Part I*, pp. 18–19.

17 *Review*, 26 October 1706, vol. III, Bk. 8, no. 128, p. 510.

18 Defoe, *History of the Union*, 'Of the Last Treaty'. p. 29.

19 [Defoe], *An Essay at Removing National Prejudices . . . Part I*, pp. 19–21.

Lest the English resist Union on the grounds that Scotland's difficulties were innate to its land or people, Defoe repeatedly emphasised that historical circumstance and hypocrisy had created the imbalance of wealth between the two neighbouring kingdoms. As he had tried to persuade Haversham, the Scots were not solely to blame for their economic plight. Since the Union of the Crowns under James I, the English had 'remov'd their Court, Engross'd their Trade, drawn off their Gentry, and thus, their Capital is Destroy'd; they wither under our Shade, and we not only keep the Sun-beams of Prosperity from them, but we drop a sort of bitter Water upon them'.[20] The *Essay* also acknowledged Scottish complaints that English policies 'exclude[d] them in Advantages as Aliens, and use[d] them as Natives in Cases to their Loss', as exemplified by the Navigation Acts and Darien fiasco. Union would mend these injustices, Defoe argued, by guaranteeing a 'Freedom of Trade' throughout Britain and by instituting 'English Articles of Possession' between Scottish landlords and their tenants, thereby ensuring prosperity and improvement for the entire island.[21] Should his English readers fear the burden of fairness, a second *Essay at Removing National Prejudices* assured them of redoubled benefits, both for England's colonial and inland commercial development, and for London's pre-eminence as the 'Emporium of Britain', the centre of wealth where 'all Circles will meet'.[22]

Although the first two essays devoted more space to economic matters, Defoe did identify objections to the co-existence of two established churches within one polity as perhaps the 'greatest Obstruction' to Union and he examined the various components of the problem.[23] He cited the Dutch and Swiss unions as successful (if not entirely apt) examples of composite settlements in order to refute the contemporary axiom which held religious pluralism to be incompatible with political stability. In keeping with the controlling theme of the essay, he blamed 'Party-prejudice', and high Anglican, anti-Presbyterian rhetoric in particular, for arousing popular jealousies with regard to Church and Kirk.[24] In response to fears, primarily Scottish ones, that incorporation might jeopardise the religious status quo, he argued that the union was 'not to

[20] *Review*, 11 December 1705, vol. II, Bk. 5, no. 120, p. 480.

[21] [Defoe], *An Essay at Removing National Prejudices . . . Part I*, p. 17–21.

[22] [Defoe], *An Essay at Removing National Prejudices Against a Union with Scotland, Part II* (London, 1706), pp. 31–2.

[23] [Defoe], *An Essay at Removing National Prejudices . . . Part I*, p. 23. Religion was 'the most Dangerous Rock of Difference, on which this Union could Split . . . ' Defoe, *History of the Union*, 'Of the Last Treaty . . . ', p. 1.

[24] [Defoe], *An Essay at Removing National Prejudices . . . Part I*, pp. 12–15. Technically, the United Provinces and Swiss cantons represented tolerant confederations and not an incorporate, dual-confessional state with a single monarch as proposed by the union treaty.

ALTER, but to CONFIRM' the present settlement in both kingdoms.[25] Above all else, Defoe tried to emphasise the common bond of Protestantism between the two kingdoms: 'The Difference in both Nations is not of Religion, but in Religious Circumstance; both are Protestant, both Orthodox in Principle, and equally opposite to Popery, and Antichristianism'.[26]

In the present crisis over union, however, Anglicans and Presbyterians were nursing their differences and not the pan-Protestant ideal which had inspired their forebears and which Defoe was trying to promote in his construction of a British national consciousness. Circumstances demanded that the treaty preserve the division of British Protestantism in perpetuity. Defoe's defence of this arrangement represented a novel application of the logic of exchange and improvement to mental and moral, as well as material, goods. While wishing that those 'worshipping the same God', and sharing the 'same faith, and the same redeemer' might agree on the 'same terms', he submitted to the fact that 'inscrutible Providence has directed otherwise', concluding

> Perhaps these things are suffer'd in the Church of Christ, for the Exercise of Charity, Forebearance, and mutual Temper, of Christians to prevent worse Inconveniences, which from the Pride of Prosperity, the Power and the Glory of an United Church, might in Conjunction with Human Infirmity, have risen in the World . . .[27]

This was no mere rationalisation on Defoe's part but an argument both Baconian and Ciceronian. Defoe embraced Bacon's programmatic sense that the natural world was to be fully explored in order to put it to use. The contention that Providence admitted ecclesiastic plurality in order to promote the exercise of Christian virtues was paralleled by his argument that God had created a world of diverse resources to encourage 'Trade', 'Dependence', and 'Mutual Assistance'.[28] Also implicit in this argument was the idea that individuals improved their moral personalities through the process of correspondence and conversation – an ethos of 'politeness', or 'sociability', generally ascribed to the third Earl of Shaftesbury, and more broadly associated with the works of Defoe, Addison, and Hume.[29] Because it might lead to conversations about the Deity, however, the trajectory of 'politeness' had a Socinian endpoint unwelcome to Trinitarians

25 [Defoe], *An Essay at Removing National Prejudices . . . Part I*, pp. 24–25.
26 [Defoe], *An Essay at Removing National Prejudices . . . Part I*, p. 17.
27 [Defoe], *An Essay at Removing National Prejudices . . . Part I*, p. 23.
28 See n 10.
29 Lawrence Klein, 'Liberty, Manners, and Politeness in Early Eighteenth-Century England', *Historical Journal*, 32, 3 (1989), 583–605; Nicholas Phillipson, *Hume* (London, 1989), ch. 2.

like Defoe: hence his occasional sallies against Arians and Deists and his accent on the Trinitarianism of both Church and Kirk throughout the course of the debate. Far more palatable to Defoe were the ecclesiastical implications of the agendas founded by Bacon and the new scientists. They had sought experiential knowledge of the natural world in order to distinguish it more clearly from the supernatural, the territory of enthusiasm. This sharp separation of the natural and supernatural worlds fostered an erastianism which was entirely compatible with the circumstances of the Union: the toleration of Trinitarian nonconformists and the acceptance of two established churches under one polity.

The 'Charity, Forebearance and mutual Temper' which Defoe had hoped for were not in evidence during the summer of 1706. His correspondence with Robert Harley reveals a growing awareness by both men that Scottish Presbyterians had been campaigning against the treaty both at home and in England. In September, Harley dispatched Defoe to Edinburgh.[30] He arrived in early October to find the Scottish Parliament already in session and mobbed daily by anti-Union protestors outside; 'The Church men . . . goeing mad', and his own two *Essays*, written to cool English passions, now reprinted and circulated to fuel Scottish ones.[31] Even before this first-hand experience with Scottish discontent, though, Defoe had introduced to the debate another weapon from his discursive arsenal.

Adapting apace to its author's changes in rhetoric and residence, the *Review*, in late September, presented its readers with a doggerel salute to 'Peace and Union' whose presence brought nations happiness, and whose absence, their destruction:

> UNION is Nature's strong Cement;
> The *Life* of *Power*, and *Soul of Government*:
> Without it, all the World's a Mob;
> Confusion's Universal Monarch of the Globe . . .
> Even Government it self must dye,
> In Wild Uncultivated Anarchy . . . [32]

At this stage, the rhetoric simply warned readers that another Anglo-Scottish conflict would result in the dissolution of government. But as public apprehension of Union by force shifted to that of Union by ratified treaty, so too did Defoe's use of this discourse.

As early as 1703, the Presbyterian minister and propagandist, James

[30] For Defoe's reports of Presbyterian machinations in London and his specific instructions to allay fears about the Kirk, see Healey, pp. 124–8.
[31] Healey, p. 137 and *passim*.
[32] *Review*, 28 September 1706, vol. III, Bk. 8, no. 116, p. 463.

Hodges, had argued that a united British parliament would not adhere to treaty provisions which protected Scottish interests. By 1706, the Scots had come to doubt completely the safety of the Kirk in the hands of a parliamentary majority composed of bishops and staunchly Anglican MPs. Probably in September, two pamphlets appeared which reiterated this distrust.[33] It must also be noted that all these works made this point in the context of promoting various schemes for a federal union which would preserve both the Scottish Parliament and Kirk. While accepting a Presbyterian case for added insurance in an Act of Security, Defoe attacked notions that incorporation would threaten the religious settlement of either nation. In a third *Essay at Removing National Prejudices*, Defoe argued that should any power, including a united British parliament, tamper with the treaty or the rights of either church, then:

> the Union is Broke, the Constitution is Overthrown . . . The fundamental is destroy'd, the Government dissolves, and the whole Island becomes a Mob, one Universal Rabble. Just as in the case of a Tyrant, dispensing with the Laws and Setting up Arbitrary Power, Property ceases, Authority dissolves, Constitution suffocates, and the National Capacity dyes.[34]

To argue that some future Parliament would risk such an action was to 'say a Parliament may be mad' enough to 'annihilat[e] their own Body'.[35]

The language reminds us that Defoe was a man of 'Revolution Principles', willing to invoke dissolution theory after most Whigs had settled upon less radical discourses in which to explain changes in government and power. Even more significant, in responding to public opinion at large and to challenges made by other able pamphleteers, Defoe had elevated the Treaty of Union to the status of fundamental law. Conversely, commentators seeking a federal union argued that in accepting the treaty, the Scottish Parliament was, in fact, violating fundamental law. The idea that a treaty might become, in effect, a social contract was a politically explosive one. In an important sense, it threatened the Scots as a people in a way that Defoe's attempts to forge the idea of a British people – as Protestant, free, commercial, and improving – had not.

33 [James Hodges], *The Rights and Interests of the Two British Monarchies, Inquir'd into, and Clear'd; with a special respect to an United or Separate State. Treatise I* (London, 1703). [George Ridpath], *Considerations upon the Union of the Two Kingdoms* . . . (London, 1706). [Andrew Fletcher?], *State of the Controversy betwixt United and Separate Parliaments* (1706).

34 [Defoe], *An Essay at Removing National Prejudices, against a Union with England. Part III* (Edinburgh, 1706), p. 12.

35 *Review*, 12 November 1706, vol. III, Bk. 8, no. 135, p. 538. Of course, this line may not have swayed many Scots who believed that in accepting incorporation, their own Parliament was destroying itself.

At the heart of the matter was the problem of the relationship between the represented and their representatives. Both Ridpath and Hodges had published pamphlets arguing that the abolition of separate parliaments challenged the fundamental law of the original rights of freeholders. Consequently, the Scottish Parliament could not ratify the present treaty without first appealing to the freeholding electorate.[36] In response to this line of argument, Defoe agreed with its first premise: 'the Right of a Freeholder is an Original, 'tis claimed by his Possession, which is to be trac'd back to God Almighty's first Donation, when he gave Man Possession of the Earth to him and his Heirs . . . from whence 'tis easy to deduce the Right of all Government in the World'.[37] But he went on to say that the treaty did not alter those rights, only their circumstances. The right to change those circumstances, to reapportion representation, rested squarely with parliament. It could alter the terms of representation for counties, towns, and corporations without their special consent and had done so on numerous occasions in the past. The treaty was merely the exercise of that authority writ large. The argument betrays an assumption on Defoe's part that parliament was not just an expression of the people's will but an embodiment of their original right. Like his description of the dissolution of government, cited above, Defoe's defence of the rights of freeholders has the Lockean ring we have been conditioned to expect in his writings. But Locke had said that the apportionment of representation rested with the crown rather than with parliament, so that invocation of Locke is insufficient if we wish to understand Defoe's emphasis upon the idea of parliament as mystical incorporation, sovereign in its authority to decide its own profile.[38]

Putting aside Defoe's theoretical beliefs for a moment, it is important to note that he blamed alternative conceptions of parliament for setting the stage for a series of practical hazards in the ratification process. Unionists successfully negotiated the first of these by rejecting early calls by the opposition for a parliamentary recess so that members could consult their constituents about the various articles. Such a delay, Defoe later reflected, might have 'furnish[ed] a Variety of Accidents to

[36] [George Ridpath], *Considerations upon the Union of the Two Kingdoms: with an Account of the Methods taken by Ancient and Modern Governments, to effect an Union* . . . (London, 1706). [James Hodges], *The Rights and Interests of the Two British Monarchies. With Special Respect to an United or Separate State. Treatise III* (London, 1706).

[37] [Defoe], *A Fourth Essay at Removing National Prejudices; with some reply to Mr. H[o]dges and some other authors, who have printed their objections against an union with England* (Edinburgh, 1706), p. 11. See also, *Review*, 19 December 1706, vol. III, Bk. 8, no. 151, pp. 602–3.

[38] John Locke, *Two Treatises of Government*, ed. Peter Laslett (Cambridge, 1967), pp. 391–2.

disappoint the whole'.[39] At this juncture, Hodges' third treatise against incorporation had appeared, which Defoe wrote to Harley 'has done more Mischief than a thousand men'.[40] Not only did it incite the 'poor people' by posing 'the dark Side of everything' and concealing 'the true Sense of things', it and other anti-incorporating pamphlets encouraged constituents to turn their 'private Letters into Publick Addresses, and those [in turn] introduc'd Mobs, Tumults, Insultings of Magistrates . . . and all manner of Popular Disorders; Till, at last, it came to downright Insurrection'.[41] However monocausal an explanation, Defoe clearly linked freeholder demands that representatives act as agents accountable to their electors with the stream of addresses of protest to Parliament and with wider public unrest. In reviewing *State of the Controversy*, Defoe could not hide his contempt for its author's assertion that 'By the Constitution of Parliaments, the Laws are to have their Rise from the Will and Humour of the People, signified by the Lords and Commons'. Such remarks, Defoe grumbled, insulted 'Parliamentary Dignity' and 'endeavour'd to stir the People to Mob, Clamour and Tumult'.[42]

Defoe too, in his day, had been accused of insulting Parliament and inciting faction, most notably after his infamous 1701 petition, *Legion's Memorial* and after his 1702 *Original Power of the Collective Body of the People of England*, a cheeky rejoinder to a Tory MP. Both of these pamphlets contain Defoe's most overt defences of the right of a people to hold their representatives to account. The non-juring polemicist, Charles Leslie was the first to tar these works with a Lockean brush and Defoe's political thought has been linked with that of Locke ever since. As Conal Condren has recently argued, however, the *Original Power* shows a considerable debt to George Lawson's *Politica sacra et civilis*. Indeed, in spite of its radical assertions of popular sovereignty, the *Original Power*, like the *Politica*, propounded a corporate conception of the people and their representatives.[43] This Lawsonian legacy helps to explain Defoe's belief that the Scottish parliament, as the embodiment of freeholder rights, had the power to transfer representation of those rights to another institution, namely a unified British parliament. There is, however, an even more direct connection between Defoe's *Original Power* and his union activities.

[39] Defoe, *History of the Union*, 'Of the Carrying on of the Treaty in Scotland', p. 3.
[40] Healey, p. 153.
[41] Defoe, *History of the Union*, 'Of . . . the Treaty in Scotland', pp. 15–22.
[42] [Fletcher?], *State of the Controversy*, p. 7. *Review*, 23 November 1706, vol. III, Bk. 8, no. 140, p. 559.
[43] Conal Condren, *George Lawson's Politica and the English Revolution* (Cambridge, 1989), pp. 166–9.

While Defoe had described members of parliament as 'an abridgement of the many volumes of the English Nation', he often elided the concept of a corporate people with that of the majority.[44] His watered down corporate theory made him very aware of the power of forms of public opinion which appeared to speak for that majority. Thus, he expended a great deal of effort to minimise and even denigrate the quality and quantity of addresses to the Scottish Parliament lest they be taken, especially by the English, as 'universal', or as proof of 'a rooted Aversion in the Generality of the *Scots* Nation against the Union'.[45] Consequently, he frequently portrayed addresses as either orchestrated and signed primarily by Jacobites, or as representing only poor and insignificant parts of the nation, or as generally exaggerated in number.[46] His overall campaign to repudiate both the forms and theory behind Scottish protest goaded the Jacobite, Patrick Abercromby, into republishing parts of the *Original Right* to embarrass its author in an avowal of Scottish rights and Scottish expression.[47] Put on the defensive, Defoe reaffirmed the right of freeholders to oppose assaults on their fundamental rights but denied that Parliament's ratification of the treaty invaded those rights in any way. Moreover, he explicitly located original right in the opinion of 'the majority', a body whose numbers were easy to manipulate but difficult to gauge. He was, however, certain that no majority of freeholders had yet appeared to constrain the House against union.[48] In 1701, Defoe's *Legion's Memorial* and his offer to append the petition with the signatures of 200,000 Englishmen was clearly intended and understood as a symbolic representation of the people. But his conception of the collective body, ambiguously presented in the *Original Right*, would be further compromised when re-used in the Scottish Union debate. In negotiating a passage through the various streams of union opinion, the language of popular sovereignty had inched a step closer toward becoming the language of majority rule.

As England's chief pamphleteer for the Union of 1707, Defoe was an active agent in, and chronicler of, negotiations which transformed two

[44] [Defoe], *The Original Power of the Collective Body of the People of England* in *A True Collection of the Writings Of the Author of The True-Born English-Man* (London, 1703), p. 139.

[45] *Review*, 10 December 1706, vol. III, Bk. 8, no. 147, p. 586.

[46] See for example *Review*, 26 November 1706, vol. III, Bk. 8, no. 141, pp. 562–3; 10 December, vol. III, Bk. 8, no. 147, p. 586.

[47] [Patrick Abercromby], *The Advantages of the Act of Security, compar'd with these of the intended union: founded on the revolution principles publish'd by Mr. Daniel De Foe* (Edinburgh, 1706).

[48] [Defoe], *A Fifth Essay, At Removing National Prejudices: with a reply to some authors, who have printed their objections against an union with England* (?Edinburgh, 1707).

kingdoms into an imperial power. The regime of William III had introduced England to a new military and financial reality and had committed its people to a greater role in protecting the European balance of power against the 'mighty Nimrod', the aspiring universal monarch, Louis XIV. Much of Defoe's pro-Union stance demonstrates his ability to perceive the rapidly changing relationship between economics and politics. For the most part, Defoe accepted these developments as necessary, if not progressive, but they demanded corresponding changes in Anglo-Scottish relations which would give new meaning to the concept of a British imperial state. In urging the English and the Scots to accept the Union, he was also encouraging them to accept a new national identity. The new British nation needed to embrace its providentially ordained and historically inevitable role as champion of a free, Protestant, and commercial world order.

The subject of identities is a sensitive one, all the more so when insiders perceive that an outsider is defining one for them, and the Scots mounted a vigorous campaign of their own to defend their sovereignty and cultural integrity. In one of the more famous defences of Scottish independence, John Hamilton, Lord Belhaven, implored his fellow members in the Edinburgh Parliament not to sign the Union treaty: 'I think I see our Ancient Mother CALEDONIA . . . attending the Fatal Blow, and breathing out her last . . . None can destroy Scotland save Scotland's self; hold your Hands from the Pen'.[49] Defoe had certain grasp of his own pen. Months of *Reviews*, over forty essays, shorter pamphlets, and poems, as well as his *History* attest to a massive political and literary effort on behalf of the Treaty of Union.

Defoe had two strategies: to address anti-Union propaganda and to promote a compelling vision of a united British nation. He conducted his assignment in three sets of discourses – providential, Baconian, and natural law – which developed in compelling ways themselves. His use of providential rhetoric, including both its inscrutable and progressive variants, placed the Union either in the path of God's direct intervention or within the indirect but divinely inspired unfolding of time. Defoe's Baconian arguments also betrayed a providential logic of improvement. Although he made occasional reference to continental thinkers during the course of the debate, this essay has focused on a subset of the natural law tradition known as 'Revolution Principles' and on Defoe's English political inheritance. All three discourses represent a central feature of Defoe's Presbyterian world view in that each in its own way could be said to support a dissenting ideology which stressed that man should exercise

[49] *The Lord Beilhaven's Speech in Parliament*, in Defoe, *History of the Union*.

his reason to understand both divine will and the world around him. At their most basic level, all three traditions accepted nature as the continuous manifestation of God's will and perceived change in the physical world as a sign of this process. They could therefore be used to explain or even justify changing material conditions in society and to argue that human relations, including political ones, would naturally develop accordingly or should be encouraged to do so. In choosing these discourses to defend the union, Defoe adopted an historical scheme which argued that socio-economic process determined the validity of political arrangements. He also could argue that the expansion of commerce was part of the divine order. What is intellectually significant in this is that the process of exchange, both material and moral, figured prominently in developing social theories of the eighteenth century, including those associated with the Scottish Enlightenment. In his Union writings, we can see Defoe the journalist participating in these efforts to understand mutuality and the historical process as principles in themselves.

10

SCOTTISH LAW, SCOTTISH LAWYERS AND THE STATUS OF THE UNION

JOHN W. CAIRNS

William Forbes, advocate, presented to the Faculty of Advocates in 1708 a proposal that he would 'write a complete body of the law of Scotland, containing the harmony thereof with, and differences from the civil and feudal laws; and shewing how far the Scots and English law do agree and differ; with incident comparative views of the modern constitutiones of other nations in Europe'. He was very concerned with English law and the effects of the Union on Scots law after 1707. Forbes explained:

> Since the happy union of the two Kingdoms into one Monarchy, such a complete body of the law of Scotland, as is proposed, may now be justly reckoned among the Desiderata, or things that are wanting, towards settling and maintaining a fair understanding and correspondence betwixt the judicatures in north and south Britain, and for facilitating the dispatch of justice; In which Judges and persons of all ranks will find their account.[1]

Forbes obtained the Faculty's approval, and wrote his Great Body, but it was never published. In fact, the work was not the sustained comparative treatise that the proposal might have led one to expect; Forbes did, however, give a brief account of the relevant English law after his discussion of each subject area of the Scots.[2] His work is none the less indicative of a new level of Scottish interest in English law after 1707.

In 1714 Forbes was elected the first Professor of Civil Law in the University of Glasgow, and he advertised in the *Scots Courant* of 8/10 September 1714 that his lectures would be on Civil and Scots law, undertaking 'to explain in his Colleges the Harmony, Analogy, and Differences betwixt the Roman Law, and the Law of Scotland; and also

I am grateful for the comments of Hector MacQueen, Neil MacCormick, John Robertson, David Sellar, and the participants at the seminar.

[1] *The Minute Book of the Faculty of Advocates, Volume 1, 1661–1712*, ed. J.M. Pinkerton, Stair Society, vol. xxix (Edinburgh, 1976), p. 277.

[2] Glasgow University Library, MSS Gen. 1246–1252.

how far either of these Laws do agree with, and differ from the Law of England'.[3] Forbes's first publication, after his theses for admission as an advocate, had been a work on bills of exchange in 1703;[4] the second edition of 1718 added in references to English Acts of Parliament, and now promised 'incident and comparative Views of the Laws and Customs of England, and other Countries'. It now also promised on its title page that 'For the Benefit of the English, our Law Terms are explain'd by these equippolent in their Law'.[5]

Scottish interest in English law was scarcely novel. Thomas Craig demonstrated in *Jus feudale*, written between 1600 and 1608, and *De unione regnorum Britanniae tractatus* of 1605 that he had some acquaintance with English law,[6] and James Dalrymple, Viscount Stair's *Institutions of the Law of Scotland* (1681) contained a number of remarks comparing English law and procedure with those of Scotland.[7] Yet, from 1707 onwards, Scots lawyers' interest in English law seems to have intensified as Forbes's interest suggests. The Copyright Act of 1709 (c.21) made access to English law easy for Scots advocates, as their Library became entitled to demand copies of English legal works. Before this Act, the Library had had very few English law books (only four in 1683),[8] and the printed Catalogue of 1692 shows them positioned awkwardly and occasionally among a wealth of civilian and canonist learning.[9] In 1712,

[3] See generally J.W. Cairns, 'The origins of the Glasgow Law School: the Professors of Civil Law, 1714–61', in P. Birks (ed.), *The Life of the Law: Proceedings of the Tenth British Legal History Conference, Oxford, 1991* (London, 1993), pp. 151–94.

[4] W. Forbes, *A Methodical Treatise, Concerning Bills of Exchange . . . according to the analogy of the Scots Law* (Edinburgh, 1703).

[5] W. Forbes, *A Methodical Treatise Concerning Bills of Exchange . . . according to the Analogy of the Law of Scotland: With incident comparative Views of the Laws and Customs of England, and other Countries* (Edinburgh, 1718).

[6] T. Craig, *Jus Feudale, tribus libris comprehensum: quibus non solum consuetudines feudales, & praediorum jura, quae in Scotia, Anglia, & plerisque Galliae locis obtinent, continentur; sed universum jus Scoticum, & omnes fere materiae juris clare & dilucide exponuntur, & ad fontes juris feudalis & civilis singula reducuntur*, ed. J. Baillie, 3rd edn (Edinburgh, 1732); and, *De unione regnorum Britanniae tractatus*, ed. C. Sanford Terry, Scottish History Society, vol. lx (Edinburgh, 1909).

[7] James, Viscount Stair, *The Institutions of the Law of Scotland Deduced from its Originals, and Collated with the Civil, Canon and Feudal Laws, and with the Customs of Neighbouring Nations in IV Books*, 2nd edn (1693), ed. D.M. Walker (Edinburgh and Glasgow, 1981); see W.D.H. Sellar, 'English law as a source [of Stair's Institutions]', in D.M. Walker (ed.), *Stair Tercentenary Studies*, Stair Society, vol. xxxiii (Edinburgh, 1981), pp. 140–50.

[8] M. Townley, *The Best and Fynest Lawers and Other Raire Bookes: A Facsimile of the Earliest List of Books in the Advocates' Library, Edinburgh with an Introduction and Modern Catalogue* (Edinburgh, 1990), pp. 25–7, 72 (nos. 15, 16, 23 and 236).

[9] *Catalogus librorum bibliothecae juris utriusque, tam civilis quam canonici, publici quam privati, feudalis quam municipalis variorum regnorum, cum historicis Graecis & Latinis, literatis & philosophis plerisque celebrioribus; a Facultate Advocatorum in Supremo Senatu Judicum in Scotia, in usum cupidae legum juventutis, constructae* (Edinburgh, 1692). I counted thirty-four English law books in the category of *libri juridici*; not all of these were on English common law as such.

the Faculty of Advocates noted that Forbes had 'brought the first volumn of his body of the laws of Great Britain nigh to a period', but that he needed a number of English treatises and case reports too complete it.[10] The works that Forbes required were standard English legal texts and reports published in the previous century; through the eighteenth century, the Library's collection of English law grew significantly because of the Copyright Act, and no advocate would have had to make such a request in 1812.

The labours of two Scots working in London provide hints of possible English interest in Scots law after 1707. It is unclear, however, to what extent their productions responded to an English demand or reflected their authors' Scottish concerns. Thus, James Innes published in 1733 in London *Idea juris Scotici*, supposedly at the request of a young man trained in English law who wished to know something about Scots law.[11] Similarly, the *Edinburgh Evening Courant* of 23 April 1745 carried an advertisement proposing the publication of *Analogia legum, or, A View of the Laws of England and Scotland, set against one another* by Patrick Turnbull of the Middle Temple. This work, however, never progressed beyond an introduction produced for purposes of advertising.[12] Turnbull had been admitted as an advocate in 1702, and had decided to pursue a career at the English bar, being admitted to the Middle Temple in 1721 and called in 1725.[13] What Turnbull proposed was described in the title of his work as 'To shew wherein those Two Laws agree and differ: designed For the Ease and better Accommodation of the Subjects of both Parts of the United Kingdom of Great Britain, in their mutual Dealings and Concerns with one another.' He explained:

> No Doubt, but few Obstructions in the Course of the Circulation of Justice amongst the People, is a Thing the most to be wished for; but I humbly conceive, that the Danger does not so much arise from the Differences of Laws in a State, as from these Differences not being known and understood as is plainly to be seen in the Laws and Customs of *Kent* and other Places; which, though different from the Laws of the rest of the Kingdom of *England*; yet when these Differences are understood, they give no Trouble at all, either to the Courts or the Suitors.
>
> To obtain the like easy Course with respect to the different Laws in

[10] *Advocates' Minute Book Volume 1*, pp. 298–9.

[11] J. Innes, *Idea juris Scotici: Or, A Summary View of the Laws of Scotland* (London, 1733).

[12] P. Turnbull, *Analogia Legum: Or, A View of The Institutes of the Laws of England and Scotland, Set One against the Other; To shew wherein those Two Laws agree and differ: Designed For the Ease and better Accommodation of the Subjects of both Parts of the United Kingdom of Great Britain, in their mutual Dealings and Concerns with one another* ([London], 1745).

[13] *Advocates' Minute Book Volume 1*, pp. 240–1; C.E.A. Bedwell, 'Scottish Middle Templars 1604–1869', *Scottish Historical Review*, 17 (1920), 100–17 at p. 104.

> *England* and *Scotland*, is the Whole of the Plot of the ensuing Treatise: In order to which I have endeavoured to set them in such a Light and Nearness to one another, that either by Concord or Discord, they may serve to illustrate one another.[14]

Events probably overtook Turnbull's proposal, and all he ever produced was a pamphlet on the controversy over the abolition of heritable jurisdictions.[15]

It is probably fair to say that English lawyers did not develop any strong interest in or concern about Scots law after the Union, though one can discover occasional allusions to it in their published works. In contrast, English law took on a great importance for Scots lawyers, and one can trace advocates such as Alexander Bayne, William Grant of Prestongrange, or Hugh Dalrymple spending time at an English Inn of Court, and occasionally being called to the English bar.[16] And it is worth noting that of the elite group of thirty-six advocates who were MPs between 1715 and 1754 no less than six had been members of an Inn of Court.[17]

There were a number of reasons for this curiosity about English law. First, English law and procedures came into use in certain areas, either by the Union itself or by subsequent statutes. Secondly, the court with ultimate jurisdiction over Scottish law suits was now the House of Lords; though it might contain sixteen representative Scots peers, there was no reason to believe they would have a predominant voice in decisions, and one of the objects of works comparing Scots law with English law and of explanations of Scottish legal terms in English terminology was obviously to expound Scots law in a way that made it intelligible to the English. Lord Bankton thus commented that 'since the union of the two kingdoms, there is such intercourse between the subjects of South and North Britain, that it must be of great moment, that the laws of both be generally understood'. This was especially so for Scotland:

> [T]he last resort for deciding on our property is now in the house of Lords, where hitherto no provision is made for having any Scots judges on the wool-packs, to inform the house, upon occasion, concerning the laws of this

14 Turnbull, *Analogia Legum*, p. xxiii.

15 P. Turnbull, *A Cursory View, of the Ancient and Present State of the Fieffs, or Tenures, In both Parts of the United Kingdom of Great-Britain* (London, [1747]).

16 *The Records of the Honourable Society of Lincoln's Inn. Vol. I. Admissions from A.D. 1420 to A.D. 1799* ([London], 1896), p. 367 (Bayne); Bedwell, 'Scottish Middle Templars', p. 104 (Grant and Dalrymple).

17 R. Sedgwick, *The House of Commons 1715–1754*, 2 vols. (London, 1970), I, p. 145. They were Archibald Grant, Andrew Mitchell, Alexander Hume Campbell, James Oswald, John Rutherford, and William Grant.

country; and we cannot be sure of having always (as at present we have) some noble lords sitting there, who are learned in the laws of Scotland . . .

It was no doubt to promote this understanding that Bankton stressed that he had 'endeavoured to render the stile agreeable to readers accustomed to the purity of the English language'.[18] This recognition of the need to understand the laws of each country led in 1710 and 1715 to fruitless proposals to establish commissions to explain the laws of each country to the other.[19] Thirdly, the law of England, with its vaunted claims to historic age and uniqueness, had an obvious intellectual fascination for the lawyers of North Britain, as the law of the wealthy, populous, and commercial country to the south where power now was based: was English law a cause of English liberty and prosperity? English lawyers, on the other hand, had none of these reasons for curiosity about Scots law. The Scots lawyers' interest in English law generally reflects the fact that South Britain was culturally and politically dominant.

The comparisons of Scots with English law, seeking out similarities and dissimilarities, that were made by Forbes and Bankton were in some respects reminiscent of the earlier Jacobean discussions of the possibility of assimilation of the laws of the two countries in which the fundamental similarity of Scots and English law was stressed. Craig's comment that 'at the present day there are no nations whose laws and institutions more closely correspond than England and Scotland . . . [and] that there is not that diversity between the two systems of law as is popularly supposed to exist' is later closely echoed by Turnbull's that '[a]s to the Parts constituent of the Bodies of the two Laws of *England* and *Scotland*, the Differences are not many nor very great; only the *Scotch* Law admits of more from the *Corpus Juris Civilis*, *Corpus Juris Canonicum*, the *Jus Feudale, &c.* than the English will acknowledge'.[20] It is likewise significant that Forbes's treatise would be described in 1712 as on the laws of Great Britain.[21] Later in the eighteenth century, Lord Kames was to stress the common historical origins of the English and Scots laws, and to advocate the writing of '[a] regular institute of the common law of this island, deducing historically the changes which that law hath undergone in the two nations'. This was a project that he considered 'must touch every Briton who wishes a compleat union', but especially Scots whose property was subject in the last resort to judges 'who have little

[18] A. MacDouall [Lord Bankton], *An Institute of the Laws of Scotland in Civil Rights: with Observations upon the Agreement or Diversity between them and the Laws of England*, 3 vols. (Edinburgh, 1751–53), I, pp. ix, vi, xi.

[19] Turnbull, *Analogia Legum*, pp. xxii–xxiii. This topic could bear further research.

[20] Craig, *De Unione*, p. 304; Turnbull, *Analogia Legum*, p. xxi.

[21] *Advocates' Minute Book Volume 1*, p. 298.

inclination, because they have scarce any means to acquire knowledge in our law'.[22]

The carefully drafted provisions of the Treaty of Union ensured that Scots law and Scottish legal institutions by and large survived. Special provisions protecting Scottish courts and Scottish private law indicate, however, that the Union was seen as a possible threat. The survey by Professor Levack of projects for unification of the laws of Scotland and England between 1603 and 1707 tends to lead to the conclusion, however, that unification was not practicably possible.[23] However much the differences between the two laws may have been minimised, the early modern state lacked the resources and political will to produce a unified law abstracted from elements of both. The superficially more practical solution of imposing English law on Scotland was politically impossible, at least in matters of private law: to have done so would have destroyed the system of land tenure on which Scottish political society was based. Such an upheaval would have destroyed the rights and privileges of the governing classes. And indeed it is remarkable how few legislative reforms in Scots private law there were in the eighteenth century. The abolition of military tenures and heritable jurisdictions, to take two examples, required the shock of the 1745 Rebellion – and even then the latter reform required payment of compensation and encountered considerable resistance.

A prominent theme of Scottish legal historiography none the less has been that the period from 1707 has seen a progressive – and regrettable – 'anglicisation' of Scots law. This has been made a historical commonplace by, most recently and notably, Lord Cooper and Professor Sir Thomas Smith. This reading of Scottish legal history has tended to focus on the House of Lords, viewed as an arrogant appeal court unsympathetic to Scots law, and on the status of certain provisions of the Treaty of Union, viewed as fundamental or entrenched, and hence as limiting the legislative competency of the Westminster Parliament. The first of these issues requires further serious exploration, but it is difficult to assert convincingly that the undoubted considerable influence of English law on Scots law was entirely or even mostly imposed by the House of Lords; the second has given rise to a vigorous debate,[24] the development of which

[22] H. Home, Lord Kames, *Historical Law-Tracts*, 4th edn (Edinburgh, 1792), pp. xii–xiii.

[23] B.P. Levack, *The Formation of the British State: England, Scotland, and the Union 1603–1707* (Oxford, 1987), pp. 68–101.

[24] See, e.g., D.J. Edwards, 'The Treaty of Union: more hints of constitutionalism', *Legal Studies*, 12 (1992), 34–41; M. Upton, 'Marriage vows of the elephant: the consitution of 1707', *Law Quarterly Review*, 105 (1989), 79–103; C.R. Munro, *Studies in Constitutional Law* (London, 1987), pp. 61–78; N. MacCormick, 'Does the United Kingdom have a constitution? Reflections on MacCormick v. Lord Advocate', *Northern Ireland Legal Quarterly*, 29 (1978), 1–20; T.B. Smith, 'The Union of 1707 as fundamental law', in *Studies Critical and Comparative* (Edinburgh, 1962), pp. 1–27.

from the time of the Union itself would prove a fruitful topic to study, but it is not a debate capable of resolution through historical scholarship, and here it will be gone beyond, or at least bypassed, as irrelevant.

Linked with the reading of Scottish legal history associated with Cooper and Smith has been the type of claim concisely expressed by Sheriff Irvine Smith: 'It was well for Scotland that she entered the Union of 1707, which laid her open to English legal influence, with a scientific system of law founded on the philosophic principles she gained from Stair.'[25] This thesis has never been the subject of serious challenge, but it is not particularly compelling. Stair's work was undoubtedly brilliant, but it is implausible that his *Institutions* alone should have preserved Scots law. Instead, his work, placing Scots law in the context of the law of nature and nations, reflected an existing, rather than created a new, Scots law and legal culture. It is therefore important to examine Scottish legal culture before 1707 in order to show how it produced Scots lawyers' interest in English law and encouraged them to use it to develop their own. It will be argued that this culture emphasised the primacy of natural law over municipal law: natural law constituted a 'fundamental' law much more than did any provision in the Treaty or Acts of Union. It was this approach to municipal law that encouraged the strong interest in English law shown by a man such as Forbes.

Scots lawyers' location of their law within the context of natural law and the law of nations in the late seventeenth and early eighteenth centuries was not limited to academic or theoretical treatises; it will be shown that the procedures of the courts required lawyers to place Scots law within this framework and to argue legal issues by referring not only to Scottish sources of law but also to the *ius naturale* and the *ius gentium*. Pleadings could thus discuss law using the language of the law of nature and nations.[26] Furthermore, as the eighteenth century progressed, in the face of inactivity by parliament to reform Scots law, lawyers such as Lord Kames (as David Lieberman has argued) favoured modernisation through the courts.[27] Pleadings may also be found discussing the law using the languages of civility and modern manners.[28]

[25] J.I. Smith, 'The rise of modern Scots law 1660–1707', in [G.C.H. Paton (ed.)], *An Introduction to Scottish Legal History*, Stair Society, vol. xx (Edinburgh, 1958), pp. 44–9 at p. 45; see also T.M. [Lord] Cooper, *The Scottish Legal Tradition*, ed. S.C. Styles, new edn (Edinburgh, 1991), p. 69; T.B. Smith, 'Strange gods: the crisis of Scots law as a civilian system', in *Studies Critical and Comparative*, pp. 72–88 at p. 73.

[26] J.W. Cairns, 'Hamesucken and the major premiss in the libel, 1672–1700: criminal law in the age of Enlightenment', in R.F. Hunter (ed.), *Justice and Crime: Essays in Honour of the Right Honourable The Lord Emslie* (Edinburgh, 1992), pp. 138–79 at pp. 171–2.

[27] D. Lieberman, *The Province of Legislation Determined: Legal Theory in Eighteenth-Century Britain* (Cambridge, 1989), pp. 144–75.

[28] Cairns, 'Hamesucken and the major premiss in the libel', pp. 166–8.

It was the foundation of law in natural law and the law of nations that helped underpin claims – of the type heard from Craig to Turnbull – that Scots law and English law were basically rather alike. Historical discussion by scholars such as Kames could also reinforce this perception of similarity. But it should be recognised that pointing out substantial similarities could as easily be used as an argument for not assimilating as for assimilating the laws of the two countries. Craig himself had argued:

> The third essential to a permanent union is, that each nation be governed in acordance with its own laws and customs; that no change be made in them, or in the established methods of judicial procedure, without the express sanction and approbation of either kingdom; that legal causes be determined in accordance with ancient practice and without appeal from the courts of one kingdom to those of the other, a procedure intolerable to both and expressly forbidden in all the examples of union which I have mentioned above.[29]

It was this type of opinion that broadly prevailed in the negotiations for the Union, whose provisions relating to the law and the courts should now be reviewed.

The provisions of the Union

The Act of Union provided that the laws regulating trade, customs and excises were to be the same in Scotland as in England.[30] The Act also required the establishment in Scotland of a Court of Exchequer 'for deciding Questions concerning the Revenues of Customs and Excises . . . having the same power and authority in such cases, as the Court of Exchequer has in England'. The English Court of Exchequer had an extensive jurisdiction at common law; such a jurisdiction was carefully excluded from the proposed new Scottish court, but it was to keep the jurisdiction over the 'power of passing Signatures, Gifts Tutories, and in other things' that was possessed by the existing Scottish Court of Exchequer.[31] A British act of 1707 established the new court, and thus introduced into the Scottish legal system a considerable body of English law and procedures. The judges of this new court were the Chief Baron and four Barons: the same complement of judges as in the English Court. Given that the procedure and law applied were English, it is unsurprising that the first Chief Baron and, through the century, always at least one

[29] Craig, *De unione*, p. 465.

[30] Act of Union, 1707, c. 7, art. 18, *Acts of the Parliaments of Scotland*, 12 vols. (Edinburgh, 1814–75), XI, pp. 406–13.

[31] Act of Union, 1707, c. 7, art. 19. On the English Court of Exchequer, see J.H. Baker, *An Introduction to English Legal History*, 3rd edn (London, 1990), pp. 56–61.

subsequent Baron were English lawyers. The scope of the use of English law, however, was carefully restricted to treasury matters; in the exercise of jurisdiction concerning private right Scots law was to be followed.[32] The new court could potentially have been a source of direct influence of English law in Scotland; but its jurisdiction was so carefully restricted, and the volume of its business so low, that it was not. Its existence, however, did require Scots lawyers to have some familiarity with English law and procedure, albeit of a limited type, and could have helped put English legal ideas into greater currency in Scotland. Detailed study of the court is wanting, however, for any certainty to be possible in this.[33]

Other than the laws of revenue, the Act of Union preserved in force existing Scots laws except in so far as contrary to or inconsistent with the Treaty of Union, but provided that they were alterable by the Parliament of Great Britain:

> With this difference betwixt the Laws concerning publick Right, Policy, and Civil Government, and those which concern private Right; That the Laws which concern publick Right Policy and Civil Government may be made the same throughout the whole United Kingdom; but that no alteration be made in Laws which concern private Right, except for evident utility of the subjects within Scotland.[34]

The Court of Session or College of Justice was preserved 'in all time coming', though 'subject . . . to such Regulations for the better Administration of Justice as shall be made by the Parliament of Great Britain'. There was a similar provision for the Court of Justiciary. The Admiralty Court and heritable admiralty jurisdictions were also preserved though subject to the Lord High Admiral or Commissioners for Admiralty of Great Britain. The inferior courts were preserved subordinate to the superior courts.[35] Heritable jurisdictions and offices and jurisdictions and offices for life were also preserved as rights of property.[36] It was provided that 'no Causes in Scotland be cognoscible by the Courts of Chancery, Queens-Bench, Common-Pleas, or any other Court in Westminster-hall; and that the said Courts, or any other of the like nature after the Union shall have no power to Cognosce, Review or Alter the Acts or Sentences of the Judicatures within Scotland, or stop the Execution of the same'.[37] The one issue that was not mentioned was

[32] Exchequer Court (Scotland) Act 1707, c.53.

[33] J. Clerk and B. Scrope, *A Historical View of the Forms and Power of the Court of Exchequer in Scotland* (Edinburgh, 1820) remains the fullest account of the court; there is a good discussion in A.J. MacLean, 'The 1707 Union: Scots law and the House of Lords', in A. Kiralfy and H.L. MacQueen (eds.) *New Perspectives in Scottish Legal History* (London, 1984), pp. 50–75 at pp. 53–7.

[34] Act of Union, art. 18. [35] Act of Union, art. 19. [36] Act of Union, art. 20.

[37] Act of Union, art. 19.

whether there would be appeals from the Scottish superior courts to the House of Lords of the new Parliament of Great Britain. The work of John MacLean has shown that it was always intended that there should be such appeals, and that the reason for them not being mentioned was not fear of Scottish reaction, but probably fear of raising once more the question of the jurisdiction of the House of Lords over certain English courts.[38] Furthermore, for some time the House of Lords entertained jursidiction over the Court of Justiciary, only later to decline it for reasons of expediency.[39]

The Union thus carefully preserved Scots law in matters of private right. The first significant change in legal regimes in Scotland came in 1708 when the English law of treason and English criminal procedure for prosecution of treason by commissions of oyer and terminer were introduced.[40] The catalyst for this legislation had been the invasion scare of that year and the lack of success of prosecutions of Jacobites in Scotland, but, despite the objection of Scots members of Parliament, it is understandable that it should have been thought desirable to have one law on treason throughout Great Britain: to impose the English law of treason on Scotland was the obvious way to achieve this, even though it was quite different from the Scots law, and the criminal procedure quite different.[41] This was also not a matter of 'private right' which could only be changed when for the evident utility of the people of Scotland.

The sources of authority in Scots Law

The sixteenth century had seen several attempts to reduce into some type of order and make accessible the variety of material drawn on by Scots lawyers. This necessitated consideration of their authority as sources. Scots lawyers by 1600 had linked law with notions of sovereignty, and had distinguished between formal and historical sources of law. The theory of sovereignty adopted by lawyers made the primary source of Scots municipal law legislation by the King and Estates of Parliament. The next source recognised was custom. Custom raises difficulties as a formal source of law. Lawyers such as Thomas Craig and Sir John Skene resolved these by identifying custom with the practice of the supreme court, the Session. The Session was known to have developed out of the

[38] MacLean, 'The 1707 Union'.

[39] A.J. MacLean, 'The House of Lords and Appeals from the High Court of Justiciary, 1707–1887', *Juridical Review* (1985), 192–226.

[40] Treason Act, 1708, c. 21.

[41] W. Ferguson, *Scotland: 1689 to the Present* (Edinburgh, 1968), pp. 57–8; B. Lenman, *The Jacobite Risings in Britain 1689–1746* (London, 1980), pp. 79–106; P.W.J. Riley, *The English Ministers and Scotland, 1707–1727* (London, 1964), pp. 119–20.

King's Council, and it may have been this connection with the King's sovereignty that permitted lawyers to recognise its authority in declaring the law by recognising rights and granting remedies. Craig, writing in 1600–1608, clearly identified the practice of the Session with custom, and, at some level, viewed its decisions as authoritative precedent creating law. And certainly from the early sixteenth century, collections of decisions of the court were made by judges, presumably for subsequent use in determining other cases.[42]

Both statutes and custom evidenced by the practice of the Session presented problems as sources. In contrast with English statutes, those of Scotland could fall into desuetude if a custom contrary to their provisions had developed: that a statute was not repealed did not mean that it was in force.[43] Furthermore, the authority of *Regiam majestatem* and the 'auld lawes' as statutes was questionable, and debated among lawyers: some accepting them as statutes, some rejecting them. Since *Regiam* had for long been treated as a major source, questioning its authority potentially could threaten much that was viewed as Scots law.[44] Collections of decisions of the Session appear to have circulated in manuscript; it was not always easy, however, to determine from them what was the custom of the court, as will be explained below. Nor were the statutes and practice of the courts always sufficient to settle any question. In the absence of law, what was to be done?

One solution was to argue from the historical origins of Scots law. Craig, for example, argued that much of Scots law originated in feudal law, and that if a solution to a legal problem were needed, and if feudal law provided that solution, then it should be adopted.[45] Craig's argument on feudal law was not one accepted by other Scots lawyers. But one source of Scots law that he recognised was also favoured by others: the customs and laws of foreign peoples.[46] His contemporary Skene also listed this as a source of Scots law.[47] Among the laws of foreign peoples, one obvious and attractive source of law was Roman law, and Skene classed it as such. What made Roman law authoritative? Craig explained:

> In a kingdom such as this, however, we are bound by the laws of the Romans only in so far as they are congruent with the laws of nature and right reason . . . Yet surely there is no greater seedbed of natural equity, no

[42] J.W. Cairns, T.D. Fergus, H.L. MacQueen, 'Legal humanism and the history of Scots law: John Skene and Thomas Craig', in J. MacQueen (ed.), *Humanism in Renaissance Scotland* (Edinburgh, 1990), pp. 48–74 at pp. 60–7.

[43] Stair, *Institutions*, pp. 87–8 (I.i.16).

[44] Cairns, Fergus and MacQueen, 'Legal humanism', pp. 61–4; Stair, *Institutions*, p. 88 (I.i.16), p. 668 (III.iv.27). The history of the use of *Regiam* requires further exploration.

[45] Craig, *Jus feudale*, p. 52 (I.viii.16).

[46] Craig, *Jus feudale*, p. 52 (I.viii.15).

[47] Cairns, Fergus and MacQueen, 'Legal humanism', p. 60.

> more fertile field of articulated reasoning and arguments from those principles of nature than the books of the Roman jurists; from which ought to be drawn, as if from the very source, what is equitable and what inequitable by nature and what most agrees and disagrees with right reason.[48]

He further commented: 'This natural law is called the good and the just, from the reason or equity of right born in us . . . to such an extent that neither the legislation of a kingdom, nor prescription even of the longest time, nor custom has any force against this law'.[49] Craig described the law of nations as 'that which ought chiefly to be observed after the reasoning and understanding of the just and the good naturally inborn in us. Whatever all nations observed ought to prevail among us whenever not against civil or municipal law.'[50] Craig accordingly put forward the view that failing statute or custom, Scots lawyers should resort to the natural law that even had primacy over municipal law and that could often be identified with Roman law, or the law of nations as evidenced by the laws of other peoples, or to feudal law as the historical source of Scots law (not necessarily authoritatively ranked in this order).

The studies of Professor Hannay and Dr Durkan have shown that many Scots advocates in the sixteenth century had trained in civil and canon law in European universities;[51] it is therefore hardly surprising that they should have turned to those laws to develop Scots law. Theories of natural law and the law of nations gave authority to the use of Roman law, but stressed that it could only be used when in itself equitable. Craig's theory of natural law is not fully worked out: for example, he did not deal adequately with the relationship of natural law to municipal law. But the type of arguments Craig presented in *Jus feudale* showed how Scots law could be developed in the absence of specific statutes or customs. Theories of sovereignty might stress statutes or customs; natural law had primacy over them.

Scottish legal culture

In the Restoration era a vital legal culture arose among the advocates in Edinburgh. One factor in this was the change in the social composition of the Faculty which increasing numbers of men from landed families joined after 1660.[52] The late Dr Rae's recent analysis of the backgrounds

[48] Craig, *Jus feudale*, p. 14 (I.ii.14). [49] Craig, *Jus feudale*, p. 50 (I.viii.7).

[50] Craig, *Jus feudale*, p. 50 (I.viii.8).

[51] R.K. Hannay, *The College of Justice: Essays on the Institution and Development of the Court of Session* (Edinburgh and Glasgow, 1933), pp. 145–7; J. Durkan, 'The French connection in the sixteenth and early seventeenth centuries', in T.C. Smout (ed.), *Scotland and Europe 1200–1850* (Edinburgh, 1986), pp. 19–44 at pp. 26–7.

[52] J.S. Shaw, *The Management of Scottish Society 1707–1764: Power, Nobles, Lawyers,*

of those who became members between 1620 and 1680 has confirmed that 'there is a subtle change in the social composition of intrants to the Faculty . . . Men from the upper classes of peers and landed gentry, who are relatively modestly represented at the beginning of the period, become the most significant group after the Restoration.[53] Instead of being a means of achieving landed status, the bar became a career for those who already had it. This increased the Faculty's authority and prestige.

Two linked projects of the Faculty in the Restoration period mark their ascent and their definition of themselves as an independent, learned corporation. The first was the creation of a Library that was to grow through the eighteenth century into one of the major European scholarly libraries. The Advocates' Library was intended not only to serve the needs of the practising bar, but also to educate young intrants and advocates generally.[54] The second was a concern to improve the education of the bar. Most advocates were admitted by examination in civil law. By 1692, such candidates first underwent private examination *viva voce* in Latin on civil law, and then had to print theses in Latin on a title of civil law that were defended publicly in a Latin disputation based on a university *disputatio pro gradu*. Finally, intrants had to read a Latin lesson before the Lords of Session. All this presupposed the competency in Latin acquired by a university education, and a reasonable, academic knowledge of civil law. This form of admission had precedents going back to 1664 and earlier, and it was obviously designed to ensure a scholarly, cultured profession. So important was this education in civil law considered to be that those few who were admitted by examination on Scots law had to pay double entry fees, and face the stigma of being admitted in a less 'honourable' way.[55]

Nor was an education in civil law narrowly conceived. In one proposal

Edinburgh Agents and English Influences (Edinburgh, 1983). pp. 21–32; N.T. Phillipson, 'Lawyers, landowners, and the civic leadership of post-Union Scotland', *Juridical Review* (1976), 97–120; and 'The social structure of the Faculty of Advocates in Scotland 1661–1840', in A. Harding (ed.), *Law-Making and Law-Makers in British History* (London, 1980), pp. 146–56.

[53] T.I. Rae, 'The origins of the Advocates' Library', in P. Cadell and A. Matheson (eds.), *For the Encouragement of Learning: Scotland's National Library 1619–1989* (Edinburgh, 1989), pp. 1–22 at p. 4.

[54] Rae, 'Origins of the Advocates' Library', pp. 16–18; J.W. Cairns, 'Sir George Mackenzie, the Faculty of Advocates, and the Advocates' Library', in G. Mackenzie, *Oratio inauguralis in aperienda juisconsultorum bibliotheca*, ed. J.W. Cairns and A.M. Cain (Edinburgh, 1989), pp. 18–35 at pp. 23–5.

[55] J.W. Cairns, 'The formation of the Scottish legal mind in the eighteenth century: themes of humanism and Enlightenment in the admission of Advocates', in N. MacCormick and P. Birks (eds.), *The Legal Mind: Essays for Tony Honoré* (Oxford, 1986), pp. 253–77.

to create a chair in 1695, it was commented that: 'The professione of the laws carys necessarly with it all the belles Letres and the knowledge of ancient and modern history'.[56] Those advocates who were educated in the Netherlands at this period did not restrict themselves to the study of civil law, and they would also often study Roman antiquities, universal history, and natural law; these were considered a necessary aspect of legal education. Depending on individual interest and taste, while in the Netherlands they might also study natural sciences, ecclesiastical history, other foreign languages, and the like.[57]

Those admitted to the bar between the Restoration and the Union were thus a well-educated and cultured group of men, of high social status, often with scholarly and scientific interests, a number of whom are known to have collected relatively large private libraries reflecting these concerns.[58] By 1700 they were, as a group, powerful and secure enough to defy the Lords of Session and to have gained control over admission to their ranks.[59]

It was this context that saw for the first time regular publication of works on Scots law, of which the best known is Stair's *Institutions*. But there were others, such as Sir George Mackenzie's many treatises on law, notably his *Laws and Customes of Scotland in Matters Criminal* (1678), his short *Institutions of the Law of Scotland* (1684), and his *Observations on the Acts of Parliament* (1686),[60] Alexander Seton of Pitmedden's *Treatise of Mutilation and Dismemberment and their Punishment* (1699),[61] and George Dallas's *System of Stiles* (1697).[62] New editions of the Scottish statutes were published in 1681 and 1682 by Sir Thomas Murray of Glendook,[63]

[56] *Advocates' Minute Book Volume I*, p. 160.

[57] *Memoirs of the Life of Sir John Clerk of Penicuik, Baronet, Baron of the Exchequer. Extracted by himself from his own Journals 1676–1755*, ed. J.M. Gray, Scottish History Society, vol. xiii (Edinburgh, 1892), pp. 13–18.

[58] Rae, 'Origins of the Advocates' Library', pp. 13–14.

[59] See generally, J.W. Cairns, 'A history of the Faculty of Advocates to 1900', *The Laws of Scotland. Stair Memorial Encyclopaedia Vol. 13* (Edinburgh, 1992), paras. 1239–85 at paras. 1247–59.

[60] On Mackenzie's works, see F.S. Ferguson, 'A bibliography of the works of Sir George Mackenzie Lord Advocate Founder of the Advocates' Library', *Edinburgh Bibliographical Society Transactions*, 1 (1935–38), 1–60. For a brief discussion, see Cairns, 'Sir George Mackenzie, the Faculty of Advocates, and the Advocates' Library'.

[61] This was published in G. Mackenzie, *The Laws and Customs of Scotland in Matters Criminal. Wherein is to be seen how the Civil Law, and the Laws and Customs of other Nations doth agree with, and supply ours . . . To this Second Edition is now added (by way of Appendix) A Treatise of Mutilation and Demembration and their Punishments, by Sir Alexander Seton of Pitmedden Knight Baronet* (Edinburgh, 1699).

[62] G. Dallas, *System of Stiles, as now practicable within the Kingdom of Scotland* (Edinburgh, 1697).

[63] *The Laws and Acts of Parliament made by King James the First, Second, Third, Fourth, Fifth, Queen Mary, King James the Sixth, King Charles the First, King Charles the Second Who now presently Reigns, Kings and Queen of Scotland. Collected, and Extracted, from the Publick Records of the said Kingdom, by Sir Thomas Murray of Glendook Knight, and*

while collections of decisions made by individuals started to be published, if in a somewhat haphazard way.[64] Furthermore, in 1681 and 1695 proposals were made to reform the statutes,[65] while between 1660 and 1700 there was very considerable and important statutory reform of the law.[66]

In the published works and statutory reforms we can see the same concerns as had exercised Craig: the relationship between the law of nature and nations and the municipal law of Scotland; sovereignty; legislation; and custom. Stair drew on a modified version of Grotius's theories of natural law to present a synthesis of Scots law and to argue for its obligatory authority. His attitude to the sources was to prefer custom to statutes and to argue that the best law appeared through practice, and it is unsurprising that he primarily founded Scots law on the decisions of the courts, of which he was to publish two volumes in 1683 and 1687, the first decisions printed in Scotland. Stair's preference for custom seems partly to reflect the emphasis he placed in government on the relationship between king and people.[67] Mackenzie's attitude was quite different: believing in the divine right of kings, he argued that statutes were 'the chief Pillars of our Law', and moreover that statutes were enacted by the king, with the estates only consenting.[68] A further reason why Mackenzie favoured statutes was their public nature: any one could read them and know the law, and in his treatise on criminal law he regretted that some

Baronet, Clerk to His Majestie's Council, Register, and Rols, by his Majestie's special warrand (Edinburgh, 1681); *The Laws and Acts of Parliament Made by King James the First, and his Royal Successors, Kings and Queen of Scotland In Two parts . . . Collected, and Extracted, from the Publick Records of the Said Kingdom, by Sir Thomas Murray of Glendook*, 2 vols. (Edinburgh, 1682, 1683).

64 *The Decisions of the Lords of Council and Session . . . Observed by Sir James Dalrymple of Stair*, 2 vols. (Edinburgh, 1683, 1687); *The Decisions of the Lords of Council and Session, in most Cases of Importance, Debated, and Brought before Them; From July 1621 to July 1642 . . . Observed by Sir Alexander Gibson of Dury* (Edinburgh, 1690).

65 Commission for revising the Laws, 1681. c.94, *Acts of the Parliaments of Scotland*, VIII, p. 356. See also *The Decisions of the Lords of Council and Session . . . Collected by the Honourable Sir John Lauder of Fountainhall*, 2 vols. (Edinburgh, 1759, 1761), I, p. 155. Act and Commission for Reviseing the Lawes and Practiques of the Kingdom, 1695, c.57, *Acts of the Parliaments of Scotland*, IX, p. 455.

66 Consider, e.g., the Courts Act, 1672; Bankruptcy Act, 1696; Blank Bonds and Trusts Act, 1696; Winter Herding Act, 1686; Prescription Acts, 1669 and 1695.

67 Stair, *Institutions*, pp. 73–94 (I.i.l–23). See, e.g., P.G. Stein, 'Stair's General Concepts: 1. The Theory of Law', *Stair Tercentenary Studies*, pp. 181–87; N. MacCormick, 'The rational discipline of Law', *Juridical Review* (1981), 146–60.

68 G. Mackenzie, *Observations on the Acts of Parliament* (Edinburgh, 1686), sig. A4r, pp. 6–7, 94, 153; and, *Institutions of the Law of Scotland*, 2nd ed. (Edinburgh, 1688), p. 5; and, *Observations upon the 18th Act of the 23rd Parliament of King James VI*, in *The Works of that Eminent and Learned Lawyer, Sir George Mackenzie of Rosehaugh*, 2 vols. (Edinburgh, 1716, 1722), II, p. 5; see Mackenzie, *Jus regium* (London, 1684) for a general account of his political theory.

crimes were not defined in statutes, as to do so would have favoured the liberty of the subject.[69] Mackenzie alluded to natural law and the law of nations in his *Institutions*, but there was no developed discussion of them as found in Stair. Similarly, in his treatise on criminal law, though he stated that the law of God was the ultimate source of Scots criminal law, there was no sophisticated discussion of natural law.[70] Given his favouring of the divine right of kings, it is unsurprising to note that he tended to found the authority of law in historical validity deriving from the age of the Scottish monarchy. This was why he privileged statutes that were enacted by the king as a source; similarly, for Mackenzie custom as a source derived its authority from the tacit acquiescence of the king and people.[71]

The political and religious conflicts of the seventeenth century were thus mirrored in disputes among the advocates about the ultimate location of sovereignty, and the need to sort out the sources of Scots law. The turn to natural law to deal with these questions was undoubtedly significant: from this time, Scottish libraries and individuals started to collect the works of Grotius and later Pufendorf, and commentaries upon them. The earliest manuscript catalogue of books in the Advocates' Library dates from 1683, and lists Grotius's treatise *De jure belli ac pacis* with Gronovius's notes published in 1680, Heinrich Henniges's commentary on Grotius published in 1671, and Samuel Rachel's *De jure naturae et gentium dissertationes* of 1676.[72] By 1692, of works on natural law, the Library included, for example, an edition of 1688 of Pufendorf's *De jure naturae et gentium libri octo* and one of 1683 of Richard Cumberland's *De legibus naturae disquisitio philosophica*.[73] Other libraries followed suit.[74] The development of the study of natural law and natural jurisprudence in Scotland is now well known in outline. Carmichael started to teach Pufendorf in Glasgow. The regius chair of Public Law and the Law of Nature and Nations was established in Edinburgh in 1707, and some, at least, of the professors taught. Moral philosophy became re-oriented to some extent around natural law.[75] Classic texts of

[69] Mackenzie, *Laws and Customes of Scotland in Matters Criminal*, in *Works*, II, pp. 53, 60–1.

[70] Mackenzie, *Institutions*, pp. 1–3; and, *Matters Criminal*, in *Works*, II, p. 53.

[71] Mackenzie, *Institutions*, p. 7 (in the lst edn he omitted to mention the King).

[72] Townley, *Best and Fynest Lawers*, pp. 58, 64, 98.

[73] *Catalogus librorum bibliothecae . . . a Facultate Advocatorum . . . constructae*, pp. 50, 65.

[74] Christine Shepherd, 'The inter-relationship between the library and teaching in the seventeenth and eighteenth centuries', in J.R. Guild and A. Law, *Edinburgh University Library 1580–1980: A Collection of Historical Essays* (Edinburgh, 1982), pp. 67–86 at pp. 72–3. The libraries of private individuals also contained many such works by the early eighteenth century.

[75] R.L. Emerson, 'Science and moral philosophy in the Scottish Enlightenment', in M.A. Stewart (ed.), *Studies in the Philosophy of the Scottish Enlightenment* (Oxford, 1990), pp.

natural law can be found not only in lawyers' libraries but also advertised in newspapers, such as Barbeyrac's edition of Grotius advertised for sale in the *Edinburgh Evening Courant* of 4/8 February 1720, and Kennet's translation of Pufendorf with Barbeyrac's notes in the *Caledonian Mercury* on 10 October 1721. Interest in these works was evidently keen.

Natural law theory allowed Stair and other Scots lawyers to produce an account of Scots law as a national law that was intellectually coherent and that related it to the laws of God, nature, and nations. It had a relevance, however, going beyond the theoretical. It had considerable practical importance for lawyers in Scotland: an importance such that, in the 1760s, the Faculty of Advocates encouraged all intrants to study it and proposed to examine them on it.[76] To understand this, it is necessary to discuss Scottish civil and criminal procedure. It was the use made of natural law and the law of nations in legal arguments that promoted the use of English law by Scots lawyers.

The practice of the courts

The two Scottish superior courts by 1707 were the Court of Session and the High Court of Justiciary, founded in 1532 and 1672 respectively. Both were developed from earlier precursors. The Faculty of Advocates had a monopoly of right of audience in both courts.[77] The forms of process in both were important and central to Scots law and need to be explained. Procedure before the Court of Session was dramatically different from procedure before the English courts of common law. Nicholas Phillipson has discussed it for the eighteenth century, focusing on how it led to delays in actions;[78] here the focus will be on how procedure left the law indeterminate in detail. Since custom, identified with the practice of the courts, was regarded as a formal source of law, this

11–36 at pp. 18–20; J. Moore and M. Silverthorne, 'Gershom Carmichael and the natural jurisprudence tradition in eighteenth-century Scotland', in I. Hont and M. Ignatieff (eds.) *Wealth and Virtue: The Shaping of Political Economy in the Scottish Enlightenment* (Cambridge, 1983), pp. 73–87; K. Haakonssen, 'Natural law and the Scottish Enlightenment', *Man and Nature: Proceedings of the Canadian Society for Eighteenth-Century Studies*, 4 (1985), pp. 47–80.

[76] J.W. Cairns, 'The influence of Smith's jurisprudence on legal education in Scotland', in P. Jones and A.S. Skinner (eds.), *Adam Smith Reviewed* (Edinburgh, 1992), pp. 168–89.

[77] College of Justice Act, 1532, c. 2, *Acts of the Parliaments of Scotland*, II, pp. 335–6; Courts Act, 1672, c. 40, *Acts of the Parliament of Scotland*, VIII, pp. 80–8; T.M. [Lord] Cooper, 'The Central Courts after 1532', in *Introduction to Scottish Legal History*, pp. 341–9; W. Croft Dickinson, 'The High Court of Justiciary', in *Introduction to Scottish Legal History*, pp. 408–12.

[78] N. Phillipson, *The Scottish Whigs and the Reform of the Court of Session 1785–1830*, Stair Society, vol. xxxvii (Edinburgh, 1990), pp. 42–61.

was of considerable importance. The following brief account will be closely derived from Phillipson's study.

As constituted in 1532, the Session consisted of the President and fourteen Senators of the College of Justice or Ordinary Lords of Session. If present, the Lord Chancellor of Scotland would preside. Until 1723, up to four extraordinary Lords of Session could be appointed by the king.[79] The effective judges were, however, the President and the fourteen Senators or Ordinary Lords of Session. The Session was divided into an Inner and an Outer Hosue. The President and the fourteen Lords sat in the Inner House, nine forming a quorum, and decisions being by majority vote. The Ordinary Lords sat in turn in the Outer House as Lord Ordinary of the week, Lord Ordinary on Oaths and Witnesses, Lord Ordinary on Bills, or Lord Ordinary on Concluded Causes. Phillipson has pointed out that most cases never went beyond the Outer House. Certain causes had to be heard before the Inner House.[80]

Actions were commenced by a libel which stated the ground of the action and concluded for a remedy. The libel or summons was served on the defender who had to give in defences. The Lord Ordinary would hear a debate on the libel and defences, and, if the facts were not at issue, pronounce an interlocutor. Parties could be ordered to prepare written memorials on the facts and the law before the judge pronounced the interlocutor. Such interlocutors could be reviewed by the judge on the basis of a written representation by one of the parties. Such a representation would normally call for written answers by the other party. There was no limit on the number of times the Ordinary could be asked to review an interlocutor. Parties could also complain of an interlocutor by reclaiming to the Inner House, which, on the basis of the reclaiming petition and printed answers to it, would confirm or recall the earlier interlocutor. Furthermore, should the Ordinary consider the cause to be one of difficulty, he could take it for advising to the Inner House.[81]

Should there be disputes over facts where witnesses were involved, the proof was taken by the Lord Ordinary on Oaths and Witnesses, who would himself examine the witnesses or issue a commission for them to be examined elsewhere. When the proof was taken, the evidence, in the form of depositions, went before the Lord Ordinary on Concluded Causes who ranked it before remitting it to the Inner House. Counsel would be heard on the evidence, and the Inner House would decide the issue.[82] From

[79] College of Justice Act, 1532, c. 2; Act 10 Geo. I, c. 19 enacted that no more extraordinary Lords be appointed to fill vacancies.

[80] Phillipson, *Reform of the Court of Session*, pp. 43–4.

[81] Phillipson, *Reform of the Court of Session*, p. 45.

[82] Phillipson, *Reform of the Court of Session*, pp. 45–6.

1686, parties and their counsel were entitled to be present at the examination of the witnesses by the judge; and from 1693 causes were advised by the Inner House in open court with the parties and their counsel present.[83]

One feature of actions was the tremendous scope for interlocutors to be reviewed, and for reclaiming motions (although only two were allowed on each interlocutor). Cases could start to seem interminable. One advocate sarcastically remarked in his pleadings:

> This Case being so remarkable an Instance of the watchful Care of Providence for an Infant against the Designs of his Grandfather and Uncle, to deprive him of his Birthright, it's hoped that the Pursuer will be excused from being very prolix in answering upon a single Point of Law now already decided eight several times uniformly in his Favour.[84]

Furthermore, it was easy to amend pleadings, so that cases could become protean, regularly changing their nature as they progressed (if that is the term) through the court. The process came largely to be written rather than oral, as memorials and condescendences multiplied arguing the law at all stages of the action.[85] William Forbes commented in 1714:

> That they [i.e. the Lords of Session] may have Time to consider weighty Cases maturely, they get them reduced into Writ by the Lawyers: And every Lord hath a Box standing upon a Table in the waiting Room of the Inner-house from Two till Four in the Afternoon, wherein all who have Papers to offer may put them by a Slit in the cover. This, tho' a mighty Advantage to the Lieges, is of late, since Informations and Bills were allowed to be printed, become an incredible Fatigue to the Lords: Who, after toiling all Day in hearing Causes, are obliged to shut themselves up to peruse and consider a Multiplicity of Papers at Night; and thereby often to want the necessary relaxation due to Nature, which visibly shortens their Days.[86]

The procedures of the court, though productive of a huge volume of legal reasoning, tended to avoid focusing on specific issues to be authoritatively determined by the court. The Inner House decided causes by voting; judges could vote one way or another for a variety of reasons. Nor did they need to give reasons for deciding to vote one way or another, and when they did, their reasons generally went unrecorded

[83] Act 1686, c.30, *Acts of the Parliaments of Scotland*, VIII, p. 599; Act 1693, c.42, *Acts of the Parliaments of Scotland*, IX, p. 305.

[84] Found quoted in J.A. Inglis, 'Eighteenth-century pleading', *Juridical Review* (OS) 19 (1907–8), 42–57, at pp. 54–5.

[85] Phillipson, *Reform of the Court of Session*, pp. 50–5.

[86] W. Forbes, *Journal of the Session* (Edinburgh, 1714), p. x.

(although they have sometimes been preserved).[87] The process thus contained legal argument by counsel, interlocutors, and the final decreet, but not necessarily any authoritative judicial pronouncement on the law. David Dalrymple, as counsel in *Millar v Robertson* in 1712, commented:

> *In Cumulo* one of your Lordships is moved by one Reason, and another by another, which Reasons, if they were examined or determined separately, would be repelled by the Plurality, which also is the Case why in most Sovereign Courts, especially in England, the Judges do resolve particular Points, which renders the Reason of the Decision clear, and makes the Precedent of greater Use in other Cases.[88]

This early, unfavourable comparison with English procedure is particularly telling. Critics directly linked this uncertainty in the law to the practices of the court:

> The difference of opinion, which could not fail to arise from the different views of the case that suggested themselves to the minds of so many Judges, gave rise often to discussions, the result of which was not always to forward the cause. Few pleas could well be brought before the Court, without plausibility enough to secure the vote of one or more of the Judges. A spirit of litigation was thus kept alive in the breasts of the parties. Among so many discordant decisions, too, the grounds of the judgment could not always be traced; and it was often difficult to decide, what had actually been held to be the law of the case.[89]

Published reports likewise generally only recounted the facts, pleadings of counsel and the relevant interlocutor or decreet: they were thus of limited value as precedents, and how they were to be understood depended much on the presentation of the case made by the reporter.

A similar situation prevailed in cases before the Justiciary Court. From 1672, this Court consisted of the Lord Justice-General, a nobleman who sat only infrequently, the Lord Justice-Clerk, and five Lords Commissioners of Justiciary appointed from the ordinary Lords of Session.[90] Actions were initiated by a libel that took the form either of an indictment (when the prosecution was at the instance of the Lord Advocate) or of criminal letters (when initiated by a private individual). The libel was served on the accused who was cited to compear at a diet of the High Court in Edinburgh or at a Circuit Court. The accused also was

[87] Phillipson, *Reform of the Court of Session*, pp. 53–4.
[88] Found quoted in Inglis, 'Eighteenth-century pleading', p. 52.
[89] [J. Ivory], *Form of Process before the Court of Session, the New Jury Court, and the Commission of Tiends*, 2 vols. (Edinburgh, 1818, 1815), I, pp. 17–18.
[90] Courts Act, 1672, c. 40.

served with a list of the witnesses against him or her and list of the men from whom the assize would be selected.[91]

The libel was in the form of a syllogism, with a major premiss, a minor premiss, and a conclusion. The major premiss specified the crime, typically by a *nomen juris* (such as murder) if there were one, stating that the crime was heinous and punishable 'by the laws of this and all well governed realms', though it could also allude to the laws of God, laws of nature and nations, and the common law (in the sense of the civil and canon laws). The minor premiss contained detailed averments which, if proved, amounted to the crime specified in the major premiss. The conclusion called for the appropriate punishment if the crime were proved.[92]

At the diet to which the panel was cited to compear, the libel was read and he or she asked to plead. On a plea of not guilty, there would normally be a debate on the relevancy of the libel. Before 1695, the panel's counsel's objection, the prosecutor's reply, the defence's duply, the prosecutor's triply, the defence's quadruply, and so on would be dictated to the Justiciary Clerk who would enter them into the record. From that date to 1747, counsel would debate *viva voce*, and then give in written informations arguing on the relevancy that would also subsequently be debated if new points were contained in them. After 1747, the *viva voce* debate on the relevancy would simply be followed by the giving in of written informations. The judges (all six, if the trial were in Edinburgh, usually two, but sometimes one, if at a Circuit Court) would then pronounce an interlocutor finding the libel relevant or irrelevant. Such interlocutor could be very simple, but sometimes it could specify questions of fact in detail for the jury to determine. A jury of fifteen would then by selected by the judges from the forty-five assizers summoned. Once the jury was empanelled, the proof followed without a break. The evidence of each witness would be summarised by the judge and dictated to the Clerk, who would enter it in the Court's Minute Book to be signed by the witness; if he or she could not sign, this would be noted, and the judge would sign. After the proof was concluded, the prosecutor and the counsel for the panel would address the jury, which would then be enclosed with instructions to return a verdict at a specified time. A simple majority sufficed. The jury could return verdicts of guilty, not guilty, or a special verdict. This last meant that the jury found specific facts proven or not proven; should such a verdict be returned, there would be a debate on whether what the jury had found proven amounted to the crime specified. If the jury returned a verdict of not guilty, the panel would be

[91] Cairns, 'Hamesucken and the major premiss in the libel', pp. 142–4; J.I. Smith, 'Criminal procedure', in *Introduction to Scottish Legal History*, pp. 426–48.

[92] Cairns, 'Hamesucken and the major premiss in the libel', p. 143.

absolved; if found guilty or the special verdict amounted to guilt, the panel would be sentenced.[93]

This procedure produced a court record which did not contain authoritative judical pronouncements on the law. All that was certain was that specific libels had been found relevant or irrelevant. This could also be complicated by the prosecutor's use of his discretion to restrict the pains of the law to an arbitrary punishment rather than capital punishment; as this was very commonly done, it could be unclear whether or not certain crimes were capital.

Statutes and customs, especially as found in the practice of the courts, caused problems as authoritative sources of Scots municipal law: the first because pre–1707 statutes could fall into desuetude, and because, after 1707, the new British parliament devoted little attention to Scots law; the second, because both the procedures and the form of the record of practice in the Session and the Justiciary Court left it unclear to some extent precisely what that custom was. Moreover, the lack of an adequate system of reporting of decisions made access, especially in civil cases, to custom difficult. Of course, this indeterminacy should not be exaggerated. Over much of the law lawyers evidently agreed on the broad outlines or principles; furthermore, the rights and duties involved in land tenure were clearly understood because they were embodied in writing, and Scotland had a sophisticated system of conveyancing and registration of titles. None the less, problems arose in the detailed working out of the broad outlines. Principles could conflict: the Session had an equitable jurisdiction as well as one at common law. Court procedure left these details unclear. Hugo Arnot commented thus on criminal law:

> There is no determined system of criminal jurisprudence in Scotland. It is a matter of doubt what is a crime in the eye of her law, and what not, also what is the punishment annexed . . . The Scots statute book is full of unrepealed laws, absurd, tyrannical and oppressive; and . . . it becomes a matter of debate whether they are gone into desuetude. There is no professed treatise on the criminal law of Scotland that either is or ought to be considered as an established authority.[94]

Study of the Justiciary Records of the eighteenth century tends to confirm Arnot's view.[95] Nor were matters generally better in civil law. The proposals to revise the laws in 1681 and 1695 in this context take on a particular importance. The commissions were not merely intended to

[93] Cairns, 'Hamesucken and the major premiss in the libel', pp. 143–4.
[94] H. Arnot, *The History of Edinburgh* (Edinburgh and London, 1779), p. 486.
[95] Cairns, 'Hamesucken and the major premiss in the libel'.

deal with statutes; it was also provided in 1681 that the commission should look at 'the Customs Consuetuds and Judiciall Practicks either in the Supream or Subalterne Courts whether Civil or Criminal, which are or have been observed as Laws or Rules of Judgement', and in 1695 the commission was instructed 'more especialy to define the pains of all Crimes not already defined by Acts of Parliament' and also:

> [T]o revise the whole Acts of Sederunt and Decisions and Practiques of the . . . Lords of Session . . . and to take notice and remark what Acts of Sederunt are in use and what Decisions should be held for Practiques to be still adverted to in Judgement, and what not As also in the case of Acts of Sederunt and Decisions or Practiques seemingly contrary to remark and give their opinion which of them shall for hereafter be observed And generally to do all and sundry other things that may best clear ascertain and establish the Practique or course of Decisions to be hereafter observed by the Lords of Session in Judgement . . .[96]

The task was so enormous it is scarcely surprising that it was not carried out. Lawyers turned to the law of nature and nations to deal with the situation.

In this context, works such as Stair's *Institutions* and Mackenzie's *Matters Criminal* were bound to take on considerable importance; yet they in themselves could decide nothing, since they were authorities only in so far as their reasoning on points was judged good. What this meant was that there was considerable scope in actions to return to first principles to argue any case in which legal points were at issue. And lawyers did so. The full title of Stair's work was: *The Institutions of the Law of Scotland Deduced from its Originals, and Collated with the Civil, Canon and Feudal Laws, and with the Customs of Neighbouring Nations in IV Books*; the full title of Mackenzie's criminal treatise was: *The Laws and Customs of Scotland in Matters Criminal: Wherein is to be seen how the Civil Law, and the Laws and Customs of other Nations do agree with, and supply ours.* These works thus placed Scots law in the context of comparative law as well as natural law. The extensive written and printed memorials and condescendences pleading on the law to which civil cases of any significance gave rise reargued the law on the same bases: pleadings would range over natural law, the historical origins of Scots law, Roman law, and the laws of neighbouring nations as demonstrating the law of nations, as well as over relevant statutes and decisions of the Session.[97] The same phenomenon is found in informations in criminal cases. So

[96] *Acts of the Parliaments of Scotland*, VIII, p. 356; IX, p. 455.

[97] The matter requires further research, but see Inglis, 'Eighteenth-century pleading', p. 53.

normal was this, that, in a model for an information in a criminal case given as a style, the argument dealt with the basis of the crime in the law of nature and the law of God, and also discussed 'the Laws of other Countries, particularly the Law of *England*' as well as Scottish authority.[98] Scots legal historians should not be inclined to see as merely ornamental the voluminous citation of civilian authorities on Roman law such as Voet, of the Roman texts themselves, and of Grotius. This would be misconceived. The form of process prevented civil litigation from focusing on specific, narrow issues for decision at law; the court records did not contain such decisions on narrow issues valuable as precedents; lawyers thus argued from natural law, the law of nations, the historical origins of Scots law, and the formal sources of Scots law.

It is therefore unsurprising that Scots lawyers were interested for practical as well as theoretical reasons in the law of nature and nations. They could not operate Scots law as a system hermetically sealed from other systems of law. They had to locate it within the theories of natural law and the law of nations.

Scots lawyers' willingness to argue from the law of nations would have made them particularly receptive to the idea of using English law in arguments. In criminal law, they may have continued to use Matthaeus's treatise *De criminibus*, but they also started to argue from Hale's *Historia placitorum coronae*.[99] In the early eighteenth century, Scots lawyers considered that civil law required to be accommodated to the genius of the nation; through the course of the eighteenth century, the focus on the need for the law to be accommodated to modern manners intensified, and arguments on what was the law could use the language of civility and manners. This seems to have made Scots lawyers more ready to turn to English law as the law of another jurisdiction with a similar political constitution, but also as the law of a more commercial country.[100] To take one example, marine insurance, vital in a trading nation, was developed, as Angelo Forte has shown, by drawing on English law.[101] English law provided a huge resource to which lawyers could turn to furnish themselves with arguments to elaborate a particular view of Scots law.

One further notable feature of Scottish litigation after 1707 was the popularity of appeals to the House of Lords. There were several reasons for this. For example, entering such an appeal stopped execution of the

[98] J. Louthian, *Form of Process Before the Court of Justiciary in Scotland* (Edinburgh, 1732), pp. 139–84.

[99] Cairns, 'Hamesucken and the major premiss in the libel', pp. 175–8.

[100] Cairns, 'Hamesucken and the major premiss in the libel', pp. 174–8.

[101] A.D.M. Forte, 'Marine insurance and risk distribution in Scotland before 1800', *Law and History Review*, 5 (1987), 393–412 at pp. 394–8.

decreet of the Lords of Session: an unsuccessful litigant thereby gained time, even if the House of Lords ultimately did not decide in his or her favour.[102] But another reason seems likely to have been the confused and unsatisfactory nature of litigation before the Session that left Scots law indeterminate. Arnot argued that one of the advantages of appeals to the House in criminal cases was that they would help remedy the unsatisfactory and indeterminate state of Scottish criminal law.[103]

Stair's *Institutions* and the other Scottish institutional works of the late seventeenth and eighteenth centuries developed out of and reflected the lively, learned legal culture of Restoration Scotland. They set out Scots law as a national law, but placed it in the context of the law of nature and nations from which they argued it derived its binding authority. Such a setting for Scots law legitimated argument from the law of nature and nations in litigation in order to develop Scots law, especially since Scots law as evidenced by the custom of the Session and of the Justiciary Court tended to be uncertain in details because of the procedures and records of those courts. From 1707 onwards, Scots lawyers turned to English law as a means of developing Scots law, because it was readily accessible, and the law of a neighbouring 'well governed realm' (to use the standard formula of the major premiss of a criminal libel). Of course, they continued to draw on more familiar Roman and civilian legal systems; but, as the eighteenth century progressed, English law came more and more to be seen as an ideal system, as the law of a commercial country, as lawyers came to be concerned with improvement in the laws. In the same way, the forms of the English courts were seen by Adam Smith as better than those of the Scots courts in producing certainty and justice in law.[104] 'Anglicisation' was thus not necessarily imposed *as such* on Scots law, but to some extent willingly adopted as modernisation.

The Union may have preserved Scots law, except when altered 'for evident utility of the subjects', but Scots lawyers' understanding of Scots law within the framework of the law of nature and nations as expounded by theorists such as Stair, led them to draw on English law to develop

[102] R.S. Tompson, 'James Greenshields and the House of Lords: a reappraisal', in W.M. Gordon and T.D. Fergus (eds.), *Legal History in the Making* (London and Rio Grande, 1991), pp. 109–24 at pp. 109–10; A.J. MacLean, 'Historical account of the jurisdiction of the House of Lords in Scotland to 1876', in *The Laws of Scotland. Stair Memorial Encyclopaedia Volume 6* (Edinburgh, 1988), pp. 330–51 (paras. 801–22) at pp. 345–6 (para. 818).

[103] Arnot, *History of Edinburgh*, pp. 481–6.

[104] J.W. Cairns, 'Adam Smith and the role of the courts in securing justice and liberty', in R.P. Malloy and J. Evensky (eds.), *Adam Smith and the Philosophy of Law and Economics* (Dordrecht, 1994), pp. 31–61.

Scots law because of the lack of reforming legislation and a court procedure that did not produce authoritative and clear precedents. The law of nature and nations could in this way be understood to be much more 'fundamental' than any provisions in the Treaty or Acts of Union. Natural law had primacy over theories of sovereignty.

Part IV

UNION AND EMPIRE IN THE EIGHTEENTH-CENTURY BRITISH WORLD

11

IRELAND WITHOUT UNION: MOLYNEUX AND HIS LEGACY

JACQUELINE HILL

THE two decades following the Glorious Revolution in England witnessed a new preoccupation with the concept of empire. A century and a half earlier, at the time of the break with Rome, England's status as an 'empire' – that is, sovereign, not subject to external or higher authority – had been affirmed.[1] In the eyes of many Englishmen, the revolution of 1688 confirmed that such sovereignty was an attribute not of the Monarchy alone but of the Kingdom or King-in-Parliament, and it was with this conviction that certain political writers in the post-revolutionary era proceeded to reflect on that other sense of empire: that of sovereignty over dependent provinces.[2]

Although there was an antiquarian strain in some of this thinking, it was driven primarily by practical considerations. The revolution itself had only been consolidated by means of a protracted and costly reconquest of Ireland, where James II had taken his stand following his flight from England. And as a result of the revolution, England had become involved, as a principal, in an even more costly and protracted European coalition against France, in the course of which tensions arose with the parliaments of both Ireland and Scotland, especially over financial and commercial issues. At a time when English opinion was convinced of the need for everyone to rally to the common cause, the Irish and Scottish parliaments displayed (to English minds) a disturbing spirit of assertiveness. This helps explain the emergence of new (and the resurrection of old) claims to the superior status of the English crown and parliament, more especially in relation to Ireland but to a lesser extent with reference to Scotland.

I am grateful to the Department of Foreign Affairs, Dublin, for a grant towards the cost of attending the Folger Institute seminar. I also wish to thank David Dickson, Raymond Gillespie, Patrick Kelly, Cadoc Leighton and John Robertson for their valuable comments on an earlier draft of this paper.

1 Act of Appeals, 1553 (24 Henry VIII, c. 12).

2 William Ferguson, 'Imperial crowns: a neglected facet of the background to the Treaty of Union of 1707', *Scottish Historical Review*, 53 (1974), 22–44 (pp. 22–3).

The articulation of such claims was facilitated by (and perhaps helped to promote) a contemporaneous shift in political discourse towards Roman and classical frames of reference, which provided a suitable setting for the discussion of concepts concerning empire, colonies, and conquest. Writers drew parallels between English and classical achievements, and this undoubtedly served to promote an 'imperial' self-image.[3] However, such an identity was not explored without a certain foreboding. For Roman history suggested that liberty (which even before 1688 was already a central element in English national identity)[4] was precarious, particularly in circumstances of imperial expansion, with its attendant inflow of riches, leading to corruption, standing armies and loss of 'virtue'. Only the cultivation of civic spirit, and the pursuit of maritime rather than territorial empire seemed likely to preserve England's 'mixed' government and stave off tyranny.[5] Where colonies or dependent provinces already existed, liberty might be safeguarded by guaranteeing the colonists the rights of Englishmen,[6] or by uniting them with England.[7] Relations between England and Scotland were to be settled on the latter basis by the Treaty of Union of 1707, an arrangement that assuaged Scottish pride by formally acknowledging that the legislative union was one between two equal Kingdoms. But in Ireland's case, talk of Union came to nothing. Ireland was left as a separate but (in English eyes)

[3] See e.g., Reed Browning, *Political and Constitutional Ideas of the Court Whigs* (Baton Rouge and London, 1982), pp. 8–9; Stephen N. Zwicker, 'England, Israel, and the triumph of Roman virtue', in Richard H. Popkin (ed.), *Millenarianism and Messianism in English Literature and Thought 1650–1800* (Leiden and New York, 1988), pp. 37–64 (pp. 37–8, 45–9). On the evolution of imperial aspirations in England, see Richard Koebner, *Empire* (New York, 1965 edn) pp. 61–81.

[4] Peter Furtado, 'National pride in seventeenth-century England', in Raphael Samuel (ed.), *Patriotism: The Making and Unmaking of British National Identity*, 3 vols. (London, 1989), I, pp. 44–56 (p. 49).

[5] This neo-republican understanding of history owed much to the influence of Machiavelli, especially as interpreted by James Harrington, and modified after the Restoration. See J.G.A. Pocock, *The Machiavellian Moment. Florentine Political Thought and the Atlantic Republican Tradition* (Princeton and London, 1975), chs 12–13; Istvan Hont, 'Free trade and the economic limits to national politics: neo-Machiavellian political economy reconsidered', in John Dunn (ed.), *The Economic Limits to Modern Politics* (Cambridge, 1990), pp. 41–120.

[6] See e.g., Charles Davenant, *Discourses on the Public Revenues, and on the Trade of England. In Two Parts* (London, 1698), in *The Political and Commercial Works of that Celebrated Writer Charles D'Avenant*, 5 vols. (London, 1771), II, pp. 35–6. Davenant used the term 'colony', as was common at the time, to mean groups emanating from a metropolitan state and settled in subject territories. Cf. 'those colonies which England has from time to time sent to conquer and possess the land, who are now properly the body politic of that kingdom [Ireland]', *Works*, II, p. 245.

[7] See the anonymous document headed 'Remarks shewing that it is not to the interest of England that Ireland should be a separate kingdom', in *Calendar of State Papers, Domestic Series* (1690–1), ed. William John Hardy (London, 1898), pp. 201–6 (p. 202).

dependent Kingdom until the shortlived era of parliamentary independence beginning in 1782, which was followed in 1800 by the Act of Union between Great Britain and Ireland.[8]

This paper sets out to examine the post-revolutionary era from the Irish perspective, or, more precisely, from the perspective of the Anglo-Irish Protestants who dominated Irish society and politics. Consideration of their predicament will be followed by a discussion of William Molyneux's *The Case of Ireland Stated*, the classic apologia for a distinct Irish Kingdom, annexed to the English Crown but not subordinate to the English parliament.[9] In particular, the significance of the issues of conquest and union for Molyneux and his contemporaries will be explored. Why did Molyneux use certain sorts of arguments to support his case and not others, and why did Ireland, unlike Scotland, fail to obtain a union at this period? Finally, an attempt will be made to evaluate Molyneux's legacy in eighteenth-century Ireland.

The Anglo-Irish predicament

The problems facing Anglo-Irish Protestants in the post revolutionary era have been explored in some detail in recent years.[10] Among the various elites in the former Stuart dominions whose privileges had been restored, confirmed or extended by the revolution, the Anglo-Irish remained particularly insecure. They had just emerged from the trauma of the Jacobite era in Ireland during which it had proved alarmingly easy to substitute Catholics for Protestants in a wide range of civil, military and ecclesiastical positions. Protestant estates, confirmed by the Cromwellian and Restoration land settlements, had been threatened, and so, in some cases, had Protestant lives. Many of those who possessed the means to do so had fled the country. Their reinstatement had only been secured by the somewhat dilatory intervention of Williamite forces from outside the country. Thus by comparison with their position when the monarchy

[8] On the Scottish Union, see Brian P. Levack, *The Formation of the British State: England, Scotland and the Union 1603–1707* (Oxford, 1987); on the Irish Union, see G.C. Bolton, *The Passing of the Irish Act of Union* (Oxford, 1966).

[9] William Molyneux, *The Case of Ireland's being Bound by Acts of Parliament in England, Stated* (Dublin, 1698). All references are to the reprint with introduction by J.G. Simms (Dublin, 1977).

[10] Patrick Kelly, 'Ireland and the Glorious Revolution: from kingdom to colony', in Robert Beddard (ed.), *The Revolutions of 1688* (Oxford, 1991), pp. 163–90; and 'The Irish Woollen Export Prohibition Act of 1699: Kearney revisited', *Irish Economic and Social History*, 7 (1980), 22–44; James I. McGuire, 'The Irish Parliament of 1692', in Thomas Bartlett and D.W. Hayton (eds.), *Penal Era and Golden Age* (Belfast, 1979), pp. 1–31; David Hayton, 'The beginnings of the undertaker system', in *Penal Era and Golden Age*, pp. 32–54. The Term 'Anglo-Irish' is used here to refer to those of English extraction but Irish birth, who conformed to the established Church of Ireland.

had been restored in 1660, the Anglo-Irish entered the Williamite era with considerably less sense of control over their own affairs.[11]

Some of this insecurity stemmed from the question of numbers. Despite considerable immigration during the 1600s, Protestants comprised less than 30 per cent of the population by 1700, and were themselves divided, with Presbyterians in certain northern counties outnumbering those who belonged to the established Church of Ireland. Despite their lack of privileges, Irish Catholics had remained far more numerous and enjoyed a much higher profile in the Restoration period than was the case in England or Scotland, which explains the facility with which a predominantly Catholic ascendancy replaced a Protestant ascendancy under James II. For this reason, the terms on which the peace between the Williamite and Irish Jacobite forces had been concluded in 1691 – the Articles of Limerick – remained an object of suspicion to Protestants. They were conscious of having exercised no influence on the settlement, regarding it as unduly indulgent (especially in respect of property rights) towards the Catholics, who might, it seemed, at any time renew their bid for power, with or without help from Jacobites abroad. These considerations helped delay the confirmation of the Articles of Limerick by the Irish parliament, and acted as one of the spurs towards the introduction of draconian penal laws, intended to copper-fasten Protestant control of land and political power.[12]

As the Anglo-Irish Protestants attempted to consolidate their battered authority inside the country, it soon emerged that this task would involve something of a challenge to the power of the executive. As James McGuire has pointed out, a quarter of a century of executive control, during which the Irish parliament had not met, had brought the Protestants to the verge of disaster; and accordingly the 1690s witnessed a vigorous effort to regain some of the initiative which had been lost in the interval.[13] Over the question of supply, the Irish House of Commons enunciated a new claim to a 'sole right' to initiate money bills and to determine how the money should be raised. Various bills, including a government money bill, deemed not to meet these conditions, were defeated in 1692. A spirit of compromise helped smooth relations between the executive and subsequent sessions of the Irish parliament, with the former recognising the latter's right to initiate legislation via a 'heads of bills' procedure, while observing the principles of Poynings'

[11] Kelly, 'Ireland and the Glorious Revolution', pp. 163–4.

[12] Kelly, 'Ireland and the Glorious Revolution', pp. 181–4; McGuire, 'The Irish Parliament of 1692', p. 3; T.W. Moody and W.E. Vaughan (eds.), *A New History of Ireland, IV: Eighteenth Century Ireland 1691–1800* (Oxford, 1986), pp. 16–21.

[13] McGuire, 'The Irish Parliament of 1692', p. 15.

Law.[14] During the decade, however, the Anglo-Irish also had to contend with periodic attacks from English woollen interests, whose own industry was going through troubled times, and who resented competition from a rival Irish industry which had sprung up since 1660 thanks to immigration by West of England cloth workers.[15]

While the 1690s witnessed a growing assertiveness on the part of the Irish parliament, there was also a good deal of interest among the Anglo-Irish in some sort of legislative union with England, particularly during the 1690s and early 1700s. Various reasons for this have been identified. Greater security against a Catholic and Jacobite threat; freedom from commercial discrimination exercised by the metropolitan parliament in response to sectional domestic pressures; security for 'the rights of Englishmen', at risk while the executive enjoyed such extensive powers; the precedent of the Anglo-Scottish union of 1707.[16] These were largely domestic considerations, but they had an international dimension. The Catholic and Jacobite threat, for instance, was one that was closely linked with contemporary fears of 'universal monarchy', or 'universal empire' emanating from the great Catholic powers. In England, the 1670s and 1680s had witnessed a growing preoccupation with the rise of France under Louis XIV as the latest manifestation of this danger. The promotion of a balance of power, and of a Europe made up of federal or confederal unions were among the strategies proposed for countering French ambitions.[17]

Similar fears about French aspirations to universal monarchy can be detected in Ireland.[18] But for the Anglo-Irish community, such fears were apt to crystallise around a more familiar bugbear: the Pope. That the Pope should loom large in their anxieties is not surprising. The Papal excommunication of Queen Elizabeth had served to encourage Irish

[14] McGuire, 'The Irish Parliament of 1692', pp. 17–20, 29; David Dickson, *New Foundations: Ireland 1660–1800* (Dublin, 1987), pp. 40–43. Poynings' Law (1494) required that before an Irish Parliament met, outline legislation must be submitted to the English King and Council: see R.D. Edwards and T.W. Moody, 'The history of Poynings' Law', *Irish Historical Studies* (*IHS*), 2 (1941), 415–24.

[15] Kelly, 'The Irish Woollen Act', pp. 24–6.

[16] James Kelly, 'The origins of the act of Union: an examination of Unionist opinion in Britain and Ireland, 1650–1800', *IHS*, 25 (1987), 236–63 (pp. 240–4); Isolde Victory, 'Colonial nationalism in Ireland, 1692–1725: from common law to natural right', PhD thesis, Trinity College, Dublin, 1984, pp. 80, 91–100. The precise kind of union envisaged (e.g., whether federal or incorporating) was rarely spelled out.

[17] J.R. Western, *Monarchy and Revolution* (London, 1972), p. 383; John Robertson, 'Union, state and empire: the European context of British Union in 1707' in Lawrence Stone (ed.), *An Imperial State at War: Britain from 1689 to 1815* (London, 1994); Steven Pincus, 'The English debate over universal monarchy', see above, pp. 43–62.

[18] See Duke of Ormond to Col. John Fitzpatrick, 3 Oct. 1681, Historical Manuscripts Commission, *Calendar of the Manuscripts of the Marquess of Ormonde*, NS 6 (London, 1911) p. 77.

Catholic rebels from the 1570s onwards, and a papal bill of 1600 had given backing (if somewhat ambiguous backing) to the rebellion of Hugh O'Neill.[19] Moreover, it was well known that the Pope had endorsed the cause of the confederate Catholics in the 1640s, and had praised Owen Roe O'Neill's efforts to extirpate heresy.[20] During the Restoration period, the reluctance of Irish Catholic leaders to take an unequivocal oath of allegiance to the restored Stuart Monarchy lent further credence to the view that the main obstacle to some measure of toleration for the Irish Catholic Church was the unwillingness of the Vatican to formally renounce its claims to temporal as well as spiritual power.[21] Looking back on the troubled events of the 1640s from the vantage point of the latest Catholic resurgence in 1689, Richard Cox, later Lord Chancellor of Ireland, wrote of the confederate Catholics, '*they were taught*, That the Pope was by Divine Right Universal Monarch and Governor of the World . . . and had Power of both Swords, to which every soul on pain of eternal Damnation was bound to give Obedience'.[22]

Worries about the malign influence of the Pope were not extinguished by Innocent XI's support for William of Orange as against James II and Louis XIV. As anxieties increased over the royal succession in the early 1700s, Archbishop Ussher's prophecies were resurrected, concerning a great persecution that (it was claimed) would befall the Protestant Churches of Europe. According to Ussher, who had allegedly foretold the Irish rebellion of 1641 and the execution of Charles I, there would be a massacre of European Protestants, inspired by the Pope. Only true believers would be preserved; but Rome would fall just when she felt herself most secure.[23] The setbacks suffered by European Protestantism in the course of the Thirty Years War, followed by a rash of princely converts to Catholicism in the second half of the seventeenth century, produced a climate of apprehension in which such apocalyptic fears could flourish.[24]

Bearing all these considerations in mind, it was natural that the

[19] R.F. Foster, *Modern Ireland, 1600–1972* (Harmondsworth, 1988), pp. 29–30, 40.

[20] Richard Cox, *Hibernia Anglicana: or, the History of Ireland from the Conquest Thereof by the English, to this Present Time.* In Two Parts (London, 1689–90), pt II, Appendix XV (pp. 55–7); [Roger Boyle], *The Answer of a Person of Quality, to a Scandalous Letter Lately Printed and Subscribed by P.W.* (Dublin, 1662), pp. 84–6.

[21] T.W. Moody, F.X. Martin and F.J. Byrne (eds.), *A New History of Ireland, III: Early Modern Ireland 1534–1691* (Oxford, 1976), pp. 429–30.

[22] Cox, *Hibernia Anglicana*, Pt II, Preface, sig. c1[a]–c1[b].

[23] Anon., *The History, Life and Death of that Most Learned and Pious Divine Bishop Usher* (London, 1712) in Anon., *Europe's Warning Piece: or, Bishop Usher's Life and Prophecies* (nd, np). James Ussher (1581–1656) had been Archbishop of Armagh: see *DNB*. The view that Popery was anti-Christ, a false religion, continued to flourish in Ireland into the 1700s. See T.C. Barnard, 'The uses of 23 October 1641 and Irish Protestant celebrations', *English Historical Review*, 106 (1991), 889–920 (p. 897).

[24] John Stoye, 'Europe and the revolution of 1688', in Beddard (ed.), *The Revolutions of 1688*, pp. 191–212 (pp. 191–5).

Anglo-Irish should cling to their links with England, and should look for even closer ties. Bishop Wetenhall of Cork was prepared to admit a royal conquest of Ireland in order to secure the relationship, and this view was particularly prevalent at the outset of the Williamite regime while memories of the Jacobite era were still fresh.[25] Others thought in terms of legislative union. For the history of the Irish parliament did not inspire much confidence in its ability to protect local interests. There was no statutory limitation on the duration of an Irish parliament such as the English parliament enjoyed; its sole right to initiate money bills was still contentious; it had not met at all between 1666 and 1689. Moreover, those pressing for the Irish parliament to become more assertive owed some of their confidence to contacts with more experienced 'Country' forces in the English parliament. All in all, some form of legislative union must have seemed an attractive way to protect Anglo-Irish interests. However, it was apparent that a union with Ireland had little appeal for English ministers. It would be a handicap from a fiscal point of view, and (as in the case of Scotland) admitting Ireland to the commercial privileges of England would be deeply unpopular at home.[26]

But if a legislative union was an unlikely blessing (and it seems that it took some time for this reality to sink in),[27] then Anglo-Irish interests had to be protected in other ways. Matters came to a head in 1697, when at the urging of West Country woollen manufacturers a bill was introduced into the English parliament to restrict the export potential of the Irish woollen industry; at much the same time, a clash occurred between the two Parliaments over the appellate jurisdiction of the Irish House of Lords.[28] This formed the background for Molyneux's intervention. His one reference to union in *The Case* ('an Happiness we can hardly hope for'[29]), suggests a realistic appraisal of the prospects for union; accordingly, all his efforts went into presenting the case for protecting and strengthening Irish parliamentary rights.

The Case of Ireland and the issue of conquest

William Molyneux was born in Dublin in 1656 into a prominent Protestant family which had been in Ireland for over a century.[30] He graduated from Trinity College, Dublin, and took up philosophy,

[25] Dickson, *New Foundations*, p. 48; Kelly, 'Ireland and the Glorious Revolution', p. 183.

[26] McGuire, 'The Irish Parliament of 1692' pp. 1–2, 14; Kelly, 'Origins of the act of Union', pp. 241–2. [27] Kelly, 'Origins of the act of Union', pp. 241–2.

[28] The first bill failed to pass: Kelly, 'The Irish Woollen Act', pp. 28, 35; Isolde Victory, 'The making of the 1720 Declaratory Act', in Gerard O'Brien (ed.), *Parliament, Politics and People* (Dublin, 1989), pp. 9–29 (pp. 9–13).

[29] Molyneux, *The Case*, p. 84.

[30] On Molyneux's life, see J.G. Simms, *William Molyneux of Dublin 1656–1698* (Dublin, 1982).

becoming a friend and correspondent of John Locke. His appointment in 1684 as chief engineer and Surveyor of the King's Buildings and Works did not survive the Jacobite era, and he spent much of 1689 and 1690 in England. Returning to Ireland after the battle of the Boyne, he subsequently represented the University in the 1692 Irish Parliament, though he took no decided part with the opposition in that or the 1695 Parliament. However, when a pamphlet war broke out in 1697/8 over moves in England to restrict the Irish woollen industry, during which it was implied that the Anglo-Irish Parliament differed little from its Jacobite predecessor, and that only 'English Conquerours' would be so indulgent as to allow it to meet at all,[31] Molyneux entered the lists on behalf of the Irish parliament, and the result was *The Case of Ireland*, published in Dublin in 1698.

It has been widely accepted that a crucial part of Molyneux's defence of Irish parliamentary rights rested on his denial that Ireland had been conquered.[32] The subject was a topical one, in view of the debate going on in England in the 1690s over whether William of Orange's spectacular intervention in English politics represented a 'conquest' of England.[33] The strong hostility among Whig spokesmen to the idea of such a conquest, reinforced by equally strong denials that the Duke of Normandy's title to the English Crown in 1066 had rested on conquest,[34] made it a promising line for Molyneux to pursue, though in the event English commentators evinced little reluctance to admit a conquest in respect of Ireland. Several followed a line hinted at by Sir Edward Coke in James I's reign: that rights of conquest extended not merely to the crown but to the parliament of England.[35] In fact, conquest was a pervasive theme in early modern European political thought.[36] It was widely acknowledged that conquest

[31] Kelly, 'The Irish Woollen Act', pp. 34–7; and 'A Pamphlet Attributed to John Toland and an Unpublished Reply by Archbishop William King', *Topoi*, 4 (1985), 81–90 (p. 85).

[32] See e.g., F.G. James, *Ireland in the Empire 1688–1770* (Cambridge MA, 1973), p. 39; Simms, *William Molyneux of Dublin*, pp. 105–6.

[33] Mark Goldie, 'Edmund Bohun and *Jus Gentium* in the Revolution Debate, 1689–1693', *Historical Journal* (hereafter *Hist. Jn*), 20 (1977), 569–86.

[34] See e.g., [?William Atwood], *Argumentum Anti-Normanicum: Or an Argument Proving, from Ancient Histories and Records, that William, Duke of Normandy, made no Absolute Conquest of England by the Sword; in the Sense of our Modern Writers* (London, 1682).

[35] In *Calvin's Case*, 1608 (Molyneux, *The Case*, p. 96). In general, Coke's authority was cited approvingly by Molyneux, but his legacy was an ambiguous one: the debate is reviewed in Martin S. Flaherty, 'The empire strikes back: *Annesley v. Sherlock* and the triumph of imperial parliamentary supremacy', *Columbia Law Review*, 87 (1987), 593–622 (pp. 596–8). I am grateful to Patrick Kelly for directing me to this article.

[36] As reflected in such works as Hugo Grotius, *De Jure Belli ac Pacis* (1625) (*Of the Rights of War and Peace, in Three Volumes. Done into English by Several Hands* (London, 1715), III, chs 5–8); John Locke, *Two Treatises of Government*, ed. Peter Laslett (Cambridge, 1988 edn), pp. 384–97. See also Mark Greengrass, 'Introduction: conquest and coalescence', in Mark Greengrass (ed.), *Conquest and Coalescence: The Shaping of the State in Early Modern Europe* (London, 1991), pp. 1–24.

(in a just war) represented one of the foundations for a legitimate title to rule (others included hereditary claims, 'compacts' and prescription).[37]

Conquest theory was important because it was widely held, on the basis of arguments derived from civil law and the law of nations, that a conquest eliminated any prior liberties or property rights of the conquered.[38] In the Irish context the issue had been a lively one throughout the seventeenth century. Sir John Davies, who, as James I's attorney-general in Ireland, was anxious that English common law should displace Irish Brehon laws, considered that 'to give Lawes to a conquered people is the principall marke and effect of a perfect Conquest'.[39] Conquest theory was also deployed to deny the validity of papal temporal jurisdiction (in the 1150s the English Pope Adrian IV had sanctioned Henry II's projected conquest of Ireland).[40] But the very fact that conquest theory was so often used to boost royal power could make it a target for critics of absolutism. One of the charges brought by the English opposition against the Earl of Strafford in 1641, supported from evidence supplied by the Irish Parliament, was that while serving as the King's minister in Ireland he had used conquest theory to claim that local privileges and liberties could only be enjoyed by royal grace, not by right.[41] Subsequently, the argument that there had indeed been a royal conquest of Ireland was occasionally used by Anglo-Irish spokesmen themselves, as for instance during the Jacobite era, to recall the Crown to its obligation to maintain Ireland as part of the royal dominions. Hence in 1689 Richard Cox, rehearsing the bases of the English Crown's titles to the kingdom of Ireland, placed conquest second only to hereditary right: 'the first is that of Descent from *Eva*, daughter of *Dermond Mac Morough* . . . whose Ancestors were Monarchs of *Ireland*: The second is by lawful Conquest in a just War'. He described Henry II as 'Conqueror and Lord of Ireland'.[42]

[37] See R. Cox's discussion of the title of the English Crown to the Kingdom of Ireland, in *Hibernia Anglicana,* pt I, p. 8; also the anonymous English Williamite tract *The Proceedings of the Present Parliament Justified by the Opinion of the Most Judicious and Learned Hugo Grotius . . . by a Lover of the Peace of his Country* (London, 1689), pp. 6–8.

[38] Grotius, *Of the Rights of War and Peace,* III, ch. 5; and see Hans S. Pawlisch, 'Sir John Davies, the ancient constitution, and civil law', *Hist. Jn,* 23 (1980), 689–702 (p. 696).

[39] Sir John Davies, *A Discoverie of the True Causes why Ireland was Never Entirely Subdued* (Dublin, 1612), in Sir John Davies, *The Complete Prose Works,* 3 vols. (vols. I & II bound together), (np, 1876), II, pp. 1–168 (pp. 63–4). It has been argued that Davies's understanding of conquest differed from the usual Tudor view: Ciaran Brady, 'The decline of the Irish kingdom', in Greengrass (ed.) *Conquest and Coalescence,* pp. 94–115 (pp. 111–12).

[40] Pawlisch, 'Sir John Davies', p. 697.

[41] J.P. Kenyon, *The Stuart Constitution 1603–1688* (Cambridge, 1969), p. 208; Moody, Martin and Byrne (eds.), *A New History of Ireland,* III, pp. 282–3.

[42] Cox, *Hibernia Anglicana,* pt I, pp. 1–2, 8. His third, fourth and fifth titles were compacts, statutes, and prescription.

Molyneux, adapting arguments devised by Locke, denied a royal title to Ireland by conquest.[43] Yet to suggest that he rejected any idea of right by conquest seems to overstate the case.[44] While he insisted that Henry II and his successors owed their Irish titles to 'Voluntary Submission' on the part of the native Irish and to a subsequent 'Compact', Molyneux made considerable use of conquest theory. 'Supposing', he suggested, '*Hen*. II had *Right* to Invade this Island . . . it was only the *Antient Race* of the *Irish*, that could suffer by this Subjugation; the *English* and *Britains*' that came over and Conquered with him, retain'd all the Freedoms and Immunities of *Free-born* Subjects'. Elsewhere, he referred to 'Conquests obtain'd by those Adventurers, who came over [to Ireland] only by the King's *License* and *Permission*, and not at all by his particular *Command*'.[45] In other words, Molyneux left room for what might be called an aristocratic conquest of Ireland.[46] This point has been obscured by a much quoted passage in *The Case*, which states that

> 'tis manifest that the great Body of the present People of *Ireland*, are the Progeny of the *English* and *Britains*, that from time to time have come over into this Kingdom; and there remains but a meer handful of the Antient *Irish* at this day; I may say, not one in a thousand . . . [47]

Various interpretations of this passage have been put forward. For J.G. Simms, Molyneux's use of the term 'People of Ireland' is to be understood as referring to the landowning classes, who, of course, were mostly of English descent. Isolde Victory saw the statement as simply disingenuous, an attempt to gloss over divisions in Irish society, which is certainly how it struck at least one English critic of *The Case*.[48] However, there were precedents for the remark. The remonstrance drawn up in 1640 by the Irish House of Commons (made up of Protestants and Catholics, Old and New English) advanced the claim that the King's 'Loyal and Dutiful People of . . . *Ireland, being now for the most part*

[43] Molyneux, *The Case*, pp. 30–3; Locke, *Two Treatises*, pp. 384–97.

[44] Caroline Robbins, *The Eighteenth-Century Commonwealthman: Studies in the Transmission, Development and Circumstances of English Political Thought from the Restoration of Charles II until the War with the Thirteen Colonies* (Cambridge MA, 1959), p. 10.

[45] Molyneux, *The Case*, pp. 30, 32, 34.

[46] Conquest theory is a neglected area in Irish historiography for the post-revolutionary period, but see Victory, 'Colonial nationalism in Ireland', pp. 46–66; also C.D.A. Leighton, *Catholicism in a Protestant Kingdom: A Study of the Irish Ancien Régime* (Dublin, 1994), in which Anglo-Irish conquest myths are discussed in terms of European myths of noble conquest (chs 2, 4, 6).

[47] Molyneux, *The Case*, p. 35.

[48] Simms, *William Molyneux of Dublin*, p. 105; Victory, 'Colonial nationalism in Ireland', p. 56; [Simon Clement], *An Answer to Mr Molyneux his Case of Ireland's Being Bound by Acts of Parliament in England, Stated: and his Dangerous Notion of Ireland's Being Under no Subordination to the Parliamentary Authority of England Refuted* (London, 1698), p. 4.

derived from British *Ancestors*, should be governed according to the Municipal and Fundamental Laws of *England*':[49] a claim substantially the same as the one Molyneux was making. It appears, therefore, that as in so much else in *The Case*, Molyneux was here making use of a well-established tradition.

What were the implications of an aristocratic conquest for Molyneux's arguments? Most obviously, Molyneux was claiming that (whatever about the native Irish), those who 'joyned with the Conqueror in a Just Invasion, have lost no Right by the Conquest'.[50] The point was also strongly made by Molyneux's contemporary, Bishop King of Derry, who (having expressed his support for a union as an ideal solution to Ireland's problems) went on to say 'I hope the English that Came into Ireland & by Conquest Inlarged the Dominion of England, Did not thereby forfeit the Liberty of English Men, which I think Consists in being Governed by Laws to which they have given their Consent'.[51] Once again, there were parallels in English thought. In the 1650s the former Bishop Goodman of Gloucester had written that 'the greatest part of the English were descended from the Normans, and in that right they might claim a liberty, that the Conquest is expired, and now they are to be governed by just laws'.[52]

None of this should be taken to imply that Molyneux or his Anglo-Irish contemporaries were seeking to overthrow the authority of the Crown: far from it. For without a King there could be no kingdom, and without a kingdom there could be no Irish parliament consisting of king, lords and commons, no ancient constitution to be inherited: Ireland would then be in the hapless condition (as it appeared to Molyneux) of the American colonists, dependent ultimately on rule 'by the *Great Council* at *Westminster*'.[53] Moreover, this remained an aristocratic age, and much of the status enjoyed by aristocracies still derived from their role as counsellors to kings, and military leaders in royal service. Another Anglo-Irish writer, Sir Francis Brewster, seeking to forestall legislation to curb the Irish woollen industry, warned the English government that such a ban was likely to fall most heavily on 'the *English* of Ireland', a people who for him possessed aristocratic qualities:

[49] As cited in Cox, *Hibernia Anglicana*, pt II, p. 61; cf. Cox's own similar remark, pt I, Preface, sig. b2^{b}.

[50] *The Case*, p. 35.

[51] King to Sir R. Southwell, 6 Jan 1697/8, in Kelly, 'A pamphlet attributed to John Toland', p. 88.

[52] Quoted in Christopher Hill, *Puritanism and Revolution* (London, 1968 edn), p. 69.

[53] Molyneux, *The Case*, p. 115. Molyneux showed little understanding of the extent to which American colonial assemblies were successfully asserting their legislative capacity; see William Simpson, *Vision and Reality: the Evolution of American Government* (London, 1978), ch. 1.

> [they] are not only most unanimous and hearty in the Interests of the present Government both in Church and State; but are a People who have been bred to Arms, and have been most of them in actual Service in the late Wars, and are all ready to appear in a very considerable Body, whenever his Majesty or his Protestant Successors shall have occasion to command them . . .[54]

It was no accident, therefore, that Molyneux was at pains to state that the Anglo-Norman conquerors of the twelfth century, while they had not come to Ireland at the command of the king, had nevertheless come by royal licence and permission; like others before him, he had no desire to claim rights descending from a free-booting band of lawless marauders.[55]

If the native Irish, according to Molyneux, had virtually disappeared from the landowning classes, thus rendering their rights in the 1690s an academic issue, the Catholics were not quite so invisible. As 'Irish Papists' they figured in *The Case* as rebels in 1641, and again in 1689, for among the arguments that Molyneux strove to refute was the claim that the money spent by England in putting down Irish rebellions entitled the English parliament to the disposal of all confiscated estates. Accordingly, Molyneux presented the seventeenth-century Irish conflicts not as wars between two countries but as 'Rebellions, or *Intestine Commotions*', in which the Catholics had risen not only against the king but also against the '*Protestants* of *Ireland*'. The latter had been instrumental in suppressing these risings, albeit 'by the Assistance of their Brethren of *England*'.[56]

This makes it much clearer that in talking about the rights of Englishmen, Molyneux was actually talking about the rights of the Protestants in Ireland. Although he did not dwell on the causes of the risings, the whole tenor of his discussion makes it apparent that he believed these were unjustified rebellions; at one point he refers to 'the Insolencies and Barbarities of the *Irish Papists*' (in 1689).[57] And here it is relevant to note that Molyneux had read the great Dutch jurist, Hugo Grotius, whose *De Jure Belli ac Pacis* (1625) contained extensive sections dealing with the rights of conquerors. Grotius was critical of those who, having been conquered, later tried to recover their liberty:

> *But he, who once vanquish'd, Revolts, is not to be call'd a Lover of Liberty, but a bold Rebellious Slave . . . For when People have been once over-power'd, and*

[54] [Sir Francis Brewster], *A Discourse Concerning Ireland and the Different Interests Thereof, In Answer to the Exon and Barnstaple Petitions* (London, 1697/8), p. 65.

[55] *The Case*, p. 32. Cf. Boyle, *The Answer of a Person of Quality*, who argued that the Protestants were 'commissionated' by the Crown to conquer the papists (p. 14).

[56] *The Case*, p. 112.

[57] *The Case*, p. 89.

have for a great while submitted, to shake off the Yoke then, is to act like Madmen and Desperadoes, and not like Friends to Liberty . . . [58]

Grotius was writing during a period of immensely destructive wars in Europe, both civil and international, and his aim was to identify general laws or principles which would minimise the occasion for war or rebellion.[59] In the Irish context, his precepts added another dimension to the self-image of the Anglo-Irish as a conquering aristocracy. Regarding themselves as descendants of those who had originally been licensed by the Crown to intervene and conquer in Ireland, they continued to pursue an aristocratic role by suppressing rebellions of a people whose propensity to revolt without warning and without just cause (according to Protestants) seemed to confirm their slavish character, and to keep alive the distinctions between conquerors and conquered. The point was reinforced by another anonymous Anglo-Irish writer (possibly Francis Annesley)[60] who also entered the debate on the woollen industry at this time. Distinguishing between 'Colonies for Trade' (whose trade he believed might legitimately be restricted by the 'Mother Kingdom'), and 'Colonies for Empire' (whose trade should be encouraged: a category into which he placed Ireland), the author commented on the latter: 'they are always planted to keep great Countries in subjection, and prevent the charge and hazard of constant standing Armies'.[61]

In all this it would be difficult to exaggerate the effect of the rebellion of 1641 on the Protestant mind. Earlier in the century, Sir John Davies had looked forward to the '*Brittish* and Irish' growing together in 'one Nation', through the salutary effects of English common law extended to all subjects in the aftermath of a complete royal conquest. He was openly critical of the Anglo-Norman aristocracy for acting like petty monarchs and failing to ensure that the native Irish had the benefits of English laws.[62] Fifty years later, in the wake of the rising, Roger Boyle, Earl of Orrery, saw matters in a much starker light. For him, the providential preservation of the Protestants despite the 'massacre' intentions of their

[58] *The Case*, p. 119; Grotius, *Of the Rights of War and Peace*, II, pp. 91–2, quoting (approvingly) the verdict of King Agrippa on the Zealots. It is relevant to note that Grotius believed that some men (and nations) were naturally framed for slavery, rather than liberty; *ibid.*, I, p. 133.

[59] On Grotius's aims, see Richard Tuck, 'The "modern" theory of natural law', in Anthony Pagden (ed.), *The Languages of Political Theory in Early-Modern Europe* (Cambridge, 1990 edn) pp. 99–119, *passim*.

[60] Rather than Sir Richard Cox, to whom it has been attributed: see Kelly, 'The Irish Woollen Act', p. 35, n47.

[61] *Some Thoughts on the Bill Depending before the Right Honourable the House of Lords, for Prohibiting the Exportation of the Woollen Manufactures of Ireland to Foreign Parts* (Dublin, 1698), pp. 8–9.

[62] Davies, *Discoverie of the True Causes*, II, pp. 85–9, 165.

enemies was evidence that the Protestants were God's chosen people, and he made blunt use of the language of conquest:

> His Majesty may rationally expect more future *obedience* and *loyalty* from *English* Protestants, than *Irish* Papists, for (1) the *English* Protestants are the *Conquerors*, the *Irish* Papists the *conquered*; and antient as well as modern experience has made it appear, the *conquered* never did (some think morally never will) love the *conqueror*; and though his Majesty should give the *Irish* Papists not the half onely, but the whole of this Kingdom: yet they will never probably forgive the *English* Protestants for conquering them, nor consequently heartily love that *Royal Authority* which first commissionated the Protestants to do it.[63]

This was written in the early years after the Restoration when it seemed quite possible that Irish Catholics might be granted some degree of toleration and perhaps regain substantial amounts of land. Orrery was spokesman for those who rejected such a policy: this explains the forceful tone. Thirty years later, in the aftermath of the Williamite forfeitures, and with several new penal laws on the statute book, Molyneux could afford to relegate the confessional issue to the background, while he concentrated on Anglo-Irish relations. Nevertheless, his references to papist rebellions suggest that his outlook had much in common with Orrery's. Whether or not the Catholics had English blood in their veins, their frequent rebellions 'against the *King* and *Protestants* of *Ireland*' rendered their lands justly forfeit, while the role of the Irish Protestants in suppressing those rebellions (as much, he claimed, for England's advantage as their own) confirmed their role as conquerors, and gave real weight to Molyneux's claim that 'Your Majesty has not in all Your Dominions a People more *United* and *Steady* to Your Interests, than the *Protestants of Ireland*'.[64]

Molyneux's choice of arguments

Molyneux's main argument in *The Case* for Irish parliamentary rights rested on an appeal to the 'ancient constitution' of Ireland; that is, to the framework of municipal laws which he took to have been in force in Ireland ever since the 'Original Compact' of Henry II's reign gave Ireland the same laws as England.[65] Hence his frequent recourse to the

[63] Boyle, *The Answer of a Person of Quality*, pp. 14, 88–93. I am grateful to Mita Choudhury for drawing this passage to my attention. On the Protestants as God's chosen people, see Nicholas Canny, 'Identity formation in Ireland: the emergence of the Anglo-Irish', in Nicholas Canny and Anthony Pagden (eds.), *Colonial Identity in the Atlantic World, 1500–1800* (Princeton, 1987), pp. 159–212 (pp. 188, 204).

[64] *The Case*, Dedication to the King, p. 18; also pp. 112–13.

[65] The Case, p. 46; Victory, 'Colonial nationalism in Ireland', ch. 2.

authority of ancient charters, precedent, and the common law. Why did Molyneux use such an argument rather than others, and how did it stand up over time?

Appeals to the ancient constitution had two main advantages for Molyneux. First (bearing in mind that he wished to win over English opinion), it was a familiar and respected argument in England, one that had been invoked a good deal during the seventeenth century in opposition to claims for the divine right of kings. It had been given a new lease of life by the Williamite revolution, which was widely interpreted by Whigs as restoring England's ancient constitution.[66] In addition, the seventeenth century had witnessed the evolution of Irish variants of the ancient constitution, including works by the Catholic lawyer Patrick Darcy in 1643, by Molyneux's father-in-law Sir William Domville in 1660, and Bishop Dopping of Meath in 1692. Indeed, it has been demonstrated that Molyneux began his work by having a new copy of Domville's tract prepared, and that one-third of *The Case* was directly based on it.[67]

The language of natural or abstract right, evidently influenced by Locke's *Two Treatises of Government* (1690), cropped up occasionally in *The Case*, but mainly to justify the claim that it was an inherent right of mankind to be ruled by consent: there was no suggestion of an appeal (past or future) to the right of resistance in the event of tyranny on the part of the ruler. Recent studies of English political thought in the late 1600s and early 1700s help explain why Molyneux made only limited use of Lockean concepts, despite his personal friendship with Locke and his evident admiration for the *Two Treatises*. Locke's claim that government was to be considered at an end if rulers threatened their subjects' lives, liberties or estates, and that thereby subjects acquired the right to resist and choose a new government or restore an old one, appeared dangerously radical to a generation which was, in general, determined to interpret the Glorious Revolution in a conservative light. Lockean theories of resistance and contract did circulate among radical Whigs during the post-revolutionary decades, but did not form part of the mainstream of English political thought;[68] only in the era of the American revolution did such ideas become more respectable, especially in America and Ireland.

[66] J.G.A. Pocock, *The Ancient Constitution and the Feudal Law* (Cambridge, 1957), pp. 188, 237–8; J.P. Kenyon, *Revolution Principles: The Politics of Party 1689–1720* (Cambridge, 1977), pp. 45, 220; R.J. Smith, *The Gothic Bequest: Medieval Institutions in British Thought, 1688–1863* (Cambridge, 1987), ch. 1.

[67] Patrick Kelly, 'The printer's copy of the MS of William Molyneux, "The Case of Ireland Being Bound by Acts of Parliament in England, Stated"', *Long Room*, 18–19 (1978–9), 7–13; Victory, 'Colonial nationalism in Ireland', p. 64.

[68] Kenyon, *Revolution Principles*, ch. 7.

But quite apart from this, it should be borne in mind that Molyneux's quarrel was not with the monarch but with the English parliament; in fact, he was prepared to argue that the pretensions of the English parliament to legislate for Ireland encroached on William's prerogative as King of Ireland.[69]

Amongst other contemporary 'opposition' languages in use in the three Kingdoms, the choice of Jacobitism was also ruled out, despite the fact that the Jacobite Parliament in Ireland had witnessed strong claims on behalf of Irish parliamentary rights. Indeed, for Protestants those claims had been a good deal too strong: a bill had been introduced into the House of Commons in 1689 for the repeal of Poynings' Law, which (among other things) preserved the subordination of the Irish parliament to the English crown. James II (still hopeful of regaining his English Kingdom, and anxious not to alienate English opinion further than necessary) had successfully opposed the bill's progress, but the move was indicative of separatist tendencies, and it is noteworthy that Molyneux was careful to make no attack on Poynings' Law. On the contrary, he invoked it to support his contention that English statutes were not binding on Ireland without consent.[70] But in any case, the implications of the restoration of a Catholic dynasty were much too fraught with danger for the established Church of Ireland, and for the existing land settlement, to tempt Molyneux in that direction. Keen to emphasise Anglo-Irish loyalty, he affirmed that 'whoever is *King of England*, is *ipso facto King of Ireland*', and conceded that if any English acts had binding force on Ireland before the Irish parliament had endorsed them, they should be acts concerning the royal succession.[71]

What may seem more suprising is the almost complete absence from Molyneux's arguments of a civic humanist or classical republican theme. His famous Anglo-Irish Whig contemporary, Robert Molesworth, was a noted exponent of such themes, in neo-Harringtonian form, as were certain other Anglo-Irish writers,[72] but *The Case* contains no eulogies of Italian city states or elective monarchies, no use of the concepts of 'virtue' and 'corruption'. The nearest Molyneux came to such thinking is contained in a passage suggesting that in Ireland and England, constitutional

[69] *The Case*, p. 127.

[70] Patrick Kelly, 'William Molyneux and the spirit of liberty in eighteenth-century Ireland', *Eighteenth-Century Ireland*, 3 (1988), 133–48 (p. 135).

[71] *The Case*, pp. 50, 102. Molyneux was referring to the 1541 Irish Act 'that the King of England, his Heirs and Successors be Kings of Ireland' (33 Henry VIII, c. 1), and to the English Bill of Rights (1 Will. & Mary, sess. 2, c. 2) which resolved that William and Mary be King and Queen of England, France and Ireland. See also Kelly, 'Ireland and the Glorious Revolution', pp. 164, 187.

[72] See Robbins, *The Eighteenth-Century Commonwealthman*, ch. 4; Pocock, *The Machiavellian Moment*, chs 12–13.

rectitude depended 'on a Right Temperament between the *Kings* and the *Peoples Rights*'.[73] Once again, it appears that such concepts were largely redundant in a discussion that was concerned with the relations between the Irish parliament and the English parliament, rather than with the relations of King, Lords and Commons; and it has been noted that the preferred solution of the neo-Harringtonian republicans to Anglo-Irish relations was a union.[74] Unlike Molyneux, they dwelled on the benefits of union at some length. Henry Maxwell, for instance, agreed with the author of *Some Thoughts* that colonies represented one means of maintaining conquered lands, avoiding the expense and threat to liberty of a standing army. But once settled, and given a constitution, they must be allowed to make their own laws, otherwise their discontent would require an army to control it. In Ireland's case, the best way to preserve the constitution would be to unite it with that of England.[75]

The impact of The Case and its legacy

By 1698 opposition groups in England were mounting an all-out attack on the Court Whig Junto, exploiting all available grievances – including the Irish woollen issue. Patrick Kelly has suggested that the inflammatory *Letter from a Gentleman in the Country* may have been intended to provoke an intemperate response from Ireland, which would fuel the fires of English discontent. If such was the intention, then the appearance of *The Case* answered admirably. For all Molyneux's reasoned tone, the work angered English MPs, and forced the Irish lobby in the English Parliament to embark on a damage limitation exercise. They prevented the book being presented to the King, and instead referred it to the House of Commons, in order to forestall an even more damaging assault on the Irish woollen industry. The Commons did not, contrary to later myth, order the book to be burned, but did condemn it as being of a piece with recent 'dangerous attempts . . . by some of your subjects of Ireland, to shake off their subjection to, and dependence on, this kingdom', not least by its proposal of union.[76]

In addition, *The Case* prompted a number of reasoned replies, most of

[73] *The Case*, p. 128.

[74] Kelly, 'Origins of the Act of Union', pp. 244–5.

[75] [Henry Maxwell], *An Essay upon an Union of Ireland with England: Most Humbly Offered to the Consideration of the Queen's Most Excellent Majesty, and Both Houses of Parliament* (Dublin, 1704), pp. 8–11.

[76] Kelly, 'The Irish Woollen Act', pp. 37–9; E. Curtis and R.B. McDowell, *Irish Historical Documents, 1172–1922* (London, 1943), pp. 183–5. On the myth of *The Case* being burned, see Victory, 'The making of the 1720 Declaratory Act', p. 21, n35. For the condemnation of union, see Kelly, 'William Molyneux and the spirit of liberty', p. 143.

which contended for the subordination of the Irish parliament to that of England, and which did not shrink from asserting that there had been an English conquest of Ireland.[77] Two types of conquest theory were employed: one derived from Grotius and the law of nations (suppression of unjustified rebellions against a legitimate ruler), and a Hobbesian variety: that since the Anglo-Irish depended ultimately on England for protection, sovereign power must reside in England.[78] Roman analogies were drawn, and Simon Clement went so far as to claim that 'in the Subduing and Settling of *Ireland*', England had closely followed 'the *Roman* Pattern'.[79] Molyneux's claim that rights derived from Henry II's 'Original Compact' had devolved on the Anglo-Irish was challenged, and Ireland's colonial status affirmed: mercantilist principles should operate in respect of Irish trade. Rather than pursuing an illusion of 'independency', the Anglo-Irish should glory in their colonial status, which guaranteed them protection from foreign and domestic enemies.[80]

The episode thus reflected the gap which had opened up since the revolution between Anglo-Irish and English perceptions of Ireland's constitutional position. For, although the response in Ireland to *The Case* was muted – inevitably so, given the condemnation that had overwhelmed it in England – the evidence suggests that Molyneux's views were widely shared there.[81] However, in the short run priority had to be given to mollifying English wrath and rebutting any suggestion that the Anglo-Irish were tainted with 'independency' or Jacobitism.

This showed up clearly over the issue of the royal succession. In 1701 the English Parliament passed an Act of Settlement, which (in default of any living descendants of Princess Anne) fixed the succession to the Crown of England, and of Ireland, on the Hanoverians. It was

[77] Only the non-juror Charles Leslie supported Molyneux, but argued that his acceptance of new oaths imposed by English statute in 1691 undermined his case. See the list of early replies in the 1977 reprint of *The Case*, Appendix B, pp. 143–4, which omits Charles Davenant's discussion in *An Essay Upon the Probable Methods of Making a People Gainers in the Balance of Trade* (London, 1699), in *Works*, II, pp. 240–59.

[78] [William Atwood], *The History, and Reasons, of the Dependency of Ireland upon the Imperial Crown of the Kingdom of England. Rectifying Mr Molineux's State of the Case of Ireland's Being Bound by Acts of Parliament in England* (London, 1698), pp. 40, 196–8, 214–15; [Simon Clement], *An Answer to Mr Molyneux*, pp. 34–41, 71–2, 109, 121–2, 152–3; Davenant, *An Essay*, *Works*, II, pp. 243, 246–8. On contemporary varieties of conquest theory, see Goldie, 'Edmund Bohun and *Jus Gentium*', pp. 570–1.

[79] [Clement], *An Answer to Mr Molyneux*, pp. 149–50; Davenant, *An Essay*, *Works*, II, p. 247. Cf. Grotius, who in discussing the Persian empire, had approved a more decentralised imperial model (*Of the Rights of War and Peace*, II, pp. 223–4).

[80] [Clement], *An Answer to Mr Molyneux*, pp. 2, 24, 165; Davenant, *An Essay*, *Works*, II, pp. 248–51. One theme was that Molyneux's distinction between kingdom and colony was spurious: whatever the name, Ireland was dependent ([Clement], *An Answer*, pp. 140–1; Davenant, *Works*, II, p. 246).

[81] Kelly, 'The Irish Woollen Act', p. 39.

this move which brought to a head relations between England and Scotland: the Scots were outraged at not having been consulted, and the Edinburgh parliament refused to accept a Hanoverian succession without conditions.[82] In Ireland, by contrast, the first parliament to meet after the Act (in 1703) displayed a markedly propitiatory spirit. In an obvious allusion to the reception of *The Case*, the House of Commons regretted that 'our Enemies . . . have misrepresented us . . . as if we thought ourselves, or desired to be, independent of the Crown of *England*', and hastened to endorse 'the Succession in the Protestant line, as the same is settled by Acts of Parliament in *England*'. Accordingly, when, shortly after this address, Robert Molesworth reported from a Commons committee, urging Queen Anne to grant 'a full Enjoyment of our Constitution, or . . . a more firm and strict Union with your Majesty's Subjects of *England*', the crucial succession issue had already been conceded.[83] Thus, while the more self-confident Scots were able to exact a union as the price of their eventual cooperation, the Anglo-Irish, loth even to appear to play the Jacobite card, could exert little effective pressure in that direction.

Notwithstanding the succession episode, and Molyneux's own death in October 1698, the confrontation between the two parliaments over commercial legislation and appellate jurisdiction continued, eventually culminating in the passing of a Declaratory Act at Westminster in 1720. This asserted the right of the (now British) parliament to legislate for Ireland, and denied the appellate jurisdiction of the Irish House of Lords. It has been argued that this statute undermined the basis of arguments from historical precedent, and prompted champions of Irish rights from the 1720s onwards to switch to natural right.[84] Two points, however, need to be borne in mind. First, while the Declaratory Act doubtless faithfully reflected the view at Westminster that the Irish parliament was subordinate to the metropolitan one, the act itself did not turn out to be a good guide to the future conduct of Anglo-Irish relations. Between the passing of the act and the granting of legislative independence in 1782 the British parliament legislated for Ireland only with great caution, and mostly on matters of an uncontentious economic or administrative nature

[82] 12 & 13 Will. III, c. 2; Ferguson, 'Imperial crowns', pp. 30–44; Robertson, 'Union, state and empire', pp. 241–2.

[83] *Journals of the House of Commons of the Kingdom of Ireland (Commons Jn Ire.)* (Dublin, 1796), II, pp. 322, 342. The Commons' resolutions were confirmed by an 'Act to make it high treason to impeach the succession of the crown, as limited by several acts of Parliament' (1703/4), 2 Anne, c. 5, in *The Statutes at Large, Passed in the Parliaments held in Ireland* (Dublin, 1765), IV, pp. 11–12.

[84] Victory, 'The making of the 1720 Declaratory Act', p. 28. But see Patrick Kelly, 'Perceptions of Locke in eighteenth-century Ireland', *Royal Irish Academy Proceedings*, 89, Sect. c (1989), 17–35 (p. 26).

which applied throughout Britain, or to the whole empire.[85] The fact was that Ireland could not be ruled without a measure of consent; in that sense the thrust of Molyneux's argument had been perfectly shrewd, and helps explain the book's enduring appeal in Ireland. In any case, the executive possessed ample alternative means of influencing Irish affairs through the operation of Poynings' Law, use of patronage, and other agencies.

Secondly, it is apparent, looking at the longer perspective of 'Patriot' claims in the eighteenth century, that an ancient constitution mode of thought, or 'common law mind' continued to find expression: though from mid-century on its champions were apt to differ from Molyneux in their attitude to Poynings' Law, finding it a badge of subordination. Charles Lucas, for instance, the most important champion of Irish rights in the middle decades of the century, made use of a rich variety of arguments based on corporate values, natural right, neo-Harringtonian republicanism, civil religion, and the ancient constitution.[86] Likewise, Henry Grattan (whose declaration of rights was eventually accepted by the Irish Parliament in 1782, and subsequently conceded by the British government) employed a variety of political arguments, but gave pride of place to rights springing from the ancient constitution and Magna Carta.[87] And there was nothing particularly outmoded about the use of such arguments at this period; R.J. Smith has noted in the English context that 'eighteenth century writers used far more of the legacy of their seventeenth century predecessors than we used to allow'.[88]

Thus *The Case* continued to appeal, in its detailed arguments as well as in its overall thrust. Indeed, it might almost be claimed that as the decades passed, and the British parliament made such limited use of the rights asserted in the Declaratory Act, Molyneux was vindicated.[89] Meanwhile, as the Irish economy began to prosper in mid-century (despite the commercial restrictions), the Irish parliament, which had been meeting regularly since the early 1700s, inevitably took on a higher profile. Accordingly, by the 1750s attitudes to legislative union were changing; no longer did such a union (attainable or not) seem to be an unmixed

[85] J.C. Beckett, *Confrontations: Studies in Irish History* (London, 1972), pp. 124–5.

[86] See e.g., Charles Lucas, *Divelina Libera: an Apology for the Civil Rights and Liberties of the Commons and Citizens of Dublin. Containing an Account of the Foundation and Constitution of this City* (Dublin, 1744); [Charles Lucas], *The Political Constitutions of Great-Britain and Ireland, Asserted and Vindicated; the Common Interest of Both Kingdoms, Demonstrated*, 2 vols. (London, 1751); also Kelly, 'William Molyneux and the spirit of liberty', p. 135. On civil religion, see Mark Goldie, 'The civil religion of James Harrington', in Pagden (ed.), *Languages of Political Theory*, pp. 197–222.

[87] Henry Grattan, *Speeches*, ed. D.O. Madden (Dublin, 1853), p. 49.

[88] Smith, *Gothic Bequest*, pp. 10, 80.

[89] Although Blackstone reaffirmed the English parliament's claims; Kelly, 'Perceptions of Locke', p. 28.

blessing. On the contrary, for those whose livelihoods depended on commerce or industry the loss of a local parliament seemed fraught with danger.[90]

Yet the appeal of legislative union had not entirely disappeared by mid-century. Quite apart from some neo-republicans from an earlier generation who championed the idea of union with Britain down to the 1750s,[91] Charles Lucas too was prepared to acknowledge that union might, in certain circumstances, be a better means of protecting liberty than the Irish parliament. Admittedly, he was writing in 1756, in the aftermath of the money bill dispute, and in the bitter knowledge that certain MPs had abandoned a Patriot stance in return for favours from the government.[92] He himself was in exile in England, having been forced to flee from Ireland to escape arrest as a result of charges arising from his populist electioneering in 1748/9. Perhaps he was never again to be so pessimistic about the prospects for liberty in Ireland, but, as he reflected on the prospect of an Irish parliament apparently content merely to register law devised by the executive, he did raise the question,

> Will it not rather be more wise and just, while any sense of Liberty remanes among the People to intitule them to inroll with the Family of Britain, with the same Care to rescue them from domestic as from foreign Destruction, and unite them effectually, as Scotland has been, with this Kingdom?[93]

In other words, it was the preservation of liberty that was the goal, and if a local parliament, and a local aristocracy, failed to perform this task, then a union must be considered. Such concerns were not confined to Ireland; fears that liberty would be lost through the corrupting effect of the executive on parliament persisted in English opposition circles down to the last decades of the eighteenth century.[94]

Vestiges of the older libertarian unionist tradition thus survived, even among Patriot politicians. But as the Irish Patriots and the Irish parliament redeemed themselves in the 1760s and 1770s by achieving

[90] Kelly, 'Origins of the act of Union', pp. 247–8; Sean Murphy, 'The Dublin anti-Union riot of 3 December 1759', in O'Brien (ed.) *Parliament, Politics and People*, pp. 49–68; Seamus Cummins, 'Extra-parliamentary agitation in Dublin in the 1760s', in R.V. Comerford, Mary Cullen, Jacqueline Hill and Colm Lennon (eds.), *Religion, Conflict and Coexistence in Ireland: Essays Presented to Monsignor Patrick J. Corish* (Dublin, 1990), pp. 118–34.

[91] Robbins, *Eighteenth-Century Commonwealthman*, ch. 5.

[92] The dispute concerned the respective rights of the Crown and the Irish Parliament to dispose of a surplus in the Irish treasury. See Declan O'Donovan, 'The Money Bill dispute of 1753', in Bartlett and Hayton (eds.), *Penal Era and Golden Age*, pp. 55–87.

[93] [Charles Lucas], *An Appeal to the Commons and Citizens of London. By Charles Lucas, the Last Free Citizen of Dublin* (London, 1756), p. 6.

[94] J.A.W. Gunn, *Beyond Liberty and Property: the Process of Self-Recognition in Eighteenth Century Political Thought* (Kingston and Montreal, 1983), ch. 1.

gains in the constitutional and commercial spheres, the lingering sense among opposition politicians that union represented a last resort for the protection of liberty was eclipsed. One sign of this change of outlook came with the publication of a new edition of *The Case* in 1782, coinciding with the winning of Irish legislative independence, in which Molyneux's reference to union as 'an Happiness we can hardly hope for' was omitted.[95]

But if union had lost its attraction, what had become of conquest? The combination of Catholic forfeitures, and stringent penal laws passed between the 1690s and the 1720s, gave a basis of security to the Anglo-Irish Protestants for the best part of a century. They were thereby enabled to act as a social and political elite, enjoy the privileges of land-ownership and (for town dwellers) to dominate corporate life. They could be all the more assured in this role because similar penal laws, which differed only in detail from their own, were to be found throughout the Hanoverian dominions, and were everywhere justified by a similar appeal to the Jacobite and French threat, the precepts of civil religion, and to the discriminatory practice of most other countries. Moreover, down to the 1770s and even beyond, contemporary political thought in Britain and America, whether inspired by ancient constitution or neo-republican ideas, remained predominantly aristocratic in outlook: what other order of society could act so effectively as a check on royal or ministerial absolutism?[96] With these new functions to the fore, there was less need for the Anglo-Irish to dwell on their more traditional role as a conquering elite.

On the other hand, there was little incentive for them to question it. And a self-image based on conquest persisted. Swift, for instance, claimed: 'One great Merit I am sure we have, which those of *English* Birth can have no Pretence to; that our Ancestors reduced this Kingdom to the Obedience of ENGLAND'. It annoyed him that English people knew little of the Anglo-Irish, regarding them 'as a sort of *Savage Irish*, whom our Ancestors conquered several Hundred Years ago'.[97] In the 1740s, Lucas went out of his way to endorse Molyneux's view that the Irish were not a conquered people (i.e., not conquered by the King); but he had no doubt that those who had broken 'solemn engagements' had been lawfully dispossessed, or that those who opposed 'the rules or laws of society'

95 1782 marked the zenith of interest in Molyneux; Kelly, 'William Molyneux and the spirit of liberty', pp. 142–3.

96 For the importance of aristocracy in eighteenth-century political thought, see Maurice Cranston, *Philosophers and Pamphleteers: Political Theorists of the Enlightenment* (Oxford, 1986), ch. 1; Gunn, *Beyond Liberty and Property*, ch. 3; J.C.D. Clark, *English Society 1688–1832* (Cambridge, 1985), ch. 2.

97 *A Letter to the Whole People of Ireland* (no. 4 of the Drapier's Letters), in Herbert Davis (ed.), *The Prose Works of Jonathan Swift*, (Oxford, 1941), X, pp. 55, 64.

should be treated as rebels. He particularly stressed the role of the Dublin freemen in suppressing such rebellions, an emphasis which reflected the growing 'aristocratic' pretensions of those who formed the body politic of the capital city.[98] In a satirical work published a decade later, Sir Richard Cox, grandson of the lord chancellor, used a metaphor from American colonial society to describe the mixture of people on the estate of 'Betty Ireland': 'They are *Whites*, *Blacks*, and *Black and White*. The *Whites* only are allowed to be *Land-holders*; but the *last* . . . pass for *Whites*, and make good their *Titles* . . . the *Blacks* . . . are ever watching for an Opportunity to make a *Riot*'.[99] By referring to those who 'pass for Whites', Cox drew attention to a contentious current issue: Catholics conforming to the established church in order to preserve their estates.[100]

If conquerors and conquered were ever to coalesce and form one people, as political theory suggested they should,[101] then conforming to the state church was evidently one means to that end, though one that never looked like affecting more than a fraction even of the propertied Catholics. By mid-century, another route seemed to be opening up, when certain Catholic spokesmen formally abandoned the language of Jacobitism and began to look for terms with the Hanoverian regime.[102] But these spokesmen faced a long, difficult campaign (not helped by many reservations among their own fellow-religionists); and in the meantime agrarian outrages in the south of Ireland helped keep alive fears of popish rebellion.[103] Accordingly, it was not until the late 1770s that any significant dismantling of the penal laws began. By 1782 most of the laws relating to freedom of worship, ownership of land, and education had been repealed. It is a measure of the vitality of traditional views that, even though they stopped short of granting Catholics any political rights, Henry Grattan could describe these reforms in 1788 as having set a people free. And he was, by contemporary standards, a friend to Catholic claims. There was little sign in the 1780s that the Anglo-Irish (with few

98 A.F. Barber and Citizen [Charles Lucas], *A Second Letter to the Free Citizens of Dublin* (Dublin, 1747), pp. 7–8; *A Third Letter to the Free-Citizens of Dublin* (Dublin, 1747), pp. 14–17; Leighton, *Catholicism in a Protestant Kingdom*, ch. 4; Jacqueline Hill, 'Corporate values in Hanoverian Edinburgh and Dublin', in R.J. Morris and R. Houston (eds), *Conflict, Identity and Economic Development, Ireland and Scotland, 1600–1939* (John Donald, forthcoming).

99 [Sir Richard Cox], *The True Life of Betty Ireland . . . Together with Some Account of Her Elder Sister Blanch of Britain* (London and Dublin, 1753), p. 22.

100 On converts, see L.M. Cullen, 'Catholics under the penal laws', *Eighteenth-Century Ireland*, I (1986), 23–36.

101 Locke thought it 'seldom' happened that conquerors and conquered 'never incorporate into one People' (*Two Treatises of Government*, p. 387).

102 Leighton, *Catholicism in a Protestant Kingdom*, ch. 5.

103 See Maureen Wall, 'The Whiteboys', in T.D. Williams (ed.), *Secret Societies in Ireland* (Dublin, 1973), pp. 13–25 (pp. 18–21).

exceptions) considered it right, safe, or desirable to go beyond this; nor did the British government take a different view.[104]

The situation was transformed in the early 1790s, when, in an increasingly counter-revolutionary atmosphere, the British government adopted a new Irish policy, based on the prescriptions of Edmund Burke. The conversion of British ministers to a policy of granting political rights to Irish Catholics – in a bid to capture them for the counter-revolutionary cause – administered a shock of such magnitude to the Irish elite that it prompted the use of a new political language. Or rather, an old language, but one which was now used in a radically new way. Assuming the leadership of a nation-wide appeal to Irish Protestants in defence of 'Protestant ascendancy',[105] Dublin corporation (with a reputation for championing Patriot causes) set out its answer to the idea of political rights for Catholics:

> One hundred years are just elapsed, since the question was tried upon an appeal to heaven, whether this country should become a Popish kingdom, governed by an arbitrary and unconstitutional Popish tyrant, and dependant upon France, or enjoy the blessings of a free Protestant government, a Protestant monarchy limited by the constitution, and an intimate connection with the free empire of Britain. The great ruler of all things decided in favour of our ancestors, he gave them victory and Ireland became a Protestant nation enjoying a British constitution. . . . we tell them [the Catholics], that the Protestants of Ireland would not be compelled by any authority whatever to abandon that political situation, which their forefathers won with their swords, and which is therefore their birthright, or to surrender their religion at the footstool of Popery.[106]

Here Molyneux's ancient constitution, with its debt to medieval ancestors who had conquered with the king, was set aside in favour of a much more recent conquest, achieved by a radical Lockean resort to arms, or 'appeal to heaven'.[107] The natural right of resistance to tyranny had been discussed in Ireland, on and off, ever since the rehabilitation of Locke's political works in the late 1770s:[108] the corporation's statement

[104] Grattan, speech on tithes, 14 Feb. 1788, in *Speeches*, p. 130, and see A.P.W. Malcomson, *John Foster: The Politics of the Anglo-Irish Ascendancy* (Oxford, 1978), p. 407. For survival of traditional views of the Catholics, see Marianne Elliott, *Wolfe Tone: Prophet of Irish Independence* (New Haven and London, 1989), ch. 7.

[105] Recent writing on the origins and meaning of the term 'Protestant ascendancy' is conveniently summarised in James Kelly, 'Eighteenth-century ascendancy: a commentary', in *Eighteenth-Century Ireland*, 5 (1990), 173–87.

[106] Sir John T. Gilbert and Lady Gilbert, *Calendar of the Ancient Records of Dublin (CARD)*, 19 vols. (Dublin, 1889–1944), XIV, pp. 287–8.

[107] 'And where the Body of the People . . . is deprived of their Right, or is under the Exercise of a power without right, and have no Appeal on Earth, there they have a liberty to appeal to Heaven . . . ' (Locke, *Two Treatises of Government*, p. 379).

[108] Kelly, 'Perceptions of Locke', pp. 27–8.

claimed that it had already been exercised. According to this view, the Williamite victory in 1690/1 signalled heaven's verdict on the conflict between the Irish Protestants and King James, and the outcome was a fixed, unalterable 'free' Protestant constitution. This, then, was the ultimate anti-absolutist statement, and hence directed not primarily against the Catholics, but against the King, or the King's ministers, who had, apparently, forgotten the political wisdom learned since Molyneux's day: that Ireland had to be ruled with the consent of her dominant elite. And, although the corporation was very far from adopting a unionist position,[109] the insistence that the Irish constitution involved an intimate connection with the 'free empire' of Britain was significant. It represented a warning to any separatists among contemporary radicals; it also indicated that, in the corporation's eyes, the transformation of 'England' into the 'British empire' had been accomplished without the loss of liberty.

Fortunately for the Catholics, the government's bombshell did not evoke the same reaction from all Protestants. Even before the government's conversion, Wolfe Tone had produced his *Argument on Behalf of the Catholics of Ireland* (August 1791) in which he called on his fellow Protestants to admit Catholics to political equality. Once the government had moved, certain mainstream opposition politicians, including, notably Henry Grattan, recognised that such a seismic shift in government policy required timely adjustments in their own position, if they were to have any hope of winning Catholic support for opposition causes in future.[110] Only five years since he had praised his fellow Protestants for repealing so many penal laws, thus setting the Catholics free, Grattan took the opportunity afforded by a debate on a Catholic relief bill to reproach them:

> The time is come when every loyal subject should be free, and every free subject loyal. It is true, the Roman Catholics will now be your fellow-subjects, but not your subjects; they will be the subjects of the king, and not the slaves of subjects, who stood, with regard to them, in the place of kings. Conquerors, or tyrants proceeding from conquerors, have scarcely ever for any length of time governed by those partial disabilities; but [for] a people so to govern itself, or rather, under the name of government so to exclude . . . a body so useful, so numerous, and that for ever; and, in the mean time, to tax them *ad libitum*, and occasionally to pledge their lives and fortunes! for what? For their disfranchisement. It cannot be done . . . Such a policy always turns on the inventor . . . What was the case of Ireland? enslaved for a century, and withered and blasted with her Protestant ascendancy . . .[111]

[109] The Dublin corporation strongly resisted Union at the time of the Act of Union and for many years thereafter, despite its exclusively Protestant composition down to 1841. See Gilbert, *CARD*, XV, pp. 81–2, XVI, p. 223.

[110] Malcomson, *John Foster*, pp. 352–5.

[111] Grattan, speech on Catholic Relief Bill, 22 Feb. 1793, *Speeches*, pp. 205, 208.

In thus identifying conquest and Protestant ascendancy with 'the case of Ireland', Grattan was (consciously or unconsciously) striking at two of the implicit assumptions of Molyneux's tract. It is doubtful whether he recognised the irony. For Molyneux's reputation – as a champion of the Irish parliamentary rights that Grattan had helped to vindicate – continued to ride high, even for advanced Protestant radicals such as Wolfe Tone.[112] Nevertheless, Grattan's attack on Protestant ascendancy was significant, emanating as it did from a politician inside Parliament, now calling on his fellow Protestants to reject a self-image which had served to sustain their ancestors for generations.

Grattan's plea failed to unite Protestants, who became increasingly polarised during the 1790s, some taking a separatist stand with the United Irishmen, and others siding with the 'Protestant ascendancy' ideals of the newly formed Orange Order. When rebellion broke out in 1798, conditions were ripe for the rebirth of unionism. Circumstances were not unlike those in the 1690s; once again, Britain was involved in an international war, once again French ambitions were to be curbed, once again there was a perceived Catholic threat in Ireland. But whereas in the 1690s that threat could be dealt with by penal laws, these had now for the most part been dismantled, and it was almost inconceivable that they would be reimposed.[113] Against this background, the insecurity felt by many Protestants could only be counteracted by a union; and in view of the international situation, government now became positively anxious to secure one.[114] Just 100 years since the English House of Commons had explicitly condemned Molyneux's tract for advocating Irish representation at Westminster, the ministerial campaign began that was to culminate in the Irish Act of Union.

Significantly, Grattan reminded his audience of their current support for the abolition of the slave trade, and asked, 'have you forgot the man at home by your side, your brother?' (*ibid.*, p. 208). At about this time the campaign for extending political rights to Catholics became known as 'emancipation' (Dickson, *New Foundations*, p. 176).

[112] Kelly, 'William Molyneux and the spirit of liberty', pp. 144–5.

[113] As noted by John Giffard, a lone Unionist in the lower house of Dublin corporation in 1800 (Gilbert, *CARD*, XV, pp. 519–20).

[114] Reopening the question of union even flushed out a unionist of the old libertarian type. Archibald Hamilton Rowan (born in London of Anglo-Irish parentage) had lived in Ireland since 1784 and was an active United Irishman until his conviction for sedition and subsequent escape to America. Baffled at Ireland's failure to show effective support for the French invasion in 1798, he wrote that he had never had the same dread of a Union as most of his friends, and that 'after one year's residence [in Ireland] . . . there was no moment that I would not have exchanged our phantom independence, for a reciprocity of rights and enjoyments with Britain'. Rowan to Rev. George Potts [probably autumn 1798], reproduced in David Dickson, 'Manuscripts of Irish domestic interest in repositories in Philadelphia', *Analecta Hibernica*, 33 (1986), 201–18 (pp. 215–16). I am grateful to David Dickson for drawing this letter to my attention.

12

THE LEGACY OF BRITISH UNION FOR THE NORTH AMERICAN COLONIES: PROVINCIAL ELITES AND THE PROBLEM OF IMPERIAL UNION

NED LANDSMAN

THE legacy of the Union of 1707 for the condition of the North American colonies is a question that was probably more notable for its absence than its prominence in eighteenth-century discussion. Even during the third quarter of that century, when British and American presses worked overtime discussing both what had been and what ought to be the relationship between Britain and her colonies, one finds surprisingly few explicit considerations of the Union – probably fewer, for example, than of the British–Irish relationship, the status of the ancient colonies of Greece and Rome or of the French and Spanish colonies in the New World, perhaps even of the condition of the Counties Palatine of the English Border. Nor did the solution chosen in 1707 – incorporation – attract the support of more than a few avowedly 'visionary' theorists such as Adam Smith, even though it would have provided one of the few available solutions to the crisis consistent with the opposing principles of sovereignty and equity. Instead, it seems that most metropolitans officially maintained a strictly imperial conception of the colonial relationship, while most colonial spokesmen endorsed a purely confederal solution that would have left the colonies in the position of smaller satellite provinces of a larger metropolitan core, a solution not so different *constitutionally* from the one that Scots by 1707 had come to reject. Thus the legacy of the Union debates for the colonies appears, on the surface at least, to have been practically nil.[1]

If we alter our perspective for the moment, and address not just the immediate ramifications of the Union debate in America, but the

[1] A recent comprehensive summary of the discussion of imperial relations is provided in Jack P. Greene, *Peripheries and Center: Constitutional Development in the Extended Polities of the British Empire and the United States 1607–1788* (Athens, Georgia, 1986).

implications of the Union itself, then the answer looks a good deal more substantial. The question then becomes one of the differences that it made that those American colonies changed from dependencies of a unified English state to provinces of an enlarged United Kingdom, in which the authority of the metropolis was partially offset for the colonies by countervailing cultural influences emanating from alternative provincial capitals. Those effects were substantial and varied. The character of the colonial population changed: a citizenry that had been predominantly English in origin became increasingly mixed, with especially fast-growing populations of Irish and German Protestants and Scots. The pattern of colonial trade altered, from a near-exclusive commerce with southern English ports towards a much broader configuration that included a rapidly expanding traffic with the outports of northern England, Scotland, and the north of Ireland. So did the pattern of colonial culture, as American ideas about religion, politics, science, and letters all were increasingly oriented towards those of Britain's other provincial cultures, especially that of Scotland, as Scots and Americans became similarly enmeshed in a cultural matrix of evangelical religion and a provincial form of Enlightenment. Moreover, the American colonists lived in an empire that was increasingly administered by provincials – Scots and Irish, but especially Scots – politically, militarily, and in matters of religion, education and trade.[2]

The last feature, deriving in part from the others, will form the principal focus of this inquiry. Traditionally, those Scots and Scots-Irish administrators have been portrayed as spokesmen for metropolitan interests and tools of empire. I would like to suggest a different view. Despite their apparently unreserved enthusiasm for the strengthening of imperial ties, the vision of empire reflected in their various activities and pronouncements looks less like an empire than an expansive commercial union, a conception rooted both in Scottish political tradition and the characteristic concerns of the provincial Enlightenment. That vision was British, in the sense of attaching rights to Britons wherever they lived; commercial, based upon a principle (if not always the practice) of mutual advantage; and responsive to the increasingly dynamic qualities of provincial society. All of those features had implications that were far from metropolitan.

A number of the views those elites expressed were shared at least in part

[2] On those developments, see my 'Provincial culture and the Empire: Scotland, the American colonies, and the development of British provincial identity', in Lawrence Stone (ed.), *An Imperial State at War: Britain from 1689 to 1815* (London, 1994). The classic statement is John Clive and Bernard Bailyn, 'England's "cultural provinces": Scotland and America', *William and Mary Quarterly*, 3rd ser., 11 (1954), 220–13.

by other participants in the imperial discussion. Their positions differed principally in the consistency with which they injected commercial values in the broadest sense into all kinds of imperial issues and – as a consequence– their unreservedly optimistic assessment of the desirability of union itself. In short, those elites established a viewpoint that differed both from that of most metropolitans and from what they considered the local and particularist perspectives of other colonials, affirming the advantages of union but asserting the claims of provincials to equal privileges within it. Their insistence upon the necessity of imperial integration accounts in large part for their marked unpopularity in the colonies. Their persistence in addressing the problem of imperial union constituted an important link between the Union debates of 1707 and the later American consideration of empire, confederation, and union that emerged in the latter part of the century.

I

The place of Scots and Scottish officials within England's overseas empire had already been at issue for several decades before the Union, owing to the growing involvement of Scots with the American colonies. The background to that involvement is well known. As recent Scottish historians have pointed out, the Union crisis was largely brought about by a growing consensus among Scotland's upper classes that their nation's economic development, and even its independence, were hindered by the perpetual neglect of Scottish interests that seemed inherent in the Union of the Crowns. The solution was economic growth through increased manufacturing coupled with expanded foreign trade.[3] It has not often been recognised how prominently the empire and the American colonies figured in that plan.

The best-known of those Scottish involvements was the Company of Scotland, which attempted to launch trading enterprises to several parts of the world, most especially Darien. In popular lore, Darien ranks as a quintessentially Scottish enterprise, accompanied by nationalistic rhetoric and the recruitment of former covenanting ministers for the colony. Yet at the outset the plan was more British than Scottish, drawing upon a British imperial vision first developed by Scottish Reformers. Much of the impetus for the company came from a London community of Scottish and English merchants endeavouring to penetrate an imperial commerce

[3] T.C. Smout, *Scottish Trade on the Eve of the Union* (Edinburgh, 1963); and Nicholas Phillipson, 'Culture and society in the 18th-century province: the case of Edinburgh and the Scottish Enlightenment', in Lawrence Stone (ed.), *The University and Society* 2 vols. (Princeton, 1975), II, pp. 407–48.

dominated by the chartered trading companies, and they counted upon considerable assistance from commercial contacts already residing in England's North American colonies. It was English rather than Scottish policy that limited English involvement in the Darien project.[4]

In fact, the Darien venture built upon the two earlier Scottish efforts to penetrate the English colonial world: a failed Covenanter colony in Carolina and a larger and more successful North-eastern and Quaker settlement in East Jersey, which together attracted well over 100 Scottish investors and nearly 1,000 settlers. Those groups shared the concerns of their countrymen for the economic development of Scotland; many of the organisers invested simultaneously in an agressive set of plans to develop mills and manufactures in Scotland, such as the New Mills cloth factory in East Lothian. But the larger point is that they established those Scottish settlements as distinct sub-settlements within English colonies, a pattern they would replicate on a smaller scale within English dominions in the West Indies, the Chesapeake, Philadelphia and New York.[5]

Thus before Darien, Scots had established a workable framework for a limited participation in England's colonial empire, allowing for settlement, administration, and trade. In East Jersey, Scots held everything from the governorship to local court positions; elsewhere they had assumed prominent positions in New York, Virginia, and the West Indies. That was only called into question by the creation of the Company of Scotland, which provoked orders from the English government prohibiting colonials from aiding the Scottish Company. Scots in East Jersey were hauled before colony courts and ordered to swear that they would not aid the Company and would give notice should any of the Darien ships appear. An act of 1696 required proprietary governments to limit office-holding to natural-born subjects of England. That was tested in the Jerseys, where a faction of English proprietors used it to remove the Scottish governor, Andrew Hamilton. Belatedly, Hamilton's position was upheld by the Attorney General, referring back to the granting of mutual naturalisation to English and Scots under the Union of the Crowns as specified in Calvin's Case (1608), thus reconfirming, before

[4] George Pratt Insh, *The Company of Scotland Trading to Africa and the Indies* (New York, 1932); Ned C. Landsman, *Scotland and its First American Colony 1683–1765* (Princeton, 1985), ch. 4; and see David Armitage, 'The Scottish vision of empire', above. On the traditions of the Scottish Reformers, see Arthur H. Williamson, *Scottish National Consciousness in the Age of James VI* (Edinburgh, 1979) and the essays in Roger A. Mason (ed.) *Scotland and England 1286-1815* (Edinburgh, 1987).

[5] George Pratt Insh, *Scottish Colonial Schemes, 1620–1686* (Glasgow, 1922); Landsman, *Scotland and its First American Colony*; and Gordon Marshall, *Presbyteries and Profits: Calvinism and the Development of Capitalism in Scotland, 1560–1707* (Oxford, 1980), Appendix.

the Union, the legitimacy of Scottish office-holding in England's colonies.[6]

The Union, then, did not so much initiate Scottish involvement with England's colonial empire as resolve its status. Few Scots, by that date, still believed that their nation could advance economically in total isolation. The entire Union debate in Scotland, as reconstructed by John Robertson, suggests that Scottish thinking about national affairs had become almost inevitably British and Unionist; the paramount question was not the desirability of union *per se* but rather the kind of union that would best protect Scottish interests from metropolitan interference. To proponents of the Treaty of Union, the answer lay in an 'incorporating union,'' as creating a single sovereign state with an undifferentiated citizenry entitled to the equal protection of British liberties. Union opponents, by contrast, drew upon continental traditions of political thought largely abandoned in parliamentary England to argue instead for one of several varieties of a reconstructed confederation as providing a greater check upon English encroachment.[7] In the aftermath of Union, Scots, much more than their English counterparts, would continue to attend to that paramount question.

II

At the outset, the Union attracted relatively little notice in America, but it was not long before its ramifications began to surface. The most dramatic of those was the rapidly growing involvement of Scots elites at all levels of colonial life. Scots quickly began to fill a great many political offices from governorships downwards: Robert Hunter in New York and New Jersey in 1710, succeeded by William Burnet and John Montgomerie; William Keith in Pennsylvania; Alexander Spotswood, William Gooch, and Robert Dinwiddie in Virginia; Gabriel Johnstone and James Glen in the Carolinas, to mention only the most prominent. Scotsmen were equally well placed in religious administration, beginning with Commissary Blair in Virginia in 1685; thereafter much of the leadership of both the colonial Anglican and Presbyterian Churches would be Scottish-born or educated. Among educational officials we could add William Smith and Francis Alison at the College of Pennsylvania, John Witherspoon at the College

[6] *Documents Relating to the Colonial History of the State of New Jersey*, ed. William A. Whitehead, *et al.* (Newark, Trenton, etc., 1880–), pp. 176–7; Brian P. Levack, *The Formation of the British State: England, Scotland and the Union 1603–1707* (Oxford, 1987), pp. 183–4, 220–2; and see William R. Brock, *Scotus Americanus: A Survey of the Sources for Links Between Scotland and America in the Eighteenth Century* (Edinburgh, 1982), ch. 2.

[7] Robertson, 'Union, state and empire: the European context of British Union in 1707', in Stone (ed.), *An Imperial State of War*.

of New Jersey at Princeton, Blair at William and Mary, and a number of others.[8]

Scots developed equally impressive commercial involvements with the colonies. They became a dominant influence not only in the tobacco trade, as is well known, but in much backcountry trading also, from the Carolinas to the far north of British America. They were a strong commercial presence also in nearly every colonial city.[9] Increasingly, the fairest prospect in all of Scotland was not the road to London, as Samuel Johnson boasted, but rather the trail from Glasgow to Port Glasgow and Greenock, the principal points of departure for America.

Let us examine a few of those Scottish-American groups in detail. At the time of his appointment to the governorships of New York and New Jersey in 1710, Robert Hunter, a native of Ayrshire, had a long background as a military man. He also had connections at court and among the literati as a friend and correspondent of Addison and Swift. During a decade in New York, Hunter attracted to the colony a number of talented young Scotsmen who would play long and influential roles there, including James Alexander, Cadwallader Colden, and Archibald Kennedy. Their backgrounds were extremely varied: Colden, a physician from southeastern Scotland, was the son of a Presbyterian clergyman, although he became an Anglican and a Tory; Alexander was a lawyer from the North-east with a Jacobite past; Kennedy, like Hunter, was an Ayrshire man with roots in the land and the law. None the less, they shared some characteristics typical of a Scottish 'lad o' pairts'. All had unusually wide-ranging interests, from science and the law to imperial administration and Indian affairs: all developed broad intercolonial contacts as well.[10]

Another prominent group of Scottish administrators turned up in the southern colonies of Virginia, South Carolina, Georgia, and especially North Carolina, following the appointment of Gabriel Johnstone as governor of that colony in 1734, and in the Virginia administrations of Spotswood, Gooch, and Dinwiddie. Included among them were a most unusual group of lower administrative officials involved in the regulation of customs and trade: Henry McCulloh, James Abercromby, and John Rutherford. After mid-century, those men would develop some of the

[8] See my 'Provincial culture and the Empire'.

[9] 'Provincial culture and the Empire', and see Jacob Price, 'The rise of Glasgow in the Chesapeake tobacco trade, *William and Mary Quarterly*, 3rd ser., II (1954), 179–99; David S. Macmillan, 'The new men' in action: Scottish mercantile and shipping operations in the North American Colonies, 1760–1825', in *Canadian Business History: Selected Studies 1497–1971* (Toronto, 1972), pp. 44–103; and Bernard Bailyn, *Voyagers to the West: A Passage in the Peopling of America on the Eve of the Revolution* (New York, 1986).

[10] See especially Mary Lou Lustig, *Robert Hunter 1666–1734: New York's Augustan Statesman* (Syracuse, 1983).

most substantial and comprehensive plans offered during that century for restructuring the imperial relationship and augmenting colonial revenues.[11]

A third group to consider were the educators, such as William Smith, Francis Alison, John Witherspoon, and William Small, along with a larger group of Scots tutors and other educators. They also came from varied origins: Smith and Small hailed from Episcopal Northeast; Alison and Witherspoon were Presbyterians, but from opposite sides of the Irish Sea and opposing positions in the politics of the Kirk. Still, all four were educated in Scotland under new curriculae established during the Scottish Enlightenment, and all devoted themselves to restructuring colonial education in accord with Enlightenment ideas in the natural sciences, political economy and moral philosophy. Moreover, all of them devoted themselves to inculcating a Whiggish philosophy of civil and religious liberty among their students.[12]

If for the moment we ignore the very considerable distinctions among those groups and consider them collectively, several important themes emerge. One was the unusual willingness of prominent and educated Scots, and to a lesser extent, Irish Protestants and English Dissenters, to involve themselves in colonial life either temporarily or permanently, the result of limited opportunities at home, an enlightened interest in America developing among the *literati*, and a general determination among Scots after mid-century to obtain for themselves a larger share of the benefits of empire. That was certainly true of merchants, ministers and placemen; it was characteristic of several other groups also, most importantly of Scottish doctors, an extraordinary talented and wide-ranging group of immigrants in the eighteenth century, including Colden, Alexander Garden, William Douglass, John Lining, John Mitchell, and a host of figures of only slightly less prominence.[13]

Another significant aspect of those Scottish and Scottish-American elites was that in general, they played a particular kind of role in America. In a variety of ways, their activities were both expansionist and integrative: establishing and consolidating both intercolonial and transatlantic networks of culture, commerce, and communications, extending the bounds of settlement and trade, and promoting the causes of colonial union and imperial reform. Thus Scottish-American doctors

[11] See especially James High, 'Henry McCulloh, progenitor of the Stamp Act', *North Carolina Historical Review*, 29 (1952), 24–38; and *The Letter Book of James Abercromby Colonial Agent 1751–1773*, ed. John C. Van Horne and George Reese (Richmond, 1991), Introduction.

[12] See especially Douglas Sloan, *The Scottish Enlightenment and the American College Ideal* (New York, 1971).

[13] C. Helen Brock, 'Scotland and American medicine', in William R. Brock, (ed.). *Scotus Americanus*, ch. 6 and Appendix.

were particularly active in the emerging American scientific community – Colden in New York, William Douglass in Massachusetts, John Mitchell in Virginia, Garden and John Lining in Carolina – and they corresponded regularly with such associates as Benjamin Franklin.[14] Scottish traders in Virginia and elsewhere were unusually active in opening up the backcountry to commerce. Some of those same merchants were important links in the emerging transatlantic evangelical community, and both merchants and evangelicals played leading roles as promoters of Scottish emigration to America.[15] Such Scottish officials as Alexander Spotswood, Wiliam Keith, and James Logan were early proponents of intercolonial co-operation, while Colden, Kennedy, Alexander, William Livingston, and others, ranked with their close ally Franklin among the most vocal advocates of the cause of provincial union after mid-century.[16]

Perhaps we should examine first the southern officials, and especially the notorious group of lower revenue officers who arrived in North Carolina during the tenure of Gabriel Johnstone – Abercromby, McCulloh, and Rutherford – and devoted so much attention to matters of colonial administration and trade. Following the appointment of the Earl of Halifax to the Board of Trade, a number of officials in England, Scotland and America at mid-century began submitting plans for tightening imperial controls over what the Board considered the excessively independent posture of the colonies.[17] The most prominent contributors to that discussion were Scots and Scottish-Americans, including the southern officials.

All of those officials were firm administration men; McCulloh was one of the first to propose a Stamp Act for America; Abercromby wrote extensively on colonial matters and argued for the importance of establishing tighter regulation of the colonies; Rutherford advocated stricter control of colonial trade. Yet for all of their talk about imperial authority, most of the suggestions they offered were less imperial than they have sometimes appeared, relying less upon the imposition of parliamentary authority over the colonies than persuasion of the benefits

[14] Raymond Phineas Stearns, *Science in the British Colonies of North America* (Chicago, 1970), *passim*.

[15] Ned. C. Landsman, 'John Witherspoon and the problem of provincial identity in Scottish evangelical culture', in Richard Sher and Jeffrey Smitten (eds.), *Scotland and America in the Age of Enlightenment* (Edinburgh, 1990), pp. 29–45.

[16] A useful discussion can be found in Max Savelle, *Seeds of Liberty: The Genesis of the American Mind* (New York, 1948), pp. 326ff, and see below; also Bruce P. Lenman, '"Garrison government"?: Governor Alexander Spotswood and empire', in Grant G. Simpson (ed.), *The Scottish Soldier Abroad 1247–1967* (Edinburgh, 1992), pp. 67–80.

[17] Jack P. Greene, '"A posture of hostility": a reconsideration of some aspects of the origins of the American Revolution', *Proceedings of the American Antiquarian Society*, 87 (1977), 27–68.

of closer imperial ties. Even the most high-handed among them approached imperial problems more from the perspective of the empire as a whole than from that of the metropolis, at least until the outbreak of colonial resistance. Thus while Henry McCulloh insisted upon the importance of standardising parliamentary regulation of the colonies and raising a revenue from them, his position differed considerably from that of many metropolitan officials. His plan for a Stamp Act, for example, which he offered during the 1750s, would have channelled all revenues into a dedicated fund reserved 'only to the use of America'. That feature was omitted from the law that was eventually enacted, and McCulloh actually opposed the tax that appeared. Moreover, he favoured administering the money through a new, centralised colonial authority, a view that would meet with much resistance in imperial circles, as we shall see.[18]

McCulloh's goal was to regularise and strengthen the imperial tie without alienating the affection of the colonists. He disavowed any intention of interfering with the liberties of the colonies, and suggested that any new imperial regulations be put in place in such a manner 'that the People there should not have too great a temptation to resist'. McCulloh largely excused the often unco-operative behaviour of the colonial assemblies, which he blamed less upon the colonists than upon unscrupulous and unregulated royal office-holders; even good governors had suffered from the 'jealousies the people entertained of their Governors', according to McCulloh, 'which arise from the Abuse of Power, which has been too frequently put in practice in the colonies'.[19]

McCulloh's position had something in common with that of another southern colonial agent and one of the more notoriously 'imperialist' administrators, the Ulster-born William Knox, agent for Georgia and Under Secretary in the Colonial Office. Like McCulloh, Knox believed in the importance of the principle of parliamentary supremacy within the empire and denied the claims of the colonists against it. But until the eve of the Revolution, Knox also recommended that Parliament not press its authority and instead employ a method the Americans seemed willing to accept, the appropriation of revenues through requisitions to individual colonies. Knox criticised George Grenville for what he considered an excessively Anglocentric view of the empire, one that measured all initiatives according to the benefits they provided to England, and argued

[18] McCulloh, *A Miscellaneous Essay Concerning the Courses Pursued by Great Britain in the Affairs of the Colonies: With Some Observations on the Great Importance of our Settlements in America, and the Trade Thereof* (London, 1755); also *Proposals for Uniting the English Colonies on the Continent of America, So as to Enable Them to Act with Force and Vigour Against their Enemies* (London, 1757).

[19] McCulloh, *Miscellaneous Essay*, pp. 65–6, 86.

that the best way to maintain the allegiance of the colonists was 'to take from them their Inclination to break away'. Knox's vision of empire included a role for Ireland as well. He recommended that both America and Ireland be granted representation in parliament, not as a matter of right – his viewpoint was consistently imperial rather than local – but as a means of further integrating the empire, using the benefits of an Irish-American commerce to increase colonial dependence upon imperial connections.[20]

Nor were Abercromby and Rutherford altogether metropolitan in their conceptions. Certainly James Abercromby was among the least sympathetic of imperial observers to the claims of the colonists to any rights beyond those of mere subjects of the realm, a position he articulated at length in his 'Examination of the Acts of Parliament Relative to the Trade and the Government of the American Colonies' in 1752. But even he measured imperial policy against a standard of mutual benefit and rejected any notion that the colonies should be governed in a manner 'more strict and severe, than what other Subjects of this Nation are'. Like McCulloh, his primary concern was for the imperial tie itself, and he proposed that any changes in the relationship be made, as far as possible, without 'breaking through the Essential part of particular Constitutions' of the colonies any more than 'absolutely necessary, to make them a part Depending on the Whole, for the good of the whole'. He emphasized the need to shape colonial policy to fit the growing 'wealth and strength' of the colonies – a phrase he used three times – which would have important ramifications for colonial policy, as we shall see.[21]

The implications of Rutherford's work were more clearly sympathetic to colonial concerns. Although the purpose of his pamphlet, *The Importance of Colonies to Great Britain*, was to advocate a stricter control upon the flow of colonial trade in order to make it more useful to Britain, the method he proposed was a system of bounties for the production of needed staples in the colonies. Rutherford contended that the only true security for the empire was a mutually beneficial commerce. The way to keep the colonies in line was to provide for their prosperity.[22]

[20] William Knox, *The Claim of the Colonies to an Exemption from Internal Taxes Imposed by Authority of Parliament, Examined* (London, 1765); *The Present State of the Nation, Particularly with Respect of its Trade, Finances, etc.* (London, 1768); and see Leland J. Bellot, *William Knox: The Life and Thought of an Eighteenth-Century Imperialist* (Austin, 1977), ch. 4.

[21] *Magna Charta For America: James Abercromby's 'An Examination of the Acts of Parliament Relative to the Trade and the Government of our American Colonies' (1752)* . . ., ed. Jack P. Greene, Charles F. Mullett, and Edward C. Papenfuse, Jr. (Philadelphia, 1986), pp. 158, 162.

[22] *The Importance of the Colonies to Great Britain, with some Hints towards Making Improvements to their Mutual Advantage* (London, 1761).

This is not to suggest that we should accept the claim of every imperial administrator to an even-handedness in his approach to the colonies. All were firm and uncompromising administation men. What matters, none the less, is that even in defending the principle of imperial sovereignty, those writers applied the perspectives of history, political economy and law to imperial affairs in a manner that assumed that the standards to be employed in an empire that was British and commercial were the rights of Britons and mutual advantage. By the middle of the eighteenth century, the application of such standards would require some new thinking about the fundamentals of imperial relations.

The implications of such an approach can be illuminated by examining the views of resident members of the Scottish-American political elite, such as Archibald Kennedy, James Alexander, Cadwallader Colden and John Mitchell. They also devoted considerable attention to imperial reform, chiefly in the form of a union of the colonies, a favourite cause also of Henry McCulloh. The most active figure in that effort was Kennedy, who published five pamphlets in favour of colonial union, making him the principal publicist of that cause. Kennnedy's ideas have been widely misunderstesood; Max Savelle labeled him a 'Tory-imperialist' for denying that the colonial assemblies possessed any rights beyond those expressly granted in their charters, making them, in essence, fiefdoms of the Crown. Yet when Kennedy's efforts are considered against the background of contemporary discussions, there is much that appears less Tory and imperial than Whig and provincial. Indeed Kennedy's understanding of imperial relations – dependence upon the Crown, independence from Parliament – would later be adopted by such American radicals as Thomas Jefferson and James Wilson.[23]

The principal effort Kennedy endorsed was the plan of union passed by the Albany Congress in 1754, based upon outlines presented by Benjamin Franklin and Thomas Hutchinson. Franklin, in his *Autobiography*, recounted discussing his draft for a union with Kennedy and James Alexander before the conference.[24] The idea for the congress had come originally from the Board of Trade, which had hoped to co-ordinate

[23] Savelle, *Seeds of Liberty*, pp. 296–9; and the following tracts by Kennedy: *Observations on the Importance of the Northern Colonies under Proper Regulations* (New York, 1750); *The Importance of Gaining and Preserving the Friendship of the Indians to the British Interest, Considered* (New York, 1751); *An Essay on the Government of the Colonies* (New York, 1752); *Serious Considerations on the Present State of the Affairs of the Northern Colonies* (New York, 1754); and *Serious Advice to the Inhabitants of the Northern-Colonies, on the Present Situation of Affairs* (New York, 1755). For Kennedy's authorship, see Lawrence C. Wroth, *An American Bookshelf 1755* (Philadelphia, 1934), pp. 118–26. Also see Milton M. Klein, 'Archibald Kennedy: imperial pamphleteer', in Lawrence H. Leder (ed.), *The Colonial Legacy*, 2 vols. (New York, 1971), II, pp. 75–106.

[24] Franklin, *The Autobiography and other Writings*, ed. Peter Shaw (New York, 1982), p. 120.

Indian relations in the colonies and improve colonial defences, but the Albany Plan went well beyond the Board's recommendations, suggesting a colonial authority with broad powers. In anticipation of the divisions of 1776, that plan foundered upon the joint opposition of the provincial assemblies, jealous of their autonomy, and parliamentary fears of colonial unity and enhanced American power.[25]

Those parliamentary fears provide the most illuminating perspective upon the efforts of Kennedy and the others. As J.M. Bumsted and Jack P. Greene have reminded us, the sudden attention to imperial matters by the Board of Trade at mid-century reflected the growing conviction within imperial circles that the American colonies were evolving on a course towards independence, and that their autonomy ought to be curbed. Kennedy, who contributed to that discussion, disagreed, arguing that the allegiance of the colonies would best be secured by 'liberty and encouragement' rather than 'oppressive laws', He continued to promote a form of union designed to further colonial competence.[26]

Part of the apprehension in metropolitan circles derived from provincial discussions of wealth and population. Benjamin Franklin offered the most famous statement, in his 1751 'Observations Concerning the Increase of Mankind', which helped popularise the notion that the rapid rate of population growth in the colonies would lead inevitably to more Britons living in America than in Britain. In fact others were suggesting much the same thing, including Kennedy. Franklin's contribution can be viewed as part of a wider debate on population in Britain at mid-century, which was largely a discussion among English Dissenters and Scots, concerned with such questions as the effects of commerce and monopoly upon religion and manners and the future position of the provinces within the empire.[27]

[25] Alison Gilbert Olson, 'The British government and the colonial Union, 1754', *William and Mary Quarterly*, 3rd ser., 17 (1960), 22–34.

[26] Kennedy, *Observations on the importance of the Northern Colonies*, p. 12; and see Greene, "'Posture of hostility"'; J.M. Bumsted, '"Things in the womb of time": ideas of American Independence, 1633 to 1763', *William and Mary Quarterly*, 3rd ser., 31 (1974), 533–64. John Murrin has pointed out that before 1763 that discussion was almost entirely British; in fact, during the period at hand, most of the participants were Scots and Scottish-Americans; see 'A roof Without walls: the dilemma of American national identity', Richard Beeman, Stephen Botein and Edward C. Carter II (eds.) *Beyond Confederation* (Chapel Hill, 1987), pp. 333–48.

[27] See especially Istvan Hont, 'The "rich country – poor country" debate in Scottish classical political economy', in Istvan Hont and Michael Ignatieff (eds.), *Wealth and Virtue: The Shaping of Political Economy in the Scottish Enlightenment* (New York, 1983), pp. 271–316; D.V. Glass, *Numbering the People: The Eighteenth-Century Population Controversy* (Farnsborough, 1973) chs 1–2; and Janet Riesman, 'Origins of American political economy', PhD thesis, Brown University, 1983, ch. 2. Franklin was probably familiar with the population debates conducted in the Philosophical Society of Edinburgh between David Hume and Robert Wallace; Franklin later joined the society. Kennedy

The population controversy was closely connected to the broader inquiry into political economy that loomed so large in the eighteenth century, especially in Scotland. At mid-century, the central figure in that discussion was not yet Adam Smith but his friend David Hume, whose economic essays did much to open up the whole question of the potential for mutually advantageous trading relations between rich and poor countries, or metropolis and province. Hume, like Franklin, offered a particularly optimistic reading of provincial potential, in essays that would be cited repeatedly in Anglo-American discussions.[28]

Kennedy, Franklin, and John Mitchell all applied that concept of mutual benefit to the relationship between Britain and its colonies. Where some metropolitan observers let their fears of colonial autonomy led them to oppose colonial growth, Kennedy and the others vigorously promoted it, arguing that such growth would benefit rather than harming imperial ties. As Kennedy wrote, 'It is the Interest of Great Britain to encourage and promote the Industry and Labour of the Plantations'. Mother countries, he continued, 'always increasse in Power in Proportion as their Colonies flourish'.[29]

If Kennedy opposed subordinating colonial interests to metropolitan authority, he was equally suspicious of the claims of the colonial assemblies. He denounced their claims of quasi-parliamentary status. They were insufficiently powerful to protect 'the Liberties and Properties of British subjects', and insufficiently resistant to the pull of faction. In that his position recalled that of Andrew Fletcher and resembled Hume's 'Idea of a Perfect Commonwealth' as well.[30]

The most optimistic analysts suggested that colonial growth would not only alter, but would eventually reverse the political relationship between Britain and its colonies, leading not towards the independence of America, as the Board of Trade had feared, but towards its ascendancy. As the population and wealth of America grew, the colonies would surpass Britain in both measures. Then, political power also, and even the seat of government, would pass across the Atlantic, resulting in a far more radical form of incorporation than had occurred in 1707. Province would become metropolis, and metropolis province. That was suggested by speculators in colonial lands, such as Archibald Grant of Monymusk, who projected America as the 'grand seat of empire and all its Concomitants'. It was recommended by Adam Smith as the ultimate

suggested an American population doubling every twenty-four years in 1750 in *Observations on the Importance of the Northern Colonies*, pp. 3–4.

[28] See especially Hont, 'The "rich country – poor country" debate', pp. 271–316.

[29] Kennedy, *Observations on the Importance of the Northern Colonies*, pp. 30–1. See also Mitchell, *The Contest in America Between Great Britain and France* (London, 1757).

[30] Kennedy, *Observations on the Importance of the Northern Colonies*, pp. 14ff.

solution to the imperial crisis, although he held out little hope that either side would agree. To William Thom of Govan, a strong promoter of Scottish emigration to America, the prospect was inevitable and highly desirable. As America grew in strength, Thom wrote, it would naturally grasp at independence. Britain, to avoid that outcome, would have to offer to transfer the capital instead.[31]

Outside of Scotland, other observers also noticed the growing centrifugal tendencies within the empire, but few agreed with Grant and Thom that events should simply be allowed to follow their natural course. Franklin initially proposed a full incorporating union between Britain and America, including the repeal of all discriminatory trade laws, but as the imperial controversy deepened, he became increasingly suspicious of British willingness to administer it fairly. Instead, he moved towards the position of most of his countrymen in favour of local autonomy and independence from Parliament. On the other side, Thomas Pownall, the former Royal Governor of Massachusetts and one of the more sympathetic of colonial administrators, suggested a more typical metropolitan view. Pownall, in 1766, argued that it was time to incorporate the American colonies into a realm, just to avoid the outcome that Grant and Thom envisioned. If a union of Great Britain and the colonies were carried out immediately, Pownall reasoned, Britain could still fix, 'while it may be so fixed, the common center in Great Britain'. Josiah Tucker thought the subordination of Britain to its colonies inevitable unless it had the good sense to declare their independence first.[32]

The introduction of such prognostications into the discussions probably impeded a solution to the eventual imperial crisis. American leaders, increasingly confident of the growing power of their own institutions and suspicious of imperial attempts to control colonial development, were reluctant to cede greater authority to a still-powerful metropolis,

[31] Thom, *Seasonable Advice to the Landholders and Farmers in Scotland* (Edinburgh, 1770), pp. 57–8; and *Present Conduct of the Chieftains and Proprietors of Lands in the Highlands of Scotland*, pp. 6–7; and see Archibald Grant, 7 March 1764, Grant of Monymusk Ms.; Scottish Record Office; Smith, *An inquiry into the Nature and Causes of the Wealth of Nations*, ed. R.H. Campbell, A.S. Skinner and W.B. Todd, 2 vols. (Oxford, 1976), II, pp. 944–7.

[32] Pownall, *The Administration of the Colonies*, 3rd edn (London, 1766), quoted in 'Thomas Pownall, 'Henry Ellis, and the spectrum of possibilities, 1763–1775', in Alison Gilbert Olson and Richard Maxwell Brown (eds.), *Anglo-American Political Relations, 1675–1775* (New Brunswick, 1970), pp. 155–86, p. 172. Shy considers the Ulster-born Ellis and his associate William Knox as the most imperial of administrators, and Pownall as among the most sympathetic to the colonial cause. Also see J.G.A. Pocock, 'Josiah Tucker on Burke, Locke, and Price: a study in the varieties of eighteenth-century conservatism', in *Virtue, Commerce and History: Essays on Political Thought at History, Chiefly in the Eighteenth Century* (New York, 1985), pp. 157–92.

whatever incorporation might portend for the future. British officials, by contrast, refrained from supporting any devolution of power to a centralised colonial authority and disdained allowing an American representation in parliament with such open-ended implications, unless they could find a way to fix the seat of authority 'while it may be so fixed', in Pownall's words. In the end, Adam Smith and William Thom were wrong. The British goverment probably did prefer losing the empire to ceding the metropolis. Thereafter, only a few visionary theorists and Loyalists would cling to the goal of reconciliation through one or another version of either a federal or an incorporating union.[33]

III

A rather different perspective upon union, empire, and liberty was provided by those Scottish clerics who came to America and involved themselves in religious and educational administration: John Witherspoon, Francis Alison, William Smith, and others. Despite their differences in background and ecclesiology, they would share some significant ideas as well. Those included a devotion to a modernised academic curriculum, a humanised, essentially Hutchesonian philosophy of morals, and a pronouncedly Whiggish rhetoric of civil and ecclesiastical liberty. From those diverse strands, they would develop a broadly commercial and cultural perspective upon the problem of imperial union that would have considerable influence in the American colonies and the United States thereafter.

Scottish educators were a popular and sought after group in early America. In part that can be attributed to the rising reputation of Scottish universities and Scottish letters in the eighteenth century; it was due also to their association with educational reform in universities that were not restricted to adherents to the ecclesiastical establishment. Those educators brought to America reformed curriculae with a special devotion to 'practical' subjects such as the natural sciences, moral and political philosophy, and the histories of Britain and its commercial partners.[34]

[33] The most persistent of those Loyalists were Joseph Galloway of Pennsylvania and William Smith, Jr. of New York, both of Scottish or partly Scottish backgrounds with close ties throughout the Scottish-American elite. See *Anglo-American Union: Joseph Galloway's Plan to Preserve the British Empire 1774–1788* (Philadelphia, 1941); 'William Smith, Jr's. Alternative to the American Revolution', ed. Robert M. Calhoon, *William and Mary quarterly*, 3rd ser., 22 (1965), 105–18. Also see J.G.A. Pocock, '1776: the revolution against Parliament', in *Virtue, Commerce, and History*, pp. 73–90.

[34] See especially Peter Jones, 'The Scottish professoriate and the polite academy, 1720–46', in Hont and Ignatieff (eds.), *Wealth and Virtue*, pp. 89–118, and Sloan, *The Scottish Enlightenment and the American College Ideal.*

They were probably best known for their teaching of moral philosophy, in which they followed one of several varieties of the 'moral sense' philosophy of Francis Hutcheson. One of the features of that philosophy was a shifting of the basis of ethical authority, not simply from divinity to human nature, but also from the dictates of traditional authorities of whatever sort to the collective conscience of a reflective citizenry. That would provide a basis for Hutcheson's well-known defence of the legitimacy of mature provinces separating from imperial authorities that had ceased to promote the welfare of their citizens.[35]

Witherspoon and Alison both borrowed extensively from Hutcheson's lectures on politics and morals in teaching what turned out to be surprisingly prominent groups of young Revolutionaries at the Colleges of New Jersey and Pennsylvania, including Charles Thomson, Thomas McKean, Francis Hopkinson, Phillip Freneau, Hugh Henry Brackenridge, and James Madison, to name only a few.[36] Perhaps more importantly, all of those educators – even such Anglicans as William Smith and William Small – lectured extensively on the topics of civil and religious liberty. Their perspective was at once Protestant and provincial, identifying political, economic and religious liberty as characteristic of, and integral to, provincial life.[37]

The discussion of liberty, of course, was nearly ubiquitous in eighteenth century Britain, but many reformed groups on both sides of the Atlantic gave that discussion a particular twist. The roots of British liberty, in their understanding, lay in Protestantism, especially Reformed Protestantism, introduced in the Reformation and secured against absolutism and Popery in 1688 and again in 1715. But neither liberty nor pure religion were to be found in equal measure throughout the empire. Rather, in the eighteenth century, the home of true religion lay in the provinces, in the Calvinistic churches of Scotland and America. Moreover, with the growth of what they considered arbitrary power at home, Reformed spokesmen increasingly came to view the colonies as the best

[35] Caroline Robbins, "'When it is that colonies may turn independent"', *William and Mary quarterly*, 3rd ser. 11 (1954), 214–51; and see T.D. Campbell, 'Francis Hutcheson: "Father" of the Enlightenment', in R.H. Campbell and Andrew S. Skinner (eds.), *Origins and Nature of the Scottish Enlightenment* (Edinburgh, 1982), pp. 167–85; and Peter J. Diamond, 'Witherspoon, Smith and the Scottish philosophy in revolutionary America', in Sher and Smitten (eds.), *Scotland and America in the Age of the Enlightenment*, pp. 115–32.

[36] David Fate Norton, 'Francis Hutcheson in America', *Studies on Voltaire and the Eighteenth Century*, 154 (1976), 1,547–68, and see below.

[37] Smith, *Discourses on Several Public Occasions During the War in America. Preached Chiefly with a View to the Explaining the Protestant Cause, in the British Colonies* (London, 1759); and, on Small, Garry Wills, *Inventing America: Jefferson's Declaration of Independence* (Garden City, New York, 1978).

refuge of liberty, the 'seat of liberty and true religion', in the words of one Scots Presbyterian.[38]

That perspective upon civil and religious liberty did much to link religious groups in the provinces, especially during the French wars at mid-century. That was reflected in the development of what Nathan Hatch has called a 'civil millennialist' rhetoric in New England, in the Presbyterian patriotism of such colonial preachers as Samuel Finley and Samuel Davies, and even in the warnings of Archibald Kennedy and Henry McCulloh about the dangers of the French threat to 'our religion, our Liberties and our Properties'. William Smith of Pennsylvania offered an Episcopalian version of that rhetoric, lamenting the reluctance of Middle Colony Anglicans to match the patriotic fervour of the New Englanders against a Catholic enemy and portraying the Church of England as the true bulwark of Protestantism and liberty.[39]

Presbyterians and other dissenters disagreed. To them, the Episcopal effort at mid-century to secure the appointment of an American bishop represented an Anglican drive for supremacy inconsistent with provincial liberty. That was challenged by Francis Alison, and his criticisms reveal some of the multi-layered quality of Presbyterian conceptions of liberty. The power to appoint such a bishop would derive from act of parliament; to concede that authority in the wake of the Stamp Act was itself a threat to political liberty. Moreover, reverting to traditional Reformed assumptions, Alison maintained that liberty and religious dissent were connected, or, as he put it, 'All the Rejecters of Episcopacy have distinguished themselves in the Cause of Liberty . . . their Principles of Church Government are Principles of Freedom'. Perhaps most importantly, Alison denied Anglican claims to authority in the colonies, or to represent a truly *national* religion at all. 'Why is Episcopacy alone honored with that name?' he asked. 'Is it because it is established by Law in England? Is not Presbyterianism also established by Law (in Scotland)? But what is this to us in America?'[40]

The last of Alison's arguments suggests the manner in which the Union itself had redefined the meaning of dissent in America. To some, that had been apparent almost from the moment of Union. Early in 1707, before

[38] John Erskine, *Shall I go To War with My American Brethren?* (London, 1769), p. 3; and see my 'John Witherspoon and the problem of provincial identity'.

[39] Smith, *Discourses on Several Public Occasions*; Kennedy, *Serious Considerations on the Present State of the Northern Colonies*, quoted in Klein, 'Archibald Kennedy', p. 103; and see Hatch, *The Sacred Cause of Liberty: Republican Thought and the Millennium in Revolutionary New England* (New Haven, 1977).

[40] *The Centinel*, ed. Elizabeth Nybakken (Newark, Delaware, 1980), pp. 87, 105. The standard treatment is Carl Bridenbaugh, *Mitre and Sceptre: Transatlantic Faiths, Ideas, Personalities, and Politics 1689–1775* (New York, 1962).

the Treaty of Union took effect, the Irish-born Presbyterian minister Francis Makemie was arrested in New York on the charge of preaching without a license from that colony's Anglican governor, Lord Cornbury. Makemie initially claimed the protection of the Toleration Act, while Cornbury denied its application in the colonies.

Makemie was still awaiting trial on 1 May of that year, when the Union took effect. Soon thereafter, the clergyman changed his defense. He now agreed that the Toleration Act did not extend beyond England's borders. Toleration implied an established Church; New York had no such establishment. There all denominations stood 'upon an equal level and bottom of liberty'. He subsequently suggested the rationale for the new defence. The new United Kingdom had no state establishment. The Anglican Church was established in England only; in Scotland, the Presbyterian Church had an equal establishment 'as highly related and annexed unto the Crown as the Church of England'. The colonies, as dominions of the Crown, were subordinate to no English Church. Makemie was aquitted by a jury and published a narrative of his trial. Thereafter, Congregationalists and Presbyterians in America would cite Makemie's case in order to dispute the claim of the English Church to special privileges within British dominions. In their view, the Union gave Presbyterians equal privileges within the dominions of the Crown and undermined Anglican assertions of supremacy beyond the bounds of England.[41]

The most comprehensive discussion of the provincial dimension of liberty was provided by Witherspoon at the College of New Jersey. Witherspoon came to America from Paisley in Scotland only eight years before independence, but during that time he worked assiduously to broaden connections between Britain and America. He inserted the literature of the Scottish Enlightenment more extensively into the College curriculum. He promoted emigration to America. He increased communications between the Presbyterian Churches in Britain and America and worked to unify the often-hostile branches in the colonial church under an essentially Scottish code of discipline. Yet when war broke out in 1775, Witherspoon would be firmly on the side of America and would take on the role of spokesman for the Scottish-American community.[42]

Witherspoon developed his conception of provincial liberty in a series

[41] *A Narrative of a New and Unusual American Imprisonment of Two Presbyterian Ministers: and Prosecution of Mr. Francis Makemie One of Them, for Preaching one Sermon at the City of New-York* (Boston, 1707), printed in *The Life and Writings of Francis Makemie*, ed. Boyd S. Schlenther (Philadelphia, 1971), pp. 193–244.

[42] See my 'Witherspoon and the problem of provincial identity'.

of essays and speeches written before and during the American Revolution. As in so much provincial discussion, his starting points were population and trade, the growth of which, in America, represented a 'progress in improvement and population so rapid as no political calculations had been able to ascertain'. He attributed that growth not to the land or the climate, but rather to 'the degree of British liberty which (the colonists) brought from home, and which pervaded more or less their several constitutions'. To Witherspoon, liberty meant something like the relative weakness of metropolitan authority in America, and he insisted that the northern colonies, those most noted for strictness in religion and 'the freest form of government', although, 'greatly inferior in soil and climate', had yet 'out-stripped the others in number of people and value of land', merely because the others were 'under the influence of appointments and authority from home'. Thus population and trade became, in effect, indices of liberty.[43]

That discussion of liberty gave a particular tone to considerations of empire and union. In Witherspoon's analyis, imperial ties were beneficial only as long as they contributed to, rather than detracted from, provincial liberty. Here he invoked the standard of mutual benefit. Borrowing especially from Hume's essays on trade, Witherspoon insisted that a resolution to the imperial conflict did not require the subjugation of America. Instead, he declared, 'I cannot believe, that the misery and subjection of any country on earth, is necessary to the happiness of another'. Rather, the 'success and increase of one nation is, or may be, a benefit to every other'.[44]

Witherspoon articulated a conception of imperial union that was cultural, commercial and confederal, based upon ties of trade and affection. His principal targets were what he described as 'narrow, selfish views', and 'local, provincial pride', and he cited in particular the refusal of Englishmen to respect the position or the interests of North Britons. On those same grounds, Witherspoon would work closely with Glasgow merchants to promote Scottish emigration to America during the 1770s. As that very time, imperial authorities at home were contemplating its restriction, to prevent both the depopulation of Scottish estates and the addition of still greater numbers to an increasingly restive America. Defending his activities, Witherspoon asked, was it a 'liberal way of thinking . . . to say that a man is an enemy to his country, while he

[43] The following discussion is drawn from a number of Witherspoon's works, chiefly 'Address to the Natives of Scotland Residing in America'; 'Letter Sent to Scotland for the Scots Magazine'; 'Part of a Speech in Congress, upon the Confederation'; 'A Few Reflections on the Federal City'; and 'The Druid'; all in *The Works of the Rev. John Witherspoon*, 4 vols. (Philadelphia, 1802, III–IV, *passim*.

[44] 'Address to the Natives of Scotland Residing in America', *Works* III, p. 55.

promotes the happiness of the great body of the people, with a small diminution of the interest of an handful?' Would not emigration contribute more to the welfare of the whole people, not only in America, but also, as the result of a mutually beneficial commerce, all of Britain?[45]

To Witherspoon, ties of culture and trade were far more effective bonds of union than formal political power. Thus by 1776, he would argue that even American independence, once completed, would not seriously disrupt a British – American connection founded upon ties of commerce and interest. Indeed, American liberty would lead to the 'peopling and enriching this great continent'. As America's natural trading partner, that would redound to Britain's benefit as well.[46]

After 1776, Witherspoon quickly became one of the most articulate spokesman for a federal union of the newly independent states. He foretold great achievements for America in framing a new government that would set an example for all mankind. He cautioned that that would amount to little without a union among the new states, to preserve their peace, security, and trade. The failure to achieve such a union would 'greatly diminish the glory and importance of the struggle', he wrote, 'whether considered as for the rights of mankind in general, or for the prosperity and happiness of this continent in future times', whereas a 'well planned confederacy among the states of America, may hand down the blessings of peace and public order to many generations'. Such a confederacy avoided the dual dangers of arbitrary rule and local particularism. Witherspoon argued that the greatest danger of war fell to powerful and aggressive empires or to small and autonomous states. By contrast, confederations, such as existed in the Netherlands, produced peace and security.[47]

The most original aspect of Witherspoon's federalism was its expansive quality. Where earlier arguments usually contrasted stable confederations with expansive imperial monarchies, Witherspoon suggested that a well-constructed confederation in America could expand through the voluntary adherence of additional states until it encompassed the whole of the continent, and as much as a quarter of the globe. That would represent 'a progress . . . in the order and perfection of human society, greater than we have yet seen'.[48]

Witherspoon's version of federalism left little room for metropolitan domination. He would come to question the necessity, or even the

[45] 'Letter Sent to Scotland for the Scots Magazine', *Works* IV, pp. 283–8.

[46] 'Address to the Natives of Scotland Residing in America'.

[47] 'Speech in Congress Upon the Confederation', *Works*, IV, pp. 347–51.

[48] 'Speech in Congress Upon the Confederation', *Works*, IV, pp. 350–1; 'Address to the Natives of Scotland Residing in America'.

desirability, of a permanent national capital, the need for which he equated with extended empires rather than confederations. He also criticised the suggestion that a metropolis ought to dictate cultural standards, such as language, contending instead that the supremacy of metropolitan English over dialects filled with Scotticisms or 'Americanisms' – a word he coined – came only from the dominant position of the metropolis and not from any inherent superiority in expression.[49]

Witherspoon's greatest influence was probably in the area of promoting political and cultural unity in Revolutionary America. His essays explicitly addressed the use of language as a cultural symbol and compiled a list of perfectly acceptable 'Americanisms', which he distinguished from local 'vulgarisms'. He surrounded himself with an unusually prolific group of cultural nationalists, including Philip Freneau, Hugh Henry Brackenridge, John Rodgers, Benjamin Rush, Robert Aitken, Thomas Paine and David Ramsay – most of them immigrants, most of them Scots. And of course his most famous student, James Madison, would adapt Hume's 'Idea of a Perfect Commonwealth' into a plan for an extended republic deriving its authority from the dispersed citizenry of regional provincial communities.[50] Through such influence the legacy of union discussions continued to play a role in early America.

Few of those arguments were unique either to Witherspoon or to Scots and Scottish-Americans; most were echoed in imperial discussions from mid-century onwards. Nor did they influence American discussions equally or importantly at all points, compared, for example, to the well-established influence of the republican and Real Whig traditions in the revolutionary movement itself. But Scots and Scottish-American elites did provide the most persistent consideration of the problems of empire and confederation and the means of protecting provincial liberties within an expansive commercial union. At particular times, such as the 1750s and 1780s, when American elites came to ponder the problem of uniting an extended provincial terrain, those discussions asssumed a considerable importance.

[49] 'A Few Reflections on the Federal City', *Works*, IV, pp. 413–19; 'The Druid', *Works*, IV, pp. 458–61.

[50] On Madison's borrowings from Hume, see especially Douglass Adair, '"That politics may be reduced to a science": David Hume, James Madison and the 10th Federalist', *Huntington Library Quarterly*, 20 (1957), 343–60; also Garry Wills, *Explaining america; The Federalist* (Garden City, New York, 1981).

13

EMPIRE, STATE AND CONFEDERATION: THE WAR OF AMERICAN INDEPENDENCE AS A CRISIS IN MULTIPLE MONARCHY

J.G.A. POCOCK

I

THERE is taking shape a pattern for the writing of British history, of particular utility to those historians whose attention is focussed on the history of political discourse. Those of the societies component of what we call 'Britain', 'the Three Kingdoms' or 'the Atlantic archipelago', whose political cohesion reached the point of generating several self-centred political discourses,[1] can be studied in both an 'internal' and an 'external' perspective. In the former case, we examine the political discourse concerned with the structure of the polity and the problems to which it gave rise; and we examine events and crises in the history of each polity as taking place in the history depicted by discourse concerning that structure. During the sixteenth and seventeenth centuries, we note, the Kingdom of England acquired characteristic patterns of discourse which shaped its history: the papal aggression, the ancient constitution, the balance of government, the balance of property; and these constructs retained paradigmatic status in English historiography so far into the modern period that, now they no longer possess that status, they have to be considered factors in shaping English history. During the same period, the Kingdom of Scotland acquired similiar patterns of historic self-shaping, but among the effects of the Union studied in this volume, these had in large part to be given up and replaced by others. This process too had long-term consequences in the history of Scottish historiography.

In the second or 'external' perspective, we examine the history of each polity as shaped by its interactions with neighbouring entities, which may

[1] The stress on the shaping of a political self owes much to recent critical and historical writing, and in particular to Richard Helgerson, *Forms of Nationhood: The Elizabethan Writing of England* (Chicago, 1992). The assumption behind the present essay is that a public, political and national 'self' may be created by many actors and authors, and legitimated by their and others' consent.

or may not have been polities or states shaped like itself (the Kingdoms of Scotland and Ireland believed themselves to possess barbarian frontiers, along which they interacted with Gaelic forms of society which they did not recognise as polities). We enquire how these interactions figured in, and helped shape, the discourse of each polity about itself, and further, whether they generated a discourse of their own, inventing and shaping the construct of a society of states. In the particular case of 'British history', we note that from at latest the early sixteenth century, there existed a discourse which spoke of 'Scotland' and 'England' as together composing an entity named 'Britain', which might possess a history of its own (the *historia majoris Britanniae*) and might be organised into a larger polity or association between polities.[2] We enquire whether there existed a discourse concerned with this 'matter of Britain', to which the term 'British political thought' might be applied with precision, instead of being employed loosely to denote the aggregate of political discourses arising in England, Scotland and elsewhere. It is now clear that we have found that such a 'discourse of Britain' did indeed take shape, but had to compete on terms often unequal with an English political discourse so intensely centred on the English political structure and its troubles that it could do no more (or less) than annex Scotland to itself and consider it part of English history, and with a Scottish discourse shaped in large measure by the need to respond to this English self-centredness. We are therefore faced with a treble structure; there is an English discourse, there is a Scottish, and there is a discourse of Britain which sometimes posits 'Britain' as a political entity, and sometimes treats it merely as a field in which political (the term includes confessional and ecclesiastical) entities interact. We deal with this problem by proposing that the history of 'Britain', or 'the Three Kingdoms', is that of a 'multiple monarchy', whose political structure is indeterminate for the reason that it is multiplex; with the consequence that such terms as 'empire' and 'confederation' have both been found applicable in discoursing of its character, and that from time to time choices have had to be made between implications arising from these terms.

It has further to be kept in mind that the 'external' perspective does not stop with the field of relationships constituting 'Britain'. The kingdoms and other entities constituting archipelagic 'Europe' interact with the kingdoms, confederations and empires constituting adjacent continental 'Europe'; they affect one another's history and create a history which they

[2] See Roger A. Mason (ed.), *Scots and Britons: Scottish Political Thought and the Union of 1603* (Cambridge, 1994). Like the present volume, this originated in a seminar conducted at the Folger Shakespeare Library for the Folger Institute Center for the History of British Political Thought.

have in common. In the case we are considering, the kingdom and empire of 'Great Britain' are shaped largely by the intervention of, and by interaction with, the imperial and maritime wars of continental 'Europe'; but they respond vigorously enough to impose themselves on the history of this entity (or society) and help to shape it. We are also concerned with a period in which these multiple histories, 'British' and 'European', extend themselves across the Atlantic[3] and play a part in involving the English and French colonies on the American seaboard in an imperial struggle for control of the interior of that continent. The relations between archipelagic and continental 'Europe' do much to remodel those between maritime, piedmont and Mississippian 'America'. Only in the period of the American Revolution is it determined that certain colonies will become 'states' and organise themselves as an 'empire' – which is at the same time a 'republic' and a new species of 'confederation' – and that an entity named 'America' will henceforth create a history (United States and Canadian) of its own making.[4]

II

The obstacle which had prevented the Union of the Crowns being more than a personal union – neither a confederation nor an incorporation of the two kingdoms[5] – was in the first place the intensity of the internal union of the Kingdom of England. The Act in Restraint of Appeals (1533) had proclaimed and enacted that this Kingdom was an 'empire' in the sense that it contained within itself absolute sovereignty over itself, so that its king (in parliament or out of it) was absolute and sovereign head of all jurisdiction both spiritual and temporal, and therefore head of the English Church as inseparable from the English body politic. 'Empire' in this sense could not be shared with another prince, at peril of mitigating the absolute separation from Rome on which Englishmen's hopes of salvation were seen to depend; and if the King of England could not conceivably share his *imperium* with the Pope, he could not share it with himself as King of Scots. The two crowns, the two realms and the two churches, should therefore become one; but the English showed themselves incapable of imagining this union as other than an annexation of the Scottish dimension, in each case, to the English. As we shall see, they

[3] The *Annual Register* in the years of the American revolution regularly treated events in the colonies in a section headed 'History of Europe'.

[4] See J.G.A. Pocock, 'States, republics and empires: the American founding in early modern perspective', in Terence Ball and J.G.A. Pocock (eds.), *Conceptual Change and the Constitution* (Lawrence, 1988), pp. 55–77.

[5] See Pocock, 'Two kingdoms and three histories? Political thought in British contexts', in Mason (ed.), *Scots and Britons*, and other essays in that volume.

were responding as much out of insecurity as out of arrogance; but they were able to claim that head and body were bound together in the English body politic by municipal laws and ecclesiastical structures generated by that body itself, which could not be given up without terminating that body's existence. The Scots were necessitated to reply that their King wore a crown as imperial as the English one, and that they had created laws and a church polity as much their own as were those of the English.[6] If they were on the whole more willing than were the English to contemplate assimilation of these structures to those of their neighbours, they drew the line at being annexed and swallowed up, and at being assimilated in the sense of digested, by the unmodified church-state of the English monarchy. The Stuart dynasty therefore found itself ruling a multiple monarchy, or more precisely a multiplicity of kingdoms, wearing at the same time the imperial crown of Scotland, the imperial crown of England, and the imperial crown of Ireland created by conquest alone and inseparably annexed to the second but not the first person of this far from perfect trinity. The age of the Three Kingdoms had begun, and it is a key problem in 'British history' to determine its character and duration.

It is possible to speak of the Three Kingdoms as constituting 'a monarchy', as we speak of the Spanish or the Austrian 'Monarchy' as a co-incidence of many crowns upon one head.[7] Since 'empire' in the Roman sense denoted a 'universal monarchy', it is also possible to describe any one of these monarchies as an 'empire', and James VI and I toyed briefly (as did the Lord Protector, Oliver Cromwell after him) with the thought of assuming the title of 'Emperor of Great Britain'. But there was the difficulty that as King of England, France and Ireland (to give that title in its partly fictional fullness) he possessed a sovereignty more 'imperial', in the sense given it by the Act in Restraint of Appeals, than any he could possess as 'emperor', and by no means capable of being shared with the latter, had that ever come to be invented (which is why it was not). We may see that the entity called 'England' was obliged to assume 'empire' in the sense of hegemony over two other kingdoms, precisely for the reason that it possessed an 'empire' in the sense of sovereignty over itself which it could not afford to share with them in a union of equals. Whether anything similar may be said of Castile in the case of the Spanish 'Monarchy' or of the Habsburg lands in the case of the

[6] Brian P. Levack, *The Formation of the British State: England, Scotland and the Union, 1603–1707* (Oxford, 1987); Bruce Galloway, *The Union of England and Scotland, 1603–08* (Edinburgh, 1986); Arthur Williamson, *Scottish National Consciousness in the Age of James VI* (Edinburgh, 1979).

[7] Anthony Pagden, *Spanish Imperialism and the Political Imagination: Studies in European and Spanish-American Social and Political Theory, 1513–1830* (New Haven, 1990).

Austrian, is not a question to be considered here.

The sovereignty or 'empire' claimed for the English Crown by the Act in Restraint of Appeals is therefore the key to English history in the age of the Three Kingdoms,[8] and in the longer period of early modern history now extended through the 'long eighteenth century' to 1832. It was a sovereignty as well ecclesiastical as civil; and to make it a 'key' to history does not mean that it was a rock-solid and unshakable consolidation of national power which of itself rendered England capable of 'empire' over the other kingdoms. On the contrary, from a date within the reign of Charles I to the end of the seventeenth century, it was shaken and very nearly shattered by a series of violent internal and external crises[9] which became known by the name of 'dissolutions of government'. These did not weaken it, so much as render the exercise of its formidable power deeply unstable; and it was this instability, coupled with the need to restore and consolidate it by any means necessary – regicide, restoration and revolution among them – which rendered impossible any sharing of English sovereignty within a wider system of multiple monarchy. The English were at times obliged to exercise 'empire' over others because they were unsure of their 'empire' over themselves.

It does not diminish the force of these statements if we suppose that the English civil wars and their long aftermath came about, not through deep-seated weaknesses in the English structure, but through the strains imposed by the task of ruling a number of monarchies.[10] However the disasters of 1642 originated, once they had come about they were cleavages between Crown and Parliament, between the King as head of the Church and that Church as many subjects perceived it; and the desperate need to restore these unities at all costs was a main cause of the revolutionary changes attempted in their nature. For this reason the English dimension of the War of Three Kingdoms (1637–52) had the character of a civil war, in which Englishmen fought each other, bitterly because unwillingly,[11] to determine the structure of a civil and ecclesiastical polity which they had thought they shared in common; whereas Scotsmen did not fight each other very much, and never to determine the character of such a polity;[12] and the diverse religious and ethnic groups

[8] In proposing the concept of this age, I find convenient the limiting dates of 1533 and 1707. Others could be proposed, and preferred; none can be cast in bronze.

[9] These could be grouped as 'the Wars of the Three Kingdoms' and held to run from 1637 to 1690, with intervals of varying duration in each kingdom when separately considered.

[10] Conrad Russell, *The Fall of the British Monarchies, 1637–42* (Oxford, 1991).

[11] Best displayed in Anthony Fletcher, *The Outbreak of the English Civil War* (New York, 1981).

[12] Argyll and Montrose, it could be argued, fought over rival interpretations of the National Covenant and the Covenanting polity. On the other hand, the Gordons and Macdonalds in Montrose's following during the only intra-Scottish war of the Three Kingdoms were engaged in the clan politics of the highland and archipelagic frontiers. See further Jane

inhabiting (but not constituting) Ireland fought each other in the absence of any shared polity at all. What we misname the Third Civil War of 1650–52 was in part a war of England against an invading King of Scots whose title the English did not challenge, even when they conquered Scotland in order to dethrone him; in part a war of religion between the saints of a British Israel and Judah, fought over the reading of a Covenant which had bound them together.

Any analysis of the great mass of printed discourse produced by the experience and memory of civil war, regicide and interregnum must lead to the conclusion that the crucial English experience in the Wars of the Three Kingdoms was that of 'the dissolution of government', and that it was remembered as the worst political experience through which England had ever passed. To say this is to pass over the brief but intense revolutionary moment of 1647–50, when there were those who saw dissolution as opening a window of opportunity to make all things new; it is to pass over the no less intense and short-lived visions of rule by liberated soldiers, visionary parliamentarians, saints in arms or out of them, and a newly forged republican citizenry, which were offered as forms of 'government' alternative to that of the historic institutions of sovereignty.[13] The discourse we have, it could be said, is that of governing elites deeply shaken but ultimately restored. But the loss it agonisedly describes is not that of the opportunity to govern so much as of the security of being governed according to law. The 'government dissolved' is primarily the Tudor sovereignty of 'empire' in church and state, exercised by king and parliament in a relationship variously described; secondly, the 'ancient constitution' held to underpin it and provide it with a history; thirdly, the condition of civil government itself, which delivers humans from the appalling responsibility to choose between forms of legitimate rule, or to choose a form of goverment where none exists and legitimate it out of no resources other than their own unaided natures.[14] 'The dissolution of government' was recalled as so dreadful an experience that it remains amazing that a powerful and

Ohlmeyer, *Civil War and Restoration in the Three Stuart Kingdoms: The Career of Randal MacDonnell, Marquis of Antrim, 1609–1683* (Cambridge, 1993); D.C. Stevenson, *Alasdair MacColla and the Highland Problem in the Seventeenth Century* (Edinburgh, 1981).

13 See William M. Lamont, 'The Puritan revolution', and J.G.A. Pocock and Gordon J. Schochet, 'The Interregnum', in Pocock (ed.), *The Varieties of British Political Thought, 1500–1800* (Cambridge, 1994).

14 Perez Zagorin, *The History of Political Thought in the English Revolution* (London, 1954); Irene Coltman, *Private Men and Public Causes: Philosophy and Politics in the English Civil War* (London; 1962); John M. Wallace, *Destiny His Choice: The Loyalism of Andrew Marvell* (Cambridge, 1968); Margaret Judson, *From Tradition to Political Reality: A Study of the Ideas set forth in Support of the Commonwealth Government in England, 1649–1653* (Hamden, CT, 1980).

cautious thinker, even in a moment of radical aberration, should have recommended it in print as a right and prerogative vested in a people who might exercise it of their own choice. The printed discourse of 1689 loses no time in denying that it has occurred.[15]

The failure even to attempt revolutionary experiment in England during the 1650s – which includes the failure to attempt creating a 'Britain' out of the conquests of Ireland and Scotland – led to the successive restorations of the English and Tudor institutions of government between 1659 and 1662.[16] In English terms, we can see that these amounted to a programme of restoring unity between crown and parliament, and (as a precondition rather than a consequence) between crown and national church; and we have a wealth of literature on the complex reasons why this programme failed and had to be re-attempted in 1688–9. There is not so much literature, either contemporary or modern, on Restoration and its failure in Scotland, and we are uncertain how far to regard it as a provincial variation on an otherwise English theme. It seems to have consisted largely of an experiment in episopacy, with some support from a nobility weary of clerical and Covenanter rule. As I have suggested elsewhere,[17] a study of 'British political thought' in the era of the Wars of the Three Kingdoms, from 1637 to 1690, would be of value.

Viewed in English terms, the Revolution of 1688-89 takes on the character of a 'second Restoration'; a reconstruction, but at the same time re-stabilisation, of the conditions under which crown, parliament and national church could co-exist.[18] There were some significant concessions on points of prerogative,[19] and of parliamentary authority in determining the succession to the crown; the Anglican clergy and squirearchy made significant changes in their position on both authority and dissent.[20] But the crown defined by the Act of Succession was stronger in its relations with parliament than the crown before 1688, and the Act of Toleration did so much to confirm as well as to mitigate the Anglican monopoly of office that it came to stand beside the Test and Corporation Acts as pillars of the Hanoverian regime.[21] So far we can go in maintaining an 'English'

15 John Kenyon, *Revolution Principles: The Politics of Party, 1689–1720* (Cambridge, 1977).

16 See Ronald Hutton, *The Restoration: A Political and Religious History of England and Wales, 1658–1667* (Oxford, 1985).

17 See n 5, above.

18 This is vigorously argued by Jonathan Scott, 'Radicalism and Restoration: the shape of the Stuart experience', *Historical Journal*, 31, 2 (1988), 453–67; see also n.23 below.

19 Lois G. Schwoerer, *The Declaration of Rights, 1689* (Baltimore, 1981).

20 John Spurr, *The Restoration Church of England, 1646–1689* (New Haven, 1992). Gordon Rupp, *Religion in England, 1688–1791* (Oxford, 1986).

21 This perspective seems to emerge forcibly from J.C.D. Clark, *English Society, 1688–1832. Ideology, Social Structure and Political Practice during the Ancien Regime* (Cambridge, 1985).

and 'internal' perspective, in considering the Revolution as produced by and giving answers to the problems of a peculiarly English history. How it might appear in the context of a Scottish, or an Irish, history 'internally' viewed is another story, or more correctly two stories. But recent historiography has forcefully reminded us that no 'internal' perspective is sufficient.[22] The event could not have happened at all if it had not happened in a 'European' context, and it was very largely its character as an event in that context which obliged its enlargement into an event occuring in a 'British' context, which (in turn) it deeply changed and helped create.

III

The problems of English politics can be made to explain the invitation to William of Orange in 1688, but do not explain his motives for accepting it, or for having a powerful armada already in readiness. These must be explained in terms of continental power politics, not excluding William's ambitions dynastic and otherwise; though we must avoid making the inane supposition that because English history cannot fully explain these events, it has therefore no autonomous existence or internal logic of its own. Nevertheless, its problems in this period were external and dynastic as well as internal and structural; the multiple monarchy of the restored Stuart brothers was so weak in the face of French power – perceived as aiming at a 'universal monarchy' – that French intervention in court and parliamentary politics was omnipresent, easier to resent than to evade.[23] William set sail with his armada intending to bring the Three Kingdoms into his anti-French alliance, and not unmindful of his wife's expectations as heir to their crowns. But it is among the many extraordinary ironies of the series of events he unchained that the Three Kingdoms were weak and distracted at the time he annexed them to his ambitions, so much so that they seemed doomed to satellite staus under French or Dutch hegemony; yet he mobilised in them a military, fiscal and political power which changed them profoundly and proved formidable, not only in furthering his objectives in continental politics, but in setting limits to English and British involvement in the pursuit of those same objectives. As the essays in this volume have amply shown, it is in this context that we

[22] Jonathan I. Israel (ed.), *The Anglo-Dutch Moment; Essays on the Glorious Revolution and its World Impact* (Cambridge, 1991); Robert Beddard (ed.), *The Revolutions of 1688: The Andrew Browning Lectures, 1988 (Oxford, 1990);* Lois G. Schwoerer (ed.), *The Revolution of 1688–89: Changing Perspectives* (Cambridge, 1992).

[23] Jonathan Scott, *Algernon Sidney and the Restoration Crisis, 1677–1683* (Cambridge, 1991).

have to understand the later events of the Union of the parliaments and the creation of the Kingdom of Great Britain.

There is an English history driven by the need to maintain the system of sovereignty laid down by the Act in Restraint of Appeals, and to avoid at all costs the disaster of renewed civil war and dissolution of government. In this context the Revolution of 1688–89 looks like a 'second Restoration', a consolidation of that sovereignty by the removal of a king who was subjecting it to too much strain. Yet the removal of a king was a desperate action, entailing the worst risks in the English historical memory, and the English were moved to run these risks only by a dynastic occurrence. William could never have sailed but for the birth of the infant prince James Francis Edward, and the chance to safeguard his wife's inheritance by proclaiming that birth spurious; and it was in the hope of maintaining the infant's rights that James II fled from his rebellious daughters, his rebellious or unco-operative subjects and the overwhelming power of the prince who had appeared in their support, and placed himself and his son under French protection. By so doing he ensured that civil war in England would not[24] be an aspect of the war of the Three Kingdoms which lasted until Limerick and Glencoe; but he left England exposed to a threat, which lasted for six decades and longer, of foreign invasion in exploitation of a contested dynastic succession. Not William alone, but his subjects and his successors, were obliged to engage the British kingdoms in European war to protect the Revolution Settlements; the European conflict of 1688–97 includes among its names that of 'the War of the English Succession'. War abroad to protect the Protestant Succession at home was necessary in order to impose stability upon the recurrent problems of English government; but James achieved a further measure of destabilisation since, by withdrawing his son and himself to France, he left the Church of England a further reminder of the paradox that the Protestant Succession was being maintained by means the Church could not wholeheartedly accept. It was a recurrent problem of English history that the Church could not quite trust its own Supreme Head, and that problem was not yet solved.

If the Revolution looks like a second Restoration in the enduring context, the *moyenne durée*, of Tudor political and ecclesiastical structures, there are other contexts in which it looks like a revolution in several meanings of the term: as I have argued elsewhere, like a *peripeteia* in the last months of 1688, like a *ridurre ai principi* in the first months of 1689,

[24] See J.G.A. Pocock, 'The Fourth English Civil War: dissolution, desertion and alternative histories in the Glorious Revolution', *Government and Opposition*, 23, 2 (1988), 151–66. A slightly shortened version is reprinted in Schwoerer (ed.), *The Revolution of 1688–89*. Also 'The significance of 1688: some reflections on Whig history', in Beddard (ed.), *The Revolutions of 1688*, pp. 271–92.

and like a *novus ordo seculorum* in a perception taking shape over the decade of the 1690s.[25] Of these terms in the vocabulary of revolution, the two first are ancient and early modern, while the third draws closer to the modern meaning of the term (perhaps growing obsolete under post-modern conditions). The needs of war on the continent obliged William and his commanders to complete the reconquest of the archipelago – Dutch and French generals campaigned in Ireland in a shared distaste for their surroundings – and then to that massive reconstruction of the English capacity to make and finance war which became known by the linked terms of 'standing army' and 'public credit', and was perceived as altering the political structure of the community and the historical conditions which connected men with their political societies. By 1698, English, Scottish and Anglo-Irish publicists were embarked upon a debate which explicitly premised that war and politics had become modern and commercial,[26] and that the European societies conducting them were structurally unlike what they had been under ancient (Greek and Roman) or medieval (Gothic and feudal) conditions. These writers further debated how far this great historical change was to be welcomed and how far dreaded, or what mixture of the two responses was appropriate and prudent.

The government of England was being transformed by the same processes that obliged it to assume a newly powerful role in the British archipelago, the European continent, the oceans beyond and the American, Indian and African regions then becoming provinces of the world system. There were many, in city as well as country, who resented the ways in which these British and particularly European involvements were incrementally altering the character of political life, and turned their resentment against the Revolution of 1688-89, which they correctly saw as the take-off point of all these developments. The war against French universal monarchy, whose necessity they need not deny, was being conducted in such a way as involved England both in the creation of an 'enormous' or 'extensive' monarchy[27] in the archipelago and in

[25] In 'Standing army and public credit: the institutions of Leviathan', in Dale F. Hoak and Mordechai Feingold (eds.), *The Revolution of 1688–89: Anglo-Dutch Perspectives on the World of William III and Mary II* (Stanford, 1994).

[26] J.G.A. Pocock, *The Machiavellian Moment: Florentine Political Thought and the Atlantic Republican Tradition* (Princeton, 1975), ch. XIII, 'Neo-Machiavellian political economy: the Augustan debate over land, trade and credit'; Istvan Hont, 'Free trade and the economic limits to national economies: neo-Machiavellian political economy reconsidered', in John Dunn (ed.), *The Economic Limits to Modern Politics* (Cambridge, 1990), pp. 41–120.

[27] The former adjective is more than once employed by David Hume, the latter by Edward Gibbon. The concepts entailed by the above sentence are examined by Eliga H. Gould, 'War, empire and the language of state formation: British imperial culture in the age of the American Revolution', Ph.D. Dissertation, Johns Hopkins University, 1992, in particular Ch. 1, 'The problem of the state in early Hanoverian Britain'.

membership of a European confederacy, swayed by Dutch, Habsburg and later Hanoverian interests, little less dangerous than Bourbon universal monarchy itself. These involvements were subjecting Englishmen to a new oligarchy made up of patronage-mongers, dissenters, stockjobbers and a military machine and national debt which fed upon one another. This polemic was shared by Old Whigs who thought the Revolution had not gone far enough, and Tories who resented the fact that it had occurred at all. Defenders of the regime, to 1789 and beyond, noted this overlap between 'commonwealth', 'patriot', and 'Jacobite' rhetoric, and drew the conclusion that republicans and absolutists were united against parliamentary monarchy, just as puritans and papists (they said) had been united in the seventeenth century. This was the point at which tensions arising from the newness and modernity of the British and European power structure which England was now obliged to maintain joined and interacted with the older tensions existing within the edifice of Tudor sovereignty in church and state; tensions which dynastic uncertainty and unhealed fissures between crown, clergy and dissent kept alive into the reign of George III.

IV

These tensions underlay the union of the parliaments which created the Kingdom of Great Britain, and helped determine the character of both. Just as in 1603, 'Britain' was a policy objective which Scots desired on the whole more than Englishmen did, but, for that reason among others, could achieve only on such terms as the English were prepared to concede; it therefore reflected the preponderance of English power over Scottish. The Scots thrust the Union on the English; the English imposed the Union on the Scots, dictating its character for the paradoxical reason that they did not really want it. Ireland remained at a distance, treated as the recently reconquered kingdom it really was; though we note the beginnings of a settler nationalism in which the Anglo-Irish claim equality with the English on the grounds that they are the conquering, not the conquered people.[28]

The more utopian schemes put forward by Andrew Fletcher – who has emerged as a major figure in the canon of Scottish political thinkers[29] – reflect the ambivalence of the Anglo-Scottish relationship. In political

[28] William Molyneux, *The Case of Ireland Being Bound by Acts of Parliament in England* (Dublin, 1698); J.G. Simms, *William Molyneux of Dublin*, ed. P.H. Kelly (Dublin: Irish Academic Press, 1982); Jacqueline Hill, 'Ireland without Union: Molyneux and his legacy', above, pp. 271–96.

[29] For this canon, see Mason, *Scots and Britons*.

practice, Fletcher strove to make the Union a confederation of two kingdoms; in his theoretical discourse, he imagined a Britain, and a Europe, which should have adopted a 'Swiss solution' and become a confederation of cantons. Implicitly, therefore, he challenged the growing presumption that Europe, archipelagic and continental, should emerge from the era of wars of religion – we may count the War of the Three Kingdoms as one such – and the threat of Habsburg or Bourbon universal monarchy, as a 'confederation' or 'republic' of powerful sovereign states, related to one another by the ties of commerce, enlightenment and even war, when conducted as *ragion di stato* and terminated by the treaties or *foedera*[30] which should form the public law of the post-imperial *confoederatio*. In Fletcher's system the units were not to be sovereign states but cantons ruled by their militias and their *landesgemeinde*. On the one hand, he joined with those who believed that monarchies maintaining armies by mortgaging their futures would prove too powerful and at the same time too unstable to preserve the peace of Europe and the liberty of the individual; on the other, the cantonal image was necessary to ensure that his confederation appeared Swiss rather than Polish, a league of republics in which free men governed one another rather than of turbulent nobles governing only their serfs and themselves. David Hume, the next great thinker in the Scottish canon, busied himself in showing that a stable and peaceable Europe could consist of powerful and wealthy sovereign states, diverse in their political structures;[31] the advice which the Swiss Rousseau tendered to Poles and Corsicans places him in the company of Andrew Fletcher, of whom he may or may not have heard. It was this confrontation between an ideology of state- building and its alternative in early modern discourse which lent a contemporary poignancy to John Robertson's seminar and its successor,[32] conducted at the Folger Library in the years of debate over Maastricht and ratification.

The English of 1707, it may be said, cared for none of these things, and it was their indifference and introspection, rather than their vaulting ambition, which ensured that the Union would be one of incorporation rather than confederation. They acquired empire, in this case at least, not

[30] It seems no accident that the major archival achievement of Anne's reign was Thomas Rymer's *Foedera* (1704–13), a collection of the external acts of the English Crown preserved among its records. See D.C. Douglas, *English Scholars* (London, 1943), pp. 285–301.

[31] David Hume, 'Of the balance of power' (*Essays, Moral, Political and Literary*, ed. Eugene F. Miller (Indianapolis, 1985), pp. 332–41). John Robertson, 'Universal monarchy and the liberties of Europe: David Hume's critique of an English Whig doctrine', in Nicholas Phillipson and Quentin Skinner (eds.), *Political Discourse in Early Modern Britain* (Cambridge, 1993), pp. 349–73.

[32] 'Empire, confederation and republic: from Atlantic dominion to American union', conducted by J.G.A. Pocock, January–April, 1992.

in the lapidary 'fit of absence of mind', but out of unwillingness to consider their relations with others in any conceptual form, with the result that these could take no other form than that of an extension of the system to which they were accustomed. They had reasons, however – it may further be said – for this extreme and now and then appalling self-centredness. They had recently acquired an imperial capacity to act as a major power by sea and land, and were divided as to whether they were happy with it; if some saw the opportunities of empire and pursued them, others saw the same opportunities and rejected them with fear and loathing; indeed, it is uncommon to find a perceptive author in whom these responses are not mixed. If we probe, and when they probed, the reasons for this powerful ambivalence, it is not long before we come upon the roots of instability within the Tudor system of sovereignty in church and state, which had caused so many dissolutions of government in the seventeenth century and were not fully removed in the eighteenth.[33] It took a long time to legitimate the Revolution Settlement, and longer than we used to suppose to legitimate the Hanoverian Succession. If this has been one of the chief lessons taught by recent historiography,[34] a corollary must be that the English response to instability old and new was immediate, instinctive and non-negotiable. The unity of crown with parliament and of both with established church must be maintained at all cost; the problem of 'empire' in the modern sense merged with that of 'empire' in the Tudor and medieval. The unified sovereign legislature which was all that stood between the English and the dissolution of government could not possibly be confederated with any other without putting its unity at risk. This was the *arcanum imperii* that determined the course of the Scottish Union; it can be argued that it also determined the course of the American Revolution. Defoe's contention that the Act of Union was fundamental law, and that to break its terms as a *foedus* would plunge both kingdoms into a dissolution of civil society,[35] was as fragile as Locke's theory of revolution, of which it was in part an elaboration. The English were well acquainted with the dissolution of government, and would on no account be threatened with it again. They were indifferent to the emotions of others because they had been too deeply wounded by their own.

[33] This would be the present writer's way of defending the 'ancien regime' thesis of J.C.D. Clark. It is not enough to point out that the Church of England's hegemony was insecure and imperfectly enforced; it was enforced, by means that included mitigation, because it was insecure.

[34] The reference is to recent work emphasising the persistence of Jacobitism: Evelyn Cruickshanks (ed.), *Ideology and Conspiracy: Aspects of Jacobitism, 1689–1759* (Edinburgh, 1982); Linda Colley, *In Defiance of Oligarchy: The Tory Party 1714–60* (Cambridge, 1982); Paul Monod, *Jacobitism and the English People, 1688–1788* (Cambridge, 1989).

[35] Katherine R. Penovich, 'From "revolution principles" to Union: Defoe's intervention in the Scottish debate', above, pp. 228–42, esp. p. 237.

V

The British single kingdom – with its newly unified crown and parliament, its dual structures of laws and churches, its conquered annexe in Ireland, its petty lordships in Man and the Channel islands not fully incorporated with either crown, its powerful trading corporations and its colonies in the Caribbean and the coasts of continental America – had been created to safeguard its own stability and act as a power in Europe (where it had in Gibraltar its first continental footing since the loss of Calais). But its two *raisons d'être* – internal sovereignty and external dominion – were not quite reconciled and therefore not quite achieved; there were fears, tensions and conflicting images. The great successes of Marlborough's wars and the defeats inflicted on Louis XIV's 'universal monarchy' brought with them the fear of entanglement in a confederacy of European powers no less 'universal' and permanent, and the fear of permanent subjection to a regime of stockjobbers, warmongers and boroughmongers; fears which could be articulated by Jacobites, commonwealthmen, and Whig or Tory opposition camarillas, with overtones threatening to the Revolution regime and the Hanoverian succession, so that the language of corruption destabilised the dynasty and drew attention to the instability of the churches. The reserve power of the English parliament and the restive counties and boroughs behind it took control, under Tory leadership, of the formidable military and financial machine built by William III and the Junto Whigs,[36] and withdrew it from its continental alliances in the manoeuvres leading to the Treaty of Utrecht; an assertion of the autonomy of the islands in the politics of Europe so decisive that it won the approval of the historian Lord Macaulay and could be praised as setting up a 'balance of power' which stabilised the European 'republic'.[37] Yet the high costs of Utrecht were seen in the succession crisis which accompanied the illness and death of Anne, and brought the Hanoverian line to the throne by a party triumph which was ruthlessly imposed on England and resisted by rebels in Scotland, and which left behind it a weakness in legitimation that two reigns could not live down.

There ensued a 'patriot' discourse – sometimes deist and sometimes

[36] The growth of this war-making and imperial machinery of state throughout the eighteenth century has been recently studied by John Brewer in *The Sinews of Power: War, Money and the English State, 1688–1783* (New York, 1989).

[37] The classic statement of Utrecht's historical importance by one of its chief British promoters is Bolingbroke's *Letters on the Study of History* (London, 1752), letters VII and VIII. For Macaulay's verdict (his *History* did not reach 1713) see his review, 'Lord Mahon's War of the Succession in Spain', *Critical and Historical Essays* (Boston: Houghton Mifflin, 1901), II, pp. 181–6. For Bolingbroke, see further Gould, n 27 above.

Anglican in England and Wales, sometimes radically covenanting in Scotland[38] – which defended the 'country' against the corrupting effects of high finance, European diplomacy, and Whig oligarchy, and responded in its own way to the growing power of commerce and imperial aggression by speaking out for a 'blue-water' policy which pursued maritime empire without European alliances and standing armies. It scarcely concealed its latent anti-Hanoverianism, and its persistent calls for reliance on the country militias were not unjustly charged with weakening the regime's military power against the Stuart exiles and their French allies, fear of which kept the spectre of 'universal monarchy' stalking the English map of Europe. It is being shown, particularly by Eliga H. Gould,[39] how in the middle decades of the eighteenth century the incursion and defeat of Prince Charles Edward coincided with the reversal of alliances as between Austria and Prussia – once so central an object of study under the name of 'the Diplomatic Revolution' – and very importantly the reorganisation of the English[40] militia as a home-defence army, to consolidate the Hanoverian regime in Great Britain and distance it from the power-conflicts of German-speaking Europe, where the anti-French cause was fatefully left in the apparently Protestant and unentangling hands of the King of Prussia.

In the opinion of Edward Gibbon, the reorganisation of the militia further coincided with the accession of George III – a 'British king' born within both the realm and the church of England – to deliver the Tory gentry (to which the Gibbons belonged) from the burden of their lingering Jacobitism and bring to the Hanoverians their support sometimes so unwavering as to be an embarrassment to Whigs.[41] In the opinion of David Hume, however, it coincided with the disastrous policies of the elder Pitt, that 'wicked madman'[42] who had doubled the national debt in pursuit of a continental empire in America, brought down on Britain the reproach of seeking 'universal monarchy' of a new kind, and left it without friends in Europe to support it against a vengeance-seeking France. The Hanoverian regime in Britain had extricated itself from one European system to make itself the centre of an Atlantic and American

[38] The history of Scottish 'patriotism' has yet to be written.

[39] 'War, empire and the language of state formation'; and 'To strengthen the King's hands: dynastic legitimacy, militia reform and ideas of national unity in England, 1745–1760', in *Historical Journal*, 34, 2 (1991).

[40] But not a Scottish; see John Robertson, *The Scottish Enlightenment and the Militia Issue* (Edinburgh, 1985).

[41] Edward Gibbon, *Memoirs of My Life*, ed. Georges A. Bonnard (New York, 1966), pp. 109–11.

[42] Hume, letter to William Strahan, 26 October 1775, in J.Y. T. Greig (ed.), *The Letters of David Hume* (Oxford, 1932), II, p. 301. See Istvan Hont, 'The rhapsody of public debt: David Hume and voluntary state bankruptcy', in Phillipson and Skinner (eds.), *Political Discourse*, pp. 321–48.

empire whose brief career dominates the history of the quarter-century following George's accession in 1760.

In the rapid and deeply confusing developments of that period, a king who had 'gloried in the name of Britain' – meaning that he was not a 'wee wee German lairdie' pledged to his Electoral interests – found himself excoriated as a puppet of villainous 'North Britons', both by aristocratic Whigs infuriated because he had taken over the cause they considered their own, and by urban demagogues whose antecedents were as Tory as they were commonwealth. The rapidity of this transformation of discourse, as well as of behaviour, indicates that the stability and even the legitimacy of the dynasty and the regime were not complete even after the extinction of Jacobitism. The early years of the reign witnessed the rallying of many English Tories to a Whig regime, and of many Scots to a Union in which what we call Enlightenment defined their place in philosophical terms;[43] its later years were to lay many seventeenth-century ghosts as the Church of England moved into unreserved support of the Georgian monarchy and the great principle of subordination. But its first quarter-century witnessed an alienation of Revolution Whigs from the monarchy, an alienation of urban crowds from monarchic and aristocratic patronage simultaneously, and an alienation of newly vocal, largely anti-trinitarian dissent (some of it originating within the Church as well as outside it) from the compromise of Test and Toleration which formed the ecclesiastical substance of the Revolution Settlement.[44] These were the 'present discontents' of England; Scotland witnessed less alienation, as did Ireland until the midpoint of the war of 1774–83; but in the larger field of 'the empire' – as the various realms, dominions and dependencies of the imperial Crown were collectively known – there arose a new crisis in multiple monarchy, which took a turn from which the epithet 'revolutionary' need not be withheld.

VI

This crisis may be thought of as arising from a change in the character and self-perception of the formerly and still consciously English colonies of the Crown on the American seaboard, excluding the Caribbean and the Gulf of St Lawrence.[45] Its crucial and revolutionary step was the

[43] Richard B. Sher, *Church and University in the Scottish Enlightenment: the Moderate Literati of Edinburgh* (Princeton, 1985).

[44] Clark *English Society*, pp. 207–8, 276, 283; Pocock (ed.), *The Varieties of British Political Thought, 1500–1800* (Cambridge, 1994), chs. 8 and 9.

[45] Jack P. Greene, *Peripheries and Center: Constitutional Development in the Extended Polities of the British Empire and the United States, 1607–1788* (Athens, Georgia, 1986 and New York, 1990) is the fullest and most illuminating study of this process.

declaration of 1776 that what had been termed 'colonies' were now to be considered, of right were, and therefore in some sense always had been, independent 'states'. From this it may be inferred, without too much simplification, that 'colonies' had been defined as something less than 'states', and now claimed that status as a step so radical that it entailed a concomitant claim to 'independence'. What then was the legal status of a 'colony', and had that status been clarified in law? Here we may find ambiguity; a colony's charter, if it had one, might authorise it to act and exist as something in the nature of a trading company, a civil corporation akin to a borough, or (to look to extremes) a body political, ecclesiastical as well as civil, subject to a crown whose authority ruled it as the same authority ruled the realm of England according to the Act in Restraint of Appeals. But there were no colonial bishops appointed by royal letters, even in Episcopalian Virginia; and bishops as spiritual peers could function only within the historical structure of the English realm. The multiplicity of churches and sects in the American colonies viewed as a whole obliges us to think of Anglo-American religious culture as in a loose sense congregational,[46] and there were sectors in which it was becoming increasingly unitarian. The structure of Tudor sovereignty did not in this sense apply.

There was a very strong sense in which colonists felt themselves to be Englishmen (whatever their ethnic origins), subjects of the crown of Great Britain and entitled to the liberties and protection of English law. But once the status of 'colonies' within the 'empire' was called in question, as it was by the policy of which the Stamp Act (1765) was part, its indeterminacy began to raise serious questions.[47] Even under royal governors, the colonies were not viceroyalties, subject kingdoms, realms or dominions, as were the components of the Spanish Monarchy; even under vigorously assertive colonial assemblies, they were not sovereign 'estates' or 'states' like those composing the Dutch republic. If they had enjoyed any such status, the British 'empire' might have acknowledged a *jus publicum* regulating relations between its component 'states' and the imperial Crown which ruled them; and that *jus* might have defined it as a 'confederation' of independent sovereignties linked through *foedera* with a central authority, as in the case of the 'Germanic body' which was both a 'confederation' and an 'empire' (though the Swiss and Dutch confederations could not be known by the latter term). But if the colonies lacked any clear

[46] The American Revolution as a war of religion is studied by J.C.D. Clark, *The Language of Liberty: Political Discourse and Social Dynamics in the Anglo-American World, 1660–1800* (Cambridge, 1993).

[47] Greene, *Peripheries and Center*, and Richard Koebner, *Empire* (Cambridge, 1961), chs. 4 and 5.

legal definition, there could be no *jus publicum* and George III enjoyed more 'empire' within the realm of Great Britain than he did in the full extent of his dominions. It came indeed to be said that there existed, or had existed, a code or consensus of informal understandings which governed the relations between crown, parliament and colonial governors and assemblies; and there were those – in fact there still are[48] – who claimed that this code enjoyed the immemorial and customary authority of an 'ancient constitution'. But Edmund Burke – who appealed eloquently for its perpetuation in the face of rival theories of empire – seems to have presented it in terms rather of the prudence of *gubernaculum* than of the binding precedents of *jurisdictio*; and the apex of the ancient constitution had long been the sovereignty of the king-in-parliament.

This 'empire', then, differed from other systems of that name in that it was not composed of sovereign or quasi-sovereign 'states' and was not held together by *pacta*, *foedera* or a *jus publicum*, but by the sovereignty of the crown in parliament, coupled with the common law in which the rights of Englishmen were held to be enshrined. It was one of those unwritten, informal arrangements in which the English believe themselves to take delight, but one which – the informal relationship between prerogative and parliamentary authority – had memorably collapsed in the previous century, and had had to be restored in the form of an unbreakable location of the royal authority in parliament (so that, it was commonly said, the crown's 'influence' had increased as its 'prerogative' had been lessened). The informal structure of 'empire' – meaning the relation of the crown to those of its dominions which were colonies but not realms – disintegrated through the 1760s and 1770s, and Edmund Burke was left appealing to the principle that it was precisely its informality which should never have been challenged, and so destroyed, by attempts at definition which he characterised as empty 'theory' for the reason that existing law was incapable of providing the answers. The reason why a problem arose to which there was no clear answer have next to be considered.

To the extent to which the individual colonist could be considered an Englishman – a definition he might insist on carrying to the fullness of its extent – he could be thought of as appealing to his rights at common law, and making this appeal to the sovereign who protected and acknowledged

[48] Greene, *Peripheries and Center*, ch. 7, pp. 144–8; John Phillip Reid, *In Defiance of the Law: The Standing Army Controversy, the Two Constitutions, and the Coming of the American Revolution* (Chapel Hill, North Carolina, 1981). Cf. Robert W. Tucker and David C. Hendrickson, *The Fall of the First British Empire: Origins of the War of American Independence* (Baltimore, 1982). For Burke's argument here, Gould, 'War, empire and the language of state formation', ch. 3, 'Leviathan abroad: the Atlantic Debate over American Taxation'.

these rights; as doing so even when, and because, the sovereign was legislating in a way he considered an infringement of them. The locus of such appeals was in parliament, but not only was the colonist unrepresented in that body; parliament was itself now part of the sovereign – the crown-in-parliament – against whose legislation he was appealing. There next arose a dimension of the problem in which the rights of the colonist were no longer vested simply in his relation as subject to the law and the sovereign, but were located in the new problematic of subordinate legislatures. He was represented, or so he might claim, in the assembly of his colony, and if his right not to be taxed without his own consent was situated there, it followed that he should not, or in a language derived from the law could not, be taxed without the consent of that assembly. But if right and representation, with which the common law unequivocally endowed him, were located in the colonial assembly, it should follow that the same law provided and regulated a process by which taxation was imposed by parliament with the consent of the colonial assemblies. This it did not do, in any sense less informal than that in which the issue had become critical before 1763; and it followed that any appeal to rights enshrined in the common law was enough to destroy that law's informal and customary character by asking it to provide guarantees more formal than it possessed the means of formulating. The essence of common law is the written (or formal) expression of unwritten (and informal) understandings.

From this dilemma there flowed two consequences. In the first place, the rights of Englishmen at common law came to be re-codified in American colonial discourse as rights by a higher law of which common law could always be described as a manifestation: a law of nations and/or of nature. It was by this route that Americans came to believe that they enjoyed the rights of Englishmen in a higher and more perfect sense than that in which Englishmen enjoyed them, and were by nature that which Englishmen were merely by history. But a higher and more ideal history was necessary in order to explain how this had come about; and the second consequence with which we have to deal was that the colonists began to provide themselves with a history in which their rights as Englishmen were seen as having been vested from the beginning in their capacity to represent themselves by a law of nature. From the writings of Richard Bland of Virginia, in the middle 1760s, there began to take shape a history which in its completed form may be stated as follows.[49] Colonists emigrating into the wilderness had taken with them the rights

[49] Greene, *Peripheries and Center*, ch. 5 and Yuhtaro Ohmori, 'The Artillery of Mr. Locke: the use of Locke's *Second Treatise* in pre-revolutionary America', PhD dissertation, Johns Hopkins University, 1988.

of Englishmen, including the rights to property, representation, and the protection of the crown, whose sovereignty they had therefore been necessitated to carry with them. On entering the wilderness, however, they had entered the state of nature, whether as that term was used by theorists of *jus civile*, to denote a condition antecedent to the establishment of civil society, or as it was used by theorists of *jus gentium*, to denote the space in which sovereign entitites were related to one another. For if rights were sufficent to generate civil sovereignty, the rights of Englishmen, transformed by the wilderness into rights of nature, had re-generated the sovereignty of the Crown of England as that of a sovereign over subjects defined by the law of nature alone.

If it were held – as by a civilian or a scholastic jurist it might not have been – that the rights-bearers negotiated with the sovereign the terms on which they would accept him as such, it followed – as for a line of colonial theorists from Bland to Jefferson[50] it came to follow – that each body of colonists had negotiated with the King of England a *pactum* or *foedus* by which he became their sovereign, but his sovereignty was exercised primarily in the assembly which represented them and their rights. If it were held – as by theorists of *jus gentium* like Grotius, Pufendorf and Vattel it was coming to be held – that between sovereigns in the state of nature there could exist only *foedera*, and that it was a question how far a system of *foedera* might develop into the *jus publicum* of a confederation like the Swiss or the German – or of Europe ideally considered as a republic of states held together by great treaties like those of Westphalia or Utrecht – then the British 'empire' might be considered a series of *pacta* between diverse civil societies and their sovereign the King of Great Britain, and a series of *foedera* which permitted the crown-in-parliament at Westminster to exercise certain powers for the good of the 'empire' as a society of civil societies, all of them 'English' in the sense in which the rights of Englishmen were the rights of nature.

To colonists, this line of argument – here abstracted and ideally expressed – had the advantage that it gave each 'colony' a legal definition and being beyond any with which the common law had hitherto endowed it, and at the same time demonstrated that rights at that law were rights by the law of nature – a proposition which, in itself, nobody could very well deny. It further supplied 'empire', as that term was used in British context, a legal definition, a common sovereignty, and a *jus publicum* with which it had not hitherto provided itself. But it did so at the price, which to colonists was not a price but an enhancement of status, of re-defining the 'empire' as a confederation; and this was a price which Englishmen,

[50] Richard Bland, *An Enquiry into the Rights of the British Colonies* (1766); Thomas Jefferson, *The Rights of British America* (1775).

and at this period to all appearances most Scots, were not willing to pay at all. This volume has been concerned with the Union of the parliaments as a great act of state which entailed the rejection of a 'confederating' in favour of an 'incorporating' union; and we have seen that the primary reason for this decision was that the 'empire' exercised by the English crown in the Westminster Parliament could 'incorporate' other bodies politic within itself, but could not 'confederate' or be confederated with them. Therefore the English (and the Scottish Unionist) response to the claims which Americans now began to put forward was, typically, that they could imagine (though they might be unwilling to effect) 'incorporating' colonies within the realm (and its 'empire') by giving them representation in the Westminster Parliament, but could never accept, and could hardly even understand, the proposal to reconstitute the 'empire' as a 'confederation'. The American Revolution is not causally a consequence of the Union of England and Scotland, but it is a consequence of a political logic contained within it.

VII

This was the logic of 'empire' in the English sense of the term. This had in 1533 meant the sovereignty of the crown in church and state; it had not then been necessary to determine in detail how far this sovereignty was exercised in parliament and how far out of it. There had ensued a series of devastating crises and 'dissolutions of government', which had led to the decision that the unity of crown with parliament and with church must be maintained at all costs, even the cost of concessions by crown to parliament and by crown-in-parliament to English dissent and Scottish distinctiveness; at the cost last named the Scots had been incorporated in 'empire' as the English understood it. There had further been set up a powerful structure of military, naval and civil power, capable of exercising imperial control within the 'extensive monarchy' of the archipelago, in the reason of state of the European 'republic of states', and on the oceans and in the American and Asian continents constituting European 'empire' in the modern sense of the term; but 'empire' in this sense was still perceived as guaranteeing the unity of crown and parliament which constituted 'empire' in the oldest sense, and guaranteed England against a recurrence of seventeenth-century disorder. Dynastic and ecclesiastical instabilities had kept the regime at risk down to a time still recent when the first American crisis began; and the rapidity with which the Jacobite menace of the 1740s had been succeeded by the 'present discontents' of the 1760s showed that the monarchy of George III was even now not perfectly legitimated. The 'growth of political stability' in England (now Britain) since 1660 had been very real, but had not reached finality.

These historical considerations were interestingly synthesised by Thomas Pownall, the successive editions of whose treatise on *The Administration of the Colonies* supply an acute commentary on the growth of the imperial crisis in the years either side of 1770.[51] Casting about for a response to the increasing demand for a definition of the colonies as legal entities within a political system, he adopted (as did others) the solution of proposing that they were (or had been) 'palatinates', in which the powers of the crown had been deputed to be exercised by local authorities. Chester, Durham and the Principality of Wales had been dominions of this order until their incorporation within the realm; the Isle of Man and the Channel Islands still were. Ireland as a kingdom by conquest occupied a different category, and Pownall did not stir up the ancient controversy as to whether the crown of Scotland had been subordinate to that of England before the incorporating union. With regard to colonies, however, he insisted that the status of palatinates was obsolete and no longer available. It had existed only under feudal conditions, when the king's personal authority was not fully incorporated with that of his realm, and the dualities of Fortescuean kingship and the King's Two Bodies had been actual and visible. About 1660, however, in a historical process which Pownall significantly associated with the Navigation Acts, these conditions had ceased; the king became incorporated with his realm in the conjoint sovereignty of King, Lords and Commons, and subjection to his authority had become subjection to his authority in parliament.[52] As subjects to the crown, therefore, colonists were subjects to the realm (so that, he might have argued, when Englishmen infuriated Americans by speaking of 'our colonies' they spoke within their rights). The flaw in this reality was that colonists were unrepresented in parliament, in the exercise of the sovereignty to which they were subject. If they could not be granted such representation, *ad hoc* agreements would have to be worked out with the assemblies in which they were represented, recognising the system's necessary imperfection and accommodating to it.

Pownall supplies us with a model which may be set up in opposition to that extractable from colonial argument as it developed between Bland and Jefferson, to show that in the imperial crisis there actually were major issues at stake. It may be doubted how many of the debaters and

[51] Thomas Pownall, *The Administration of the Colonies, wherein their Rights and Constitution are Discussed and Stated* London, 1764; five editions by 1774).

[52] Pownall, *Administration of the Colonies*, 4th edn. (1768), rep. (New York, 1971), pp. 138–40, 172–3.

spectators understood them; the history of the controversy can easily be written as one of incomprehension on both sides. The absence – which Pownall was trying to supply – of a clear legal concept of a colony as a subordinate political society led to the controversy's being conducted as a debate between local varieties of Englishmen, possessing the same rights and appealing to the same law and the same sovereign; and on this perspective it was easy to arrive at the position, upheld by Edmund Burke, that there were no debatable issues and the mistake lay in trying to debate them. This is, rather strangely, the position of many American historians, who contend that the issues could have been resolved and it was only the purblindness of British ministers which prevented this happening. It is curious to see them arguing that the foundation of their republic, and its new birth of freedom, were not inevitable but could (and should?) have been avoided. The advantage of the argument being advanced in this essay is that it provides the American revolution with a measure of historical logic. The development of the colonies into self-conscious political societies, and the arguments they adopted to declare themselves such, led them to propose, in effect, the conversion of the 'empire' into a 'confederation'. There was nothing illogical about this, since it was possible for an association of states to be both, and Grotius, Pufendorf and Vattel were inscribed as names in the American pantheon because they showed this to be possible. But in addressing such proposals to the British crown-in-parliament, the colonists were dealing with an entity to which the term 'empire' denoted its own sovereignty and its own unity, which must be maintained at all costs as the only guarantee against its own dissolution, as well as the only guarantee of its continuing imperial power. They thus found themselves contending with the ghost of history, with that terrifying 'rhinoceros charging out of the past', of which Jonathan Scott has so wittily and eloquently written.[53]

The colonial argument came to set up the image of a series of quasi-contractual *foedera* or relationships between each colony, considered as a 'people' seated in the state of nature, and the crown of England (later Great Britain); relations with the crown which were not essentially, but at best contingently, subordinate to the authority of parliament. They claimed in short to be subject to the crown but not to the crown-in-parliament; and Pownall had much of the authority of English history on his side when he sought to show them that this claim was historically obsolete, since the civil wars, followed by the growth of commerce and modern 'empire', had ensured that crown and parliament were so irrevocably incorporated in one another that colonies were necessarily

[53] Jonathan Scott, *Algernon Sidney and the Restoration Crisis, 1677–83* (Cambridge, 1991), pp. xiii–xiv, 26–49.

subordinate to their conjoint sovereignty, and could only aspire (perhaps in vain) to be represented in its exercise. But the unity of crown and parliament was recent: no older than 1660 in Pownall's projection, and perhaps a century younger if we listen to Edward Gibbon; and the extinction of the Jacobite threat did not mean that it had ceased to be fragile. In appealing to the crown but not to parliament, the colonists came to be seen as separating the two; they were unwittingly raising the spectre of Bolingbroke's Patriot King, supposed to have guided, through sinister maternal and Scottish familiars, the unwise steps of George III in separating himself from the natural leaders of his parliament. The radical populism of much American language aligned the colonists with those, in London and elsewhere,[54] who thought the solution lay in an appeal, from monarchy and aristocracy alike, to the people as repository of all patriot virtue; but the Americans were not appealing to the English or British people, so much as they were claiming to be peoples in their own right. In pursuit of this claim, they set up a confederal relation which they supposedly enjoyed with the crown; this was to separate the king's personal from his parliamentary authority, with the result that those to whom it mattered above all to maintain the unity of crown and parliament could, perhaps must, respond that the American argument simultaneously did the work of Tories who would exalt the King above the two houses and of republicans who would reduce him to a mere 'duke of Venice'. It was already a staple of Whig argument that Jacobites and republicans were allied against the sovereignty of crown and parliament, as had been the papists and puritans of old. In the first three decades of George III's reign, all these ghosts were gibbering in the streets (which is not to say that new things in British politics were not appearing at the same time).

VIII

This is to present the crisis leading to American independence as a crisis in multiple monarchy: not indeed in the multiple monarchy of the Three Kingdoms, but in the very specific and self-conscious structure of the English monarchy and its realm and empire, occurring when colonies which had not been legally defined as distinct political societies laid claim to that status and began defining themselves, in their own terms, as what they ended by terming 'states'. If they had been 'states' within a legally defined 'empire' with a *jus publicum*, there might still have been a crisis

[54] John Sainsbury, *The Disaffected Patriots: London Supporters of Revolutionary America, 1769–1782* (Kingston and Montreal, 1987); Colin Bonwick, *English Radicals and the American Revolution* (Chapel Hill, 1977).

leading to independence, but it would have been of a different character to the one which in fact occurred. We have seen that they began, but did not complete, shaping a concept of empire as confederation, in which each component contained the seeds of its own sovereignty and enjoyed its own relation with the crown as a sovereign shared by all. This was not so much unacceptable as unintelligible to the politicians and publicists of the Kingdom of Great Britain, less because they had an alternative concept of their 'empire' over colonies than because they had none to speak of, and employed the term 'empire' to mean their sovereignty over themselves, of which they had assumed the colonists to form part. This sovereignty was lodged in the king-in-parliament, and the confederal theory of empire looked like a design to separate the two. James VI and I had strenuously objected to finding himself the head of two bodies or the husband of two wives,[55] but the seraglio formed of twenty or more independent legislatures was one from which George III had little need to escape, since he never entered it and scarcely recognised that it was there. The Anglo-British response to the semi-articulated trends in colonial argument was less rejection than incomprehension. So far was George from aiming at the status of a Patriot King that he instinctively aligned his authority with that of parliament, and resolutely upheld the conjoint sovereignty of both. This increased the fears of those among his subjects, both colonial and metropolitan, who saw him either as a prisoner of the corruption of parliament, or as aiming through his sinister advisers at corrupting it himself. The bogey of the Patriot King returned to haunt him, most of all when – for once in the history of the English monarchy – he acted as a conqueror, and in the Quebec Act[56] used statute to enact a *pactum concessionis* with his newly acquired Francophone subjects, guaranteeing to them – to the horror and dismay of Protestants in both Ireland and America – the continued exercise of priestly and feudal authority. The image of monarchial tyranny thus both reinforced and partly concealed the image of absolute parliamentary sovereignty which was the true target of American arguments.

The crown, nevertheless, anchored itself in parliament, and therefore in a Tudor and parliamentary conception of 'empire'; it rejected, perhaps without ever comprehending, an American conception of 'empire' as confederation, in which every legislative assembly should represent a distinct 'people' or civil society – or, as the term was coming to be used, a

[55] Mason, *Scots and Britons* and Jenny Wormald, 'The creation of Britain: multiple kingdoms or core and colonies?', *Transactions of the Royal Historical Society*, Sixth Series, II (1992), 175–94.

[56] Philip Lawson, *The Imperial Challenge: Quebec and Britain in the Age of the American Revolution* (Kingston and Montreal, 1989).

'state' – enjoying its own relationship with the crown. All attempts to negotiate without resolving this conflict having failed – this is not to say that none could have succeeded – the revolutionary breaking point was reached in the Declaration of Independence; a document which enacts a great many positions, easier for us to understand once we recognise that it operates as much within a discourse of *jus gentium* as within one of *jus civile*.[57] Stating its objective initially as that of announcing the separation of one 'people', the American, from another, the British, it employs a Lockean language framed to ground government in the 'people' in order to assert the equality of all 'peoples' with one another, and therefore the right of any 'people' to withdraw from the ties linking it with another. The implication can only be that there has existed a relationship between as many 'peoples' as there are colonies with delegates at Philadelphia and the 'people' (evidently a single one) of Great Britain; that the ties existing between them have been those provided by the authority of the Crown, now about to be declared dissolved; and that each 'people' has possessed and still possesses the authority to generate its own government, and to enter if it chooses into *pacta* and *foedera* with the Crown as furnishing it both with civil authority and with ties linking it with the other peoples of a confederate empire.

The Declaration proceeds to employ a Lockean language of dissolution of government, with which it indicts the King for misgovernment, pronounces him at war with those of his peoples who are party to the action the Congress is now taking, and declares his government over them dissolved. It is presumed, however, that they existed, and possessed both governments and the capacity to generate them, antecedently of the royal government; and the consequence must be that it is less the civil government of the colonies which is being dissolved, than the authority of the crown as providing a shared government, or 'empire', over a confederation of many 'peoples'. The British 'empire' is being proclaimed a confederation by the same act as proclaims that confederation dissolved. In consequence, the Declaration concludes, 'these united colonies' are now, and of right ought to be, 'independent states', The phrase 'of right' strongly suggests that they have always been 'states', or at least civil societies possessing the capacity to enter into contracts of government, and into treaties with other societies and peoples equal with themselves. It is the American solution to the English failure to furnish colonies with a clearly defined legal and civil status; very English, both in its use of the term 'right' to appeal to immemorial antiquity and in its adaptation to American purposes of the Act in Restraint of Appeals' claim that the

[57] See further Pocock, n 44 above.

realm is an 'empire, and so hath been reputed in the world', possessing an absolute and sovereign capacity to govern itself.

But since what is being dissolved is not the civil government of a society so much as the ties between a number of civil societies, it is primarily the crown's capacity to constitute and regulate these external relationships which is being declared at an end; the language of Locke is being injected into the language of Grotius, Pufendorf and Vattel. The matter does not quite end there, since through the governors it appoints the crown has been claiming executive authority in the civil government of each colony. In declaring this at an end and enjoining each colony to set about replacing it, Congress is effecting in each colony a limited revolution on the scale of 1688;[58] a partial dissolution of government, or of one component thereof, which does not amount to a dissolution of the authority composing civil society. It goes further than 1688 in declaring the crown itself deposed, and enjoining each colony to embark on the republican road of replacing it; the republican component in American history is activated from this moment; but what is being dissolved is a relation between a number of civil societies, and if 'dissolution of government' leads to a 'state of nature', the latter term denotes not the human condition that precedes civil government, but the 'state of nature' in which civil governments exist with respect to one another. Americans, the Declaration pronounces, henceforth consider the British government and people 'as we hold the rest of mankind, enemies in war and in peace friends'. It is the language of the *jus belli ac pacis*, and for the moment it is a declaration of war. The war may be terminated by a peace treaty or *foedus*, but not by a *confoederatio* or decision to share and obey a common *imperium*; for that is what has just been declared dissolved.

Implicit in all this is an acknowledgement of the position articulated by Pownall, that the crown, parliament and people of Great Britain are so far incorporated with one another that they cannot be considered apart. There is no indictment of George III's government of his kingdom, no suggestion that this is to be dissolved; those English radicals who threatened the King with such language were grievously disappointed by the word reaching them from Philadelphia.[59] The Declaration of Independence set out to separate one 'people' from another, with the result that all its Lockean indictments of royal misgovernment necessarily implied the existence of a royal government so far incorporated with the British 'people' that to cast off one was to cast off the other. At this point the confederate theory of empire collapsed, since it could not be maintained that the English, or by

[58] Willi Paul Adams, *The First American Constitution: Republican Ideology and the Making of the State Constitutions in the Revolutionary Era* (Chapel Hill, 1980).
[59] Sainsbury, *The Disaffected Patriots*, pp. 127–31.

now the Scottish, people recognised the crown only, or primarily, as the link between them and other peoples. The indictment of George III barely conceals an indictment of both parliament and the people represented by it. Deep down in the language of the Declaration may be uncovered an acceptance both of the Fortescuean theory of English kingship and the 'incorporating' rather than 'confederating' character of the Union of 1707. The American 'people' recognised the 'British people' even as it defined itself by defying them.

IX

This essay has traced the history of a crisis in multiple monarchy, arising too late in British history to be solved in the terms – themselves very imperfectly formulated – taking shape around that concept. Interestingly, its language was English rather than British; the idioms in which colonial writers from Bland to Jefferson put forward their concept of empire as confederation owed little to Andrew Fletcher[60] or any of the debaters of Union in 1603 or 1707, and it is something of a puzzle to tell where (other than in the European classics of *jus gentium*) they laid hold of them. When the concept was put to the English, and by this time to the Scots or North Britons, it encountered quite insuperable obstacles, the reasons for which lie so deep in English history as well as in that of Union that it is fair to speak of the American crisis as one in which the English, to say nothing more of the still nascent British,[61] were obliged to defend themselves as they thought their history had shaped them. It was necessary to maintain at all costs the conjoint sovereignty of the crown-in-parliament; the more so as the American crisis came when, and perhaps because, the relations between crown, parliament and people were for domestic reasons quite sharply destabilised. To unite the colonies with parliament by representation was one means of acheiving this overriding purpose; to subject the colonies to parliament by imperial and military power was another; to rid parliament of the colonies by recognising their independence was a third, and from the start there were imperial realists, like David Hume and Josiah Tucker,[62] who wanted to take this route. To compromise the unity

[60] Awareness of his argument for a confederating union may be detected in the Scot John Witherspoon; Greene, *Peripheries and Center*, pp. 155, 172. For Witherspoon see further Richard Sher and Jeffrey Smitten (eds.), *Scotland and America in the Age of the Enlightenment* (Princeton, 1990), section I, chs. 1–6; and Ned Landsman, 'The legacy of British Union for the North American colonies: provincial elites and the problem of imperial union', above, pp. 314–17.

[61] Linda Colley, *Britons: Forging the Nation, 1707–1837* (New Haven, 1992).

[62] Pocock, *Virtue, Commerce and History: Essays in Political Thought and History, chiefly in the eighteenth century* (Cambridge, 1985), chs. 7, 9.

of crown and parliament by sharing the crown with other parliaments was an alternative not considered, except in a further case which we have yet to consider.

With the recognition of American independence in 1783, there began to be an American history in which the ambiguities of the Declaration of 1776 had to be confronted. In what sense were the united colonies now united states? Had the thirteen of them merely entered a state of nature in respect to one another, in which what held them together were merely the *foedera* which might constitute an alliance or a confederation, and might or might not constitute a *jus publicum*? What could have been meant by the Declaration's constitution of an 'American people' forming a single entity, and how was it possible for that people to have manifested itself in thirteen distinct states? Was it conceivable that the unitary people enjoyed sovereignty, and that the multiple states existed only as its 'empire' defined them? Out of these linguistic puzzles it was a practical, indeed an imperial, necessity for James Madison to formulate a science of federal government, inclusive of Alexander Hamilton's pronouncement that the United States formed 'an empire perhaps the most interesting in the world'.[63] It may have been in large part Americans' enduring perception of themselves as still Englishmen, enjoying rights at common law which there must be a sovereign to protect and enforce, which led to the blend of states' rights with national government characterising the Federalist synthesis. In this process, however, the thesis that each colony was a state, whose political autonomy was visible in its own separate and distinct history, disappeared from the discourse of Federalism as rapidly as it had been invented to form part of the discourse of Independence. Once Congress affirmed the authority to create the territories which should become states, it exerted an imperial power of telling each 'people' where and how it might create itself; the empire of liberty was indeed an empire.[64]

As for the kingdoms and dominions which remained in the allegiance of George III, the loss of thirteen colonies was a painful but not a revolutionary experience; it diminished the territorial extent of empire without compelling its relocation in the structure of political authority, and the fashionable analogy with the decline and fall of Rome was false from the start. American war can only be seen as producing a hardening, to the point of ruthlessness, of the sovereign power of crown, parliament and all that they stood for. If some perceived a potentially revolutionary

[63] The second sentence of *The Federalist*, no. 1, in any edition.

[64] Peter S. Onuf, *The Origins of the Federal Republic: jurisdictional controversies in the United States, 1775–1787* (Philadelphia, 1983).

situation in 1780,[65] this must be seen as leading to counter-revolution in 1783-84, when the crown recovered control in parliament and never lost it again. The aristocracy took on more of the character of an imperial, military and administrative elite;[66] it faced the challenges of the French revolution with its mind made up and its dissenters marginalised. Slowly and painfully over the next quarter-century, it recovered the European position it had lost in 1763-83; it took part in another grand alliance against another universal monarchy, and mistrustfully entered into a restoration of the republic of European states in and after the Congress of Vienna. It enlarged its maritime and extra-European hegemonies in ways that gave rise to two new imperial discourses: the Anglo-Indian, which debated whether empire in South Asia was necessarily despotic because exercised over subjects naturally or historically incapable of liberty;[67] the Anglo-Canadian, in which the French-speaking province of Lower Canada and the Loyalist colonies of Upper Canada and the Maritimes entered upon the complex discourses of sovereignty which constitute 'Canadian political thought'.[68] There as elsewhere on the planet, 'crown colonies' of British settlers began exploring non-American routes towards 'responsible' and 'representative' government.[69]

There remained one zone in which the history of the Three Kingdoms continued to shape 'British history'. If the Union of the parliaments succeeded to the point where the American crisis produced no crisis in Scotland, and something like a 'British' nationality can be seen taking shape, we need to increase the attention we give to the series of developments in which the Anglo-Irish gentry formed themselves into a patriot militia and claimed for their parliament something not unlike what some Americans claimed for their own assemblies: union with an imperial crown of its own, distinct from the crown and parliament of Great Britain. Immediately there were those who declared that the only possible solution was the opposite: the complete incorporation of Ireland within the parliamentary monarchy of the United Kingdom.[70] From this point the historian of 'British political thought' needs to begin tracing the complex history of the various Irish political discourses – patriot,

[65] Herbert Butterfield, *George III, Lord North and the People* (London, 1949).

[66] Gould, 'War, empire and the language of state formation', ch. 5, 'The invention of the British ancien regime'.

[67] Rolando Minuti, 'Proprietà della Terra e Dispotismo Orientale: aspetti di un dibattio sull' India nella seconda metà del settecento', in *Materiali per una storia della cultura giuridica*, 8, 2 (1978), 29–176.

[68] There is as yet no coherent history of this body of discourse. I am indebted to James Tully and Paul Romney for such understanding as I have of it.

[69] Mark Francis, *Governors and Settlers: Images of Authority in the British Colonies, 1820–1860* (Cambridge, 1992).

[70] Josiah Tucker, *A Treatise Concerning Civil Government* (London, 1781), pp. 96–101.

unionist and United Irish; Protestant, Catholic and Presbyterian; Jacobin, Orange and Nationalist – and to begin conducting them toward a third Union: the fateful Act of 1801, without which the legislation of 1829-32, bringing an end to the Revolution Settlement in Great Britain, could hardly have occurred[71] and the relations of the United Kingdom with Ireland could not have assumed their modern form. This volume has studied British history largely from a Scottish angle of approach; the present essay has sought to exhibit it in an English and American perspective. Do we not need to return to the archipelago and (following the lead given by Jacqueline Hill) examine its Irish dimension?

[71] Clark, *English Society*, pp. 383–420.

INDEX

(includes citations by author)

9096486R00229

Printed in Great Britain
by Amazon.co.uk, Ltd.,
Marston Gate.